How [redacted]n Wesley Longman make your Western Civilization course more successful?

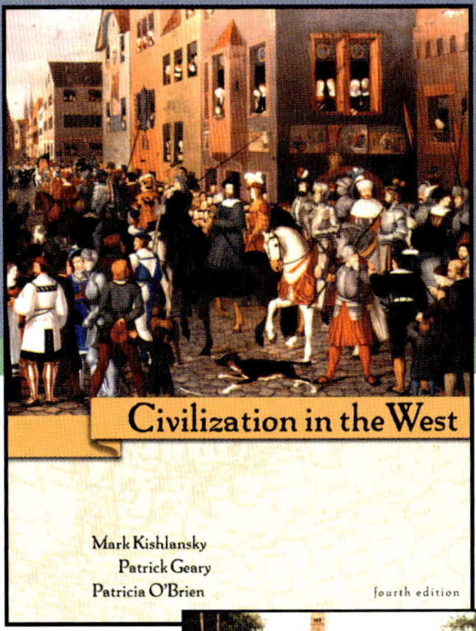

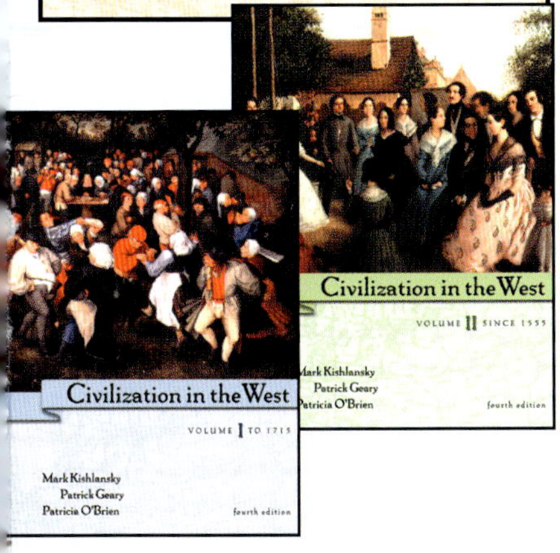

First, by offering you an excellent textbook.

Civilization in the West seamlessly blends social and political history into a scintillating narrative that brings to life the history of all groups and peoples who have created the enduring legacy that is Western Civilization. With a strong map program, a full-color comprehensive timeline, end-of-chapter website URLs, and much more, *Civilization in the West* captures student interest and helps them explore and appreciate the rich and complex history of Western Civilization.

But an excellent textbook isn't the only thing you'll need for a successful course. Addison Wesley Longman also provides you with an extensive selection of supplementary materials.

- Do your students struggle with geography?
- Do you have trouble engaging your students?
- Do your students have poor study habits?
- Would you be interested in primary or secondary sources?
- Would you be interested in using Penguin paperbacks?
- Would you be interested in additional Instructor Resources?

If you answered "yes" to any of these questions, then turn the page to see what Addison Wesley Longman has to offer you and your students...

Addison Wesley Longman

If your students are struggling with geography...

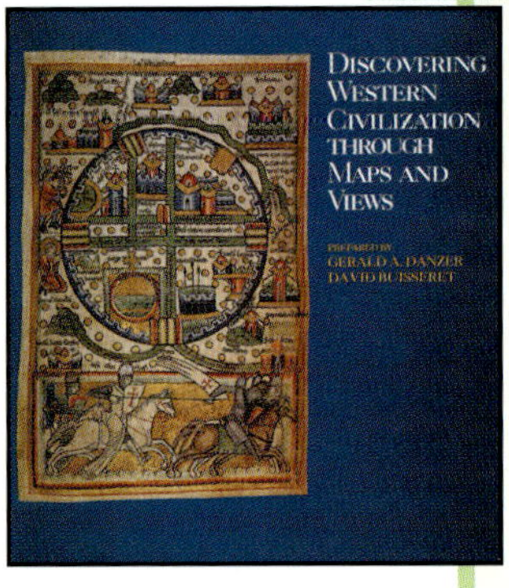

Discovering Western Civilization Through Maps and Views

by Gerald Danzer, *University of Illinois at Chicago*

This comprehensive and innovative set of over 100 four-color transparencies is bound with introductory materials and contains a detailed commentary on each map.

0-673-53596-7

Mapping Western Civilization

A workbook created for use in conjunction with *Discovering Western Civilization Through Maps and Views* that is designed to teach students to interpret and analyze cartographic materials as historical documents.

FREE when bundled. 0-673-53774-9

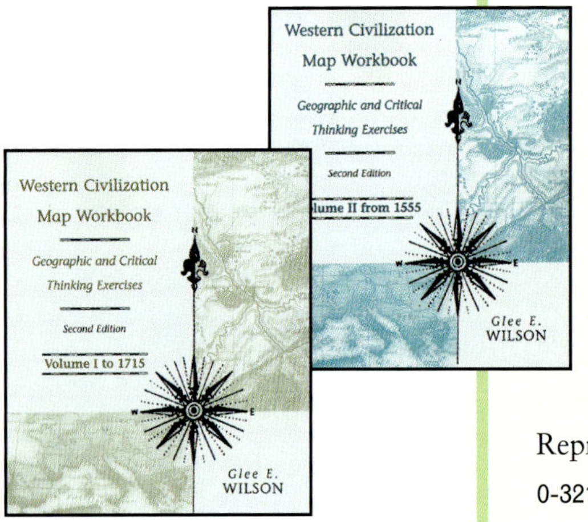

Western Civilization Map Workbooks

by Glee Wilson, *Kent State University*

Consists of two volumes that include map exercises and questions designed to test and establish geographic literacy and to build critical thinking skills.

Volume I: 0-321-01878-8; Volume II: 0-321-01877-X

Text-specific Map Overhead Transparencies

Representing maps from *Civilization in the West, 4/e.*

0-321-08150-1

If your students' study habits are poor...

Everything You Need to Know about Your History Course

by Sandra Mathews-Lamb, *Nebraska Wesleyan University*

Shows students how to become better history students. Provides direction on how to take good notes, how to write a paper, how to read maps, graphs, and charts, how to read primary and secondary source documents, and much more.

Free when bundled. 0-321-06628-6

The StudyWizard CD-ROM

by Paul Bischoff, *Oklahoma State University*

Helps students learn the major facts and concepts of Western Civilization through drill and practice exercises and diagnostic feedback. Provides students with individual, self-paced review of text material using multiple-choice, short-answer, and true/false questions, and detailed feedback.

Free when bundled. 0-321-08152-8

Study Guide

by Paul Bischoff, *Oklahoma State University*

Two volumes contain learning objectives, chapter overviews, and self-testing study questions for each chapter of the text.

Volume I: 0-321-08148-X; Volume II: 0-321-08147-1

Interactive Edition CD-ROM for *Civilization in the West, 4/e*

Includes a complete study guide.

Free when bundled. 0-321-08166-8

Researching Online, 4/e

by David Munger, Daniel Anderson, Bret Benjamin, Christopher Busiel and Bill Paredes-Holt

Practical, indispensable guide to the internet with a simple, step-by-step format that guides students through the array of possibilities and pitfalls that await them on the internet.

Free when bundled. 0-321-08408-X

If you are interested in primary and secondary source collections...

Sources of the West: Readings in Western Civilization, 4/e

by Mark Kishlansky

Presents a well-balanced selection of constitutional documents, political theory, philosophy, imaginative literature, and social description to raise significant issues for classroom discussions or lectures. By reading the voices of the past, students can connect them to the present; learn to understand and respect other cultures; and think critically about history. Includes the introductory essay "How to read a Document," designed to show students how to read, understand, and appreciate primary sources.

Volume I: 0-321-07677-X; Volume II: 0-321-07718-0

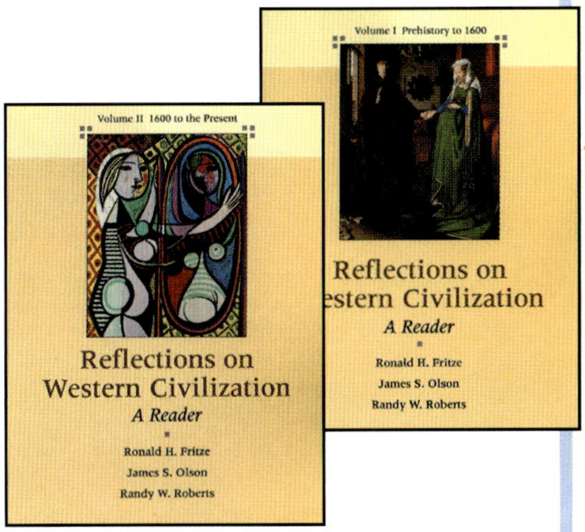

Reflections on Western Civilization

by Ronald Fritze, Randy Roberts, and James Olson

A collection of original documents and historical articles that explores European history from prehistory to the present, blending social, political, religious, and military history.

Volume I, Prehistory to 1600: 0-673-38403-9;

Volume II, 1600 to the Present: 0-673-38404-7

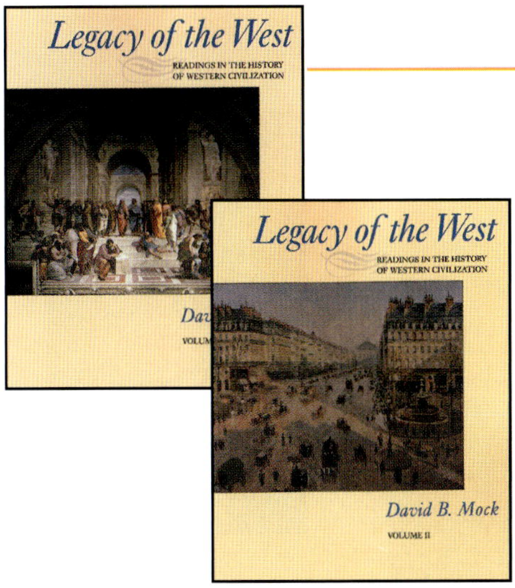

Legacy of the West

by David Mock

Immerses students in the works of those writers whose ideas contributed to the development of Western culture and institutions. Through its wide selection of readings, this collection shows how European history is directly tied to the heritage of Western civilization.

Volume I: 0-673-46999-9; Volume II: 0-673-99000-1

If you are interested in using Penguin paperbacks..

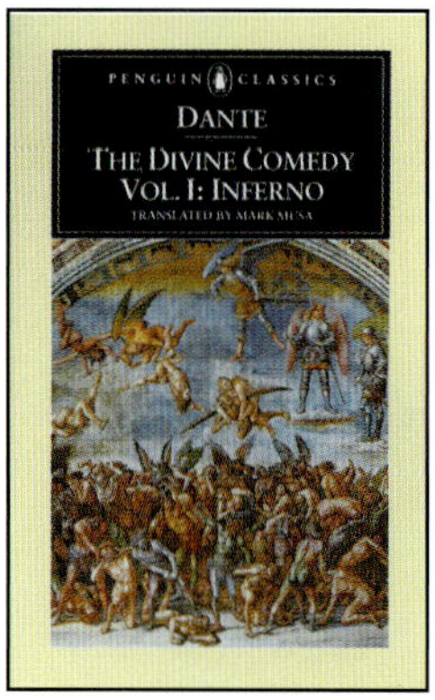

The partnership between Penguin Putnam Inc. and Longman offers your students a discount on the titles below when you bundle them with any Longman survey. The Penguin titles available are:

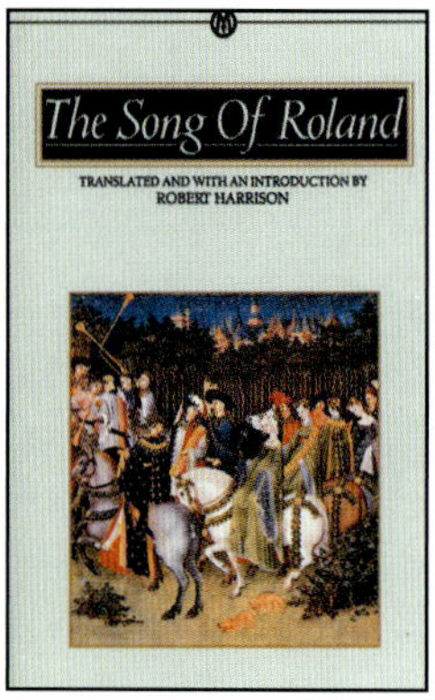

Anonymous, *The Song of Roland*
Dante, *The Divine Comedy: Vol I: Inferno*
Descartes, *Discourse on Method and the Meditations*
Machiavelli, *The Prince*
Marx and Engels, *The Communist Manifesto*
Mill, *On Liberty*
Orwell, *1984*
Plato, *The Republic*
Rousseau, *The Social Contract*
Solzhenitsyn, *One Day in the Life of Ivan Denisovich*
Tacitus, *The Histories*
Voltaire, *Candide, Zadig and Selected Stories*
Herodotus, *Herodotus: The Histories*
Benvenuto Cellini, *Benvenuto Cellini Autobiography*
Cervantes, *Don Quixote*
More, *Utopia*
Polo, *The Travels*
Dos Passos, Three Soldiers

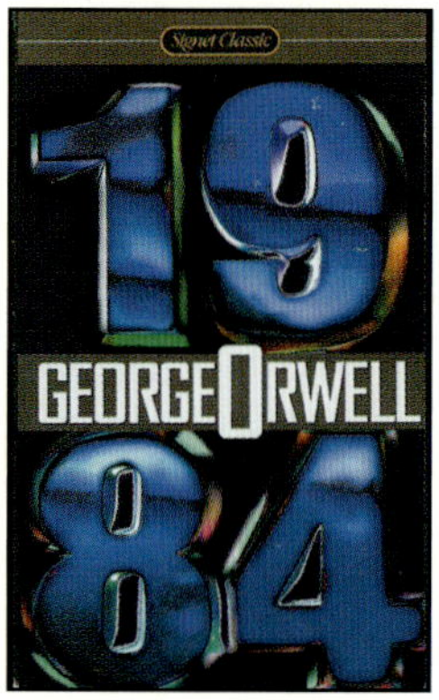

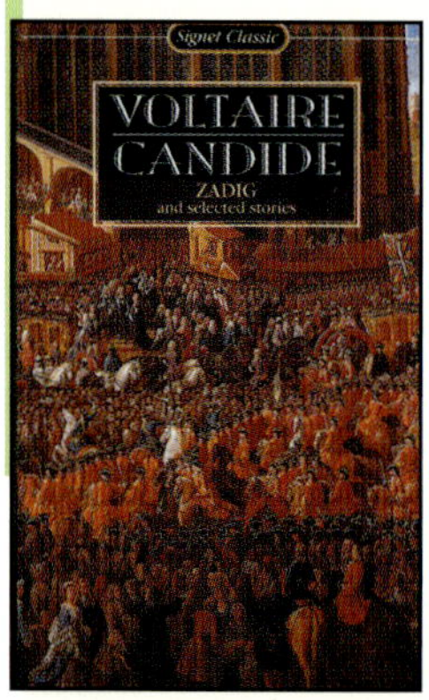

If you are interested in additional Instructor Resources...

Instructor's Manual

by David Mock, *Tallahassee Community College*

Contains chapter overviews, points for mastery, points for further discussion, and lecture supplements, making it a great tool for instructors.

0-321-08149-8

Test Bank

Provides professors with multiple choice, true/false, and essay questions that are keyed to topic, difficulty level, cognitive type, and relevant text page.

0-321-08146-3

TestGen CD-ROM

A flexible, easy-to-master computer test bank that includes all of the test items in the printed test bank and allows professors to edit existing questions and add their own items.

0-321-08154-4

CIVILIZATION IN THE WEST

FOURTH EDITION

VOLUME B: FROM 1350 TO 1850

MARK KISHLANSKY
HARVARD UNIVERSITY

PATRICK GEARY
UNIVERSITY OF CALIFORNIA, LOS ANGELES

PATRICIA O'BRIEN
UNIVERSITY OF CALIFORNIA, RIVERSIDE

Longman

New York San Francisco Boston
London Toronto Sydney Tokyo Singapore Madrid
Mexico City Munich Paris Cape Town Hong Kong Montreal

Publisher: Priscilla McGeehon
Development Manager: Lisa Pinto
Senior Development Editor: Dawn Groundwater
Executive Marketing Manager: Sue Westmoreland
Media Supplement Editor: Mark Toews
Supplement Editor: Jennifer Ackerman
Production Manager: Donna DeBenedictis
Project Coordination, Text Design, and Electronic Page Makeup: Elm Street Publishing Services, Inc.
Cover Designer/Manager: John Callahan
Cover Illustration: Goya Y Lucientes, *The Burial of the Sardine,* Real Academia de Bellas Artes de San Fernando, Madrid, Spain/Giraudon, Paris/Superstock
Photo Researcher: Jullie Chung/Photosearch, Inc.
Manufacturing Buyer: Al Dorsey
Printer and Binder: Quebecor World/Versailles
Cover Printer: The Lehigh Press, Inc.

For permission to use copyrighted material, grateful acknowledgment is made to the copyright holders on pp. C-1 to C-3, which are hereby made part of this copyright page.

Library of Congress Cataloging-in-Publication Data

Kishlansky, Mark A.
Civilization in the West / Mark Kishlansky, Patrick Geary, Patricia O'Brien.—4th ed.
p. cm.
Includes bibliographical references and index.
ISBN 0-321-06680-4 (single v.)—ISBN 0-321-07082-8 (p-copy)
1. Civilization, Western—History. I. Geary, Patrick J., 1948– II. O'Brien, Patricia, 1945– III. Title.

CB245.K546 2001
909'.09821—dc21

00-029962

Please visit our website at http://www.awl.com/Kishlansky

ISBN 0-321-06680-4 (single volume edition)
ISBN 0-321-07084-4 (volume I)
ISBN 0-321-07086-0 (volume II)
ISBN 0-321-07088-7 (volume A)
ISBN 0-321-07090-9 (volume B)
ISBN 0-321-07092-5 (volume C)

1 2 3 4 5 6 7 8 9 10—ARV—03 02 01 00

CONTENTS

Maps and Geographical Tours *viii*

Chronologies, Genealogies, and Figures *ix*

Documents *ix*

Supplements *x*

Preface *xi*

CHAPTER 11

THE ITALIAN RENAISSANCE *353*

A CIVIC PROCESSION *354*
RENAISSANCE SOCIETY *356*
- The Environment *356*
- Production and Consumption *358*
- The Experience of Life *359*
- The Quality of Life *362*

RENAISSANCE ART *364*
- An Architect, a Sculptor, and a Painter *364*
- Renaissance Style *367*
- Michelangelo *368*

RENAISSANCE IDEALS *370*
- Humanists and the Liberal Arts *371*
- Machiavelli and Politics *373*

THE POLITICS OF THE ITALIAN CITY-STATES *375*
- The Five Powers *376*
- Venice: A Seaborne Empire *377*
- Florence: Spinning Cloth into Gold *379*
- The End of Italian Hegemony, 1450–1527 *381*

QUESTIONS FOR REVIEW *386*
SUGGESTIONS FOR FURTHER READING *386*
DISCOVERING WESTERN CIVILIZATION ONLINE *387*

SPECIAL FEATURE
The Fall of Constantinople *382*

DOCUMENTS
- On the Family *361*
- The Renaissance Man *371*
- The Lion and the Fox *374*
- The Siege of Constantinople *384*

CHAPTER 12

THE EUROPEAN EMPIRES *388*

PTOLEMY'S WORLD *389*
EUROPEAN ENCOUNTERS *391*
- A Passage to India *391*
- *Mundus Novus* *393*
- The Spanish Conquests *397*
- The Legacy of the Encounters *400*

GEOGRAPHICAL TOUR
Europe in 1500 *403*
- Eastern Boundaries *404*
- Central Europe *405*
- The West *406*

THE FORMATION OF STATES *407*
- Eastern Configurations *408*
- The Western Powers *410*

THE DYNASTIC STRUGGLES *419*
- Power and Glory *419*
- The Italian Wars *420*

QUESTIONS FOR REVIEW *424*
SUGGESTIONS FOR FURTHER READING *424*
DISCOVERING WESTERN CIVILIZATION ONLINE *426*

SPECIAL FEATURE
Isabella of Castile *394*

DOCUMENTS
- A Momentous Discovery *396*
- The Halls of Montezuma *399*
- Last Words *412*
- The Kingdom of France *414*

CHAPTER 13

THE REFORM OF RELIGION 427

SOLA SCRIPTURA 428
THE INTELLECTUAL REFORMATION 430
- The Print Revolution 430
- Christian Humanism 431
- The Humanist Movement 432
- The Wit of Erasmus 433

THE LUTHERAN REFORMATION 435
- The Spark of Reform 435
- Martin Luther's Faith 437
- Lutheranism 439
- The Spread of Lutheranism 442

THE PROTESTANT REFORMATION 443
- Geneva and Calvin 444
- The English Reformation 446
- The Reformation of the Radicals 449

THE CATHOLIC REFORMATION 453
- The Spiritual Revival 453
- Loyola's Pilgrimage 456
- The Counter-Reformation 458
- The Empire Strikes Back 460

QUESTIONS FOR REVIEW 462
SUGGESTIONS FOR FURTHER READING 462
DISCOVERING WESTERN CIVILIZATION ONLINE 464

SPECIAL FEATURE
The Reformation and the War of the Common Man 450

DOCUMENTS
- A Dutch Wit 434
- Luther on Marriage 440
- The Eternal Decree 444
- Heavenly Vision 455

CHAPTER 14

EUROPE AT WAR, 1555–1648 465

THE MASSACRE OF THE INNOCENTS 466
THE CRISIS OF THE WESTERN STATES 468
- The French Wars of Religion 468
- One King, Two Faiths 472
- The World of Philip II 476
- The Burgundian Inheritance 477
- The Revolt of the Netherlands 480

THE STRUGGLES IN EASTERN EUROPE 483
- Kings and Diets in Poland 484
- Muscovy's Time of Troubles 485
- The Rise of Sweden 486

THE THIRTY YEARS' WAR, 1618–1648 489
- Bohemia Revolts 490
- The War Widens 491
- The Long Quest for Peace 495

QUESTIONS FOR REVIEW 497
SUGGESTIONS FOR FURTHER READING 497
DISCOVERING WESTERN CIVILIZATION ONLINE 499

SPECIAL FEATURE
The Monstrous Regiment of Women 470

DOCUMENTS
- Catholics and Huguenots 473
- Cannibals 480
- War Is Hell 490
- Fire and Sword 493

CHAPTER 15

THE EXPERIENCES OF LIFE IN EARLY MODERN EUROPE, 1500–1650 500

HAYMAKING 501
ECONOMIC LIFE 503
- Rural Life 503
- Town Life 507
- Economic Change 510

SOCIAL LIFE 513
- Social Constructs 514
- Social Structure 515
- Social Change 518
- Peasant Revolts 520

PRIVATE LIFE 523
- The Family 523
- Communities 527
- Popular Beliefs 530

QUESTIONS FOR REVIEW 536
SUGGESTIONS FOR FURTHER READING 536
DISCOVERING WESTERN CIVILIZATION ONLINE 538

SPECIAL FEATURE
Sex and the Married Man 532

DOCUMENTS
Living by One's Wits *505*
The Peasants' Revolt *522*
A Feminine Perspective *524*
The Devil's Due *531*

CHAPTER 16

THE ROYAL STATE IN THE SEVENTEENTH CENTURY *539*

FIT FOR A KING *540*
THE RISE OF THE ROYAL STATE *542*
Divine Kings *542*
The Court and the Courtiers *544*
The Drive to Centralize Government *546*
The Taxing Demands of War *548*
THE CRISES OF THE ROYAL STATE *550*
The Need to Resist *551*
The Right to Resist *553*
The English Civil War *556*
The English Revolutions *558*
THE ZENITH OF THE ROYAL STATE *563*
The Nature of Absolute Monarchy *564*
Absolutism in the East *566*
The Origins of French Absolutism *570*
Louis le Grand *571*
QUESTIONS FOR REVIEW *574*
SUGGESTIONS FOR FURTHER READING *574*
DISCOVERING WESTERN CIVILIZATION ONLINE *576*

SPECIAL FEATURE
"King Charles's Head" *560*

DOCUMENTS
A Glimpse of a King *544*
A Short, Sharp Shock *559*
Fathers Know Best *565*
A Close Shave *569*

CHAPTER 17

SCIENCE AND COMMERCE IN EARLY MODERN EUROPE *577*

REMBRANDT'S LESSONS *578*
THE NEW SCIENCE *580*
Heavenly Revolutions *580*
The Natural World *584*
Science Enthroned *590*
EMPIRES OF GOODS *592*
The Marketplace of the World *593*
Consumption Choices *595*
Dutch Masters *598*
Mercantile Organization *600*
THE WARS OF COMMERCE *604*
The Mercantile Wars *605*
The Wars of Louis XIV *606*
The Colonial Wars *610*
QUESTIONS FOR REVIEW *612*
SUGGESTIONS FOR FURTHER READING *612*
DISCOVERING WESTERN CIVILIZATION ONLINE *614*

SPECIAL FEATURE
The Trials of Galileo *586*

DOCUMENTS
Stargazing *582*
The Telescope *584*
Eastern Traders *602*
Defining Commerce *605*

CHAPTER 18

THE BALANCE OF POWER IN EIGHTEENTH-CENTURY EUROPE *615*

CALLING THE TUNE *616*
GEOGRAPHICAL TOUR
Europe in 1714 *618*
Expansion in the West *619*
Realignment in the East *623*
THE RISE OF RUSSIA *624*
The Reforms of Peter the Great *625*
Life in Rural Russia *626*
The Enlightened Empress Catherine *627*
THE TWO GERMANIES *632*
The Rise of Prussia *633*
Austria Survives *634*
The Politics of Power *637*
THE GREATNESS OF GREAT BRITAIN *640*
The British Constitution *640*
Parties and Ministers *642*
America Revolts *643*

QUESTIONS FOR REVIEW *646*
SUGGESTIONS FOR FURTHER READING *647*
DISCOVERING WESTERN CIVILIZATION ONLINE *648*

SPECIAL FEATURE
Catherine before She Was Great *628*

DOCUMENTS
Childhood Traumas *630*
A King's-Eye View *634*
Military Discipline *636*
Unalienable Rights *646*

CHAPTER 19

CULTURE AND SOCIETY IN EIGHTEENTH-CENTURY EUROPE *649*

HAPPY FAMILIES *650*
EIGHTEENTH-CENTURY CULTURE *652*
The Enlightenment *652*
The Spirit of the Enlightenment *653*
The Impact of the Enlightenment *659*
EIGHTEENTH-CENTURY SOCIETY *661*
The Nobility *661*
The Bourgeoisie *663*
The Masses *671*
QUESTIONS FOR REVIEW *682*
SUGGESTIONS FOR FURTHER READING *682*
DISCOVERING WESTERN CIVILIZATION ONLINE *684*

SPECIAL FEATURE
Giving Birth in the Eighteenth Century *672*

DOCUMENTS
The All-Knowing *653*
The Human Condition *655*
Of the People *657*
The Good of All *659*

CHAPTER 20

THE FRENCH REVOLUTION AND THE NAPOLEONIC ERA, 1789–1815 *685*

ADMIRING THE AMERICAN REVOLUTION *686*
THE CRISIS OF THE OLD REGIME IN FRANCE, 1715–1788 *688*
Louis XV's France *688*
Louis XVI and the National Debt *689*
The Three Estates *691*
THE FIRST STAGE OF THE FRENCH REVOLUTION, 1789–1792 *694*
Taking Politics to the People *694*
Convening the Estates-General *696*
The Storming of the Bastille *698*
The Revolution of the Peasantry *698*
Women on the March *700*
The Revolution Threatened *701*
EXPERIMENTING WITH DEMOCRACY: THE REVOLUTION'S SECOND STAGE, 1792–1799 *703*
Declaring Political Rights *703*
The Second Revolution: The Revolution of the People *704*
"Terror is the Order of the Day" *705*
The End of the Revolution *710*
THE REIGN OF NAPOLEON, 1799–1815 *711*
Bonaparte Seizes Power *711*
Napoleon at War with the European Powers *712*
The First Empire and Domestic Reforms *714*
Decline and Fall *716*
QUESTIONS FOR REVIEW *718*
SUGGESTIONS FOR FURTHER READING *718*
DISCOVERING WESTERN CIVILIZATION ONLINE *720*

SPECIAL FEATURE
The Guillotine and Revolutionary Justice *706*

DOCUMENTS
"What Is the Third Estate?" *697*
On Revolutionary Government *709*
The Civil Code of the *Code Napoléon* *715*

CHAPTER 21

INDUSTRIAL EUROPE *721*

PORTRAIT OF AN AGE *722*
THE TRADITIONAL ECONOMY *724*
Farming Families *724*
Rural Manufacture *726*
The Agricultural Revolution *728*
THE INDUSTRIAL REVOLUTION IN BRITAIN *731*

Britain First 732
Minerals and Metals 734
Cotton Is King 737
The Iron Horse 740
Entrepreneurs and Managers 744
The Wages of Progress 747
THE INDUSTRIALIZATION OF THE CONTINENT 752
Industrialization Without Revolution 753
Industrialization and Union 756
The Lands That Time Forgot 758
QUESTIONS FOR REVIEW 761
SUGGESTIONS FOR FURTHER READING 761
DISCOVERING WESTERN CIVILIZATION ONLINE 762

SPECIAL FEATURE
Industry and the Environment 748

DOCUMENTS
The Wealth of Britain 740
The Sin of Wages 746
Exploiting the Young 751
The Slavery of Labor 758

CHAPTER 22

POLITICAL UPHEAVALS AND SOCIAL TRANSFORMATIONS, 1815–1850 763

POTATO POLITICS 764

GEOGRAPHICAL TOUR
Europe in 1815 766
The Congress of Vienna 766
The Alliance System 771
THE NEW IDEOLOGIES 772
The New Politics of Preserving Order 772
Romanticism and Change 776
Reshaping State and Society 778
PROTEST AND REVOLUTION 782
Causes of Social Instability 782
The Revolutions of 1830 784
Reform in Great Britain 788
Workers Unite 789
Revolutions Across Europe, 1848–1850 792
QUESTIONS FOR REVIEW 797
SUGGESTIONS FOR FURTHER READING 797
DISCOVERING WESTERN CIVILIZATION ONLINE 799

SPECIAL FEATURE
The Birth of the Prison 774

DOCUMENTS
Young Italy (1832) 778
The Communist Manifesto 780
Flora Tristan and the Rights of Working Women 791

Credits C-1
Index I-1

MAPS AND GEOGRAPHICAL TOURS

Largest Cities in Western Europe, ca. 1500 *357*
Italy, 1494 *375*
Portuguese Explorations *391*
Voyages of Discovery and World Empires, 1550 *400*
Geographical Tour: Europe in 1500 *403*
  Eastern Europe *404*
  Central Europe *405*
  Western Europe *406*
The Unification of France *413*
The Travels of Ferdinand and Isabella *418*
The Italian Wars *421*
The Spread of Printing *430*
The Spread of Lutheranism *442*
Religious Divisions of Europe, ca. 1555 *461*
Religious Divisions in France *468*
The Habsburg Empire Under Philip II *476*
The Revolt of the Netherlands, 1555 *482*
The Revolt of the Netherlands, 1609 *482*
Eastern Europe, ca. 1550 *484*
The Rise of Russia *486*
The Rise of Sweden *487*
Population Loss in Germany During the Thirty Years' War *494*
The Peace of Westphalia, Europe, 1648 *495*
Grain Supply and Trade in Sixteenth-Century Europe *508*
Population Density in Europe, ca. 1600 *511*
Witchcraft Persecutions *535*
The English Civil War *557*
Russia Under Peter the Great *567*
Dutch Trade Routes, ca. 1650 *593*
France Under Louis XIV *606*
War of the Spanish Succession *609*
The Treaty of Utrecht, Europe 1714 *611*
The Seven Years' War *612*
Geographical Tour: Europe in 1714 *618*
  The Americas *619*
  India and the East Indies *620*
  Great Britain and the Low Countries *621*
  France and Spain *621*
  The Holy Roman Empire *622*
  Russia and Sweden *623*
The Expansion of Prussia *632*
The Partition of Poland *639*
The British Empire, ca. 1763 *644*
Cereal Crops *676*
Revolutionary France *695*
Napoleon's Empire *713*
Population Growth in Europe, 1800–1850 *725*
The European Linen Industry *729*
Great Britain: Canals and Navigable Rivers *732*
Great Britain: Coal and Iron Ore Deposits *734*
Great Britain: Textile Centers *738*
Great Britain: Railroads, ca. 1850 *742*
Great Britain: Manufacturing Centers *745*
The Industrial Revolution on the Continent *753*
Geographical Tour: Europe in 1815 *766*
  France *767*
  United Netherlands *767*
  Italian Peninsula *768*
  The German Confederation *769*
  Saxony *770*
  Poland *770*
Quadruple Alliance *771*
Holy Alliance *771*
Revolutions of 1830 and 1848 *793*

CHRONOLOGIES, GENEALOGIES, AND FIGURES

Chronology: The Reformation and the Counter-Reformation *459*
Genealogy: The House of Valois and Bourbon of France *474*
Chronology: The French Wars of Religion *475*
Genealogy: The Family of Charles V *479*
Chronology: Revolt of the Netherlands *483*
Genealogy: The Jagiellon Monarchy of Poland *485*
Genealogy: The House of Vasa of Sweden *488*
Chronology: The Thirty Years' War *494*
European Population Data *551*
War and Peace in Europe, 1598–1650 *563*
Genealogy: Tsars of Russia *566*
Epicycle and Eccentric Circles *581*
Tea Imports in England *596*
Genealogy: The Spanish Succession *608*
Chronology: The New European Powers *645*
Chronology: Major Works of the Enlightenment *661*
Chronology: The French Revolution *711*
Chronology: The Reign of Napoleon *716*
Yield Ratios for Grain Crops, 1400–1800 *731*
Chronology: The Alliance System *772*
Chronology: Protest and Revolution *796*

DOCUMENTS

On the Family *361*
The Renaissance Man *371*
The Lion and the Fox *374*
The Siege of Constantinople *384*
A Momentous Discovery *396*
The Halls of Montezuma *399*
Last Words *412*
The Kingdom of France *414*
A Dutch Wit *434*
Luther on Marriage *440*
The Eternal Decree *444*
Heavenly Vision *455*
Catholics and Huguenots *473*
Cannibals *480*
War Is Hell *490*
Fire and Sword *493*
Living by One's Wits *505*
The Peasant's Revolt *522*
A Feminine Perspective *524*
The Devil's Due *531*
A Glimpse of a King *544*
A Short, Sharp Shock *559*
Fathers Know Best *565*
A Close Shave *569*
Stargazing *582*
The Telescope *584*
Eastern Traders *602*
Defining Commerce *605*
Childhood Traumas *630*
A King's-Eye View *634*
Military Discipline *636*
Unalienable Rights *646*
The All-Knowing *653*
The Human Condition *655*
Of the People *657*
The Good of All *659*
"What Is the Third Estate?" *697*
On Revolutionary Government *709*
The Civil Code of the *Code Napoléon* *715*
The Wealth of Britain *740*
The Sin of Wages *746*
Exploiting the Young *751*
The Slavery of Labor *758*
Young Italy (1832) *778*
The Communist Manifesto *780*
Flora Tristan and the Rights of Working Women *791*

SUPPLEMENTS

FOR QUALIFIED COLLEGE ADOPTERS

Companion Website (*www.awl.com/Kishlansky*)

Instructors can take advantage of the online course companion that supports this text. The instructor section of the website includes portions of the instructor's manual, teaching links, downloadable images from the text, and Syllabus Builder, our comprehensive course management system.

Discovering Western Civilization through Maps and Views

Created by Gerald Danzer, University of Illinois at Chicago—the recipient of the American History Association's James Harvey Robinson Prize for his work in the development of map transparencies—and David Buissert, this set of 140 four-color acetates is a unique instructional tool. It contains an introduction on teaching history through maps and a detailed commentary on each transparency. The collection includes cartographic and pictorial maps, views and photos, urban plans, building diagrams, and works of art. Available to qualified college adopters.

Instructor's Resource Manual

Prepared by David B. Mock of Tallahassee Community College, this thorough Instructor's Manual includes an introductory essay on teaching Western civilization and a bibliographic essay on the use of primary sources for class discussion and analytical thinking. Each chapter contains a chapter summary, key terms, geographic and map items, and discussion questions.

Test Bank

Developed by John Paul Bischoff of Oklahoma State University, the Test Bank contains more than 1200 multiple-choice, matching, and completion questions. Multiple-choice items are referenced by topic, text page number, and type (factual or interpretive).

TestGen EQ Computerized Testing System

This flexible easy-to-master computerized testing system includes all of the test items in the printed test bank. The friendly interface allows instructors to easily edit, print, and expand item banks. Tests can be printed in several different formats and can include figures such as graphs and tables. Available for Windows and Macintosh computers.

Transparencies

This set of transparencies contains *all* the maps from the text, bound together with reproducible map exercises in a binder.

FOR STUDENTS

Companion Website (*www.awl.com/Kishlansky*)

The online course companion provides a wealth of resources for students using *Civilization in the West.* Students can access chapter summaries, practice test questions, web links for every chapter, interactive web activities, and more!

Interactive Edition CD-ROM for *Civilization in the West*

This unique CD-ROM take students beyond the printed page, offering them a complete multimedia learning experience. It contains the full text of the book on CD-ROM, with contextually placed media icons—audio, video, photos, figures, web links, practice tests, primary sources, and more—that link students to additional content directly related to key concepts in the text. FREE when packaged with the text.

StudyWizard Computerized Tutorial

Written by Paul Bischoff of Oklahoma State University, this interactive program helps students learn major facts and concepts through drill and practice exercises and diagnostic feedback. Available on dual platform CD-ROM and floppy disks, StudyWizard provides immediate correct answers and the text page number on which the material is discussed.

Study Guide

Compiled by John Paul Bischoff of Oklahoma State University, this Study Guide is available in two volumes and offers for each chapter a summary; a glossary list; map and geography questions; and identification, multiple-choice, and critical-thinking questions.

Western Civilization Map Workbooks

Prepared by Glee Wilson of Kent State University, these two volumes include map exercises designed to test and reinforce basic geographic literacy and to build critical thinking skills. Available shrink-wrapped at no cost with any Longman survey text.

Mapping Western Civilization: Student Activities

Written by Gerald Danzer of the University of Illinois at Chicago, this free map workbook for students is designed as an accompaniment to Discovering Western Civilization through Maps and Views. It features exercises designed to teach students to interpret and analyze cartographic materials as historical documents. The instructor is entitled to a free copy for each copy of the text purchased from Longman.

PREFACE

In planning *Civilization in the West,* our aim was to write a book that students would *want* to read. Throughout our years of planning, writing, revising, rewriting, and meeting together, this was our constant overriding concern. Would students read our book? Would it be effective in conveying information while stimulating the imagination? Would it work for a variety of Western civilization courses with different levels and formats? It was not easy to keep this concern in the forefront throughout the long months of composition, but it was easy to receive the reactions of scores of reviewers to this simple question: "Would students *want* to read these chapters?" Whenever we received a resounding "No!" we began again—not just rewriting, but rethinking how to present material that might be complex in argument or detail or that might simply seem too remote to engage the contemporary student. Although all three of us were putting in long hours in front of word processors, we quickly learned that we were engaged in a teaching rather than a writing exercise. And though the work was demanding, it was not unrewarding. We hope that you will recognize and come to share with us the excitement and enthusiasm we felt in creating this text. We have enjoyed writing it, and we want students to enjoy reading it.

Judging from the reactions to our first three editions, they have. We have received literally hundreds of cards and letters from adopters and users of *Civilization in the West.* The response has been both overwhelming and gratifying. It has also been constructive. Along with praise, we have received significant suggestions for making each subsequent edition stronger. Topics such as the Crusades, the Enlightenment, and imperialism have been reorganized to present them more clearly. Subjects such as the ancient Hebrews, Napoleon, and German unification have been given more space and emphasis. New features have been added to freshen the book and keep abreast of current scholarship, and more than 100 excerpts from primary sources are presented to give students a feel for the concreteness of the past. We believe that the fourth edition of *Civilization in the West* not only preserves the much-praised quality of its predecessors but also enhances it.

APPROACH

We made a number of decisions early in the project that we believed contributed to our goal. First, we were *not* writing an encyclopedia on Western civilization. Information was not to be included in a chapter unless it related to the themes of that chapter. There was to be no information for information's sake, and each of us was called upon to defend the inclusion of names, dates, and events whenever we met to critique one another's chapters. We found, to our surprise, that by adhering to the principle that information included must contribute to or illustrate a particular point or dominating theme, we provided as much, if not more, material than books that habitually list names, places, and dates without any other context.

Second, we were committed to integrating the history of ordinary men and women into our narrative. We believe that isolated sections, placed at the end of chapters, that deal with the experiences of women or minority groups in a particular era profoundly distort historical experience. We called this technique *cabooseing,* and whenever we found ourselves segregating women or families or the masses, we stepped back and asked how we might recast our treatment of historical events to account for a diversity of actors. How did ordinary men, women, and children affect the course of historical events? How did historical events affect the fabric of daily life for men and women and children from all walks of life? We tried to rethink critical historical problems of civilization as gendered phenomena. To assist us in the endeavor, we engaged two reviewers whose sole responsibility was to evaluate our chapters for the integration of those social groups into our discussion.

We took the same approach to the coverage of central and Eastern Europe that we did to women and minorities. Even before the epochal events of 1989 that returned this region to the forefront of international attention, we realized that in too many textbooks the Slavic world was treated as marginal to the history of Western civilization. Thus, with the help of a specialist reviewer, we worked to integrate more of the history of Eastern Europe into our text than is found in most others, and to do so in a way that presented the regions, their cultures and their institutions, as integral rather than peripheral to Western civilization.

To construct a book that students would *want* to read, we needed to develop fresh ideas about how to involve them with the material, how to transform them from passive recipients to active participants. We borrowed from computer science the concept of being "user-friendly." We wanted to find ways to stimulate the imagination of the student, and the more we experimented with different techniques, the more we realized that the most effective way to do this was visually. It is not true that contemporary students cannot be taught effectively by the written word; it is only true that they cannot be taught as effectively as they can by the combination of words and images. From the beginning, we realized that a text produced in full color was essential to the features we most wanted to use: the pictorial chapter openers; the large number of maps; the geographical tours of Europe at certain times in history; and the two-page special feature in every chapter, each with its own illustration.

FEATURES

It is hard to have a new idea when writing a textbook. So many authors have come before, each attempting to do something more effective, more innovative than his or her predecessor. However, we feel that the following features enhance students' understanding of Western civilization.

Pictorial Chapter Openers

It is probably the case that somewhere there has been a text that has used a chapter-opening feature similar to the one we use here. What we can say with certainty is that nothing else we experimented with, no other technique we attempted, has had such an immediate and positive impact on our readers or has so fulfilled our goal of involving the students in learning as our *pictorial chapter openers*. An illustration—a painting, a photograph, a picture, an artifact, an edifice—appears at the beginning of each chapter, accompanied by text through which we explore the picture, guiding students across a canvas or helping them see in an artifact or a piece of architecture details that are not immediately apparent. It is the direct combination of text and image that allows us to achieve this effect, to "unfold" both an illustration and a theme. In some chapters we highlight details, pulling out a section of the original picture to take a closer look. In others we attempt to shock the viewer into the recognition of horror or of beauty. Some chapter-opening images are designed to transport students back in time, to make them ask the question "What was it like to be there?" All of the opening images have been chosen to illustrate a dominant theme within the chapter, and the dramatic and lingering impression they make helps reinforce that theme.

Geographical Tours of Europe

We have taken a similar image-based approach to our *presentation of geography*. When teachers of Western civilization courses are surveyed, no single area of need is cited more often than that of geographical knowledge. Students simply have no mental image of Europe, no familiarity with those geophysical features that are a fundamental part of the geopolitical realties of Western history. We realized that maps, carefully planned and skillfully executed, would be an important component of our text. To complement the standard map program of the text, we have added a special geographical feature, the "Geographical Tours of Europe." Six times throughout the book, we pause in the narrative to take a tour of Europe. Sometimes we follow an emperor as he tours his realm; sometimes we examine the impact of a peace treaty; sometimes we follow the travels of a merchant. Whatever the thematic occasion, our intention is to guide the student around the changing contours of the geography of Western history. In order to do this effectively, we have worked with our cartographer to develop small, detailed maps to complement the overview map that appears at the beginning of each tour section. We know that only the most motivated students will turn back several pages to locate on a map a place mentioned in the text. Using small maps allows us to integrate maps directly into the relevant text, thus relieving students of the sometimes frustrating experience of attempting to locate not only a specific place on a map but perhaps even the relevant map itself. The great number of maps throughout the text, the specially designed tour-of-Europe geographical feature, and the ancillary programs of map transparencies and workbook exercises combine to provide the strongest possible program for teaching historical geography.

Special Feature Essays

The third technique we have employed to engage students with historical subjects is the two-page *special feature* that appears in each chapter. The special features focus on a single event or personality chosen to enhance the student's sense that history is something that is real and alive. The features are written more dramatically and sympathetically, with a greater sense of wonder than would be appropriate in the body of the text. The prose style and the accompanying illustration are designed to captivate the reader. To help the student relate personally and directly to a historical event, we have highlighted figures such as Hypatia of Alexandria, Isabella of Castile, and nineteenth-century Zimbabwe political heroes Nehanda and Kagubi.

Discovering Western Civilization Online

Fourth, *Discovering Western Civilization Online,* new to this edition, encourages students to further explore Western Civilization. These resources link students to documents, images, and cultural sites not currently included in the text.

Primary Sources

Finally, *Civilization in the West* contains selections from primary sources designed to stimulate students' interest in history by allowing them to hear the past speak in its own voice. We have tried to provide a mixture of "canonical" texts along with those illustrating the lives of ordinary people in order to demonstrate the variety of materials that form the building blocks of historical narrative. Each selection is accompanied by an explanatory headnote that identifies the author and work and provides the necessary historical context. Most of the extracts relate directly to discussion within the chapter, thus providing the student with a fuller understanding of a significant thinker or event.

CHANGES IN THE NEW EDITION

In the fourth edition, we have made significant changes in both content and pedagogical enhancements.

Content Changes

Chapter 22: Political Upheavals and Social Transformations, 1815–1850 was reorganized to present new ideologies before social instability and revolutions.

New pictorial essays were developed for the fourth edition as well. Chapter 20: The French Revolution and the Napoleonic Era opens with a pictorial on the admiration for the American Revolution.

New primary source documents were also added to this edition. Chapter 20 has two new documents on revolutionary government and the *Code Napoléon*; Chapter 22 includes a new document on Flora Tristan and the rights of working women.

Learning Enhancements

In an effort to respond to the latest developments in university education, we have developed a new feature that encourages students to continue learning about Western civilization through the vast World Wide Web. Located at the end of each chapter, *Discovering Western Civilization Online* prompts students to explore a particular topic or period and link it to specific documents, maps, or cultural sites not currently included in the text itself. A companion website, www.awl.com/Kishlansky, updates these resources as necessary.

To strengthen the map program, detailed annotations accompany both the standard maps and the Geographical Tours. Our goal was to create annotations that are more meaningful than standard captions, capturing for the reader significant points and major ideas about shifting borders, diffusions of cultural innovations and religions, wars and battles, and the impact of treaties.

To make the book more accessible to students, additional headings have been incorporated to allow easier comprehension and mastery of a chapter's main ideas. These headings create more compact segments on which students may concentrate and reinforce their ability to retain key information.

There are many new features in our text and much that is out of the ordinary. But there are important traditional aspects of the narrative itself that also require mention. *Civilization in the West* is a mainstream text in which most of our energies have been placed in developing a solid, readable narrative of Western civilization that integrates coverage of women and minorities into the discussion. We have highlighted personalities while identifying trends. We have spotlighted social history, both in sections of chapters and in separate chapters, while maintaining a firm grip on political developments. We hope that there are many things in this book that teachers of Western civilization will find valuable. But we also hope that there are things here with which you will disagree, themes that you can develop better, arguments and ideas that will stimulate you. A textbook is only one part of a course, and it is always less important than a teacher. What we hope is that by having done our job successfully, we will have made the teacher's job easier and the student's job more enjoyable.

ACKNOWLEDGMENTS

We want to thank the many conscientious historians who gave generously of their time and knowledge to review our manuscript. We would like to thank the reviewers of the first three editions as well as those of the current edition. Their valuable critiques and suggestions have contributed greatly to the final product. We are grateful to the following:

Achilles Aavraamides, *Iowa State University*; Meredith L. Adams, *Southwest Missouri State University*; Arthur H. Auten, *University of Hartford*; Suzanne Balch-Lindsay, *Eastern New Mexico University*; Sharon Bannister, *University of Findlay*; John W. Barker, *University of Wisconsin*; Patrick Bass, *Mount Union College*; William H. Beik, *Northern Illinois University*; Patrice Berger, *University of Nebraska*; Lenard R. Berlanstein, *University of Virginia*; Raymond Birn, *University of Oregon*; Donna Bohanan, *Auburn University*; Werner Braatz, *University of Wisconsin, Oshkosh*; Thomas A. Brady, Jr., *University of Oregon*; Anthony M. Brescia, *Nassau Community College*; Elaine G. Breslaw, *Morgan State University*; Ronald S. Brockway, *Regis University*; April Brooks, *South Dakota State University*; Daniel Patrick Brown, *Moorpark College*; Ronald A. Brown, *Charles County Community College*; Blaine T. Browne, *Broward Community College*; Kathleen S. Carter, *High Point University*; Robert Carver, *University of Missouri, Rolla*; Edward J. Champlin, *Princeton University*; Stephanie Evans Christelow, *Western Washington University*; Sister Dorita Clifford, BVM, *University of San Francisco*; Gary B. Cohen, *University of Oklahoma*; Jan M. Copes, *Cleveland State University*; John J. Contreni, *Purdue University*; Tim Crain, *University of Wisconsin, Stout*; Norman Delaney, *Del Mar College*; Samuel E. Dicks, *Emporia State University*; Frederick Dumin, *Washington State University*; Laird Easton, *California State University, Chico*; Dianne E. Farrell, *Moorhead State University*; Margot C. Finn, *Emory University*; Allan W. Fletcher, *Boise State University*; Elizabeth L. Furdell, *University of North Florida*; Thomas W. Gallant, *University of Florida*; Frank Garosi, *California State University, Sacramento*; Lorne E. Glaim, *Pacific Union College*; Joseph J. Godson, *Hudson Valley Community College*; Sue Helder Goliber, *Mount St. Mary's College*; Manuel G. Gonzales, *Diablo Valley College*; Louis Haas, *Duquesne University*; Eric Haines, *Bellevue Community College*; Paul Halliday, *University of Virginia;* Margaretta S. Handke, *Mankato State University*; David A. Harnett, *University of San Francisco*; Paul B. Harvey, Jr., *Pennsylvania State University*; Neil Heyman, *San Diego State University*; Daniel W. Hollis, *Jacksonville State University*; Kenneth G. Holum, *University of Maryland*; Patricia Howe, *University of St. Thomas;* David Hudson, *California State University, Fresno;* Charles Ingrao, *Purdue University*; George F. Jewsbury, *Oklahoma State University*; Donald G. Jones, *University of Central Arkansas*; William R. Jones, *University of New Hampshire*; Richard W. Kaeuper, *University of Rochester*; David Kaiser, *Carnegie-Mellon University*; Jeff Kaufmann, *Muscatine Community College*; Carolyn Kay, *Trent University*; William R. Keylor, *Boston University*; Joseph Kicklighter, *Auburn University*; Charles L. Killinger, III, *Valencia Community College*; Alan M. Kirshner, *Ohlone College*; Alexandra Korros, *Xavier University*; Cynthia Kosso, *Northern Arizona University*; Lisa M. Lane, *Mira Costa College*; David C. Large, *Montana State University*; Bryan LeBeau, *Creighton University*; Donna J. Maier, *University of Northern Iowa*; Margaret Malamud, *New Mexico State University*; Roberta T. Manning, *Boston College*; Lyle McAlister, *University of Florida*; Therese M. McBride, *College of the Holy Cross*; David K. McQuilkin, *Bridgewater College*; Victor V. Minasian, *College of Marin*; David B. Mock, *Tallahassee Community College*; Robert Moeller, *University of California, Irvine*; Pierce C. Mullen, *Montana State University*; John A. Nichols, *Slippery Rock University*; Thomas F. X. Noble, *University of Virginia*; Bruce K. O'Brien, *Mary Washington College*; Dennis H. O'Brien, *West Virginia University*; Maura O'Connor, *University of Cincinnati*; Richard A. Oehling, *Assumption College*; James H. Overfield, *University of Vermont*; Catherine Patterson, *University of Houston*; Sue Patrick, *University of Wisconsin, Barron County*; Peter C. Piccillo, *Rhode Island College*; Peter O'M. Pierson, *Santa Clara University*; Theophilus Prousis, *University of North Florida*; Marlette Rebhorn, *Austin Community College*; Jack B. Ridley, *University of Missouri, Rolla*; Constance M. Rousseau, *Providence College*; Thomas J. Runyan, *Cleveland State University*; John P. Ryan, *Kansas City Community*

College; Joanne Schneider, *Rhode Island College*; Steven Schroeder, *Indiana University of Pennsylvania*; Steven C. Seyer, *Lehigh County Community College*; Lixin Shao, *University of Minnesota, Duluth*; George H. Shriver, *Georgia Southern University*; Ellen J. Skinner, *Pace University*; Bonnie Smith, *University of Rochester*; Patrick Smith, *Broward Community College*; James Smither, *Grand Valley State University*; Sherill Spaar, *East Central University*; Charles R. Sullivan, *University of Dallas*; Peter N. Stearns, *Carnegie-Mellon University*; Saulius Suziedelis, *Millersville University*; Darryl B. Sycher, *Columbus State Community College*; Roger Tate, *Somerset Community College*; Donna L. Van Raaphorst, *Cuyahoga Community College*; James Vanstone, *John Abbot College*; Steven Vincent, *North Carolina State University*; Richard A. Voeltz, *Cameron University*; Faith Wallis, *McGill University*; Eric Weissman, *Golden West College*

Each author also received invaluable assistance and encouragement from many colleagues, friends, and family members over the years of research, reflection, writing, and revising that went into the making of this text.

Mark Kishlansky thanks Ann Adams, Robert Bartlett, Ray Birn, David Buisseret, Ted Cook, Frank Conaway, Constantine Fasolt, James Hankins, Katherine Haskins, Richard Hellie, Matthew Kishlansky, Donna Marder, Mary Beth Rose, Victor Stater, Jeanne Thiel, and the staffs of the Joseph Regenstein Library, the Newberry Library, and the Widener and Lamont Libraries at Harvard.

Patrick Geary wishes to thank Mary, Catherine, and Anne Geary for their patience, support, and encouragement; he also thanks Anne Picard, Dale Schofield, Hans Hummer, and Richard Mowrer for their able assistance throughout the project.

Patricia O'Brien thanks Elizabeth Sagias for her encouragement and enthusiasm throughout the project and Robert Moeller for his keen eye for organization and his suggestions for writing a gendered history.

All the authors thank Dawn Groundwater, development editor, and Ginger Yarrow, project editor at Elm Street Publishing Services, Inc., for producing a beautiful book.

Mark Kishlansky
Patrick Geary
Patricia O'Brien

CHAPTER

11 THE ITALIAN RENAISSANCE

- A CIVIC PROCESSION
- RENAISSANCE SOCIETY
  - The Environment
  - Production and Consumption
  - The Experience of Life
  - The Quality of Life
- RENAISSANCE ART
  - An Architect, a Sculptor, and a Painter
  - Renaissance Style
  - Michelangelo
- RENAISSANCE IDEALS
  - Humanists and the Liberal Arts
  - Machiavelli and Politics
- THE POLITICS OF THE ITALIAN CITY-STATES
  - The Five Powers
  - Venice: A Seaborne Empire
  - Florence: Spinning Cloth into Gold
  - The End of Italian Hegemony, 1450–1527

A Civic Procession

IT IS 25 APRIL 1444, the day Venice celebrates its patron, Saint Mark, with a procession through the square that bears his name. Processions are a common form of civic ritual by which a community defines itself. The special features that identify Venice for its citizens are all on display. City flags and emblems are mounted on poles, and clothes bear the insignia of various orders and groups. The procession recreates all forms of communal life. Here are the religious orders (the white-clad brothers of the Confraternity of Saint John are passing before us now), and the civic leaders can be seen just behind them. Musicians entertain both marchers and onlookers. A band files by on the right. The procession is orderly, but it is by no means contrived. It is not staged, as would be a modern ceremony, and this is evident in the relaxed attitude of ordinary citizens who gather in the middle of the square. There is no apparent drama to observe, and they walk and talk quite naturally. So, too, do the participants. In the lower left-hand corner of the painting shown here, some friars are reading music; at the lower right, members of the confraternity carry their candles negligently.

Yet this painting, *The Procession of the Relic of the Holy Cross* (1496) by Gentile Bellini (ca. 1429–1507), was commissioned to commemorate a miracle rather than a civic procession. On the evening before Saint Mark's day, a visiting merchant and his son were touring the square when the boy fell and cracked his skull. The doctors who treated him regarded the case as hopeless and prepared the father for his son's

death. The next morning, the Brothers of the Confraternity of Saint John paraded their relic of a piece of the cross on which Jesus was crucified. The merchant approached the golden altarpiece containing the relic, dropped to his knees, and prayed that Saint Mark would miraculously cure his son. He is the red-clad figure kneeling just to the right of center, where the line of brothers breaks. The next day the boy revived.

The Brothers of Saint John commissioned Bellini to commemorate the event. He came from the most distinguished family of painters in Venice. His father, Jacopo, had studied in Florence and had brought his sons into his workshop as young boys. Until the age of thirty, Gentile worked on his father's commissions, learning the difficult craft of painting. Art was a family business in fifteenth-century Italy. The large workshops, with their master and apprentices, turned out vast canvasses with assembly-line precision. The master created the composition and sketched it; his skilled assistants, like the Bellini brothers, worked on the more complex parts; and young apprentices painted backgrounds. The master was first and foremost a businessman, gaining commissions to sustain his family and his workers. The Bellinis were connected to the Confraternity of Saint John, and it was only natural that Gentile would receive the lucrative contract.

Although *The Procession of the Relic of the Holy Cross* was designed to recreate a central moment in the history of the confraternity, it is not the confraternity that dominates the picture. Miracles were part of civic life, and each town took pride in the special manifestations of heavenly care that had taken place within it. Thus it is Venice that is the centerpiece of Bellini's canvas. Dominating the painting is the Basilica of San Marco, with its four great horses over the center portico and the winged lion—the city's symbol—on the canopy above. The procession emanates from the duke's palace to the right of the church, and the great flags of the city are seen everywhere. By the end of the fifteenth century, Venice was one of the greatest powers on earth, the center for international trade and finance. Home to the largest concentration of wealthy families anywhere in Europe, it could well afford the pomp and splendor of its processions. The achievements of God and the achievements of humans blend together in this painting as they blended together in that era of remarkable accomplishments that historians call the Renaissance.

RENAISSANCE SOCIETY

Perhaps the most surprising result of the Black Death was the way in which European society revived itself in the succeeding centuries. Even at the height of the plague, a spirit of revitalization was evident in the works of artists and writers. Petrarch (1304–1374), the great humanist poet and scholar, was among the first to differentiate the new age in which he was living from two earlier ones: the classical world of Greece and Rome, which he admired, and the subsequent Dark Ages, which he detested. That spirit of self-awareness is one of the defining characteristics of the Renaissance. "It is but in our own day that men dare boast that they see the dawn of better things," wrote Matteo Palmieri (1406–1475). Like many others, Marsilio Ficino (1433–1499), a Florentine physician and philosopher who translated Plato and dabbled in astrology, dubbed his times a golden age: "This century, like a golden age, has restored to light the liberal arts, which were almost extinct: grammar, poetry, rhetoric, painting, sculpture, architecture, and music." The Renaissance was a new age by self-assertion. In that self-assertion, wave after wave of artistic celebration of the human spirit found its wellspring and created a legacy that is still vibrant 500 years later.

What was the Renaissance? A French word for an Italian phenomenon, *renaissance* literally means "rebirth." The word captures both the emphasis on humanity that characterized Renaissance thinking and the renewed fascination with the classical world. But the Renaissance was an age rather than an event. There is no moment at which the Middle Ages ended, and late medieval society was artistically creative, socially well developed, and economically diverse. Yet eventually the pace of change accelerated, and it is best to think of the Renaissance as an era of rapid transitions. Encompassing the two centuries between 1350 and 1550, it passed through three distinct phases. The first, from 1350 to 1400, was characterized by a declining population, the uncovering of classical texts, and experimentation in a variety of art forms. The second phase, from 1400 to 1500, was distinguished by the creation of a set of cultural values and artistic and literary achievements that defined Renaissance style. The large Italian city-states developed stable and coherent forms of government, and the warfare between them gradually ended. In the final period, from 1500 to 1550, invasions from France and Spain transformed Italian political life, and the ideas and techniques of Italian writers and artists radiated to all points of the Continent. Renaissance ideas and achievements spread throughout western Europe and were particularly important in Holland, but they are best studied where they first developed, on the Italian peninsula.

The Environment

The Italian peninsula differed sharply from other areas of Europe in the extent to which it was urban. By the late Middle Ages nearly one in four Italians lived in a town, in contrast to one in ten elsewhere. Not even the plague did much to change that ratio. There were more Italian cities and more people in them. By 1500, seven of the ten largest cities in the West were in Italy. Naples, Venice, and Milan, each with a population of more than 100,000, led the rest. But not every city was a great metropolis, and it was the numerous smaller towns, with populations nearer to 1000, that gave the Italian peninsula its urban character. Cities also served as convenient centers of judicial and ecclesiastical power.

Cities acted as central places around which a cluster of large and small villages was organized. Urban areas, especially the small towns, provided markets for the agricultural produce of the countryside and for the manufactured goods of the urban artisans. It was in the cities that goods and services changed hands. This allowed for the specialization in agricultural and industrial life that increased both productivity and wages. Cities also caught the runoff of rural population, especially the surplus of younger sons and daughters who could not be accommodated on the farms. Cities grew by migration rather than by natural increase, and immigrants flooded into them. Thus the areas surrounding a city were critical to its prosperity and survival. The urban system was a network of cities encompassed by towns and encircled by rural villages. Florence, the dominant city in the region of Tuscany, exemplifies that relationship. Although it possessed two-thirds of its region's wealth, Florence contained only 14 percent of the regional population. The surrounding countryside was agriculturally rich because marketing costs were low and demand for foodstuffs was high. Smaller cities channeled their local produce and trade to Florence.

Although cities may have dominated Renaissance Italy, by present standards they were small in both area and population. Despite the city's wealth, great banks,

Largest Cities in Western Europe, ca. 1500. There were as many large cities in the Italian peninsula as in all of the rest of Western Europe.

magnificent palaces, and piazzas, a person could walk across fifteenth-century Florence in less than half an hour. In 1427 its population was 37,000, only half its pre-plague size. Most Italian cities contained large fields for agricultural production, and within the outer walls of Florence were gardens and fields of grain. Inside the inner city walls the people crowded together into tightly packed quarters. The intensity of the stench from raw sewage, rotting foodstuffs, and animals being brought to slaughter was equaled only by the din made by hoofs and wooden cartwheels on paving stones.

Urban populations were organized far differently from rural ones. On the farms, the central distinctions involved ownership of land. Some farmers owned their estates outright and left them intact to their heirs. Others were involved in a sharecropping system by which absentee owners of land supplied working capital in return for half of the farm's produce. A great gulf in wealth separated owners from sharecroppers, but within the groups the gaps were not as great. There were gradations, but those ordinarily were temporary conditions that bad harvests, generous dowries, or divided inheritances balanced out over time.

In the city, however, distinctions were based first on occupation, which largely corresponded to social position and wealth. Cities began as markets, and the privilege to participate in the market defined citizens. City governments provided protection for consumers and producers by creating monopolies through which standards for craftsmanship were maintained and profits for craftsmen were guaranteed. The monopolies were called guilds or companies. Each large city had its own hierarchy of guilds. At the top were the important manufacturing groups—clothiers, metalworkers, and the like. Just below them were bankers, merchants, and the administrators of civic and Church holdings. At the bottom were grocers, masons, and other skilled workers. Roughly speaking, all of those within the guild structure, from bottom to top, lived comfortably. Yet the majority of urban inhabitants were not members of guilds. Many managed to eke out a living as wage laborers; many more were simply destitute. As a group, the poor constituted as much as half of the entire population. Most were dependent upon civic and private charity for their survival.

The disparities between rich and poor were overwhelming. The concentration of wealth in the hands of an ever-narrowing group of families and favored guilds characterized every large city. One reason for that was the extreme instability of economic life. Prices and wages fluctuated wildly in response to local circumstance. After an epidemic of plague, wages climbed and the prices of consumer goods tumbled. A bad harvest sent food prices skyrocketing. Only those able to even out the extreme swings by stockpiling goods in times of plenty and consuming them in times of want were safe. Capital, however initially accumulated, was the key to continued wealth. Monopolies ensured the profitability of trade and manufacturing, but only those with sufficient capital could engage in either. In Florence, for example, 10 percent of the families controlled 90 percent of the wealth, with an even more extreme concentration at the top. The combined wealth of the richest 100 Florentine families was greater than the combined wealth of 87 percent of the city's population.

Cloth making was a major contributor to European economic growth during the Middle Ages. In this 1470 portrait of Cloth Merchants' Street in Bologna, a tailor (center) measures a prospective client.

Production and Consumption

The concentration of wealth and the way in which it was used defined Renaissance economy. Economic life is bound up in the relationship between resources and desires, or, as economists would have it, supply and demand. The late medieval economy, despite the development of international banking and long-distance trade, was still an economy of primary producers: between 70 and 90 percent of Europe's population was involved in subsistence agriculture. Even in Italy, which contained the greatest concentration of urban areas in the world, agriculture predominated. The manufacture of clothing was the only other significant economic activity. Moreover, most of what was produced was for local consumption rather than for the marketplace. The relationship between supply and demand was precisely measured by the full or empty stomach. Even in good times, more than 80 percent of the population lived at subsistence level with food, clothing, and shelter their only expenses. Thus, when the market economy of the Renaissance is discussed, it actually is the circumstances of the few rather than the many that is under discussion.

The defining characteristic of the early Renaissance economy was population change. Recurring waves of plague kept population levels low for more than a century. Between 1350 and 1450, one in every six years was characterized by an unusually high mortality rate. At the end of that period, for example, Florence's population was only a quarter of what it had been at the beginning. The dramatic reduction in population depressed economic growth. Until 1460 the major sectors of the economy were stagnant. The general economy did not revive until the sustained population increase toward the end of the fifteenth century. Until then, in both agriculture and manufacturing, supply outstripped demand.

On the farms, overabundance resulted from two related developments, the concentration of surviving farmers on the best land and the enlargement of their holdings. In the shops, finished products outnumbered the consumers who survived the epidemics. Overproduction meant lower prices for basic commodities, and the decline in population meant higher wages for labor. The result was that, at the lowest levels of society, survivors found it easier to earn their living and even to create a surplus than had their parents. For a time, the lot of the masses improved.

But for investors, such economic conditions meant that neither agriculture nor cloth making were particularly attractive. Expensive investments in land or equipment for sharecropping were paid back in inexpensive grain. High wages for the few surviving skilled workers brought a return only in cheap cloth. In such circumstances, consumption was more attractive than investment. It was not merely the perceived shortage in profitable investments that brought on the increase in conspicuous consumption during the fifteenth century. In the psychological atmosphere created by unpredictable, swift, and deadly epidemics, luxurious living seemed an appropriate response. Moreover, although tax rates increased, houses and personal property remained exempt, making luxury goods attractive investments. Even those at the lowest levels of society eagerly purchased whatever their meager means permitted.

For those reasons, the production and consumption of luxuries soared. By the middle of the fourteenth century, Florence was known for its silks and jewelry as much as for its cloth. Venice became a European center for the glass industry, especially for the finely ground glass that was used in eyeglasses. Production of specialty crops such as sugar, saffron, fruits, and high-quality wine expanded. International trade increasingly centered on acquiring Eastern specialities, resulting in the serious outflow of gold and silver that enriched first the Byzantine and then the Ottoman emperors.

The Experience of Life

Luxury helped improve a life that for rich and poor alike was short and uncertain. Nature was still people's most potent enemy. Renaissance children who survived infancy found their lives governed by parentage and by gender. In parentage, the great divide was between those who lived with surplus and those who lived at subsistence. The first category encompassed the wealthiest bankers and merchants down to those who owned their own farms or engaged in small urban crafts. The vast majority of urban and rural dwellers comprised the second category. About the children of the poor we know very little other than that their survival was unlikely. If they did not die at birth or shortly afterward, they might be abandoned—especially if female—to the growing number of orphanages in the cities, waste away from lack of nutrition, or fall prey to ordinary childhood diseases for which there were no treatments. Eldest sons were favored; younger daughters were disadvantaged. In poor families, however, this favoritism meant little more than early apprenticeship to day labor in the city or farm labor in the countryside. Girls were frequently sent out as domestic servants far from the family home.

Childhood. Children of the wealthy had better chances for survival than did children of the poor. For children of the wealthy, childhood might begin with "milk parents," life in the home of the family of a wet nurse who would breast-feed the baby through infancy. Only the very wealthy could afford a live-in wet nurse, which would increase the child's chances of survival. Again, daughters were more likely to be sent far from home and least likely to have their nursing supervised. The use of wet nurses not only emancipated parents from the daily care of infants, it also allowed them to resume sexual relations. Nursing women refrained from sex in the belief that it affected their milk.

During the period between weaning and apprenticeship, Renaissance children lived with their families. There was no typical Renaissance family. Nuclear families—parents and their children under one roof—were probably more common than extended families, which might include grandparents and other relatives. But the composition of the family changed over the course of the life cycle and included times in which married children or grandparents were present and other times when a single parent and small children were the only members. Moreover, even nuclear families commonly contained stepparents and stepchildren as well as domestic servants or apprentices. Thus a child returning to the parental household was as likely to form emotional bonds with older siblings as with parents.

The family was an economic unit as well as a grouping of relatives. Decisions to abandon children, to send them away from the household when very young, or to take in domestic servants were based on economic calculations. In the competition for scarce resources, the way in which children were managed might determine the survival of the family unit. Sons could expect to be apprenticed to a trade, probably between the ages of 10 and 13. Most, of course, learned the crafts of their fathers, but not necessarily in their father's shop. By adolescence those fortunate boys, who might have had some rudimentary schooling, were earning token wages that contributed to family income. Sons inherited the family business and its most important possessions—tools of the trade or beasts of labor for the farm. Inheritance customs varied. In some places only the eldest son received the equipment of the family occupation; in others, such as Tuscany, all the sons shared it. Still, in the first 15 years of life, the most-favored children would have spent between one-third and one-half of their time outside the household in which they had been born.

Old Man with a Child *by the Florentine painter Domenico del Ghirlandaio (1449–1494).*

Marriage and the Family. Expectations for daughters centered on their chances of marriage. For a girl, dowry was everything. If a girl's father could provide a handsome one, her future was secure; if not, the alternatives were a convent, which would take a small bequest, or a match lower down the social scale, where the quality of life deteriorated rapidly. Daughters of poor families entered domestic service in order to have a dowry provided by their masters. The dowry was taken to the household of the husband. There the couple resided until they established their own separate family. If the husband died, it was to his parental household that the widow returned.

Women married in late adolescence, usually around the age of 20. Among the wealthy, marriages were perceived as familial alliances and business transactions rather than love matches. The dowry was an investment on which fathers expected a return, and while the bride might have some choice, it was severely limited. Compatibility was not a central feature in matchmaking. Husbands were, on average, ten years older than their wives and likely to leave them widows. In the early fifteenth century, about one-fourth of all adult women in Florence were widows, many without prospects of remarriage.

Married women lived in a state of nearly constant pregnancy. Alessandra Strozzi, whose father was one of the wealthiest citizens of Florence, married at the age of 16, gave birth to eight children in ten years, and was widowed at the age of 25. Not all pregnancies produced children. The rates of miscarriages and stillbirths were very high, and abortions and infanticide were not unknown. Only among the families who hovered between surplus and subsistence is there any evidence of attempts to control pregnancies. The efforts, which relied upon techniques such as the rhythm method and withdrawal, were not particularly effective. The rhythm method was especially futile because of the misunderstanding of the role of women in conception. It was not yet known that the woman contained an egg that was fertilized during conception. Without this knowledge it was impossible to understand the cycle of ovulation. Practically speaking, family size was limited

ON THE FAMILY

Leon Battista Alberti wrote a number of important tracts that set out the general principles of a subject, including On Architecture, *which was considered the basic text for 300 years. His writings on the family bring insight into the nature of a patriarchal, male-dominated institution.*

THEY SAY THAT IN CHOOSING A WIFE ONE LOOKS FOR BEAUTY, parentage, and riches.... Among the most essential criteria of beauty in a woman is an honorable manner. Even a wild, prodigal, greasy, drunken woman may be beautiful of feature, but no one would call her a beautiful wife. A woman worthy of praise must show first of all in her conduct, modesty, and purity. Marius, the illustrious Roman, said in that first speech of his to the Roman people: "Of women we require purity, of men labor." And I certainly agree. There is nothing more disgusting than a coarse and dirty woman. Who is stupid enough not to see clearly that a woman who does not care for neatness and cleanliness in her appearance, not only in her dress and body but in all her behavior and language, is by no means well mannered? How can it be anything but obvious that a bad-mannered woman is also rarely virtuous? We shall consider elsewhere the harm that comes to a family from women who lack virtue, for I myself do not know which is the worse fate for a family, total celibacy or a single dishonored woman. In a bride, therefore, a man must first seek beauty of mind, that is, good conduct and virtue.

In her body he must seek not only loveliness, grace, and charm but must also choose a woman who is well made for bearing children, with the kind of constitution that promises to make them strong and big. There's an old proverb, "When you pick your wife, you choose your children." All her virtues will in fact shine brighter still in beautiful children. It is a well-known saying among poets: "Beautiful character dwells in a beautiful body." The natural philosophers require that a woman be neither thin nor very fat. Those laden with fat are subject to coldness and constipation and slow to conceive. They say that a woman should have a joyful nature, fresh and lively in her blood and her whole being. They have no objections to a dark girl. They do reject girls with a frowning black visage, however. They have no liking for either the undersized or the overlarge and lean. They find that a woman is most suited to bear children if she is fairly big and has limbs of ample length. They always have a preference for youth, based on a number of arguments which I need not expound here, but particularly on the point that a young girl has a more adaptable mind. Young girls are pure by virtue of their age and have not developed any spitefulness. They are by nature modest and free of vice. They quickly learn to accept affectionately and unresistingly the habits and wishes of their husbands.

From Leon Battista Alberti, *On the Family*.

on the one end by late marriages and on the other by early deaths.

Life experiences differed for males. Men married later—near the age of 25 on the farms, nearer the age of 30 in the cities—because of the cost of setting up in trade or on the land. Late marriage meant long supervision under the watchful eye of father or master, an extended period between adolescence and adulthood. The reputation that Renaissance cities gained for homosexuality and licentiousness must be viewed in light of the advanced age at which males married. The level of sexual frustration was high, and its outlet in ritual violence and rape was also high.

The establishment of one's own household through marriage was a late rite of passage, considering the expectations of early death. Many men, even those with families, never succeeded in setting up separately from their fathers or elder brothers. Men came of age at 30 but were thought to be old by 50. Thus for men marriage and parenthood took place in middle age rather than in youth. Valued all their lives more highly than their sisters, male heads of households were the source of all power in their domiciles, in their shops, and in the state. They were responsible for overseeing every aspect of the upbringing of their children, even choosing wet nurses for their infants and spouses for their daughters. But their wives were essential partners who governed domestic life. Women labored not only at the hearth, but in the fields and shops as well. Their economic contribution to the well-being of the family was critical, both in the dowry they brought at marriage and in the labor they contributed to the household. If their wives died, men with young children remarried quickly. While there were many bachelors, there were few widowers.

In most cases death came suddenly. Epidemic diseases, of which plague was the most virulent, struck with fearful regularity. Even in the absence of a serious outbreak, there were always deaths in town and country attributable to the plague. Epidemics struck harder at the young—children and adolescents, who were the majority of the population—and hardest in the summer months, when other viruses and bacteria weakened the population. Influenza must have been the second largest cause of death, although that can only be speculated in the absence of proper records. Medical treatment was more likely to hasten death than to prolong life. Lorenzo de' Medici's physician prescribed powdered pearls for the Florentine ruler's gout. After that Lorenzo complained more of stomach pains than of gout. Marsilio Ficino, in his popular medical tract, "How to Prolong Your Life," recommended drinking liquefied gold during certain phases of the moon. Such remedies revealed a belief in the harmony of nature and the healing power of rare substances. The remedies were not silly or superstitious, but they were not effective either. Starvation was rare, less because of food shortage than because the seriously undernourished were more likely to succumb to disease than to famine. In urban areas, the government would intervene to provide grain from public storehouses at times of extreme shortage; in the countryside large landholders commonly exercised the same function.

The Quality of Life

Although life may have been difficult during the Renaissance, it was not unfulfilling. Despite constant toil and frequent hardship, people of the Renaissance had reason to believe that their lives were better than those of their ancestors and that their children's lives would be better still. On the most basic level, health improved and, for those who survived plague, life expectancy increased. Better health was related to better diet. Improvement came from two sources: the relative surplus of grain throughout the fifteenth century and the wider variety of foods consumed. Bread remained the most widely consumed foodstuff, but even subsistence consumers were beginning to supplement their diet with meat and dairy products. There was more pork and lamb in the diet of ordinary people in the fifteenth century than there would be for the next 400 years. At the upper levels of society, sweet wine and citrus fruits helped offset the lack of vegetables. The diversification of diet resulted from improvements in transportation and communication, which brought more goods and services to a growing number of towns in the chain that linked the regional centers to the rural countryside.

But the towns and cities contributed more than consumer goods to Renaissance society. They also introduced a new sense of social and political cohesiveness. The city was something to which people belonged. In urban areas they could join social groups of their own choosing and develop networks of support not possible in rural environments. Blood relations remained the primary social group. Kin were the most likely source of aid in times of need, and charity began at home. Kin groups extended well beyond the immediate

Detail from a fifteenth-century Florentine painted wedding chest shows a procession of young people participating in a ductio ad maritum, *the installation of a new bride in her husband's home.*

family, with both cousins and in-laws laying claim to the privileges of blood. The urban family could also depend upon the connections of neighborhood. In some Italian cities, wealth or occupation determined housing patterns. In others, such as Florence, rich and poor lived side by side and identified themselves with their small administrative unit and with their local church. Thus they could participate in relationships with others both above and below them on the social scale. From their superiors they gained connections that helped their families; from their inferiors they gained devoted clients. The use of both in such important functions as godparenting demonstrates how the urban family built a complex set of social relations.

As in the Middle Ages, the Church remained the spatial, spiritual, and social center of people's lives. There was not yet any separation between faith and reason. The Church provided explanations for both the mysterious and the mundane. It offered comfort for the present life and for the life to come. The rituals of baptism, marriage, and burial that measured the passage of life were performed. The Church was also the source of the key symbols of urban society. The flags of militia troops, the emblems of guilds, the regalia of the city itself were all adorned by recognizable religious symbols. The Church preserved holy relics, such as the piece of the true cross in Venice, that were venerated for their power to protect the city or to endow it with particular skills and resources. Through its holy days as much as through its rituals, the Church helped channel leisure activities into community celebrations.

A growing sense of civic pride and individual accomplishment were underlying characteristics of the Italian Renaissance, enhanced by the development of social cohesion and community solidarity that both Church and city-state fostered. It is commonly held that the Renaissance was both elitist and male dominated, that it was an experience separate from that of the society at large. There can be no question that it was the rich who commissioned works of art and that it was the highly skilled male craftsmen who executed them. But neither lived in a social vacuum. The Renaissance was not the result of the efforts of a privileged few. Family values that permitted early apprenticeships in surrogate households and that emphasized the continuity of crafts from one generation to the next made possible the skilled artists of the Renaissance cities. The stress on the production of luxury goods placed higher value upon individual skills and therefore upon excellence in workmanship. Church and state sought to express social values through representational art. One of the chief purposes of wall murals was to instruct the unlettered in religion, to help them visualize the central episodes in Christian history and thus increase the pleasure they derived from their faith. The grandiose architecture and statuary that adorned central places were designed to enhance civic pride, nurture loyalty, and communicate the protective power of public institutions.

For ordinary people, the world of the Renaissance was not much different from the world of the Middle Ages. Although urban areas grew, providing a wider

This painting by Botticelli (1444–1510) shows the wedding banquet that celebrated the marriage of Nastagio delgi Oresti and the daughter of Paulo Tvaversaro.

variety of occupations and a varied material life, most people continued to scratch a meager living from the soil. The crucial difference from generation to generation was the degree of infectious diseases and the rate of rising or falling population. For the lucky ones there was surplus, for the unfortunate there was dearth. Within those confines men were privileged over women, having greater security and status and monopolizing power. But the tightly knit organization of family life protected the weak and the poor, while the church provided faith, hope, and charity.

Renaissance Art

In every age, artistic achievement represents a combination of individual talent and predominant social ideals. Artists may be at the leading edge of the society in which they live, but it is the spirit of that society that they capture in word or song or image. Artistic disciplines also have their own technical development. Individually, Renaissance artists were attempting to solve problems of perspective and three-dimensionality that had defeated their predecessors. But the particular techniques or experiments that interested them owed as much to the social context as they did to the artistic one. For example, the urban character of Italian government led to the need for civic architecture—public buildings on a grand scale. The celebration of individual achievement led to the explosive growth of portraiture. Not surprisingly, major technological breakthroughs were achieved in both areas. Nor should the brilliance of the artists themselves be underestimated. To deny genius is to deprecate humanity. What needs to be explained is not the existence of a Leonardo or a Michelangelo but their coexistence.

The relationship between artist and social context was all the more important in the Renaissance, when artists were closely tied to the crafts and trades of urban society and to the demands of clients who commissioned their work. Although it was the elite who patronized art, it was skilled tradesmen who produced it. Artists normally followed the pattern of any craftsman, an apprenticeship begun as a teenager and a long period of training and work in a master's shop. That form of education gave the aspiring artist a practical rather than a theoretical bent and a keen appreciation for the business side of art. Studios were identified with particular styles and competed for commissions from clients, especially the Church. Wealthy individuals commissioned art as investments, as marks of personal distinction, and as displays of public piety. They got what they paid for, usually entering into detailed contracts that stipulated the quality of materials and the amount of work done by the master. Isabella d'Este (1474–1539), one of the great patrons of Renaissance artists, wrote hundreds of letters specifying the details of the works she commissioned. She once sent an artist threads of the exact dimensions of the pictures she had ordered. Demand for art was high. The vast public works projects needed buildings, the new piazzas (public squares) and palazzos (private houses) needed statuary, and the long walls of churches needed murals.

The survival of so many Renaissance masterpieces allows the reconstruction of the stages by which the remarkable artistic achievements of the era took place. Although advances were made in a variety of fields during the Renaissance, the three outstanding areas were architecture, sculpture, and painting. While modern artists would consider each a separate discipline, Renaissance artists crossed their boundaries without hesitation. Not only could the artists work with a variety of materials, their intensive and varied apprenticeships taught them to apply the technical solutions of one field to the problems of another. Few Renaissance artists confined themselves to one area of artistic expression, and many created works of enduring beauty in more than one medium. Was the greatest achievement of Michelangelo his sculpture of David, his paintings on the ceiling of the Sistine Chapel, or his design for the dome of Saint Peter's? Only a century of interdisciplinary cross-fertilization could have prepared the artistic world for such a feat.

An Architect, a Sculptor, and a Painter

The century that culminated in Michelangelo's extraordinary achievements began with the work of three Florentine masters who deeply influenced one another's development: Brunelleschi (1377–1446), Donatello (1386–1466), and Masaccio (1401–1428). In the Renaissance, the dominant artistic discipline was architecture. Buildings were the most expensive investment patrons could make, and the technical knowledge necessary for their successful construction was immense. Not only did the architect design a building, he also served as its general contractor, its construction supervisor, and its inspector. Moreover, the architect's design determined the amount and the scale of the statuary

Florence Cathedral was begun by Arnolfo di Cambio in 1296. The nave was finished about 1350 and the dome, designed by Brunelleschi, was added in the 1420s. This view shows the dome and the apse end of the cathedral.

and decorative paintings to be incorporated. By 1400 the Gothic style of building had dominated western Europe for more than two centuries. Its pointed arches, vaulted ceilings, and slender spires had simplified building by removing the heavy walls formerly thought necessary to support great structures. Gothic construction permitted greater height, a characteristic especially desirable in cathedrals, which stretched toward the heavens. But although the buildings themselves were simplified, the techniques for erecting them became more complex. By the fifteenth century, architects had turned their techniques into an intricate style. They became obsessed by angular arches, elaborate vaultings and buttresses, and long, pointed spires.

It was Brunelleschi who decisively challenged the principles of Gothic architecture by recombining its basic elements with those of classical structures. His achievement was less an innovation than a radical synthesis of old and new. Basing his designs on geometric principles, Brunelleschi reintroduced planes and spheres as dominant motifs. His greatest work was the dome on the cathedral in Florence, begun in 1420. His design was simple but bold. The windows at the base of the dome of the cathedral illustrate Brunelleschi's geometric technique. Circular windows are set inside a square of panels, which in turn are set inside a rectangle. The facades are dominated by columns and rounded arches, proportionally spaced from a central perspective. Brunelleschi is generally credited with having been the first Renaissance artist to have understood and made use of perspective, though it was immediately put to more dramatic effect in sculpture and painting.

The sculptor's study was the human form in all of its three-dimensional complexity. The survival of Roman and Hellenistic pieces, mostly bold and muscular torsos, meant that the influence of classical art was most direct in sculpture. Donatello translated the classical styles into more naturalistic forms. His technique is evident in the long flowing robes that distinguish most of his works. Donatello sculpted the cloth, not in the stylized angularity of the past in which the creases were as sharp as sword blades, but in the natural fashion in which cloth hung. Donatello also revived the freestanding statue, which demanded greater attention to human anatomy because it was viewed from many angles. *Judith Slaying Holofernes* (1455) is an outstanding example of Donatello's use of geometric proportion and perspective. Each side of the piece captures a different vision of Judith in action. In addition, Donatello led the revival of the equestrian statue, sculpting the Venetian captain-general Gattamelata for a public square in Padua. The enormous bronze horse and rider (1445–1450) borrowed from surviving first- and second-century Roman models but relied upon the standpoint of the viewer to achieve its overpowering effect. The use of linear perspective was also a characteristic of Donatello's dramatic works, such as the breathtaking altar scenes of the miracles of Saint Anthony in Padua, which resemble nothing so much as a canvas cast in bronze.

The altar scenes clearly evince the unmistakable influence of the paintings of Masaccio. Although he lived fewer than 30 years, Masaccio created an enduring legacy. His frescoes in the Brancacci Chapel in Florence were studied and sketched by all the great artists of the next generation, who unreservedly praised his naturalism. What most claims the attention of the modern viewer is Masaccio's shading of light and

Donatello's bronze statue Judith Slaying Holofernes *symbolized the Florentines' love of liberty and hatred of tyranny.*

shadow and his brilliant use of linear perspective to create the illusion that a flat surface has three dimensions. Masaccio worked with standard Christian themes, but he brought an entirely novel approach to them all. In an adoration scene he portrayed a middle-aged Madonna and a dwarfish baby Jesus; in a painting of Saint Peter paying tribute money he used his own likeness as the face of one of the Apostles. His two best-known works are *The Expulsion of Adam and Eve* (ca. 1427) and *The Holy Trinity* (1425). In *The Expulsion of Adam and Eve,* Masaccio has left an unforgettable

In this fresco, The Expulsion of Adam and Eve *(ca. 1425), Masacchio's mastery of perspective helps create the illusion of movement, as an angel drives the grieving Adam and Eve out of paradise into the world.*

image of the fall from grace in Eve's primeval anguish. Her deep eyes and hollow mouth are accentuated by casting the source of light downward and shading what otherwise would be lighted. In *The Holy Trinity,* Masaccio provides the classic example of the use of linear perspective. In the painting, the ceiling of a Brunelleschi-designed temple recedes to a vanishing point beyond the head of God, creating the simultaneous illusion of height and depth.

Renaissance Style

By the middle of the fifteenth century, a recognizable Renaissance style had triumphed. Florence continued to lead the way, although ideas, techniques, and influences had spread throughout the Italian peninsula and even to the north and west. The outstanding architect of the period was Leon Battista Alberti (1404–1472), whose treatise *On Building* (1452) remained the most influential work on the subject until the eighteenth century. Alberti consecrated the geometric principles laid down by Brunelleschi and infused them with a humanist spirit. He revived the classical dictum that a building, like a body, should have an even number of supports and, like a head, an odd number of openings, which furthered precise geometric calculations in scale and design. But it was in civic architecture that Alberti made his most significant contributions. There he demonstrated how classical forms could be applied to traditional living space by being made purely decorative. His facade of the Palazzo Rucellai uses columns and arches not as building supports, but as embellishments that give geometric harmony to the building's appearance.

No sculptor challenged the preeminence of Donatello for another 50 years, but in painting there were many contenders for the garlands worn by Masaccio. The first was Piero della Francesca (ca. 1420–1492) who, though trained in the tradition of Masaccio, broke new ground in his concern for the visual unity of his paintings. From portraits to processions to his stunning fresco *The Resurrection* (ca. 1463), Piero concentrated upon the most technical aspects of composition. He was influenced by Alberti's ideas about the geometry of form, and it is said that his measurements and calculations for various parts of *The Resurrection* took more time than the painting itself. Another challenger was Sandro Botticelli (1445–1510), whose classical themes, sensitive portraits, and bright colors set him apart from the line of Florentine painters with whom he studied. His mythologies, *The Birth of Venus* and *Spring* (both ca. 1478), depart markedly from the naturalism inspired by Masaccio. Botticelli's paintings have a dreamlike quality, an unreality highlighted by the beautiful faces and lithe figures of his characters.

Botticelli's Primavera *(Spring), also called* Garden of Venus. *Venus, in the center, is attended by the three Graces and by Cupid, Flora, Chloris, and Zephyr. Botticelli's figures have a dreamlike quality, an unreality highlighted by their beautiful faces and lithe figures.*

Botticelli's concern with beauty and personality is also seen in the paintings of Leonardo da Vinci (1452–1519), whose creative genius embodied the Renaissance ideal of the "universal man." Leonardo's achievements in scientific, technical, and artistic endeavors read like a list of all of the subjects known during the Renaissance. His detailed anatomical drawings and the method he devised for rendering them, his botanical observations, and his engineering inventions (including models for the tank and the airplane) testify to his unrestrained curiosity. His paintings reveal the scientific application of mathematics to matters of proportion and perspective. The dramatic fresco *The Last Supper* (ca. 1495–1498), for example, takes the traditional scene of Jesus and his disciples at a long table and divides it into four groups of three, each with its own separate action, leaving Jesus to dominate the center of the picture by balancing its two sides. Leonardo's psychological portrait *La Gioconda* (1503–1506), popularly called the Mona Lisa, is quite possibly the best-known picture in the Western world.

From Brunelleschi to Alberti, from Masaccio to Leonardo da Vinci, Renaissance artists placed a unique stamp upon visual culture. By reviving classical themes, geometric principles, and a spirit of human vitality, they broke decisively from the dominant medieval traditions. Art became a source of individual and collective pride, produced by masters but consumed by all. Cities and wealthy patrons commissioned great works of art for public display. New buildings rose everywhere, adorned with the statues and murals that still stand as a testimony to generations of artists.

Leonardo da Vinci's La Gioconda, *or* Mona Lisa.

Michelangelo

The artistic achievements of the Renaissance culminated in the creative outpourings of Michelangelo Buonarroti (1475–1564). It is almost as if the age itself had produced a summation of how it wished to be remembered. Uncharacteristically, Michelangelo came from a family of standing in Florentine society and gained his apprenticeship over the opposition of his father. He claimed to have imbibed his love of sculpture from the milk of his wet nurse, who was the wife of a stonecutter. In 1490, Michelangelo gained a place in the household of Lorenzo de' Medici, thus avoiding the long years of apprenticeship during which someone else's style was implanted upon a young artist.

In 1496, Michelangelo moved to Rome. There his abilities as a sculptor brought him a commission from a French cardinal for a religious work in the classical style, which Michelangelo named the *Pietà*. Although it was his first attempt at sculpting a work of religious art, Michelangelo would never surpass it in beauty or composition. The *Pietà* created a sensation in Rome, and by the time that Michelangelo returned to Florence in 1501, at the age of 26, he was already acknowledged as one of the great sculptors of his day. He was immediately commissioned to work on an enormous block of marble that had been quarried nearly a half-century before and had defeated the talents of a series of carvers. He worked continuously for three years on his *David* (1501–1504), a piece that completed the union between classical and Renaissance styles. Michelangelo's giant nude gives eloquent expression to his belief that the human body was the "mortal veil" of the soul.

Although Michelangelo always believed himself to be primarily a sculptor, his next outstanding work was in the field of painting. In 1508, Pope Julius II commissioned Michelangelo to decorate the small ceremonial chapel that had been built next to the new papal residence. The initial plan called for figures of the 12 apostles to adorn the ceiling, but Michelangelo soon launched a more ambitious scheme: to portray, in an extended narrative, human creation and those Old Testament events that foreshadowed the birth of Jesus. Everything about the execution of the Sistine Chapel paintings was extraordinary. First, Michelangelo framed his scenes within the architecture of a massive classical temple. In this way he was able to give the impression of having flattened the rounded surface on which he worked. Then, on the two sides of the central panels, he represented figures of Hebrew prophets and pagan Sybils as sculptured marble statues. Finally, within the center panels came his fresco scenes of the events of the creation and of human history from the Fall to the Flood. His representations were simple and compelling: the fingers of God and Adam nearly touching; Eve with one leg still emerging from Adam's side; the half-human snake in the temptation. All are majestically evocative.

The *Pietà*, the *David*, and the paintings of the Sistine Chapel were the work of youth. Michelangelo's crowning achievement—the building of Saint Peter's—was undertaken at the age of 71. The purpose of the church was to provide a suitable monument for the grave of Saint Peter. The basework had already been laid, and drawings for the building's completion had been made 30 years earlier by Donato Bramante. Michelangelo altered the plans in an effort to bring more light inside the church and provide a more majestic facade outside. His main contribution, however, was the design of the great dome, which centered the interior of the church on Saint Peter's grave. More than the height, it is the harmony of Michelangelo's design that creates the sense of the building thrusting upward like a Gothic cathedral of old. The dome on Saint Peter's was the largest then known and provided the model, in succeeding generations, for Saint Paul's Cathedral in London and the U.S. Capitol building in Washington, D.C.

Michelangelo, Pietà *(1498–1499). The sculptor's contract for the piece called for it to be "the most beautiful work in marble which exists today in Rome." Michelangelo made several trips to Carrara to find the highest quality marble for the* Pietà.

Renaissance art served Renaissance society. It reflected both its concrete achievements and its visionary ideals. It was a synthesis of old and new, building upon classical models, particularly in sculpture and architecture, but adding newly discovered techniques and skills. Demanding patrons such as Pope Julius II, who commonly interrupted Michelangelo's work on the Sistine Chapel with criticisms and suggestions, fueled the remarkable growth in both the quantity and quality of Renaissance art. When Giorgio Vasari (1511–1574) came to write his *Lives of the Great Painters, Sculptors, and Architects* (1550), he found more than 200 artists worthy of distinction. But Renaissance artists did more than construct and adorn buildings or celebrate and beautify spiritual life. Inevitably their work expressed the ideals and aspirations of the society in which they lived, the new emphasis upon learning and knowledge; upon the here and now rather than the hereafter; and, most importantly, upon humanity and its capacity for growth and perfection.

The creation of Adam and Eve, a detail from Michelangelo's frescoes on the ceiling of the Sistine Chapel. The Sistine frescoes had become obscured by dirt and layers of varnish and glue applied at various times over the years. In the 1980s they were cleaned to reveal their original colors.

RENAISSANCE IDEALS

Renaissance thought went hand in glove with Renaissance art. Scholars and philosophers searched the works of the ancients to find the principles on which to build a better life. They scoured monastic libraries for forgotten manuscripts, discovering among other things Greek poetry and history, the works of Homer and Plato, and Aristotle's *Poetics*. Their rigorous application of scholarly procedures for the collection and collation of those texts was one of the most important contributions of the Renaissance intellectuals who came to be known as humanists. Humanism developed in reaction to an intellectual world that was centered on the Church and dominated by otherworldly concerns. Humanism was secular in outlook, though by no means was it antireligious.

Humanists celebrated worldly achievements. Pico della Mirandola's *Oration on the Dignity of Man* (1486) is the best known of a multitude of Renaissance writings influenced by the discovery of the works of Plato. Pico believed that people could perfect their existence on earth because humans were divinely endowed with the capacity to determine their own fate: "O highest and most marvelous felicity of man! To him it is granted to have whatever he chooses, to be whatever he wills."

Thus humanists studied and taught the humanities—the skills of disciplines such as philology, the art of language, and rhetoric, the art of expression. Although they were mostly laypeople, humanists applied their learning to both religious and secular studies. Humanists were not antireligious. Although they reacted strongly against Scholasticism (see Chapter 14), they were heavily indebted to the work of medieval churchmen, and most were devoutly religious. Nor were they hostile to the Church. Petrarch, Leonardo Bruni, and Leon Battista Alberti were all employed by the papal court at some time in their careers, as was Lorenzo Valla, the most influential of

THE RENAISSANCE MAN

Giorgio Vasari celebrated the creativity of the artists who made Italy the center of cultural activity in the later Middle Ages. His commemoration of their achievements through the medium of biographies helped to create the aura that still surrounds Renaissance art.

THE MOST HEAVENLY GIFTS seem to be showered on certain human beings. Sometimes supernaturally, marvelously, they all congregate in one individual. Beauty, grace, and talent are combined in such bounty that in whatever that man undertakes, he outdistances all other men and proves himself to be specially endowed by the hand of God. He owes his pre-eminence not to human teaching or human power. This was seen and acknowledged by all men in the case of Leonardo da Vinci, who had, besides the beauty of his person (which was such that it has never been sufficiently extolled), an indescribable grace in every effortless act and deed. His talent was so rare that he mastered any subject to which he turned his attention. Extraordinary strength and remarkable facility were here combined. He had a mind of regal boldness and magnanimous daring. His gifts were such that his celebrity was worldwide, not only in his own day, but even more after his death, and so will continue until the end of time.

Leonardo was frequently occupied in the preparation of plans to remove mountains or to pierce them with tunnels from plain to plain. By means of levers, cranes, and screws, he showed how to lift or move great weights. Designing dredging machines and inventing the means of drawing water from the greatest depths were among the speculations from which he never rested. Many drawings of these projects exist which are cherished by those who practice our arts....

Leonardo, with his profound comprehension of art, began many things that he never completed, because it seemed to him that perfection must elude him. He frequently formed in his imagination enterprises so difficult and so subtle that they could not be entirely realized and worthily executed by human hands. His conceptions were varied to infinity. In natural philosophy, among other things, he examined plants and observed the stars—the movements of the planets, the variations of the moon, and the course of the sun....

From Giorgio Vasari, *Lives of the Most Eminent Painters, Sculptors, and Architects.*

the humanists. Their interest in human achievement and human potential must be set beside their religious beliefs. As Petrarch stated quite succinctly: "Christ is my God; Cicero is the prince of the language I use."

Humanists and the Liberal Arts

The most important achievements of humanist scholars centered on ancient texts. It was the humanists' goal to discover as much as had survived from the ancient world and to provide texts of classical authors that were as full and accurate as possible.

Studying the Classical World. Although much was already known of the Latin classics, few of the central works of ancient Greece had been uncovered. Humanists preserved that heritage by reviving the study of the Greek language and by translating Greek authors into Latin. After the fall of Constantinople in 1453, Italy became the center for Greek studies as Byzantine scholars fled the Ottoman conquerors. Humanists also introduced historical methods in studying and evaluating texts, establishing principles for determining which of many manuscript copies of an ancient text was the oldest, the most accurate, and the least corrupted by copyists. That was of immense importance in studying the writings of the ancient Fathers of the Church, many of whose manuscripts had not been examined for centuries. The humanists' emphasis upon the humanistic disciplines fostered new educational ideals. Along with the study of theology, logic, and natural philosophy that had dominated the medieval university, humanist scholars stressed the importance of grammar, rhetoric, moral philosophy,

A miniature portrait of Petrarch is seen within the illuminated initial A in a manuscript of the poet's treatise De remediis utriusque fortunae *(Remedies Against Fortune).*

and history. They believed that the study of the "liberal arts" should be undertaken for its own sake. That belief gave a powerful boost to the ideal of the perfectability of the individual that appeared in so many other aspects of Renaissance culture.

Humanists furthered the secularization of Renaissance society through their emphasis on the study of the classical world. The rediscovery of Latin texts during the later Middle Ages spurred interest in all things ancient. Petrarch, who is rightly called the father of humanism, revered the great Roman rhetorician Cicero above all others. For Petrarch, Cicero's legacy was eloquence. He stressed that in his correspondence with the leading scholars of his day and taught it to those who would succeed him. From 1350 to 1450, Cicero was the dominant model for Renaissance poets and orators. Petrarch's emphasis upon language led to efforts to recapture the purity of ancient Latin and Greek, languages that had become corrupted over the centuries. The leading humanist in the generation after Petrarch was Leonardo Bruni (1370–1444), who was reputed to be the greatest Greek scholar of his day. He translated both Plato and Aristotle and did much to advance mastery of classical Greek and foster the ideas of Plato in the late fifteenth century.

Philology and Lorenzo Valla. The study of the origins of words, their meaning and their proper grammatical usage may seem an unusual foundation for one of the most vital of all European intellectual movements. But philology was the humanists' chief concern, and can be best illustrated by the work of Lorenzo Valla (1407–1457). Valla was brought up in Rome, where he was largely self-educated, although according to the prescriptions of the Florentine humanists. Valla entered the service of Alfonso I, king of Naples, and applied his humanistic training to affairs of state. The kingdom of Naples bordered on the Papal States, and its kings were in continual conflict with the papacy. The pope asserted the right to withhold recognition of the king, a right that was based upon the jurisdictional authority supposedly ceded to the papacy by the Emperor Constantine in the fourth century. The so-called Donation of Constantine had long been a matter of dispute, and its authenticity had been challenged frequently in the Middle Ages. But those challenges were made on political grounds, and the arguments of papal supporters were as strenuous as those of papal opponents. Valla settled the matter definitively. Applying historical and philological critiques to the text of the Donation, Valla proved that it could not have been written earlier than the eighth century, 400 years after Constantine's death. He exposed words and terms that had not existed in Roman times, such as *fief* and *satrap,* and thus proved beyond doubt that the Donation was a forgery and papal claims based upon it were without merit.

Valla's career demonstrates the impact of humanist values on practical affairs. Although humanists were scholars, they made no distinction between an active and a contemplative life. A life of scholarship was a life of public service. They saw their studies as means of improving themselves and their society: "Man is born in order to be useful to man." That civic humanism is best expressed in the writings of Leon Battista Alberti (1404–1472), whose treatise *On the Family* (1443) is a classic study of the new urban values, especially prudence and thrift. Alberti extolled the virtues

Portrait of Baldesar Castiglione *by Raphael.*

of "the fatherland, the public good, and the benefit of all citizens." An architect, a mathematician, a poet, a playwright, a musician, and an inventor, Alberti was one of the great virtuosi of the Renaissance.

Alberti's own life might have served as a model for the most influential of all Renaissance tracts, Baldesar Castiglione's *The Courtier* (1528). While Alberti directed his lessons to the private lives of successful urban families, Castiglione (1478–1529) directed his to the public life of the aspiring elite. In Castiglione's view, the perfect courtier was as much born as made: "Besides his noble birth I would have the Courtier endowed by nature not only with talent and beauty of person and feature, but with a certain grace and air that shall make him at first sight pleasing." Everything that the courtier did was to maintain his pleasing grace and his public reputation. *The Courtier* was an etiquette book, and in it Castiglione prescribed every detail of the education necessary for the ideal state servant, from table manners to artistic attainments. Although each talent was to be acquired through careful study and application, it was to be manifested with *sprezzatura,* a natural ease and superiority that was the essence of the gentleman.

Machiavelli and Politics

At the same time that Castiglione was drafting a blueprint for the idealized courtier, Niccolò Machiavelli (1469–1527) was laying the foundation for the realistic sixteenth-century ruler. No Renaissance work has been more important or more controversial than Machiavelli's *The Prince* (1513). Its vivid prose, its epigrammatic advice—"Men must either be pampered or crushed"—and its clinical dissection of power politics have attracted generation after generation of readers. With Machiavelli began the science of politics.

Machiavelli came from an established Florentine family and entered state service as an assistant to one of his teachers, who then recommended him for the important office of secretary to the Council of Ten, the organ of Florentine government that had responsibility

Portrait of Niccolò Machiavelli, who expounded his theory of statecraft in The Prince.

THE LION AND THE FOX

Niccolò Machiavelli wrote The Prince *in 1513 while he was under house arrest. It is one of the classics of Western political theory in which the author separates the political from the moral.*

EVERYONE UNDERSTANDS HOW PRAISEWORTHY it is in a prince to keep faith, and to live uprightly and not craftily. Nevertheless we see, from what has taken place in our own days, that princes who have set little store by their word, but have known how to overreach men by their cunning, have accomplished great things, and in the end got the better of those who trusted to honest dealing.

Be it known, then, that there are two ways of contending—one in accordance with the laws, the other by force; the first of which is proper to men, the second to beasts. But since the first method is often ineffectual, it becomes necessary to resort to the second. A prince should, therefore, understand how to use well both the man and the beast.... But inasmuch as a prince should know how to use the beast's nature wisely, he ought of beasts to choose both the lion and the fox; for the lion cannot guard himself from the toils, nor the fox from wolves. He must therefore be a fox to discern toils, and a lion to drive off wolves.

To rely wholly on the lion is unwise; and for this reason a prudent prince neither can nor ought to keep his word when to keep it is hurtful to him and the causes which led him to pledge it are removed. If all men were good, this would not be good advice, but since they are dishonest and do not keep faith with you, you in return need not keep faith with them.

From Niccolò Machiavelli, *The Prince*.

for war and diplomacy. There Machiavelli received his education in practical affairs. His special interest was in the militia, and he was an early advocate of organizing and training Florentine citizens to defend the city rather than hiring mercenaries. He drafted position papers on the tense international situation that followed the French invasion of Italy in 1494. Machiavelli devoted all his energies and his entire intellect to his career. He was a tireless correspondent, and he began to collect materials for various tracts on military matters. He also planned out a prospective history in which to celebrate the greatness of the Florentine republic that he served.

But as suddenly as Machiavelli rose to his position of power and influence, he fell from it. The militia that he had advocated and in part organized was soundly defeated by the Spaniards, and the Florentine republic fell. Machiavelli was summarily dismissed from office in 1512 and was imprisoned and tortured the following year. Released and banished from the city, he retired to a small country estate and turned his restless energies to writing. Immediately he began work on what became his two greatest works, *The Prince* and the *Discourses on Livy* (1519).

Machiavelli has left a haunting portrait of his life in exile, and it is important to understand how intertwined his studies of ancient and modern politics were.

> On the coming of evening, I return to my house and enter my study; and at the door I take off the day's clothing, covered with mud and dust, and put on garments regal and courtly; and reclothed appropriately, I enter the ancient courts of ancient men, where, received by them with affection, I feed on that food which only is mine and which I was born for. For four hours of time I do not feel boredom, I forget every trouble, I do not dread poverty, I am not frightened by death; entirely I give myself over to them.

In this state of mind *The Prince* was composed.

The Prince is a handbook for a ruler who would establish a lasting government. It attempts to set down principles culled from historical examples and contemporary events to aid the prince in attaining and maintaining power. By study of those precepts and by their swift and forceful application, Machiavelli believed that the prince might even control fortune itself. *The Prince* is purely secular in content and philosophy. Where the medieval writer of a manual for princes would have stressed the divine foundations of the state, Machiavelli asserted the human bases: "The chief foundations on which all states rest are good laws and good arms." What made *The Prince* so remarkable in its day, and what continues to enliven debate over it, is that Machiavelli was able to separate all ethical considerations from his analysis. Whether that resulted from cynicism or from his own expressed desire for realism, Machiavelli uncompromisingly instructed the would-be ruler to be half man and half beast—to conquer neighbors, to murder enemies, and to deceive friends. Steeped in the humanist ideals of fame and *virtù*—a combination of virtue and virtuosity, of valor, character, and ability—he sought to reestablish Italian rule and place government upon a stable, scientific basis that would end the perpetual conflict among the Italian city-states.

The careers of Lorenzo Valla and Niccolò Machiavelli both illustrate how humanists were able to bring the study of the liberal arts into the service of the state. Valla's philological studies had a vital impact on diplomacy; Machiavelli's historical studies were directly applicable to warfare. Humanists created a demand for learning that helps account for the growth of universities, the spread of literacy, and the rise of printing. They also created a hunger for knowledge that characterized intellectual life for nearly two centuries.

Italy, 1494, showing the largest of the city-states. The city-states were among the most wealthy urban areas in the world.

THE POLITICS OF THE ITALIAN CITY-STATES

Like studs on a leather boot, city-states dotted the Italian peninsula. They differed in size, shape, and form. Some were large seaports, others small inland villages; some cut wide swaths across the plains, others were tiny islands. The absence of a unifying central authority in Italy, resulting from the collapse of the Holy Roman Empire and the papal schism, allowed ancient guilds and confraternities to transform themselves into self-governing societies. By the beginning of the fifteenth century the Italian city-states were the center of power, wealth, and culture in the Christian world.

That dominion rested on several conditions. First, Italy's geographical position favored the exchange of resources and goods between the East and the West. Until the fifteenth century, and despite the crusading efforts of medieval popes, the East and the West fortified each other. A great circular trade had developed, encompassing the Byzantine Empire, the North African coastal states, and the Mediterranean nations of western Europe. The Italian peninsula dominated the circumference of that circle. Its port cities, Genoa and Venice especially, became great maritime powers through their trade in spices and minerals. Second, just beyond the peninsula to the north lay the vast and populous territories of the Holy Roman Empire. There the continuous need for manufactured goods, especially cloths and metals, was filled by long caravans that traveled from Italy through the Alps. Milan specialized in metal crafts. Florence was a financial capital as well as a center for the manufacture of fine luxury goods. Finally, the city-states and their surrounding areas were agriculturally self-sufficient.

Because of their accomplishments, there has been a tendency to think of the Italian city-states as small nations. Even the term *city-state* implies national identity. Each city-state governed itself according to its own rules and customs, and each defined itself in isolation from the larger regional or tribal associations that once prevailed. Indeed, the struggles of the city-states against one another speak eloquently of their local self-identification. Italy was neither a nation nor a people.

The Five Powers

Although there were dozens of Italian city-states, by the early fifteenth century five had emerged to dominate the politics of the peninsula. In the south was the kingdom of Naples, the only city-state governed by a hereditary monarchy. Its politics were mired by conflicts over its succession, and it was not until the Spaniard Alfonso I of Aragon (1442–1458) secured the throne in 1443 that peace was restored. Bordering Naples were the Papal States, whose capital was Rome but whose territories stretched far to the north and lay on both sides of the spiny Apennine mountain chain that extends down the center of the peninsula. Throughout the fourteenth and early fifteenth centuries, the territories under the nominal control of the Church were largely independent and included such thriving city-states as Bologna, Ferrara, and Urbino. Even in Rome the weakened papacy had to contend with noble families for control of the city.

The three remaining dominant city-states were clustered together in the north. Florence, center of Renaissance culture, was one of the wealthiest cities of Europe before the devastations of the plague and the sustained economic downturn of the late fourteenth century. The city itself was inland and its main waterway, the Arno, ran to the sea through Pisa, whose subjugation in 1406 was a turning point in Florentine history. Nominally Florence was a republic, but during the fifteenth century it was ruled in effect by its principal banking family, the Medici.

To the north of Florence was the duchy of Milan, the major city in Lombardy. It too was landlocked, cut off from the sea by Genoa. But Milan's economic life was oriented northward to the Swiss and German towns beyond the Alps, and its major concern was preventing foreign invasions. The most warlike of the Italian cities, Milan was a despotism, ruled for nearly two centuries by the Visconti family.

The last of the five powers was the republic of Venice. Ideally situated at the head of the Adriatic Sea, Venice became the leading maritime power of the age. Until the fifteenth century, Venice had been less interested in securing a landed empire than in dominating a seaborne one. Its outposts along the Greek and Dalmatian coasts, and its favored position in Constantinople, were the source of vast mercantile wealth. The republic was ruled by a hereditary elite—headed by an elected doge, who was the chief magistrate of Venice—and a variety of small elected councils.

The political history of the Italian peninsula during the late fourteenth and early fifteenth centuries is one of unrelieved turmoil. Everywhere, the governments of the city-states were threatened by foreign invaders, internal conspiracies, or popular revolts. By the middle of the fifteenth century, however, two trends were

Ambrogio Lorenzetti, The Allegory of Good Government *(1338–39), a fresco series Lorenzetti created to depict allegorically good and bad government in the Italian communes. Shown here is the enthroned Commune of Siena holding the orb and scepter and surrounded by Faith, Hope, and Charity. Justice, at left, dispenses rewards and punishments through the winged figures representing Commutative and Distributive Justice. Below, Concordia presides over the twenty-four members of the Great Council of the Sienese Republic.*

apparent amid the political chaos. The first was the consolidation of strong centralized governments within the large city-states. The governments took different forms but yielded a similar result—internal political stability. The return of the popes to Rome after the Great Schism restored the pope to the head of his temporal estates and began a long period of papal dominance over Rome and its satellite territories. In Milan, one of the great military leaders of the day, Francesco Sforza (1401–1466), seized the reins of power. The succession of King Alfonso I in Naples ended a half century of civil war. In both Florence and Venice, the grip that the political elite held over high offices was tightened by placing greater power in small advisory councils and, in Florence, by the ascent to power of the Medici family. That process, known as the rise of signorial rule, made possible the establishment of a balance of power within the Italian peninsula.

It was the leaders of the Italian city-states who first perfected the art of diplomacy. Constant warfare necessitated continual alliances, and by the end of the fourteenth century the large city-states had begun the practice of keeping resident ambassadors at the major seats of power. That enhanced communication, a principal challenge in Renaissance diplomacy, and also provided leaders with accurate information about the conditions of potential allies and enemies. Diplomacy was both an offensive and a defensive weapon, especially because the city-states hired their soldiers as contract labor. The mercenary armies, whose leaders were known as *condottieri* from the name of their contract, were both expensive and dangerous to maintain. If they did not bankrupt their employers, they might desert them or, even worse, turn on them.

Venice: A Seaborne Empire

Water was the source of the prosperity of Venice. Located at the head of the Adriatic Sea, the city was formed by a web of lagoons. Through its center snaked the Grand Canal, whose banks were lined with large and small buildings that celebrated its civic and mercantile power. At the Piazza San Marco stood the vast palace of the doge, elected leader of the republic, and the Basilica of Saint Mark, a domed church built in the Byzantine style. At the Rialto were the stalls of the bankers and moneylenders, less grand perhaps but no less important. There, too, were the auction blocks for the profitable trade in European slaves, eastern European serfs, and battlefield captives who were sold into service in Egypt or Byzantium. On the eastern edge of the island city was the Arsenal, erected in the twelfth century to house the shipbuilding and arms manufacturing industries. Three centuries later it was the industrial marvel of the world, where the Venetian great galleys were constructed with assembly-line precision.

Its prosperity based on trade rather than conquest, Venice enjoyed many natural advantages. Its position at the head of the Adriatic permitted access to the raw materials of both the East and the West. The rich Alpine timberland beyond the city provided the hardwoods necessary for shipbuilding. The hinterland population were steady consumers of grain, cloth, and the new manufactured goods—glass, silk, jewelry, and cottons—that came pouring onto the market in the later Middle Ages.

But the success of Venice owed more to its own achievements than to its rich inheritances. "It is the most triumphant city I have ever seen," wrote the Frenchman Philippe de Commynes at the end of the fifteenth century. The triumph of the Venetian state was the triumph of dedicated efficiency. The heart of its success lay in the way in which it organized its trade and its government. The key to Venetian trade was its privileged position with the Byzantine Empire. Through a treaty with the Byzantines, Venetian traders gained a competitive edge in the spice trade with the East. Venetians were the largest group of resident Europeans in Constantinople, and their personal contacts with eastern traders were an important part of their success. The spice trade was so lucrative that special ships were built to accommodate it. The galleys were constructed at public expense and doubled as the Venetian navy in times of war. By controlling the ships, the government strictly regulated the spice trade. Goods imported into or exported from Venice had to be carried in Venetian ships and be consigned by Venetian merchants. The trade in spices was carefully organized in other ways as well. Rather than allow the wealthiest merchants to dominate it, as they did in other cities, Venice specified the number of annual voyages and sold shares in them at auction based on a fixed price. The practice allowed big and small merchants to gain from the trade and encouraged all merchants to find other trading outlets.

Like its trade, Venetian government was also designed to disperse power. Although it was known as the Most Serene Republic, Venice was not a republic in the sense that the term is used today; rather, it was an oligarchy—a government administered by a restricted group. Political power was vested in a Great Council whose membership had been fixed at the end of the thirteenth century. All males whose fathers enjoyed the privilege of membership in the Great Council were registered at birth in the "Book of Gold" and became members of the Great Council when adults. There were no further distinctions of rank within the nobility, whose members varied widely in wealth and intermarried freely with other groups in the society. From the body of the Great Council, which numbered about 2500 at the end of the fifteenth century, was chosen the Senate—a council about one-tenth the size, whose members served a one-year term. It was from the Senate that the true officers of government were selected: the doge, who was chosen for life; and members of a number of small councils, who administered affairs and advised the doge. Members of the councils were chosen by secret ballot in an elaborate process by which nominators were selected at random. Terms of office on the councils were extremely short in order to limit factionalism and to prevent any individual from gaining too much power. Venetian-style republicanism was admired throughout Europe.

Giotto di Bondone (1266–1336), Death and Funeral of Saint Francis. *Giotto's paintings provided a bridge between the medieval era and the early Renaissance.*

With its mercantile families firmly in control of government and trade, Venice created an overseas empire in the east during the thirteenth and fourteenth centuries. Naval supremacy, based largely on technological advances that made long-distance and winter voyages possible, allowed the Venetians to offer protection to strategic outposts in return for either privileges or tribute. But in the fifteenth century, Venice turned to the west. In a dramatic reversal of its centuries-old policy, it began a process of conquest in Italy, an empire on terra firma, as Venetian islanders called it. There were several reasons for this new policy. First, the Venetian navy was no longer the unsurpassed power that it once had been. More importantly, mainland expansion offered new opportunities for Venice. Not all Venetians were traders, and the new industries that were being developed in the city could readily benefit from control of mainland markets. So could those Venetian nobles employed to administer the conquered lands. They argued persuasively that the supply of raw materials and foodstuffs on which Venetian trade ultimately depended should be secured by the republic itself. Most decisively of all, opportunity was knocking. In Milan, Visconti rule was weakening and the Milanese territories were ripe for picking.

Venice reaped a rich harvest. For the first half of the fifteenth century, the Most Serene Republic engaged in unremitting warfare. Its successes were remarkable. It pushed out to the north to occupy all the lands between the city and the Habsburg territories; it pushed to the east until it straddled the entire head of the Adriatic; and it pushed to the west almost as far as Milan itself. Venetian victories resulted from both the traditional use of hired mercenaries and from the Venetians' own ingenuity at naval warfare. Although Venice was creating a landed empire, the course of expansion, especially in Lombardy, was along river routes. At the Arsenal were built new oared vessels armed with artillery for river sieges. Soon the captured territories were paying for continued expansion. The western conquests in particular brought large populations under Venetian control, which, along with their potential as a market, provided a ready source of taxation. By the end of the fifteenth century, the mainland dominions of Venice were contributing nearly 40 percent of the city's revenue at a cost far smaller than that of the naval empire a century earlier. Venice had become the most powerful city-state in Italy.

Florence: Spinning Cloth into Gold

"What city, not merely in Italy, but in all the world ... is more proud in its palazzi, more bedecked with churches, more beautiful in its architecture, more imposing in its gates, richer in piazzas, happier in its wide streets, greater in its people, more glorious in its citizenry, more inexhaustible in wealth, more fertile in its fields?" So boasted the humanist Coluccio Salutati (1331–1406) in 1403 during one of the most calamitous periods in Florentine history. Salutati's boastings were not unusual; the Florentines' mythical view of their homeland as savior of Christianity and as heir to the republican greatness of Rome was everywhere apparent. And it seemed to be most vigorously expressed in the city's darkest moments.

Florentine prosperity was built on two foundations: money and wool. Beginning in the thirteenth century, Florentine bankers were among the wealthiest and most powerful in the world. Initially their position was established through support of the papacy in its long struggle with the Holy Roman Empire. Florentine financiers established banks in all the capitals of Europe and the East, though their seats in Rome and Naples were probably most important. In the Middle Ages, bankers had served more functions than simply handling and exchanging money. Most were also tied to mercantile adventures and underwrote industrial activity. So it was in Florence, where international bankers purchased high-quality wool to be manufactured into the world's finest woven cloth. At its height before the plague, the cloth industry employed nearly 30,000 workers, providing jobs at all levels of society, from the rural women who spun the wool into yarn at piecework wages to the highly paid weavers and dyers whose skills made Florentine cloth so highly prized.

The activities of both commerce and cloth manufacture depended on external conditions, and thus the wealth of Florence was potentially unstable. In the mid-fourteenth century instability came with the plague that devastated the city. Nearly 40 percent of the entire population was lost in the single year 1348, and recurring outbreaks continued to ravage the already weakened survivors. Loss of workers and loss of markets seriously disrupted manufacturing. By 1380, cloth production had fallen to less than a quarter of pre-plague levels. On the heels of plague came wars. The property of Florentine bankers and merchants abroad was an easy target. Thirty years of warfare with Milan, interrupted by only a single decade of peace (1413–1423), resulted in total bankruptcy for many of the city's leading commercial families. More significantly, the costs of warfare, offensive and defensive, created a massive public debt. Every Florentine of means owned shares of the debt, and the republic was continually devising new methods for borrowing and staving off crises of repayment. Small wonder that the republic turned for aid to the wealthiest banking family in Europe, the Medici.

The ability of the Medici to secure a century-long dynasty in a government that did not have a head of state is just one of the mysteries surrounding the history of the remarkable family. Cosimo de' Medici (1389–1464) was one of the richest men in Christendom when he returned to the city in 1434 after a brief exile. His leading position in government rested upon supporters who were able to gain a controlling influence on the Signoria, the ruling Council in Florence's republican form of government. Cosimo built his party carefully, recruiting followers among the artisans whom he employed and even paying delinquent taxes to maintain the eligibility of his voters. Most importantly,

Painted terra-cotta bust of Lorenzo de' Medici by Andrea del Verrocchio.

A view of Florence in 1490.

emergency powers were invoked to reduce the number of citizens qualified to vote for the Signoria until the majority were Medici backers.

Cosimo was a practical man. He raised his children along humanist principles and was a great patron of artists and intellectuals. He collected books and paintings, endowed libraries, and spent lavishly on his own palace, the Palazzo Medici, which after his death was transformed into the very center of Florentine cultural life. Cosimo's position as an international banker brought him into contact with the heads of other Italian city-states and enabled him to negotiate peace treaties.

It was Cosimo's grandson Lorenzo (1449–1492) who linked the family's name to that of the age. Lorenzo was trained to office as if he had been a prince rather than a citizen of a republic. His own father ruled for five years and used his son as a diplomat in order to acquaint him with the leaders of Europe. Diplomacy was Lorenzo's greatest achievement. He held strong humanist values instilled in him by his mother, Lucrezia Tornabuoni, who organized his education. He wrote poetry and drama and even entered competitions for architectural designs. But Lorenzo's chief contribution to artistic life as it reached its height in Florence was to facilitate its production. He brought Michelangelo and other leading artists to his garden; he brought Pico della Mirandola and other leading humanists to his table. He secured commissions for Florentine artists throughout the Italian peninsula, ensuring the spread of their influence and the continued regeneration of artistic creativity in Florence itself.

Lorenzo was generally regarded as the leading citizen of Florence, and that was true in terms of both his wealth and his influence. He did not rule from high office, though he maintained the party that his grandfather had built and even extended it through wartime emergency measures. His power was based on his personality and reputation, a charisma enhanced when he survived an assassination attempt in which his brother was killed. His diplomatic abilities were the key to his survival. Almost immediately after Lorenzo came to power, Naples and the papacy began a war with Florence, a war that was costly to the Florentines in both taxation and lost territory. In 1479, Lorenzo traveled to Naples and personally convinced the Neapolitan king to sign a separate treaty, which restored the Italian balance of power and ensured continued Medici rule in Florence. Soon Lorenzo even had a treaty with the pope that allowed for the recovery of lost territories and the expansion of Florentine influence. But two years after his death, the Italian peninsula was plunged into wars that turned it from the center of European civilization into one of its lesser satellites.

The End of Italian Hegemony, 1450–1527

In the course of the Renaissance, western Europe was Italianized. For a century the city-states dominated the trade routes that connected the East and the West. Venetian and Genoese merchants exchanged spices and minerals from the Black Sea to the North Sea, enriching the material life of three continents. They brought wool from England and Spain to the skilled artisans in the Low Countries and Florence. Italian manufactures such as Milanese artillery, Florentine silk, and Venetian glass were prized above all others. The ducat and the florin, two Italian coins, were universally accepted in an age when every petty prince minted his own money. The Italian peninsula exported culture in the same way that it exported goods. Humanism quickly spread across the Alps, aided by the recent invention of printing (which the Venetians soon dominated), while Renaissance standards of artistic achievement were known worldwide and everywhere imitated. The city-states shared their technology as well. The compass and the navigational chart, projection maps, double entry bookkeeping, eyeglasses, the telescope—all profoundly influenced what could be achieved and what could be hoped for. In this spirit, Christopher Columbus—a Genoese seaman—successfully crossed the Atlantic under the Spanish flag, and Amerigo Vespucci—a Florentine merchant—gave his name to the newly discovered continents.

Political and Military Unrest. But it was not in Italy that the rewards of innovation or the satisfactions of achievement were enjoyed. There the seeds of political turmoil and military imperialism, combined with the rise of the Ottoman Turks, were to reap a not-unexpected harvest. In 1454, the five powers agreed to the Peace of Lodi, which established two balanced alliances, one between Florence and Milan, the other between Venice and Naples. The states, along with the papacy, pledged mutual nonaggression, a policy that lasted for nearly 40 years. But the Peace of Lodi did not bring peace. It only halted the long period in which the major city-states struggled against one another. Under cover of the peace, the large states continued the process of swallowing up their smaller neighbors and creating quasi-empires. It was a policy of imperialism as aggressive as that of any in the modern era. Civilian populations were overrun, local leaders exiled or exterminated, tribute monies taken, and taxes levied. Each of the five states either increased its mainland territories or strengthened its hold upon them.

By the end of the fifteenth century the city-states eyed one another greedily and warily. Each expected the others to begin a peninsulawide war for hegemony and took the steps that ultimately ensured the contest. Perhaps the most unusual aspect of the imperialism of the city-states was that it had been restricted to the Italian peninsula. Each of the major powers shared the dream of recapturing the glory that was Rome. Although the Venetians had expanded abroad, their acquisitions had not come through conquest or occupation. In their Greek and Dalmatian territories, local law and custom continued to govern under the benevolent eye of Venetian administrators. But in their mainland territories, the Venetians were as ruthless as the Florentines were in Pisa or as Cesare Borgia was in

Paolo Uccello, Niccolò da Tolentino at the Battle of San Romano *(ca. 1435–1450). The painting represents the early stages of a 1432 battle between the Florentines and the Sienese at San Romano. The Florentine condottiere, Niccolò da Tolentino, on a white horse, dominates the center of the scene.*

The Fall of Constantinople

The prayers of the devout were fervent on Easter Sunday in 1453. The Christians of Constantinople knew that it was only a matter of time before the last remaining stronghold of the Byzantine Empire came under siege. For decades the ring of Ottoman conquests had narrowed around the holy city until it alone stood out against the Turkish sultan. Constantinople, the bridge between Europe and Asia, was tottering. The once teeming center of Eastern Christianity had never recovered from the epidemics of the fourteenth century, and now dwindling revenues matched the dwindling population.

Perhaps it was that impoverishment that had kept the Turks at bay. Constantinople was still the best-fortified city in the world. Shaped like the head of a horse, it was surrounded by water on all but one side, and that side was protected by two stout rings of walls separated by a trench lined with stones. No cannon forged in the West could dent the battlements, and no navy could hope to force its way through the narrow mouth of the Golden Horn. Thus an uneasy peace existed between sultan and emperor. It was shattered in 1451 with the accession of a new sultan, the 19-year-old Mehmed II. Mehmed's imagination was fired by the ancient prophecies that a Muslim would rule the East. Only Constantinople was a fitting capital for such an empire, and Mehmed immediately began preparations for its conquest.

In 1452 Mehmed had constructed a fortress at the narrow mouth of the Bosporus and demanded tribute from all ships that entered the Golden Horn. The Byzantine emperor sent ambassadors to Mehmed to protest that aggression; Mehmed returned their severed heads. When the first Venetian convoy refused to lower its sails, Mehmed's artillery efficiently sank one of the galleys with a single shot. The Turks now controlled access to the city for trade and supplies. An attack the following spring seemed certain.

The emperor appealed far and wide for aid: to the Venetians and Genoese to protect their trade and to the pope to defend Christianity. The Europeans were willing, but as yet they were unable. They did not think that the Ottomans could assemble an army before summer. By then an Italian armada could dislodge the Ottoman fortress and reinforce the city with trained fighting men.

But they hadn't reckoned with Mehmed. While the Italians bickered over the cost of the expedition and Christians everywhere made ready to celebrate Holy Week, the Ottomans assembled a vast army of fighters and laborers and a huge train of weapons and supplies. Among them was the largest cannon ever cast, with a 26-foot barrel that shot a 1200-pound ball. Fifty teams of oxen and 200 men took two months to pull it in place.

Mehmed's forces—which eventually numbered more than 150,000, of which 60,000 were soldiers—assembled around the walls of Constantinople on 5 April. During the next week a great flotilla sailed up the Bosporus and anchored just out of reach of the Byzantine warships in the Golden Horn. A census taken inside the city revealed that there were only 7000 able-bodied defenders—about 5000 Greek residents and 2000 foreigners, mostly Genoese and Venetians. The Italians were the only true soldiers among them.

Although the defenders were vastly outnumbered, they still held the military advantage. As long as their ships controlled the entrance to the Golden Horn, they could limit the Ottoman attack to only one side of the city, where all of the best defenders could be massed. The Byzantines cast a boom—an iron chain supported by wooden floats—across the mouth of the Horn to forestall a naval attack. By the middle of April, the Turks had begun their land assault. Each day great guns pounded the walls of the city, and each night residents worked frantically to repair the damage. Everyone contributed. Old women wove baskets in which children carried stones. Monks and nuns packed mud and cut branches to shore up the breaches in the wall. The Turks suffered heavily each time they attempted to follow a cannon shot with a massed charge, but the attack took its toll among the defenders as well. No one was safe from the flaming arrows and catapulted stones flung over the city's walls. Choking black smoke filled the air as the huge cannon shook the foundations of the city and treated its stout stone walls as if they were plaster.

Nevertheless, for the first month of siege the defenders held their own.

The stubborn defense of the city infuriated Mehmed. As long as there was only one point of attack, the defenders could resist indefinitely. The line of assault had to be extended, and this could only be done by sea. With the boom effectively impregnable and with Italian seamen superior to the Turks, the prospects seemed dim. But what could not be achieved by force might be achieved by intelligence. Mehmed devised a plan to carry a number of smaller ships across land and then to float them behind the Christian fleet. Protected by land forces, the ships could be used as a staging point for another line of attack. Thousands of workers built huge wooden rollers, which were greased with animal fat. Under cover of darkness and the smoke of cannon fire, 72 ships were pulled up the steep hills and pushed down into the sea. Once they were safely anchored, a pontoon bridge was built and cannons were trained on the seaward walls of the city.

By then the city had withstood siege for nearly six weeks without any significant reinforcement. At the end of May there was a sudden lull. A messenger from the sultan arrived to demand surrender. The choice was clear. If the city was taken by force, the customary three days of unrestricted pillage would be allowed; if it yielded, the sultan pledged to protect the property of all who desired to remain under his rule. The emperor replied feebly that no one who had ever laid siege to Constantinople had enjoyed a long life. He was ready to die in defense of his capital.

On 30 May the final assault began. Mehmed knew that his advantage lay in numbers. First, he sent in waves of irregular troops, mostly captured slaves and Christians, who suffered great losses and were finally driven back by the weakened defenders. Next, better-trained warriors attacked and widened the breaches made by the irregulars. Finally came the crack Janissaries, the sultan's elite warriors, disciplined from birth to fight. It was the Janissaries who found a small door left open at the base of the wall. In they rushed, quickly overwhelming the first line of defenders and battering their way through the weaker second walls. By dawn the Ottoman flag was raised over the battlements and the sack of Constantinople had begun.

There was no need for the customary three days of pillage. By the end of the first day there was nothing left worth taking. The churches and monasteries had been looted and defaced, the priests and nuns murdered or defiled, and thousands of civilians had been captured to be sold into slavery. Large areas of the city smoldered from countless fires. The bastion of Eastern Christendom was no more.

THE SIEGE OF CONSTANTINOPLE

Mehmed II (1432–1481) was one of the great military geniuses of world history. He consolidated the expansion of the Ottoman Empire in Asia Minor and in 1453 organized the siege of Constantinople. He personally directed the combined land and naval assault and brilliantly improvised the tactics that led to the fall of the city. The fall of Constantinople to the Ottomans was a watershed. Kritovoulos was a Greek who entered the service of Mehmed II, probably after the siege. Though he was not an eyewitness of the fall of Constantinople, he gathered numerous accounts together in composing his history. In this selection he refers to the defenders of the city as Romans because Constantinople was what remained of the Roman Empire.

SULTAN MEHMED CONSIDERED IT NECESSARY in preparation for his next move to get possession of the harbor and open the Horn for his own ships to sail in. So, since every effort and device of his had failed to force the entrance, he made a wise decision, and one worthy of his intellect and power. It succeeded in accomplishing his purpose and in putting an end to all uncertainties.

He ordered the commanders of the vessels to construct as quickly as possible glideways leading from the outer sea to the inner sea.... He brought up the ships and placed large cradles under them, with stays against each of their sides to hold them up. And having under-girded them well with ropes, he fastened long cables to the corners and gave them to the soldiers to drag, some of them by hand, and others by certain machines and capstans.

So the ships were dragged along very swiftly. And their crews, as they followed them, rejoiced at the event and boasted of it. Then they manned the ships on the land as if they were on the sea. Some of them hoisted the sails with a shout, as if they were setting sail, and the breeze caught the sails and bellied them out. Others seated themselves on the benches, holding the oars in their hands and moving them as if rowing. And the commanders, running along by the sockets of the masts with whistlings and shouting, and with their whips beating the oarsmen on the benches, ordered them to row. The ships, borne along over the land as if on the sea, were some of them being pulled up the ascent to the top of the hill while others were being hauled down the slope into the harbor, lowering the sails with shouting and great noise.

It was a strange spectacle, and unbelievable in the telling except to those who actually did see it—the sight of ships borne along on the mainland as if sailing on the sea, with their crews and their sails and all their equipment. I believe this was a much greater feat than the cutting of a canal across at Athos by Xerxes, and much stranger to see and to hear about.

The Romans, when they saw such an unheard-of thing actually happen, and warships lying at anchor in the Horn—which they never would have suspected—were astounded at the impossibility of the spectacle, and were overcome by the greatest consternation and perplexity. They did not know what to do now, but were in despair. In fact they had left unguarded the walls along the Horn for a distance of about thirty stadia, and even so they did not have enough men for the rest of the walls, either for defense or for attack, whether citizens or men from elsewhere. Instead, two or even three battlements had but a single defender.

And now, when this sea-wall also became open to attack and had to be guarded, they were compelled to strip the other battlements and bring men there. This constituted a manifest danger, since the defenders were taken away from the rest of the wall while those remaining were not enough to guard it, being so few.

From Kritovoulos, *The History of Mehmed the Conqueror.*

Romagna when he consolidated the Papal States by fire and sword. Long years of siege and occupation had militarized the Italian city-states. Venice and Florence balanced their budgets on the backs of their captured territories, Milan had been engaged in constant war for decades, and even the papacy was militarily aggressive.

The Italian Decline. The Italians were no longer alone. The most remarkable military leader of the age was not a Renaissance *condottiere* but an Ottoman prince, Mehmed II (1451–1481), who conquered Constantinople and Athens and threatened Rome itself. The rise of the Ottomans (whose name is derived from that of Osman, their original tribal leader) is one of the most compelling stories in world history. Little more than a warrior tribe at the beginning of the fourteenth century, 150 years later the Ottomans had replaced stagnant Byzantine rule with a virile and potent empire. First they gobbled up towns and cities in a wide arc around Constantinople. Then they fed upon the Balkans and the eastern kingdoms of Hungary and Poland. By 1400, they were a presence in all the territory that stretched from the Black Sea to the Aegean; by 1450, they were its master.

Venice was most directly affected by the Ottoman advance. Not only was its favored position in eastern trade threatened, but during a prolonged war at the end of the fifteenth century, the Venetians lost many of their most important commercial outposts. Ottoman might closed off the markets of eastern Europe. Islands in the Aegean Sea and seaports along the Dalmatian coast fell to the Turks in alarming succession. By 1480, Venetian naval supremacy was a thing of the past. (See "The Fall of Constantinople," pp. 382–383.)

The Italian city-states might have met this challenge from the east had they been able to unite in opposing it. Successive popes pleaded for holy wars to halt the advance of the Turks, which was compared in officially inspired propaganda to an outbreak of plague. The fall of Constantinople in 1453 was an event of epochal proportions for Europeans, many believing that it foreshadowed the end of the world. "A thing terrible to relate and to be deplored by all who have in them any spark of humanity. The splendor and glory of the East has been captured, despoiled, ravaged and completely sacked by the most inhuman barbarians," the Venetian doge was informed. Yet it was Italians rather than Ottomans who plunged the Italian peninsula into the wars from which it never recovered.

The Wars of Italy (1494–1529) began when Naples, Florence, and the Papal States united against Milan. At first the alliance seemed little more than another shift in the balance of power. But rather than call upon Venice to redress the situation, the Milanese leader, Ludovico il Moro, sought help from the French. An army of French cavalry and Swiss mercenaries, led by Charles VIII of France (1483–1498), invaded the Italian peninsula in 1494. With Milanese support, the French swept all before them. Florence was forced to surrender Pisa, a humiliation that led to the overthrow of the Medici and the establishment of French sovereignty. The Papal States were next to be occupied, and within a year Charles had conquered Naples without engaging the Italians in a single significant battle. Unfortunately, the Milanese were not the only ones who could play at the game of foreign alliances. Next, it was the turn of the Venetians and the pope to unite and call upon the services of King Ferdinand of Aragon and the Holy Roman Emperor. Italy was now a battleground in what became a total European war for dynastic supremacy. The city-states used their foreign allies to settle old scores and to extend their own mainland empires. At the turn of the century Naples was dismembered. In 1509, the pope conspired to organize the most powerful combination of forces yet known against Venice. All the "terra firma" possessions of the Most Serene Republic were lost, but by a combination of good fortune and skilled diplomacy Venice itself survived. Florence was less fortunate, becoming a pawn first of the French and then of the Spanish. The final blow to Italian hegemony was the sack of Rome in 1527, when German mercenaries fulfilled the fears of what the "infidels" would do to the Holy City.

Surveying the wreckage of the Italian wars, Machiavelli ended *The Prince* with a plea for a leader to emerge to restore Italian freedom and recreate the unity of the ancient Roman republic. He concluded with these lines from Petrarch:

> *Then virtue boldly shall engage*
> *And swiftly vanquish barbarous rage,*
> *Proving that ancient and heroic pride*
> *In true Italian hearts had never died.*

The revival of "ancient and heroic pride" fueled the Italian Renaissance. The sense of living in a new age, the spirit of human achievement, and the curiosity and wonderment of writers and artists all characterized the Renaissance. The desire to recreate the glories of Rome was not Machiavelli's alone. It could be seen in the palaces of the Italian aristocracy; in the papal rebuilding of the Holy City; and in the military ambitions of princes. But the legacy of empire, of "ancient and heroic pride," had passed out of Italian hands.

Questions for Review

1. What social and cultural conditions were peculiar to the Italian peninsula, and how might those conditions have contributed to the Renaissance?
2. What were the principal characteristics of the Renaissance style in the visual arts?
3. What is humanism, and why was the study of languages so important to the humanists?
4. In what ways did the ideas of Niccolò Machiavelli reflect the reality of politics in the city-states of Renaissance Italy?

Suggestions for Further Reading

General Reading

Paul Grendler, ed., *Encyclopedia of the Renaissance* (New York: Scribners, 1999). A valuable reference work for all aspects of the Renaissance.

Ernst Breisach, *Renaissance Europe 1300–1517* (New York: Macmillan, 1973). A solid survey of the political history of the age.

* P. Burke, *Culture and Society in Renaissance Italy* (Princeton, NJ: Princeton University Press, 1999). A good introduction to social and intellectual developments.

* Eugenio Garin, ed., *Renaissance Characters* (Chicago: University of Chicago Press, 1991). Studies of prototypical Renaissance figures from courtiers to courtesans by leading historians.

J. R. Hale, ed., *A Concise Encyclopedia of the Italian Renaissance* (Oxford, England: Oxford University Press, 1981). A treasure trove of facts about the major figures and events of the era.

* Denys Hay, *The Italian Renaissance* (Cambridge, England: Cambridge University Press, 1977). The best first book to read, an elegant interpretive essay.

Renaissance Society

* M. Aston, *The Fifteenth Century: The Prospect of Europe* (London: Thames & Hudson, 1968). A concise survey of continental history, well written and illustrated.

* Carlo Cipolla, *Before the Industrial Revolution: European Society and Economy, 1000–1700* (New York: W. W. Norton, 1976). A sweeping survey of social and economic developments across the centuries.

* J. R. Hale, *Renaissance Europe: The Individual and Society* (Berkeley: University of California Press, 1978). A lively study that places the great figures of the Renaissance in their social context.

D. Herlihy and C. Klapiche-Zuber, *The Tuscans and Their Families* (New Haven, CT: Yale University Press, 1985). A difficult but rewarding study of the social and demographic history of Florence and its environs.

* Margaret L. King, *Women of the Renaissance* (Chicago: University of Chicago Press, 1991). The most recent study by a leading women's historian.

* Christiane Klapiche-Zuber, *Women, Family, and Ritual in Renaissance Italy* (Chicago: University of Chicago Press, 1985). A sparkling collection of essays on diverse topics in social history from wet nursing to family life.

Louis Haas, *The Renaissance Man and His Children: Childbirth and Early Childhood in Florence 1300–1600,* (New York: St. Martins Press, 1998). The nature of childhood in the Renaissance studied through Florentine sources.

* Harry Miskimin, *The Economy of Early Renaissance Europe, 1300–1460* (Englewood Cliffs, NJ: Prentice-Hall, 1969). A detailed scholarly study of economic development.

Renaissance Art

* Michael Baxandall, *Painting and Experience in Fifteenth Century Italy* (Oxford, England: Oxford University Press, 1972). A study of the relationship between painters and their patrons and of how and why art was produced.

Frederick Hartt, *History of Italian Renaissance Art* (Englewood Cliffs, NJ: Prentice-Hall, 1974). The most comprehensive survey, with hundreds of plates.

* Howard Hibbard, *Michelangelo* (New York: Harper & Row, 1974). A compelling biography of an obsessed genius.

* Michael Levey, *Early Renaissance* (London: Penguin, 1967). A concise survey of art, clearly written and authoritative.

* Linda Murray, *High Renaissance and Mannerism* (London: Thames & Hudson, 1985). The best introduction to late Renaissance art.

Roberta Olson, *Italian Renaissance Sculpture* (New York: Thames and Hudson, 1992). The best introduction to the subject, well illustrated and easy to read.

John Pope-Hennessy, *Introduction to Italian Sculpture* (New York: Phaidon, 1972). A thorough analysis of the development of sculpture, carefully illustrated.

* Rudolph Wittkower, *Architectural Principles in the Age of Humanism* (New York: W. W. Norton, 1971). A difficult but rewarding study of Renaissance architecture.

Renaissance Ideals

* Hans Baron, *The Crisis of the Early Italian Renaissance* (Princeton, NJ: Princeton University Press, 1966). One of the most influential intellectual histories of the period.

* Ernst Cassirer, ed., *The Renaissance Philosophy of Man* (Chicago: University of Chicago Press, 1948). An outstanding selection of writings from the leading Renaissance humanists.

George Holmes, *The Florentine Enlightenment,* 2nd ed. (Oxford: Clarendon Press, 1992). A new edition of the best study of intellectual developments in Florence.

Albert Rabil, ed., *Renaissance Humanism* (Philadelphia: University of Pennsylvania Press, 1988). A multiauthored, multivolume collection of essays on humanism, with all of the latest scholarship.

* Quentin Skinner, *Machiavelli* (Oxford, England: Oxford University Press, 1981). A brief but brilliant biography.

The Politics of the Italian City-States

* Gene Brucker, *Florence, The Golden Age 1138–1737* (Berkeley: University of California Press, 1998). The best single-volume introduction to Florentine history with excellent illustrations.

* J. R. Hale, *Florence and the Medici* (London: Thames & Hudson, 1977). A compelling account of the relationship between a city and its most powerful citizens.

* Frederic C. Lane, *Venice: A Maritime Republic* (Baltimore, MD: Johns Hopkins University Press, 1973). A complete history of Venice that stresses its naval and mercantile developments.

* Charles Stinger, *The Renaissance in Rome* (Bloomington, IN: University of Indiana Press, 1998). A thorough account of one of the great ages in the history of Rome.

* Lauro Martines, *Power and Imagination: City-States in Renaissance Italy* (New York: Alfred A. Knopf, 1979). An important interpretation of the politics of the Italian powers.

* Eugene E. Rice, Jr., *The Foundations of Early Modern Europe, 1460–1559* (New York: W. W. Norton, 1970). The best short synthetic work.

* Indicates paperback edition available.

Discovering Western Civilization Online

To further explore the Italian Renaissance, consult the following World Wide Web sites. Since Web resources are constantly being updated, also go to *www.awl.com/Kishlansky* for further suggestions.

Renaissance Society

www.history.evansville.net/renaissa.html#Resources
A site of links to a wide array of subjects relating to the era of the Renaissance. A good starting point.

www.mega.it/eng/egui/epo/secrepu.htm
The history of the Florentine republic with links to major tourist attractions and buildings. Brief biographies of important Florentine citizens can also be found.

www.siue.edu/COSTUMES/COSTUME5_INDEX.HTML
A site devoted to the history of dress. This page shows examples both of the clothing worn by different classes as well as in different countries during the fifteenth and sixteenth centuries.

Renaissance Art

www.online.anu.edu.au/ArtHistory/renart/pics.art/index_1.html
A pictorial guide to the major artists of the Italian Renaissance and their works. Thumbnail representations lead to links on specific pieces.

CHAPTER

12 THE EUROPEAN EMPIRES

- PTOLEMY'S WORLD
- EUROPEAN ENCOUNTERS
  - A Passage to India
  - *Mundus Novus*
  - The Spanish Conquests
  - The Legacy of the Encounters
- GEOGRAPHICAL TOUR EUROPE IN 1500
  - Eastern Boundaries
  - Central Europe
  - The West
- THE FORMATION OF STATES
  - Eastern Configurations
  - The Western Powers
- THE DYNASTIC STRUGGLES
  - Power and Glory
  - The Italian Wars

Ptolemy's World

FOR MORE THAN A THOUSAND YEARS, educated Europeans thought of the world as it had been described by Ptolemy in the second century. Most of their knowledge came from guesswork rather than observation. The world was a big place when you had to cross it on foot or by four-legged beast, or in small rickety vessels that hugged the shoreline as they sailed. Those without education lived in a world bounded by their farm or their village and thought of neighboring cities as faraway places. There were few experiences to pass from generation to generation, and those that were handed down changed from fact to fancy in the retelling. The people of the Renaissance probably knew less for certain about the planet they inhabited than had the Greeks, and the Greeks knew precious little. But lack of knowledge did not cause confusion. People who lived at the end of the fifteenth century knew enough to conduct their affairs and to dream their dreams.

The map shown here depicts the image of the world that Ptolemy bequeathed, the world that the Renaissance inherited with Ptolemy's calculations and writings.

The first thing to note is that it is shaped like a sphere. Although popular myth, confirmed by common sense, held that the world was flat and that one could theoretically fall off its edges, educated Europeans understood that it was spherical. Ptolemy had portrayed the earth as an irregular semicircle divided into degrees of longitude, beginning with 0° in the west, where Europe was situated, and progressing to 180° in the east. His construction of latitude was less certain, for less was known (then as now) about the extreme north and south. But Ptolemy did locate an equator, somewhat off center, and he portrayed as accurately as he could what was known of the European landmass. Scandinavia, in the north, and England and Ireland, set off from the Continent and from each other, are readily visible. The contours of Spain in the southwest are clear, though distorted. As the ancient world centered on the Mediterranean (literally, "in the middle of the earth"), it was the area most accurately reconstructed. Italy, Greece, and Asia Minor are easily recognizable, while France and Spain stretch out of shape like taffy. The size of the Mediterranean is grossly overestimated, its coastline occupying nearly a quarter of the map.

Africa, too, is swollen. It spans the too-wide Mediterranean and then balloons out to cover the entire southern hemisphere. Its eastern portions stretch into Asia, though so little is certain that they are labeled *terra incognita*—unknown lands. Europe, Africa, and Asia are the only continents. They are watered by a single ocean whose name changes with the languages of its neighboring inhabitants. Most remarkable of all is the division of the earth's surface. Land covers three-quarters of it. This was the world as it was known in 1400, and this was why the ensuing century would be called the age of exploration.

EUROPEAN ENCOUNTERS

There were many reasons why the map of the world shown on page 389 changed in the early sixteenth century. The sixteenth century was an age of exploration in many ways. Knowledge bequeathed from the past created curiosity about the present. Technological change made long sea voyages possible, and the demands of commerce provided incentives. Ottoman expansion on the southern and eastern frontiers of the Continent threatened access to the goods of the East on which Europeans had come to rely. Spices were rare and expensive, but they were not merely luxuries. While nobles and rich merchants consumed them lavishly to enhance their reputations of wealth and generosity, spices had many practical uses. Some acted as preservatives, others as flavorings to make palatable the rotting foodstuffs that were the fare of even the wealthiest Europeans. Others were used as perfumes to battle the noxious gases that rose from urban streets and invaded homes and workplaces. The drugs of the East, the nature of which we can only guess at, helped soothe chronic ill health. The demand for all of the "spices" continued to rise at a greater rate than their supply. There was more than a fortune to be made by anyone who could participate in the trade.

Eastern spices were expensive. Most European manufactured goods had little utility in the East. Woven wool, which was the staple of western industry, was too heavy to be worn in eastern climes. Both silk and cotton came from the East and were more expertly spun there. Even western jewelry relied upon imported stones. While metalwork was an attractive commodity for export, the dilemma of the arms trade was as acute then as it is now. Providing Ottomans or other Muslims with weapons to wage holy wars against Christian Europe posed problems of policy and morality. And once the Ottomans began to cast great bronze cannons of their own, European arms were less eagerly sought. Western gold and silver flowed steadily east. As supplies of precious metals dwindled, economic growth in Europe slowed. Throughout the fifteenth century, ever larger amounts of western specie were necessary to purchase ever smaller amounts of eastern commodities. Europe faced a severe shortage of gold and silver, a shortage that threatened its standard of living and its prospects for economic growth. The search was on to discover new sources of gold.

A Passage to India

It was the Portuguese who made the first dramatic breakthroughs in exploration and colonization. Perched on the southwestern tip of Europe, Portugal was an agriculturally poor and sparsely populated nation. Among its few marketable commodities were fish and wine, which it traded with Genoese and Venetian galleys making their voyages to northern Europe. Portugal's North African trade was more lucrative, but extended warfare between Christians and Muslims had made it unreliable. The Portuguese had long been sea explorers, especially in the Atlantic Ocean, where they had established bases in the Azores and Madeira islands. Their small ships, known as caravels, were ideal for ocean travel, and their navigators were among the most skillful in the world. Yet they were unable to participate in the lucrative Mediterranean trade in bullion and spices until the expanding power of the Ottomans threatened the traditional eastern sea routes.

Portuguese explorers moved gradually down the coast of Africa and ultimately reached western India in their search for gold, spices, and slaves.

Prince Henry the Navigator made no voyages himself. He spent his life directing exploration along the western coast of Africa from his base at Sagres, at the extreme southwestern tip of Portugal.

Prince Henry the Navigator. In the early fifteenth century, the Portuguese gained a foothold in northern Africa and used it to stage voyages along the continent's unexplored western coast. Like most explorers, the Portuguese were motivated by an unselfconscious mixture of faith and greed. Establishing southern bases would enable them to surround their Muslim enemies and give them access to the African bullion trade. The Portuguese navigator Bartolomeu Dias (ca. 1450–1500) summarized those goals succinctly: "To give light to those who are in darkness and to grow rich." Under the energetic leadership of Prince Henry the Navigator (1394–1460), the Portuguese pushed steadily southward. Prince Henry studied navigational techniques, accumulated detailed accounts of voyages, and encouraged the creation of accurate maps of the African coastline. What was learned on one trip was applied to the next. Soon the Portuguese were a power in the West African trade in slaves and gold ore. Black slaves became a staple of the African voyages, with nearly 150,000 slaves imported in the first 50 years of exploration. Portugal became the first European nation in which black slavery was common. Most slaves were used as domestics and laborers in Portugal; others were sent to work the lucrative sugar plantations that Prince Henry had established on the island of Madeira.

Prince Henry's systematic program paid off in the next generation. By the 1480s Portuguese outposts had reached almost to the equator, and in 1487 Bartolomeu Dias rounded the tip of Africa and opened the eastern African shores to Portuguese traders. The aim of the enterprises was access to Asia rather than Africa. Dias might have reached India if his crew had not mutinied and forced him to return home. A decade later, Vasco da Gama (ca. 1460–1524) rounded the Cape of Good Hope and crossed into the Indian Ocean. His journey took two years, but when he returned to Lisbon in 1499 laden with the most valuable spices of the East, Portuguese ambitions were achieved. Larger expeditions followed, one of which, blown off course, touched the South American coast of Brazil. Brazil was soon subsumed within the Portuguese dominions.

The Asian Trade. The Portuguese came to the East as traders rather than as conquerors. Building on their experience in West Africa, they developed a policy of establishing military outposts to protect their investments and subduing native populations only when necessary. Their achievements resulted more from determination than from technological superiority, though their initial displays of force, like da Gama's attack on Calicut in 1503, terrified the Asian rulers who controlled the spice trade. Throughout the East the Portuguese took advantage of local feuds to gain allies, and they established trading compounds that were easily defensible. The Portuguese general Alfonso de Albuquerque (1453–1515) understood the need for strategically placed garrisons and conquered the vital ports of the Middle East and India. By the first decade of the sixteenth century, the Portuguese were masters of a vast empire, which spanned both the eastern and western coasts of Africa and the western shores of India. Most importantly, the Portuguese controlled Ceylon and Indonesia, the precious Spice

Islands from which came cloves, cinnamon, and pepper. Almost overnight, Lisbon became one of the trading capitals of the world, tripling in population between 1500 and 1550.

It was northern Europe that was to harvest what Portugal had sown. The long voyages around Africa were costly and dangerous. Portugal produced no valuable commodities and had to exchange bullion for spices. Moreover, the expense of maintaining a far-flung empire ate into the profits of trade at the same time that the increased volume necessary to make the voyages worthwhile drove down spice prices. Between 1501 and 1505, more than 80 ships and 7000 men sailed from Portugal to the East. The vast commitment was underwritten by Flemish, German, and Italian bankers. Soon Antwerp replaced Lisbon as the marketplace for Asian spices. Ironically, it was in the accidental discovery of Brazil rather than in Asia that the Portuguese were rewarded for the enterprise of their explorers.

This sixteenth-century map of Java and the Moluccas shows European traders bartering for spices. At the upper left, a ship laden with the rich cargo sails for markets in Europe.

Mundus Novus

While most of Portugal's resources were devoted to the Asian trade, those of the Spanish kingdom came to be concentrated in the New World. Although larger and richer than its eastern neighbor, Spain had been segmented into a number of small kingdoms and principalities and divided between Christians and Muslims. Not until the end of the fifteenth century, when the crowns of Aragon and Castile were united and the Muslims expelled from Granada, could the Spanish concentrate their resources. By then they were far behind in establishing commercial enterprises. With Portugal dominating the African route to India, Queen Isabella of Castile was persuaded to take an interest in a western route by a Genoese adventurer, Christopher Columbus (ca. 1446–1506). That interest resulted in one of the greatest accidents of history. (See "Isabella of Castile," pp. 394–395.)

Christopher Columbus. Like all well-informed people of his day, Columbus believed that the world was round. By carefully calculating routes and distances, he concluded that a western track would be shorter and less expensive than the path that the Portuguese were breaking around Africa. Columbus's conclusions were based partly on conventional knowledge and partly on his own self-assurance. All were wholly erroneous. He misjudged the size of the globe by 25 percent and the distance of the journey by 400 percent. But he persevered against all odds. Columbus sailed westward into the unknown in 1492, and on 12 October he landed in the Bahamas, on an island that he named San Salvador. He had encountered a *Mundus Novus*, a New World.

Initially, Columbus's discovery was a disappointment. He had gone in search of a western passage to the Indies and he had failed to return to Spain laden with eastern spices. Despite his own belief that the islands he had discovered lay just off the coast of Japan, it was soon apparent that he had found an altogether

Isabella of Castile

"It is bittersweet to reign" was the motto of her predecessor, Henry IV. It was also the legacy of Isabella of Castile. She was beloved in life and revered after death; indeed, until recently there was a movement to have her canonized as a saint in the Catholic church. Her achievements were staggering. Her reign ended nearly a half century of internecine and dynastic warfare in Castile. Through her marriage to Ferdinand of Aragon she united the two largest kingdoms on the Spanish peninsula. With their combined resources, Isabella and Ferdinand were able to accomplish what their predecessors had only dreamed of for 500 years: the final reconquest of Spanish lands held by the Moors. By her financial support to a Genoese explorer named Christopher Columbus, Isabella gained for Castile title to the richest discovery in history.

But those accomplishments were not without cost. For Isabella, a united Spain was a Catholic Spain. The reconquista was conducted as a holy war of Christian against Muslim. It was as brutal as it was successful. Isabella was directly involved in planning the military campaign and attending to the details of logistics and strategy. She ended centuries of religious diversity by expelling both the Muslims and the Jews. She also accepted the need to purify Catholicism and encouraged the work of the Inquisition in examining the beliefs of converts known as *conversos*. That resulted in the exile or execution of thousands of former Muslims and Jews and blackened forever the reputation of the Spanish church.

Isabella of Castille was not raised to rule. She had two older brothers and was given a "woman's" education as a child. While her brother Alfonso struggled with Latin and French, she was taught only Castilian. While he learned to wield a sword, she learned to manipulate a needle. Isabella mastered sewing and the decorative arts of needlepoint and embroidery. Even as queen she sewed Ferdinand's shirts as a mark of respect and wifely devotion. But if she accepted the education that was offered to her, she had a streak of independence as well. She loved to hunt and refused to give up horses for donkeys as befitted a noblewoman. She also refused to accept the husband that her half-brother Henry IV had chosen for her. Isabella was a valuable pawn in the international game of diplomacy. She had a reputation for great beauty—her strawberry-blond hair and turquoise eyes were uncommon and much admired in Spain—and that, plus the fact that she had been named heir to the Castilian throne in 1468, brought a number of suitors. Henry betrothed her to Alfonso of Portugal, but Isabella had set her heart on Ferdinand of Aragon. In 1469, the two teenagers eloped, setting off a succession crisis in Castile and ultimately a civil war for the crown in which Isabella triumphed.

Ferdinand and Isabella enjoyed three decades of a happy marriage. Despite their travels, they were nearly inseparable. They ruled their kingdoms as partners and shared the joys and sorrows of their days. They endured the death of their only son, Juan, in 1497, and of his sister Isobel the following year. Three girls outlived their mother, but the eldest, Isabella's heir, Juana, had exhibited such erratic behavior that she was widely believed mentally incompetent. Her claims to the throne were ultimately set aside. Their youngest daughter, Catherine, the queen's favorite, was married to an English prince in 1501. Her mother would not live to see her divorced by Henry VIII.

At the time of their marriage, neither Ferdinand nor Isabella could have known that the union of their crowns was the first step in making Spain the most powerful nation in Europe. The two economies were complementary: Aragon with its long Mediterranean coastline was mercantile and Castile with its vast plain and fertile valleys was agricultural. Both were to benefit by the reconquest of Granada, which joined Spain's Atlantic and Mediterranean seaboards in the southeast. Isabella herself directed the military campaign. During eight years of battle, she guided Christian forces from the front, organizing supplies, reinforcements, and arms. She took special care of the wounded, setting up hospital tents that she visited. "The dead weigh on me heavily," she confessed to Ferdinand, "but they could not have gone better employed." Isabella was present at the siege of Granada, viewing the battlements personally and receiving the surrendered keys to the city on 2 January 1492.

The conquest of Granada drove the Muslims south into North Africa. It completed one part of the queen's program for religious unity. The second part was accomplished by decree. In April 1492, all Jews were given three months to depart the Spanish kingdoms. They were prohibited from removing arms, horses, or precious metal, making them not only homeless, but destitute. From the beginning of her reign, Isabella had persecuted the Jewish minority in her realm. They were made to wear distinguishing badges and denied civil rights that they had long enjoyed. At the same time, the work of the Spanish Inquisition under the direction of the zealous Cardinal Tomás de Torquemada had increased anti-Semitic tensions within Castile. Using threats and torture, Torquemada exposed loyal conversos as secret Jewish agents. He encouraged confiscation of converso property and attacks against Jewish communities. Although the queen at first intervened to maintain civic order, she, too, believed that the Jews constituted a disloyal fifth column within her state. But as long as she was at war with the Muslims, she needed Jewish financiers and administrators.

Once the war had ended, expulsion followed. Paradoxically, the first of the representatives of the old wealth of Castile boarded ship on the same day as a Genoese explorer, Christopher Columbus, set sail under the Castilian flag to uncover the new wealth of Castile. Columbus had approached Isabella twice before, but on both occasions his proposals had been rejected. Isabella's councillors were opposed both to Columbus's plan of sailing west to reach the Indies and to the concessions he demanded should he be successful. Although crown finances were depleted by the war and Isabella did not wish to bargain with an Italian adventurer, she realized that she would risk little to gain much. The decision was the most important of her reign. Through the discoveries made by Columbus and his successors, Castile reaped the greatest windfall in European history.

A MOMENTOUS DISCOVERY

Christopher Columbus seemingly needs no introduction. His name has forever been associated with the European discovery of the New World, although the meaning of that discovery has continually been contested. In the summer of 1492, Columbus sailed west from the Canary Islands believing that he would reach the coast of China. Instead he landed on an island in the Caribbean. This passage, from a letter addressed to the royal treasurer of Spain, contains his first impressions of the people he encountered.

A LETTER ADDRESSED TO THE NOBLE LORD RAPHAEL SANCHEZ, Treasurer to their most invincible Majesties, Ferdinand and Isabella, King and Queen of Spain, by Christopher Columbus, to whom our age is greatly indebted, treating of the islands of India recently discovered beyond the Ganges, to explore which he had been sent eight months before under the auspices and at the expense of their said Majesties.

The inhabitants of both sexes in this island, and in all the others which I have seen, or of which I have received information, go always naked as they were born, with the exception of some of the women, who use the covering of a leaf, or small bough, or an apron of cotton which they prepare for that purpose. None of them are possessed of any iron, neither have they weapons, being unacquainted with, and indeed incompetent to use them, not from any deformity of body (for they are well-formed), but because they are timid and full of fear.

They carry however in lieu of arms, canes dried in the sun, on the ends of which they fix heads of dried wood sharpened to a point, and even these they dare not use habitually; for it has often occurred when I have sent two or three of my men to any of the villages to speak with the natives, that they have come out in a disorderly troop, and have fled in such haste at the approach of our men, that the fathers forsook their children and the children their fathers. This timidity did not arise from any loss or injury that they had received from us; for, on the contrary, I gave to all I approached whatever articles I had about me, such as cloth and many other things, taking nothing of theirs in return: but they are naturally timid and fearful. As soon however as they see that they are safe, and have laid aside all fear, they are very simple and honest, and exceedingly liberal with all they have; none of them refusing any thing he may possess when he is asked for it, but on the contrary inviting us to ask them. They exhibit great love towards all others in preference to themselves: they also give objects of great value for trifles, and content themselves with very little or nothing in return.

Such are the events which I have briefly described. Farewell.

Lisbon, the 14th of March.
CHRISTOPHER COLUMBUS,
Admiral of the Fleet of the Ocean.

Christopher Columbus, *Letter from the First Voyage* (1493).

unknown landmass. Columbus's own explorations and those of his successors continued to focus on discovering a route to the Indies. That was all the more imperative once the Portuguese succeeded in finding the passage around Africa. Rivalry between the two nations intensified after 1500, when the Portuguese began exploring the coast of Brazil. In 1494, the Treaty of Tordesillas had confined Portugal's right to the eastern route to the Indies as well as to any undiscovered lands east of an imaginary line fixed west of the Cape Verde Islands. That entitled Portugal to Brazil; the Spanish received whatever lay west of the line. At the time few doubted that Portugal had the better of the bargain.

But Spanish-backed explorations soon proved the value of the new lands. Using the Caribbean islands as a staging ground, successive explorers uncovered the vast coastline of Central and South America. In 1513, Vasco Núñez de Balboa (1475–1517) crossed the land passage in Panama and became the first European to view the Pacific Ocean. The discovery of this ocean refueled Spanish ambitions to find a western passage to the Indies.

A woodcut depicting Christopher Columbus's landing on the island of Hispaniola.

Magellan. In 1519, Ferdinand Magellan (ca. 1480–1521), a Portuguese mariner in the service of Spain, set sail in pursuit of Columbus's goal of reaching the Spice Islands by sailing westward. His voyage, which he did not live to complete, remains the most astounding of the age. After making the Atlantic crossing, Magellan resupplied his fleet in Brazil. Then his ships began the long southerly run toward the tip of South America, though he had no idea of the length of the continent. Suppressing mutinies and overcoming shipwrecks and desertions, Magellan finally found the straits that still bear his name. That crossing was the most difficult of all; the 300 miles took 38 terrifying days to navigate.

The Pacific voyage was equally remarkable. The sailors went nearly four months without taking on fresh food or water. Survival was miraculous. "We drank yellow water and often ate sawdust. Rats were sold for half a ducat a piece."

When Magellan finally reached land, in the Philippines, his foolhardy decision to become involved in a local war cost him his life. It was left to his navigator, Sebastian Elcano (ca. 1476–1526), to complete the journey. In 1522, three years and one month after setting out, Elcano returned to Spain with a single ship and 18 survivors of the crew of 280. But in his hold were spices of greater value than the cost of the expedition, and in his return was practical proof that the world was round.

The circumnavigation of Magellan and Elcano brought to an end the first stage of the Spanish exploration of the New World. Columbus's dreams were realized, but the vastness of the Pacific Ocean made a western passage to the Indies uneconomical. In 1529, the Spanish crown relinquished to the Portuguese its claims to the Spice Islands for a cash settlement. By then, trading spices was less alluring than mining gold and silver.

The Spanish Conquests

At the same moment that Magellan's voyage closed one stage of Spanish exploration, the exploits of Hernando Cortés (1485–1547) opened another. The Spanish colonized the New World along the model of their reconquest of Spain. Individuals were given control over land and the people on it in return for military service. The interests of the crown were threefold: to convert the natives to Christianity; to extend sovereignty over new dominions; and to gain some measure of profit from the venture. The colonial entrepreneurs had a singular interest—to grow rich. By and large, the colonizers came from the lower orders of Spanish society. Even the original captains and governors were drawn from groups, like younger sons of the nobility, that would have had little opportunity for rule in Castile. They undertook great risks in expectation of great rewards. Ruthlessness and greed were their universal qualities.

Thus many of the protective measures taken by the crown to ensure orderly colonization and fair treatment of the natives were ineffective in practice. During the first decades of the sixteenth century, Spanish captains and their followers subdued the Indian populations of the Caribbean islands and put them to work on the agricultural haciendas that they had carved out for themselves. As early as 1498, Castilian women began arriving in the New World. Their presence helped change the character of the settlement towns from wild frontier garrisons to civilized settlements. Younger daughters of the lesser nobility, guided and guarded by chaperones, came to find husbands among the successful conquistadores. Some of the women ultimately inherited huge estates and participated fully in the forging of Spanish America.

A sixteenth-century Indian drawing of Cortés marching on the Aztec capital at Tenochtitlán. Cortés, the bearded figure third from right, is accompanied by the Indian princess Malinche, who served as his interpreter, and the Moorish servant Estevancio. Barefoot soldiers and Indian porters bring up the rear.

Life on the hacienda, even in relative ease with a Castilian wife and family, did not always satisfy the ambitions of the Spanish colonizers. Hernando Cortés was one such conquistador. Having participated in the conquest of Cuba, Cortés sought an independent command to lead an expedition into the hinterland of Central America, where a fabulous empire was rumored to exist. Gathering a force of 600 men, Cortés sailed across the Gulf of Mexico in 1519; established a fort at Vera Cruz, where he garrisoned 200 men; and then sank his boats so that none of his company could turn back. With 400 soldiers, he began his quest. The company marched 250 miles through steamy jungles and over rugged mountains before glimpsing the first signs of the great Aztec civilization.

The Aztec empire was a loose confederation of native tribes that the Aztecs had conquered during the previous century. They were ruled by the emperor Montezuma II (1502–1520) from his capital at Tenochtitlán, a marvelous city built of stone and baked clay in the middle of a lake. Invited to an audience with the Aztec emperor, Cortés and his men saw vast stores of gold and silver.

The conquest of the Aztecs took almost a year. Nearly 100,000 natives from the tribes that the Aztecs had conquered supported the Spanish assault. Cortés's cavalry terrified the Aztecs. They had never seen horses or iron armaments. Cortés also benefited from the Aztec practice of taking battlefield captives to be used in religious sacrifices. That allowed many Spanish soldiers, who would otherwise have been killed, to be rescued and to fight again.

By 1522, Cortés was master of an area larger than all of Spain. But the cost in native lives was staggering. In 30 years a population of approximately 25 million had been reduced to less than 2 million. Most of the loss was due to exposure to European diseases like smallpox, typhoid, and measles, against which the natives were helpless. Their labor-intensive system of agriculture could not survive the rapid decrease in population, and famine followed pestilence.

This tragic sequence was repeated everywhere the Europeans appeared. In 1531, Francisco Pizarro (ca. 1475–1541) matched Cortés' feat when he conquered the Peruvian empire of the Incas. That conquest vastly

The Aztecs were a collection of tribal peoples who created a flourishing network of city-states in the Valley of Mexico. Once a population of 25 million people, Cortes' conquest and the introduction of European diseases reduced that number to just two million three decades later.

THE HALLS OF MONTEZUMA

Bernal Díaz del Castillo (ca. 1492–1581) was one of the soldiers who accompanied Hernando Cortés on the conquest of the Aztecs. Díaz wrote The True History of the Conquest of New Mexico *to refute what he regarded as inaccurate accounts of the conquest. In this passage he describes the Aztec gods from a Christian point of view and shows how difficult it was for the Europeans to understand the different cultures they were encountering.*

THEN CORTÉS SAID TO MONTEZUMA ... "Your Highness is indeed a great prince, and it has delighted us to see your cities. Now that we are here in your temple, will you show us your gods?"

Montezuma replied that he would first have to consult with his priests. After he had spoken with them, he bade us enter a small tower room, a kind of hall where there were two altars with very richly painted planks on the ceiling. On each altar there were two giant figures, their bodies very tall and stout. The first one, to the right, they said was Uichilobos, their god of war. It had a very broad face with monstrous, horrible eyes, and the whole body was covered with precious stones, gold, and pearls that were stuck on with a paste they make in this country out of roots. The body was circled with great snakes made of gold and precious stones, and in one hand he held a bow and in the other some arrows. A small idol standing by him they said was his page; he held a short lance and a shield rich with gold and precious stones. Around the neck of Uichilobos were silver Indian faces and things that we took to be the hearts of these Indians, made of gold and decorated with many precious blue stones. There were braziers with copal incense, and they were burning in them the hearts of three Indians they had sacrificed that day. All the walls and floor were black with crusted blood, and the whole place stank.

To the left stood another great figure, the height of Uichilobos, with the face of a bear and glittering eyes made of their mirrors, which they call *tezcal.* It was decorated with precious stones the same as Uichilobos, for they said that the two were brothers. This Tezcatepuca was the god of hell and had charge of the souls of the Mexicans. His body was girded with figures like little devils, with snakelike tails. The walls were so crusted with blood and the floor was so bathed in it that in the slaughterhouses of Castile there was no such stink. They had offered to this idol five hearts from the day's sacrifices....

Our captain said to Montezuma, half laughingly, "Lord Montezuma, I do not understand how such a great prince and wise man as yourself can have failed to come to the conclusion that these idols of yours are not gods, but evil things—devils is the term for them...."

The two priests with Montezuma looked hostile, and Montezuma replied with annoyance, "Señor Malinche, if I had thought that you would so insult my gods, I would not have shown them to you. We think they are very good, for they give us health, water, good seedtimes and weather, and all the victories we desire. We must worship and make sacrifices to them. Please do not say another word to their dishonor."

From Bernal Díaz, *The True History of the Conquest of New Mexico* (1552–1568).

extended the territory under Spanish control and became the true source of profit for the crown when a huge silver mine was discovered in 1545 at Potosí in what is now southern Bolivia. The gold and silver that poured into Spain in the next quarter century helped support Spanish dynastic ambitions in Europe. During the course of the sixteenth century, more than 200,000 Spaniards migrated across the ocean. Perhaps one in ten were women who married and set up families. In succeeding generations, the settlers created huge haciendas built on the forced labor of black African slaves, who proved better able to endure the rigors of mining and farming than did the natives.

The Legacy of the Encounters

By the seventeenth century, long-distance trade had begun to integrate the regions of the world into a single marketplace. Slaves bought in Africa mined silver in South America. The bullion was shipped to Spain, where it was distributed across Europe. Most went to Amsterdam to settle Spanish debts, Dutch bankers having replaced the Italians as the paymasters of Europe. From Holland the silver traveled east to the Baltic Sea—the Dutch lifeline where vital stores of grain and timber were purchased for home consumption. Even more of this African-mined Spanish silver, traded by the Dutch, was carried to Asia to buy spices in the Spice Islands, cottons in India, and silk in China. Millions of ounces of silver flowed from South America to Asia via the European trading routes. On the return voyage, Indian cottons were traded in Africa to purchase slaves for the South American silver mines.

Gold, God, and Glory. Gold, God, and glory neatly summarized the motives of the European explorers. Perhaps it is not necessary to delve any further. The gold of Africa and the silver of South America enriched the western nations. Christian missions arose wherever the European empires touched down: among Africans, Asians, and Native Americans. And glory there was in plenty. The feats of the European explorers were recounted in story and song. The *Lusiads* (1572) by Luiz de Camões (ca. 1524–1580), one of the greatest works of Portuguese literature, celebrated the new age. "They were men of no ordinary stature, equally at home in war and in dangers of every kind: they founded a new kingdom among distant peoples, and made it great." In the achievement of exploration and conquest, the modern world had finally surpassed the ancients. "Let us hear no more then of Ulysses and Aeneas and their long journeyings, no more of Alexander and Trajan and their famous victories. My theme is the daring and renown of the Portuguese, to whom Neptune and Mars alike give homage."

The feats of exploration were worthy of celebration. In less than 50 years, tenacious European seafarers

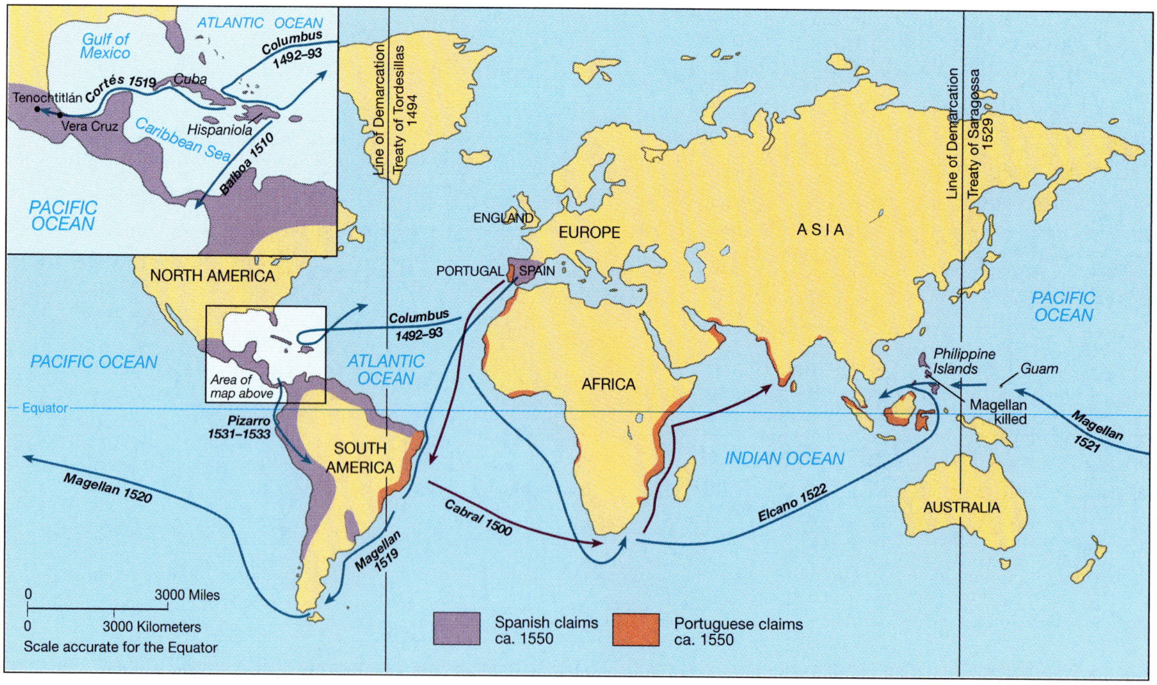

Voyages of discovery and the claims of Spain and Portugal to overseas empires. Pope Alexander VI divided the New World between the two Iberian powers.

This French navigator has come ashore to use an early navigating instrument in order to avoid the inaccurate readings obtained on a rolling deck.

found passages to the east and continents to the west. In doing so they overcame terrors both real and imagined. Hazardous journeys in uncharted waters took their toll in men and ships. The odds of surviving a voyage of exploration were no better than those of surviving an epidemic of plague. Nearly two-thirds of da Gama's crew perished on the passage to India. The 40 men that Columbus left on Hispaniola, almost half his company, disappeared without a trace. Only one of the five ships that set out with Magellan in 1519 returned to Spain. "If you want to learn how to pray, go to sea" was a Portuguese proverb that needed no explanation.

However harsh was reality, fantasy was more terrifying still. Out of sight of land for three months, da Gama's crew brooded over the folk wisdom of the sea: that the earth was flat and the ships would fall off its edge; that the green ocean was populated by giant monsters. As they approached the equator, they feared that the water would become so hot it would boil them alive and the sun so powerful it would turn their skin black. Sailors to the New World expected to find all manner of horrible creations. Cyclopes and headless one-legged torsos were popularized in drawings, while cannibals and giants were described in realistic detail by the earliest voyagers. No wonder mutiny was a constant companion of exploration.

Yet all of the fanciful inhibitions were overcome. So too were those inhibitions over which the explorers had more control. The expansion of Europe was a feat of technology. Advances in navigational skills, especially in dead reckoning and later in calculating latitude from the position of the sun, were essential preconditions for covering the distances that were to be traveled. So were the more sophisticated ship designs. The magnetic compass and the astrolabe were indispensable tools. New methods for the making of maps and charts, and the popular interest in them, fueled both ambitions and abilities. It was a mapmaker who named the newly found continents after Amerigo Vespucci (1451–1512), the Italian explorer who voyaged to Brazil for the Portuguese. It may have been an accident that Columbus found the New World, but it was no coincidence that he was able to land in the same place three more times.

European Reflections. Riches and converts, power and glory, all came in the wake of exploration. But in the process of exploring new lands and new cultures, Europe also discovered itself. It learned something of its own aspirations. Early Portuguese voyagers went in quest of the mythical Prester John, a saintly figure who was said to rule a heaven on earth in the middle of Africa. The first children born on Madeira were named Adam and Eve, though that slave plantation of sugar and wine was an unlikely Garden of Eden. The optimism of those who searched for the fountain of youth in the Florida swamps was not only that they would find it there, but that a long life was worth living.

Contact with the cultures of the New World also forced a different kind of thinking about life in the old one. The French essayist Michel de Montaigne (1533–1592) was less interested in the perceptions of Native Americans than he was of his own compatriots when he recorded this encounter: "They have a way in their language of thinking of men as halves of one another. They noticed among us some men gorged to the full with things of every sort while their other halves were beggars at their doors. They found it

Contact with cultures of the New World forced Europeans into a different way of thinking about the old world. In this detail from The Cognoscenti, *a seventeenth century Flemish painting, English scholars and navigators examine European encounters with new lands and new cultures.*

strange that these poverty stricken halves should suffer such injustice." The supposed customs of strange lands also provided the setting for one of the great works of English social criticism, Sir Thomas More's *Utopia* (1516).

Europe also discovered and revealed a darker side of itself in the age of exploration. Accompanying the boundless optimism and assertive self-confidence that made so much possible was a tragic arrogance toward and callous disregard of native races. Portuguese travelers described Africans as "dog-faced, dog-toothed people, satyrs, wild men, and cannibals." Such attitudes helped justify enslavement. The European conquests were both brutal and wasteful. The Dominican priest Bartolomé de Las Casas (1474–1566) championed the cause of the native inhabitants at the court of the Spanish kings. His *Apologetic History of the Indies* (1550) highlighted the complexity of native society even as he witnessed its destruction. The German artist Albrecht Dürer (1471–1528) marveled at the "subtle ingenuity of the men in those distant lands" after viewing a display of Aztec art.

But few Europeans were so enlightened about native society. Although Europeans encountered heritages that were in some ways richer than their own, only the most farsighted westerners could see that there was more value in the preservation of the heritages than in their demolition. The Portuguese spice trade did not depend upon the indiscriminate destruction of eastern ports. The obliteration of millions of Aztecs and Incas was not a necessary result of the fever for gold and silver. The destruction was wanton. It revealed the

Europe in 1500. While the western part of Europe had taken on its modern features, central and eastern Europe continued to change their boundaries.

rapaciousness, greed, and cruelty of the Portuguese and Spanish conquerors. Those were the impulses of the Crusades rather than of the Renaissance. The Iberian *reconquista*—the holy war against the Muslims by which the Iberian Peninsula was won back into Christian hands—was replayed throughout South America with tragic results.

GEOGRAPHICAL TOUR
EUROPE IN 1500

Just as the map of the world was changing as a result of the voyages of exploration, so the map of Europe was changing as a result of the activities of princes. The early sixteenth century was the age of the prince, the first great stage of nation building that would last for the next 300 years. The New Monarchies, as they are sometimes called, consolidated territories that were divided culturally, linguistically, and historically. The states of Europe were political units, and they were forged by political means: by diplomacy, by marriage, and, most commonly, by war. The national system that we take for granted when thinking about Europe is a relatively recent development. Before we can observe its beginnings, we must first have a picture of Europe as it existed in 1500. At that time it was composed of nearly 500 distinct political units.

Europe is a concept. Like all concepts, it is difficult to define. The vast plain that stretches from the

Netherlands to the steppes of Russia presents few natural barriers to migration. Tribes had been wandering across the plain for thousands of years, slowly settling into the more fertile lands to practice their agriculture. Only in the south did geographical forces stem the flow of humanity. The Carpathian Mountains created a basin for the settlement of Slavic peoples that extended down to the Black Sea. The Alps provided a boundary for French, Germanic, and Italian settlements. The Pyrenees defined the Iberian Peninsula, with a mixture of African and European peoples.

Eastern Boundaries

In the East, three great empires had created the political geography that could be said to define a European boundary: the Mongol, the Ottoman, and the Russian. During the early Middle Ages, Mongol warriors had swept across the Asian steppes and conquered most of central and southern Russia. By the sixteenth century, the Mongol empire was disintegrating, its lands divided into a number of separate states called *khanates*. The khanate of the Crimea, with lands around the northern shores of the Black Sea, created the southeastern border of Europe.

Eastern Europe before the consolidation of Russia. The Duchy of Lithuania had reached the height of its power and stretched from the Baltic to the Black Sea.

The Ottoman territories defined the southern boundary. By 1450, the Ottomans controlled all of Byzantium and Greece, dominating an area from the Black Sea to the Aegean. Fifty years later, they had conquered nearly all the lands between the Aegean and the Adriatic seas. A perilous frontier was established on the Balkan Peninsula. There the principalities of Moldavia, Wallachia, Transylvania, and Hungary held out against the Ottomans for another quarter century before being overrun.

The Russian state defined the eastern boundary of Europe. Russia too had been a great territorial unit in the Middle Ages, centered at Kiev in the west and stretching eastward into Asia. The advance of the Mongols in the thirteenth century had contracted the eastern part of Russia, and its western domains had disintegrated under the practice of dividing the ruling prince's inheritance among his sons. In 1500, Europe reached as far east as the principality of Muscovy. There the heritage of East and West mingled. In some periods of history, Russia's ties with the West were most important; at other times, Russia retreated into isolation from Europe.

The northern borders of eastern Europe centered on the Baltic Sea, one of the most important trading routes of the early modern era. On the northern coasts lay the Scandinavian nations of Sweden, Norway, and Denmark. Those loosely confederated nations had a single king throughout the fifteenth century. Denmark, the southernmost of the three, was also the richest and most powerful. It enjoyed a favorable trading position on both the North and Baltic seas and social and economic integration with the Germanic states on its border. On the southern side of the Baltic Sea lay the dominions of the Teutonic Knights, physically divided by the large state of Poland-Lithuania. The Teutonic territories, in the valuable Baltic region of Prussia, had been colonized by German crusaders in the thirteenth century.

Poland-Lithuania comprised an enormous territory that covered the length of Europe from the Baltic to the Black Sea. The crowns of the two nations had been joined at the end of the fourteenth century, and their dynastic history was tied up with the nations of Bohemia and Hungary to their west and south. While Bohemia was increasingly drawn into the affairs of central Europe, Hungary remained more eastern in orientation, partly because the Bohemians gave nominal allegiance to the Holy Roman Emperor and partly because the Ottoman conquests had engulfed a large part of the Hungarian territories. At the end of the fifteenth century, Poland, Lithuania, Bohemia, and Hungary were all ruled by the same family, the Jagiellons.

Mongols and Ottomans to the south, Russians in the east, Scandinavia in the north, Poland-Lithuania in the center, and Hungary in the west: such were the contours of the eastern portion of Europe. Its lands were, on the whole, less fertile than those farther west, and its climate was more severe. It was a sparsely populated region. Its wealth lay in the Baltic fisheries, in the Hungarian and Bohemian silver mines, and in the enormous Russian forests, where wood and its by-products were plentiful. Except in the southern portions of Poland and central Bohemia, the region was agriculturally poor. The eastern territories had been resettled during the population crisis of the early fourteenth century. Then, native Slavs were joined by German colonizers from the West and Asian conquerors from the East. The clash of races did much to define the political history of eastern Europe.

Central Europe

The middle of the continent was defined by the Holy Roman Empire and occupied almost entirely by Germanic peoples. In length, the empire covered the territory from the North and Baltic seas to the Adriatic and the Mediterranean, where the Italian city-states were located. In width, it stretched from Bohemia to Burgundy. Politically, central Europe comprised a bewildering array of principalities, Church lands, and free towns. By the end of the fifteenth century, the Holy Roman Empire was an empire in name only. The large states of Brandenburg, Bohemia, and Bavaria resembled the political units of the east. In the south, the Alps provided an effective physical boundary, which allowed the Archduchy of Austria and the Swiss Confederation to follow their own separate paths. Stretching across the center of the empire, from the Elbe River to the North Sea, were a jumble of petty states. Great cities such as Nuremberg and Ulm in the south, Bremen and Hamburg in the north, and Frankfurt and Cologne in the west were free municipalities. Large sections of the northwestern part of the empire were governed by the Church through resident bishops. Farther to the west were the prosperous Low Countries: Holland and its port of Amsterdam, Brabant and its port of Antwerp. In the southwest, the empire

Central Europe showing the boundaries of the Holy Roman Empire.

extended in some places as far as the Rhone River and included the rich estates of Luxembourg, Lorraine, and Burgundy.

The riches of the empire made it the focal point of Europe. Nearly 15 million people lived within its borders. Its agriculture varied from the olive- and wine-producing areas in the southwest to the great granaries in its center. Rich mineral deposits and large reserves of timber made the German lands industrially advanced. The European iron industry was centered there, and the empire was the arms manufacturer for the western world. The empire was also a great commercial center, heir to the Hanseatic League of the Middle Ages. Its northern and western ports teemed with trade, and its merchants were replacing the Italians as the leading international bankers.

Like the empire, the Italian peninsula was divided into a diverse collection of small city-states. During the course of the fifteenth century, five city-states had emerged as most powerful (see Chapter 11). In the north were Florence, Venice, and the Duchy of Milan. In the south was Rome, spiritual center of Catholicism and residence of the pope. Although Roman and papal governments were separate jurisdictions, in fact their fates were bound together. Papal lands stretched far to the north of Rome, and wars to defend or expand them were Roman as well as papal ventures. The kingdom of Naples—the breadbasket of the Mediterranean—occupied the southernmost part of Italy and included the agriculturally rich island of Sicily.

The West

The Iberian Peninsula, the French territories, and the British Isles formed the westernmost borders of Europe. Separated from France in the north by the Pyrenees, the Iberian Peninsula is surrounded by the Atlantic Ocean and the Mediterranean Sea on the west and east. But neither its protective mountain barrier nor its ample coastline was its most significant geographical feature during its formative period. Rather, it was the fact that Iberia is separated from North Africa only by the easily navigable Strait of Gibraltar. During the Middle Ages, the peninsula was overrun by North African Muslims, whom the Spanish called Moors. From the eighth to the fifteenth centuries, Iberian history was dominated by the reconquista—the recapture and re-Christianization of the conquered territories. The reconquest was finally completed in 1492, when the Moors were pushed out of Granada and the Jews were expelled from Spain. At the end of the fifteenth century, the Iberian Peninsula contained several separate kingdoms. The most important were Portugal—the only Continental nation to have the same borders in 1500 as it does today—on the western coast; Aragon, with its Mediterranean ports of Barcelona and Valencia; and Castile, the largest of the Iberian states. The marriage of King Ferdinand of Aragon and Queen Isabella of Castile in 1469 had joined the crowns of Aragon and Castile, but the two kingdoms remained separate.

Western Europe was already consolidated into nation states.

The remnants of ancient Gaul were also favored by a maritime location. Like those of Iberia, French coasts are located along the Mediterranean Sea and the Atlantic Ocean. France's eastern boundaries touched the empire; its southern mountain border touched Spain. To the northwest, Britain was less than 30 miles from France across the English Channel. Toward the end of the fifteenth century, France was still divided into many smaller fiefs. The royal domain centered on Paris and extended to Champagne in the east and Normandy in the west. South of this area, however, from Orléans to Brittany, were principalities that had long been contested between England and France. Nor was the rich central plain yet integrated into the royal domain. Agriculturally, French lands were the richest in Europe. France enjoyed both Mediterranean and Atlantic climates, which suited the growing of the widest variety of foodstuffs. Its population of approximately 13 million was second only to that of the empire.

Across the Channel lay Britain (composed of England, Scotland, and Wales) and Ireland. Britain had been settled by an array of European colonizers—Romans, Danes, Angles, and Saxons—before being conquered in the eleventh century by the French Normans. From that time, it was protected by the rough waters of the English Channel and the North Sea and allowed to develop a distinct cultural and political heritage. Wales to the west and Scotland to the north were still separate nations at the beginning of the sixteenth century. Both were mountainous lands with harsh climates and few natural advantages. They were sparsely populated. Although Ireland, too, was sparsely populated, it contained several rich agricultural areas especially suited for dairying and grazing.

In 1500, Europe exhibited a remarkable diversity of political and geographical forms. Huge states in the east, tiny principalities in the center, emerging nations in the west, all seemingly had little in common. There was as yet no state system and no clear group of dominant powers. The western migration of the Germanic peoples appeared to be over, but their consolidation was as yet unimagined. The Iberians struggled to expel the Moors, the Hungarians to hold back the Ottomans. Everywhere one looked there was fragmentation and disarray. Yet in less than a half century the largest empire yet known in the West would be formed. States would come to be consolidated and dynasties established all over the Continent. And with the rise of the state would come the dream of dominion, an empire over all of Europe.

THE FORMATION OF STATES

It was Machiavelli who identified the prince as the agent of change in the process of state formation. He believed that the successful prince could bring unity to his lands, security to his borders, and prosperity to his subjects. The unsuccessful prince brought nothing but ruin.

A process as long and as complex as the formation of nations is not subject to the will of individuals. Factors as diverse as geography, population, and natural resources are all decisive. So too are the structures through which human activity is channeled. The ways in which families are organized and wealth is transmitted from generation to generation can result in large estates with similar customs or small estates with varying ones. The manner in which social groups are formed and controlled can mean that power is centralized or dispersed. The beliefs of ordinary people and the way they practice them can define who is a part of a community and who is not. All those elements and many others have much to do with the way in which European states began to take shape at the end of the fifteenth century. Despite the complexities, the simple truth of Machiavelli's observations should not be forgotten: in the first stages of the consolidation of European nations, the role of the prince was crucial.

Indeed, in the middle of the fifteenth century there were many factors working against the formation of large states in Europe. The most obvious involved simple things such as transportation and communication. The distance that could be covered quickly was very small. In wet and cold seasons, travel was nearly impossible. The emperor Charles V sat in Burgundy for two months awaiting a favorable wind to take him to his newly inherited kingdom of Spain. Similarly, directives from the center of the states to the localities were slow to arrive and slower still to be adopted. Large areas were difficult to control and to defend. Distinct languages or dialects also made for difficulties in communication. Only the most educated could use Latin as a common written language. Separate languages contributed to separate cultures. Customary practices, common ancestry, and shared experiences helped define a sense of community through which small states defined themselves.

To the natural forces that acted to maintain the existence of small units of government were added invented ones. To succeed, a prince had to establish supremacy over a number of rivals. For the most part, states were inherited. In some places it was customary to follow the rule of primogeniture—inheritance by the eldest son. In others, estates were split among sons, or among children of both sexes. Some traditions, like those of the French, excluded inheritance through women; others, like the Castilian, treated women's claims as equal to men's. Short lives meant prolonged disputes about inheritance. Rulers had to defend their thrones from any number of rivals with strong claims to legitimacy.

So, too, did rulers have to defend themselves from the ambitions of their mightiest subjects. Dukes could dream only one dream. The constant warfare of the European nobility was one of the central features of the later Middle Ages. To avoid resort to arms, princes and peers entered into all manner of alliances, using their children as pawns and the marriage bed as the chessboard. Rulers also faced independent institutions within their states, powerful organizations that had to be won over or crushed. The long process of taming the Church was well advanced by the end of the fifteenth century and about to enter a new stage. Fortified towns presented a different problem. They possessed both the manpower and wealth necessary to raise and maintain armies. They also jealously guarded their privileges. Rulers who could not tax their towns could not rule their state. Finally, most kingdoms had assemblies that represented the propertied classes, especially in matters of taxation. Some, such as the English

Parliament and the Spanish Cortes, were strong; others, such as the Imperial Diet and the French Estates-General, were weak. But everywhere they posed an obstacle to the extension of the power of princes.

In combination, such factors slowed and shaped the process of state formation. But neither separately nor together were they powerful enough to overcome it. The fragmentation of Europe into so many small units of government made some consolidation inevitable. There were always stronger and weaker neighbors, always broken successions and failed lines. The practice of dynastic marriage meant that smaller states were continually being inherited by the rulers of larger ones. If the larger state was stable, it absorbed the smaller one. If not, the smaller state would split off again to await its next predator or protector. As the first large states took shape, the position of smaller neighbors grew ever more precarious.

That was especially true by the end of the fifteenth century because of the increase in the destructive power of warfare. Technological advances in cannonry and in the skills of gunners and engineers made medieval fortifications untenable. The fall of Constantinople was as much a military watershed as it was a political one. Gunpowder decisively changed battlefield tactics. It made heavy armor obsolete and allowed for the development of a different type of warfare. Lightly armored horses and riders could not only inflict more damage upon one another, but they were now mobile enough to be used against infantry. Infantry armed with long pikes or small muskets became the crucial components of armies that were growing ever larger. Systems of supply were better, sources of small arms were more available, and the rewards of conquest were more tangible. What could not be inherited or married could be conquered.

Eastern Configurations

The interplay of factors that encouraged and inhibited the formation of states is most easily observed in the eastern parts of Europe. There the different paths taken by Muscovy and Poland-Lithuania stand in contrast. At the beginning of the sixteenth century, the principality of Muscovy was the largest European political unit. Muscovy had established itself as the heir to the ancient state of Russia through conquest, shrewd political alliances, and the good fortune of its princes to be blessed with long reigns. Muscovy's growth was phenomenal. Under Ivan III, "the Great" (1462–1505), Muscovy expanded to the north and west. During a long series of wars it annexed Novgorod and large parts of Livonia and Lithuania. Its military successes were almost unbroken, but so too were its diplomatic triumphs. Ivan the Great preferred pacification to conquest, though when necessary he could conquer with great brutality. Between 1460 and 1530, Muscovy increased its landed territory by 1.5 million square miles.

A number of factors led to the rise of Muscovy. External threats had diminished. First, the deterioration of the Mongol empire that had dominated south-central Russia allowed Ivan to escape the yoke of Mongol rule that the Russian princes had worn for centuries. Second, the fall of Constantinople made Muscovy the heir to eastern Christendom, successor to the Roman and Byzantine empires. Ivan's marriage to Sophia, niece of the last emperor of Byzantium, cemented the connection. Sophia brought both Italian artisans and Byzantine customs to the Russian court, helping Ivan open his contacts with the wider world.

Territorial conquests and the decline of Byzantium were not the only important features of the consolidation of the Muscovite state. Ivan the Great was fortunate in having no competitors for his throne. He was able to use other social groups to help administer the new Muscovite territories without fear of setting up a rival to power. Ivan extended the privileges of his nobility and organized a military class that received land as a reward for fidelity. He also developed a new theory of sovereignty that rested on divine rather than temporal power. Traditionally, Russian princes ruled their lands by patrimony. They owned both estates and occupants. Ivan the Great extended that principle to cover all lands to which there was an ancient Russian claim and combined it with the religious authority of the Orthodox church. Both he and his successors ruled with the aid of able Church leaders who were usually part of the prince's council.

Ivan the Terrible. What made the expansion of Muscovy so impressive was that land once gained was never lost. The military and political achievements of Ivan the Great were furthered by his son Vasili and his more famous grandson Ivan IV, "the Terrible" (1533–1584). Ivan IV defeated the Mongols on his southeastern border and incorporated the entire Volga river basin into Muscovy. But his greatest ambition was to gain a port on the Baltic Sea and establish a northern outlet for commerce. His objective was to conquer

Livonia. Nearly three decades of warfare between Muscovy and Poland-Lithuania—with which Livonia had allied itself—resulted in large territorial gains, but Muscovy always fell short of the real prize. And Ivan's northern campaigns seriously weakened the defense of the south. In 1571, the Crimean Tartars advanced from their territories on Muscovy's southwestern border and inflicted a powerful psychological blow when they burned the city of Moscow. Although the Tartars were eventually driven off Muscovite soil, expansion in both north and south was at an end for the next 75 years.

By the reign of Ivan IV, Muscovite society was divided roughly into three groups: the hereditary nobility known as the boyars, the military service class, and the peasantry who were bound to the land. There was no large mercantile presence in Muscovy and its urban component remained small. The boyars, who were powerful landlords of great estates, owed little to the tsar. They inherited their lands and did not necessarily benefit from expansion and conquest. Members of the military service class, on the other hand, were bound to the success of the crown. Their military service was a requirement for the possession of their estates, which were granted out of lands gained through territorial expansion. Gradually, the new military service class grew in power and prestige, largely at the expense of the older boyars. Ivan IV used members of the military service class as legislative advisors and elevated them in his parliamentary council (the Zemsky Sobor), which also included representatives of the nobility, clergy, and towns.

Unlike his grandfather, Ivan IV had an abiding mistrust of the boyars. They had held power when he was a child, and it was rumored that his mother had been poisoned by them. It was in his treatment of the boyars that he earned the nickname "the Terrible." During his brutal suppression of supposed conspiracies, several thousand families were massacred by Ivan's own orders and thousands more by the violent excesses of his agents. Ivan constantly imagined plots against himself, and many of the men who served him met horrible deaths. He also forcibly relocated boyar families, stripping them of their lands in one place but granting them new lands elsewhere. The practice made their situation similar to that of the military service class, who owed their fortunes to the tsar.

All those measures contributed to the breakdown of local networks of influence and power and to a disruption of local governance. But they also made possible a system of central administration, one of Ivan IV's most important achievements. He created departments of state to deal with the various tasks of administration, which resulted in more efficient management of revenues and of the military. Ivan IV promoted the interests of the military service class over those of the boyars, but he did not destroy the nobility. New boyars were created, especially in conquered territories, and those new families owed their positions and loyalty to the prince. Both the boyars and the military benefited from Ivan's policy of binding the great mass of people to the land. Russian peasants had few political or economic rights in comparison to those of western peasants, but during the early sixteenth century even the meager rights Russian peasants had were curtailed. The right of peasants to move from the estate of one lord to that of another was suspended, all but binding the peasantry to the land. The serfdom made possible the prolonged absence of military leaders from their estates and contributed to the creation of the military service class. But it also made imperative the costly system of coercing agricultural and industrial labor. In the long term, serfdom retarded the development of the

A delegation of Russian boyars bearing gifts visited the Holy Roman Emperor Maximilian II in 1576 in order to seek his aid against Poland-Lithuania.

Muscovite economy by removing incentive from large landholders to make investments in commerce or to improve agricultural production.

Poland-Lithuania. The growth of an enlarged and centralized Muscovy stands in contrast to the experiences of Poland-Lithuania during the same period. At the end of the fifteenth century, Casimir IV (1447–1492) ruled the kingdom of Poland and the grand duchy of Lithuania. His son Vladislav II ruled Bohemia (1471–1516) and Hungary (1490–1516). Had the four states been permanently consolidated they could have become an effective barrier to Ottoman expansion in the south and Russian expansion in the east. But the union of crowns had never been the union of states. The union of crowns had taken place during the previous century by political alliances, diplomatic marriages, and the consent of the nobility. Such arrangements kept peace among the four neighbors, but it kept any one of them from becoming a dominant partner.

While the Polish-Lithuanian monarchs enjoyed longevity similar to that of the Muscovites, those who ruled Hungary and Bohemia were not so fortunate: by the sixteenth century a number of claimants to both crowns existed. The competition was handled by diplomacy rather than war. The accession of Vladislav II, for example, was accompanied by large concessions, first to the Bohemian towns and later to the Hungarian nobility. The formal union of the Polish and Lithuanian crowns in 1569 also involved the decentralization of power and the strengthening of the rights of the nobility in both countries. In the end, the states split apart. The Russians took much of Lithuania, the Ottomans much of Hungary. Bohemia, which in the fifteenth century had been ruled more by its nobles than its king, was absorbed into the Habsburg territories after 1526.

There were many reasons why a unified state did not appear in east-central Europe. In the first place, external forces disrupted territorial and political arrangements, and wars with the Ottomans and the Russians absorbed resources. Second, the princes faced rivals to their crowns. Although Casimir IV was able to place his son on the thrones of both Bohemia and Hungary, he managed to do so against the powerful claims of the Habsburg princes, who continued to intrigue against the Jagiellons. The contests for power necessitated concessions to leading citizens, which decreased the ability of the princes to centralize their kingdoms or to effect real unification among them. The nobility of Hungary, Bohemia, and Poland-Lithuania all developed strong local interests that increased over time. In Bohemia, Vladislav II was king in name only, and even in Poland the nobility won confirmation of its rights and privileges from the monarchy. War, rivalries for power, and a strong nobility prevented any one prince from dominating the area as the princes of Muscovy dominated theirs.

The Western Powers

Just as in the east, there was no single pattern to the consolidation of the large western European states. They, too, were internally fragmented and externally imperiled. While England had to overcome the ruin of

A miniature painted by a Krakow artist about 1510 depicts the final act of the coronation rite. The king in majesty is surrounded by his court while a Te Deum is sung. The knights in the foreground bear the standards of Poland and Lithuania.

decades of civil war, France and Spain faced the challenges of invasion and occupation. Western European princes struggled against powerful institutions and individuals within their states. Some they conquered, others they absorbed. Each nation formed its state differently: England by administrative centralization, France by good fortune, and Spain by dynastic marriage. Yet in 1450 few imagined that any one of these states would succeed.

The Taming of England. Alone among European states, England suffered no threat of foreign invasion during the fifteenth century. The island fortress might easily have become the first consolidated European state were it not for the ambitions of the nobility and the weakness of the crown. For thirty years, the English aristocracy fought over the spoils of a helpless monarch. The Wars of the Roses (1455–1485), as they came to be called, were as much a free-for-all among the English peerage as they were a contest for the throne between the houses of Lancaster and York. At their center was an attempt by the dukes of York to wrest the crown from the mad and ineffective Lancastrian king Henry VI (1422–1461). All around the edges was the continuation of local and family feuds that had little connection to the dynastic struggle.

Three decades of intermittent warfare had predictable results. The houses of Lancaster and York were both destroyed. Edward IV (1461–1483) succeeded in gaining the crown for the House of York, but he was never able to wear it securely. When he died, his children, including his heir, Edward V (1483), were placed in the protection of their uncle Richard III (1483–1485). It was protection that they did not survive. The two boys disappeared, reputedly murdered in the Tower of London, and Richard declared himself king. Richard's usurpation led to civil war, and he was killed by the forces of Henry Tudor at the battle of Bosworth Field in 1485. By the end of the Wars of the Roses, the monarchy had lost both revenue and prestige, and the aristocracy had stored up bitter memories for the future.

It was left to Henry Tudor to pick up the pieces of the kingdom. As legend has it, he picked up the crown off a bramble bush. The two chief obstacles to his determination to consolidate the English state were the power of the nobility and the poverty of the monarchy. No English monarch had held secure title to the throne for more than a century. Henry Tudor, as Henry VII (1485–1509), put an end to the dynastic instability at once. He married Elizabeth of York, in whose heirs would rest the legitimate claim to the throne. Their children were indisputable successors to the crown. He also began the long process of taming his overmighty subjects. Traitors were hung and turncoats rewarded. He and his son Henry VIII (1509–1547) adroitly created a new peerage, which soon was as numerous as the old feudal aristocracy. The new nobles owed their titles and loyalty to the Tudors. They were favored with offices and spoils and were relied upon to suppress both popular and aristocratic rebellions.

Holbein's last portrait of Henry VIII, painted in 1542. Henry made England into one of the world's greatest naval powers but embroiled the kingdom in a series of costly foreign wars. He married six times in an effort to produce a legitimate male heir.

LAST WORDS

Anne Boleyn was the second wife of Henry VIII and the mother of Elizabeth I. Henry's desire to have a son and his passion for Anne resulted in his divorce from Catherine of Aragon and England's formal break with the Roman Catholic Church. When Anne bore only a daughter, she too became dispensable. She was convicted of adultery and incest and executed in 1536. Here are her last words.

GOOD FRIENDS, I am not come here to excuse or to justify myself, for as much as I know full well that aught that I could say in my defense doth not appertain unto you, and that I could draw no hope of life from the same. But I come here only to die, and thus to yield myself humbly to the will of the King my lord. And if in my life I did ever offend the King's grace, surely with my death I do now atone for the same. And I blame not my judges, nor any other manner of person, nor anything save the cruel law of the land by which I die. But be this, and be my faults as they may, I beseech you all, good friends, to pray for the life of the King my sovereign lord and yours, who is one of the best princes on the face of the earth, and who hath always treated me so well that better could not be; wherefore I submit to death with a good will, humbly asking pardon of the world.

Anne Boleyn, scaffold speech.

Henry VIII was even more ruthless than his father. He preferred the chopping block to the peace treaty. In 1450, there were nine English dukes; by 1525, there were only two. With both carrot and stick, the Tudors tamed the peerage.

The financial problems of the English monarchy were not so easily overcome. In theory and practice an English king was supposed to live "of his own," that is, off the revenues from his own estates. In normal circumstances, royal revenue did not come from the king's subjects. The English landed classes had established the principle that only on extraordinary occasions were they to be required to contribute to the maintenance of government. The principle was defended through their representative institution—the Parliament. When the kings of England wanted to tax their subjects, they had first to gain the assent of Parliament. Although Parliaments did grant requests for extraordinary revenue, especially for national defense, they did so grudgingly. The English landed elites were not exempt from taxation, but they were able to control the amount of taxes they paid.

The inability of the crown to extract its living from its subjects made it more dependent on the efficient management of its own estates. Thus English state building depended upon the growth of centralized institutions that could oversee royal lands and collect royal customs. Gradually, medieval institutions such as the Exchequer were supplanted by newer organs that were better able to adjust to modern methods of accounting, record keeping, and enforcement. Henry sent ministers to view and value royal lands. He ordered the cataloging and collection of feudal obligations. Ship cargoes were inspected thoroughly and every last penny of customs charged. Whether Henry's reputation for greed and rapacity was warranted, it was undeniable that he squeezed as much as could be taken from a not very juicy inheritance. His financial problems limited both domestic and foreign policy.

It was not until the middle of the next reign that the English monarchy was again solvent. As a result of his dispute with the papacy, Henry VIII confiscated the enormous wealth of the Catholic church, and with one stroke solved the crown's monetary problems (see Chapter 13). But the real contribution that Henry and his chief minister, Thomas Cromwell (ca. 1485–1540), made to forming an English state was the way in which the windfall was administered. Cromwell accelerated the process of centralizing government that had begun under Edward IV. He divided administration according to its functions by creating separate departments of state, modeled upon courts. The new departments were responsible for record keeping, revenue collection, and law enforcement. Each had a distinct jurisdiction and a permanent, trained staff. Cromwell coordinated the work of the distinct departments by expanding the power of the Privy Council, which included the heads of the administrative bodies. Through a long evolution, the Privy Council came to serve as the king's executive body. Cromwell also saw the importance of Parliament as a legislative body. Through Parliament, royal policy could be turned into statutes that had the assent of the political nation. If Parliament was well managed, issues that were potentially controversial could be defused. Laws passed by Parliament were more easily enforced locally than were proclamations issued by the king. By the end of Henry VIII's reign, the English monarchy was strong enough to withstand the succession of a child king, precisely the circumstance that had plunged the nation into civil war a century earlier.

The Unification of France. Perhaps the most remarkable thing about the unification of France is that it took place at all. The forces working against the consolidation of a French state were formidable. France was surrounded by aggressive and powerful neighbors with whom it was frequently at war. Its greatest nobles were semi-independent princes who were constant rivals for the throne and consistent opponents of the extension of royal power. The French people were deeply suspicious of the pretensions of the monarchy. Provincialism was not simply negative; it was a fierce pride of and loyalty toward local customs and institutions that had deep roots within communities. Furthermore, France was splintered by profound regional differences. The north and south were divided by culture and by language (the *langue d'oc* in the south and the *langue d'oïl* in the north). As late as the fifteenth century, a French king needed a translator to communicate with officials from his southern lands.

The first obstacles that were overcome were the external threats to French security. For more than a century, the throne of France had been contested by the kings of England. The so-called Hundred Years' War, which was fought intermittently between 1337 and 1453, originated in a dispute over the inheritance of the French crown and English possessions in Gascony in southern France (see Chapter 10). The war was fought on French soil, and by the early fifteenth century English conquests in north-central France extended from Normandy to the borders of the Holy Roman Empire. Two of the largest French cities, Paris and Bordeaux, were in English hands.

The problems posed by the Hundred Years' War were not just those of victory and defeat. The struggle between the kings of England and the kings of France allowed French princes and dukes, who were nominally vassals of the king, to enhance their autonomy by making their own alliances with the highest bidder. When the English were finally driven out of France in the middle of the fifteenth century, the kings of France came into a weakened and divided inheritance.

Nor was England the only threat to the security of the French monarchy. On France's eastern border, in a long arching semicircle, were the estates of the dukes of Burgundy. The dukes of Burgundy and the kings of France shared a common ancestry—both were of the House of Valois. Still, the sons of brothers in one generation were only cousins in the next, and the two branches of the family grew apart. The original Burgundian inheritance was in the southeast, centered at Dijon. A good marriage and good fortune brought to the first duke the rich northern province of Flanders. For the next hundred years, the aim of the dukes of Burgundy was to unite their divided estates. While England and France were locked in deadly embrace,

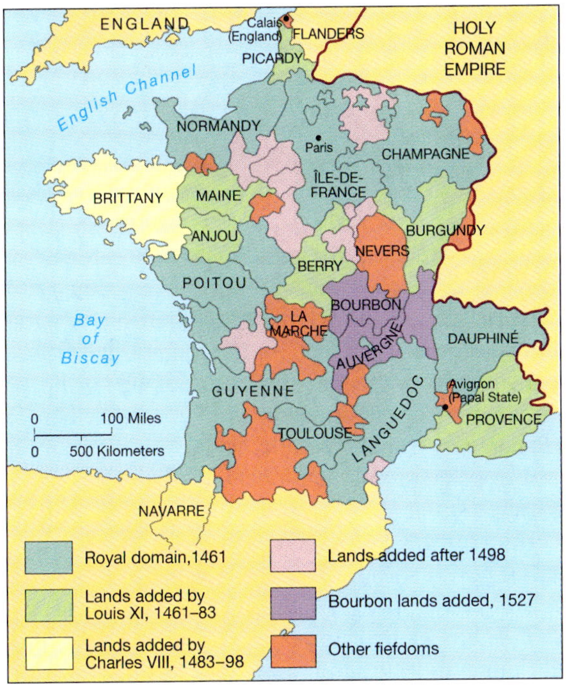

The Unification of France. Notice how France grew piecemeal rather than by acquiring large additions of adjacent estates.

THE KINGDOM OF FRANCE

Claude de Seyssel (ca. 1450–1519) was a legal scholar and professor at the University of Turin. He came from the duchy of Savoy, a small state that mixed French and Italian peoples and culture. Seyssel thus learned about the French monarchy as an outsider and wrote The Monarchy of France *as a book of counsel for French kings. In this passage he explains and defends the Salic law, which prohibited legitimate title to the French throne from passing through a woman. The legal documents that supposedly established Salic law were fakes.*

WITHOUT GOING TOO DEEPLY INTO THE DISPUTES OF THE PHILOSOPHERS, we may presuppose three kinds of political rule: monarchy under a single person, aristocracy under a certain number of the better sort, and democracy the popular state. Of these, according to the true and most widespread opinion, monarchy is the best if the prince is good and has the sense, the experience, and the good will to govern justly. That rarely comes to pass, however, because with such authority and license it is hard to follow the right course and hold fairly the balance of justice. The second state seems the more reasonable and praiseworthy since it is more lasting, better founded, and easier to bear, being comprised of the persons selected by the assembly or a part of them. Such persons are, moreover, subject to corruption and change, at least to the extent that, when there are several bad and inadequate men among them, the better sort, being their superiors, can repress their boldness and thwart their unreasonable enterprises. As to the popular state, it has always been turbulent, dangerous, and hostile to the better sort. Nevertheless, the aristocratic state is often transformed into oligarchy, a monopoly by covetous and ambitious folk, who, though chosen as the wisest and most prudent of the people to rule and to govern the people well, care only for their particular profit. So when all is said, none of these states can possibly be perpetual, for ordinary in the course of time they get worse, especially when they go on growing, so that often one [by disorder] rises from the other.

Burgundy systematically grew. It absorbed territory from both the Holy Roman Empire and France. To little pieces gained through marriages were added little pieces taken through force. As the second half of the fifteenth century began, the court of the duke of Burgundy was the glittering jewel of Europe, the heir of the Italian Renaissance. Wealthy and powerful, it stood poised to achieve what had once only been dreamed: the unification of the Burgundian lands. The conquest of Lorraine finally connected the ducal estates in one long, unbroken string.

But it was a string stretched taut. The power of Burgundy threatened its neighbors in all directions. Both France and the empire were too weak to resist its expansion, but the confederation of Swiss towns to the southwest of Burgundy was not. Fearing a Burgundian advance against them, a number of independent Swiss towns pooled their resources to raise a large army. In a series of stunning military victories, Swiss forces repelled the Burgundians from their lands and demolished their armies. Charles the Bold, the last Valois duke of Burgundy, fell at the Battle of Nancy in 1477. His estates were quickly dismembered. France recovered its ancestral territories, including Burgundy, and through no effort of its own was now secure on its eastern border.

The king most associated with the consolidation of France was Louis XI (1461–1483). He inherited an estate exhausted by warfare and civil strife. More by chance than by plan, he vastly extended the territories under the dominion of the French crown and, more importantly, subdued the nobility. Louis XI was as cunning as he was peculiar. In an age in which royalty was expressed through magnificence, Louis sported an old felt hat and a well-worn coat. His enemies constantly underestimated his abilities, which earned him the

The first special trait that I find good is that this realm passes by masculine succession and, by virtue of the law which the French call Salic, cannot fall into the hands of a woman. This is excellent, for by falling into the feminine line it can come into the power of a foreigner, a pernicious and dangerous thing, since a ruler from a foreign nation is of a different rearing and condition, of different customs, different language, and a different way of life from the men of the lands he comes to rule. He ordinarily, therefore, wishes to advance those of his nation, to grant them the most important authority in the handling of affairs, and to prefer them to honors and profits. Moreover, he always has more love for and faith in them and so conforms more to their customs and ways than to the customs of the land to which he has newly come, whence there always follows envy and dissension between the natives and the foreigners and indignation against the princes, as has often been seen by experience, and is seen all the time. When the succession goes from male to male, the heir is always certain and is of the same blood as those who formerly ruled, so the subjects have the very same love and reverence for him as for his predecessors. Even though he be related only distantly and the dead king have daughters, yet without deviation or scruple the people turn to him as soon as the other has ceased to be, and there is no disturbance or difficulty. So it went at the death of King Charles VIII and of King Louis XII recently deceased. Although in former times there were great quarrels and differences on such occasions, which brought great wars, persecutions, and desolations to the realm, nevertheless, these differences were not the reason for the troubles but the pretext, although well known to be frivolous and ill founded. In the end matters must have been redressed and so established that there can never again be dissensions and difficulties on this score. [In order to demonstrate what I said about the perfection of the monarchy of France I have included in this account] the state of France as it is now, joining the old laws, customs, and observances with the new and more recent.

From Claude de Seyssel, *The Monarchy of France* (1515).

nickname "the Spider." But during the course of his reign, Louis XI gradually won back what he had been forced to give away. Years of fighting both the English and each other left the ranks of the French aristocracy depleted. As blood spilled on the battlefields, the stocks of fathers and sons ran low. Estates, to which no male heirs existed, fell forfeit to the king. In that manner, the crown absorbed Anjou and Maine in the northwest and Provence in the south. More importantly, Louis XI ultimately obtained control of the two greatest independent fiefs, Brittany and Orléans. He managed the feat by arranging the marriage of his son Charles to the heiress of Brittany and of his daughter Jeanne to the heir of Orléans. When in 1527 the lands of the duke of Bourbon fell to the crown, the French monarch ruled a unified state.

The consolidation of France was not simply the result of the incorporation of diverse pieces of territory into the domain of the king. More than in any other state, the experience in France demonstrated how a state could be formed without the designs of a great leader. Neither Louis XI nor his son Charles VIII (1483–1498) was a nation builder. Louis's main objective was always to preserve his estate. His good fortune saved him from the consequences of many ill-conceived policies. But no amount of luck could make up for Louis's failure to obtain the Burgundian Low Countries for France after the death of Charles the Bold in 1477. The marriage of Mary of Burgundy to Maximilian of Habsburg was one of the great turning points in European history. It initiated the struggle for control of the Low Countries that endured for more than two centuries.

The long years of war established the principle of royal taxation that was so essential to the process of state building in France. It enabled the monarchy to raise money for defense and for consolidation. Because of the strength of the nobles, most taxation fell only on the commoners, the so-called third estate. The *taille* was a direct tax on property from which the nobility and clergy were exempt. The *gabelle* was a consumption tax on the purchase of salt in most parts of the kingdom, and the *aide* was a tax on a variety of commodities, including meat and wine. The consumption taxes were paid by all members of the third estate no matter how poor they might be. Although there was much complaint about taxes, the French monarchy established a broad base for taxation and a high degree of compliance long before any other European nation.

Along with money went soldiers, fighting men necessary to repel the English and to defend the crown against rebels and traitors. Again the French monarchy was the first to establish the principle of a national army, raised and directed from the center but quartered and equipped regionally. From the nobility were recruited the cavalry, from the towns and countryside the massive infantry. Fortified towns received privileges in return for military service to the king. Originally, towns were required to provide artillery, but constant troubles with the nobility had led the kings of France to establish their own store of heavy guns. The towns supplied small arms, pikes, and swords, and later pistols and muskets. By the beginning of the sixteenth century, the French monarch could raise and equip an army of his own.

Taxation and military obligation demanded the creation and expansion of centralized institutions of government. It was the most difficult development in the period of state formation in France. The powers of royal agents were constantly challenged by the powers of regional nobles. It is easy to exaggerate the extent of the growth of central control and to underestimate the enduring hold of regional and provincial loyalties. Even the crown's absorption of estates did not always end local privileges and customs. France was not a nation and was hardly a state by the start of the sixteenth century. But despite continued regional autonomy, a beginning had been made.

King Ferdinand of Aragon and Queen Isabella of Castille often traveled the length of their kingdoms, making personal contact with their subjects.

The Marriages of Spain. Before the sixteenth century there was little prospect of a single nation emerging on the Iberian Peninsula. North African Muslims, called Moors, occupied the province of Granada in the south, while the stable kingdom of Portugal dominated the western coast. The Spanish peoples were divided among a number of separate states. The two most important were Castile, the largest and wealthiest kingdom, and Aragon, which was composed of a number of quasi-independent regions, each of which maintained its own laws and institutions. Three religions and four languages (not including dialects) widened the political divisions. Furthermore, the different states had different outlooks. Castile was, above all, determined to subjugate the last of Islamic Spain and to convert its large Jewish population to Christianity. Aragon played in the high-stakes game for power in the Mediterranean, claiming sovereignty over Sicily and Naples and exercising that sovereignty whenever it could.

A happy teenage marriage brought together the unhappy kingdoms of Castile and Aragon. When Ferdinand of Aragon and Isabella of Castile secretly exchanged wedding vows in 1469, both their homelands were rent by civil war. In Castile, Isabella's brother, Henry IV (1454–1474), struggled unsuccessfully against the powerful Castilian nobility. In Aragon, Ferdinand's father, John II (1458–1479), faced a revolt by the rich province of Catalonia on one side and the territorial ambitions of Louis XI of France on the other. Joining the heirs increased the resources of both kingdoms. Ferdinand took an active role in the pacification of Castile, while Castilian riches allowed him to defend Aragon from invasion. In 1479, the two crowns were united and the Catholic monarchs, as they were called, ruled the two kingdoms jointly. But the unification of the crowns of Castile and Aragon was not the same as the formation of a single state between them. Local privileges were zealously guarded, especially in Aragon, where the representative institutions of the towns—the Cortes—were aggressively independent. Their attitude is best expressed in the oath of the townspeople of Saragossa: "We accept you as our king provided you observe all our liberties and laws; and if not, not." The powerful Castilian nobility never accepted Ferdinand as their king and refused him the crown after Isabella's death.

But Ferdinand and Isabella (1479–1516) took the first steps toward forging a Spanish state. Their most notable achievement was the final recovery of the lands that had been conquered by the Moors. For centuries, the Spanish kingdoms had fought against the North African Muslims, who had conquered large areas of the southern peninsula. The reconquista was characterized by short bursts of warfare followed by long periods of wary coexistence. By the middle of the fifteenth century, the Moorish territory had been reduced to the province of Granada, but civil strife in Castile heightened the possibility of a new Moorish offensive. "We no longer mint gold, only steel," was how a Moorish ruler replied to Isabella's demand for the traditional payment of tribute money. The final stages of the reconquista began in 1482 and lasted for a decade. The struggle was waged as a holy war and was financed in part by grants from the pope and the Christian princes of Europe. It was a bloody undertaking. The Moorish population of nearly 500,000

Hans Holbein the Younger, The Ambassadors *(1533). On the left is Jean de Dinteville, French ambassador to England. To the right is Bishop Georges de Selve, ambassador to the Emperor, the city of Venice, and the pope.*

was reduced to 100,000 before the town of Granada finally fell and the province was absorbed into Castile.

The reconquista played an important part in creating a national identity for the Christian peoples of Spain. In order to raise men and money for the war effort, Ferdinand and Isabella mobilized their nobility and town governments and created a central organization to oversee the invasion. Ferdinand was actively involved in the warfare, gaining the respect of the hostile Castilian nobles in the process. The conquered territories were used to reward those who had aided the effort, though the crown maintained control and jurisdiction over most of the province. But the idea of the holy war also had a darker side and an unanticipated consequence. The Jewish population that had lived peacefully in both Castile and Aragon became another object of hostility. Many Jews had risen to prominence in government and in skilled professions. Others, who had accepted conversion to Christianity and were known as *conversos*, had become among the most powerful figures in Church and state.

Both groups were now attacked. The conversos fell prey to a special Church tribunal created to examine their sincere devotion to Catholicism. This was the Spanish Inquisition, which, though it used traditional judicial practices—torture to gain confessions, public humiliation to show contrition, and burnings at the stake to maintain purity—used them on a scale never before seen. Thousands of conversos were killed, and many more families had their wealth confiscated to be

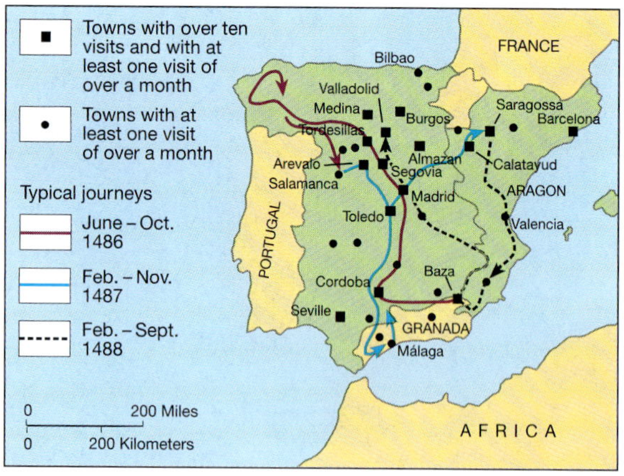

The travels of Ferdinand and Isabella. Early modern monarchs did not reside solely in a capital city but moved around their territories to consolidate their power and assure the loyalty of their subjects.

used for the reconquista. In 1492, the Jews themselves were expelled from Spain. Although the reconquista and the expulsion of the Jews inflicted great suffering upon victims and incalculable loss to the Castilian economy, both events enhanced the prestige of the Catholic monarchs.

In many ways, Ferdinand and Isabella had trodden the paths of the medieval monarchy. They relied upon personal contact with their people more than upon the use of a centralized administration. They frequently dispensed justice personally, sitting in court and accepting petitions from their subjects. Quite remarkably, they had no permanent residence and traveled the length and breadth of their kingdoms. Isabella is said to have visited every town in Castile, and it is entirely possible that a majority of the population of both kingdoms actually saw their monarchs at one time or another. Queen Isabella was venerated in Castile, where women's right to inheritance remained strong. Ferdinand's absences from Aragon were always a source of contention between him and the Cortes of the towns, yet he was careful to provide regents to preside in his absence and regularly returned to visit his native kingdom. He was not an absentee monarch.

The joint presence of Ferdinand and Isabella in the provinces of Spain was symbolic of the unity that they wanted to achieve. Despite the great obstacles, they were intent on bringing about a more permanent blending. Ferdinand made Castilian the official language of government in Aragon and even appointed Castilians to Aragonese posts. He and Isabella actively encouraged the intermarriage of the two aristocracies and the expansion of the number of wealthy nobles who held land in both kingdoms. A single coinage, stamped with the heads of both monarchs, was established for both kingdoms. Nevertheless, the measures did not unify Spain or erase the centuries' long tradition of hostility among the diverse Iberian peoples.

It was left to the heirs of Ferdinand and Isabella to forge together the Spanish kingdoms, and the process was a painful one. The hostility to a foreign monarch that both the Castilian nobility and the Aragonese towns had shown to Ferdinand and Isabella increased dramatically at the accession of their grandson, who became the Emperor Charles V (1516–1556). Charles had been born and raised in the Low Countries, where he ruled over Burgundy and the Netherlands. Through a series of dynastic accidents, he became heir to the Spanish crown with its possessions in the New World and to the vast Habsburg estates that included Austria.

Charles established his rule in Spain gradually. For a time he was forced to share power in Castile and to suppress a disorganized aristocratic rebellion.

Because of his foreign obligations, Charles was frequently absent from Spain. During those periods he governed through regents and royal councils that did much to centralize administration. Although Castile and Aragon had separate councils, they were organized similarly and had greater contact than before. Charles V realized the importance of Spain, especially of Castile, in his empire. He learned Castilian and spent more time there than in any other part of his empire, calling it "the head of all the rest." Like Ferdinand and Isabella, he traveled throughout Castile and Aragon; unlike them, he established a more permanent bureaucratic court, modeled on that of Burgundy, and placed able Spaniards at the head of its departments. That smoothed over the long periods when Charles was abroad, especially the thirteen years between 1543 and 1556.

Yet neither his personal efforts to rule as a Spanish monarch nor those of his able administrators were the most important factor in uniting the Spanish kingdoms of Iberia. Rather it was the fact that Charles V brought Spain to the forefront of European affairs in the sixteenth century. Spanish prowess, whether in arms or in culture, became a source of national pride that helped erode regional identity. Gold and silver from the New World helped finance Charles's great empire. Whether or not he dreamed of uniting all of Europe under his rule, Charles V fulfilled nearly all of the ancient territorial ambitions of the Spanish kingdoms. In Italy, he prosecuted Aragonese claims to Sicily and Naples; in the north he held on firmly to the kingdom of Navarre, which had been annexed by Ferdinand and which secured Spain's border with France. In the south, he blocked off Ottoman and Muslim expansion. The reign of Charles V ushered in the dawn of Spain's golden age.

THE DYNASTIC STRUGGLES

The formation of large states throughout Europe led inevitably to conflicts among them. Long chains of marriages among the families of the European princes meant that sooner or later the larger powers would lay claim to the same inheritances and test the matter by force. Thus the sixteenth century was a period of almost unrelieved general warfare that took the whole of the Continent as its theater. Advances in technology made war more efficient and more expensive. They also made it more horrible. The use of artillery against infantry increased the number of deaths and maiming injuries, as did the replacement of the arrow with the bullet. As the size of armies increased, so did casualties. Nearly 60,000 men met at Marignano in 1515, where it took 30 French cavalry charges and 28 consecutive hours of battle before the Swiss infantry was driven from the field. The slaughter of French nobility at Pavia in 1525 was the largest in a century, while the Turkish sultan Suleiman the Magnificent recorded the burial of 24,000 Hungarian soldiers after the battle of Mohacs in 1526.

Power and Glory

The frequency with which offensive war was waged in the sixteenth century raises a number of questions about the militaristic values of the age. Valor remained greatly prized—a Renaissance virtue inherited from the crusading zeal and chivalric ideals of the Middle Ages. Princes saw valor as a personal attribute and sought to do great deeds. Ferdinand of Aragon and Francis I of France (1515–1547) won fame for their exploits in war. Charles the Bold and Louis II of Hungary were less fortunate: their battlefield deaths led to the breakup of their states. Wars were fought to further the interests of princes rather than the interests of national sovereignty or international Christianity. Wars certainly were not fought in the interests of their subjects. States were an extension of a prince's heritage: what rulers sought in battle was a part of the historical and familial rights that defined themselves and their subjects. The wars of the sixteenth century were dynastic wars.

Along with desire came ability. The New Monarchs were capable of waging war. The very definition of their states involved the ability to accumulate territories and to defend them. Internal security depended upon locally raised forces or hired mercenaries. Both required money, which was becoming available in unprecedented quantities as a result of the increasing prosperity of the early sixteenth century and the windfall of gold and silver from the New World. Professional soldiers, of whom the Swiss and Germans were the most noteworthy, sold their services to the highest bidders. Developments in transport and supply enabled campaigns to take place far from the center of a state.

Titian, *Charles V on Horseback* (1548). *The portrait commemorates the Emperor's victory in the Battle of Mülberg in 1547. The portrait is less that of a victorious hero, but rather that of a forceful individual girded to contend against his enemies.*

Finally, communications were improving. The need for knowledge about potential rivals or allies had the effect of expanding the European system of diplomacy. Resident agents were established in all the European capitals, and they had a decisive impact upon war and peace. Their dispatches formed the most reliable source of information about the strengths of armies or the weaknesses of governments, about the birth of heirs or the death of princes.

Personality also played a part in the international warfare of the early sixteenth century. The three most consistent protagonists—Charles V, Francis I, and Henry VIII—were of similar age and outlook. Each came unexpectedly to his throne in the full flush of youth, eager for combat and glory. The three were self-consciously rivals, each jealous of the other's successes, each triumphant in the other's failures. Henry VIII and Francis I held wrestling bouts when they met in 1520. Francis I challenged Charles V to single combat after the French king's humiliating imprisonment in Madrid in 1526. As the three monarchs aged together, their youthful wars of conquest matured into strategic warfare designed to maintain a continental balance of power.

The Italian Wars

The struggle for supremacy in Europe in the sixteenth century pitted the French House of Valois against the far-flung estates of the Habsburg empire. Yet the wars took place in Italy. The rivalries among the larger Italian city-states proved fertile ground for the newly consolidated European monarchies. Both French and Spanish monarchs had remote but legitimate claims to the kingdom of Naples in southern Italy. In 1494, the French king, Charles VIII, took up an invitation from the ruler of Milan to intervene in Italian affairs. His campaign was an unqualified, if fleeting, success. He marched the length of the Iberian Peninsula, overthrew the Medici in Florence, forced the pope to open the gates of Rome, and finally seized the crown of Naples. The occupation was accomplished without a single great battle and lasted until the warring Italian city-states realized that they had more to fear from the French than from one another. Once that happened, Charles VIII beat a hasty retreat. But the French appetite for Italian territory was not sated. Soon a deal was struck with Ferdinand of Aragon to divide the kingdom of Naples in two. In the end, Spain wound up with all of Naples and France was left with nothing but debts and grievances.

Thus, when Francis I came to the French throne and Charles V to the Spanish, Naples was just one of several potential sources of friction. Not only had Ferdinand betrayed the French in Naples, he had also broken a long-standing peace on the Franco-Spanish border by conquering the independent but French-speaking kingdom of Navarre. Francis could be expected to avenge both slights. Charles, on the other hand, was the direct heir of the dukes of Burgundy. From his childhood he had longed for the restoration of his ancestral lands, including Burgundy itself, which had been gobbled up by Louis XI after the death of Charles the Bold. Competition between Francis and

Jean Clouet, Portrait of Francis I *(16th century). Rivalry between Francis and Charles V plunged Europe into decades of war.*

Charles became all the more ferocious when Charles's grandfather, the Holy Roman Emperor Maximilian I (1486–1519), died in 1519. Both monarchs launched a vigorous campaign for the honor of succeeding him.

For nearly a century the Holy Roman Emperor had come from the Austrian ruling family, and there was little reason to believe that Charles V, who now inherited the Habsburg lands in Austria and Germany, would not also succeed to the eminent but empty dignity. Nevertheless, the electors were willing to be bribed by French agents who supported Francis's candidacy, and even by English agents who supported Henry VIII. Charles spent the most of all, and his eventual election not only aggravated the personal animosity among the monarchs, but added another source of conflict in Italy. When Louis XII (1498–1515) succeeded Charles VIII as king of France, he had laid claim to the duchy of Milan through an interest of his wife's, though he was unable to enforce it. Francis I proved more capable. In 1515, he stunned all of Europe by crushing the vaunted Swiss mercenaries at the battle of Marignano. But the duchy of Milan was a territory under the protection of the Holy Roman Emperor, and it soon appealed for Imperial troops to help repel the French invaders. Milan was strategically important to Charles V, as it was the vital link between his Austrian and Burgundian possessions. Almost as soon as he took up the imperial mantle, Charles V was determined to challenge Francis I in Italy.

The key to such a challenge was the construction of alliances among the various Italian city-states and most especially with England, whose aid both Charles and Francis sought to enlist in the early 1520s. Henry VII had found foreign alliances a ready source of cash, and he was always eager to enter into them as long as they did not involve raising armies and fighting wars. Henry VIII was made of sterner stuff. He longed to reconquer France and to cut a figure on the European

The Italian wars with key battle sites. Italy was overrun in the sixteenth century and became a battleground for the dynastic struggles of the French, the Spanish, and the Imperial forces.

The Field of the Cloth of Gold, the lavish setting for the meeting between Henry VIII and Francis I in June 1520. The fountain in the foreground provides free wine for all.

scene. Despite the fact that his initial Continental adventures had emptied his treasury without fulfilling his dreams, Henry remained eager for war. He was also flattered to find himself the object of attention by both Valois and Habsburg emissaries. Charles V made two separate trips to London, while Henry crossed the Channel in 1520 to meet Francis I in one of the gaudiest displays of conspicuous consumption that the century would witness, appropriately known as the Field of the Cloth of Gold.

The result of the diplomatic intrigues was an alliance between England and the Holy Roman Empire. English and Burgundian forces would stage an invasion of northern France while Spanish and German troops would again attempt to dislodge the French forces from Italy. The strategy worked better than anyone could have imagined. In 1523, Charles's forces gained a foothold in Milan by taking the heavily fortified town of Pavia. Two years later Francis was ready to strike back. At the head of his own royal guards, he massed Swiss mercenaries and French infantry outside Pavia and made ready for a swift assault. Instead, a large imperial army arrived to relieve the town, and in the subsequent battle the French suffered a shattering defeat. Francis I was captured.

The victory at Pavia, which occurred on Charles V's twenty-fifth birthday, seemingly made him master of all of Europe. His ally Henry VIII urged an immediate invasion and dismemberment of France and began raising an army to spearhead the attack. But Charles's position was much less secure than it appeared. The Ottomans threatened his Hungarian territories, and the Protestants threatened his German lands. He could not afford a war of conquest in France. His hope now was to reach an agreement with Francis I for a lasting European peace, and for that purpose the French king was brought in captivity to Madrid.

It is doubtful that there was ever any real chance for peace between Habsburg and Valois after the battle of Pavia. Francis's personal humiliation and Charles's military position were both too strong to allow for a permanent settlement in which Habsburgs ruled in Milan and Naples. But it was neither political nor personal considerations that were the source of another 30 years of continuous European warfare. Rather it was Charles's demand that Burgundy be returned to him. Although Francis was hardly in a position to bargain, he held out on this issue for as long as possible and secretly prepared a disavowal of the final agreement before it was made. By the Treaty of Madrid in 1526,

Francis I yielded Burgundy and recognized the Spanish conquest of Navarre and Spanish rule in Naples. The agreement was sealed by the marriage of Francis to Charles's sister, Eleanor of Portugal. But marriage was not sufficient security for such a complete capitulation. To secure his release from Spain, Francis was required to leave behind as hostages his seven- and eight-year-old sons until the treaty was fulfilled. For three years, the children languished in Spanish captivity.

No sooner had he set foot upon French soil than Francis I renounced the Treaty of Madrid. Despite the threat that it posed to his children, Francis argued that the terms had been extracted against his will, and he even gained the approval of the pope for violating his oath. Setting France on a war footing, he began seeking new allies. Henry VIII, disappointed with the meager spoils of his last venture, switched sides. So too did a number of Italian city-states, including Rome. Most importantly, Francis I entered into an alliance with the Ottoman sultan, Suleiman the Magnificent (1520–1566), whose armies were pressing against the southeastern borders of the Holy Roman Empire. In the year following Pavia, the Ottomans secured an equally decisive triumph at Mohács, captured Budapest, and threatened Vienna, the eastern capital of the Habsburg lands. Almost overnight Charles V had been turned from hunter into hunted. The Ottoman threat demanded immediate attention in Germany, the French and English were preparing to strike in the Low Countries, and the Italian wars continued. In 1527, Charles's unpaid German mercenaries stormed through Rome, sacked the papal capital, and captured the pope. Christian Europe was mortified.

The struggle for European mastery ground on for decades. The Treaty of Cateau-Cambresis in 1559 brought to a close 60 years of conflict. In the end the French were no more capable of dislodging the Habsburgs from Italy than were the Habsburgs of forcing the Ottomans out of Hungary. The great stores of silver that poured into Castile from the New World were consumed in the fires of Continental warfare. In 1557, both France and Spain declared bankruptcy to avoid foreclosures by their creditors. For the French, the Italian wars were disastrous. They seriously undermined the state's financial base, eroded confidence in the monarchy, and thinned the ranks of the ruling nobility. The adventure begun by Charles VIII in search of glory brought France nearly to ruin. It ended with fitting irony. After the death of Francis I, his son Henry II (1547–1559) continued the struggle. Henry never forgave his father for abandoning him in Spain, and he sought revenge on Charles V, who had been his jailer. He regarded the Treaty of Cateau-Cambrésis as a victory and celebrated it with great pomp and pageantry. Among the feasts and festivities were athletic competitions for the king's courtiers and attendants. Henry II entered the jousting tournament and was killed there.

The sixteenth-century army of the Ottoman Turks under Suleiman the Magnificent was the most feared military power in the West. Most of the Ottoman soldiers were cavalry, armed only with bows, lances, and swords, but the Turks also possessed cannons and other modern weapons.

Charles V died in his bed. The long years of war made clear that the dream to dominate Europe could only be a dream. He split apart his empire and granted to his brother, Ferdinand I (1558–1564), the Austrian and German lands and the mantle of the Holy Roman Empire. To his son Philip II (1556–1598) he ceded the Low Countries, Spain and the New World, Naples, and his Italian conquests. In 1555, Charles abdicated all of his titles and retired to a monastery to live out his final days. The cares of an empire that once stretched from Peru to Vienna were lifted from his shoulders. Beginning with his voyage to Castile in 1517, he had made ten trips to the Netherlands, nine to Germany, seven to Italy, six to Spain, four to France, two to England, and two to Africa. "My life has been one long journey," he told those who witnessed him relinquish his crowns. On 21 September 1558, he finally rested forever.

Questions for Review

1. What impulses in European society were revealed by the global exploration and conquests of the Portuguese and the Spanish?
2. What qualities characterized the "New Monarchies" and what are some of the best examples of such princely states?
3. How and why did the experience of political and territorial unification differ in England, France, and Spain?
4. How did war between the great European monarchies contribute to unity within each?

Suggestions for Further Reading

General Reading

* G. R. Potter, ed., *The New Cambridge Modern History.* Vol. I, *The Renaissance, 1493–1520* (Cambridge: Cambridge University Press, 1957). Comprehensive survey of political history written by renowned scholars.

* Denys Hay, *Europe in the Fourteenth and Fifteenth Centuries* (London: Longman, 1966). A good first survey of political history.

* Richard Mackenney, *Sixteenth Century Europe* (London: Macmillan, 1993). An accessible survey of the period that is well written and imaginatively organized.

* Eugene Rice, *The Foundations of Early Modern Europe, 1460–1559* (New York: Norton, 2d ed., 1994). An outstanding synthesis.

* T. A. Brady, H. A. Oberman, and J. D. Tracy, eds., *Handbook of European History, 1400–1600* (Leiden: E. J. Brill, 1996). The first volume of this compendium contains essays on every aspect of European society by acknowledged experts.

European Encounters

C. R. Boxer, *The Portuguese Seaborne Empire, 1415–1825* (London: Hutchinson, 1968). The best history of the first of the explorer nations.

J. R. S. Phillips, *The Medieval Expansion of Europe* (Oxford: Oxford University Press, 1988). An engaging account of medieval travel myths and their impact upon European expansion.

Felipe Fernandez-Armesto, *Before Columbus: Exploration and Colonization from the Mediterranean to the Atlantic, 1229–1492* (London: Macmillan, 1987). A comprehensive survey. Difficult but rewarding.

Patricia Seed, *Ceremonies of Possession in Europe's Conquest of the New World, 1492–1640* (Cambridge: Cambridge University Press 1995). An anthropological view of the encounters between Europeans and native Americans.

* Felipe Fernandez-Armesto, *Columbus* (Oxford: Oxford University Press, 1991). The best of the new studies. Reliable, stimulating, and up-to-date.

* Samuel Morison, *Christopher Columbus, Mariner* (New York: New American Library, 1985). A biography by an historian who repeated the Columbian voyages.

* Kirkpatrick Sale, *The Conquest of Paradise: Christopher Columbus and the Columbian Legacy* (New York: Plume Publishers, 1991). An entertaining and infuriating account. Very readable and very controversial.

* Dan O'Sullivan, *Age of Discovery, 1400–1550* (London: Longman, 1984). Best short synthetic work.

Valerie Flint, *The Imaginative Landscape of Christopher Columbus* (Princeton, NJ: Princeton University Press, 1992). A study of what Columbus and his contemporaries knew about the geography of the world.

* Lyle McAlister, *Spain and Portugal in the New World, 1492–1700* (Minneapolis: University of Minnesota Press, 1984). The most up-to-date history of the great South American empires.

John Thornton, *Africa and Africans in the Making of the Atlantic World* (Cambridge: Cambridge University Press, 1992). The African effect on the development of the West.

* Sanjay Subrahmanyam, *The Career and Legend of Vasco Da Gama* (Cambridge: Cambridge University Press, 1998). A full length study of da Gama and Portuguese culture in the age of discovery.

* J. H. Parry, *The Age of Reconnaissance* (New York: New American Library, 1963). A survey of technological and technical changes that made possible the European discovery of America.

* J. H. Elliott, *The Old World and the New, 1492–1650* (Cambridge: Cambridge University Press, 1970). A brilliant look at the reception of knowledge about the New World by Europeans.

* Anthony Pagden, *Lords of All the World: Ideologies of Empire in Spain, Britain and France, c. 1500–c. 1800* (New Haven, CT: Yale University Press, 1995). A fresh look at the ideas behind the European encounter with the new world.

* Bernard Lewis, *Cultures in Conflict* (London: Oxford University Press, 1995). The religious struggle in the merging of the New and Old Worlds.

* A. W. Crosby, *The Columbian Exchange: Biological and Cultural Consequences of 1492* (Westport, CT: Greenwood Press, 1972). An argument about the medical consequences of the transatlantic encounter.

Geographical Tour: Europe in 1500

* N. J. G. Pounds, *An Historical Geography of Europe, 1500–1800* (Cambridge: Cambridge University Press, 1990). A remarkable survey of the relationship between geography and history.

* Daniel Waley, *Later Medieval Europe* (London: Longman, 1985). A good brief account.

The Formation of States

J. H. Shennan, *The Origins of the Modern European State, 1450–1725* (London: Hutchinson, 1974). An analytic account of the rise of the state.

* Bernard Guenée, *States and Rulers in Later Medieval Europe* (London: Basil Blackwell, 1985). An engaging argument about the forces that helped shape the state system in Europe.

* Brian Downing, *The Military Revolution and Political Change: Origins of Democracy and Autocracy in Early Modern Europe* (Princeton, NJ: Princeton University Press, 1992). A sociological study of the effects military change had on early modern states.

* Norman Davies, *God's Playground: A History of Poland* Vol. 1, *The Origins to 1795* (New York: Columbia University Press, 1982). The best treatment in English of a complex history.

* Orest Subtelny, *Ukraine: A History* (Toronto: University of Toronto Press, 1988). A compendious history of a people and their domination by their neighbors—from the earliest times to the twentieth century.

* Richard Pipes, *Russia Under the Old Regime* (London: Weidenfeld and Nicolson, 1974). A magisterial account.

* Robert O. Crummey, *The Formation of Muscovy, 1304–1613* (London: Longman, 1987). The best one-volume history.

* J. R. Lander, *Government and Community, England, 1450–1509* (Cambridge, MA: Harvard University Press, 1980). A comprehensive survey of the late fifteenth century.

* S. B. Chrimes, *Henry VII* (Berkeley: University of California Press, 1972). A traditional biography of the first Tudor.

* C. D. Ross, *The Wars of the Roses* (London: Thames and Hudson, 1976). The best one-volume account.

* G. R. Elton, *Reform and Reformation, England, 1509–1558* (Cambridge, MA: Harvard University Press, 1977). A survey by the dean of Tudor historians.

Richard Vaughan, *Valois Burgundy* (Hampden, CT: Shoe String Press, 1975). An engaging history of a vanished state.

* Paul M. Kendall, *Louis XI: The Universal Spider* (New York: Norton, 1971). A highly entertaining account of an unusual monarch.

* R. J. Knecht, *French Renaissance Monarchy* (London: Longman, 1984). A study of the nature of the French monarchy and the way it was transformed in the early sixteenth century.

* John Lynch, *Spain, 1516–1598: From Nation State to World Empire* (Cambridge, MA: Blackwell, 1994). The most up-to-date survey.

* L. P. Harvey, *Islamic Spain, 1250–1500* (Chicago: University of Chicago Press, 1990). A detailed political history of Islamic rule in Spain before the reconquista.

* J. H. Elliot, *Imperial Spain, 1469–1716* (New York: Mentor, 1963). Still worth reading for its insights and examples.

Henry Kamen, *The Spanish Inquisition: A Historical Revision* (New Haven, CT: Yale University Press, 1998). The most recent assessment of the power and activities of the Inquisition.

The Dynastic Struggles

* J. R. Hale, *War and Society in Renaissance Europe* (Baltimore, MD: Johns Hopkins University Press, 1986). Assesses the impact of war on the political and social history of early modern Europe.

M. F. Alvarez, *Charles V* (London: Thames and Hudson, 1975). An accessible biography of the most remarkable man of the age.

* Martyn Rady, *The Emperor Charles V* (London: Longman, 1988). An excellent brief introduction that includes documents and a recent bibliography.

Otto Von Habsburg, *Charles V* (New York: Praeger Publishers, 1970). A classic study.

* R. J. Knecht, *Renaissance Warrior and Patron: The Reign of Francis I* (Cambridge: Cambridge University Press, 1996). A full history of the reign lavishly illustrated.

David Potter, *A History of France 1460–1560* (London: Macmillan, 1995). A reliable survey that connects medieval and early modern developments.

* R. J. Knecht, *Francis I* (Cambridge: Cambridge University Press, 1982). A compelling study by the leading scholar of sixteenth-century France.

* J. J. Scarisbrick, *Henry VIII* (Berkeley: University of California Press, 1968). The definitive biography.

* E. W. Ives, *Anne Boleyn* (Oxford: Blackwell, 1986). A gripping biography of an ill-fated queen.

* Paperback edition available.

Discovering Western Civilization Online

To further explore the European empires, consult the following World Wide Web sites. Since Web resources are constantly being updated, also go to *www.awl.com/Kishlansky* for further suggestions.

European Encounters

www.win.tue.nl/cs/fm/engels/discovery/
A site devoted to all ages of discovery with maps, short biographies, and time lines. There are links to the writings of Columbus, Cortés, and others of the early voyagers.

www1.minn.net/~keithp/
Everything you ever wanted to know about Christopher Columbus.

www.castellobanfi.com/features/story_3.html
A site devoted to the food and drink associated with a long ocean voyage in the fifteenth century.

www.fordham.edu/halsall/sbook1z.html
Dozens of primary sources relating to the voyages of discovery.

CHAPTER

13 THE REFORM OF RELIGION

- *SOLA SCRIPTURA*
- **THE INTELLECTUAL REFORMATION**
  - The Print Revolution
  - Christian Humanism
  - The Humanist Movement
  - The Wit of Erasmus
- **THE LUTHERAN REFORMATION**
  - The Spark of Reform
  - Martin Luther's Faith
  - Lutheranism
  - The Spread of Lutheranism
- **THE PROTESTANT REFORMATION**
  - Geneva and Calvin
  - The English Reformation
  - The Reformation of the Radicals
- **THE CATHOLIC REFORMATION**
  - The Spiritual Revival
  - Loyola's Pilgrimage
  - The Counter-Reformation
  - The Empire Strikes Back

Sola Scriptura

"IN THE BEGINNING WAS THE WORD, and the word was with God, and the word was God." In no other period of European history was this text of the apostle John so appropriate. Men and women shared a consuming desire to hear and to read the Word of God as set down in the Bible. In the early sixteenth century, Europeans developed an insatiable appetite for the Bible. Scriptures rolled off printing presses in every shape and form, from the great vellum tomes of Gutenberg pictured here to pocket Bibles that soldiers carried into battle. They came in every imaginable language. Before 1500 there were 14 complete Bibles printed in German, 4 each in Italian, French, and Spanish, 1 in Czech, and even 1 in Flemish. There were hundreds more editions in Latin, the official Vulgate Bible first translated by Saint Jerome in the fourth century. Whole translations and editions of the Bible were only part of the story. Separate sections, especially the Psalms and the first books of the Old Testament, were printed by the thousands. There were 24 French editions of the Old Testament before an entirely new translation appeared in 1530. When Martin Luther began his own German translation of the Bible in 1522, it immediately became an international best-seller. In 25 years it went into 430 editions. It is estimated that 1 million German Bibles were printed in the first half of the sixteenth century—a time when Europe had a German-speaking population of about 15 million people, 90 percent of whom were illiterate.

Bible owning was no fad. It was but one element in a new devotional outlook that was sweeping the Continent and that would have far-reaching consequences for European society during the next 150 years. A renewed spirituality was everywhere to be seen. It was expressed in a desire to change the traditional practices and structures of the Roman church. It was expressed in a desire to have learned and responsible ministers to tend to the needs of their parishioners. It was expressed in a desire to establish godly families, godly cities, and godly kingdoms. Sometimes it took the form of sarcasm and bitter denunciations; sometimes it took the form of quiet devotion and pious living. The need for reform was everywhere felt; the demand for reform was everywhere heard. It came from within the Roman church as much as from without.

The inspiration for reform was based on the Word of God. Scholars, following humanist principles, worked on biblical translations in an attempt to bring a purer text to light. Biblical commentary dominated the writings of churchmen as never before. Woodcut pictures depicting scenes from the life of Jesus or from the Old Testament were printed in untold quantities for the edification of the unlettered. For the first time, common people could, in their own dwellings, contemplate representations of the lives of the saints. Many of the Bibles that were printed in vernacular—that is, in the languages spoken in the various European states rather than in Latin—were interleaved with illustrations of the central events of Christian history. Preachers spoke to newly aware audiences and relied on biblical texts to draw out their message. Study groups, especially in urban areas, proliferated so that the literate could read and learn together. Bible reading became a part of family life, one that mothers and fathers could share with their children and their servants. *Sola Scriptura*—by the word alone—became the battle cry of religious reform.

THE INTELLECTUAL REFORMATION

There is nothing as powerful as an idea whose time has come. But the coming of ideas has a history as complex as the ideas themselves. In the early sixteenth century, reformers throughout western Europe preached new ideas about religious doctrine and religious practice. At first the ideas took the form of a sustained critique of the Roman Catholic church, but soon they developed a momentum of their own. Some reformers remained within traditional Catholicism; others moved outside and founded new Protestant churches. Whether Catholic or Protestant, wherever the movement for religious reform appeared it was fed by new ideas. But if new ideas were to supplant old ones, they had to be communicated—not only heard and repeated but accurately recorded and understood. That was made possible by the development of the technology of printing, which appeared in Germany in the late fifteenth century and rapidly spread across Europe in the succeeding decades. Yet printing was as much a result as it was a cause of the spread of ideas. The humanist call for a return to the study of the classics and for the creation of accurate texts, first heard in Italy, aroused scholars and leaders in all of the European states. Their appetite for manuscripts exhausted the abilities of the scribes and booksellers who reproduced texts. Printing responded to that demand.

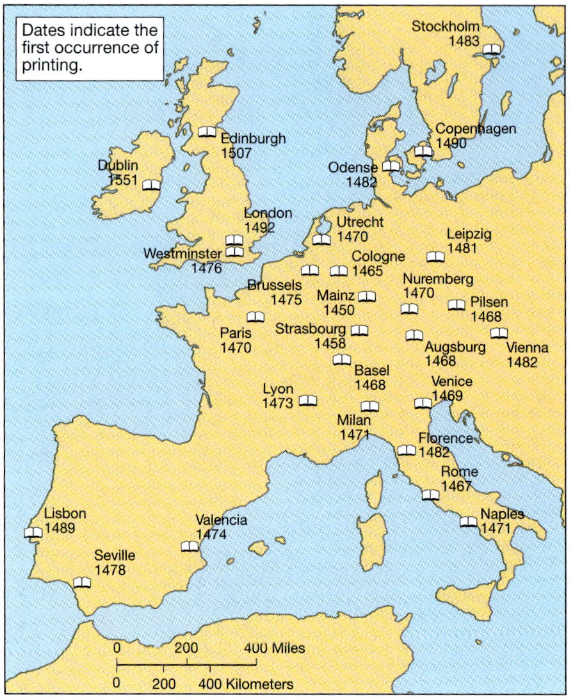

The Spread of Printing. Printing was entirely an urban phenomenon with presses established in the largest cities in Europe.

The Print Revolution

The development of printing did not cause religious reform, but it is difficult to see how reform would have progressed in its absence. The campaign to change the doctrine and practice of Catholicism was waged through the press, with millions of flyers and pamphlets distributed across Europe to spread the new ideas. One-third of all books sold in Germany between 1518 and 1525 were written by Luther. But the ways in which printing came to be used by religious reformers could hardly have been foreseen by the artisans, bankers, and booksellers who together created one of the true technological revolutions in Western history.

Printing was not invented. It developed as a result of progress made in a number of allied industries, of which papermaking and goldsmithing were the most important. Scholars and university students needed copies of manuscripts. Their need led to the development of a trade in bookselling that flourished in almost every university town. The process of reproduction was slowed by difficulties in obtaining the sheep and calfskins on which the manuscripts were written. It took the skins of 300 sheep to produce a single Bible. In the early fifteenth century, copyists began to substitute paper made from linen rags for the expensive vellum skins. A number of German artisans experimented with using movable metal type to make exact reproductions of manuscripts on paper. Paper took a better impression and provided an absolutely smooth surface, which was essential for pressing the image. In the 1450s, in Mainz, Johannes Gutenberg (ca. 1400–1468) and his partners succeeded and published their famous Bibles.

The association of early printing with goldsmithing resulted from the high level of technical skill that was necessary to create the hard metal stamps from which the softer metal type was produced. Printing was an expensive business. The investment in type and in paper was considerable. Only the press itself was cheap. Any corn or wine press could be used to bring

An early print shop. The man at the right operates the screw press while an apprentice (center) stacks the printed sheets. The men at the left are setting type for the next impression.

the long flat sheets of paper down upon a wooden frame filled with ink-coated metal type. Booksellers initially put up the capital needed to cast the stamps, mold the type, and buy the paper. They bound the printed pages and found the markets to distribute them. At first sales were slow. Printed books were considered inferior to handwritten manuscripts. Nor at first were printed books less expensive. Bibles like those printed by Gutenberg were major investments, equivalent to purchasing a house today. Many printing shops quickly went bankrupt as they misjudged their markets and were unable to pay back their loans.

Still, once it was begun, printing spread like wildfire. By 1480, more than 110 towns had established presses, most in Italy and Germany. After that the pace quickened. By the beginning of the sixteenth century, Venice and Paris were the centers of the industry, with the Paris presses producing more than three hundred new titles annually. Most of the early printed works were either religious or classical. Bibles, church service books, and the commentaries of the church fathers were most common. Cicero topped the list of classical authors.

What is most amazing about the printing revolution is how rapidly printing came to be a basic part of life. In the first 40 years after the presses began, perhaps as many as 20 million books were produced and distributed. Printing changed the habits of teachers and students, and therefore the possibilities of education. It altered the methods by which the state conducted its business. It affected both legal training and legal proceedings. Compilations of laws could now be widely distributed and more uniformly enforced. Printing had a similar effect on the development of scientific study. The printing press popularized the discoveries of the New World and contributed to the reproduction of more accurate charts and maps, which in turn facilitated further discovery. Printing also helped standardize language—both Latin and vernacular—by frequent repetition of preferred usage and spelling. Perhaps most importantly, printing created an international intellectual community whose ideas could be dispersed the length and breadth of the Continent. The printing press enhanced the value of ideas and of thinking. Nothing could be more central to the reform of religion.

Christian Humanism

Many of the ideas that spread across Europe as the result of the printing revolution originated in Italian humanism (see Chapter 11). The revival of classical literature, with its concern for purity in language and eloquence in style, was one of the most admired achievements of the Renaissance. Students from all over Europe who descended upon Italian universities to study medicine and law came away with a strong dose of philology, rhetoric, moral philosophy, and the other liberal arts. Their heads were filled with the new learning. By the beginning of the sixteenth century, the force of humanism was felt strongly in northern and western Europe, where it was grafted to the dominant strains of traditional theological teaching. The combination was a new and powerful intellectual movement known as Christian humanism.

Although the humanism of the north differed from that of the Italian city-states, this is not to say that northern humanists were Christians and Italian humanists were not. But Italian intellectual interests were in secular subjects, especially in mastering classical languages and in translating classical texts. Italian humanists had established techniques for the recovery of accurate texts and had developed principles for compiling the scholarly editions that now poured forth from the printing presses. Christian humanists applied the techniques to the study of the authorities and texts of the Church. Most of the new humanists had been trained in Italy, where they devoted themselves to the mastery of Greek and Latin. They had imbibed the idea that scholars, using their own critical faculties, could establish the authority of texts and the meaning of words. Building upon the patient work of their predecessors and the advantages offered by printing, the new generation of humanists brought learning to educated men and women throughout Europe.

Christian humanism was a program of reform rather than a philosophy. It aimed to make better Christians through better education. Humanists were especially interested in the education of women. "For what is more fruitful than the good education and order of women, the one half of all mankind," wrote Thomas More (1478–1535). Humanists helped found schools for girls and advocated that they be trained in the same subjects as boys. Thomas More raised his daughters to be among the educated elite of England, and they enjoyed international renown. The Spanish humanist Juan Luis Vives (1492–1540) wrote *The Instruction of a Christian Woman* (1523), a handbook for women of the elite orders commissioned by Catherine of Aragon. Renowned women scholars even held places at Italian universities. Humanist educational principles posed an implicit challenge to Roman Catholicism. Schools had once been the monopoly of the Church, which used them to train clergymen. The Church had founded them and kept them afloat in good times and in bad. Literacy itself had been preserved over the centuries so that the gospel could be propagated.

By the sixteenth century those purposes had been transformed. Schools now trained many who were not destined for careers in the Church, and literacy served the needs of the state, the aristocracy, and the merchant classes. More importantly, as the humanists perfected their techniques of scholarship, the Church continued to rely upon traditional methods of training and traditional texts. The dominant manner of teaching at the schools and universities was known as Scholasticism. Passages of biblical texts were studied through the commentaries of generations of church fathers. Rote memorization of the opinions of others was more highly valued than critical thinking. Argument took place by formal disputation of questions on which the church fathers disagreed. Disputed questions became more and more obscure. Even if Scholastics did not debate the question, "How many angels can dance on the head of a pin?" it seemed to many humanists that they might as well have. The Vulgate Bible was used throughout western Christendom. It was now a thousand years old.

The Humanist Movement

Many humanist criticisms of Church teaching focused on its failure to inspire individuals to live a Christian life. Humanist writers were especially scathing about popular practices that bordered on superstition, such as pilgrimages to holy places or the worship of relics from the early history of the Church. Such beliefs became the butt of popular humor: "If the fragments [of the Lord's Cross] were joined together they would seem a full load for a freighter. And yet the Lord carried his whole cross." Christian humanists wanted to inspire Christians. As the great Dutch humanist Desiderius Erasmus observed, "To be learned is the lot of only a few; but no one is unable to be a Christian, no one is unable to be pious." The ironic strain in humanist writing is most closely associated with Erasmus, but it is also visible in the humanist social criticism of Sir Thomas More's *Utopia*.

Christian humanism was an international movement. The humanists formed the elite of the intellectual world of the sixteenth century, and their services were sought by princes and peers as well as by the most distinguished universities. In fact, the New

Monarchs supported the humanists and protected them from their critics. Marguerite of Navarre, sister of Francis I, was an accomplished writer who frequently interceded on behalf of the leading French humanists. Ferdinand of Aragon, Henry VIII, and the Holy Roman Emperors Maximilian I and Charles V all brought humanists to their courts and aided their projects. Maria of Hungary and Mary and Elizabeth Tudor were trained in humanist principles and participated in humanist literary achievements. That support was especially important for educational reform. Under the influence of the French humanist Jacques Lefevre d'Étaples (ca. 1455–1536), Francis I established the College de France; under the direction of Cardinal Jiménez de Cisneros, the University of Alcala was founded in Spain. Throughout northern Europe, professorships in Greek and Latin were endowed at universities to help further the study of classical languages.

The centerpiece of humanist reforms was the translation of Christian texts. Armed with skills in Greek and Latin, informed by scholars of Hebrew and Aramaic, humanist writers prepared new editions of the books of the Bible and of the writings of the early church fathers. Their favorite method was side-by-side translation. The Polyglot—literally "many languages"—Bible that was produced in 1522 at the University of Alcala took a team of scholars 15 years to complete. They gathered together copies of all known biblical manuscripts and rigorously compared their texts. They established the principle that inconsistencies among Latin manuscripts were to be resolved by reference to Greek texts, and difficulties in Greek texts by reference to Hebrew texts. The result was six elegantly printed volumes that allowed scholars to compare the texts. The Old Testament was printed in three parallel columns of Hebrew, Latin Vulgate, and Greek. The New Testament was printed in double columns, with the Greek text on one side and the Vulgate on the other. The Greek edition of the Bible and its establishment as a text superior to the Vulgate caused an immediate sensation throughout humanist and Church circles.

The Wit of Erasmus

Although the Polyglot Bible contained the first completed Greek edition of the New Testament, it was not the first published one. That distinction belongs to the man whose name is most closely associated with the idea of Christian humanism: Desiderius Erasmus of Rotterdam (ca. 1466–1536). Orphaned at an early age, Erasmus was educated by the Brothers of the Common Life, a lay brotherhood that specialized in schooling children and preparing them for a monastic life. Marked out early by his quick wit, pleasant though strong personality, and extraordinary intellectual gifts, Erasmus entered a monastery and was then allowed to travel to pursue his studies, first in France and then in England.

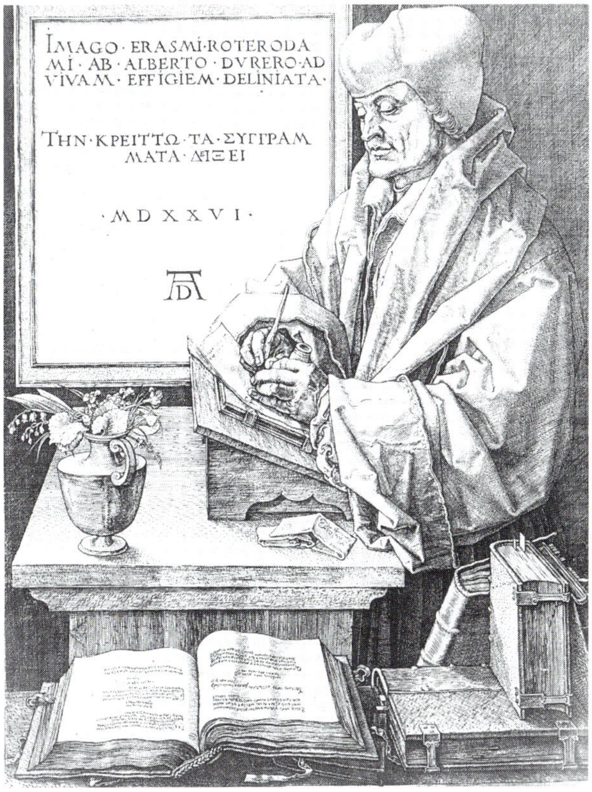

An engraving of Erasmus by the German master Albrecht Dürer. The title, the date, and the artist's name appear in Latin behind the philosopher. The Greek inscription reads: "His writings depict him even better."

In England, Erasmus learned of new techniques for instructing children both in classical knowledge and in Christian morals, and he became particularly interested in the education of women. He dedicated a number of his later writings to women patrons who were accomplished humanist scholars. While in England, Erasmus decided to compose a short satire on the lines of his

A DUTCH WIT

In Praise of Folly (1500) was a witty satire on the abuses to be found in the Catholic church. Desiderius Erasmus wrote it on a lark to be presented to his friend, Sir Thomas More, on whose name its Greek title puns. It was probably the first best-seller of the age of printing.

THESE VARIOUS FORMS OF FOOLISHNESS so pervade the whole life of Christians that even the priests themselves find no objection to admitting, not to say fostering, them, since they do not fail to perceive how many tidy little sums accrue to them from such sources. But what if some odious philosopher should chime in and say, as is quite true: "You will not die badly if you live well. You are redeeming your sins when you add to the sum that you contribute a hearty detestation of evil doers: then you may spare yourself tears, vigils, invocations, fasts, and all that kind of life. You may rely upon any saint to aid you when once you begin to imitate his life."

As for the theologians, perhaps the less said the better on this gloomy and dangerous theme, since they are a style of man who show themselves exceeding supercilious and irritable unless they can heap up six hundred conclusions about you and force you to recant; and if you refuse, they promptly brand you as a heretic—for it is their custom to terrify by their thunderings those whom they dislike. It must be confessed that no other group of fools are so reluctant to acknowledge Folly's benefits toward them, although I have many titles to their gratitude, for I make them so in love with themselves that they seem to be happily exalted to the third heaven, whence they look down with something like pity upon all other mortals, wandering about on the earth like mere cattle.

From Erasmus, *In Praise of Folly.*

conversations with Thomas More, extolling what was silly and condemning what was wise. The result was *In Praise of Folly* (1509), a work that became one of the first best-sellers in publishing history.

Before his visit to England, Erasmus had worked solely on Latin translations, but he came to realize the importance of recovering the Greek texts of the early church fathers. At the age of 30, he began the arduous task of learning ancient Greek and devoted his energies to a study of the writings of Saint Jerome, the principal compiler of the Vulgate, and to preparing an edition of the Greek text of the Bible. Erasmus's New Testament and his edition of the writings of Saint Jerome both appeared in 1516. Coming from the pen of the most renowned intellectual in Europe, they were an immediate success.

Erasmus devoted his life to restoring the direct connection between the individual Christian and the textual basis of Christian doctrine. Although he is called the father of biblical criticism, Erasmus was not a theologian. He was more interested in the practical impact of ideas than in the ideas themselves. His scathing attacks upon the Scholastics, popular superstition, and the pretensions of the traditionalists in the Church and the universities all aimed at the same goal: to restore the experiences of Christ to the center of Christianity. Many of Erasmus's popular writings were how-to books—how to improve one's manners, how to speak Latin properly, how to write letters—he even propounded 22 rules on how to lead a Christian life. Although his patrons were the rich and his language was Latin, Erasmus also hoped to reach men and women lower down the social order, those whom he believed the Church had failed to educate. "The doctrine of Christ casts aside no age, no sex, no fortune or position in life. It keeps no one at a distance." He hoped that his biblical translations would comfort others in the same way that they had comforted him. "I would to God that the plowman would sing a text of the Scripture at his plow and that the weaver would hum [it] to the tune of his shuttle. I wish that the traveler would expel the weariness of his journey with this pastime. I wish that all communication of the Christian would be of the Scriptures."

THE LUTHERAN REFORMATION

On the surface, the Roman Catholic church appeared as strong as ever at the end of the fifteenth century. The growth of universities and the spread of the new learning had helped create a better-educated clergy. The printing press proved an even greater boon to the Church than it had to the humanists by making widely available both instructional manuals for priests and up-to-date service books for congregations. The prosperity of European societies enhanced the prosperity of the Church. In Rome, successive late medieval popes had managed to protect Church interests in the wake of the disintegration of the autonomous power of the Italian city-states. That was a remarkable feat. Popes had become first diplomats and then warriors in order to repel French and Spanish invaders. Although Rome had been invaded, it had never been conquered. And it was more beautiful than ever, as the greatest artists and artisans of the Renaissance had built and adorned its churches. Pilgrims came in the hundreds of thousands to bask in its glory. On the surface all was calm.

Yet everywhere in Europe the cry was for reform. Reform the venal papacy and its money-sucking bishops. Reform the ignorant clergy and the sacrilegious priests. Raise up the fallen nuns and the wayward friars. Wherever people turned, they saw abuses. Parish livings were sold to the highest bidder to raise money. That was simony. Rich appointments were given to the kinsmen of powerful Church leaders rather than to those most qualified. That was nepotism. Individual clergymen accumulated numerous positions whose responsibilities they could not fulfill. That was pluralism. Some priests who took the vow of chastity lived openly with their concubines. Some mendicants who took the vow of poverty dressed in silk and ate from golden plates.

Yet the cry for reform that pierced the states of Europe at the beginning of the sixteenth century was a cry not so much of anguish as of hope. It came at a moment when people from all walks of life demanded greater spiritual fulfillment and held those whose vocation it was to provide such fulfillment to higher standards of achievement. It was expectation rather than experience that powered the demands for reform.

The Spark of Reform

Europe was becoming more religious. The signs of religious fervor were everywhere. Cities hired preachers to expound the gospel. Pilgrims to the shrines of saints clogged the roadways every spring and summer. It is estimated that 140,000 people visited the relics at Aachen on one day in 1496. Rome remained the greatest attraction, but pilgrims covered the Continent. The shrine of the apostle Saint James at Compostela in Spain was believed to cure the ill. Endowments of masses for the dead increased. Henry VII of England provided money for 10,000 masses to be said for his soul. Even moderately well-to-do city merchants might bequeath funds for several hundred. The chantries, where such services were performed, became overburdened by the "arithmetical piety," as there were neither enough priests nor enough altars to supply the demand.

People wanted more from the Church than the Church could possibly give them. Humanists condemned visits to the shrines as superstitious; pilgrims demanded that the relics be made more accessible. Reformers complained of pluralism; the clergy complained that they could not live on the salary of a single office. In one English diocese, 60 percent of all parish incomes were inadequate to live on. Civic authorities demanded that the established Church take greater responsibility for good works; the pope demanded that civic authorities help pay for them.

Contradiction and paradox dominated the movements for reform. Although the most vocal critics of the Church complained that its discipline was too lax, for many ordinary people its demands were too rigorous. The obligations of penance and confession weighed heavily upon them. Church doctrine held that sins had to be washed away before the souls of the dead could enter heaven. Until then they suffered in purgatory. Sins were cleansed through penance—the performance of acts of contrition assigned after confession. Despite the rule that confession must be made at least annually, it is doubtful if many Catholics entered the confessional for years on end. This is not to say that they were unconcerned about their sins or did not desire to do penance for them. Rather, it was the ordeal of the confession itself that kept many people away. "Have you skipped mass? Have you dressed proudly? Have you thought of committing adultery? Have you insulted or cursed your parents? Have you failed to offer prayers, give alms, and endow masses for departed parents?" These were just a few of the uncomfortable questions that priests were instructed to pose in confession. In towns, merchants were asked about their trading practices, shopkeepers about the quality of their goods. Magistrates were questioned about their attitudes to the clergy, intellectuals about their attitudes to the pope.

Thus it is hardly surprising that the sale of indulgences became a popular substitute for penance and confession. An indulgence was a portion of the treasury of good works performed by righteous Christians throughout the ages. They could be granted to those who desired to atone for their sins. Strictly speaking, an indulgence supplemented penance rather than substituted for it. It was effective only for the contrite—for sinners who repented of their sins. But as the practice of granting indulgences spread, the subtle distinction largely disappeared. Indulgences came to be viewed as pardons and the gift given to the Church in return as payment. "So soon as coin in coffer rings, the soul from purgatory springs." Indulgences were bought by the living to cleanse the sins of the dead, and some people even bought indulgences in anticipation of sins they had not yet committed.

By the sixteenth century, to limit abuses by local Church authorities, only the pope, through his agents, could grant indulgences. And their sale had become big business. Indulgences were one of the first items printed on Gutenberg's press. Popes used special occasions to offer an indulgence for pilgrimages to Rome or for contributions to special papal projects. Other indulgences were licensed locally, usually at the shrines of saints or at churches that contained relics, which was one reason why pilgrimages became increasingly popular. Frederick III, "the Wise" (1463–1525), ruler of Saxony, was one of the largest collectors of relics in Europe. At its height, his collection contained 17,000 different items, including a branch of Moses' burning bush, straw from Christ's manger, and 35 fragments of the true cross. Together, his relics carried remission for sins that would otherwise have taken more than a quarter of a million years in purgatory to be cleansed.

The indulgence controversy was a symptom rather than a cause of the explosion of feelings that erupted in the small German town of Wittenberg in the year 1517. In that year, the pope was offering an indulgence to help finance the rebuilding of Saint Peter's Basilica in Rome. The pope chose Prince Albert of Brandenburg (1490–1545) to distribute the indulgence in Germany, and Albert hired the Dominican friar Johann Tetzel (ca. 1465–1519) to preach its benefits. Tetzel offered little warning about the theological niceties of indulgences to those who paid to mitigate their own sins or alleviate the suffering of their ancestors whose souls resided in purgatory.

An anonymous caricature of Johann Tetzel, whose sale of an indulgence inspired Martin Luther's Ninety-five Theses. Tetzel answered with 122 theses of his own but was rebuked and disowned by the Catholics.

Enthusiasm for the indulgence spread to the neighboring state of Saxony, where Frederick banned its sale. His great collection of relics carried their own indulgences, and Tetzel offered unwelcome competition. But Saxons flocked into Brandenburg to make their purchases. By the end of October, Tetzel was not very far from Wittenberg Castle, where Frederick's relics were housed. On All Saints' Day the relics would be opened to view and, with the harvest done, one of the largest crowds of the year would gather to see them. On the night before, Martin Luther (1483–1546), a professor of theology at Wittenberg University, posted on the door of the castle church Ninety-five Theses attacking indulgences and their sale.

Aside from the timing of Luther's action, there was nothing unusual about the posting of theses. In the Scholastic tradition of disputation, scholars presented propositions, or theses, for debate and challenged all comers to argue with them in a public forum. Luther's theses were controversial, but—as that was the whole point of offering them for discussion—they were meant to be. Only circumstance moved Luther's theses from the academic to the public sphere. Already there was growing concern among clergy and theologians about Tetzel's blatant sale of indulgences. Hordes of purchasers believed that they were buying unconditional remission of sin. In the late summer and early fall of 1517, the frenzy to buy indulgences had reached gold-rush proportions, and individual priests and monks began to sound the alarm: an indulgence without contrition was worthless.

Luther's theses focused that concern and finally communicated it beyond the walls of the church and university. The theses were immediately translated into German and spread throughout the Holy Roman Empire by humanists who had long criticized practices such as the sale of indulgences as superstitious. Prospective buyers became wary; past purchasers became angry. They had been duped again by the Church, by the priests who took their money, and by the Italian pope who cared nothing for honest, hard-working Germans. But Prince Albert and the pope needed the income. They could not stand by while sales collapsed and anticlerical and antipapal sentiment grew. Luther and his theses would have to be challenged.

Martin Luther's Faith

Martin Luther was not a man to challenge lightly. Although he was only an obscure German professor, he had already marked himself out to all who knew him. In his youth, Luther was an exceptionally able student whose father sent him to the best schools in preparation for a career in law. But Martin had his own ideas about his future, which were made more vivid when he was nearly struck by lightning. Against the wishes of his father, he entered an Augustinian monastery, wholeheartedly followed the strict program of his order, and was ordained a priest in 1507. Intellectually gifted, he went on to study at the university, first at Erfurt and then at Wittenberg, where he received his doctorate and was appointed to the theology faculty in 1512.

A professor at the age of 29, he also served as priest at the castle church, where he preached each week. He attracted powerful patrons in the university and gained a reputation as an outstanding teacher. He began to be picked for administrative posts and became overseer of 11 Augustinian monasteries. His skills in disputation were so widely recognized that he was sent to Rome to argue a case on behalf of his order. Each task he was given he fulfilled beyond expectation; at every step he proved himself ready to go higher.

In all outward appearances, Luther was successful and contented. But beneath this tranquil exterior lay a soul in torment. As he rose in others' estimation, he sank in his own. Through beating and fasting he mortified his flesh. Through vigil and prayer he nourished his soul. Through study and contemplation he honed his intellect. Still he could find no peace. Despite his devotion, he could not erase his sense of sin; he could not convince himself that the righteousness God demanded of him was a righteousness he could achieve. "I was one who terribly feared the last judgment and who nevertheless with all my heart wished to be saved."

Knowledge of his salvation came to Luther through study. His internal agonies led him to ponder over and

Martin Luther.

over again the biblical passages that described the righteousness of God. In the intellectual tradition in which he had been trained, that righteousness was equated with law. The righteous person either followed God's law or was punished by God's wrath. It was that understanding that tormented him. "I thought that I had to perform good works till at last through them Jesus would become a friend and gracious to me." But no amount of good works could overcome Luther's feelings of guilt for his sins. Like a man caught in a net, the more he struggled the more entangled he became. For years he wrestled with his problem. Almost from the moment he began lecturing in 1512 he searched for the key to the freedom of his own soul.

Even before he wrote his Ninety-five Theses, Luther had made the first breakthrough by a unique reading of the writings of Saint Paul. "I pondered night and day until I understood the connection between the righteousness of God and the sentence 'The just shall live by faith.' Then I grasped that the justice of God is the righteousness by which through grace and pure mercy, God justifies us through faith. Immediately I felt that I had been reborn and that I had passed through wide open doors into paradise!" Finally he realized that the righteousness of God was not a burden that humans carried, but a gift that God bestowed. It could not be earned by good works but was freely given. It was this belief that fortified Luther during his years of struggle with both civil and Church powers.

Over the next several years, Luther refined his spiritual philosophy and drew out the implications of his newfound beliefs. His religion was shaped by three interconnected tenets. First came justification by faith alone—*sola fide*. An individual's everlasting salvation came from faith in God's goodness rather than from the performance of good works. Sin was ever present and inescapable. It could not be washed away by penance, and it could not be forgiven by indulgence. Second, faith in God's mercy came only through the knowledge and contemplation of the Word of God—*sola scriptura*. All that was needed to understand the justice and mercy of God was contained in the Bible, the sole authority in all things spiritual. Reading the Word, hearing the Word, expounding upon and studying the Word—that was the path to faith, and through faith to salvation. Third, all who believed in God's righteousness and had achieved their faith through the study of the Bible were equal in God's eyes. No longer was it necessary for men and women to renounce their worldly existence and take up a life consumed by spiritual works. Neither pope nor priest, neither monk nor nun, could achieve a higher level of spirituality than the most ordinary citizen. The priesthood was of all believers. Each followed his or her own calling in life and found his or her own faith through Scripture. Ministers and preachers were valuable because they could help others learn God's Word. But they could not confer faith.

Luther's spiritual rebirth and the theology that developed from it posed a fundamental challenge to the Roman Catholic church. The doctrine of justification by faith alone called into question the Church's emphasis upon the primacy of works—that is, receiving the sacraments administered by the priests and performing acts of charity and devotion. The doctrine that faith was achieved through Scripture weakened the mediating power of the Church by making salvation an individual rather than a collective event. The doctrine of the equality of all believers struck at the vast establishment of religious houses as well as the spiritual hierarchy of the Church from the lowest priest to the pope. Although for centuries the Roman Catholic church had met doctrinal challenges and had absorbed many seemingly unorthodox ideas, Luther's theology could not be among them. It struck too deeply at the roots of belief, practice, and structure. If Luther was right, then the Roman Catholic church must be wrong.

Yet for all of the transforming power of the apparently simple ideas, it was not Luther alone who initiated the reform of religion. His obsession with salvation was based on the same impulse that had made indulgences so popular. Before Luther, countless thousands strove for salvation. Justification by faith alone provided an alternative to the combination of works and faith that many Roman Catholics found too difficult to fulfill. Luther's insistence that faith comes only through the study of the Word of God was facilitated by the new learning and the invention of printing. The printing press prepared the ground for the dissemination of his thought as much as it disseminated it. That was a result of the Renaissance. Luther's hope for the creation of a spiritual elite, confirmed in their faith and confident of their salvation, readily appealed to the citizens of hundreds of German towns who had already made of themselves a social and economic elite. That was a result of the growth of towns. The idea of the equality of all believers meant that all were equally responsible for fulfilling God's commandments. That set secular rulers on an equal footing with the pope at a moment in Western history when they were already challenging papal power in matters of both Church and state. That was a result of the formation of states. For all of the painful soul-searching by which he came to his shattering insight, there was embodied in Luther the culmination of changes of which he was only dimly aware.

Lutheranism

The first to feel the seriousness of Luther's challenge to the established order was the reformer himself. The head of his order, a papal legate, and finally the Emperor Charles V all called for Luther to recant his views on indulgences. Excommunicated by Pope Leo X in 1521, Luther was ordered by Charles V to appear before the diet, or assembly, in Worms. The emperor demanded that Luther retract his teachings. Infuriatingly, Luther replied that, if he could be shown the places in the Bible that contradicted his views, he would gladly change them. "I cannot and I will not retract anything, since it is neither safe nor right to go against conscience. I cannot do otherwise." In fact, during the three years between the posting of his theses and his appearance before the emperor, Luther came to conclusions much more radical than his initial attack on indulgences. Preparing to contend with papal representatives about the pope's right to issue indulgences, Luther came to believe that the papacy was a human rather than a divine invention. Therefore he denounced both the papacy and the general councils of the Church. In his *Address to the Christian Nobility of the German Nation* (1520), he called upon the princes to take the reform of religion into their own hands. No longer was there hope of compromise. Charles V declared Luther an enemy of the empire. In both Church and state he was now an outlaw.

But Luther had attracted powerful supporters as well as powerful enemies. Prince Frederick III of Saxony consistently intervened on his behalf, and the delicate international situation forced Luther's chief antagonists to move more slowly than they might have wanted. The pope hoped first to keep Charles V off the imperial throne and then to maintain a united front with the German princes against him. Charles V, already locked in his lifelong struggle with the French, needed German military support and peace in his German territories. Those factors consistently played into Luther's hands.

Lucas Cranach the Elder's 1521 portrait of Martin Luther shows Luther in the disguise of the horseman's garb and long beard he adopted while in hiding from his enemies in 1521–1522.

While pope and emperor were otherwise occupied, Luther refined his ideas and thus was able to hold his own in the theological debates in which he won important converts. More importantly, as time passed Luther's reputation grew, not only in Germany, but all over Europe. Between 1517 and 1520 he published 30 works, all of which achieved massive sales. Yet Luther alone could not sustain what came to be called Lutheranism. The Roman Catholic church had met heresy before and knew how to deal with it. What

LUTHER ON MARRIAGE

Martin Luther wrote thousands of pages of theological and devotional literature in establishing a new religious movement. His simple style and everyday examples made his message accessible to hundreds of thousands of ordinary people. In this selection from his tract On Good Works *(1520), he compares the relationship of the husband and wife to that of the Christian and Christ.*

WE CAN UNDERSTAND THIS WHOLE MATTER [of good works] by an obvious human example. When husband and wife are fond of one another and live together in love and in confidence in one another, and each believes truly in the other, who shall teach them how they should act, what they should do or leave undone, say or not say, think or not think? Their own insight tells them all that need be, and more too. There is no distinction in their "works" for one another. They do the long, hard, and heavy tasks as willingly as the slight and easy things, and moreover they act with glad, peaceful, and secure hearts and are altogether free and unconstrained. But when doubt comes they begin to ask what is best, and begin to distinguish between their acts in order to gain the other's favor, and go about with troubled and heavy hearts, perhaps well-nigh in despair or driven to downright desperation.

So the Christian who lives in confidence toward God knows what things he should do, and does all gladly and freely, not with a view to accumulating merit and good works, but because it is his great joy to please God and to serve him without thought of reward, contented if he but do God's will. On the contrary, he who is not at one with God, or is in doubt, will begin to be anxious how he may satisfy God and justify himself by his works. He runs off on a pilgrimage to St. James of Compostella, to Rome, to Jerusalem—here, there, anywhere; prays to St. Bridget, or some other saint, fasts this day and that, confesses here and confesses there, asks this man and that, but finds no peace.

From Martin Luther, *On Good Works*.

turned Luther's theology into a movement—which after 1529 came to be known as Protestantism—was the support he received among German princes and within German cities.

Princes and Cities. There were many reasons that individual princes turned to Luther's theology. First and foremost was sincere religious conviction. Matters of the hereafter were a pressing concern in a world in which the average life span was 30 years and nearly all natural phenomena were inexplicable. And they were more pressing still among the educated elites inspired by the new learning and confident of their power to reason critically. Yet there were secular reasons as well. The formation of large states had provided a model for civil government. On a smaller scale, German princes worked to centralize their administration, protect themselves from predatory neighbors, and increase their revenues. They had long suffered under the burden of papal exactions. Taxes and gifts flowed south to a papacy dominated by Italians. Luther's call for civil rulers to lead their own churches meant that civil rulers could keep their own revenues.

The Reformation spread particularly well in the German cities, especially those the emperor had granted the status of freedom from the rule of any prince. Once Protestant ideas were established, entire towns adopted them. The cities had long struggled with the tension of the separate jurisdictions of state and Church. Much urban property was owned by the Church and thus exempt from taxation and law enforcement, and the clergy constituted a significant proportion of urban populations. Reformed religion stressed the equality of clergy and laity, and thus the indisputable power of civil authorities. Paradoxically, it was because the cities contained large numbers of priests that Luther's ideas reached them quickly. Many of his earliest students served urban congregations and began to develop doctrines and practices that, though based on Luther's ideas, were adapted to the circumstances of city life. The reform clergy became integrated into the life of the city in a way that the Catholic clergy had not. They married the daughters of citizens, became citizens themselves, and trained their children in the guilds. Moreover, the imperial free cities were also the center of the printing trade and home to many of the most noted humanists who were initially important in spreading Luther's ideas.

Luther's message held great appeal for the middle orders in the towns. While it was necessary for the leader of a state to support reform if it was to survive, in the cities it was the petty burghers, lesser merchants, tradesmen, and artisans who led the movements that ultimately gained the approval of city governments. The groups resented the privileges given to priests and members of religious orders who paid no taxes and were exempt from the obligations of citizenship. The level of anticlericalism, always high in Germany, was especially acute in cities that were suffering economic difficulties. Pressure from ordinary people and petty traders forced town leaders into action. The evangelism of reforming ministers created converts and an atmosphere of reform. Support from members of the ruling oligarchy both mobilized the pressures and capitalized upon them. Town governments secured their own autonomy over the church, tightening their grip upon the institutions of social control and enhancing the social and economic authority of their members. Once Protestant, city governments took over many of the religious houses, often converting them into schools or hostels for the poor. Former monks were allowed to enter trades and to become citizens. Former nuns were encouraged to marry. Luther himself married an ex-nun after the dissolution of her convent.

A portrait of Marguerite de Valois, queen of Navarre, the cultured and talented sister of King Francis I.

The Appeal for Women. Religious reform appealed to women as well as men, but it affected them differently. Noblewomen were among the most important defenders of Protestant reformers, especially in states in which the prince opposed it. Marguerite of Navarre (1492–1549), sister of Francis I, frequently intervened with her brother on behalf of individual Lutherans who fell afoul of Church authorities. She created her own court in the south of France and stocked it with both humanists and Protestants. Her devotional poem *Mirror of the Sinful Soul* (1533) inspired women reformers and was translated into English by Elizabeth I. Mary of Hungary (1505–1558) served a similar role in the Holy Roman Empire. Sister of both Charles V and Ferdinand I, queen of Hungary and later regent of the Netherlands, she acted as patron to Hungarian reformers. Although Mary was more humanist than Protestant, Luther dedicated an edition of the Psalms to her, and she read a number of his works. Her independent religious views infuriated both of her brothers. Bona (1493–1558), wife of Sigismund I of Poland, was especially important in eastern reform. An Italian by birth, Bona was a central figure in spreading both Renaissance art and humanist learning in Poland. She became one of the largest independent landowners in the state and initiated widespread agricultural and economic reforms. Her private confessor was one of Poland's leading Protestants.

Luther's reforms also offered much to women who were not so highly placed in society. The doctrine of the equality of all believers put men and women on an equal spiritual footing, even if it did nothing to break the male monopoly of the ministry. But the most important difference that Protestantism made to ordinary women was in the private rather than the public sphere. Family life became the center of faith when salvation was removed from the control of the Church. Luther's marriage led him to a deeper appreciation of the importance of the wife and mother in the family's spirituality. "Next to God's word there is no more precious treasure than holy matrimony."

By following humanist teaching on the importance of educating women of the upper orders and by encouraging literacy, the reformers did much that was uplifting. Girls' schools were founded in a number of German cities, and townswomen could use their newly acquired skills in their roles as shopkeepers, family accountants, and teachers of their children. But there were losses as well as gains. The attack on the worship of saints, and especially of the Virgin Mary, removed female images from religion. Protestantism was male dominated in a way that Catholicism was not. Moreover, the emphasis upon reading the Bible tended to reinforce the image of women as weak and inherently sinful. The dissolution of the convents took away from women the one institution that valued their gender and allowed them to pursue a spiritual life outside marriage.

The Spread of Lutheranism

By the end of the 1520s, the Holy Roman Empire was divided between cities and states that accepted reformed religion and those that adhered to Roman Catholicism. Printing presses, traveling merchants, and hordes of students who claimed—not always accurately—to have attended Luther's lectures or sermons spread the message. Large German communities across northern Europe, mostly founded as trading outposts, became focal points for the penetration of reformist ideas. In Livonia, the Teutonic Knights established a Lutheran form of worship that soon took hold all along the shores of the Baltic. Lutheran-inspired reformers seized control of the Polish port city of Gdansk, which they held for a short time, while neighboring Prussia officially established a Lutheran church. Polish translations of Luther's writings were disseminated into Poland-Lithuania, and Protestant communities were established as far south as Krakow.

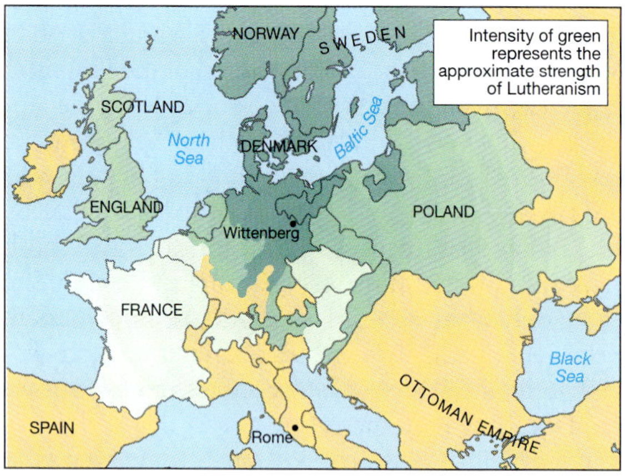

The Spread of Lutheranism from Germany to Scandinavia, Central Europe, and England. Protestant ideas took hold almost exclusively in Northern Europe.

Merchants and students carried Luther's ideas into Scandinavia, but there the importance of political leaders was crucial. Christian III (1534–1559) of Denmark had been present at the Diet of Worms when Luther made his famous reply to Charles V. Christian was deeply impressed by the reformer, and after a ruinous civil war, he confiscated the property of the Catholic church in Denmark and created a reformed religion under Luther's direct supervision.

Paradoxically, Lutheranism came to Sweden as part of an effort to throw off the yoke of Danish dominance. There, too, direct connection with Luther provided the first impulses. Olaus Petri (1493–1552) had studied at Wittenberg and returned to preach Lutheran doctrine among the large German merchant community in Stockholm. He was a trained humanist who used both Erasmus's Greek New Testament and Luther's German one to prepare his Swedish translation (1526). When Gustav I Vasa (1523–1560) led a successful uprising against the Danes and became king of Sweden, he encouraged the spread of Protestant ideas and allowed Petri to continue his Swedish translations of the mass and the Lutheran service. Under the protection of the monarchy, Lutheranism flourished in Scandinavia, where it remains the dominant religion to this day.

Luther's impact extended into central Europe. Bohemia had had a reforming tradition of its own that antedated Luther. Although the teachings of Jan Hus (1373–1415) had been condemned by the Catholic church, Hussitism was in fact the all but established religion in most parts of Bohemia. Ferdinand was bound by law to allow its moderate practice. Hussites had already initiated many of the reforms insisted upon by Luther: the mass was said in Czech, and the Bible had been translated into the vernacular. Most importantly, the laity took the wine as well as the bread at communion. Hussites believed that communion in both forms was mandated by the Bible. That was the real issue that separated them from Roman Catholics, for the Hussites refused to accept the traditional view that the authority of either the pope or the general council of the Church could alter God's command. On all those issues, Hussites and Lutherans shared a common program. But the Hussites were conservative in almost everything else. While the German communities in Bohemia accepted the core of Lutheran doctrine, most Czechs rejected justification by faith alone and maintained their own practices.

As important as Protestant ideas were in northern and central Europe, it was in the Swiss towns of the Holy Roman Empire that they proved most fertile. Here was planted the second generation of reformers, theologians who drew radical new conclusions from Luther's insights. In the east, Huldrych Zwingli (1484–1531) brought reformed religion to the town of Zurich. Educated at the University of Basel and deeply influenced by humanist thought early in his career, Zwingli was a preacher among the Swiss mercenary troops that fought for the empire. In 1516, he met Erasmus in Basel and under his influence began a study of the Greek writings of the church fathers and of the New Testament. Zwingli was also influenced by reports of Luther's defiance of the pope, for his own antipapal views were already developing. Perhaps most decisively for his early development, in 1519 Zwingli was stricken by plague. In his life-and-death struggle he came to a profoundly personal realization of the power of God's mercy.

Those experiences became the basis for the reform theology Zwingli preached in Zurich. He believed that the Church had to recover its earlier purity and to reject the innovations in practices brought in by successive popes and general councils. He stressed the equality of believers, justification by faith alone, and the sufficiency of the gospel as authority for church practice. He attacked indulgences, penance, clerical celibacy, prayers to the Virgin, statues and images in churches, and a long list of other abuses. He also stressed that the mass was to be viewed as a commemorative event rather than one that involved the real presence of Christ. He preferred to call the service the Lord's Supper. His arguments were so effective that the town council adopted them as the basis for a reform of religion.

The principles Zwingli preached quickly spread to neighboring Swiss states. He participated in formal religious disputations in both Bern and Basel. In both places, his plea for a simple, unadorned religious practice met widespread approval. Practical as well as theological, Zwingli's reforms were carried out by the civil government with which he allied himself. That was not the same as the protection that princes had given to Lutherans. Rather, in the places that came under Zwingli's influence there was an important integration of church and state. Zwingli organized a formal military alliance of the Protestant Swiss towns. For him, the Bible carried a social message, and it is fitting that he died on the battlefield defending the state. He stressed the divine origins of civil government and the importance of the magistrate as an agent of Christian reform: "A church without the magistrate is mutilated and incomplete." That theocratic idea—that the leaders of the state and the leaders of the church were linked together—became the basis for further social and political reform.

THE PROTESTANT REFORMATION

By the middle of the 1530s, Protestant reform had entered a new stage. Luther did not intend to form a new religion; his struggle had been with Rome. Before he could build, he had to tear down—his religion was one of protest. Most of his energy was expended in attack and counterattack. The second generation of reformers faced a different task. The new reformers were the church builders who had to systematize doctrine for a generation that had already accepted religious reform. Their challenge was to draw out the logic of reformed ideas and to create enduring structures for reformed churches. The problems they faced were as much institutional as doctrinal. How was the new church to be governed in the absence of the traditional hierarchy? How could discipline be enforced when members of the reformed community went astray? What was the proper relationship between the community of believers and civil authority? Whatever the failings of the Roman Catholic church, it had ready answers to those critical questions. The first generation of reformers had thrown out the stagnant bathwater of ecclesiastical abuses; it was left to the

THE ETERNAL DECREE

John Calvin was born in France but led the Reformation in the Swiss town of Geneva. He was one of the leaders of the second generation of reformers, whose task was to refine the structure of church doctrine. Calvinism was propounded in the Institutes of the Christian Religion *(1534), from which this section on the doctrine of predestination is taken.*

WE MUST BE CONTENT WITH THIS—that such gifts as it pleased the Lord to have bestowed upon the nature of man he vested in Adam; and therefore when Adam lost them after he had received them, he lost them not only from himself but also from us all.... Therefore from a rotten root rose up rotten branches, which sent their rottenness into the twigs that sprang out of them; for so were the children corrupted in their father that they in turn infected their children....

And the apostle Paul himself expressly witnesseth that therefore death came upon all men, because all men have sinned and are wrapped in original sin and defiled with the spots thereof. And therefore the very infants themselves, since they bring with them their own damnation from their mothers' womb, are bound not by another's but by their own fault. For although they have not as yet brought forth the fruits of their own iniquity, yet they have the seeds thereof inclosed within them; yea, their whole nature is a certain seed of sin, therefore it cannot but be hateful and abominable to God....

Predestination we call the eternal decree of God, whereby he has determined with himself what he wills to become of every man. For all are not created to like estate; but to some eternal life and to some eternal damnation is foreordained. Therefore as every man is created to the one or the other end, so we say that he is predestinate either to life or to death.

From John Calvin, *Institutes of the Christian Religion.*

second generation to discover if they had thrown out the baby and the bathtub as well.

Geneva and Calvin

The Reformation came late to Geneva. In the sixteenth century, Geneva was under the dual government of the Duchy of Savoy, which owned most of the surrounding rural areas, and the Catholic bishop of the town, who was frequently a Savoy client. The Genevans also had their own town council, which traditionally struggled for power against the bishop. By the 1530s the council had gained the upper hand. The council confiscated Church lands and institutions, secularized the Church's legal powers, and forced the bishop and most of his administrators to flee the city. War with Savoy inevitably followed, and Geneva would certainly have been crushed into submission had it not been for its alliance with neighboring Bern, a potent military power among the Swiss towns.

Geneva was saved and was free to follow its own course in religious matters. Under Zwingli's influence, Bern had become Protestant, and it might have been expected that Geneva would adopt that model even though French rather than German was the predominant language of the city. Some Protestant preachers arrived in Geneva to propagate reformed religion, and after a public disputation the town council abolished the mass. In 1536, the adult male citizens of the city voted to become Protestant. But as yet there was no reformer in Geneva to establish a Protestant program and no clear definition of what that program might be.

Martin Luther had started out to become a lawyer and ended up a priest. John Calvin started out to become a priest and ended up a lawyer. The difference tells much about each man. Calvin (1509–1564) was born in France, the son of a bishop's secretary. His education was based on humanist principles, and he learned Greek and Hebrew, studied theology, and received a legal degree from the University of Orléans. Around the age of 20 he converted to Lutheranism. He described the experience as "unexpected," but it had predictable results. Francis I had determined to root Protestants out of France, and Calvin fled Paris. Persecution of Protestants continued in France, and one of Calvin's close friends was burned for heresy. The events left an indelible impression upon him. In 1535, he left France for Basel, where he wrote and published the first edition of his *Institutes of the Christian Religion* (1536), a defense of French Protestants against persecution. Directed to Francis I, it set out "the whole sum of godliness and whatever it is necessary to know of the doctrine of salvation." Calvin returned briefly to France to wind up his personal affairs and then decided to settle in Strasbourg, where he could retire from public affairs and live out his days as a scholar.

To Calvin, providence guided all human action. He could have no better evidence for that belief than what happened next. War between France and the Holy Roman Empire clogged the major highways to Strasbourg. Soldiers constantly menaced travelers, and Protestants could expect the worst from both sides. Thus Calvin and his companions detoured around the armies and passed through Geneva. How Calvin's presence there came to be known remains a mystery, but when Guillaume Farel (1489–1565), one of Geneva's leading Protestant reformers, heard of it, he quickly made his way to the inn where Calvin was staying. Farel implored Calvin to remain in Geneva and lead its reformation. Calvin was not interested. Farel tried every means of persuasion he knew until, in exasperation, Farel declared that God would curse Calvin's retirement if, Calvin wrote, "I should withdraw and refuse to help when the necessity was so urgent. By this imprecation I was so terror-struck that I gave up the journey that I had undertaken." For a quarter of a century, Calvin labored to bring order to the Genevan church.

Calvin's greatest contributions to religious reform came in church structure and discipline. He had studied the writings of the first generation of reformers and accepted without question justification by faith alone and the biblical foundation of religious authority. Like

This painting depicts a Calvinist service in Lyon, France, in 1564. The sexes are segregated, and the worshipers are seated according to rank. An hourglass times the preacher's sermon.

Luther and Zwingli, he believed that salvation came from God's grace. But more strongly than his predecessors he believed that the gift of faith was granted only to some and that each individual's salvation or damnation was predestined before birth. "We call predestination God's eternal decree. For all are not created in equal condition; rather, eternal life is foreordained for some, eternal damnation for others." The doctrine of predestination was a traditional one, but Calvin emphasized it differently and brought it to the center of the problem of faith. "Many are called but few are chosen," Calvin quoted from the Bible. Those who were predestined to salvation, "the elect," were obliged to govern; those who were predestined to damnation were obliged to be governed. Thus, for the church that Calvin erected, discipline was the central concern.

Calvin structured the institution of the Genevan church in four parts. First were the pastors who preached the Word to their congregations. There were fewer than 10 pastors in Geneva in the early 1540s and fewer than 20 by the time of Calvin's death—a far cry from the 500 priests who administered the sacraments there under Catholicism. While the pastors preached, the doctors, the second element in Calvin's church, studied and wrote. The doctors were scholars who mastered the difficult portions of the Bible and who increased the stock of learned pastors by their teaching. In the beginning, Calvin was the only Genevan doctor, but after he helped to establish the University of Geneva in 1559, there was a ready supply of learned theologians.

Pastors and doctors made up the top tier of the official church; deacons and elders the lower. Deacons, the third element in Calvin's four-part structure, were laymen chosen by the congregation to oversee the institutions of social welfare run by the church. Those institutions included the hospitals and schools that cared for the sick and the poor and instructed the young. The last element was the elders of the church, who were its governors in all moral matters. They were the most controversial part of Calvin's establishment and the most fundamental. They had the power to discipline. Chosen from among the elite of the city, the 12 elders enforced the strict Calvinist moral code that extended into all aspects of private life. The elders and the pastors met each week in a body known as the consistory to examine violations of God's laws; for them was reserved the ultimate sanction of excommunication. Offenses ranged from trivial superstitions—a woman wrapping a walnut containing a spider around the neck of her sick husband—to cases of blasphemy. Sexual offenses were the most common. Adultery and fornication were vigorously suppressed, and prostitutes, who had nearly become a recognized guild in the early sixteenth century, were expelled from Geneva.

The structure that Calvin gave to the Genevan church soon became the basis for reforms throughout the Continent. The Calvinist church was self-governing, independent of the state, and therefore capable of surviving and even flourishing in a hostile environment. Expanded in several subsequent editions, *The Institutes of the Christian Religion* became the most influential work of Protestant theology. It had begun as an effort to extend Protestantism to France, and Calvin never abandoned hope that his homeland would be converted. Waves of Calvinist-educated pastors returned to France in the mid-sixteenth century and established churches along Calvinist lines. Calvinism spread north to Scotland and the Low Countries, where it became the basis for Dutch Protestantism, and east to Poland, where it flourished in Lithuania and Hungary. It reached places untouched by Luther and revitalized reform where Lutheranism had been suppressed. Perhaps its greatest impact was in Britain, where the Reformation took place not once but twice.

The English Reformation

The king of England wanted a divorce. Henry VIII had been married to Catherine of Aragon (1485 –1536) as long as he had been king, and she had borne him no male heir to carry on his line. Catherine of Aragon had done her duty: in ten years she had given birth to six children and endured several miscarriages. Yet only one daughter, Mary, survived. Nothing so important as the lack of a male heir could happen by accident, and Henry came to believe that it was God's punishment for his marriage. Catherine had been married first to Henry's older brother, who had died as a teenager, and there was at least one scriptural prohibition against marrying a brother's wife. A papal dispensation had been provided for the marriage, and now Henry wanted a papal dispensation for an annulment. For three years his case ground its way through the papal courts. Catherine of Aragon was the aunt of the Emperor Charles V, and the emperor had taken her side in the controversy. With imperial power in Italy at its height, the pope was content to hear all of the complex legal and biblical precedents argued at leisure.

By 1533, Henry could wait no longer. He had already impregnated Anne Boleyn (ca. 1507–1536), one of the ladies-in-waiting at his court. If the child—which Henry was certain would be a boy—was to be legitimate, a marriage would have to take place at once. Legislation was prepared in Parliament to prevent papal interference in the decisions of England's courts, and Thomas Cranmer (1489–1556), archbishop of Canterbury, England's highest ecclesiastical officer, agreed to annul Henry's first marriage and celebrate his second. That was the first step in a complete break with Rome. Under the guidance of Thomas Cromwell (ca. 1485–1540), the English Parliament passed statute after statute that made Henry supreme head of the church in England and owner of its vast wealth. Monasteries were dissolved and a Lutheran service was introduced. England's first reformation came as a result of the "King's Great Matter." On 7 September 1533, Anne Boleyn gave birth not to the expected son, but to a daughter, the future Queen Elizabeth I.

The Church of England. Henry's reformation was an act of state, but the English Reformation was not. There was an English tradition of dissent from the Roman church that stretched back to the fourteenth century and that had survived even the most determined efforts to suppress it. Anticlericalism was especially virulent in the towns, where citizens refused to pay fees to priests for performing services such as burial. And humanist ideas flourished in England, where Thomas More, John Colet, and a host of others supported both the new learning and its efforts to reform spiritual life. The English were as susceptible as other Europeans to Luther's ideas, which crossed the Channel with German merchants and English travelers. Luther's attack on ritual and the mass and his emphasis on Scripture and faith echoed the lost Lollard program and found many recruits in London and the northern port towns.

Protestantism had grown slowly in England because it had been vigorously repressed. Like Francis I and Charles V, Henry VIII had viewed actual attacks on the established church as potential attacks on the established state. The consolidation of the Tudor monarchy was too recent for him not to be concerned with its stability. Henry had earned the title "Defender of the Faith" from the pope in 1521 for authoring an attack on Luther. Bonfires of Lutheran books had lighted the English skies. Small groups of Protestants at Cambridge and Oxford universities had been sniffed out and hunted down by Henry's agents. Some had made public recantations; some had fled to the Continent; one—Thomas Bilney—went to the stake. The first published English translation of the New Testament, made by William Tyndale in 1525, had to be smuggled into England. As sensitivity to the abuses of the Church grew and Lutheran ideas spread, official censorship and persecution sharpened.

Henry's divorce unleashed a groundswell of support for religious change. The king's own religious beliefs remained a secret, but Anne Boleyn and Thomas Cromwell sponsored Lutheran reforms and Thomas Cranmer put them into practice. Religion was legislated through Parliament, and the valuable estates of

Portrait of Anne Boleyn, the second wife of Henry VIII, by an unknown artist. Anne lost favor with Henry when she delivered a daughter instead of the son he expected. Anne made other enemies at court, and in 1536 was convicted of adultery and beheaded.

the Church were sold to the gentry. The practices found favor with both the legal profession and the landed elites and made Protestantism more palatable among those conservative groups. It was in the reign of Edward VI (1547–1553), Henry's son by his third wife, that the central doctrinal and devotional changes were made. Although they were Protestant in tenor, there remained compromises and deliberate ambiguities. The chantries were abolished, and with them masses for the dead. Church service was now conducted in English, and the first two English prayer books were created. The mass was reinterpreted along Zwinglian lines and became the Lord's Supper, the altar became the communion table, and the priest became the minister. Preaching became the center of the church service, and concern over the education of learned ministers resulted in commissions to examine and reform the clergy.

Beginning in the 1530s, state repression turned against Catholics. Those who would not swear the new oaths of allegiance or recognize the legality of Henry VIII's marriage suffered for their beliefs as the early Protestants had suffered for theirs. Thomas More and more than 40 others paid with their lives for their opposition. Others took up arms against the government, marrying economic and political grievances to religious ones. An uprising in the north in 1536, known as the Pilgrimage of Grace, posed the most serious threat to the English Crown since the Wars of the Roses. Gentry and common people opposed the dissolution of the monasteries and feared for provision for their spiritual needs. Henry's ability to suppress the Pilgrimage of Grace owed more to his political power than to the conversion of his governing classes to Protestantism. Edward VI's government faced a similar uprising in 1549 when it attempted to introduce a new and more Protestant prayer book. Catholicism continued to flourish in England, surviving underground during the reigns of Henry and Edward and reemerging under Mary I (1553–1558).

The Successors of Henry VIII. Mary Tudor was her mother's child. The first woman to rule England, she held to the Catholic beliefs in which Catherine of Aragon had raised her, and she vowed to bring the nation back to her mother's church. When Edward VI died, the English ruling elite opted for political legitimacy rather than religious ideology in supporting Mary against a Protestant pretender to the throne. The new queen was as good as her word. She reestablished papal sovereignty, abolished Protestant worship, and introduced a crash program of education in the universities to train a new generation of priests. The one thing that Mary could not achieve was restoration of monastic properties and Church lands: they had been scattered irretrievably and any attempt at confiscation from the landed elite would surely have been met with insurrection. Mary had to be content with reestablishing orthodoxy. She fought fire with fire. Catholic retribution for the blood of their martyrs was not long in coming. Cranmer and three other bishops were burned for heresy, and more than 270 others, mostly commoners, were consigned to the flames.

Nearly 800 Protestants fled the country rather than suffer a similar fate. The Marian exiles, as they came to be called, settled in a number of reformed communities, Zurich, Frankfurt, and Geneva among them. There they imbibed the second generation of Protestant ideas, especially Calvinism, and from there they began a propaganda campaign to keep reformed religion alive in England. It was the Marian exiles who were chiefly responsible for the second English reformation, which began in 1558 when Mary died and her half-sister, Elizabeth I (1558–1603), came to the throne.

Under Elizabeth, England returned to Protestantism. The rapid reversals of established religion were more than disconcerting to laity and clergy alike. Imagine the experience of ordinary churchgoers. For all their lives they had prayed to the Virgin Mary for aid and comfort. One day all images of the Virgin disappeared from the church. The Latin mass was replaced by a whole new English service. Then the Latin mass returned and back came the images of the Virgin. Five years later the Virgin was gone again and the English service was restored. Imagine the plight of a clergyman who questioned the vow of chastity in the 1540s. Prohibited from marrying under Henry VIII, he was encouraged to marry under Edward VI. When Mary came to the throne, he had to put his wife aside and deny the legitimacy of his children. At Elizabeth's accession he was married again—if he could find his wife and if she had not taken another husband. The Elizabethan reforms put an end to those uncertainties.

But what was reestablished was not what had come before. Even the most advanced reforms during Edward's reign now seemed too moderate for the returning exiles. Against Elizabeth's wishes, the English church adopted the Calvinist doctrine of predestination and the simplification (but not wholesale reorganization) of the structure of the church. But it did not become a model of thoroughgoing reformation. The Thirty-nine Articles (1563) continued the English tradition of compromising points of disputed doctrine and of maintaining traditional practices wherever possible. The Calvinism that the exiles learned abroad was more demanding than the Calvinism that the queen practiced at home.

The Reformation of the Radicals

Schism breeds schism. That was the stick with which Catholic church and civil authorities beat Luther from the beginning. By attacking the authority of the established church and flouting the authority of the established state, he was fomenting social upheaval. It was a charge to which he was particularly sensitive. He insisted that his own ideas buttressed rather than subverted authority, especially civil authority, under whose protection he had placed the Church. As early as 1525, peasants in Swabia appealed to Luther for support in their social rebellion. They based some of their most controversial demands, such as the abolition of tithes and labor service, on biblical authority. Luther offered them no comfort. "Let every person be subject to the governing authorities with fear and reverence," he quoted from the Bible while instructing rebels to lay down their arms and await their just rewards in heaven.

But Luther's ideas had a life of their own. He clashed with Erasmus over free will and with Zwingli over the mass. Toward the end of his life he felt he was holding back the floodgates against the second generation of Protestant thinkers. Time and again serious reformers wanted to take one or another of his doctrines further than he was willing to go himself. The water was seeping in everywhere. (See "The Reformation and the War of the Common Man," pp. 450–451.)

The most dangerous threat to the establishment of an orthodox Protestantism came from groups who were described, not very precisely, as Anabaptists. *Anabaptist* was a term of abuse. Although it identified people who practiced adult baptism—literally, "baptism again"—the label was mainly used to tar religious opponents with the brush of extremism. For more than a hundred years it defined the outcast from the Protestant fold. New ideas were branded Anabaptist to discredit them; religious enthusiasts were labeled Anabaptists to expel them. Catholics and Protestants both used the term to describe what they were not, and thereby defined what they were.

Anabaptists appeared in a number of German and Swiss towns in the 1520s. Taking seriously the doctrine of justification by faith, Anabaptists argued that only believers could be members of the true church of God. Those who were not of God could not be members of his church. While Catholics, Lutherans, and Calvinists

Among the Protestant victims executed during the reign of Mary I was Thomas Cranmer. Convicted of heresy, he was burned at the stake in Oxford in 1556.

The Reformation and the War of the Common Man

FOR THREE DAYS, Thomas Müntzer preached to the inhabitants of the central German city of Frankenhausen and to the thousands of peasants who had gathered within its walls. The Lord was ready to smite the nobility, the princes, the oppressors of the common man with the sword of Gideon. Throughout the spring of 1525, the peasants of Thuringia had risen against their landlords. So had those in the Black Forest, in southwestern Germany, and on the Swiss borders. The Thuringian peasants had had remarkable success. They had seized control of the town of Mühlhausen where Müntzer was instrumental in creating an "eternal council" of those who accepted the doctrines of the Reformation, displacing those who followed the secular lords and the Catholic bishops. In April, the peasant army, which numbered more than 10,000, burned monasteries and stormed castles, forcing the capitulation of feudal overlords until only the powerful Counts of Mansfeld held out against them.

Flushed with the victories, Müntzer prepared for his final triumph. In Frankenhausen he unfurled his banner of battle, which depicted a rainbow of light that was the covenant through which the common people would secure their salvation. God would send this shield to his chosen instruments, Müntzer promised. As he preached, a powerful army gathered to oppose him and preparations for battle were made throughout the early hours of 15 May. At daybreak, a glorious rainbow arched over the town.

Beginning in the autumn of 1524, Germany was convulsed by peasant revolts. The risings were spontaneous reactions to the increasing burden of imperial taxation, feudal dues, and ecclesiastical tithes. Such revolts were not unknown in south and central Germany, but never before had they occurred with such frequency and never before had they been underpinned by religious enthusiasm. In five short years, the message of individual salvation preached by Luther and his followers had led to radical social and political conclusions. In Swabia, isolated rebellions against monastic lords led to the calling of a "peasant parliament" and the formulation of a program of social change known as the Twelve Articles.

Although the Articles complained of traditional feudal grievances—disputes over the boundaries of forests, the use of common meadows, rights of hunting, fishing, and foraging—they were justified through an appeal to the Bible and the common obligations that Christians held toward one another. "The purpose of all the peasants' articles is to hear the Gospel and live according to it.... [Those] who ask for the Gospel as their teaching and rule of life should not be called disobedient or rebellious." The first of the Twelve Articles was that each community be allowed to choose its own pastor, the last, "that if any of the articles be incompatible with the Word of God, then we will abandon them." Thus justified, the Peasants War spread and isolated local rebellions became joined together through the adoption of the Twelve Articles as common demands.

The Twelve Articles were moderate in substance and in many places they formed the basis of negotiation over tithes and feudal dues. Central and southwestern Germany was a tangle of overlapping and conflicting political jurisdictions and in places the risings of peasants were co-opted by dispossessed noblemen and impoverished Imperial knights. Demobilized mercenaries became the military leaders of peasant bands, which were formed into coordinated military units. The Swabian forces grew to almost 12,000 including thousands of hardened mercenaries who posed a threat so impressive that the professional army of the Swabian League offered them a truce rather than a battle. But in other places, the Articles were nothing other than a symbol for the bitter class warfare between lords and tenants that had flared intermittently for decades. Tax collectors, estate agents, and petty nobles were put to the sword when they could be captured, especially in Franconia, which was the scene of great violence.

In Thuringia, the Peasants War assumed a Utopian face. Inspired by Müntzer and other apoca-

Radical Thomas Müntzer advocated taking up arms against governments that persecuted Protestants. He chastised Luther, calling him "Dr. Pussyfoot" because Luther did not support him in the Peasants' Revolt of 1525.

lyptic preachers, an attempt was made to form peasants and townsmen into an "eternal league of God" that called for the abolition of all feudal relations, the destruction of the Catholic church, and the abolition of private property. The union was more apparent than real, as the miners, town dwellers, and rural peasantry had different grievances and different experiences. Nevertheless, Müntzer and his allies were able to form a large but undisciplined army that ransacked religious establishments and noble estates and carried away as much booty as possible to be "redistributed" from the rich to the poor. They gained political control in Mühlhausen and military control in Frankenhausen where, on 15 May 1525, the day of the rainbow, Müntzer defied the aristocratic forces that arrayed against him claiming that he would "catch all of the bullets of the enemy in the sleeves of his coat."

By noontime, however, the morning rainbow had cleared away and great hopes proved no match for great guns. At the second volley of the nobles' artillery the peasant forces broke and ran. The slaughter was horrific. Within a few hours more than 5000 peasants and townspeople lay slain, Frankenhausen was sacked, and Thomas Müntzer was taken prisoner and soon after beheaded. The military tide had turned decisively and in the succeeding months tens of thousands of peasants were killed in revenge. On some few estates the bargains struck on the basis of the Twelve Articles held, but on many others the condition of the common man on earth was not improved by the dreams of religious reformers.

incorporated all members of society into the church, Anabaptists excluded all but true believers. As baptism was the sacrament through which entry into the church took place, Anabaptists reasoned that it was a sacrament for adults rather than infants. Although the practice was as much symbolic as substantive, it was a practice that horrified others. Infant baptism was a core doctrine for both Catholics and Protestants. It was one of only two sacraments that remained in reformed religion. It symbolized the acceptance of Christ, and without it eternal salvation was impossible. Luther, Zwingli, and Calvin agreed that infant baptism was biblical in origin and all wrote vigorously in its defense. It was a doctrine with practical import. Unbaptized infants who died could not be accepted in heaven, and infant mortality was appallingly common.

Thus the doctrine of Anabaptism posed a psychological as well as a doctrinal threat to the reformers. But the practice of adult baptism paled in significance to many of the other conclusions that religious radicals derived from the principle of *sola scriptura*—by the Word alone. Some groups argued the case that since true Christians were only those who had faith, all others must be cast out of the church. Those true Christians formed small separate sects. Many believed that their lives were guided by the Holy Spirit, who directed them from within. Both men and women could give testimony of revelations that appeared to them or of mystical experiences. Some went further and denied the power of civil authority over true believers. They would have nothing to do with the state, refusing to pay taxes, perform military obligations, or give oaths: "The Sword must not be used by Christians even in self-defense. Neither should Christians go to law or undertake magisterial duties." Some argued for the community of goods among believers and rejected private property. Others literally followed passages in the Old Testament that suggested polygamy and promiscuity.

Wherever they settled, the small bands of believers were persecuted to the brutal extent of the laws of heresy. Catholics burned them, Protestants drowned them, and they were stoned and clubbed out of their communities. Although Anabaptists were never a large group within the context of the Protestant churches, they represented an alternative to mainstream views—whether Lutheran or Calvinist—that was both attractive and persistent. There was enough substance in their ideas and enough sincerity in their patient sufferings that they continued to recruit followers as they

Anabaptist leaders persecuted at Münster endured the torture of being confined in cages hung from the church belfry.

were driven from town to town, from Germany into the Swiss cities, from Switzerland into Bohemia and Hungary.

There, on the eastern edges of the Holy Roman Empire, the largest groups of Anabaptists finally settled. Although all practiced adult baptism, only some held goods in common or remained pacifist. Charismatic leaders such as Balthasar Hubmaier (1485–1528) and Jacob Hutter (d. 1536) spread Anabaptism to Moravia in southern Bohemia, where they converted a number of the nobility to their views. They procured land for their communities, which came to be known as the Moravian Brethren. The Moravian Anabaptists ultimately split on the question of pacifism when the advancing Turkish armies posed the problem starkly. Anabaptists remained a target of official persecution, and Hubmaier, Hutter, and a number of other leaders met violent deaths. But the Moravian communities were able to survive and to spread their movement throughout Hungary and Poland. Independent groups existed in England and throughout northwest Europe, where Menno Simons (1496–1561), a Dutch Anabaptist, spent his life organizing bands of followers who came to be known as Mennonites.

THE CATHOLIC REFORMATION

Like a rolling wave, Protestant reform slapped up across the face of Europe, but the rock of the Roman Catholic church endured. Although pieces of the universal church crumbled away in northern Germany, Switzerland, Bohemia, Scandinavia, England, and Scotland, the dense mass remained in southern Germany, Italy, Poland-Lithuania, Spain, France, and Ireland. Catholics felt the same impulses toward a more fulfilling religious life as did Protestants and complained of the same abuses of clerical, state, and papal powers. But the Catholic response was to reform the Church from within. A new personal piety was stressed, which led to the founding of additional spiritual orders. The ecclesiastical hierarchy became more concerned with pastoral care and initiated reforms of the clergy at the parish level. The challenge of converting other races, Asians and Native Americans especially, led to the formation of missionary orders and to a new emphasis on preaching and education. Protestantism itself revitalized Catholicism. Pope and emperor met the challenge of religious reform with all of the resources at their disposal. If anything, Roman Catholicism was stronger at the end of the era of religious reformation than it had been at the beginning.

The Spiritual Revival

The quest for individual spiritual fulfillment dominated later medieval Roman Catholicism. Erasmus, Luther, and Zwingli were all influenced by a Catholic spiritual movement known as the New Piety. It was propagated in Germany by the Brethren of the Common Life, a lay organization that stressed the importance of personal meditation upon the life of Jesus. *The Imitation of Christ* (1427), the central text of the New Piety, commonly attributed to Thomas à Kempis (1379–1471), was among the most influential works of the later Middle Ages, with 70 editions printed before 1500. The Brethren taught that a Christian life should be lived according to Jesus' dictates as expressed in the Sermon on the Mount. They instructed their pupils to lead a simple ascetic life with personal devotion at its core. Those were the lessons that the young Erasmus found so liberating and the young Luther so stifling.

The New Piety, with its emphasis on a simple personal form of religious practice, was a central influence upon Christian humanism. It is important to realize that humanism developed within the context of Catholic education and that many churchmen embraced the new learning and supported educational reform or patronized works of humanist scholarship. The Polyglot Bible, the first new translation project of the sixteenth century, was organized by Cardinal Jiménez de Cisneros (1436–1517), Archbishop of Toledo and Primate of Spain. The greatest educational reformer in England, John Colet (1467–1519), was dean of Saint Paul's, London's cathedral church. Without any of his famed irony, Erasmus dedicated his Greek Bible to the pope. Although they set out to reform education and to provide better texts through which Christian learning could be accomplished, the leading Christian humanists remained within the Catholic church even after many of their criticisms formed the basis of Protestant reforms.

The combination of piety and humanism imbued the ecclesiastical reforms initiated by Church leaders. Archbishop Jiménez de Cisneros, who also served as Inquisitor-General of the Spanish Inquisition, undertook a wide-ranging reorganization of Spanish religious life in the late fifteenth century. He tackled the

Tintoretto, Crucifixion *(1565). Tintoretto's composition, dominated by the figure of the crucified Christ at the center, looking down as if from heaven, suggests the spiritual renewal and peak of religious feeling that marked the Catholic Reformation in Europe.*

Herculean task of reforming the parish clergy in his diocese. He emphasized the need for priests to explain the gospel to their congregations and to instruct children in Church doctrine. Jiménez de Cisneros also initiated reforms in the religious houses, especially within his own Franciscan order. Although not every project was successful, Jiménez de Cisneros's program took much of the sting out of Protestant attacks on clerical abuse, and there was never a serious Protestant movement in Spain.

The most influential reforming bishop was Gian Matteo Giberti (1495–1543) of Verona. Like Jiménez de Cisneros, Giberti believed that a bishop must be a pastor rather than an administrator. After a period of service in Rome, Giberti returned to live in his diocese and made regular visits to all of its parishes. Using his own frugal life as an example, Giberti rigorously enforced vows, residency, and the pastoral duties of the clergy. "The priests in this diocese are marked men; the unworthy are removed from their offices; the jails are full of their concubines; sermons for the people are preached incessantly and study is encouraged," came the report after one of his tours. He founded almshouses to aid the poor and orphanages to house the homeless. In Verona, Giberti established a printing press, which turned out editions of the central works of Roman Catholicism, especially the writings of Augustine.

The most important indication of the reforming spirit within the Roman church was the foundation of new religious orders in the early sixteenth century. Devotion to a spiritual life of sacrifice was the chief characteristic of the lay and clerical orders that had flourished throughout the Middle Ages. In one French diocese, the number of clergy quadrupled in the last half of the fifteenth century, and while entrants to the traditional orders of Franciscans and Dominicans did not rise as quickly, the growth of lay communities such as the Brethren of the Common Life attested to the continuing appeal of Catholic devotionalism.

Devotionalism was particularly strong in Italy, where a number of new orders received papal charters. The Capuchins were founded by the Italian peasant Matteo de Bascio (ca. 1495–1552). He sought to follow the strictest rule of the life of Saint Francis of Assisi, a path that even the so-called Observant Franciscans had found too arduous. Bascio won admiration for his charitable works among the poor and the victims of the plague in the late 1520s and ultimately secured approval for the establishment of a

HEAVENLY VISION

Teresa of Ávila was a Carmelite nun whose life became a model of spirituality for Spanish Catholics in the seventeenth century. She founded a number of monasteries and convents and wrote popular devotional literature. Her autobiography was published after her death.

MY LOVE OF, AND TRUST IN, OUR LORD, after I had seen Him in a vision, began to grow, for my converse with Him was so continual. I saw that, though He was God, He was man also; that He is not surprised at the frailties of men; that He understands our miserable nature, liable to fall continually, because of the first sin, for the reparation of which He had come. I could speak to Him as a friend, though He is my Lord, because I do not consider Him as one of our earthly lords, who affect a power they do not possess, who give audience at fixed hours, and to whom only certain persons may speak. If a poor man have any business with these, it will cost him many goings and comings, and currying favour with others, together with much pain and labour before he can speak to them. Ah, if such a one has business with a king! Poor people, not of gentle blood, cannot approach him, for they must apply to those who are his friends; and certainly these are not persons who tread the world under their feet; for they who do this speak the truth, fear nothing, and ought to fear nothing; they are not courtiers, because it is not the custom of a court, where they must be silent about those things they dislike, must not even dare to think about them, lest they should fall into disgrace.

O my Lord! O my King! who can describe Thy Majesty? It is impossible not to see that Thou art Thyself the great Ruler of all, that the beholding of Thy Majesty fills men with awe. But I am filled with greater awe, O my Lord, when I consider Thy humility and the love Thou hast for such as I am. We can converse and speak with Thee about everything whenever we will; and when we lose our first fear and awe at the vision of Thy Majesty, we have a greater dread of offending Thee—not arising out of the fear of punishment, O my Lord, for that is as nothing in comparison with the loss of Thee!

From *The Life of St. Theresa of Ávila* (1611).

small community devoted to penance and good works. In contrast, the Theatines were established by a group of well-to-do Italian priests who also wanted to lead a more austere devotional existence than was to be found in the traditional orders. Like the Capuchins, they accepted a life of extreme poverty, in which even begging was only a last resort. Their small house in Rome became a center for intellectual spirituality that nurtured two subsequent popes. Throughout Italy, spiritual groups coalesced, some to become permanent orders like the Capuchins and Theatines, some to remain loose affiliations.

The spiritual revival spread all over Catholic Europe and was not limited to male orders. In Spain, Saint Teresa of Ávila (1515–1582) led the reform of the Carmelites. From an early age she had had mystical visions and had entered a convent near her home. But her real spiritual awakening came when she was 40. She believed that women had to withdraw totally from the world around them in order to achieve true devotion. Against the wishes of the male superiors of her order, she founded a convent to put her beliefs into practice and began writing devotional tracts such as *The Way of Perfection* (1583). Teresa was ultimately granted the right to establish convents throughout Castile, and she supervised the organization of 16 religious houses for women. In 1535, Angela Merici (ca. 1474–1540) established another female order. The Ursulines were one of the most original of the new foundations, composed of young unmarried girls who remained with their families but lived chaste lives devoted to the instruction of other women. The group met monthly and submitted to the discipline of a superior, but otherwise they rejected both the cloistered

The Council of Trent met from 1545–1563 and corrected a number of abuses of the Church, including the sale of indulgences, and stressed the obligations of priests and bishops to preach to their congregations. No concessions, however, were made to Protestants. This painting is attributed to Titian.

monastic life and vows. The Ursuline movement, begun in northern Italy, spread into France and helped provide women with education and with moral role models.

Loyola's Pilgrimage

At first sight, Saint Ignatius Loyola (1491–1556) appears an unlikely candidate to lead one of the most vital movements for religious reform in the sixteenth century. The thirteenth child of a Spanish noble family, Loyola trained for a military life in the service of Castile. He began his career as an administrative official and then became a soldier. In 1521, he was one of the garrison defenders when the French besieged Pamplona. A cannonball shattered his leg, and he was carried home for a long enforced convalescence. There he slowly and carefully read the only books in the castle, a life of Jesus and a history of the saints. His reading inspired him. Before he had sought glory and renown in battle. But when he compared the truly heroic deeds of the saints to his own vainglorious exploits, he decided to give his life over to spirituality.

Loyola was not a man to do things by halves. He resolved to model his life on the sufferings of the saints about whom he had read. He renounced his worldly goods and endured a year-long regimen of physical abstinence and spiritual nourishment in the town of Manresa. He deprived himself of food and sleep for long periods and underwent a regimen of seven hours of daily prayer, supplemented by nearly continuous religious contemplation. "But when he went to bed, great enlightenment, great spiritual consolations often came to him, so that he lost much of the time he had intended for sleeping." During that period of intense concentration he first began to have visions, which later culminated in a mystical experience in which Jesus called him directly to his service.

Like Luther, Loyola was tormented by his inability to achieve grace through penance, but unlike Luther he redoubled his efforts. At Manresa, Loyola encountered *The Imitation of Christ*, which profoundly influenced his conversion. He recorded the techniques he used during this vigil in *The Spiritual Exercises*, which

Rubens' (1577–1640), The Miracles of Saint Ignatius Loyola. *Founder of the Society of Jesus, Loyola prepared his Jesuit recruits for an active, rather than a contemplative, life.*

became a handbook for Catholic devotion. In 1523, crippled and barefoot, he made a pilgrimage to Jerusalem, where he intended to stay and battle the infidel. But he was dissuaded from that course and returned to Spain intent upon becoming a priest.

By this time, Loyola had adopted a distinctive garb that attracted both followers and suspicion. Twice the Spanish ecclesiastical authorities summoned him to be examined for heresy. In 1528, he decided to complete his studies in France. Education in France brought with it a broadening of horizons that was so important in the movement that Loyola was to found. He entered the same college that Calvin had just left, and it is more than likely that he came into contact with the Protestant and humanist ideas that were then in vogue. Given his own devotional experiences, Protestantism held little attraction. While in France, Loyola and a small group of his friends decided to form a brotherhood after they became priests. They devoted themselves to the cure of souls and took personal vows of poverty, chastity, and obedience to the pope. On a pilgrimage to Rome, Loyola and his followers again attracted the attention of ecclesiastical authorities. Loyola explained his mission to them and

A Spanish wood carving showing St. Ignatius Loyola, the founder of the Society of Jesus.

in 1540 won the approval of Pope Paul III to establish a new holy order, the Society of Jesus.

Loyola's Society was founded at a time when the spiritual needs of the church were being extended beyond the confines of Europe. Loyola volunteered his followers, who came to be known as Jesuits, to serve in the remotest parts of the world, and that offer was soon accepted. One disciple, Francis Xavier (1506–1552), was sent to Portugal, where he embarked on an expedition to the East. For ten years, Xavier made converts to Catholicism in the Portuguese port cities in the East, and then in India and Japan. Other Jesuits became missionaries to the New World, where they offered Christian consolation to the Native American communities. By 1556, the Society of Jesus had grown from 10 to 1000 and Loyola had become a full-time administrator in Rome.

Loyola never abandoned the military images that had dominated his youth. He thought of the world as an all-consuming struggle between the forces of God and Satan: "It is my will to conquer the whole world and all of my enemies." He enlisted his followers in military terms. The Jesuits were "soldiers of God" who served "beneath the banner of the Cross." Loyola's most fundamental innovation in those years was the founding of schools to train recruits for his order. Jesuit training was rigorous. The period of the novitiate was extended and a second period of secular education was added. Since they were being prepared for an active rather than a contemplative life, Jesuits were not cloistered during their training. At first Loyola wanted to train only those who wanted to be missionaries. When that proved impractical, Jesuit schools were opened to the laity and lay education became one of the Jesuits' most important functions. Loyola lived to see the establishment of nearly a hundred colleges and seminaries and the spread of his order throughout the world. He died while at prayer.

The Counter-Reformation

The Jesuits were both the culmination of one wave of Catholic reform and the advance guard of another. They combined the piety and devotion that stretched from medieval mysticism through humanism, diocesan reforms, and the foundations of new spiritual orders. But they also represented an aggressive Catholic response that was determined to meet Protestantism head on and repel it. This was the Church Militant. Old instruments like the Inquisition were revived, and new weapons such as the Index of prohibited books were forged. But the problems of fighting Protestantism were not only those of combating Protestant ideas. Like oil and water, politics and religion failed to combine. The emperor and the hierarchy of the German church, where Protestantism was strong, demanded thoroughgoing reform of the Catholic church; the pope and the hierarchy of the Italian church, where Protestantism was weak, resisted the call. As head of the Catholic church, the pope was distressed by the spread of heresy in the lands of the empire. As head of a large Italian city-state, the pope was consoled by the weakening of the power of his Spanish rival. Brothers in Christ, pope and emperor were mortal enemies in everything else. Throughout the Catholic states of

Germany came the urgent cry for a reforming council of the Church. But the voices were muffled as they crossed the Alps and made their way down the Italian peninsula.

At the instigation of the emperor, the first serious preparations for a general council of the Church were made in the 1530s. The papacy warded it off. The complexities of international diplomacy were one factor—the French king was even less anxious to bring peace to the empire than was the pope—and the complexities of papal politics were another. The powers of a general council in relation to the powers of the papacy had never been clarified. Councils were usually the product of crises, and crises were never the best times to settle constitutional matters. Hard cases make bad law. After the advent and spread of Protestantism, successive popes had little reason to believe that in that gravest crisis of all a council would be mindful of papal prerogatives. In fact, Catholic reformers were as bitter in their denunciations of papal abuses as were Protestants. The second attempt to arrange a general council of the Church occurred in the early 1540s. Again the papacy warded it off.

Those factors ensured that when a general council of the Church did finally meet, its task would not be an easy one. The emperor wanted the council in Germany; the pope wanted it in Italy. The northern churches, French and German alike, wanted reforms of the papacy; the papacy wanted a restatement of orthodox doctrine. The Spanish church wanted reform along the principles set down by Jiménez de Cisneros—for example, that bishops must be made resident in their dioceses. The papacy needed bishops to serve as administrators in Rome. Many princes whose states were divided among Catholics and Protestants wanted compromises that might accommodate both. Ferdinand I, King of Bohemia, saw the council as an opportunity to bring the Hussites back into the fold. He wanted to allow the laity to take communion in both kinds and the clergy to marry. Charles V and the German bishops wanted the leading Protestant church authorities to offer their own compromises on doctrine that might form a basis for reuniting the empire. The papacy wanted traditional Church doctrine reasserted.

The general council of the Church that finally met in Trent from 1545 to 1563 thus had nearly unlimited potential for disaster. It began in compromise—Trent was an Italian town under the government of the emperor—but ended in total victory for the views of the papacy. For all of the papacy's seeming weaknesses—the defections of England and the rich north German territories cut into papal revenues and Italy was under Spanish occupation—an Italian pope always held the upper hand at the council. Fewer than a third of the delegates came from outside Italy. The French looked upon the council suspiciously and played only a minor role, and the emperor forbade his bishops to attend after the council moved to Bologna. While 270 bishops attended one or another of the council's sessions, 187 of them were Italians.

Yet for all of the difficulties, the councillors at Trent made some real progress. They corrected a number of abuses, of which the sale of indulgences was the most substantive. They formulated rules for the better regulation of parish priests and stressed the obligation of priests and bishops to preach to their congregations. Following the work of Jiménez de Cisneros and Giberti, they emphasized the pastoral function of the clergy. On the heels of the success of the Jesuits, they ordered seminaries to be founded in all dioceses where there was not already a university so that priests could

CHRONOLOGY

The Reformation and the Counter-Reformation

1517	Luther writes his Ninety-five Theses
1521	Luther is excommunicated and declared an enemy of the empire; Henry VIII receives title Defender of the Faith
1523	Zwingli expounds his faith in formal disputation
1533	Henry VIII divorces Catherine of Aragon, marries Anne Boleyn, and breaks with the church of Rome
1536	Calvin publishes *Institutes of the Christian Religion*
1540	Loyola receives papal approval for Society of Jesus
1545–1563	Council of Trent
1553	Mary I restores Catholicism in England
1563	Elizabeth I enacts the Thirty-nine Articles, which restores Protestantism to England

Bernini (1598–1680), The Ecstasy of Saint Teresa of Ávila. *Teresa experienced mystical visions at an early age and as an adult believed that women had to withdraw from the world to achieve true devotion.*

receive sufficient education to perform their duties. They prepared a new modern and uniform Catholic service and centralized and updated the Index of prohibited books to include Protestant writings from all over the Continent.

The Council of Trent made no concessions to Protestants, moderate or radical. The councillors attempted to turn back every doctrinal innovation of the previous 40 years. Although Protestant theologians attended one of the council's sessions, their views were totally repudiated and efforts at compromise, which were supported by a number of Catholics on the council, were rejected. The councillors upheld justification by faith and works over justification by faith alone. They confirmed the truth of Scripture and the traditions of the Church against Scripture alone. They declared the Vulgate the only acceptable text of the Bible and encouraged vast bonfires of Greek and Hebrew Scriptures in an effort to undo the great scholarly achievements of the humanists. They reaffirmed the seven sacraments and the doctrine of the miracle of the Eucharist. They upheld clerical celibacy. The redefinition of traditional Roman Catholicism drew the doctrinal lines clearly and ended decades of confusion. But it also meant that the differences between Catholics and Protestants could now be settled only by the sword.

The Empire Strikes Back

Warfare dominated the reform of religion almost from its beginning. The burnings, drownings, and executions by which both Catholics and Protestants attempted to maintain religious purity were but raindrops compared to the sea of blood that was shed in sieges and on battlefields beginning in the 1530s. Neither side was capable of waging an all-out war against the other, but they fought intermittently for 25 years. The Catholic divisions were clear. The Holy Roman Empire continued to be engaged in the west with its archenemy France, and in the south with the ever-expanding Ottoman Empire. Charles V needed not only peace within his own German realms, but also positive support for his offensive and defensive campaigns. He could never devote his full resources to suppressing Protestant dissent.

Yet there was never a united Protestant front to suppress. The north German towns and principalities that accepted Lutheranism in the 1520s had had a long history of warfare among themselves. Princes stored up grievances from past wars and contested inheritances; cities stored up jealousies from commercial rivalries and special privileges. Added to that was the division between Luther and Zwingli over doctrinal issues that effectively separated the German and Swiss components of the Reformation from each other. Each faction formed its own political league, and the division almost certainly cost Zwingli his life in 1531, when Zurich was left to stand by itself against imperial allies.

Although both the Protestant and the Catholic sides were internally weak, it was the greater responsibilities of Charles V that allowed for the uneasy periods of peace. Each pause gave the Protestant reformers new life. Lutheranism continued to spread in the northern part of the Holy Roman Empire, and Zwinglian reform

The Religious Divisions of Europe, ca. 1555. Prior to 1520, all of Europe was Roman Catholic.

in the south. Charles V asked the papacy to convoke a general council and the Protestants to stop evangelizing in new territories. But Protestant leaders were no more capable of halting the spread of the Reformation than were Catholics. Thus each violation of each uneasy truce seemed to prove treachery. In 1546, just after Luther's death, both sides raised armies in preparation for renewed fighting. In the first stage of war, Charles V scored a decisive victory, capturing the two leading Protestant princes and conquering Saxony and Thuringia, the homeland of Lutheran reform.

Charles V's greatest victories were always preludes to his gravest defeats. The remaining Protestant princes were driven into the arms of the French, who placed dynastic interests above religious concerns. Again Europe was plunged into general conflict, with the French invading the German states from the west, the Turks from the south, and the Protestant princes from the north. Charles V, now an old and broken man, was forced to flee through the Alps in the dead of winter and was brought to the bargaining table soon after. Through the Peace of Augsburg in 1555, the emperor agreed to allow the princes of Germany to establish the religion of their people. Protestant princes would govern Protestant states, Catholic princes Catholic states. The Peace of Augsburg ended 40 years of religious struggle in Germany.

In 1547, the then-victorious Charles V stood at the grave of Martin Luther. Luther had been buried in the shadow of the church in which he had been baptized, and now other shadows darkened his plot. Imperial troops were masters of all Saxony and were preparing to turn back the religious clock in Luther's homeland. The emperor was advised to have Luther's body exhumed and burned to carry out 25 years too late the Edict of Worms that had made Luther an outlaw from church and state. But Charles V was no longer the self-confident young emperor who had been faced down by the Saxon monk on that long-ago day. Popes had come and gone, and his warrior rivals Francis I and

Henry VIII were both dead. He alone survived. He had little stomach for the petty revenge that he might now exact upon the man who more than any other had ruined whatever hope there might have been for a united empire dominant over all of Europe. "I do not make war on dead men," Charles declared as he turned away from the reformer's grave. But the ghosts of Luther and Zwingli, of Calvin and Ignatius of Loyola were not so easily laid to rest. For another century, they would haunt a Europe that could do nothing else but make war on dead men.

Questions for Review

1. How did humanism prepare the way for the Reformation?
2. What motivated Martin Luther?
3. What were the differences between the reforming ideas of Luther, Zwingli, and Calvin?
4. How did the Catholic church respond to the challenges posed by the Protestant Reformation?

Suggestions for Further Reading

General Reading

* G. R. Elton, ed., *The New Cambridge Modern History.* Vol. II, *The Reformation, 1520–1559* (Cambridge: Cambridge University Press, 1958). A multiauthored study of the Protestant movement, with sections on social and political life.

* Owen Chadwick, *The Reformation* (London: Penguin Books, 1972). An elegant and disarmingly simple history of religious change.

* Euan Cameron, *The European Reformation* (Oxford: Oxford University Press, 1991). The most up-to-date survey of the Reformation period. Difficult but rewarding.

* Carter Lindberg, *The European Reformations* (London: Blackwells, 1996). A crisp survey that stresses the religious dimensions of the reformations across Europe.

* A. Pettegree, ed., *The Early Reformation in Europe* (Cambridge: Cambridge University Press, 1992). Scholarly essays on the differing reactions to the Reformation throughout Europe.

* Steven Ozment, *The Age of Reform, 1250–1550* (New Haven: CT: Yale University Press, 1980). An important interpretation of an epoch of religious change.

The Intellectual Reformation

Lucien Febvre and Henri Martin, *The Coming of the Book* (Atlantic Highlands, NJ: Humanities Press, 1976). A study of the early history of bookmaking.

* E. Eisenstein, *The Printing Revolution in Early Modern Europe* (Cambridge: Cambridge University Press, 1983). An abridged edition of a larger work that examines the impact of printing upon European society.

* R. W. Scribner, *For the Sake of Simple Folk* (Cambridge: Cambridge University Press, 1994). A study of the impact of the Reformation on common people. Especially good on the iconography of reform.

* Richard Marius, *Thomas More* (New York: Alfred A. Knopf, 1984). A recent reinterpretation of the complex personality of England's greatest humanist.

* Roland Bainton, *Erasmus of Christendom* (New York: Charles Scribner's Sons, 1969). Still the best starting point and most compelling biography.

Richard L. DeMolen, *Erasmus* (New York: St. Martin's Press, 1974). Selections from Erasmus's writings.

The Lutheran Reformation

* Francis Oakley, *The Western Church in the Later Middle Ages* (Ithaca, NY: Cornell University Press, 1979). A study of the spiritual and intellectual state of the Roman Catholic church on the eve of the Reformation.

* Hajo Holborn, *A History of Modern Germany.* Vol. I, *The Reformation* (New York: Alfred A. Knopf, 1964). A widely respected account in a multivolume history of Germany. Especially strong on politics.

* R. W. Scribner, *The German Reformation* (Atlantic Highlands, NJ: Humanities Press, 1986). An excellent introduction, especially to the social history of the Reformation.

* Roland Bainton, *Here I Stand* (New York: New American Library, 1968). The single most compelling biography of Luther.

* John Dillenberger, *Martin Luther: Selections from His Writings* (New York: Doubleday, 1961). A comprehensive selection from Luther's vast writings.

* Heiko Oberman, *Luther: Man Between God and the Devil* (New York: Doubleday, 1992). English translation of one of the best German biographies of Luther. Sets Luther within the context of late medieval spirituality.

Richard Marius, *Martin Luther: The Christian between God and Death* (Cambridge, MA: Harvard University Press, 1999). An up-to-date, readable biography that stresses the inner life of the great German reformer.

* Bernd Moeller, *Imperial Cities and the Reformation* (Durham, NC: Labyrinth Press, 1982). A central work that defines the connection between Protestantism and urban reform.

* Alister E. McGrath, *Reformation Thought: An Introduction*, 2d ed. (New York: Basil Blackwell, 1993). A useful general work that explains the central doctrines of the Protestant Reformation, from Luther to the radical reformers.

* Lyndal Roper, *The Holy Household: Women and Morals in Reformation Augsburg* (Oxford: Oxford University Press, 1991). The best work to show the impact of the Reformation on family life and women.

* R. Po-chia Hsia, ed., *The German People and the Reformation* (Ithaca, NY: Cornell University Press, 1988). A collection of essays exploring the social origins of the Reformation.

* G. R. Potter, *Huldrych Zwingli* (New York: St. Martin's Press, 1984). A difficult but important study of the great Swiss reformer.

* W. P. Stephens, *Zwingli* (Oxford: Oxford University Press, 1994). A thorough introduction to the ideas of one of the great reformers.

The Protestant Reformation

E. William Monter, *Calvin's Geneva* (London: John Wiley & Sons, 1967). A social and political history of the birthplace of Calvinism.

T. H. L. Parker, *John Calvin: A Biography* (Philadelphia: The Westminster Press, 1975). The classic study.

* William Bousma, *John Calvin* (Oxford: Oxford University Press, 1988). A study that places Calvin within the context of the social and intellectual movements of the sixteenth century.

* McGrath Alister, *A Life of John Calvin: A Study in the Shaping of Western Culture* (Cambridge, MA: Basil Blackwell, 1990). Follows Calvin's influence on modern society.

* John Dillenberger, *John Calvin: Selections from His Writings* (New York: Doubleday, 1971). A comprehensive collection.

* J. J. Scarisbrick, *Henry VIII* (Berkeley: University of California Press, 1968). The classic biography of the larger-than-life monarch.

* A. G. Dickens, *The English Reformation*, 2d ed. (London: Batsford, 1989). The classic study of reform in England, newly updated.

* Rosemary O'Day, *The Debate on the English Reformation* (London: Methuen, 1986). A survey of conflicting views by eminent scholars.

* J. J. Scarisbrick, *The Reformation and the English People* (Oxford: Blackwell, 1984). A work that argues for the gradual acceptance of Protestantism in the English Reformation.

* Peter Marshall, *The Impact of the English Reformation, 1500–1640* (London: Arnold, 1997). A collection of critical essays on the reformation in England and its long-term influence.

George H. Williams, *The Radical Reformation*, 2d ed. (Kirksville, MO: Sixteenth Century Journals Publishers, 1992). The most comprehensive synthesis of the first generation of radical Protestants, now brought up to date.

Claus-Peter Clasen, *Anabaptism, A Social History, 1525–1618* (Ithaca, NY: Cornell University Press, 1972). An important study of the Anabaptist movement.

* Steven Ozment, *Protestants: The Birth of a Revolution* (New York: Doubleday, 1992). An accessible study of the origins of Protestant beliefs and the impact of Protestant ideas among ordinary people.

The Catholic Reformation

Jean Delumeau, *Catholicism Between Luther and Voltaire* (Philadelphia: Westminster Press, 1977). An important reinterpretation of the Counter-Reformation.

* Carlos Eire, *From Madrid to Purgatory* (Cambridge: Cambridge University Press, 1995). A brilliant study of the Spanish culture of death during the Counter-Reformation.

* John C. Olin, *The Autobiography of St. Ignatius Loyola* (New York: Harper & Row, 1974). The best introduction to the founder of the Jesuits.

* W. W. Meissner, *Ignatius of Loyola: The Psychology of a Saint* (New Haven, CT: Yale University Press, 1994). A searching study of the founding spirit of the Counter-Reformation.

* J. O'Malley, *The First Jesuits* (Cambridge, MA: Harvard University Press, 1995). An in-depth, scholarly study of the foundation and beliefs of the Jesuits.

* Martin D. W. Jones, *The Counter Reformation: Religion and Society in Early Modern Europe* (Cambridge: Cambridge University Press, 1995). A readable and reliable account of the progress of the counter-reformation.

* A. D. Wright, *The Counter-Reformation* (New York: St. Martin's Press, 1984). A comprehensive survey.

* A. G. Dickens, *The Counter-Reformation* (London: Thames and Hudson, 1968). An excellent introduction, handsomely illustrated.

* Paperback edition available.

Discovering Western Civilization Online

To further explore the reform of religion, consult the following World Wide Web sites. Since Web resources are constantly being updated, also go to *www.awl.com/Kishlansky* for further suggestions.

The Lutheran Reformation

www.wittenberg.de/e/seiten/personen/luther.html
A site devoted to Martin Luther and the city of Wittenberg. Texts of the famous Ninety-five Theses and other of Luther's writings as well as pictures of locations associated with the Lutheran reformation.

The Protestant Reformation

www.educ.msu.edu/homepages/laurence/reformation/index.htm
The Reformation guide is the best starting place for information about all aspects of the Protestant Reformation. Dozens of links to follow.

www.tudor.simplenet.com
A site with links to a variety of subjects relating to England under the Tudors. Biographies of the kings and queens, bibliographies, maps, and documents.

www.mun.ca/rels/hrollmann/reform/pics/pics.html
Contemporary pictures of leading reformers and the places associated with the Protestant reformation. Excellent reproductions, especially from woodcuts.

www.fordham.edu/halsall/mod/modsbook02.html
Sources for both the Reformation and Counter-Reformation with links to other valuable sites.

CHAPTER

14

EUROPE AT WAR, 1555–1648

- THE MASSACRE OF THE INNOCENTS
- THE CRISES OF THE WESTERN STATES
  - The French Wars of Religion
  - One King, Two Faiths
  - The World of Philip II
  - The Burgundian Inheritance
  - The Revolt of the Netherlands
- THE STRUGGLES IN EASTERN EUROPE
  - Kings and Diets in Poland
  - Muscovy's Time of Troubles
  - The Rise of Sweden
- THE THIRTY YEARS' WAR, 1618–1648
  - Bohemia Revolts
  - The War Widens
  - The Long Quest for Peace

The Massacre of the Innocents

"War is one of the scourges with which it has pleased God to afflict men," wrote Cardinal Richelieu (1585–1642), the French minister who played no small part in spreading the scourge. War was a constant of European society and penetrated to its very core. It dominated all aspects of life. It enhanced the power of the state; it defined gender roles; it consumed lives and treasure and commodities ravenously. War affected every member of society from combatants to civilians. There were no innocent bystanders. Grain in the fields was destroyed because it was food for soldiers; houses were burned because they provided shelter for soldiers. Civilians were killed for aiding the enemy or holding out against demands for their treasure and supplies. Able-bodied men were taken forcibly to serve as conscripts, leaving women to plant and harvest as best as they could.

There was nothing new about war in the middle of the sixteenth century. The early part of the century had witnessed the dynastic struggle between the Habsburgs and the House of Valois as well as the beginnings of the religious struggle between Catholics and Protestants. But the wars that dominated Europe from 1555 to 1648 brought together the worst of both of the conflicts. War was fought on a larger scale, it was more brutal and more expensive, and it claimed more victims, civilians and combatants alike. During this century, war extended throughout the Continent. Dynastic strife, rebellion, and international rivalries joined together with the ongoing struggle over religion. Ambition and faith were an explosive mixture. The French endured 40 years of civil war; the Spanish, 80 years of fighting with the Dutch. The battle for hegemony in the east led to dynastic strife for decades on end as Poles, Russians, and Swedes pressed their rival claims to each other's crowns. Finally, in 1618, the separate theaters of war came together in one of the most brutal and terrifying episodes of destruction in European history: the Thirty Years' War.

Neither the ancient temple nor the Roman costume can conceal the immediacy of the picture shown here. It is as painful to look at now as it was when it was created more than 350 years ago. Painted by Nicolas Poussin (1594–1665) at the height of the Thirty Years' War, *The Massacre of the Innocents* remains a horrifying composition of power, terror, and despair. The cruel and senseless slaughter of the innocent baby that is about to take place is echoed throughout the canvas. In the background between the executioner's legs can be seen a mother clasping her own child tightly and anticipating the fall of the sword. In the background on the right, another mother turns away from the scene and carries her infant to safety. In the foreground strides a mother holding her dead child. She tears at her hair and cries in anguish. To a culture in which the image of mother and child—of Mary and Jesus—was one of sublime peacefulness and inexpressible joy, the contrast could hardly be more shocking.

The picture graphically displays the cruelty of the soldier, the helplessness of the child, and the horror of the mother. By his grip on the mother's hair and his foot on the baby's throat, the warrior shows his brute power. The mother's futile effort to stop the sword illustrates her powerlessness. She scratches uselessly at the soldier's back. Naked, the baby boy raises his hands as if to surrender to the inevitable, as if to reinforce his innocence.

To study Europe at war, we must enter into a world of politics and diplomacy, of issues and principles, of judgment and error. We must talk about armies in terms of their cost and numbers, of generals

in terms of their strategy and tactics, and of battles in terms of winners and losers. There can be no doubt that the future of Europe was decisively shaped by the century of wholesale slaughter during which dynastic and religious fervor finally ran its course. The survival of Protestantism, the disintegration of the Spanish empire, the rise of Holland and Sweden, the collapse of Poland and Muscovy, the fragmentation of Germany— all were vital transformations whose consequences would be felt for centuries. History cannot avoid telling this story, untangling its causes, narrating its course, or revealing its outcome. But neither should history avoid facing its reality. Look again at the painting by Poussin.

THE CRISES OF THE WESTERN STATES

"Un roi, une foi, une loi"—one king, one faith, one law. That was a prescription that members of all European states accepted without question in the sixteenth century. Society was an integrated whole, equally dependent upon monarchical, ecclesiastical, and civil authority for its effective survival. A European state could no more tolerate the presence of two churches than it could the presence of two kings. But the Reformation had created two churches.

In Germany, where the problem first arose, the Peace of Augsburg (1555) enacted the most logical solution. The religion of the ruler was to be the religion of the subjects. Princes, town governments, and bishops would determine faith. Not surprisingly, the policy was more convenient for rulers than for the ruled. Sudden conversions of princes, a hallmark of Protestantism, threw the state into disarray. Those closely identified with Catholicism and those who firmly believed in its doctrines had no choice but to move to a neighboring Catholic community and begin again. Given the dependence of ordinary people upon networks of kin and neighbors, enforced migration was devastating. Protestant minorities in Catholic states suffered the same fate. The enmity between the two groups came as much from bitter experience as from differences of belief.

Thus compromises that might have brought Protestants back into a reformed Catholic church were doomed from the start. Doomed too was the practical solution of toleration. To the modern mind, toleration seems so logical that it is difficult to understand why it took over a century of bloodshed before it came to be grudgingly accepted by those countries most bitterly divided. But toleration was not a practical solution in a society that admitted no principle of organization other than one king, one faith. In such a world, toleration was more threatening than warfare. Pope Clement VIII (1592–1605) described liberty of conscience as "the worst thing in the world." Those who advocated limited forms of toleration were universally despised. Those occasions during which toleration was a reluctant basis for a cease-fire were moments for catching breath before resuming the struggle for total victory. Only Poland-Lithuania, Hungary, and a few German states experimented with religious toleration during the sixteenth century.

Religious Divisions in France during the Wars of Religion. Protestantism flourished away from Paris and in lands that had a long history of rebellions against the French crown.

The crises of the western European states that stretched from the middle of the sixteenth century to the middle of the seventeenth were as much internal and domestic as they were external and international. In France, a half century of religious warfare sapped the strength of both the monarchy and the nation. In Spain, the protracted revolt of the Netherlands drained men, money, and spirit from the most powerful nation in Europe. Decades of intermittent warfare turned the golden age of Spain to lead and hastened the decline of the Spanish empire. Each crisis had its own causes and its own history. Yet it was no coincidence that they occurred together or that they starkly posed the conflict between the authority of the state and the conscience of the individual. The century between the Peace of Augsburg (1555) and the Peace of Westphalia (1648) was the century of total war.

The French Wars of Religion

No wars are more terrible than civil wars. They tear at the very fabric of society, rending its institutions and destroying the delicate web of relationships that underlie all communal life. The nation is divided; communities break into factions; families are destroyed. Civil wars are wars of passion. Issues become elevated into causes and principles that form the rallying cry of heroic self-sacrifice or wanton destruction. Civil wars feed on themselves. Each act of war becomes an outrage to be revenged, each act of revenge a new outrage. Passions run deep and, however primitive, the rules for the civilized conduct of war are quickly broken. The loss of lives and property is staggering, but the loss of communal identity is greater still. Generations pass before societies recover from their civil wars. Such was the case with the French wars of religion.

Calvinism in France. Protestantism came late to France. It was not until after Calvin reformed the church in Geneva and began to export his brand of Protestantism that French society began to divide along religious lines. By 1560 there were more than 2000 Protestant congregations in France, whose membership totaled nearly 10 percent of the French population. Calvin and his successors concentrated their efforts on large provincial towns and had their greatest success among the middle ranks of urban society, merchants, traders, and artisans. They also found a receptive audience among aristocratic women, who eventually converted their husbands and their sons.

The wars of religion, however, were brought on by more than the rapid spread of Calvinism. Equally important was the vacuum of power that had been created when Henry II (1547–1559) died in a jousting tournament. Surviving Henry were his extraordinary widow, Catherine de Médicis, three daughters, and four sons, the oldest of whom, Francis II (1559–1560), was only 15. Under the influence of his beautiful young wife, Mary, Queen of Scots, Francis II allowed the Guise family to dominate the great offices of state and to exclude their rivals from power. The Guises controlled the two most powerful institutions of the state, the army and the Church.

The Guises were staunchly Catholic, and among their enemies were the Bourbons, princes of the blood with a direct claim to the French throne but also a family with powerful Protestant members. The revelation of a Protestant plot to remove the king from Paris provided the Guises with an opportunity to eliminate their most potent rivals. The Bourbon duc de Condé, the leading Protestant peer of the realm, was sentenced to death. But five days before Condé's execution, Francis II died and Guise power evaporated. The new king, Charles IX (1560–1574), was only ten years old and firmly under the grip of his mother, Catherine de Médicis, who now declared herself regent of France. (See "The Monstrous Regiment of Women," pp. 470–471.)

Catherine de Médicis (1519–1598), the wife of Henry II of France, was the real power behind the throne during the reigns of her sons Charles IX (1560–1574) and Henry III (1574–1589). Her overriding concern was to ensure her sons' succession and to preserve the power of the monarchy.

The Saint Bartholomew's Day Massacre. Condé's death sentence convinced him that the Guises would stop at nothing to gain their ambitions. Force would have to be met with force. Protestants and Catholics alike raised armies, and in 1562 civil war erupted. Because of the tangle of motives among the participants, each side in the struggles had different objectives. Catherine wanted peace and was willing to accept almost any strategy for securing it. War weakened the state and weakened loyalty to the monarch. At first she negotiated with the Bourbons, but she was ultimately forced to accept the fact that the Guises were

The Monstrous Regiment of Women

"To promote a woman to bear rule, superiority, dominion or empire above any realm, nation, or city is repugnant to nature, contumely to God, and the subversion of good order, of all equity and justice." So wrote the Scottish theologian John Knox (1513–1572) in *The First Blast of the Trumpet Against the Monstrous Regiment of Women* (1558). Although he made his points more emphatically than many others, Knox was only repeating the commonplace notions of his day. He could quote Aristotle and Aquinas as well as a host of secular authorities to demonstrate female inadequacies: "Nature, I say, doth paint them forth to be weak, frail, impatient, feeble, and foolish." He could quote Saint Paul along with the ancient Fathers of the Church to demonstrate the "proper" place of women—"Man is not of the woman, but the woman of the man."

But no stacking up of authorities, no matter how numerous or revered, could erase the fact that all over Europe in the sixteenth century women could and did rule. In the Netherlands, Mary, Queen of Hungary (1531-1552), and Margaret of Parma (1559–1567) were successful regents. Jeanne d'Albret (1562–1572) was queen of the tiny state of Navarre, territory claimed by both France and Spain but kept independent by that remarkable woman. Catherine de Médicis (1560–1589), wife of one king of France and mother of three others, was the effective ruler of that nation for nearly 30 years. Mary, Queen of Scots (1542–1587), was the nominal ruler of Scotland almost from her birth. England was ruled by two very different women, the Catholic Mary I (1553–1558) and her Protestant half-sister Elizabeth I (1558–1603).

The problems faced by this long list of queens and regents were more than just the ordinary cares of government. The belief that women were inherently inferior in intelligence, strength, and character was so pervasive that, for men like Knox, a woman ruler was almost a contradiction in terms. Yet this was not the view taken by everyone, and female rule had its defenders as well as its detractors. One set of objections was overcome by the traditional medieval theory of the two bodies of the monarch. That argument was developed to reconcile the divine origins and functions of monarchs with their very real human frailties. In the theory of the two bodies, there was the body natural and the body politic. Both were joined together in the person of the ruler, but the attributes of each could be separated. Rule of a woman did nothing to disrupt this notion. In fact, it made it easier to argue that the frailties of the body natural of a woman were in no way related to the strengths of the body politic of a monarch.

While such ideas might help a female ruler win the acceptance of her subjects, they did little to invigorate her own sense of her role. Female rulers often strained against the straitjacket that definitions of gender placed them in. When angered, Elizabeth I would proclaim that she had more courage than her father, Henry VIII, "though I am only a woman." Mary, Queen of Scots, once revealed that her only regret was that she "was not a man to know what life it was to lie all night in the fields or to walk with a buckler and a broadsword." Some queens assumed

masculine traits, riding in armor or leading forces to battle. Elizabeth's presence in armor at the threat of the landing of the Spanish Armada was viewed as one of the heroic moments of her reign. Other women rulers combined characteristics that were usually separated by gender definitions. Margaret of Parma was considered one of the most accomplished horse riders of her day. After leading her courtiers through woods and fields at breakneck speed, she would then attend council meetings and work on her needlepoint. Mary, Queen of Scots, loved hawking, a traditional kingly sport, in the Scottish wilds. After relishing the hawk's destruction of its prey, she liked to negotiate matters of state by beginning with tears and entreaties and ending with accusations and threats. The effect was more than disconcerting.

Women were no more or less successful as rulers than were men. Women's achievements, like men's, depended upon strength of character and the circumstances of the times. All the women rulers of the sixteenth century had received outstanding educations. Whether raised Catholic or Protestant, each was trained in Latin as well as modern languages, in the liberal arts, and in fine arts. Mary and Elizabeth Tudor of England wrote poetry and played musical instruments with considerable accomplishment. Mary, Queen of Scots, who was raised at the court of France, was considered particularly apt at learning, praise not often accorded a foreigner by the French. Catherine de Médicis, orphaned as an infant, was raised in convents and instructed in the new learning by Italian nuns. It was said that her political instincts were in her blood: Machiavelli had dedicated *The Prince* to her father. Marguerite of Navarre chose one of the leading French humanists to supervise the training of her daughter, Jeanne d'Albret.

Mary, Queen of Scots, was the only one of the female rulers born to rule. She was the sole survivor of her father, who died shortly after her birth. Mary and Elizabeth Tudor came to their thrones after the death of their younger brother Edward VI; Mary of Hungary and Margaret of Parma came to theirs as princesses of the House of Habsburg. The rule of Catherine de Médicis was the most unexpected of all. Her vigorous husband, Henry II, died during a jousting tournament, and her eldest son, Francis II, husband of Mary, Queen of Scots, died the following year. Instead of retirement as a respected queen dowager (the widow of a previous king), Catherine de Médicis was forced into the vortex of French politics to protect the rights of her ten-year-old son, Charles IX.

For most of the queens and regents, marriage was of central importance to their position. Both Mary, Queen of Hungary, and Mary, Queen of Scots, married kings whose reigns were exceedingly brief. Lewis of Hungary died at the battle of Mohács in 1526, just four years after Mary had become his queen. Mary, Queen of Scots, was widowed even sooner, and throughout the rest of her remarkable career schemed to remarry. To strengthen her claim to the throne of England, she married the Scottish Lord Darnley. When he proved unsatisfactory to her plans, she plotted his murder and then married one of his assassins. When that husband died, she sought a match with a powerful English lord who might help her capture Elizabeth's throne. The intrigues finally led to her execution in England in 1587. Mary Tudor married Philip II of Spain in hope of reestablishing Catholicism in England through a permanent alliance with the most powerful Catholic state in Europe. Her dreams went unfulfilled when she failed to produce an heir, and the throne passed to her sister, Elizabeth, who, alone among the women rulers of the period, did not marry.

Unfortunately, the accomplishments of women rulers did little to dispel prejudices against women as a whole or to alter the definition of gender roles. Except for Mary, Queen of Scots, whose principal achievement was to provide an heir to the English throne, all the queens and regents of the sixteenth century were successful rulers. Margaret of Parma steered the careful middle course in the conflict between Spain and the Netherlands. She opposed the intervention of the Duke of Alba, and, had her advice been followed, the 80 years of war between Spain and the Netherlands might have been avoided. Catherine de Médicis held the crown of France on the heads of her sons, navigated the treacherous waters of civil war, and provided the model for religious toleration that finally was adopted in the Edict of Nantes. Elizabeth I of England became one of the most beloved rulers in that nation's history. A crafty politician who learned to balance the factions at her court and who turned the aristocracy into a service class for the crown, she brought nearly a half century of stability to England at a time when the rest of Europe was in flames.

more powerful. The Guises wanted to suppress Protestantism and eliminate Protestant influence at court. They were willing to undertake the task with or without the king's express support.

Once the wars began, the leading Protestant peers fled the court, but the position of the Guises was not altogether secure. Henry Bourbon, king of Navarre, was the next in line to succeed to the throne should Charles IX and his two brothers die without male heirs. Henry had been raised in the Protestant faith by his mother, Jeanne d'Albret, whose own mother, Marguerite of Navarre, was among the earliest protectors of the French Protestants. The objectives of the Huguenots, as the French Calvinists came to be called, were less clear-cut. The townspeople wanted the right to practice their faith, the clergy wanted the right to preach and make converts, and the nobility wanted their rightful place in local government. Almost from the beginning, the Huguenots were on the defensive, fighting to preserve what they already had and to avoid annihilation.

The inconclusive nature of the early battles might have allowed for the pragmatic solution sought by Catherine de Médicis had it not been for the assassination of the duc de Guise in 1563 by a Protestant fanatic. That act added a personal vendetta to the religious passions of the Catholic leaders. They encouraged the slaughter of Huguenot congregations and openly planned the murder of Huguenot leaders. Protestants gave as good as they got. In open defiance of Valois dynastic interests, the Guises courted support from Spain, while the Huguenots imported Swiss and German mercenaries to fight in France. Noble factions and irreconcilable religious differences were pulling the government apart.

By 1570 Catherine was ready to attempt another reconciliation. She announced her plans for a marriage between her daughter Margaret and Henry of Navarre, a marriage that would symbolize the spirit of conciliation between the crown and the Huguenots. The marriage was to take place in Paris during August 1572. The arrival of Huguenot leaders from all over France to attend the marriage ceremony presented an opportunity of a different kind to the Guises and their supporters. If leading Huguenots could be assassinated in Paris, the Protestant cause might collapse and the truce that the wedding signified might be turned instead into a Catholic triumph.

Saint Bartholomew was the apostle that Jesus described as a man without guile. Ironically, it was on his feast day that the Huguenots who had innocently come to celebrate Henry's marriage were led like lambs to the slaughter. On 24 August 1572, the streets of Paris ran red with Huguenot blood. Although frenzied, the slaughter was inefficient. Henry of Navarre and a number of other important Huguenots escaped the carnage and returned to their urban strongholds. In the following weeks, the violence spread from Paris to the countryside and thousands of Protestants paid for their beliefs with their lives. Until the French Revolution, no event in French history would evoke as much passion as the memory of the Saint Bartholomew's Day Massacre.

One King, Two Faiths

The Saint Bartholomew's Day Massacre was a transforming event in many ways. In the first place, it prolonged the wars. A whole new generation of Huguenots now had an emotional attachment to the continuation of warfare: their fathers and brothers had been mercilessly slaughtered. By itself, the event was shocking enough; in the atmosphere of anticipated reconciliation created by the wedding, it screamed out for revenge. And the target for retaliation was no longer limited to the Guises and their followers. By accepting the results of the massacre, the monarchy sanctioned it and spilled Huguenot blood on itself. For more than a decade, Catherine de Médicis had maintained a distance between the crown and the leaders of the Catholic movement. That distance no longer existed.

The Theory of Resistance. The Huguenots could not continue to maintain the fiction that they were fighting against the king's evil advisers rather than against the king. After Saint Bartholomew's Day, Huguenot theorists began to develop the idea that resistance to a monarch whose actions violated divine commandments or civil rights was lawful. For the first time, Huguenot writers provided a justification for rebellion. Perhaps most importantly, a genuine revulsion against the massacres swept the nation. A number of Catholic peers now joined with the Huguenots to protest the excesses of the crown and the Guises. Those Catholics came to be called *politiques* from their desire for a practical settlement of the wars. They were led by the duc d'Anjou, next in line to the throne after Henry III (1574–1589) became king.

Against them, in Paris and a number of other towns, the Catholic League was formed, a society that pledged its first allegiance to religion. The League took up

CATHOLICS AND HUGUENOTS

The Edict of Nantes (1598) was a milestone in the development of religious toleration in Europe. It was granted by King Henry IV to the Huguenots at the end of the French wars of religion. The Edict of Nantes established the rights of Protestants and was in effect for nearly a century.

WE ORDAIN THAT THE CATHOLIC, APOSTOLIC AND ROMAN RELIGION shall be restored and re-established in all places and districts of this our kingdom and the countries under our rule, where its practice has been interrupted, so that it can be peacefully and freely practiced there, without any disturbance or hindrance. We forbid very expressly all persons of whatever rank, quality or condition they may be, under the aforesaid penalties, to disturb, molest or cause annoyance to clerics in the celebration of the Divine worship....

And in order not to leave any cause for discords and disputes between our subjects, we have permitted and we permit those of the so-called Reformed religion to live and dwell in all the towns and districts of this our kingdom and the countries under our rule, without being annoyed, disturbed, molested or constrained to do anything against their conscience, or for this cause to be sought out in their houses and districts where they wish to live, provided that they conduct themselves in other respects according to the provisions of our present Edict....

From the Edict of Nantes.

where the Saint Bartholomew's Day Massacre left off, and the slaughter of ordinary people who unluckily professed the wrong religion continued. Matters grew worse in 1584, when Anjou died. With each passing year it was becoming apparent that Henry III would produce no male heir. After Anjou's death, the Huguenot Henry of Navarre was the next in line for the throne. Catholic Leaguers talked openly of altering the royal succession and began to develop theories of lawful resistance to monarchical power. By 1585, when the final civil war began—the war of the three Henrys, named for Henry III, Henry Guise, and Henry of Navarre—the crown was in the weakest possible position. Paris and the Catholic towns were controlled by the League, the Protestant strongholds by Henry of Navarre. King Henry III could not abandon his capital

Painting of the Saint Bartholomew's Day Massacre. The massacre began in Paris on 24 August 1572, and the violence soon spread throughout France.

GENEALOGY

The Houses of Valois and Bourbon of France

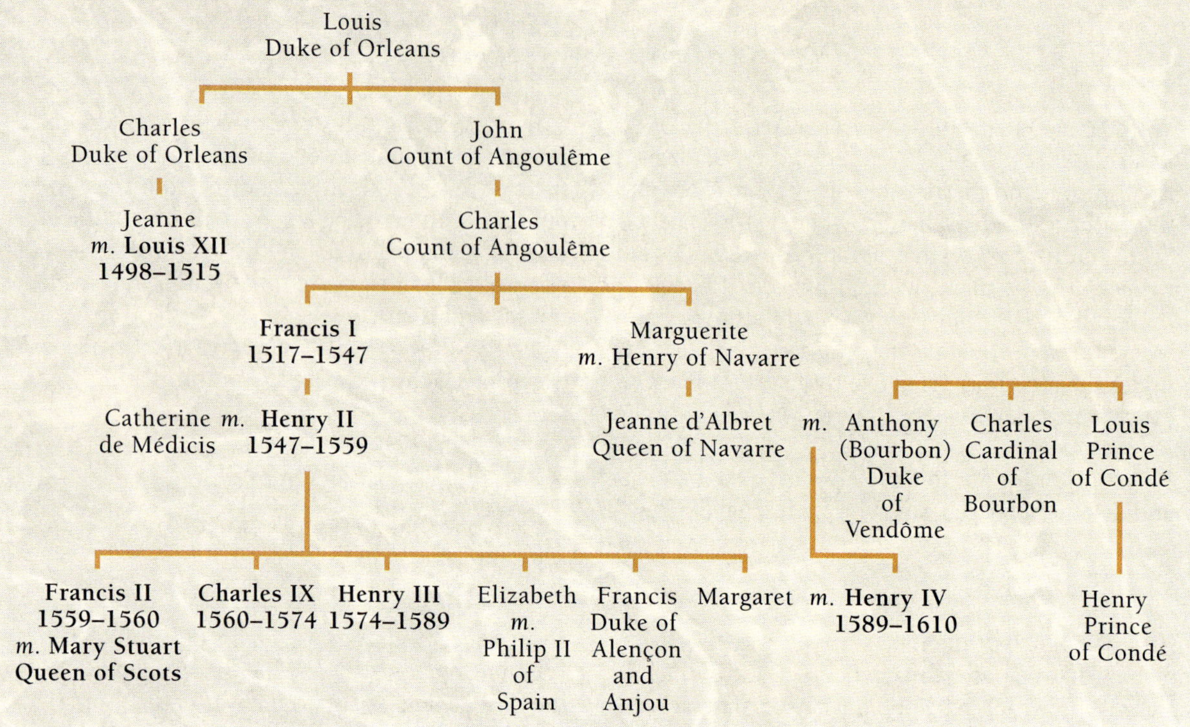

or his religion, but neither could he gain control of the Catholic party. The extremism of the Leaguers kept the politiques away from court, and without the politiques, there could be no settlement.

In December 1588, Henry III summoned Henry Guise and Guise's brother to a meeting in the royal bedchamber. There they were murdered by the king's order. The politiques were blamed for the murders—revenge was taken on a number of them—and Henry III was forced to flee his capital. Paris was still firmly in the hands of the League, and Henry was in danger of becoming a king without a country. He made a pact with Henry of Navarre, and together royalist and Huguenot forces besieged Paris. All supplies were cut off from the city and only the arrival of a Spanish army prevented its fall. In 1589, Catherine de Médicis died, her ambition to reestablish the authority of the monarchy in shambles, and in the same year a fanatic priest gained revenge for the murder of the Guises by assassinating Henry III.

Henry IV. Now Henry of Navarre came into his inheritance. After nearly 30 years of continuous civil war, it was certain that a Huguenot could never rule France. The League had already proclaimed a Catholic rival as king, and the pope excommunicated Henry of Navarre and absolved France from loyalty to him. If Henry was to become king of all France, he would have to become a Catholic king. It is not clear when Henry made the decision to accept the Catholic faith—"Paris is worth a mass," he reportedly declared—but he did not announce his decision at once. Rather he strengthened his forces, tightened his bonds with the politiques, and urged his countrymen to expel the Spanish invaders. He finally made his conversion public and in 1594 was crowned Henry IV (1589–1610). A war-weary nation was willing to accept the sincerity of its new king rather than endure a seemingly endless struggle. Even the Leaguers were exhausted. Their claimant to the throne had died, and they were now seen as rebels rather than patriots. War had sapped both their treasuries and their spirit. Most of the leading peers on both sides were nearly bankrupt, and Henry IV was willing to pay large cash settlements to all those who would return to their estates and pledge allegiance to him.

Resistance to the reestablishment of the monarchy continued for several years, but Henry IV was a strong and capable ruler. He declared war on Spain to unite his nation against foreign aggression, and he carefully reestablished the balance of aristocratic factions at his court. The League collapsed, and moderate Catholics rallied around the king. Although Huguenots and Calvinists everywhere were shocked by Henry's conversion, they were hardly in a position to wage a successful war against their former leader. Henry's accession gave them their first real hope for an enduring settlement with the crown.

In 1598, Henry proclaimed the Edict of Nantes, which granted limited toleration to the Huguenots. It was the culmination of decades of attempts to find a solution to the existence of two religions in one state. It was a compromise that satisfied no one, but it was a compromise that everyone could accept. One king, two faiths was as apt a description of Henry IV as it was of the settlement. Yet neither Henry's conversion nor the

CHRONOLOGY

The French Wars of Religion

1559	Death of Henry II
1560	Protestant duc de Condé sentenced to death
1562	First battle of wars of religion
1563	Catholic duc de Guise assassinated; Edict of Amboise grants limited Protestant worship
1572	Saint Bartholomew's Day massacre
1574	Accession of Henry III
1576	Formation of Catholic League
1584	Death of duc d'Anjou makes Henry of Navarre heir to throne
1585	War of the three Henrys
1588	Duc de Guise murdered by order of Henry III
1589	Catherine de Médicis dies; Henry III assassinated
1594	Henry IV crowned
1598	Edict of Nantes

Religious warfare in France was brutal and only ceased with the accession of Henry IV.

Edict of Nantes stilled the passions that had spawned and sustained the French wars of religion. Sporadic fighting between Catholics and Huguenots continued, and fanatics on both sides fanned the flames of religious hatred. Henry IV survived 18 attempts on his life before he was finally felled by an assassin's knife in 1610, but by then he had reestablished the monarchy and brought a semblance of peace to France.

The World of Philip II

By the middle of the sixteenth century, Spain was the greatest power in Europe. The dominions of Philip II (1556–1598) of Spain stretched from the Atlantic to the Pacific; his continental territories included the Netherlands in the north and Milan and Naples in Italy. In 1580, Philip became king of Portugal, uniting all the states of the Iberian Peninsula. With the addition of Portugal's Atlantic ports and its sizable fleet, Spanish maritime power was now unsurpassed. Spain was also a great cultural and intellectual center. The fashions and tastes of its golden age dominated all the courts of Europe.

Great power meant great responsibilities, and few monarchs took their tasks more seriously than did Philip II. Trained from childhood for the cares of office, he exceeded all expectations. Philip II earned his reputation as "King of Paper" by maintaining a grueling work schedule. Up at eight and at mass soon afterward, he met with his advisers and visitors on official business until noon. After a brief lunch, he began the real business of the day, the study of the mountains of papers that his empire generated. Although summaries were prepared of the hundreds of documents he handled each day, Philip II frequently read and annotated the longer originals. No detail was too small to escape his attention. His workday often lasted ten hours or longer. Even when he was traveling, his secretaries carried huge chests of state papers that Philip studied in his carriage and annotated on a portable desk that always accompanied him.

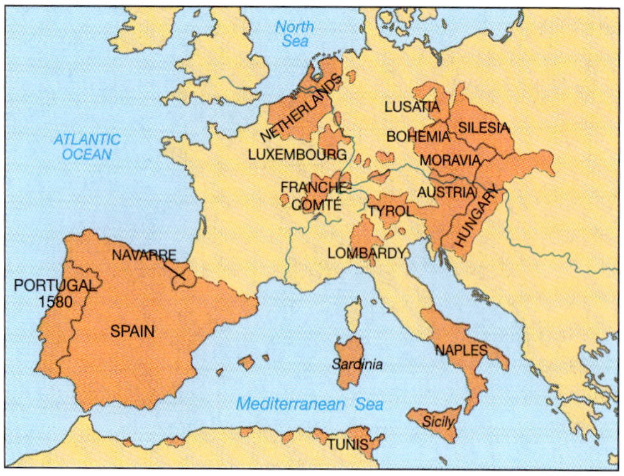

The combined territories of the Spanish and Austrian Habsburgs during the reign of Philip II. Charles V had divided his estates to make it easier for them to be governed.

There was good reason why the slightly stooped king appeared as if he had the weight of the world on his shoulders. In the Mediterranean, Spain alone stood out against the expansion of Ottoman power. The sultan's navy continually threatened to turn the Mediterranean into a Turkish lake, while his armies attempted to capture and hold Italian soil. All Europe shuddered at the news of each Ottoman advance. Popes called for holy wars against the Turks, but only Philip heeded the cry. From nearly the moment that he inherited the Spanish crown, he took up the challenge of defending European Christianity. For more than a decade, Philip maintained costly coastal garrisons in North Africa and Italy and assembled large fleets and larger armies to discourage or repel Turkish invasions. The sparring could not go on indefinitely, and in 1571 both sides prepared for a decisive battle. A combined Spanish and Italian force of more than 300 ships and 80,000 men met an even larger Ottoman flotilla off the coast of Greece. The Spanish naval victory at Lepanto was considered one of the great events of the sixteenth century, celebrated in story and song for the next 300 years. Although the Turks continued to menace the Mediterranean islands, Lepanto marked the end of Ottoman advances.

If Philip II saw himself as a Christian monarch fending off the advance of the infidel, he also saw himself as a Catholic monarch fending off the spread of heresy. There can be no doubt of Philip's personal devotion to Catholicism or of his oft-expressed conviction, "I would prefer to lose all my dominions and a hundred lives if I had them rather than be lord over heretics." The lives that were to be lost in battling heretics were numbered not in hundreds, but in hundreds of thousands. Philip II came to the throne at just the moment that Calvinism began its rapid growth in northern Europe. He supported the Catholic cause in France throughout the civil wars, sending money, advisers, and ultimately an army to relieve Paris. His ambassadors urged Catherine de Médicis and her sons to take the most repressive measures against the Huguenots, including the Saint Bartholomew's Day Massacre.

Philip was equally aggressive against English Protestants. For a brief time he had been king in England through his marriage to Mary I (1553–1558). He encouraged Mary's efforts to restore the Catholic church in England and supported her policies of repression. When Mary died and Elizabeth I (1558–1603) rejected his marriage proposal, his limited rule in England came to an end. From then on, England and Spain entered a long period of hostility. English pirates raided Spanish treasure ships returning to Europe, and Elizabeth covertly aided both French and Dutch Protestants. Finally, in 1588, Philip decided upon invasion. A great fleet set sail from the Portuguese coast to the Netherlands, where a large Spanish army stood waiting to be conveyed to England.

El Greco, The Adoration of the Name of Jesus *(ca. 1580). The painting is an allegory of the Holy League of Spain, Venice, and the papacy. The League's victory over the Turks in the naval battle at Lepanto in 1571 halted the Ottoman advance in Europe. The figures kneeling at the bottom of the painting are Philip II of Spain, the doge of Venice, and the pope.*

The Spanish Armada was composed of more than 130 ships, many of them the pride of the Spanish and Portuguese navies. They were bigger and stronger than anything possessed by the English, whose forces were largely merchant vessels hastily converted for battle. But the English ships were faster and more easily maneuverable in the unpredictable winds of the English Channel. They also contained guns that could easily be reloaded for multiple firings, while the Spanish guns were designed to discharge only one broadside before hand-to-hand combat ensued. With those advantages the English were able to prevent the Armada from reaching port in the Netherlands and to destroy many individual ships as they were blown off course. The defeat of the Spanish Armada was less a military than a psychological blow to Philip II: he could more easily replace ships than restore confidence in Spanish power.

The Burgundian Inheritance

Confidence was all the more necessary when Philip II faced the gravest crisis of his reign: the revolt of the Netherlands. Although Philip's father, Charles V, had amassed a great empire, he had begun only as the duke of Burgundy. Charles's Burgundian inheritance encompassed a diverse territory in the northwestern corner of Europe. The 17 separate provinces of the territory were called the Netherlands, or the Low Countries, because of the flooding that kept large portions of them under water. The Netherlands was one of the richest and most populous regions of Europe, an international leader in manufacturing, banking, and commerce. Antwerp and Amsterdam were bustling port cities with access to the North Sea; inland were the prosperous industrial towns of Ghent and Brussels. The preeminence of the Netherlands was all the more remarkable because the provinces themselves were divided geographically, culturally, and linguistically. Rivers, lakes, and flooded plains separated the southern provinces, where French was the background and language of the inhabitants, from the northern ones, where Germans had settled and Dutch was spoken. Charles V attempted to unify the provinces by removing them from the jurisdiction of the Holy Roman Empire and establishing a separate regency under his eldest son, Philip II. Thus the future of the Netherlands was tied to Spain and the New World when Philip II set sail for Castile in 1559 to claim the crown of Spain.

Although Philip II had every intention of returning to the Low Countries, in fact the Netherlands had seen the last of their king. Philip left his half-sister, Margaret of Parma, as regent, providing her with a talented group of Spanish administrators to carry out policies that were to be formulated in Madrid. As Philip's own grasp on the affairs of the Netherlands loosened, so did the loyalty of the native nobility to the absent monarch. The resentments that built up were traditional ones—hostility to foreigners, distrust of royal advisers, and contempt for policies that lacked understanding of local conditions. All of the discontents came together over Philip's religious policies.

The Low Countries had accepted the Peace of Augsburg in a spirit of conciliation in which it was never intended. There Catholics, Lutherans, Anabaptists, and Calvinists peaceably coexisted. As in France, the situation changed dramatically with the spread of Calvinism. The heavy concentration of urban populations in the Low Countries provided the natural habitat for Calvinist preachers, who made converts across the entire social spectrum. As Charles V, Holy Roman Emperor, he may have made his peace with Protestants, but as Charles I, king of Spain, he had not. Charles V had maintained the purity of the Spanish Catholic church through a sensible combination of reform and repression.

Philip II intended to pursue a similar policy in the Low Countries. With papal approval he initiated a scheme to reform the hierarchy of the Church by

This painting by an unknown artist depicts the clash between the Spanish and English fleets during the Armada invasion in 1588.

GENEALOGY

The Family of Charles V

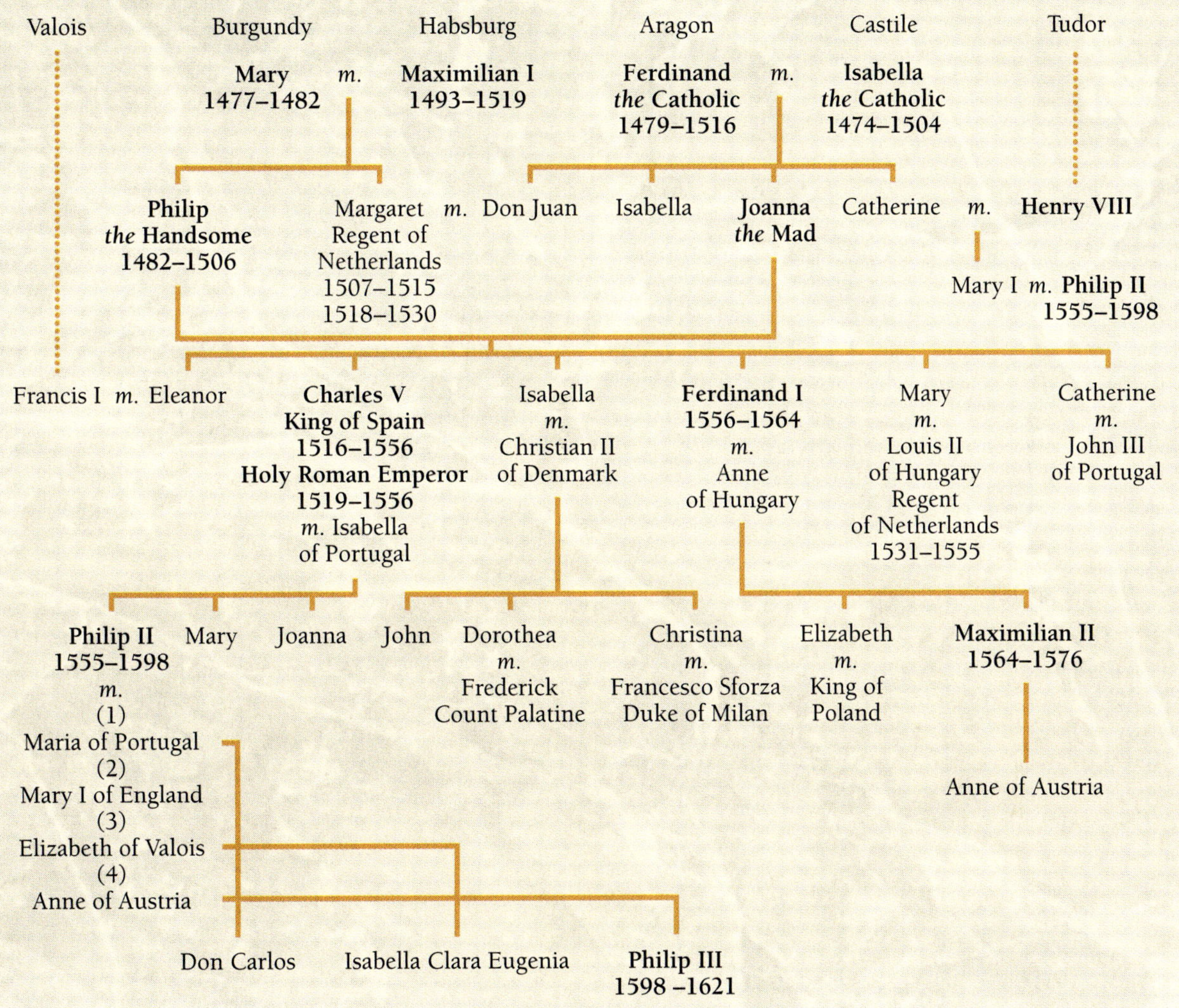

expanding the number of bishops, and he invited the Jesuits to establish schools for orthodox learning. Simultaneously, he strengthened the power of the Inquisition and ordered the enforcement of the decrees of the Council of Trent. The Protestants sought the protection of their local nobility who—Catholic or Protestant—had their own reasons for opposing Provincial nobility, and magistrates resented both the policies that were being pursued and the fact that they disregarded local autonomy. Town governors and noblemen refused to cooperate in implementing the new laws. Leading Protestants such as Prince William of Orange, one of the largest landholders in the Netherlands, and Count Egmont, an outstanding military leader, urged Margaret to adopt a policy of toleration along the lines of the Peace of Augsburg and made clear that they would resign from office rather than support anything else.

CANNIBALS

Michel de Montaigne (1533–1592) came from a wealthy family in the Bordeaux region of France and ultimately inherited the chateau from which his name derives. Before his early retirement he worked in the legal profession. His Essays (1572–1588) combined humanist learning with the new philosophy of skepticism. The following excerpt, from "Of Cannibals," shows both his penetrating intelligence and his detached observation of the world around him.

THESE NATIONS, THEN, seem to me barbarous in this sense, that they have been fashioned very little by the human mind, and are still very close to their original naturalness. The laws of nature still rule them, very little corrupted by ours; and they are in such a state of purity that I am sometimes vexed that they were unknown earlier, in the days when there were men able to judge them better than we. I am sorry that Lycurgus and Plato did not know of them; for it seems to me that what we actually see in these nations surpasses not only all the pictures in which poets have idealized the golden age and all their inventions in imagining a happy state of man, but also the conceptions and the very desire of philosophy....

For the rest, they live in a country with a very pleasant and temperate climate, so that according to my witnesses it is rare to see a sick man there; and they have assured me that they never saw one palsied, bleary-eyed, toothless, or bent with age. They are settled along the sea and shut in on the land side by great high mountains, with a stretch about a hundred leagues wide in between. They have a great abundance of fish and flesh which bear no resemblance to ours, and they eat them with no other artifice than cooking.

They have their wars with the nations beyond the mountains, further inland, to which they go quite naked, with no other arms than bows or wooden swords ending in a sharp point, in the manner of the tongues of our boar spears. It is astonishing what firmness they show in their combats, which never end but in slaughter and bloodshed; for as to routs and terror, they know nothing of either.

Each man brings back as his trophy the head of the enemy he has killed, and sets it up at the entrance to his dwelling. After they have treated their prisoners well for a long time with all the hospitality they can think of, each man who has a prisoner calls a great assembly of his acquaintances. He ties a rope to one of the prisoner's arms by the end of which he holds him, a few steps away, for fear of

The Revolt of the Netherlands

The passive resistance of nobles and magistrates was soon matched by the active resistance of the Calvinists. Unable to enforce Philip's policy, Margaret and her advisers agreed to a limited toleration. But in the summer of 1566, before it could be put into effect, bands of Calvinists unleashed a storm of iconoclasm in the provinces, breaking stained glass windows and statues of the Virgin and the saints, which they claimed were idolatrous. Catholic churches were stormed and turned into Calvinist meeting houses. Local authorities were helpless in the face of determined Calvinists and apathetic Catholics; they could not protect Church property. Iconoclasm gave way to open revolt. Fearing social rebellion, even the leading Protestant noblemen took part in suppressing the riots.

Rebellion and War. In Spain, the events in the Netherlands were treated for what they were: open rebellion. Despite the fact that Margaret had already restored order, Philip II was determined to punish the rebels and enforce the heresy laws. A large military force under the command of the Duke of Alba (1507–1582)—whose record of success was matched only by his record of brutality—was sent from Spain as an army of occupation. As befit a warrior who had made his reputation leading imperial troops against the Lutherans, Alba gave no quarter to the Protestants of the Netherlands. "Everyone must be made to live in being hurt, and gives his dearest friend the other arm to hold in the same way; and these two, in the presence of the whole assembly, kill him with their swords. This done, they roast him and eat him in common and send some pieces to their absent friends. This is not, as people think, for nourishment, as of old the Scythians used to do; it is to betoken an extreme revenge. And the proof of this came when they saw the Portuguese, who had joined forces with their adversaries, inflict a different kind of death on them when they took them prisoner, which was to bury them up to the waist, shoot the rest of their body full of arrows, and afterward hang them. They thought that these people from the other world, being men who had sown the knowledge of many vices among their neighbors and were much greater masters than themselves in every sort of wickedness, did not adopt this sort of vengeance without some reason, and that it must be more painful than their own; so they began to give up their old method and to follow this one.

I am not sorry that we notice the barbarous horror of such acts, but I am heartily sorry that, judging their faults rightly, we should be so blind to our own. I think there is more barbarity in eating a man alive than in eating him dead; and in tearing by tortures and the rack a body still full of feeling, in roasting a man bit by bit, in having him bitten and mangled by dogs and swine (as we have not only read but seen within fresh memory, not among ancient enemies, but among neighbors and fellow citizens, and what is worse, on the pretext of piety and religion), than in roasting and eating him after he is dead....

So we may well call these people barbarians, in respect to the rules of reason, but not in respect to ourselves, who surpass them in every kind of barbarity.

Their warfare is wholly noble and generous, and as excusable and beautiful as this human disease can be; its only basis among them is their rivalry in valor. They are not fighting for the conquest of new lands, for they still enjoy that natural abundance that provides them without toil and trouble with all necessary things in such profusion that they have no wish to enlarge their boundaries. They are still in that happy state of desiring only as much as their natural needs demand; anything beyond that is superfluous to them.... Truly here are real savages by our standards, for either they must be thoroughly so, or we must be; there is an amazing distance between their character and ours.

From Montaigne, "Of Cannibals."

Portrait of Philip II by Alonso Sánchez Coello (ca. 1582). Philip tried for 12 years to suppress rebellion in the Protestant Netherlands, and he sent troops to aid Catholic forces in battle with the Huguenots in France. He fared badly in his attempts to deal with England, his Spanish Armada suffering a humiliating defeat in 1588 that marked the beginning of the decline of Spanish power.

constant fear of the roof breaking down over his head," he wrote.

Alba lured Count Egmont and other Protestant noblemen to Brussels, where he publicly executed them in 1568. He also established a military court to punish participants in the rebellion, a court that came to be called the Council of Blood. The Council handed down more than 9000 convictions, a thousand of which carried the death penalty. As many as 60,000 Protestants fled beyond Alba's jurisdiction. Alba next made an example of several small towns that had been implicated in the iconoclasm. He allowed his soldiers to pillage the towns at will before slaughtering their entire populations and razing them to the ground. By the end of 1568, royal policy had gained a sullen acceptance in the Netherlands, but the hostilities did not end. For the next 80 years, with only occasional truces, Spain and the Netherlands were at war.

The Protestants Rebel. Alba's policies drove Protestants into rebellion. That forced the Spanish government to maintain its army by raising taxes from those provinces that had remained loyal. Soon the loyal provinces too were in revolt, not over religion, but over taxation and local autonomy. Tax resistance and fear of an invasion from France left Alba unprepared for the series of successful assaults Protestants launched in the northern provinces during 1572. Protestant generals established a permanent base in the northwestern provinces of Holland and Zeeland. By 1575 the Protestants had gained a stronghold that they would never relinquish. Prince William of Orange assumed the leadership of the two provinces that were now united against the tyranny of Philip's rule.

Spanish government was collapsing all over the Netherlands. William ruled in the north and the States-General, a parliamentary body composed of representatives from the separate provinces, ruled in the south. Margaret of Parma had resigned in disgust at Alba's tactics, and Alba had been relieved of his command when his tactics had failed. No one was in control of the Spanish army. The soldiers, who had gone years with only partial pay, now roamed the southern provinces looking for plunder. Brussels and Ghent both had been

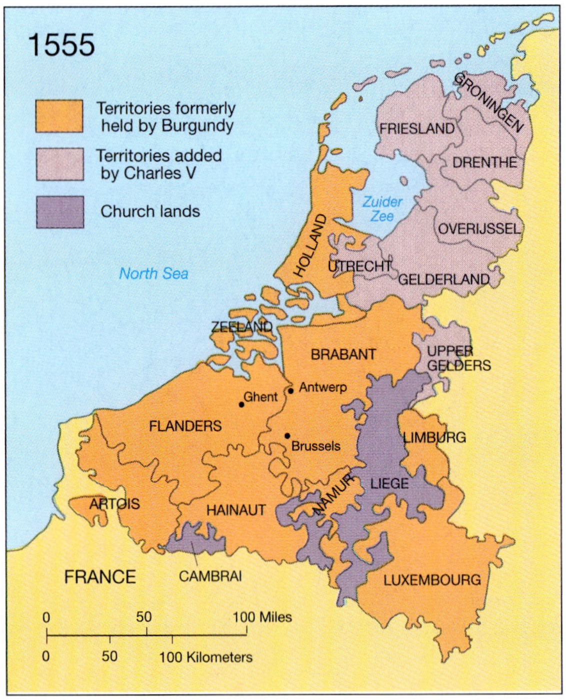

The Revolt of the Netherlands,1555. The consolidation of the low countries under Charles V. Charles brought together lands with different languages, cultures, and forms of government.

The Revolt of the Netherlands, 1609. By the beginning of the seventeenth century, the union had broken apart and the northern provinces had won independence from Spain.

targets, and in 1576 the worst atrocities of all occurred when mutinous Spanish troops sacked Antwerp. One of the wealthiest cities in Europe, home to the most important mercantile and banking establishments in the world, Antwerp was torn apart like a roasted pig. The rampage lasted for days. When it ended, more than 7000 people had been slaughtered and nearly a third of the city burned to the ground.

The "Spanish fury" in Antwerp effectively ended Philip's rule over his Burgundian inheritance. The Protestants had established a permanent home in the north. The States-General had established its ability to rule in the south, and Spanish policy had been totally discredited. To achieve a settlement, the Pacification of Ghent of 1576, the Spanish government conceded local autonomy in taxation, the central role of the States-General in legislation, and the immediate withdrawal of all Spanish troops from the Low Countries. Five southern provinces pledged to remain Catholic and to accept the authority of the king's regent. The rift between the provinces was soon followed by a permanent split. In 1581, one group of provinces voted to depose Philip II, while a second group decided to remain loyal to him.

The troops of Philip II of Spain under the Duke of Alba inflicted countless cruelties on the people of the Netherlands.

CHRONOLOGY

Revolt of the Netherlands

1559	Margaret of Parma named regent of the Netherlands
1566	Calvinist iconoclasm begins revolt
1567	Duke of Alba arrives in Netherlands and establishes Council of Blood
1568	Protestant Count Egmont executed
1572	Protestants capture Holland and Zeeland
1573	Alba relieved of his command
1576	Sack of Antwerp; pacification of Ghent
1581	Catholic and Protestant provinces split
1585	Spanish forces take Brussels and Antwerp
1609	Twelve Years' Truce

Philip II refused to accept the dismemberment of his inheritance and refused to recognize the independent Dutch state that now existed in Holland. Throughout the 1580s and 1590s, military expeditions attempted to reunite the southern provinces and to conquer the northern ones. But Spanish military successes in the south were outweighed by the long-term failure of their objectives in the north. In 1609, Spain and the Netherlands concluded the Twelve Years' Truce, which tacitly recognized the existence of the state of Holland. By the beginning of the seventeenth century, Holland was not only an independent state, it was one of the greatest rivals of Spain and Portugal for the fruits of empire.

THE STRUGGLES IN EASTERN EUROPE

In eastern Europe, dynastic struggles outweighed the problems created by religious reform. Muscovy remained the bulwark of Eastern Orthodox Christianity, immune from the struggles over the Roman faith. Protestantism did spread into Poland-Lithuania, but unlike its reception in the west, its presence was tolerated by the Polish state. The spread of dissent was checked not by repression, but by a vigorous Catholic reformation led by the Jesuits. The domestic crises in the east were crises of state rather than of church. In Muscovy, the disputed succession that followed the death of Ivan the Terrible plunged the state into anarchy and civil war. Centuries of conflict between Poland-Lithuania and Muscovy came to a head with the Poles' desperate gamble to seize control of their massive eastern neighbor. War between Poland-Lithuania and Muscovy inevitably dominated the politics of the entire region. The Baltic states, of which Sweden was to become the most important, had their own ambitions for territory and economic gain. They soon joined the fray, making alliances in return for concessions and conquering small pieces of the mainland.

Kings and Diets in Poland

Until the end of the sixteenth century, Poland-Lithuania was the dominant power in the eastern part of Europe. It was economically healthy and militarily strong. Through its Baltic ports, especially Gdansk, Poland played a central role in international commerce and a dominant role in the northern grain trade. The vast size of the Polish state made defense difficult, and during the course of the sixteenth century it had lost lands to Muscovy in the east and to the Crimean Tartars in the south. But the permanent union with Lithuania in 1569 and the gradual absorption of the Baltic region of Livonia more than compensated for the losses. Matters of war and peace, of taxation and reform, were placed under the strict supervision of the Polish Diet, a parliamentary body that represented the Polish landed elite. The Diet also carefully controlled religious policy. Roman Catholicism was the principal religion in Poland, but the state tolerated numerous Protestant and Eastern creeds. In the Warsaw Confederation of 1573, the Polish gentry vowed, "We who differ in matters of religion will keep the peace among ourselves."

The biological failure of the Jagiellon monarchy in Poland ended that nation's most successful line of kings. Without a natural heir, the Polish nobility and gentry, who officially elected the monarch, had to peddle their throne among the princes of Europe. When Sigismund III (1587–1632) was elected to the Polish throne in 1587, he was also heir to the crown of Sweden. Sigismund accepted the prohibitions

Eastern Europe (ca. 1550) after the consolidation of Russia and the growth of Poland. The eastern part of Europe was still sparsely populated and economically underdeveloped.

GENEALOGY

The Jagiellon Monarchy of Poland

Casimir IV Jagiellon *m.* Elizabeth of Habsburg
1445–1492

John I Albert 1492–1501
Alexander I 1501–1506
Sigismund I 1506–1548 *m.* Bona Sforza

Sigismund II 1548–1572
John III Vasa of Sweden *m.* Catherine

Sigismund III 1587–1632

against religious repression that were outlined in the Warsaw Confederation, but he actively encouraged the establishment of Jesuit schools, the expansion of monastic orders, and the strengthening of the Roman Catholic church.

All those policies enjoyed the approval of the Polish ruling classes. But the Diet would not support Sigismund's efforts to gain control of the Swedish crown, which he inherited in 1592 but from which he was deposed three years later. If Sigismund triumphed in Sweden, all Poland would get was a part-time monarch. The Polish Diet consistently refused to give the king the funds necessary to invade Sweden successfully. Nevertheless, Sigismund mounted several unsuccessful campaigns against the Swedes that sapped Polish money and manpower.

Muscovy's Time of Troubles

The wars of Ivan the Great and Ivan the Terrible in the fifteenth and sixteenth centuries were waged to secure agricultural territory in the west and a Baltic port in the north; both objectives came at the expense of Poland-Lithuania. But following the death of Ivan the Terrible in 1584, the Muscovite state began to disintegrate. For years it had been held together only by conquest and fear. Ivan's conflicts with the boyars, the hereditary nobility, had created an aristocracy unwilling and unable to come to the aid of his successors. By 1601, the crown was plunged into a crisis of legitimacy known as the Time of Troubles. Ivan had murdered his heir in a fit of anger and left his half-witted son to

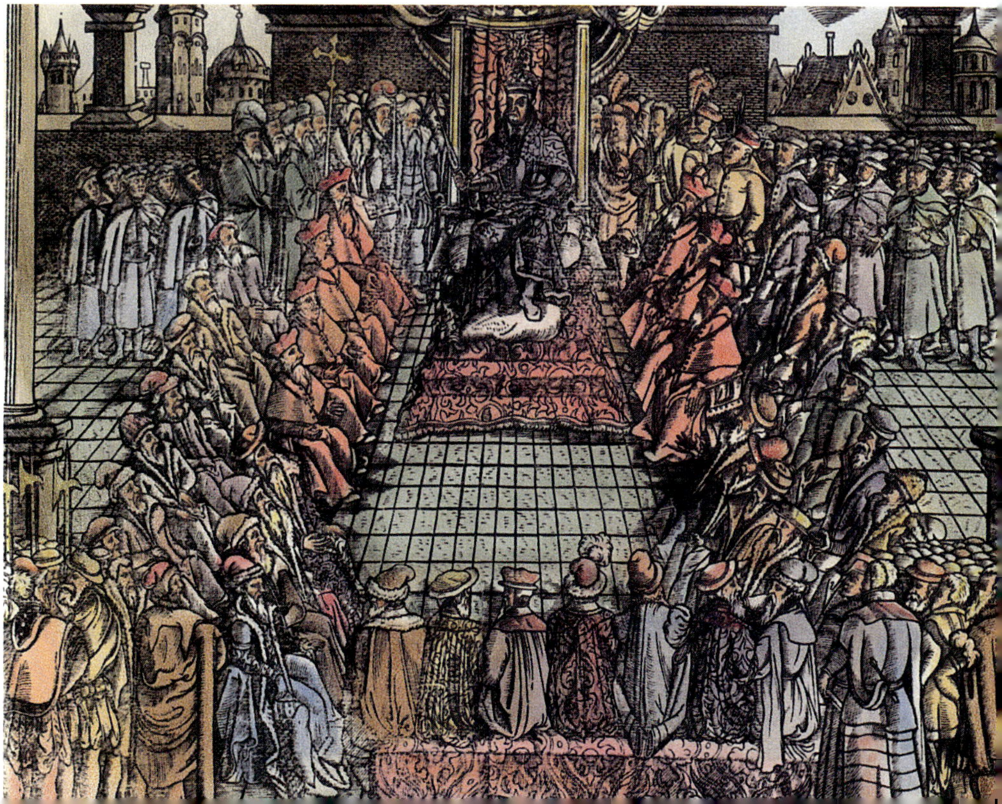

An assembly of the Polish Diet, the parliamentary body composed of the landed elite. On the throne is Sigismund III. Rivalry among the magnates weakened the Diet, and conflicts with the elected monarchs were frequent.

inherit the throne, which led to a vacuum of power at the center as well as a struggle for the spoils of government. Private armies ruled great swaths of the state and pretenders to the crown—all claiming to be Dimitri, the lost brother of the last legitimate tsar—appeared everywhere. Ambitious groups of boyars backed their own claimants to the throne. So, too, did ambitious foreigners who eagerly sought to carve up Muscovite possessions.

Muscovy's Time of Troubles was Poland's moment of opportunity. While anarchy and civil war raged, Poland looked to regain the territory that it had lost to Muscovy during the previous century. Sigismund abandoned war with Sweden in order to intervene in the struggle for the Russian crown. Polish forces crossed into Muscovy and Sigismund's generals backed one of the strongest of the false Dimitris, but their plan to put him on the throne failed when he was assassinated. Sigismund used the death of the last false Dimitri as a pretext to assert his own claim to the Muscovite crown. More Polish forces poured across the frontier. In 1610, they took Moscow and Sigismund proclaimed himself tsar, intending to unite the two massive states.

Michael Romanov was chosen to be tsar in 1613. His father, the Patriarch Philaret of Moscow, acted as joint ruler with Michael until the patriarch's death in 1633.

The Rise of Russia. Russia grew through the addition of large units of territory comprising millions of square acres.

The Russian boyars, so long divided, now rose against the Polish enemy. The Polish garrison in Moscow was starved into submission, and a native Russian, Michael Romanov (1613–1645), was chosen tsar by an assembly of landholders, the Zemsky Sobor. He made a humiliating peace with the Swedes—who had also taken advantage of the Time of Troubles to invade Muscovy's Baltic provinces—in return for Swedish assistance against the Poles. Intermittent fighting continued for another 20 years. In the end, Poland agreed to peace and a separate Muscovite state, but only in exchange for large territorial concessions.

The Rise of Sweden

Sweden's rise to power during the seventeenth century was as startling as it was swift. Until the Reformation, Sweden had been part of the Scandinavian confederation ruled by the Danes. Although the Swedes had a measure of autonomy, they were very much a junior

The Rise of Sweden. For the only time in its history, Sweden acquired territories on the European mainland.

partner in Baltic affairs. Denmark controlled the narrow sound that linked the Baltic with the North Sea, and its prosperity derived from the tolls it collected on imports and exports. When, in 1523, Gustav I Vasa led the uprising of the Swedish aristocracy that ended Danish domination, he won the right to rule over a poor, sparsely populated state with few towns or developed seaports. The Vasas ruled Sweden in conjunction with the aristocracy. Although the throne was hereditary, the part played by the nobility in elevating Gustav I Vasa (1523–1560) gave the nobles a powerful voice in Swedish affairs. Through the council of state, known as the Rad, the Swedish nobility exerted a strong check on the monarch. Sweden's aggressive foreign policy began accidentally. When in the 1550s the Teutonic Knights found themselves no longer capable of ruling in Livonia, the Baltic seaports that had been under their dominion scrambled for new alliances. Muscovy and Poland-Lithuania were the logical choices, but the town of Reval, an important outlet for Russian trade near the mouth of the Gulf of Finland, asked Sweden for protection. After some hesitation, since the occupation of territory on the southern shores of the Baltic would involve great expense, Sweden fortified Reval in 1560. A decade later, Swedish forces captured Narva, farther to the east, and consolidated their hold on the Livonian coast. By occupying the most important ports on the Gulf of Finland, Sweden could control a sizable portion of the Muscovite trade.

Now only two obstacles prevented them from dominating trade with Muscovy: Archangel in the north and Riga in the south. In the 1580s, the Muscovites established a port at Archangel on the White Sea. With the new port they opened a trading route to the west, around northern Scandinavia. Sweden benefited from the White Sea trade by claiming the northern portions of the Scandinavian peninsula necessary to make the trade secure. In all of their dealings with Muscovy, the Swedes sought further privileges at Archangel while laying plans for its conquest. Riga was a problem of a different sort. As the Swedes secured the northern Livonian ports, more of the Muscovy trade moved to

A Livonian peasant. Livonia was conquered by Ivan the Terrible in his campaign of 1563 but was soon reclaimed by the Poles. In 1660 Livonia became part of the Swedish empire. Livonia was originally inhabited by the Livs, a Finnish people.

the south and passed through Riga, which would have to be captured or blockaded if the Swedes were to control commerce in the eastern Baltic.

Sigismund's aggressive alliance with the Polish Jesuits persuaded the Swedish nobility that he would undermine their Lutheran church. Sigismund was deposed in favor of his uncle Charles IX (1604–1611). War with Poland resulted from Sigismund's efforts to regain the Swedish crown. The Swedes used the opportunity to blockade Riga and to occupy more Livonian territory. The Swedish navy was far superior to any force that the Poles could assemble, but on land Polish forces were masters. The Swedish invasion force suffered a crushing defeat and had to retreat to its coastal enclaves. The Poles now had an opportunity to retake all of Livonia but, as always, the Polish Diet was reluctant to finance Sigismund's wars. Furthermore, Sigismund had his eyes on a bigger prize. Rather than follow up its Swedish victory, Poland invaded Muscovy.

Meanwhile, the blockade of Riga and the assembly of a large Swedish fleet in the Baltic threatened Denmark. The Danes continued to claim sovereignty over Sweden and took the opportunity of the Polish-Swedish conflict to reassert it. In 1611, under the energetic leadership of the Danish king Christian IV (1588–1648), Denmark invaded Sweden from both the east and the west. The Danes captured the towns of Kalmar and Alvsborg and threatened to take Stockholm. To end the Danish war, Sweden accepted humiliating terms in 1613. Sweden renounced all claims to the northern coasts and recognized Danish control of the Arctic trading route.

Paradoxically, the setbacks became the springboard for Swedish success. Fear of the Danes led both the English and the Dutch into alliances with Sweden. The countries all shared Protestant interests, and the English were heavily committed to the Muscovy trade, which was still an important part of Swedish commerce. Fear of the Poles had a similar effect upon Muscovy. In 1609, the Swedes agreed to send 5000 troops to Muscovy to help repel the Polish invasion. In return, Muscovy agreed to cede to Sweden its Baltic possessions. That was accomplished in 1617, giving Sweden complete control of the Gulf of Finland.

In 1611, during the middle of the Danish war, Charles IX died and was succeeded by his son Gustavus Adolphus (1611–1632). Unlike his father and cousin before him, who had come by chance to the Swedish throne, Gustavus Adolphus was raised to be king. Gruff and affable by turns, he was one of the leading Protestant princes of his day, in every way a match for Christian IV of Denmark. Gustavus's greatest skills were military. He inherited an ample navy and an effective army. Unlike nearly every other European state, Sweden raised its forces from its own citizens. Gustavus's predecessors had made important innova-

GENEALOGY

The House of Vasa of Sweden

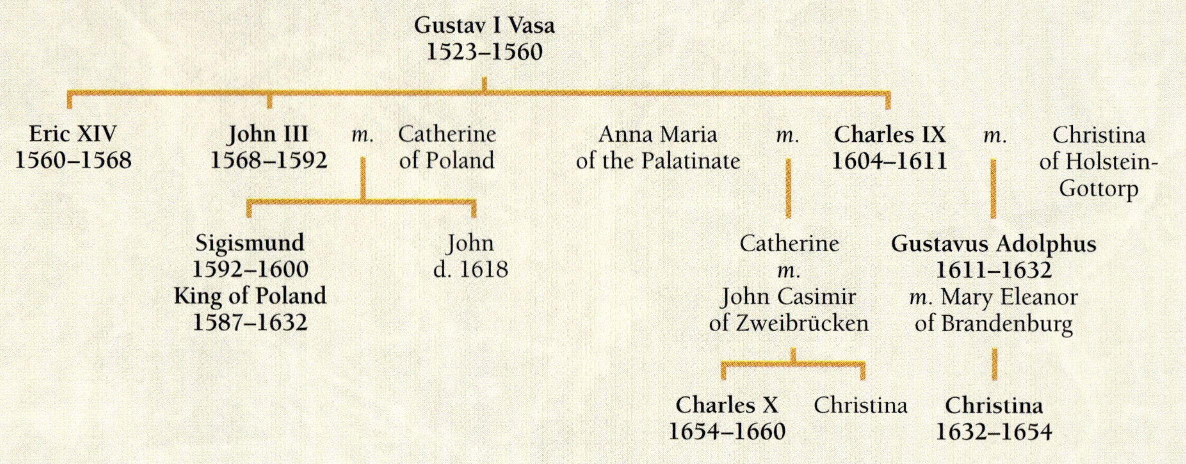

tions in the training of soldiers and in their battlefield tactics. Those the new king improved upon. He introduced new weapons such as the light mobile gun and reshaped his army into standard-size squadrons and regiments, which were easier to administer and deploy.

The calamitous wars inherited from his father occupied Gustavus during the early years of his reign. He was forced to conclude the humiliating peace with the Danes in 1613 and to go to war with the Russians in 1614 in order to secure the Baltic coastal estates that had been promised in 1609. Gustavus's first military initiative was to resume war with Poland in order to force Sigismund to renounce his claim to the Swedish throne. In 1621, Gustavus landed in Livonia and within two weeks had captured Riga, the capstone of Sweden's Baltic ambitions. Occupation of Riga increased Swedish control of the Muscovy trade and deprived Denmark of a significant portion of its customs duties. Gustavus now claimed Riga as a Swedish port and successfully demanded that ships sailing from there pay tolls to Sweden rather than Denmark. The capture of Riga firmly established Sweden as a coequal Baltic power.

By the mid-seventeenth century, the Sweden of Gustavus Adolphus was well on its way to international prominence. The capture of Riga gave Sweden complete control of the eastern Baltic and ended Polish pretensions to the Swedish throne. A negotiated settlement with the Danes over the collection of tolls enhanced Swedish prestige and increased Sweden's commercial prosperity. Moreover, Gustavus's marriage into the family of the Protestant rulers of Prussia gave Sweden a presence in Germany as well. For the time being, Sweden faced east. But the storm clouds of religious warfare were already bursting over the Holy Roman Empire. Gustavus Adolphus now took his place among the Protestant princes of Europe, and Sweden ranked among the leading Protestant powers.

THE THIRTY YEARS' WAR, 1618–1648

Perhaps it was just a matter of time before the isolated conflicts that dotted the corners of Europe were joined together. In 1609 Spain and the Dutch Republic had signed a truce that was to last until 1621. In more than 40 years of nearly continuous fighting, the Dutch had carved out a state in the northern Netherlands. They used the truce to consolidate their position and increase their prosperity, largely at the expense of Spain and Portugal. Thus, to the insult of rebellion was added the injury of commercial competition. Spain had reluctantly accepted Dutch independence, but Philip III (1598–1621) never abandoned the objective of recovering his Burgundian inheritance. By the start of the seventeenth century, Philip had good reasons for hope. Beginning in the 1580s, Spanish forces had reconquered the southern provinces of the Netherlands. The prosperous towns of Brussels, Antwerp, and Ghent were again under Spanish control, and they provided a springboard for another invasion.

The Twelve Years' Truce gave Spain time to prepare for the final assault. During this time, Philip III attempted to resolve all of Spain's other European conflicts so that he could then give full attention to a resumption of the Dutch war. Circumstance smiled upon his efforts. In 1603, the pacific James I (1603–1625) came to the English throne. Secure in his island state, James I desired peace among all Christian princes. He quickly concluded the war with Spain that had begun with the

Marie de Médicis, the widow of Henry IV, with her son Louis XIII.

WAR IS HELL

No source has better captured the brutality of the Thirty Years' War than the novel Simplicissimus *(1669). In a series of loosely connected episodes, the hero (whose name means "the simplest of the simple") is snatched from his village to serve in marauding armies whose confrontations with local villagers are usually more horrifying than the episode narrated here.*

THESE TROOPERS WERE EVEN NOW READY TO MARCH, and had the pastor fastened by a rope to lead him away. Some cried, "Shoot him down, the rogue!" Others would have money from him. But he, lifting up his hands to heaven, begged, for the sake of the Last Judgment, for forbearance and Christian compassion, but in vain; for one of them rode down and dealt him such a blow on the head that he fell flat, and commended his soul to God. Nor did the remainder of the captured peasants fare any better. But even when it seemed these troopers, in their cruel tyranny, had clean lost their wits, came such a swarm of armed peasants out of the wood, that it seemed a wasps'-nest had been stirred. And these began to yell so frightfully and so furiously to attack with sword and musket that all my hair stood on end; and never had I been at such a merrymaking before: for the peasants of the Spessart and the Vogelsberg are as little wont as are the Hessians and men of the Sauerland and the Black Forest to let themselves be crowed over on their own dunghill. So away went the troopers, and not only left behind the cattle they had captured, but threw away bag and baggage also, and so cast all their booty to the winds lest themselves should become booty for the peasants: yet some of them fell into their hands. This sport took from me well-nigh all desire to see the world, for I thought, if 'tis all like this, then is the wilderness far more pleasant.

From Hans Von Grimmelshausen, *The Adventurous Simplicissimus.*

invasion of the Spanish Armada and entered into negotiations to marry his heir to a Spanish princess. In 1610, the bellicose Henry IV of France was felled by an assassin's knife. French plans to renew war with Spain were abandoned with the accession of the eight-year-old Louis XIII (1610–1643). As the sands of the Twelve Years' Truce ran out, Spain and the Netherlands readied for war. But not even the greatest empire in Europe could control its own destiny. War was in the air all over the Continent, and not everyone could wait until 1621.

Bohemia Revolts

The Peace of Augsburg had served the German states well. The principle that the religion of the ruler was the religion of the state complicated the political life of the Holy Roman Empire, but it also pacified it. Although rulers had the right to enforce uniformity on their subjects, in practice many of the larger states tolerated more than one religion. By the beginning of the seventeenth century, Catholicism and Protestantism had achieved a rough equality within the German states, symbolized by the fact that of the seven electors who chose the Holy Roman Emperor, three were Catholic, three Protestant, and the seventh was the emperor himself, acting as king of Bohemia. The situation was not unwelcome to the leaders of the Austrian Habsburg family who succeeded Emperor Charles V. By necessity, the eastern Habsburgs were more tolerant than their Spanish kinfolk. Protestants fought the Ottomans with as much zeal as did Catholics, and the Ottomans were the empire's more potent enemy. The unofficial policy of toleration not only helped the Austrian Habsburgs defend their state, it allowed them to expand it. The head of their house was elected king of Bohemia and king of Hungary, both states with large Protestant populations.

A Fatal Election. In 1617, Mathias, the childless Holy Roman Emperor, began making plans for his cousin, Ferdinand Habsburg, to succeed him. In order to ensure a Catholic majority among the electors, the emperor relinquished his Bohemian title and pressed for Ferdinand's election as the new king of Bohemia. Ferdinand was Catholic, very devout, and very committed. He had been educated by Jesuits and practiced what had been preached to him. On his own estates, Ferdinand abandoned the policy of toleration. Jesuit schools were founded and the precepts of the Council of Trent were enforced. Protestant preachers were barred from their offices, Protestant books were publicly burned, and thousands of common people were forced to flee, many into nearby Bohemia, where Protestants constituted the majority of the population.

Thus Ferdinand's election as king of Bohemia was no foregone conclusion. Although in the end the Protestant nobles of Bohemia could not prevent his election, they forced the new king to accept the strictest limitations upon his political and religious powers. But once elected, Ferdinand had not the slightest intention of honoring the provisions that had been thrust upon him. His opponents were equally strong willed. When Ferdinand violated Protestant religious liberties, a group of noblemen marched to the royal palace in Prague in May 1618, found two of the king's chief advisers, and hurled them out of an upper-story window. The officials' lives—if not their dignity—were preserved by the pile of manure in which they landed.

The Defenestration of Prague, as the incident came to be known, initiated a Protestant counteroffensive throughout the Habsburg lands. Fear of Ferdinand's policies led to Protestant uprisings in Hungary as well as Bohemia. Those who seized control of the government declared Ferdinand deposed and the throne vacant, but they had no candidate to accept their crown. When Emperor Mathias died in 1619, the stalemate was broken. Ferdinand succeeded to the imperial title as Ferdinand II (1619–1637) and Frederick V, one of the Protestant electors, accepted the Bohemian crown.

Frederick V, the "Winter King." Frederick was a sincere but weak Calvinist whose credentials were much stronger than his abilities. His mother was a daughter of Prince William of Orange and his wife, Elizabeth, a daughter of James I of England. It was widely believed that it was Elizabeth's resolution that she would "rather eat sauerkraut with a King than roast meat with an Elector" that decided the issue. No decision could have been more disastrous for the fate of Europe. Frederick ruled a geographically divided German state known as the Palatinate. One hundred miles separated the two segments of his lands, but both were strategically important. The Lower Palatinate bordered on the Catholic Spanish Netherlands and the Upper Palatinate on Catholic Bavaria.

Once Frederick accepted the Bohemian crown, he was faced with a war on three fronts. It was over almost before it began. Ferdinand II had no difficulty enlisting allies to recover the Bohemian crown, since he could pay them with the spoils of Frederick's lands. Spanish troops from the Netherlands occupied the Lower Palatinate, and Bavarian troops occupied the Upper Palatinate. Frederick, on the other hand, met rejection wherever he turned. Neither the Dutch nor the English would send more than token aid—both had advised him against breaking the imperial peace. The Lutheran princes of Germany would not enter into a war between Calvinists and Catholics, especially after Ferdinand II promised to protect the Bohemian Lutherans.

At the Battle of the White Mountain in 1620, Ferdinand's Catholic forces annihilated Frederick's army. Frederick and Elizabeth fled north, first to Denmark and then to Holland. Bohemia was left to face the wrath of Ferdinand, the victorious king and emperor. The retribution was horrible. Mercenaries who had fought for Ferdinand II were allowed to sack Prague for a week. Elective monarchy was abolished, and Bohemia became part of the hereditary Habsburg lands. Free peasants were enserfed and subjected to imperial law. Those nobles who had supported Frederick lost their lands and their privileges. Calvinism was repressed and thoroughly rooted out, consolidating forever the Catholic character of Bohemia. Frederick's estates were carved up and his rights as elector transferred to the Catholic duke of Bavaria. The Battle of the White Mountain was a turning point in the history of central Europe.

The War Widens

For the Habsburgs, religious and dynastic interests were inseparable. Ferdinand II and Philip III of Spain fought for their beliefs and for their patrimony. Their victory gave them more than they could have expected: Ferdinand swallowed up Bohemia and strengthened his position in the empire, and Philip gained possession of a vital link in his supply route between Italy and the Netherlands. The Habsburgs were now more dangerous than ever. Ferdinand's aggressive Catholicism threatened the Protestant princes of Germany, who prudently began to seek allies outside the empire. Spanish expansion threatened France. The occupation of the Lower Palatinate placed a ring of Spanish armies around the French borders from the Pyrenees to the Low Countries. The French too searched for allies. But French opinion remained divided over which was the greater evil: Spain or Protestantism.

The Danes Respond. Frederick, now in Holland, refused to accept the judgment of battle. He lobbied for a grand alliance to repel the Spaniards from the Lower Palatinate and to restore the religious balance in the empire. Although his personal cause met with little sympathy, his political logic was impeccable, especially after Spain again declared war upon the Dutch in 1621. A grand Protestant alliance—secretly supported by the French—brought together England, Holland, a number of German states, and Denmark. It was the Danes who led this potentially powerful coalition. In 1626, a large Danish army under the command of King Christian IV engaged imperial forces on German soil. But Danish forces could not match the superior numbers and the superior leadership of the Catholic mercenary forces under the command of the ruthless and brilliant Count Albrecht von Wallenstein (1583–1634). In 1629, the Danes withdrew from the empire and sued for peace.

If the Catholic victory at the White Mountain in 1620 threatened the well-being of German Protestantism, the Catholic triumph over the Danes threatened its survival. More powerful than ever, Ferdinand II determined to turn the religious clock back to the state of affairs that had existed when the Peace of Augsburg was concluded in 1555. He demanded that all lands that had then been Catholic but had since become Protestant be returned to the fold. He also proclaimed that as the Peace of Augsburg made no provision for the toleration of Calvinists, they would no longer be tolerated in the empire. Those policies together constituted a virtual revolution in the religious affairs of the German states, and they proved impossible to impose. Ferdinand succeeded in only one thing—he united Lutherans and Calvinists against him.

Protestant Gains. In 1630, King Gustavus Adolphus of Sweden decided to enter the German conflict. To protect Swedish interests, he reasoned, he must defend the Protestant states of northern Germany. Moreover, France was willing to pay much of the cost of a war against Ferdinand. The French too felt the pressure of increasing imperial and Spanish power. Gustavus Adolphus had more success gaining the support of Catholic France than he did gaining the support of the Protestant German princes. Saxony and Brandenburg, the two largest states, feared the consequences of

Gustavus Adolphus of Sweden, shown at the battle of Breitenfeld in 1631. The battle was the first important Protestant victory of the Thirty Years' War. Gustavus died on the battlefield at Lützen in the following year.

FIRE AND SWORD

No event of the Thirty Years' War had a greater effect on public opinion than the annihilation of the Protestant city of Magdeburg, in 1631. Dozens of pamphlets and woodcuts, including this anonymous account, detailed the slaughter of civilians and the devastation of property. It was commonly believed that neither a human nor an animal escaped the destruction.

THUS IT CAME ABOUT THAT THE CITY and all its inhabitants fell into the hands of the enemy, whose violence and cruelty were due in part to their common hatred of the adherents of the Augsburg Confession, and in part to their being imbittered by the chain shot which had been fired at them and by the derision and insults that the Magdeburgers had heaped upon them from the ramparts.

Then was there naught but beating and burning, plundering, torture, and murder. Most especially was every one of the enemy bent on securing much booty. When a marauding party entered a house, if its master had anything to give he might thereby purchase respite and protection for himself and his family till the next man, who also wanted something, should come along....

Thus in a single day this noble and famous city, the pride of the whole country, went up in fire and smoke; and the remnant of its citizens, with their wives and children, were taken prisoners and driven away by the enemy with a noise of weeping and wailing that could be heard from afar, while the cinders and ashes from the town were carried by the wind to Wanzleben, Egeln, and still more distant places....

renewed war. Gustavus believed that he could defend the north German states from Ferdinand's aggression and by doing so protect Sweden's Baltic empire. "I seek not my own advantage in this war, nor any gain save the security of my Kingdom," he lectured the reluctant Germans. It was a farsighted strategy. In fact, the only thing he could not foresee when he landed in Germany early in 1630 was how successful his intervention would be.

While Gustavus Adolphus struggled to construct his alliance, imperial forces continued their triumphant progress. In 1631 they besieged, captured, and put to the torch the town of Magdeburg. In a war noted for cruelty between combatants and atrocities against civilians, the destruction of Magdeburg set new standards. Perhaps three-fourths of the 40,000 inhabitants of the town were slaughtered—"in the midst of a horrible din of heart-rending shrieks and cries they were tortured and put to death in so cruel a manner that no words would suffice to describe nor no tears to bewail it," was the report in one pamphlet. The sack of Magdeburg marked a turning point in Protestant fortunes. It gave the international Protestant community a unifying symbol that enhanced Gustavus's military efforts. Hundreds of pamphlets, woodcuts, and newspaper accounts brought the horror of Magdeburg home to Protestants throughout the Continent. Brandenburg and Saxony joined Gustavus Adolphus, not only enlarging his forces, but allowing him to open a second front in Bohemia. He would soon have 140,000 men under his command, only 13,000 of whom were Swedish. In the autumn of 1631, the combination overwhelmed the imperial armies. Gustavus won a decisive triumph at Breitenfeld, while the Saxons occupied Prague. For the first time since 1618, Protestant forces were ascendant, and they brought the war into the Catholic heartland of the empire.

Gustavus Adolphus lost no time in pressing his advantage. The Swedes marched west to the Rhine, easily conquering the richest of the Catholic cities and retaking the Lower Palatinate. In early 1632, Protestant forces plundered Bavaria. It was the Bavarian ruler Maximilian who had gained most from the years of war. His troops had occupied the Upper Palatinate, and he had received Frederick's rights as imperial elector in return for support of Ferdinand. Moreover, Maximilian had played a double game of negotiating with the French for neutrality and with the emperor for the

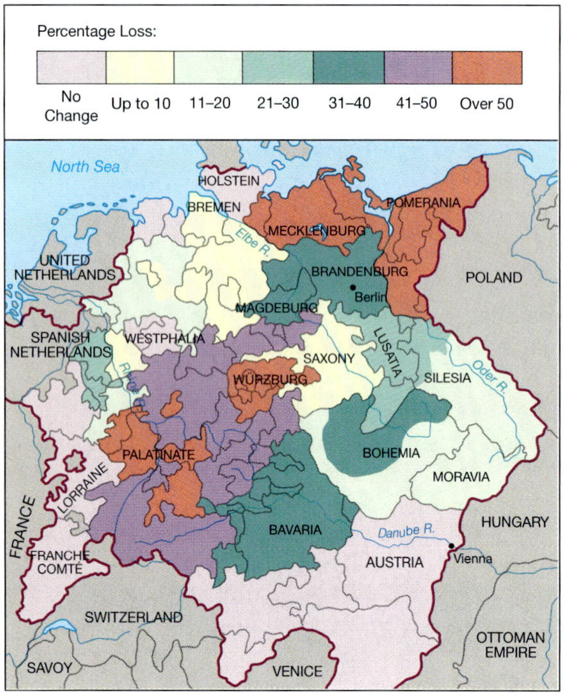

Population loss in Germany during the Thirty Years' War. It was the most devastating war in European history before the twentieth century.

CHRONOLOGY

The Thirty Years' War

1618	Defenestration of Prague
1619	Ferdinand Habsburg elected Holy Roman Emperor; Frederick of the Palatinate accepts the crown of Bohemia
1620	Catholic victory at battle of White Mountain
1621	End of Twelve Years' Truce; war between Spain and Netherlands
1626	Danes form Protestant alliance under Christian IV
1627	Spain declares bankruptcy
1630	Gustavus Adolphus leads Swedish forces into Germany
1631	Sack of Magdeburg; Protestant victory at Breitenfeld
1632	Protestant victory at Lützen; death of Gustavus Adolphus
1635	France declares war on Spain
1640	Portugal secedes from Spain
1643	Battle of Rocroi; French forces repel Spaniards
1648	Peace of Westphalia

spoils of victory. So there was poetic justice when Maximilian's state was invaded, his castles looted, and his lands plundered. But there was no justice at all for the wretched inhabitants of that stronghold of German Catholicism. Town and countryside were laid waste. Not until the winter of 1632 did the armies of Gustavus and Wallenstein finally meet. At the battle of Lützen the Swedes won the field but lost their beloved king. Wounded in the leg, the back, and the head, Gustavus Adolphus died. In less than two years he had decisively transformed the course of the war and the course of Europe's future. Protestant forces now occupied most of central and northern Germany. Ferdinand's ability to redraw the religious map of the empire was at an end.

The siege of Magdeburg, 1631. The sack of the city by the Imperial troops of Tilly's army was one of the most barbarous incidents of the brutal Thirty Years' War.

The Long Quest for Peace

The Thirty Years' War was barely half over when Gustavus Adolphus fell at Lützen. But from that time forward, its central European phase receded in importance. The final stages of the war involved the resumption of the century-old struggle between France and Spain. When the Twelve Years' Truce expired in 1621, Spain again declared war upon the Dutch. Philip III's hopes of concentrating all his resources against Holland had been disappointed by the outbreak of war in central Europe. Not until after the Bohemian revolt had been repressed did the Spanish army begin the long, laborious process of besieging the well-fortified and well-defended towns of the Netherlands. The resumption of war in the Netherlands, combined with the continued successes of Habsburg forces in central Europe, convinced Louis XIII and his chief minister, Cardinal Richelieu, that the time for active French involvement in European affairs was at hand. Throughout the early stages of the war, France had secretly aided anti-Habsburg forces. The time had come to take an open stand. In 1635, France declared war on Spain.

Neither country was prepared for large-scale military action, and neither could afford it. The war resembled nothing so much as two punch-drunk fighters pounding each other, both receiving as much punishment as they inflicted. France took the offensive first, invading the Spanish Netherlands. In 1636, a Spanish

The Peace of Westphalia, 1648, recognized the new boundaries of European states that included an independent Portugal and United Netherlands. It also recognized the growth of the Ottoman Empire into the Balkans.

army struck back, pushing to within 25 miles of Paris before it was repelled. Both sides soon began to search for a settlement, but pride prevented them from laying down their gloves. Spain toppled first. Its economy in shambles and its citizens in revolt over high prices and higher taxes, it could no longer maintain its many-fronted war. The Swedes again defeated imperial forces in Germany, the Dutch destroyed much of Spain's Atlantic fleet in 1639, and the Portuguese rose up against the union of crowns that had brought them nothing but expense and the loss of crucial portions of their empire. In 1640, the Portuguese regained their independence. In 1643, Spain gambled once more on a knockout blow against the French. But at the battle of Rocroi, exhausted French troops held out and the Spanish invasion failed.

By then the desire for peace was universal. Most of the main combatants had long since perished: Philip III, ever optimistic, in 1621; Frederick V, an exile to the end, in 1632; Gustavus Adolphus, killed at Lützen in the same year; Wallenstein, murdered by order of Ferdinand II in 1634; Ferdinand himself in 1637; and Louis XIII in 1643, five days before the French triumph at Rocroi. Those who succeeded them had not the same passions, and after so many decades the longing for peace was the strongest emotion on the Continent. But the tangle of wars and alliances was not easily unsnarled, and those who saw themselves as victors at one stage or another still sought desperately for their spoils. Some wanted to reconstruct the political world as it had existed in 1618, others to reestablish it as it was after the first round of Catholic victories in 1627. The Swedes, who had gained most from the struggle—they now occupied much of northern Germany and, after a brief war with Denmark, much territory in the western Baltic as well—wanted to settle things largely as they stood. Fighting persisted as each effort to reach a universal peace failed. Finally, at the beginning of 1648, Spain and the Netherlands concluded their 80 years of fighting. The bilateral agreement broke the logjam. One by one, the combatants agreed to end their hostilities with one another, and soon the stage was set for a Continentwide settlement.

A series of agreements, collectively known as the Peace of Westphalia, established the outlines of the political geography of Europe for the next century. Its focus was on the Holy Roman Empire, and it reflected Protestant successes in the final two decades of war. Sweden gained further territories on the Baltic, making it master of the north German ports. France, too, gained in territory and prestige. It kept the vital towns in the Lower Palatinate through which Spanish men and material had moved, and though it did not agree to come to terms with Spain immediately, France's fear of encirclement was at an end. The Dutch gained statehood through official recognition by Spain and through the power they had displayed in building and maintaining an overseas empire.

Territorial boundaries were reestablished as they had existed in 1624, giving the Habsburgs control of both Bohemia and Hungary. The independence of the Swiss cantons was now officially recognized, as were the rights of Calvinists to the protection of the Peace of Augsburg, which again was to govern the religious affairs of the empire. Two of the larger German states were strengthened to balance the emperor's power. Bavaria was allowed to retain the Upper Palatinate, and Brandenburg, which ceded some of its coastal territory to Sweden, gained extensive territories in the east.

The emperor's political control over the German states was also weakened. German rulers were given independent authority over their states, and the imperial Diet, rather than the emperor, was empowered to settle disputes. Thus weakened, future emperors ruled in the Habsburg territorial lands with little ability to control, influence, or even arbitrate German affairs. The judgment that the Holy Roman Empire was neither holy, nor Roman, nor an empire was now irrevocably true.

The Peace of Westphalia put the pieces of the map of European states back together. Protestantism and Catholicism now coexisted and there was to be little further change in the geography of religion. The northwest of Europe—England, Holland, Scandinavia, and the north German states—was Protestant, while the south was Catholic. The empire of the German peoples was at an end, the Austro-Hungarian empire at a beginning. Holland and Sweden had become international powers; Spain and Denmark faded from prominence. Muscovy began a long period of isolation from the west, attempting to restore a semblance of government to its people. But if the negotiators at Westphalia could resolve the political and religious ambitions that gave rise to a century of nearly continuous warfare, they could do nothing to eradicate the effects of war itself. The devastation of humanity in the name of God with which the reform of religion had begun was exhausted. The costs were horrific. The population of Germany fell from 15 million in 1600 to 11 million in 1650. The armies brought destruction of all kinds in their wake. Plague again raged in Europe—the town of Augsburg lost 18,000 inhabitants in the early 1630s. Famine, too, returned to a continent that 50 years earlier had been self-sufficient in grain. The war played havoc with all of the economies that it touched. Inflation, devaluation of coinage, and huge public and private debts were all directly attributable to the years of fighting. And the toll taken on the spirit of those generations that never knew peace is incalculable.

Questions for Review

1. How was Henry IV able to bring peace to France after decades of civil war?
2. What were the political and religious connections between the Armada launched against England by Philip II and the revolt of the Netherlands?
3. How did Sweden rise to become one of Europe's great powers in the first half of the seventeenth century?
4. How did religion help spark and spread the Thirty Years' War?
5. What were the effects of the Peace of Westphalia on political arrangements in the heart of Europe?

Suggestions for Further Reading

General Reading

* J. H. Elliott, *Europe Divided, 1559–1598* (New York: Harper & Row, 1968). An outstanding synthesis of European politics in the second half of the sixteenth century.

* Geoffrey Parker, *Europe in Crisis, 1598–1648* (London: William Collins and Sons, 1979). An up-to-date study of European states in the early seventeenth century.

* M. S. Anderson, *The Origins of the Modern European State System, 1494–1618* (London: Longman, 1998). A survey of developments stressing war and diplomacy across all of Europe.

* Richard Bonney, *The European Dynastic States, 1494–1660* (Oxford: Oxford University Press, 1991.) The most up-to-date introduction to the period, by a noted historian of France.

* Jan de Vries, *The European Economy in an Age of Crisis* (Cambridge: Cambridge University Press, 1976). A comprehensive study of economic development, including long-distance trade and commercial change.

* Richard Dunn, *The Age of Religious Wars, 1559–1715* (New York: Norton, 1979). A well-written survey of early modern society.

* H. G. Koenigsberger, *Early Modern Europe* (London: Longman, 1987). A general overview designed for beginning students.

The Crises of the Western States

J. H. M. Salmon, *Society in Crisis* (New York: St. Martin's Press, 1975). The best single-volume account of the French civil wars; difficult but rewarding.

* Mack Holt, *The French Wars of Religion, 1562–1629* (Cambridge: Cambridge University Press, 1995). The wars of religion seen in a long perspective.

N. M. Sutherland, *The Massacre of St. Bartholomew and the European Conflict* (London: Macmillan, 1973). Argues the case for the importance of Spanish influence on the massacre and the course of the wars of religion.

Robert Kingdon, *Myths about the St. Bartholomew's Day Massacres, 1572–76* (Cambridge, MA: Harvard University Press, 1988). A study of the impact of a central event in the history of France.

David Buisseret, *Henry IV* (London: Allen & Unwin, 1984). A stylish biography of a problematic personality.

* Mark Greengrass, *France in the Age of Henri IV* (London: Longman, 1984). An important synthesis of French history in the early seventeenth century.

Geoffrey Parker, *Philip II* (Boston: Little, Brown, 1978). The best introduction.

* Garrett Mattingly, *The Armada* (Boston: Houghton Mifflin, 1959). Still the classic account, despite recent reinterpretations.

Colin Martin and N. G. Parker, *The Spanish Armada* (London: Hamilton Press, 1988). A recent study based on archaeological finds and a fresh look at the evidence.

* John Lynch, *Spain, 1516–1598: From Nation State to World Empire* (Cambridge, MA: Blackwell, 1994). The most up-to-date survey.

* M. J. Rodriguez-Salgado, *The Changing Face of Empire, Charles V, Philip II and Habsburg Authority* (Cambridge: Cambridge University Press, 1988). A study of the connections between the Spanish and Austrian empires in the sixteenth century.

* Henry Kamen, *Spain, 1469–1714* (London: Longman, 1983). A recent survey with up-to-date interpretations.

* A. W. Lovett, *Early Habsburg Spain* (Oxford: Oxford University Press, 1986). An accessible survey of the recent work on sixteenth century Spain.

* Geoffrey Parker, *The Dutch Revolt* (London: Penguin Books, 1977). An outstanding account of the tangle of events that comprised the revolts of the Netherlands.

* Pieter Geyl, *The Revolt of the Netherlands* (London: Ernest Benn, 1962). Still worth reading for its passion and enthusiasm.

* Jonathan Israel, *The Dutch Republic and the Hispanic World, 1606–1661* (Oxford: Clarendon, 1986). A panoramic survey of the stormy relations between Empire and Republic.

* C. V. Wedgwood, *William the Silent, William of Nassau, Prince of Orange, 1533–1584* (New York: Norton, 1968). A stylish biography.

* Peter Limm, *The Dutch Revolt, 1559–1648* (London: Longman, 1989). A brief introduction with source excerpts.

James D. Tracy, *Holland Under Habsburg Rule, 1506–1566* (Berkeley: University of California Press, 1990). A history of the political formation of the Dutch state.

* Penry Williams, *The Later Tudors* (Oxford: Oxford University Press, 1995). The newest survey in the Oxford history of England.

* J. A. Guy, *Tudor England* (Oxford: Oxford University Press, 1988). A magisterial survey by the leading scholar of Tudor England.

* Wallace Maccaffrey, *Elizabeth I* (New York: Edward Arnold, 1993). The latest scholarly biography.

* Alison Weir, *Elizabeth the Queen* (London: J. Cape, 1998). A lively biography of the great queen.

W. E. F. Reddawaay, et al., eds., *The Cambridge History of Poland to 1696* (Cambridge: Cambridge University Press, 1950). A difficult but thorough narrative of Polish history.

Michael Roberts, *Gustavus Adolphus and the Rise of Sweden* (London: English Universities Press, 1973). A highly readable account of Sweden's rise to power.

The Struggles in Eastern Europe

* S. F. Platonov, *The Time of Troubles* (Lawrence: University Press of Kansas, 1970). A good narrative of the disintegration of the Muscovite state.

Maureen Perrie, *Pretenders and Popular Monarchisms in Early Modern Russia* (Cambridge: Cambridge University Press, 1995). Recent scholarship on the Time of Troubles, focusing on the royal impostors.

Stewart Oakley, *War and Peace in the Baltic, 1560–1790* (New York: Routledge, 1992). A solid account of military history during the period of Sweden's rise.

David Kirby, *Northern Europe in the Early Modern Period: The Baltic World, 1492–1772* (London: Longman, 1990). The best single volume on Baltic politics.

Michael Roberts, *The Swedish Imperial Experience* (Cambridge: Cambridge University Press, 1979). Reflections on Swedish history by the preeminent historian of early modern Sweden.

The Thirty Years' War

* C. V. Wedgwood, *The Thirty Years' War* (New York: Doubleday, 1961). An heroic account; the best narrative history.

* Geoffrey Parker, ed., *The Thirty Years' War* (London: Routledge & Kegan Paul, 1984). A multiauthor account that views the war from a variety of vantage points.

* Peter Limm, *The Thirty Years' War* (London: Longman, 1984). An excellent brief survey with documents.

* Josef Polisensky, *Tragic Triangle* (Prague: Charles University Press, 1991). The origins of the Thirty Years' War from the Bohemian point of view.

* J. H. Elliott, *Richelieu and Olivares* (Cambridge: Cambridge University Press, 1984). A comparison of statesmen and statesmanship in the early seventeenth century.

* Paperback edition available.

Discovering Western Civilization Online

To further explore Europe at war, consult the following World Wide Web sites. Since Web resources are constantly being updated, also go to *www.awl.com/Kishlansky* for further suggestions.

The Crisis of the Western States

www.fordham.edu/halsall/mod/modsbook1.html#Conflict
Links to documents on the French wars of religion, the invasion of the Spanish Armada, and the Thirty Years' War.

www.metalab.unc.edu/wm/paint/tl/north-ren/
Links to pictures and portraits from the late sixteenth and early seventeenth centuries.

www.metalab.unc.edu/wm/paint/auth/bruegel/death.jpg
A site depicting Peter Brueghel's *Triumph of Death,* one of the most evocative paintings of the destruction wrought by warfare in early modern Europe.

The Thirty Years' War, 1618–1648

www.yale.edu/lawweb/avalon/westphal.htm
The full text of the Treaty of Westphalia that ended the Thirty Years' War.

CHAPTER

15

THE EXPERIENCES OF LIFE IN EARLY MODERN EUROPE, 1500–1650

- HAYMAKING
- ECONOMIC LIFE
  - Rural Life
  - Town Life
  - Economic Change
- SOCIAL LIFE
  - Social Constructs
  - Social Structure
  - Social Change
  - Peasant Revolts
- PRIVATE LIFE
  - The Family
  - Communities
  - Popular Beliefs

Haymaking

IT IS SUMMER IN THE LOW COUNTRIES. The trees are full, the meadows green; flowers rise in clumps and bushes hang heavy with fruit. The day has dawned brightly for haymaking. Yesterday the long meadow was mowed, and today the hay will be gathered and the first fruits and vegetables of the season harvested. From throughout the village families come together to labor. Twice each summer the grass is cut, dried, and stacked. Some of it will be left in the fields for the animals until autumn; some will be carried into large lofts and stored for the winter.

The scene of communal farming shown here was repeated with little variation throughout Europe in the early modern era. The village pictured is fairly prosperous with at least three horses and a large wheeled cart in view. Horses were still a luxury for farmers; they could be used for transportation as well as labor, but they were weaker than oxen and had to be fed grain rather than grass. The houses of the village also suggest comfort. The one at the far right is typical. It contains one floor for living and a loft for storage. The chimney separates a kitchen in the back from the long hall where the family works, sleeps, and entertains itself. The bed—it was not uncommon for there to be only one for the whole family— would be near the fireplace, and would be restuffed with straw after the harvest. The long end of the hall,

farthest from heat and light, would be home to the family's animals once winter set in. But in summer it was a luxurious space where children could play or parents could claim a little privacy.

The church is easily distinguished by its steeple and is made of brick. The steeple has 16 windows, probably all set with expensive glass and even some stained glass. The church would have been built over several generations at considerable cost to the villagers. Even the most prosperous houses in the far meadow are made of timber and thatch. The layout of the buildings shows how the village must have grown. The original settlement was all on the rise above the church. The houses nearer the center of the picture were added later, perhaps to allow the sons of the more prosperous village farmers to begin their own families before their parents' deaths.

In the center of the scene are a large number of laborers. Four men with pitchforks load the cart while two women sweep the hay that falls back into new piles. Throughout the field, men and women, distinguished only by their clothing, rake hay into large stacks for successive loadings of the cart. At least 25 individuals work at these tasks. Men perform the heaviest work of loading the haycart and hammering the scythes while men and women share all the other work. Although no children appear in the scene, some are undoubtedly at work picking berries and beans.

The scenes of physical labor remind us that the life of ordinary people in the early modern period was neither romantic nor despondent, neither quaint nor primitive. It had its own joys and sorrows, its own triumphs and failures, its own measures of progress and decay. By today's standards, a sixteenth-century prince endured greater material hardships than a twentieth-century welfare recipient. There was no running water, no central heating, no lavatories, no electricity. There was no relief for toothache, headache, or numbing pain. Travel was dangerous and exhausting. There was no protection from the open air, and many nights were spent on the bare ground. Waiting for winds to sail was more tedious than waiting to board a plane. Entertainment was sparse, and the court jester would have been little match for stereo and video. But though we cannot help but be struck by these differences, we will not understand very much about the experiences of life in sixteenth-century Europe if we judge it by our own standard of living. We must exercise our historical imagination if we are to appreciate the conditions of early modern European society.

Economic Life

There was no typical sixteenth-century European. Travelers' accounts and ambassadors' reports indicate that contemporaries were constantly surprised by the habits and possessions of other Europeans. Language, custom, geography, and material conditions separated peoples in one place from those in another. Contrasts between social groups were more striking still. A Muscovite boyar had more in common with an English nobleman than either had with his country's peasants. A Spanish goldsmith and a German brass maker lived remarkably similar lives when compared to that of a shepherd anywhere in Europe. No matter how carefully historians attempt to distinguish between country and town life, between social or occupational groups, or between men and women, they are still smoothing out edges that are very rough, still turning individuals into aggregates, still sacrificing the particular for the general. No French peasant family ever had 3.5 children even if, on average, they all did. There was no typical sixteenth-century European.

But there were experiences that most Europeans shared and common structures through which their activities were channeled that separated them from their predecessors and their successors. There was a distinctive sixteenth-century experience that we can easily discern and that they could dimly perceive. Much of it was a natural progression in which one generation improved upon the situation of another. Agriculture increased: more land was cleared, more crops were grown, and better tools were crafted. Some of the experience was natural regression. Irreplaceable resources were lost: more trees were felled, more soil was eroded, and more fresh water was polluted. But some of what was distinctive about sixteenth-century life resulted from dynamic changes in economic and social conditions. The century-long population explosion and increase in commodity prices fundamentally altered people's lives. Not since the Black Death had Europe experienced so thorough a transformation in its economic development and its social organization. Change and reactions to change became dominant themes of everyday life.

Rural Life

In the early modern era, as much as 90 percent of the European population lived on farms or in small towns in which farming was the principal occupation. Villages were small and relatively isolated, even in densely populated regions such as Italy and the Low Countries. They might range in size from 100 families, as was common in France and Spain, to fewer than 20 families, which was the average size of Hungarian villages. The villages, large or small, prosperous or poor, were the bedrock of the sixteenth-century state. A surplus peasant population fed the insatiable appetite of towns for laborers and of crowns for soldiers. The manor, the parish, and the rural administrative district were the institutional infrastructures of Europe. Each organized the peasantry for its own purposes. Manorial rents supported the lifestyle of the nobility; parish tithes supported the works of the Church; local taxes supported the power of the state. Rents, tithes, and taxes easily absorbed more than half of the wealth produced by the land. From the remaining half, the peasants had to make provisions for their present and their future.

To survive, the village community had to be self-sufficient. In good times there was enough to eat and some to save for the future. Hard times meant hunger and starvation. Both conditions were accepted as part of the natural order, and both occurred regularly. One in every three harvests was bad; one in every five was disastrous. Bad harvests came in succession. Depending upon the soil and crop, between one-fifth and one-half of the grain harvested had to be saved as seed for the next planting season. When hunger was worst, people faced the agonizing choice of eating or saving their seed corn.

The Sixteenth-Century Household. Hunger and cold were the constant companions of the average European. In Scandinavia and Muscovy, winter posed as great a threat to survival as did starvation. There the stove and garments made from animal fur were essential requirements, as were the hearth and the woolen tunic in the south. Everywhere in Europe, homes were inadequate shelter against the cold and damp. Most were built of wood and roofed in thatch. Inside walls were patched with dried mud and sometimes covered with bark or animal skins. Windows were few and narrow. Piled leaves or straw, which could easily be replaced, covered the ground and acted as insulation. The typical house was one long room with a stone hearth at the end. The hearth provided both heat and light and belched forth soot and smoke through a brick chimney.

This picture, painted in 1530, shows farmworkers threshing grain. The figure at the door seems to be an overseer. He has just sold a sack of grain, indicating the transition from a system of self-sufficient manors to a market economy.

People had relatively few household possessions. The essential piece of furniture was the wooden chest, which was used for storage. A typical family could keep all of its belongings in the chest, which could then be buried or carried away in times of danger. The chest had other uses as well. Its flat top served as a table or bench or as a sideboard on which food could be placed. Tables and stools were becoming more common during the sixteenth century, though chairs were still a great luxury. Most domestic activities, of which cooking, eating, and sleeping were dominant, took place close to the ground, and squatting, kneeling, and sitting were the usual postures of family members. In areas in which spinning, weaving, and other domestic skills were an important part of the family's economy, a long bench was propped against the wall, usually beneath a window. Bedsteads were also becoming more common as the century wore on. They raised the straw mattresses off the ground, keeping them warmer and drier. All other family possessions related to food production. Iron spits and pots, or at least metal rings and clamps for wooden ones, were treasured goods that were passed from generation to generation. Most other implements were wooden. Long-handled spoons; boards known as trenchers, which were used for cutting and eating; and one large cup and bowl were the basic stock of the kitchen. The family ate from the long trencher and passed the bowl and cup. Knives were essential farm tools that doubled for kitchen and mealtime duty, but forks were still a curiosity.

The scale of life was small, and its pace was controlled by the limits that nature imposed. It was a civilization of daylight—up at dawn, asleep at dusk; long working hours in summer, short ones in winter. For most people, the world was bounded by the distance that could be traveled on foot. Those who stayed all their lives in their rural villages may never have seen more than a hundred other people at once or have heard any noise louder than a human voice and terrifying thunder. Their wisdom—hard won and carefully preserved—was of the practical experience necessary

LIVING BY ONE'S WITS

The Life of Lazarillo des Tormes (1554) is among the first modern novels, one of a variety of sixteenth-century Spanish stories that are called picaresque after the wandering beggars that are their heroes. Although the picaresque novel was a fictional account, much of the descriptive detail accurately portrays the social conditions for the vast majority of the Spanish population in the so-called Golden Age.

WE BEGAN OUR JOURNEY, and in a few days he taught me thieves' jargon, and when he saw me to be of a good wit, was well pleased, and used to say: "Gold or silver I cannot give thee, but I will show thee many pointers about life." And it was so; for after God this man gave me my life, and although blind lighted and guided me in the career of living.

He used to carry bread and everything else in a linen sack which closed at the mouth with an iron ring and a padlock and key, and when he put things in and took them out, it was with so much attention, so well counted, that the whole world wouldn't have been equal to making it a crumb less. But I would take what stingy bit he gave me, and finish it in less than two mouthfuls. After he had fastened the lock and stopped worrying about it, thinking me to be engaged in other things, by a little seam, which I unsewed and sewed up again many times in the side of the sack, I used to bleed the miserly sack, taking out bread—not measured quantities but good pieces—and slices of bacon and sausage; and thus would seek a convenient time to make good the devilish state of want which the wicked blind man left me in.

When we ate he used to put a little jug of wine near him. I would quickly seize it and give it a couple of silent kisses and return it to its place; but this plan didn't work long, for he noticed the deficiency in his draughts, and in order to keep his wine safe, he never after let go the jug, but kept hold of the handle. But there is no lode-stone that draws things to it so strongly as I with a long rye straw, which I had prepared for that purpose, and placing which in the mouth of the jug, I would suck up the wine to a fare-ye-well. But the villain was so clever that I think he heard me; and from then on he changed procedure and set his jug between his legs and covered it with his hand, and thus drank secure.

We were at Escalona, town of the Duke of that ilk, in an inn, and he gave me a piece of sausage to roast. When he had basted the sausage and eaten the basting, he took a maravedi from his purse and bade me fetch wine from the tavern. The devil put the occasion before my eyes, which, as the saying is, makes the thief; and it was this: there lay by the fire a small turnip, rather long and bad, and which must have been thrown there because it was not fit for the stew. And as nobody was there at the time but him and me alone, as I had an appetite whetted by having got the toothsome odour of the sausage inside me (the only part, as I knew, that I had to enjoy myself with), not considering what might follow, all fear set aside in order to comply with desire—while the blind man was taking the money out of his purse, I took the sausage, and quickly put the above-mentioned turnip on the spit, which my master grasped, when he had given me the money for the wine, and began to turn before the fire, trying to roast what through its demerit had escaped being boiled. I went for the wine, and on the way did not delay in despatching the sausage, and when I came back I found the sinner of a blind man holding the turnip ready between two slices of bread, for he had not yet recognized it, because he had not tried it with his hand. When he took the slices of bread and bit into them, thinking to get part of the sausage too, he found himself chilled by the chilly turnip.

From *Lazarillo des Tormes.*

to survive the struggle with nature. That was the most important legacy that parents left their children.

Reliance on Agriculture. Peasant life centered on agriculture. Technology and technique varied little across the continent, but there were significant differences depending upon climate and soil. The lives of those who grew crops contrasted with the experiences of those who raised animals. Across the great plain, the breadbasket that stretched from the Low Countries to Poland-Lithuania, the most common form of crop growing was still the three-field rotation system. In that method, winter crops such as wheat or rye were planted in one field; spring crops such as barley, peas, or beans were planted in another; and the third field was left fallow. More than 80 percent of what was grown on the farm was consumed on the farm. In most parts of Europe, wheat was a luxury crop, sold at market rather than eaten at home. Wheat bread was prized for its taste, texture, and white color. Rye and barley were the staples for peasants. Those grains were cheaper to grow, had higher yields, and could be brewed as well as baked. Most of the grain was baked into the coarse black bread that was the monotonous fare of the peasant diet. Two to three pounds a day for an adult male was an average allotment when grain was readily available. Beer and gruels of grain and skimmed milk or water flavored with fruit juice supplemented peasant fare. In one form or another, grain provided more than 75 percent of the calories in a typical diet.

An illustration for the month of December from a sixteenth-century Book of Hours *shows pig-killing and baking. The loaves were prepared in individual homes and baked in communal ovens.*

The warm climate and dry weather of Mediterranean Europe favored a two-crop rotation system. With less water and stronger sunlight, half the land had to be left fallow each year to restore its nutrients. There fruit, especially grapes and olives, was an essential supplement to diet. With smaller cereal crops, wine replaced beer as a nutritious beverage. The fermentation of grapes and grain into wine and beer also provided convenient ways of storing foodstuffs, a constant problem during the winter and early spring. Wine and olive oil were also luxury products and were most commonly exchanged for meat, which was less plentiful on southern European farms.

Animal husbandry was the main occupation in the third agricultural area of Europe, the mountainous and hilly regions. Sheep were the most common animal that Europeans raised. Sheep provided the raw material for almost all clothing, their skins were used for parchment and as window coverings, and they were a ready source of inexpensive meat. They were bred in hundreds of thousands, migrating across large areas of grazing land, especially in western Europe, where their wool was the main export of both England and Spain. Pigs were domestic animals prevalent in woodland settlements. They foraged for food and were kept, like poultry, for slaughter. Cattle, on the other hand, were essential farm animals. "The fundamentals of the home," wrote the Spanish poet Luis de Leon (1527–1591), "are the woman and the ox, the ox to plow and the woman to manage things." In the dairying areas of Europe, cattle produced milk, cheese, and butter; in Hungary and Bohemia, the great breeding center of the continent, they were raised for export; and most everywhere else they were used as beasts of burden.

Because agriculture was the principal occupation of Europeans, land was the principal resource. Most land was owned, not by those who worked it, but by lords who let it out in various ways. The land was still divided into manors, and the manor lord, or seigneur, was still responsible for maintaining order, administering justice, and arbitrating disputes. Although the personal bonds between lords and tenants were gradually loosening, political and economic ties were as strong as ever. Lords were not necessarily individual members of the nobility; in fact, they were more commonly the Church or the State. In western Europe, peasants generally owned between a third and a half of the land they worked, while eastern European peasants owned little if any land. But by the sixteenth century, almost all peasants enjoyed security of tenure on the land they worked. In return for various forms of rents, they used the land as they saw fit and could hand it down to their children. Rents were only occasionally paid in coin, although money rents became more common as the century progressed. More frequently, the lord received a fixed proportion of the yield of the land or received labor from the peasant. Labor service was being replaced by monetary payments in northern and western Europe, but it continued in the east, where it was known as the *robot*. German and Hungarian peasants normally owed two or three days' labor on the lord's estate each week, while Polish peasants might owe as many as four days. Labor service tied the peasants to the land they worked. Eastern European peasants were less mobile than peasants in the west, and as a result towns were fewer and smaller in the east.

Although the land in each village was set out in large fields so that crops could be rotated, families owned their own pieces within the field, usually in scattered strips that they plowed, manured, and planted individually. There were also large common fields used as pasture, as well as common woodlands where animals foraged, fuel was gathered, and game hunted. Even the common fields and woodlands were not shared equally. Those who held the most land in the fields possessed greater shares of the commons. Villagers disputed frequently over rights to sticks and branches of trees and over the number of sheep or cows that could be grazed in the meadows, especially when resources were scarce.

Farm work was ceaseless toil. Six or seven times a year farmers tilled the fields to spread animal manure below the surface of the soil. While most villages possessed metal plows, the team of draught animals was the single essential component for farming. The births of foals and calves were more celebrated events than the births of children; the death of an ox or horse was a catastrophe that could drive a family into debt or from the land entirely. Calamities lurked everywhere, from rain and drought to locusts and crows. Most farms could support only one family at subsistence level, and excess sons and daughters had to fend for themselves, either through marriage in the village or by migration to a town.

Town Life

In the country, men and women worked to the natural rhythm of the day: up at the cock's crow, at work in the cooler hours, at rest in the hotter ones. Rain and cold kept them idle; sunlight kept them busy. Each season brought its own activity. In the town the bell tolled every hour. In the summer the laborers gathered at the town gates at four in the morning, in the winter at seven. The bell signaled the time for morning and afternoon meals as well as the hour to lay down tools and return home. Wages were paid for hours worked: 7 in winter, as many as 16 in June and July.

The Heart of Commerce. In all towns there was an official guild structure that organized and regulated labor. Rules laid down the requirements for training, the standards for quality, and the conditions for exchange. Only those officially sanctioned could work in trades, and each trade could perform only specified tasks. In the German town of Nuremberg, a sword maker could not make knives nor could a pin maker make thimbles. Specialization went even further in London, Paris, and other large cities.

While the life of the peasant community turned on self-sufficiency, that of the town turned on interdependence. Exchange was the medium that transformed labor and skill into food and shelter. The town was one large marketplace in which the circulation of goods dictated the survival of the residents. Men and women in towns worked as hard as did those on farms, but town dwellers received a more varied and more comfortable life in return. However, that did not mean that hunger and hardship were unknown in towns. Urban poverty was endemic and grew worse as the century wore on. In most towns, as much as a quarter of the entire population might be destitute, living from casual day labor, charity, or crime. But even for those people, food was more readily available in greater varieties than in the countryside, and the institutional network of support for the poor and homeless was stronger. In Lyon, the overseers of the poor distributed a daily ration of a pound and a half of bread, more than half of what a farm laborer would consume. The urban poor more often fell victim to disease than to starvation.

In the early sixteenth century, the port city of Antwerp became Europe's leading commercial center. The city's rulers adopted tolerant policies that encouraged economic activity, including international trade with Spanish and Portuguese territories in the Americas. The bustling crowd in the marketplace reflects the city's status as a center of commerce.

Grain Supply and Trade in Sixteenth-Century Europe. There were two distinct trading routes in northern Europe centering on the Baltic Sea and in southern Europe centering on the Mediterranean Sea.

Towns were distinguished by the variety of occupations that existed within them. The preparation and exchange of food dominated small market towns. Peasants would bring in their finest produce for sale and exchange it for vital manufactured goods such as iron spits and pots for cooking or metal and leather tools for farm work. In smaller towns, there was as much barter as sale; in larger places, money was exchanged for commodities. Women dominated the food trades in most market towns, trading, buying, and selling in the shop fronts that occupied the bottom story of their houses. Because of their skills in food preparation, they were better able to obtain the best prices and advantageously display the best goods. In the small towns, men divided their time between traditional agricultural pursuits—there were always garden plots and even substantial fields attached to towns—and manufacturing. Half of the households in the Spanish town of Ciudad Real derived their income entirely from farming. Almost every town made and distributed to the surrounding area some special product that drew to the town the wealth of the countryside.

The Work Force. In larger towns, the specialization of labor was more intense and wage earning more essential. Large traders dominated the major occupations such as baking, brewing, and cloth manufac-

Van Schwanerburg (1537–1614), The Spinners. *Workers spinning and weaving wool. Labor in large towns was often specialized into occupations like baking, brewing, and cloth manufacture.*

ture, leaving distribution in the hands of the family economy, where there might still be a significant element of bartering. Piecework handicrafts became the staple for less prosperous town families, who prepared raw materials for the large manufacturers or finished products before their sale. Occupations were usually organized geographically, with metal- or glassworking taking place in one quarter of the town, brewing or baking in another. There was a strong family and kin network to the occupations, as each craft required long years of technical training, which was handed down from parents to children.

In large towns there were also specialized trades performed by women. There were 55 midwives in Nuremberg in the middle of the sixteenth century, and a board of women chosen from among the leading families of the town supervised their work. Nursing the sick was a logical extension of those services and also appears to have been an exclusively female occupation. So, too, was prostitution, which was an officially sanctioned occupation in most large towns in the early modern era. There were town brothels, situated in specified districts, subject to taxation and government control. Public bathhouses, which employed skilled women workers, served as unofficial brothels for the upper ranks of urban society. They too were regulated, especially after the first great epidemic of venereal disease in the early sixteenth century.

Most town dwellers, however, lived by unskilled labor. The most lucrative occupations were strictly controlled, so those who flocked to towns in search of employment usually hired themselves out as day laborers, hauling and lifting goods onto carts or boats, stacking materials at building sites, or delivering water and food. After the first decades of the century, the supply of laborers exceeded the amount of work to occupy them and town authorities were constantly attempting to expel them. The most fortunate might succeed in becoming servants.

Domestic service was a critical source of household labor. Even families on the margins of subsistence employed servants to undertake the innumerable household tasks, which allowed parents to pursue their primary occupations. Everything was done by hand and on foot, and extra pairs of each were essential. In Münster at mid-century, there were 400 servants for 1000 households. Domestics were not apprentices, though they might aspire to become apprentices to the trade followed in the family with whom they lived. If they had kinship bonds in the town, apprenticeship was a likely outcome. But more commonly, domestics remained household servants, frequently changing employers in hope of more comfortable housing and better food. Their lives were always precarious. Any number of circumstances, from the death of their employer to allegations of misconduct, could cost them their places. Male servants were scapegoats for missing household items; female servants were vulnerable to sexual assaults.

Just as towns grew by the influx of surplus rural population, they sustained themselves by the import of surplus agricultural production. Most towns owned tracts of land, which they leased to peasants or farmed by hired labor. The town of Nuremberg controlled 25 square miles of forest and farmlands, while the region around Toledo was inhabited by thousands of peasants who paid taxes and rents to city landlords. Agriculture was the fourth largest occupation in the Spanish city of Barcelona, which had a population of more than 35,000 in the early sixteenth century. All towns had municipal storehouses of grain to preserve their inhabitants from famine during harvest failures. Grain prices were strictly regulated and frequently subsidized to ensure that laborers were adequately fed. The diet of even a casual laborer would have been envied by an average peasant. Male grape pickers in Stuttgart received meat, soup, vegetables, wine, and beer; females received soup, vegetables, milk, and bread. In addition they received their wages. It is hardly surprising that towns were enclosed by thick walls and defended by armed guards.

Economic Change

Over the course of the sixteenth century, the European population increased by about a third, with much of the growth taking place in the first 50 years. Rough estimates suggest the rise to have been from about 80 to 105 million. Patterns of growth varied by region. The population of the eastern part of Europe seems to have increased more steadily across the century, while western Europe experienced a population explosion in the early decades. The population of France may have doubled between 1450 and 1550, from 10 to 20 million. The population of England nearly doubled between 1500 and 1600, from more than 2 million to more than 4 million. Castile, the largest region in Spain, grew 50 percent in 50 years. Europe had finally recovered from the devastation of the Black Death, and by 1600 its population was greater than it had ever been. Demographic growth was even more dramatic in the cities. In 1500, only four cities had populations greater than 100,000; in 1600, there were eight. Naples grew from 150,000 to 280,000, and both Paris and London to more than 200,000 inhabitants. Fifteen large cities more than doubled their populations, with London experiencing a phenomenal 400 percent increase.

The rise in population dramatically affected the lives of ordinary Europeans. In the early part of the century, the first phase of growth brought prosperity. The land was still not farmed to capacity, and extra hands meant increased productivity. As there was uncultivated land that could be plowed, convenient room for new housing, and enough commons and woodlands to be shared, the population increase was a welcome development. Even when rural communities began to reach their natural limits as people's needs pressed against nature's resources, opportunity still existed in the burgeoning towns and cities. At first the cycle was beneficial. Surplus on the farms led to economic growth in the towns. Growth in the towns meant more opportunities for those on the farms. More food supported more workers, and more workers produced more goods and services, which were exchanged for more food.

The first waves of migrants to the towns found opportunity everywhere. Even the most lucrative textile and provisioning trades were recruiting new members, and apprenticeships were easy to find. A shortage of casual labor kept wages at a decent rate. Successful migrants encouraged kin from their villages to move to the towns and sponsored their start in trade or service. For a while, rural families did not have to make elaborate preparations to provide for their younger sons and daughters: they could be sent to the towns. Instead of saving every extra penny to give their children a start in life, farmers could purchase some luxury goods or expand their landholdings.

Such an opportunity could not last. With more mouths to feed, more crops had to be planted. Since the most productive land was already under the plow, new fields were carved from less fertile areas. In some villages, land was taken from the common waste, the woodlands or scrublands that were used for animal forage and domestic fuel. The land was less suitable for crops, and it became unavailable for other important uses. In Spain, for example, the land that was reclaimed came at the expense of sheep grazing, which reduced the size of the flocks of sheep and damaged both the domestic and the foreign wool trade. It also reduced the amount of fertilizer available for enriching the soil. In England and the Low Countries, large drainage projects were undertaken to reclaim land for crops. In the east, so-called forest colonies sprang up, clearing space in the midst of woodlands for new farms. Colonization of areas in Poland-Lithuania, Muscovy, and the Ukraine can be compared to the overseas ventures of Spain and Portugal.

By midcentury there was a natural limit to the number of workers who could profitably engage in any given trade, and those safely in were pulling the ladder up behind them. Town governments came under pressure from the guilds to enforce apprenticeship requirements that had been relaxed during the period of growth. Guilds raised fees for new entrants and designated only a small number of places where their goods could be purchased. Most apprenticeships were limited to patrimony: one son for each full member. Such restrictions meant that newly arrived immigrants could enter only into the less profitable small crafts.

As workers continued to flood into the towns, real wages began to fall, not only among the unskilled but throughout the work force. A black market in labor developed to take advantage of the surplus population. In terms of purchasing power, the wages of a craftsman in the building trade in England fell by one-half during the sixteenth century. A French stonemason, a highly paid skilled laborer, could buy 33 pounds of bread with his daily wage in 1480; by 1550 he could buy fewer than 10. Peasants in the French region of Languedoc who hired out for farm labor lost 56 percent of their purchasing power during the century. Only reapers, who were the physically strongest agricultural laborers, appear to have kept pace with inflation; grape pickers, among the least skilled, endured declines of up to 300 or 400 percent.

Population Density in Europe, ca. 1600. Most people lived in the western part of the continent on its coastal areas.

The fall in real wages took place against a backdrop of inflation that has come to be called the Price Revolution. Between 1500 and 1650, cereal prices increased between five- and sixfold, manufactured goods between two- and threefold. Most of the rapid increase came in the second half of the sixteenth century, a result of both population growth and the import of precious metals from the New World. Sixteenth-century governments understood little about the relationship between money supply and prices. Gold and silver from America flooded the international economy, raising commodity prices. As prices rose so did the deficits of the state, which was the largest purchaser of both agricultural and manufactured goods. With huge deficits, states began to devalue their coins in the mistaken belief that this would lower their debt. But debased coinage resulted in still higher prices, and higher prices resulted in greater debt. The Price Revolution was felt throughout the Continent and played havoc with government finances, international trade, and the lives of ordinary people.

A 500 percent inflation in agricultural products over a century is not much by modern standards. Compounded, the rate averages less than 2 percent a year. But the Price Revolution did not take place in a modern society or within a modern market economy. In the sixteenth century, that level of rising prices disrupted everything. In the Spanish town of Seville, almost all buildings were rented on 99-year leases to the families who lived and worked in them. That was a fairly common practice throughout Europe. It meant that a landlord who rented a butcher shop and living quarters in 1501 could not raise the rent until 1600! Similarly, lords frequently held the right to purchase agricultural produce at specified prices. That system, similar to today's commodity market, helped both lords and peasants plan ahead. It assured the lord a steady supply and the peasant a steady market. But it assumed steady prices. Until the middle of the seventeenth century, the king of England had the right to purchase wheat at prices set 300 years earlier.

Thus an enduring increase in prices created profound social dislocation. Some people became destitute; others became rich beyond their dreams. The towns were particularly hard hit, for they exchanged manufactured goods for food and thus suffered when grain prices rose faster than those of other commodities. Landholders who derived their income from rents were squeezed; those who received payment in kind reaped a windfall of more valuable agricultural goods. Peasants were largely protected from the rise in food prices, but they were not insulated from its consequences. As long as they consumed what they raised, the nominal value of commodities was of no great matter. But if some part of their subsistence had to be obtained by labor, they were in grave peril.

There was now an enormous incentive to produce a surplus for market and to begin to specialize in particular grains that were in high demand. Every small scrap of land that individual peasant families could

Joris Hoefnagel, Wedding Feast at Bermondsey *(ca. 1590). In this painting of an Elizabethan wedding feast, as depicted by the Flemish painter Joris Hoefnagel, bakers and violinists usher in the wedding party to the feast. In the background in the left of the picture is the imposing Tower of London.*

The new money economy inspired this satirical portrait by Quentin Massys. It shows a moneylender counting his receipts while his wife is distracted from her Bible by the pile of coins. Many such merchants won fame and power and even titles.

bring under cultivation would now yield foodstuffs that could be exchanged for manufactured luxury goods. The tendency for all peasants to hold roughly equivalent amounts of land abruptly ceased. The fortunate could become prosperous by selling their surplus. The unfortunate found ready purchasers for their strips and common rights. Villagers began to be divided into those who held large amounts of land and sold their surplus at a profit and those who held small amounts of land and hired out as laborers to their more fortunate neighbors.

The beneficial cycle now turned vicious. Those who had sold out and left the land looking for prosperity in the towns were forced to return to the land as agrarian laborers. In western Europe, they became the landless poor, seasonal migrants without the safety net of rooted communal life. In eastern Europe, labor service enriched the landed nobility, who were able to sell stores of grain in the export market. They used the law to tie the peasants to the land in order to ensure that grain would be cultivated for the market. Poland-Lithuania became a major supplier of cereals to northern Europe, and Gdansk became the most important agricultural seaport in the world. But agricultural surplus from the east could not make up for the great shortfall in the west. By the beginning of the seventeenth century, the western European states faced a crisis of subsistence. Everyone was hungry; many were starving.

SOCIAL LIFE

Social organization combines elements of tradition, belief, and function, but the elements are so fused together that it is impossible to determine where one ends and the other begins. Society is a human construct, subject to the strengths and frailties of its creators. The basic assumption of sixteenth-century European society was inequality, and its basic form of social organization was stratification. The group, rather than the individual, was the predominant unit in society. The first level of the social order was the family and the household; then came the village or town community; and finally the gradations of ranks and orders of society at large. Elaborate rituals helped define membership in each of the groups, from the marriage ceremony to the initiation rites of citizens and to the processions and ceremonial displays of the nobility. All stressed the significance of the rights and obligations of different levels of society. Each group had its own place in the social order and each performed its own essential function. Society was the sum of its parts.

The traditional social organization was severely tested over the course of the early modern period. Economic change reshaped ideas of mobility and drew sharper distinctions between rural and urban life. The growth of towns and their domination of the countryside around them challenged beliefs about the primacy of agricultural production and the subordinate nature of trade and commerce. The rise to new wealth and prominence of some social groups challenged traditional elites' hold on power and prestige. The transformation of landholding patterns in the villages challenged the stability of rural communities. The rising numbers of both urban and rural poor challenged the institutions of charitable relief and posed the threat of crime and disorder. Eventually those developments led to bloody confrontations between social groups.

Social Constructs

Hierarchy was the dominant principle of social organization in the early modern era. Hierarchy existed at every level, from the basic distinction between lords and commoners to the fastidious complexity of the ranks of the nobility. The hierarchy of masters, journeymen, and apprentices dominated trades; trades themselves existed in a hierarchy. In the hierarchy of civic government, each official held a place in an ascending order, up to the elite of councillors and mayors. On the land was the hierarchy of freeholder, laborer, and leaseholder among the peasants. The family itself was hierarchically organized, with the wife subordinate to her husband, the children to their parents, and the apprentices and servants to their master and mistress. "All things observe degree, priority and place," Shakespeare wrote of both natural and human order in *Troilus and Cressida* (1601–1602). "Take but degree away, untune that string, and hark what discord follows."

Hierarchy was a principle of orderliness that helped govern social relations. It is tempting to approach hierarchy through wealth, to divide groups and individuals into rich and poor. Many gradations in the sixteenth-century social hierarchy corresponded to levels of wealth, but they were threshold levels rather than absolute levels. Lords, by definition, did not engage in manual labor. They were wealthier than peasants. The governing elites of towns needed sufficient wealth to neglect their own affairs while occupied in public service. They were wealthier than wage earners. But the ranks of the nobility cannot be explained by gradations of wealth among nobles, and there were many rich town dwellers who were not members of the governing elite.

Status, rather than wealth, determined the social hierarchy. It conferred privileges and exacted responsibilities according to rank. Status was everywhere apparent. It was confirmed in social conventions such as bowing and hat doffing. In towns and cities the clothing that people were allowed to wear—even the foods that they were allowed to eat—reflected status. Status was signified in titles: not just in the ranks of the nobility or between nobles and commoners, but even in ordinary communities masters and mistresses, goodmen and goodwives, squires and ladies, adopted the English equivalents of European titles. The acceptance of status was an everyday, uncomplicated, unreflective act, similar to stopping at a red light. Inequality was a fact of European social life that was as unquestioned as it was unquestionable.

Images that people used to describe both the natural world and their social world reinforced the functional

An illumination from a sixteenth-century manuscript shows a prosperous Venetian merchant entertaining visitors at his mainland country estate.

nature of hierarchy. The first, and most elaborate image, was that of the Great Chain of Being. The Great Chain was a description of the universe in which everything had a place, from God at the top of the chain to inanimate objects like rocks at the bottom. Complex accounts of the chain listed the seven orders of angels, the multiple ranks of humans, even the degrees of animals and plants, from which lions emerged as kings of the jungle. Spanish botanists were dispatched to the New World to help identify the unknown flora and fauna in terms of their places in the chain. Native Americans were first thought to be the lost tribes of Israel, as they were the only humans missing from traditional accounts of the chain. For ordinary people, the Great Chain of Being expressed the belief that all life was interconnected, that every link was a part of a divinely ordered universe and was as necessary as every other.

The second metaphor used to describe society stressed the notion of interdependency even more strongly. It was the image of the Body Politic. In the Body Politic, the head ruled, the arms protected, the stomach nourished, and the feet labored. The image described a small community as well as a large state. In the state, the king was the head, the Church the soul, the nobles the arms, the artisans the hands, and the peasants the feet. Each performed its own function, and each function was essential to the health of the body. The Body Politic was an organic unity of separate parts working harmoniously for a common goal. Like the Great Chain of Being, it was a profoundly conservative concept of social organization. Taken literally, it precluded the idea of social mobility, of people rising or falling from one group to another.

Social Structure

The Great Chain of Being and the Body Politic were static concepts of social organization. But in the early modern era, European society was in a state of dynamic change. Fundamentally, all European societies were divided into nobles and commoners. That basic distinction existed throughout the Continent, although relationships between the two orders differed from place to place.

The Nobles. Nobility was a legal status that conferred certain privileges upon its holders. The first was rank and title, a well-defined place at the top of the social order that was passed from one generation to the next. Each rank had its own privileges and each was clearly demarcated from the next by behavior, dress, and title. The escutcheon—the coat of arms—was a universally recognized symbol of rank and family connection. The coat of arms was woven in garments; emblazoned on windows, carriages, and household goods; and displayed on banners during formal processions. Although there were various systems of title in use across the Continent and the nobility of one state could not claim noble privileges in another state, the hierarchy of prince, duke, earl, count, and baron was roughly standard.

Because rulers conferred the titles on individuals, elevating some to higher ranks and others from commoner to noble, the nobility was a political order as well as a social one. Political privileges were among the nobility's most important attributes. In many countries, the highest offices of the state and the military were reserved for members of the nobility. In Poland, for example, all offices were held by noblemen. It was a privilege that could work both ways, either restricting officeholders to those already ennobled or, as in town councils in France and Spain, ennobling those who achieved certain offices. The nobility was also granted rights of political participation in the deliberative bodies of the state. In England, the peerage was defined as all those who were summoned to the House of Lords. In most parts of central Europe, the nobility alone composed the diets that advised the monarch. In the empire, the rank of imperial free knights allowed the nobility to separate itself entirely from the jurisdiction of towns or individual principalities.

Finally, members of the nobility held economic privileges, a result both of their rank and of their role as lords on the lands they owned. In almost every state, the nobility was exempt from most taxation. That was an area in which the interests of the nobles conflicted directly with those of the ruler. The larger the number of tax exemptions for the nobility, the stronger was its power in relation to the monarch. Tax exemptions of the nobility were most extensive in eastern and central Europe. There the crowns were elective rather than hereditary, allowing the nobles to bargain their support. The Polish nobility was exempt from the salt tax, the alcohol tax, and all internal tolls and customs. As Polish agriculture developed into an export industry, exemption from tolls gave the nobility a competitive advantage over merchants in the marketing of goods. The Hungarian nobility was exempt from all direct taxes, including the land tax. The nobility in western

Europe enjoyed fewer immunities but not necessarily less valuable ones. French nobles were exempt from the taille, Spanish nobles from the hearth tax. As French nobles had vast incomes and Spanish nobles' houses had many hearths, both were important exclusions. The English nobility enjoyed no exemptions from direct taxation, but then there was little direct taxation from which to be exempted. The most important English taxes were on exports of wool and cloth, and thus fell on merchants rather than landholders.

Privileges implied obligations. Initially the nobility was the warrior caste of the state and its primary obligations were to raise, equip, and lead troops into battle. Much of the great wealth that nobles possessed was at the service of the ruler during times of war, and war was a perpetual activity. By the sixteenth century, the military needs of the state had far surpassed the military power of its nobility. Warfare had become a national enterprise that required central coordination. Nobles became administrators as much as warriors, though it is fair to say that many did both. The French nobility came to be divided into the nobility of the sword and the nobility of the robe—that is, warriors and officeholders. The old military nobility could hardly understand the new service nobility. "I have continually been astounded," one of them remarked, "that so many young men could thus amuse themselves in a law court, since ordinarily youthful blood is boiling." A glorious battlefield death was still an ideal for most of Europe's noblemen.

Nobles also had the obligation of governing at both the national and the local level. At the discretion of the ruler, they could be called to engage in any necessary occupation, no matter how disruptive to their economic or family affairs. On their land, they administered their estates and settled the disputes of their tenants. In times of want they were expected to provide for the needy, in times of dearth for the hungry. There was an obligation of good lordship that was implicitly understood, if not always explicitly carried out, between lord and peasant.

Town Elite and Gentry. The principal distinction in sixteenth-century society was between lord and commoners, but it was not the only one. In both town and countryside a new social group was emerging. It had neither the legal nor the social privileges of nobility, but it performed many of the same functions. Over

Georges de La Tour, The Fortune Teller. *In the painting, which serves as a warning to the naive about the wicked ways of the world, a fashionably dressed young innocent is drawn into the snare of the wily fortune teller.*

the course of the century the group carved out a place that was clearly distinct from that of the commoners, even if it was not clearly identical to the lords. It was most evident in the towns, for the towns remained a separate unit of social organization in most states. Towns enjoyed many of the same political and economic privileges as the nobility. In many states, the towns sent representatives to meet with the nobles and the king and were the most important part of national deliberative assemblies such as the English Parliament, the French Estates, or the Spanish Cortes. Towns were granted legal rights to govern their own citizens, to engage in trade, and to defend themselves by raising and storing arms. Although they paid a large share of most taxes, towns also received large tax concessions.

Yet, as individuals, members of the town elite held no special status in society at large. Some were among the richest people in the state—great bankers and merchants who were wealthier than dukes—but they had to devise their own systems of honor and prestige. In Venice, the *Book of Gold* distinguished the local elite from the ranks of ordinary citizens. Members of the "Old Families," who monopolized the highest civic offices, ruled Nuremberg. In France and Spain, some of the highest officers of leading towns were granted noble status, such as the "honored citizens" of Barcelona who were ennobled by King Ferdinand of Aragon. German burghers, as prosperous townsmen were called, remained caught in a state between noble and common, despised from above because they worked with their hands, envied from below for their wealth and comfort. In Münster, many withdrew from urban affairs and sought the privileges of the lower nobility.

Marinus van Reymerswaele, The Two Tax Gatherers. *The figure on the left is a city treasurer who is posting in the book an account of the city's revenues from taxes on wine, beer, fish, and other commodities. The painting is probably a satirical composition intended to expose the iniquity of covetousness, usury, or extortion.*

In rural society, the transformation of agricultural holdings in many places also created a group that fit uncomfortably between lords and commoners. The accumulation of larger and larger estates through purchase from the nobility, the state, or the Church made lords—in the sense of landowners with tenants—out of many who were not lords in rank. They received rents and dues from their tenants, administered their estates, and preserved the so-called moral economy that sustained the peasants during hard times. In England, the group came to be known as the gentry, and there were parallel groups in Spain, France, and the empire. The gentry aspired to the privileges of the nobility. In England, members of the gentry had the right to have a coat of arms and could be knighted. But knighthoods were not hereditary and did not confer membership in the House of Lords. In Spain, the caballeros and hidalgos gained noble privileges but were still of lower status than the grandees. The gentry aped the habits of the nobility, often outdoing nobles in lavish displays of wealth and spending.

Social stratification did not only apply to the wealthy groups within European societies. Although it is more difficult to reconstruct the principles upon which rural communities based their complicated systems of status and order, there can be no doubt that systems existed and that they helped create the bonds that tied communities together. In many German villages, a principal distinction was between those who held land in the ancient part of the settlement—the *Esch*—and those who held land in those areas into which the village had expanded. The *Esch* was normally the best land, and thus the distinction was likely to correlate with the relative wealth of the two groups. But interestingly, the holders of the *Esch* were tied to the lord of the estate, while holders of the less desirable lands were free peasants. There freedom to move from place to place was less valued than the right to live in the heart of the village.

Just the opposite set of values prevailed in English villages, where freeholders were in the most enviable position. They led the movements to break up the common fields for planting and were able to initiate legal actions against their lord. They might not have the best lands in the village, but whenever village land was converted to freehold, unfree tenants would go into debt to buy it. Increasingly, French peasants came to own the land that they farmed. They protested against the very title of *villein,* claiming that its older association with serfdom discouraged others from trading with those so labeled. The relationship of free and unfree went even further in Muscovy, where thousands of starving laborers sold themselves into slavery. Perhaps as much as 10 percent of the population of Muscovy accepted their loss of freedom and became domestic slaves of the military and noble orders.

In towns, the order of rank below the elite pertained as much to the kind of work that one performed as it did to the level at which it was undertaken. The critical division in town life was between those who had the freedom of the city—citizens—and those who did not. Citizenship was restricted to membership in certain occupations and was closely regulated. It could be purchased, especially by members of learned professions whose services were becoming vital in the early modern era, but most citizenship was earned by becoming a master in one of the guilds after a long period of apprenticeship and training. Only males could be citizens. In Germany, the feminine equivalent for the word used to denote a male citizen in good standing meant "prostitute"! But women who were married to citizens enjoyed their husbands' privileges, and widows of citizens could pass the privileges to their new husbands when they remarried. In both town and countryside, the privileges and obligations of each social group were the glue that held communities together.

Social Change

In the sixteenth century, social commentators believed that change was transforming the world in which they lived. In 1600, a Spanish observer blamed the rise of the rich commoners for the ills of the world: "They have obtained a particular status, that of a self-made group; and since they belong neither to the rich nor to the poor nor to the middle, they have thrown the state into the confusion we now see it in." An Englishman commenting on the rise of the gentry could give no better definition of its status than to say that a gentleman was one who lived like a gentleman. The challenge that the new nobility of the robe posed to the old nobility of the sword poisoned relations between the two segments of the French ruling elite. The military service class in Muscovy, who were of more use to the Muscovite princes than were the traditional landed nobility, posed an even greater threat to the privileges of the boyars.

The New Rich. Pressures on the ruling elites of European society came from above as well as below. The expansion of the state and the power of the prince frequently came as a result of direct conflict with the nobility. Only in east-central Europe—in Hungary, Bohemia, and Poland-Lithuania, where towns were small and urban elites weak—did the consolidation of the state actually enhance the privileges of the traditional noble orders.

There were many reasons why the traditional European social hierarchy was transformed during the course of the early modern era. In the first place, population increase necessitated an expansion of the ruling orders. With more people to govern, there had to be more governors who could perform the military, political, and social functions of the state. The traditional nobility grew slowly, as titles could be passed to only one son and intermarriage within the group was very high. Second, opportunities to accumulate wealth expanded dramatically with the Price Revolution. Traditionally, wealth was calculated in land and tenants rather than in the possession of liquid assets such as gold and silver. But with the increase in commodity prices, surplus producers could rapidly improve their economic position. What previously might have taken a generation or two of good fortune to amass could now be gathered seemingly overnight. Moreover, state service became a source of unlimited riches. The profits to be made from tax collecting, officeholding, or administering the law could easily surpass those to be made from landholding, especially after the economic downturn at the end of the century. The newly rich clamored for privileges, and many were in a position to lobby rulers effectively for them. Across European society the nobility grew, fed from fortunes made on the land, in trade, and in office.

The New Poor. Social change was equally apparent at the bottom of the social scale, but there it could not be so easily absorbed. The continuous population growth created a group of landless poor who squatted in villages and clogged the streets of towns and cities. Although poverty was not a new development of the early modern era, its growth created new problems. Rough estimates suggest that as many as a quarter of all Europeans were destitute. That was a staggering figure in great cities. There were tens of thousands of destitute people in London or Paris, where, it was observed, "the crowds of poor were so great that one could not pass through the streets."

Traditionally, local communities cared for their poor. Widows, orphans, and the handicapped, who would normally constitute over half the poor in a village or town, were viewed as the "deserving poor," worthy of the care of the community through the Church or through private almsgiving. Catholic communities such as Venice created a system of private charity that paralleled the institutions of the Church. Although Protestant communities took charity out of the control of the church, they were no less concerned about the plight of the deserving poor. In England, a special tax, the poor rate, supported the poor and provided them with subsistence until they remarried or found employment. Perhaps the most elaborate system of all existed in the French town of Lyon where all the poor were registered and given identity cards. Each Sunday they would receive a week's worth of food and money. Young girls were provided with dowries, and young boys were taught crafts. Vagrants from the surrounding countryside were given one week's allotment to enable them to travel on. But Lyon's enlightened system was only for the deserving poor, and as the century progressed it was overwhelmed.

Charity began at home—it was an obligation of the community. But as the sixteenth century progressed, the number of people who lived on the margins of subsistence grew beyond the ability of the local community to care for them. Perhaps more importantly, many of those who now begged for alms fell outside the traditional categories of the deserving poor. In England, they were called the sturdy beggars, men and women capable of working but incapable of finding more than occasional labor. To support themselves and their families, they left their native communities in search of employment and thus forfeited their claims on local charity. Most wound up in the towns and cities, where they slept and begged in the streets. Some disfigured themselves to enhance their abilities as beggars. As strangers they had no claim on local charity; as able-bodied workers they had no claim on local sympathy.

Feeding the Hungry *by Cornelius Buys, 1504. A maidservant is doling out small loaves to the poor and the lame at the door of a wealthy person's home. The poor who flocked to the towns were often forced to rely on charity to survive.*

Poor mothers abandoned their newborn infants on the steps of foundling hospitals or the houses of the rich. It is estimated that 10 percent of all newborn babies in the Spanish city of Valladolid were abandoned.

The problem of crime complicated the problems of poverty and vagrancy. Increasing population and increasing wealth equaled increasing crime; the addition of the poor to the equation aggravated the situation. The poor, destitute outsiders to the community, without visible means of support, were the easiest targets of official retribution. Throughout the century, numerous European states passed vagrancy laws in an effort to alleviate the problem of the wandering poor. In England, the poor were whipped from village to village until they were returned home. The sturdy beggars were branded with the letter *V* on their chests to identify them as vagrants, and therefore as potential criminals. Both Venetian and Dutch vagrants were regularly rounded up for galley service, while vagrants in Hungary were sold into slavery. Physical mutilation was used in an ineffective method of deterrence; thieves had fingers chopped off—which made it impossible for them to perform manual labor, and thus likely to steal again. Sexual offenses were criminalized—especially bastardy, since the birth of illegitimate children placed an immediate burden on the community. Prostitutes, who had long been tolerated and regulated in towns, were now persecuted. Rape increased. Capital punishment was reserved for the worst crimes—murder, incest, and grand larceny being most common—but, not surprisingly, executions were carried out mostly on outsiders to the community, with single women, the poor, and the vagrant being the most frequent victims.

Peasant Revolts

The economic and social changes of the sixteenth century bore serious consequences. Most telling was the upswing of violent confrontations between peasants and their lords. There was more than one difference between rich and poor in sixteenth-century society, but when conflict arose between them the important difference was that the wealthy controlled the means of coercion: the military and the law. Across Europe, and with alarming regularity, peasants took up arms to defend themselves from what they saw as violations of traditional rights and obligations. Peasant revolts were not hunger riots. Although they frequently occurred in periods of want, after bad harvests or marauding armies had impoverished villages, peasant revolts were not desperate attacks against warehouses or grain silos. Nor did those who took part in them form undisciplined mobs. Most revolts chose leaders, drew up petitions of grievances, and organized the rank and file into a semblance of military order. Leaders were literate—usually drawn from the lower clergy or minor gentry rather than from the peasantry—political demands were moderate, and tactics were sophisticated. But peasant revolts so profoundly threatened the social order that they were met with the severest repression. Confronted with the execution of their estate agents, rent strikes, and confiscation of their property, lords responded as if they were at war. Veteran soldiers and trained mercenaries were called out to fight peasant armies composed mostly of raw recruits. The results were horrifying.

Agrarian Changes. It is essential to realize that while peasants revolted against their lords, fundamentally their anger and frustration were products of agrarian changes that could be neither controlled nor understood. As population increased and market production expanded, many of the traditional rights and obligations of lords and peasants became oppressive. One example is that of forest rights. On most estates, the forests surrounding a village belonged to the lord. Commonly the village had its own woodlands in which animals foraged and fuel and building material were available. As the population increased, more farms came into existence. New land was put under the plow, and grain fields pressed up against the forest. There were more animals in the village, and some of them were let loose to consume the young sprouts and saplings. Soon there was not enough food for the wild game that was among the lord's most valuable property. So the game began to feed on the peasants' crops, which were now placed so appetizingly close to the forests. It was a capital crime for a peasant to kill wild game, but peasants couldn't allow the game to consume their crops.

A similar conflict arose over enclosing crop fields. An enclosure was a device—normally a fence or hedge that surrounded an area—to keep a parcel of land separate from the planted strips of land owned by the villagers. The parcel could be used for grazing animals or raising a specialty crop for the market. But an enclosure destroyed the traditional form of village agriculture, whereby decisions on which crops to plant were made communally. It became one of the chief grievances of

Rebellious peasants carrying a standard called the Banner of the Shoe surround a knight.

the English peasants. But while enclosures broke up the old field system in many villages, they were a logical response to the transformation of land ownership that had already taken place. As more land was accumulated by fewer families, it made less sense for them to work widely scattered strips all over the village. If a family could consolidate its holdings by swaps and sales, it could gain an estate large enough to be used for both crops and grazing. An enclosed estate allowed wealthy farmers to grow more luxury crops for market or to raise only sheep on a field that had once been used for grain.

Enclosure was a process that both lord and rich peasant undertook, but it drove the smallholders from the land and was thus a source of bitter resentment for the poorer peasants. It was easy to protest the greed of the lords who, owning the most land, were the most successful enclosers. But enclosures were more a result of the process in which villages came to be characterized by a very small elite of large landholders and a very large mass of smallholders and landless poor. It was an effect rather than a cause.

From Hungary to England, peasant revolts brought social and economic change into sharp relief. A call for a crusade against Ottoman advances in 1514 provided the opportunity for Hungarian peasants to revolt against their noble landlords. Thousands dropped their plowshares and grasped the sword of a holy war. However, in fact, war against the Ottomans did not materialize. Instead, the mobilized peasants, under the leadership of disaffected army officers and clergymen, issued grievances against the labor service that they owed to their lords as well as numerous violations of customary agricultural practices. Their revolt turned into a civil war that was crushed with great brutality. In England, severe economic conditions led to a series of revolts in 1549. Participants in the Western Rising, who succeeded in storming the town of Exeter, also combined religious and economic grievances. Cornish rebels added a social dimension with their slogan "Kill the gentlemen." In eastern England, Ket's Rebellion arose from peasant opposition to enclosure. The rebels occupied Norwich, the second largest city in the realm, but their aspirations were for reform rather than revolution. They, like the Hungarian peasants, were crushed by well-trained forces.

Uprising in Germany. The complexity of the peasants' problems is perhaps best revealed in the series of uprisings that are known collectively as the German Peasants' War. It was by far the most widespread peasant revolt of the sixteenth century, involving tens of thousands of peasants, and it combined a whole series of agrarian grievances with an awareness of the new

THE PEASANTS' REVOLT

In 1524 and 1525, a series of local protests over economic conditions coalesced into one of the largest concerted peasant uprisings in German history. The Peasants' Revolt was not a disorganized uprising of the hungry and dispossessed, but rather a carefully coordinated movement that attempted to win widespread social reforms. The Twelve Articles of the Peasants of Swabia show both the nature of the peasants' grievances and their ability to articulate them.

The First Article. First, it is our humble petition and desire, as also our will and resolution, that in the future we should have power and authority so that each community should choose and appoint a pastor, and that we should have the right to depose him should he conduct himself improperly. The pastor thus chosen should teach us the gospel pure and simple, without any addition, doctrine, or ordinance of man.

The Second Article. According as the just tithe is established by the Old Testament and fulfilled in the New, we are ready and willing to pay the fair tithe of grain.... We will that for the future our church provost, whomsoever the community may appoint, shall gather and receive this tithe....

The Tenth Article. In the tenth place, we are aggrieved by the appropriation by individuals of meadows and fields which at one time belonged to a community. These we will take again into our own hands....

Conclusion. In the twelfth place, it is our conclusion and final resolution that if any one or more of the articles here set forth should not be in agreement with the word of God, as we think they are, such article we will willingly retract if it is proved really to be against the word of God by a clear explanation of the Scripture.

From the Twelve Articles of the Peasants of Swabia.

religious spirit preached by Martin Luther. Luther condemned both lords and peasants: the lords for their rapaciousness, the peasants for their rebelliousness. Although he had a large following among the peasants, his advice that earthly oppression be passively accepted was not followed. The Peasants' War was directed against secular and ecclesiastical lords, and the rebels attacked both economic and religious abuses. Their combination of demands, such as the community's right to select its own minister and the community's right to cut wood freely, attracted a wide following in the villages and small towns of southern and central Germany. The printed demands of the peasantry, the most famous of which was the Twelve Articles of the Peasants of Swabia (1525), helped spread the movement far beyond its original bounds. The peasants organized themselves into large armies led by experienced soldiers. Initially they were able to besiege castles and abbeys and plunder lords' estates. Ultimately, those movements that refused compromise were ruthlessly crushed. By conservative estimates, more than 100,000 peasants were slaughtered during and after the war, many to serve as warning against future uprisings.

At base, the demands of the peasantry addressed the agrarian changes that were transforming German villages. Population growth was creating more poor villagers who could only hire out as laborers but who demanded a share of common grazing and woodlands. Because the presence of the poor increased the taxable wealth of the village, they were advantageous to the lord. But the strain they placed on resources was felt by both the subsistence and the surplus farmers. Tensions within the village were all the greater because the landless members were the kin of the landed—sons and daughters, brothers and sisters. If they were to be settled properly on the land, then the lord would have to let the village expand. If they were to be kept on the margins of subsistence, then the more prosperous villagers would have to be able to control their numbers and their conduct. In either case, the peasants needed more direct responsibility for governing the village than existed in their traditional relationship with their lord. Thus the grievances of the peasants of Swabia demanded release of the village peasantry from the status of serfs. They wanted to be allowed to move off the land, to marry out of the village without penalty, and to be free of the death taxes that further impoverished their children. The concessions would make it easier for the excess population to adjust to new conditions. They also wanted stable rents fixed at fair rates, a limit placed on labor service, and a return to the ancient customs that governed relations between lords and peasants. All the proposals were backed by an appeal to Christian principles of love and charity. They were profoundly conservative.

The demands of the German peasants reflected a traditional order that no longer existed. In many places, the rents and tithes that the peasants wanted to control no longer belonged to the lords of the estates. They had been sold to town corporations or wealthy individuals who purchased them as an investment and expected to realize a fair return. Most tenants did enjoy stable and fixed rents, but only on their traditional lands. As they increased their holdings, perhaps to keep another son in the village or to expand production for the market, they were faced with the fact that rents were higher and land more expensive than it had been before. Marriage fines, death duties, and labor service were oppressive, but they balanced the fact that traditional rents were very low. In many east German villages, peasants willingly increased their labor service for a reduction in their money rents. It was hardly likely that they could have both. If the peasants were being squeezed, and there can be little doubt that they were, it was not only the lords who were doing the squeezing. The Church took its tenth, the state increased its exactions, and the competition for survival and prosperity among the peasants themselves was ferocious. Peasants were caught between the jaws of an expanding state and a changing economy. When they rebelled, the jaws snapped shut.

PRIVATE LIFE

The great events of the sixteenth century—the discovery of the New World, the consolidation of states, the increasing incidence and ferocity of war, the reform of religion—all had profound impact on the lives of ordinary people. There could be no private life separate from the developments. However slowly they penetrated to isolated village communities, however intermittent their effect, they were inextricably bound up with the experiences and the worldview of all Europeans. The states offered more protection and demanded more resources. Taxes increased, and tax collecting became more efficient. Wars took village boys and made them soldiers. Armies brought devastation to thousands of communities. The New World offered new opportunities, brought new products, and increased the wealth of the Continent. Religious reform, both Protestant and Catholic, penetrated into popular beliefs and personal piety. All the sweeping changes blurred the distinction between public and private life.

Still, the transformations wrought by political and intellectual developments were not necessarily the most important ones in people's lives. The lives of most Europeans centered on births and deaths, on the harvest, and on the social relations in their communities. For them, great events were the successful crop, the marriage of an heir, or the festivals that marked the progress of the year. Their beliefs were based as much on the customs they learned as children as on the religion they learned at church. Their strongest loyalties were to family and community rather than to church or state.

The Family

Sixteenth-century life centered on the family. The family was a crucial organizing principle for Europeans of all social ranks, and it served a variety of functions. In the most obvious sense, the family was the primary kin group. European families were predominantly nuclear, composed of a married couple and their children. In western Europe, a small number of families contained the adult siblings of the family head, uncles and aunts who had not yet established their own families. That pattern was more common in the east, especially in Hungary and Muscovy, where taxation was based on households and thus encouraged extended families. There several nuclear families might live under the same roof. Yet however families were composed, kinship had a wider orbit than just parents and children. In-laws, step-relations, and cousins were considered part of the kin group and could be called upon for support in a variety of contexts, from charity to employment and business partnerships. In towns, such family connections created large and powerful clans.

A FEMININE PERSPECTIVE

Arcangela Tarabotti was born in Venice in the early seventeenth century. Her family did not have the means to provide her with a sufficient dowry, so she was sent to live in a Catholic convent, where she unhappily remained for the rest of her life. She wrote two major works. The first, Monastic Hell, *gives the flavor of her attitude toward her fate. The second was* Innocence Undone, *from which the following excerpt is taken.*

SINCE WOMAN IS THE EPITOME OF ALL PERFECTIONS, she is the last of the works of God, as far as material creation is concerned, but otherwise she dates from the beginning, and is the first-generated of all creatures, generated by the breath of God himself, as the Holy Spirit inferred, through the mouth of Solomon in the Ecclesiastes where he introduces the Most Holy Virgin to sing of herself: *The Lord possessed me in the beginning of his ways, before he made any thing from the beginning.*

This creature, although a woman, did not need to be made with a rib taken from man, because, so to speak, she was born before the beginning of time as well as before men, who, blinded by their ambition to dominate the world alone, astutely fail to mention this infallible truth, that the woman has existed in the Divine mind from the beginning. *I was set up from eternity, and of old before the earth was made. The depths were not as yet, and I was already conceived.*

They cannot deny the fact, although their malice prevents them from speaking it openly; but let us try to make them admit, in accordance with the Holy Scriptures rather than with some ill-informed preachers, that the woman made the man perfect and not vice versa.

After the Supreme Being created the world and all the animals (as I have said before), the text says *And God saw all the things that he had made; and they were very good.* Foreseeing that the man without woman would be the compendium of all imperfections, God said: *It is not good for man to be alone: let us make him a help like unto himself.* And therefore he created a companion for him that would be the universal glory of humanity and make him rich with merits.

Almighty God, having kept the creation of the woman as the last act of his wonderful work, desired to bestow privileges upon her, reinforce her graces and gladden the whole world with her splen-

In a different sense, family was lineage, the connections between preceding and succeeding generations. That was an important concept among the upper ranks of society, where ancient lineage, genuine or fabricated, was a valued component of nobility. That concept of family imparted a sense of stability and longevity in a world in which individual life was short. Even in peasant communities, however, lineage existed in the form of the family farm, that is, the strips in the field that were passed from generation to generation and named for the family that owned them. The village's fields and landmarks also bore the names of individual families, and membership in one of the ancient families of the village was a mark of social distinction.

The family was also an economic unit. In this sense, family overlapped with the household—all those who lived under the same roof, including servants and apprentices. In its economic functions, the family was the basic unit for the production, accumulation, and transmission of wealth. Occupation determined the organization of the economic family. Every member of the household had his or her own functions that were essential to the survival of the unit. Tasks were divided by gender and by age, but there was far more intermixture than is traditionally assumed. On farms, women worked at nearly every occupation with the exception of mowing and plowing. In towns, they were vital to the success of shops and trades, though they were denied training in the skilled crafts. As laborers, they worked in the town fields—for little more than half the wages of men performing the same tasks—and in carrying and delivering goods and materials. Children contributed to the economic vitality of the household from an early age.

dour. If the supreme Architect's greatness, wisdom and love towards us shone brightly in his other works, he planned to make the woman, this excellent last addition to his splendid construction, capable of filling with wonder whoever looked at her. He therefore gave her the strength to subdue and dominate the proudest and wildest hearts and hold them in sweet captivity by a mere glance or else by the power of her pure modesty. God formed Man, who is so proud, in the field of Damascus; and from one of his ribs he formed woman in the garden of Eden.

If I were not a female, I would deduce from this that the woman, both because of her composition and because of the place in which she was created, is nobler, gentler, stronger and worthier than the man.

What is true strength anyway, if not domination over one's feelings and mastery over one's passions? And who is better at this than the female sex, always virtuous and capable of resisting every temptation to commit or even think evil things? Is there anything more fragile than your head? Compare it to the strength of a rib, the hard bone that is the material from which we were created, and you will be disappointed. Anyone knows that women show more strength than men when they conceive and give birth, by tirelessly carrying all that weight around for nine months.

But you cruel men, who always go around preaching evil for good and good for evil, you pride yourselves in your strength because, like the inhuman creatures you are, you fight and kill each other like wild beasts.... Thus, if strength is the ability to bear misfortunes and insults, how can you call yourselves strong when you shed other people's blood sometimes for no reason at all and take the life of innocent creatures at the slightest provocation of a word or a suspicion?

Strength is not mere violence; it requires an indomitable soul, steadfast and constant in Christian fortitude. How can you, o most inconstant ones, ever boast of such virtù? Improperly and deceitfully you have called yourselves virtuous, because only those who fill the world with people and virtù can be called strong.

And those are women. Listen to Solomon, whose words about women reinforce my argument: *Strength and dignity are her clothing.*

From Tarabotti, *Innocence Undone.*

Finally, the family was the primary unit of social organization. In the family children were educated and the social values of hierarchy and discipline were taught. Authority in the family was strictly organized in a set of three overlapping categories. At the top was the husband, head of the household, who ruled over his wife, children, and servants. All members of the family owed obedience to the head. The family was like "a little commonwealth," as English writers put it, in which the adult male was the governor and all others the governed. But two other categories of relationships in the family dispersed the authority. Children owed obedience to their parents, male or female. In this role, the wife and mother was governor as well as governed. Similarly, servants owed obedience to both master and mistress. Male apprentices were under the authority of the wife, mother, and mistress of the household. The importance of the family as a social unit was underscored by the fact that people unattached to families attracted suspicion in sixteenth-century society. Single men were often viewed as potential criminals; single women as potential prostitutes. Both lived outside the discipline and social control of families.

Although the population of Europe was increasing in the early modern era, families were not large. Throughout northern and western Europe, the size of the typical family was two adults and three or four children. Late marriages and breast-feeding helped control family size: the former restricted the number of childbearing years while the latter increased the space between pregnancies. Women married around age 25, men slightly later. A woman could expect about 15 fertile years and seven or eight pregnancies if neither she nor her husband died in the interim. Only three or

Peasant Family *(ca. 1640), a realistic scene of peasant life in France by the genre painter Louis Le Nain.*

four children were likely to survive beyond the age of ten. In her fertile years, a woman was constantly occupied with infants. She was either about to give birth or about to become pregnant. If she used a wet nurse rather than feed her own babies, as many women in the upper ranks of society did, then she was likely to have 10 or 12 pregnancies during her fertile years and correspondingly more surviving children.

Constant pregnancy and child care may help explain some of the gender roles that men and women assumed in the early modern era. Biblical injunctions and traditional stereotypes help explain others. Pregnant or not, women's labor was a vital part of the domestic economy, especially until the first surviving children were strong enough to assume their share. The woman's sphere was the household. On the farm, she was in charge of the preparation of food, the care of domestic animals, the care and education of children, and the manufacture and cleaning of the family's clothing. In towns, women supervised the shop that was part of the household. They sold goods, kept accounts, and directed the work of domestics or apprentices. Mothers trained their daughters to perform the tasks in the same way that fathers trained their sons to work the fields or ply their craft.

The man's sphere was public—the fields in rural areas, the streets in towns. Men plowed, planted, and did the heavy reaping work of farming. They made and maintained essential farm equipment and had charge of the large farm animals. They marketed surplus produce and made the few purchases of equipment or luxury goods. Men performed the labor service that was normally due the lord of the estate, attended the local courts in various capacities, and organized the affairs of the village. In towns, men engaged in heavy labor, procured materials for craft work, and marketed their product if it was not sold in the household shop. Only men could be citizens of the towns or full members of most craft guilds, and only men were involved in civic government.

The separation of men and women into the public and the domestic spheres meant that marriage was a blending of complementary skills. Each partner brought to the marriage essential knowledge and abilities that were fundamental to the economic success of the union. Except in the largest towns, nearly everyone was married for at least a part of his or her life. Remarriage was more common for men than women, however, because a man continued to control the family's property after the death of his wife, whereas a widow might have only a share of it after bequests to children and provisions for apprentices. In the French town of Nantes, a quarter of the annual weddings were remarriages.

While male roles were constant throughout the life cycle, as men trained for and performed the same occupations from childhood to death, female roles varied greatly depending upon the situation. While under the care of fathers, masters, or husbands, women worked in the domestic sphere; once widowed, they assumed the public functions of head of household. Many women inherited shops or farmland; most became responsible for the placement and training of their children. But because of the division of labor upon which the family depended and because of the inherent social and economic prejudices that segregated public and domestic roles, widows were particularly disadvantaged. The most fortunate among them remarried—"The widow weeps with one eye and casts glances with the other," an English proverb held. Their financial and personal independence from men, prized today, was a millstone in the early modern world.

Communities

Despite its central place in all aspects of sixteenth-century life, the family was a fragile and impermanent institution. Even without divorce—permitted in Protestant communities, though never very common—marriages were short. The early death of one of the partners abbreviated the life of the natural family. New marriage partners or social welfare to aid the indigent was sought from within the wider community. On the farm, that community was the rural village; in the town, it was the ward, quarter, or parish in which the family lived. Community life must not be romanticized. Interpersonal violence, lawsuits, and feuds were extraordinarily common in both rural and urban communities. The community was not an idyllic haven of charity and love, where everyone knew and respected neighbors and worked toward a common goal. Like every other aspect of society, the community was socially and economically stratified, gender roles were segregated, and resources were inequitably divided. But the community was the place where people found their social identity. It provided marriage partners for its families, charity for its poor, and a local culture for all of its inhabitants.

Identities and Customs. The two basic forces that tied the rural community together were the lord and the priest. The lord set conditions for work and property ownership that necessitated common decision making on the part of the village farmers. The lord's presence, commonly in the form of an agent, could be both a positive and a negative force for community solidarity. Use of the common lands, the rotation of labor service, and the form in which rents in kind were paid were all decisions that had to be made collectively. Village leadership remained informal, though in some

In an age of high infant mortality and short life expectancy, women were expected to bear many children to ensure family continuity. This embroidery depicts a mother with her thirteen daughters.

villages headmen or elders bargained with the lord's agent or resolved petty disputes among the villagers. Communal agreement was also expressed in communal resistance to violations of custom or threats to the moral economy. All those forms of negotiation fused individual families into a community. So, too, in a different way did the presence of the parish priest or minister, who attended all the pivotal events of life—birth, marriage, and death. The church was the only common building of the community; it was the only space that was not owned outright by the lord or an individual family. The scene of village meetings and ceremonies, it was the center of both spiritual and social life. The parish priest served as a conduit for all the news of the community and the focal point for the village's festive life. In rural communities, the church was the only organization to which people belonged.

Communities were bound together by the authorities who ruled them and by their common activities. But they were also bound together by their own social customs. Early modern communities used a number of ceremonial occasions as opportunities for expressing solidarity and confirming, in one way or another, the values to which they adhered. In rural parishes there was the annual perambulation, a walk around the village fields that usually occurred before planting began. It was led by the priest, who carried with him any particularly sacred objects that the parish possessed. Behind him followed the village farmers, in some places all members of the village who were capable of walking the distance. The perambulation had many purposes. The priest blessed the fields and prayed for a bountiful crop; the farmers surveyed their own strips and any damage that had been done to the fields during the winter; the community defined its geographical space in distinction to the space of others; and all the individuals who took part reaffirmed their shared identity with others in the village.

In towns, ceremonial processions were far more elaborate. Processions might take place on saints' days in Catholic communities or on anniversaries of town liberties. The order of the march, the clothing worn by the participants, and the objects displayed reflected the strict hierarchies of the town's local organizations. In Catholic towns, the religious orders led the town governors in their robes of office. Following the governors were the members of guilds, each guild placed according to its rank of importance and each organized by masters, journeymen, and apprentices. In some towns, the wives of citizens marched in procession; in others, they were accorded special places from which to view the ceremony. Village and civic ceremonies normally ended with communal feasting and dancing, which were the most popular forms of recreation.

Jan van Eyck, The Marriage of Giovanni Arnolfini and Giovanna Cenami. *This outstanding fifteenth-century painting of a nuptial scene teems with symbols, including the religious symbols of the rosary, the roundels on the mirror frame, and the post of the chair. The little dog in the foreground may represent fidelity, and the candles in the chandelier may be a symbol of marriage. The mirror reflects the image of two witnesses, who would have been standing where spectators viewing the picture would stand. The inscription on the wall, "Jan van Eyck was here, 1434," suggests that one of the figures is a self-portrait of the artist.*

Weddings and Festivals. Not all ceremonial occasions were so formal. The most common ceremony was the wedding, a rite of passage that was simultaneously significant to the individual, the family, and the community. The wedding was a public event that combined a religious ceremony and a community procession with feasting and festivity. It took different forms in different parts of Europe and in different social groups. But whether eastern or western, noble or common, the wedding was celebrated as the moment when the couple entered fully into the community. Marriage involved more than just the union of bride and groom. Parents were a central feature in the event, both in arranging the economic aspects of the union—dowry and inheritance—and in approving the occasion. Many couples were engaged long before they were married, and in many places it was the engagement that was most important to the individuals and the wedding that was most important to the community. One German townsman described how he "had taken a wife but they have not held the wedding yet."

Traditional weddings involved the formal transfer of property, an important event in rural communities, where the ownership of strips of land or common rights concerned everyone. The bridal dowry and the groom's inheritance were formally exchanged during the wedding, even if both were small. The public procession—"the marriage in the streets" as it was sometimes called in towns—proclaimed the union throughout the community and was considered to be as important as the religious ceremony. It was followed by a feast as abundant as the families of bride and groom could afford. In peasant communities, gifts of food for the feast were as common as were gifts to the couple. There were always provisions made that excess food should be sent to the poor or unfortunate after the wedding.

Weddings also legitimated sexual relations. Many of the dances and ceremonies that followed the feast symbolized the sexual congress. Among German burghers it was traditional for the bride to bring the bed to her new home, and bridal beds were passed from mothers to daughters. Among the nobility, the consummation of the marriage was a vital part of the wedding, for without it the union could be annulled. Finally, the marriage inaugurated both bride and groom into new roles in the community. Their place at the wedding table next to their parents elevated them to the status of adults.

Other ceremonies were equally important in creating a shared sense of identity within the community. In both town and countryside, the year was divided by a number of festivals that defined the rhythm of toil and rest. They coincided with both the seasonal divisions of agricultural life and the central events of the Christian

Carnivals were occasions for games and feasting. A Carnival on the Feast Day of Saint George in a Village Near Antwerp, *painted around 1605 by Abel Grimmer, shows the revels of the villagers presided over by the religious figure on the banner at the right.*

calendar. There was no essential difference between the popular and Christian elements in festivals, however strongly the official church insisted upon one. Christmas and Easter were probably the most widely observed Christian holidays, but Carnival, which preceded Lent, was a frenzied round of feasts and parties that resulted in a disproportionate number of births nine months later. The Twelve Days of Christmas, which inaugurated the slow, short days of winter, were only loosely attached to the birth of Jesus and were even abolished by some Protestant churches. The rites of May, which celebrated the rebirth of spring, were filled with sexual play among the young adults of the community. Youth groups went "a-Maying" by placing flowers at the homes of marriageable girls, electing a Queen of the May, and dancing and reveling before the hard work of planting. All Hallows' Eve was a celebration for the community's dead, whose spirits were believed to have wandered the village on that night, visiting kin and neighbors.

Festivals helped maintain the sense of community that might be weakened during the long months of increased work or enforced indoor activity. They were first and foremost celebrations in which feasting, dancing, and play were central. But they also served as safety valves for the pressures and conflicts that built up over the year. There were frequently group and individual sports, such as soccer or wrestling, which served to channel aggressions. Village elders would arbitrate disputes, and marriage alliances or property transactions would be arranged.

Festivals further cemented the political cohesion of the community. Seating arrangements reflected the hierarchy of the community, and public punishment of offenders reinforced deference and social and sexual mores. Youth groups, or even the village women, might band together to shame a promiscuous woman or to place horns on the head of a cuckolded husband. Sometimes a man who had been beaten or abused by his wife, or who had simply failed to enforce obedience from her, was forced to ride backward on a horse or donkey to symbolize the misrule in his family. At such processions, which the French called *charivaris* and the English *skimmingtons*, rough music was played and the offense of the individual or couple was elaborately recreated. (See "Sex and the Married Man," pp. 532–533.) Such forms of community ritual worked not only to punish offenders but also to reinforce the social and sexual values of the village as a whole.

Popular Beliefs

Ceremony and festival are reminders that sixteenth-century Europe was still a preliterate society. Despite the introduction of printing and the millions of books that were produced during the period, the vast majority of Europeans conducted their affairs without the benefit of literacy. Their culture was oral and visual. They had need of an exact memory, and they developed a shorthand of adages, charms, and spells that helped them organize their activities and pass down their knowledge. It is difficult for us to recreate that mental world, in which almost all natural events were unpredictable and in which there was little certainty. Outside a small circle of intellectuals, there was little effective knowledge about either human or celestial bodies. The mysteries of the sun, moon, and stars were as deep as those of health and sickness. But ordinary people did not live in a constant state of terror and anxiety. They used the knowledge they did have to form a view of the universe that conformed to their experiences and that responded to their hopes. Although many of their beliefs seem mere superstitions, they allowed people to form a coherent explanation of the natural world and of their relationship to it.

Magical Practices. The people's beliefs blended Christian teaching and folk wisdom with a strong strain of magic. Popular belief in magic could be found everywhere in Europe, and it operated in much the same way as science does today. Only skilled practitioners could perform magic. It was a technical subject that combined expertise in the properties of plants and animals with theories about the composition of human and heavenly bodies. It had its own language, a mixture of ancient words and sounds with significant numbers and catchphrases. Magicians specialized: some concentrated on herbs and plants, others on the diseases of the body. Alchemists worked with rocks and minerals, astrologers with the movement of the stars. Witches were thought to understand the properties of animals especially well. The witches of Shakespeare's *Macbeth* chanted their exotic recipe for witch's gruel:

> *Eye of newt and toe of frog,*
> *Wool of bat and tongue of dog,*
> *Adder's fork and blindworm's sting,*
> *Lizard's leg and owlet's wing,*
> *For a charm of powerful trouble,*
> *Like a hell-broth boil and bubble.*

THE DEVIL'S DUE

Evidence of the supernatural world abounded for the people of premodern Europe. Natural disasters such as plague and human disasters such as war promoted fear of witchcraft. When the world seemed out of balance and the forces of good retreated before the forces of evil, people sought someone to blame for their troubles. Witches were an obvious choice. Accused witches were most commonly women on the margins of society. Once brought before the authorities, many admitted their traffic with Satan, especially under torture. The Witch Hammer *is a set of detailed instructions for the rooting out of witches, including procedures to induce their confessions.*

THE METHOD OF BEGINNING AN EXAMINATION BY TORTURE IS AS FOLLOWS: First, the jailers prepare the implements of torture, then they strip the prisoner (if it be a woman, she has already been stripped by other women, upright and of good report). This stripping is lest some means of witchcraft may have been sewed into the clothing—such as often, taught by the Devil, they prepare from the bodies of unbaptized infants, [murdered] that they may forfeit salvation. And when the implements of torture have been prepared, the judge, both in person and through other good men zealous in the faith, tries to persuade the prisoner to confess the truth freely; but, if he will not confess, he bids attendants make the prisoner fast to the strappado or some other implement of torture. The attendants obey forthwith, yet with feigned agitation. Then, at the prayer of some of those present, the prisoner is loosed again and is taken aside and once more persuaded to confess, being led to believe that he will in that case not be put to death.

But if, neither by threats nor by promises such as these, the witch cannot be induced to speak the truth, then the jailers must carry out the sentence, and torture the prisoner according to the accepted methods, with more or less of severity as the delinquent's crime may demand. And, while he is being tortured, he must be questioned on the articles of accusation, and this frequently and persistently, beginning with the lighter charges—for he will more readily confess the lighter than the heavier. And, while this is being done, the notary must write down everything in his record of the trial—how the prisoner is tortured, on what points he is questioned, and how he answers.

And note that, if he confesses under the torture, he must afterward be conducted to another place, that he may confirm it and certify that it was not due alone to the force of the torture.

But, if the prisoner will not confess the truth satisfactorily, other sorts of tortures must be placed before him, with the statement that, unless he will confess the truth, he must endure these also. But, if not even thus he can be brought into terror and to the truth, then the next day or the next but one is to be set for a *continuation* of the tortures—not a *repetition,* for they must not be repeated unless new evidence be produced....

And during the interval, before the day assigned, the judge, in person or through approved men, must in the manner above described try to persuade the prisoner to confess, promising her (if there is aught to be gained by this promise) that her life shall be spared.

The judge shall see to it, moreover, that throughout this interval guards are constantly with the prisoner, so that she may not be left alone; because she will be visited by the Devil and tempted into suicide.

From *The Witch Hammer.*

Magical practices appealed to people at all levels of society. The wealthy favored astrology and paid handsomely to discover which days and months were the most auspicious for marriages and investments. So-called cunning men predicted the future for those of the lower orders who would not be able to give an astrologer such vital information as the date of their birth or to pay exorbitant fees. The poorest villagers

Sex and the Married Man

ON 27 MAY 1618 the peace of the small hamlet of Quemerford, in the west of England, was shattered by the appearance of a large crowd from the neighboring market town of Calne. Men marched with fowling pieces and muskets to a cacophony of drums, clanging pots, whistles, and shouts. Among them, on a red horse, rode an outlandishly costumed man—a smock covering his body; on his head a nightcap with two long shoehorns tied to his ears; and on his face a false beard made from a deer's tail. The crowd escorted the rider to the home of Thomas Mills, who worked in Calne as a cutler. There they stopped. Guns were discharged into the air; an even greater clamor of rough music arose from drums, pipes, and metal objects; and when Mills opened his door, members of the crowd waved aloft the horns of goats or rams mounted on sticks. Then a few strong men entered the house; seized hold of his wife, Agnes; and dragged her to a village mud hole where she was ducked and covered in filth. She was rescued from being set on the horse and ridden to Calne.

That event, known as a skimmington in the west of England and a charivari in France, was a shaming ritual. It was an element of popular culture that took place against the wishes of local authorities and without their connivance. Its purpose was twofold: to identify and punish sexual misconduct and to maintain the male-dominated gender system. The shaming rituals resulted from conduct that the male members of the community believed threatened local order (few women are known to have taken part in the events). In France, most charivaris were conducted against husbands who were beaten by their wives; in England, many skimmingtons were directed against husbands whose wives had been unfaithful. In both they were designed to shame men into disciplining women and to warn women to remain obedient.

Although skimmingtons and charivaris differed from place to place, all contained similar elements which were designed to invert normal behavior in one way or another. The rough music symbolized the disharmony of a household in which the woman dominated, either by her physical conduct—adultery or husband beating—or her verbal conduct—cursing or abusing her husband or other men. The music was made with everyday objects rather than instruments, and pots and pans were universally present. The "riding" of the husband was another common feature. In many rituals, the "husband," played by a neighbor, was placed facing the tail of the horse or donkey to symbolize the backwardness of his behav-

ior. In some, a "wife," also acted by a neighbor, rode behind the man and beat him with a stick or, in England, with the long-handled ladle used to skim cream that was known as a skimmington. In the end, the real husband or wife was captured, the man to ride in shame throughout the town, the woman to be sat on a cucking stool and dunked in water.

The presence of horns on the male riding the horse and on sticks carried by members of the crowd or worn atop their heads was the universal symbol of adultery. The cuckold—a word derived from the name of a promiscuous female bird—was an object of derision throughout European society. Codes of conduct from noble to peasant stressed the importance of female sexual fidelity in maintaining the purity of bloodlines and the order of the household. The cuckold was shorn of his masculinity; he had lost his "horns," in common parlance. His personal indignity was a cause for jest and insult, but the disorderliness implicit in the conduct of his wife was a cause for community concern. In local society, reputation was equated with personal worth, and no one had less reputation than the cuckold. Among the nobility, duels were fought over the slightest suggestion of a wife's unfaithfulness, while among ordinary folks the raising of the forefinger and pinkie—the sign of horns—initiated brawls.

The skimmington or charivari combined festive play with the enforcement of social norms. It was rough justice, as the objects of shame were allowed neither explanation nor defense. They were guilty by common fame, that is, by the report of their neighbors and the gossip of the local alehouse rather than by any examination of evidence. Women who yelled at their husbands were sometimes assumed to have beaten them; women who had beaten their husbands were assumed to have cuckolded them. The crimes were all interrelated, and protestations of innocence were useless. The crowds that gathered to perform the ceremony usually had bolstered their courage at the local tavern, and among them were village toughs and those who held grudges against the targeted family. Assault, property damage, and theft occasionally accompanied a skimmington. But most of the crowd was there to have a bit of sport and revel in the discomfort of the victims. Their conduct was the inverse of a legal procedure, as disorderly as the conduct of those to be punished. However, their purpose was not to turn the world upside down, but to set it right side up again by restoring the dominance of husbands over wives.

While shaming rituals like the charivari and the skimmington had a long history in Europe, they seem to have exploded into prominence in the late sixteenth and early seventeenth centuries. Population pressures and economic hardship are two conventional explanations for why there were greater local tensions during that period. Skimmingtons and charivaris frequently had rough edges, with some participants motivated by hatred or revenge. But it is also likely that there were more inversion rituals because there was more inversion. Women were taking a larger role in economic affairs and were becoming increasingly literate and active in religion, especially in Protestant countries. Assertive, independent women threatened the male-dominated social order as much as demographic and social change. That the threats were most identified with sexual misconduct and with the stripping of a husband's masculinity was hardly surprising. The image of the obedient female was conventionally the image of chastity. Thus the image of the independent female had to become one of promiscuity. Through the use of skimmingtons and charivaris, men attempted to restore norms of sexual conduct and gender relations that were increasingly under attack. As one English poet put it:

Ill fares the hapless family that shows
A cock that's silent, and a Hen that crows.
I know not which live more unnatural lives,
Obedient husbands, or commanding wives.

A German manuscript of 1464 shows an astrologer "diagnosing and prognosticating." The interest of astrologers in the heavens foreshadowed the rise of the science of astronomy in the sixteenth and seventeenth centuries.

sought the aid of herbalists to help control the constant aches and pains of daily life. Sorcerers and wizards were called upon in more extreme circumstances, such as a threatened harvest or matters of life and death. The magicians competed with the remedies offered by the Church. Special prayers and visits to the shrines of particular saints were believed to have similar curative value. Magical and Christian beliefs did not oppose each other; they existed on a continuum and were practiced simultaneously. In some French villages, for example, four-leaf clovers were considered especially powerful if they were found on a particular saint's day. It was not until the end of the century, when Protestant and Catholic leaders condemned magical practices and began a campaign to root them out, that magic and religion came into conflict.

Magical practices served a variety of purposes. Healing was the most common, and many "magical" brews were effective remedies of the minor ailments for which they were prescribed. Most village magicians were women because it was believed that women had unique knowledge and understanding of the body. Women were also familiar with the properties of the herbs from which most remedies were derived. Magic was also used for predictive purposes. Certain charms and rituals were believed to have the power to affect the weather, the crops, and even human events. As always, affairs of the heart were as important as those of the stomach. Magicians advised the lovesick on potions and spells that would gain them the object of their desires. Cats were particularly associated with love spells, as were the petals of certain flowers. "He loves me, he loves me not" was more than a child's game. Magic was believed to have the power to alter the course of nature, and it could be used for both good and evil purposes.

The Witchcraft Craze. Magic for evil was black magic, or witchcraft, which utilized beliefs in the presence of spiritual forces in nature. Witches were believed to possess special powers that put them into contact with the devil and the forces of evil, which they could then use for their own purposes. Belief in the prevalence of good and evil spirits was Christian as well as magical. But the Church had gradually consigned the operation of the devil to the afterlife and removed his direct agency from earthly affairs. Beginning in the late fifteenth century, Church authorities began to prosecute large numbers of suspected witches. By the end of the sixteenth century, there was a continentwide witchcraze. Unexplained misfortune or simple malice could set off accusations that might include dozens or even hundreds of suspected witches. Confessions were obtained under torture, as were further accusations. In the period from 1550 to 1650, there were more than 30,000 prosecutions in Germany alone.

Witches were usually women, most often those unmarried or widowed. Although male sorcerers and wizards were thought to have powers over evil spirits, by the sixteenth century it was females who served as the mediators between humans and the diabolical. In a sample of more than 7000 cases of witchcraft prosecuted in early modern Europe, more than 80 percent of the defendants were women. There is no clear explanation why women fulfilled this important and powerful role. Belief in women's special powers over the body through their singular ability to give birth is certainly one part of the explanation, for many stories about the origins of witches suggest that they were children fathered by the devil and left to be raised by women. The sexual element of union with the devil and the common belief that older women were sexually aggressive combined to threaten male sexual dominance.

Women were most often accused of witchcraft. This painting, Witches Assembly, *is by Frans Francken (1581–1642).*

Witches were also believed to have peculiar physical characteristics. A group of Italian witches, male and female, were distinguished by having been born with a caul (a membrane around their heads that was removed after birth). Accused witches were strip-searched to find the devil's mark, which might be any bodily blemish. Another strand of explanation lies in the fact that single women existed on the fringes of society, isolated and exploited by the community at large. Their occult abilities thus became a protective mechanism that gave them a function within the community while they remained outside it.

It is difficult to know how important black magical beliefs were in ordinary communities. Most of the daily magic that was practiced was the mixture of charms, potions, and prayers that mingled magical, medical, and Christian beliefs. But as the century progressed, more and more notice was taken of black magic. Misfortunes that befell particular families or social groups were blamed upon the activities of witches. The campaign of the established churches to root out magic was largely directed against witches. The churches transposed witches' supposed abilities to communicate with the devil into the charge that they worshipped the devil. Because there was such widespread belief in the presence of diabolical spirits and in the capabilities

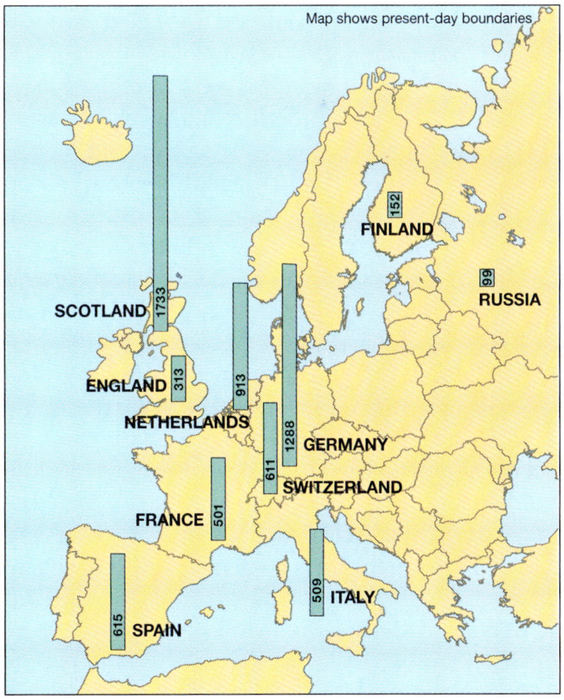

Witchcraft Persecutions. There were more trials for witchcraft in Calvinist Scotland than in all of Spain and France combined.

of witches to control them, Protestant and Catholic church courts could easily find witnesses to testify in support of the charges against individual witches. Yet wherever sufficient evidence exists to understand the circumstances of witchcraft prosecutions, it is clear that the community itself was under some form of social or economic stress. Sacrificing a marginal member of the community might have been the means to restore village solidarity.

Population growth, economic diversification, and social change characterized life in early modern Europe. It was a century of extremes. The poor were getting poorer and the rich were getting richer. The early part of the century has been called the golden age of the peasantry; the later part has been called the crisis of subsistence. At all levels of the social scale, the lives of grandparents and grandchildren were dramatically different. For surplus producers, the quality of life improved throughout the century. The market economy expanded. Agricultural surplus was exchanged for more land and a wider variety of consumer goods. Children could be provided with an education, and domestic and agricultural labor was cheap and plentiful. For subsistence producers, the quality of life eroded. In the first half of the century, their diet contained more meat than it would for the next 300 years. Their children could be absorbed on new farms or sent to towns where there was a shortage of both skilled and unskilled labor. But gradually the outlook turned bleak. The land could support no more new families, and the towns needed no more labor. As wages fell and prices rose, peasants in western Europe were caught between the crushing burdens of taxation from lord, state, and church and the all-too-frequent catastrophes of poor harvests, epidemic disease, and warfare. In eastern Europe, the peasantry was tied to the land in a new serfdom that provided minimum subsistence in return for the loss of freedom and opportunity. When peasants anywhere rose up against those conditions, they were cut down and swept away like new-mown hay.

Questions for Review

1. What physical forces and social customs shaped the everyday life of Europe's rural population?
2. What was the nature of demographic change in the sixteenth century, and what was its impact on the European economy?
3. How are the terms "stratification," "hierarchy," and "status" useful for understanding social relations in early modern Europe?
4. How were the different roles of men and women within the family reflected in the different lives of men and women in the wider community?

Suggestions for Further Reading

General Reading

Henry Kamen, *European Society, 1500–1700* (London: Hutchinson, 1984). A general survey of European social history.

* Robert Mandrou, *Introduction to Modern France* (New York: Harper & Row, 1977). Explores a variety of subjects in French social history from the mental to the material world.

* Peter Laslett, *The World We Have Lost: Further Explored* (New York: Scribners, 1984). One of the pioneering works on the family and population history of England.

* George Huppert, *After the Black Death* (Bloomington: Indiana University Press, 1986). An up-to-date and detailed study of social history in all parts of the Continent.

Economic Life

* Fernand Braudel, *Civilization and Capitalism: The Structures of Everyday Life* (New York: Harper & Row, 1981). Part of a larger work filled with fascinating detail about the social behavior of humankind during the early modern period.

Emmanuel Le Roy Ladurie, *The French Peasantry, 1450–1660* (London: Scholar Press, 1987). A complex study of the lives of the French peasantry.

* Gerald Strauss, *Nuremberg in the Sixteenth Century* (New York: John Wiley & Sons, 1966). A political and social history of a typical German town.

David Palliser, *Tudor York* (Oxford: Oxford University Press, 1979). A study of the second largest English urban area and its decline in the sixteenth century.

* Natalie Z. Davis, *Society and Culture in Early Modern France* (Stanford, CA: Stanford University Press, 1975). A collection of compelling essays drawn from the author's research on the French town of Lyon.

* Judith Bennett, *Ale, Beer, and Brewsters: Women's Work in a Changing World* (Oxford:Oxford University Press, 1996).

An important study of the role of women in one of the most traditional trades.

* Carlo Cipolla, ed., *Fontana Economic History of Europe*. Vol. 2, *The Sixteenth and Seventeenth Centuries* (London: Harvester Press, 1977). A multiauthored compendium of information and analysis on all aspects of European economic life.

* Peter Kriedte, *Peasants, Landlords and Merchant Capitalists* (Cambridge: Cambridge University Press, 1983). A Marxist interpretation of the transformations of the European economy.

Hermann Kellenbenz, *The Rise of the European Economy* (London: Weidenfeld and Nicolson, 1976). A general survey of economic life with good material from Scandinavian and German sources.

Social Life

* E. M. W. Tillyard, *The Elizabethan World Picture* (New York: Harper & Row, 1960). The classic account of the social constructs of English society.

* Arthur Lovejoy, *The Great Chain of Being* (New York: Random House, 1959). An intellectual history of an idea through its centuries of development.

* Jonathan Dewald, *The European Nobility 1400–1800* (Cambridge: Cambridge University Press, 1996). An outstanding survey based on a wide range of sources.

Michael Bush, *Noble Privilege* (New York: Holmes & Meier, 1983). An analytic account of the types of privileges enjoyed by the European nobility, based on wide reading.

Antoni Maczak, Henryk Samsonowicz, and Peter Burke, eds., *East-Central Europe in Transition* (Cambridge: Cambridge University Press, 1985). Essays by leading historians of eastern Europe, most of which focus upon economic development.

Michael Weisser, *The Peasants of the Montes* (Chicago: University of Chicago Press, 1972). A study of the lives of the Spanish peasants who lived in the shadow of Toledo.

* Margaret Spufford, *Contrasting Communities* (Cambridge: Cambridge University Press, 1974). A detailed reconstruction of three English villages that explores social, economic, and religious life in the late sixteenth and early seventeenth centuries.

* Edward Muir, *Ritual in Early Modern Europe* (Cambridge: Cambridge University Press, 1997). A fascinating account of the transformations in concepts of time and the body in early modern Europe.

* R. Scribner and G. Benecke, *The German Peasant War, 1525* (London: Allen & Unwin, 1979). Essays by leading scholars on different aspects of the most important of all peasant revolts.

* Peter Blickle, *The Revolution of 1525* (Baltimore, MD: Johns Hopkins University Press, 1981). A provocative interpretation of the causes and meaning of the German Peasants' War.

* Yves-Marie Bercé, *Revolt and Revolution in Early Modern Europe* (New York: St. Martin's Press, 1987). A study of the structure of uprisings throughout Europe by a leading French historian.

Private Life

* Roger Chartier, ed., *A History of Private Life*. Vol. 3, *Passions of the Renaissance* (Cambridge, MA: Harvard University Press, 1989). A lavishly illustrated study of the habits, mores, and structures of private life from the fifteenth to the eighteenth centuries.

* Michael Mitterauer and Reinhard Sieder, *The European Family* (Chicago: University of Chicago Press, 1982). A sociological survey that presents the varying ways in which European families were structured.

* Ralph Houlbrooke, *The English Family, 1450–1700* (London: Longman, 1984). A thorough survey of family history for the society that has been most carefully studied.

* Jean-Louis Flandrin, *Families in Former Times* (Cambridge: Cambridge University Press, 1976). Studies of kinship, household, and sexuality by one of the leading French family historians.

* Beatrice Gottlieb, *The Family in the Western World From the Black Death to the Industrial Age* (Oxford: Oxford University Press, 1994). An outstanding introduction to the transformations in the lives of families.

* Paul Zumthor, *Daily Life in Rembrandt's Holland* (Stanford, CA: Stanford University Press, 1994). A fascinating recovery of the lives of ordinary people.

* A. T. Van Deursen, *Plain Lives in a Golden Age* (Cambridge: Cambridge University Press, 1991). A study of Dutch popular culture and religious belief that makes excellent use of the visual arts.

Merry Wiesner, *Working Women in Renaissance Germany* (New Brunswick, NJ: Rutgers University Press, 1986). A survey of women's work in Germany and the ways in which it changed during the sixteenth century.

* Margaret Sommerville, *Sex and Subjection* (London: Macmillan, 1995). The origins of modern views on women.

Anthony Fletcher, *Gender, Sex and Subordination in England, 1500–1800* (New Haven, CT: Yale University Press, 1995). A sensitive reading of relations between men and women in the early modern world.

* David Cressy, *Birth, Marriage, and Death: Ritual, Religion, and the Life-Cycle in Tudor and Stuart England* (Oxford: Oxford University Press, 1997). The best single volume on the history of the English family.

* Merry E. Wiesner, *Women and Gender in Early Modern Europe* (Cambridge: Cambridge University Press, 1993). The best introduction to European women's history.

Brian Pullan, *Rich and Poor in Renaissance Venice* (Cambridge, MA: Harvard University Press, 1971). A massive history of social classes in Venice with a detailed account of poverty and vagrancy.

* Robert Jutte, *Poverty and Deviance in Early Modern Europe* (Cambridge: Cambridge University Press, 1994). The poor, crime, and criminality.

* Peter Burke, *Popular Culture in Early Modern Europe* (New York: Harper & Row, 1978). A lively survey of cultural activities among the European populace.

* R. Muchembled, *Popular Culture and Elite Culture in France, 1400–1750* (Baton Rouge: Louisiana State University Press, 1985). A detailed treatment of the practices of two conflicting cultures.

* R. A. Houston, *Literacy in Early Modern Europe* (London: Longman, 1988). How literacy and education became part of popular culture from 1500 to 1800.

* D. Underdown, *Revel, Riot, and Rebellion* (Oxford: Oxford University Press, 1985). An engaging study of popular culture and its relationship to social and economic structures in England.

* Keith Thomas, *Religion and the Decline of Magic* (New York: Scribners, 1971). A gargantuan descriptive and anecdotal account of the forms of religious and magical practice in England.

* Jean Delumeau, *Sin and Fear* (New York: St. Martin's Press, 1990). A cultural history of emotion based on a dazzling study of mainly Catholic writers.

* Brian Levack, *The Witch-Hunt in Early Modern Europe* (London: Longman, 1987). A study of the causes and meaning of the persecution of European witches in the sixteenth and seventeenth centuries.

Stuart Clark, *Thinking with Demons: The Idea of Witchcraft in Early Modern Europe* (Oxford: Oxford University Press, 1997). A sensitive reading of the sources for the study of witchcraft.

* Paperback edition available.

Discovering Western Civilization Online

To further explore life in early modern Europe, consult the following World Wide Web sites. Since Web resources are constantly being updated, also go to *www.awl.com/Kishlansky* for further suggestions

Social Life

www.fordham.edu/halsall/mod/modsbook04.html
A site with links to sources, pictures, and accounts of everyday life in early modern Europe. A good place to start.

www.fordham.edu/halsall/mod/17france-soc.html
Documents illustrating social conditions in early modern France.

Private Life

www.kenyon.edu/projects/margin/witch.htm
A site with links to sources concerning European witchcraft. Suggestions for further reading and a brief overview of the subject.

CHAPTER

16 THE ROYAL STATE IN THE SEVENTEENTH CENTURY

- **FIT FOR A KING**
- **THE RISE OF THE ROYAL STATE**
  - Divine Kings
  - The Court and the Courtiers
  - The Drive to Centralize Government
  - The Taxing Demands of War
- **THE CRISES OF THE ROYAL STATE**
  - The Need to Resist
  - The Right to Resist
  - The English Civil War
  - The English Revolutions
- **THE ZENITH OF THE ROYAL STATE**
  - The Nature of Absolute Monarchy
  - Absolutism in the East
  - The Origins of French Absolutism
  - Louis le Grand

Fit for a King

BEHOLD VERSAILLES: the greatest palace of the greatest king of the greatest state in seventeenth-century Europe. Everything about it was stupendous, a reflection of the grandeur of Louis XIV and of France. Sculptured gardens in dazzling geometric forms stretched for acres, scenting the air with exotic perfumes. Nearly as beautiful as the grounds were the 1400 fountains, especially the circular basins of Apollo and Latona, the sun god and his mother. The hundreds of water jets that sprayed at Versailles defied nature as well as the senses, for the locale was not well irrigated and water had to be pumped through elaborate mechanical works all the way from the Seine. Gardens and fountains provided the setting for the enormous palace with its hundreds of rooms for both use and show. Five thousand people, a tenth of whom served the king alone, inhabited the palace. Thousands of others flocked there daily.

Most lived in the adjacent town, which had grown from a few hundred people to more than 40,000 in a single generation. The royal stables quartered 12,000 horses and hundreds of carriages. The cost of all that magnificence was equally astounding. Fragmentary accounts indicate that construction costs were more than 100 million French pounds. Louis XIV ordered the official receipts burned.

Like the marble of the palace, nature itself was chiseled to the requirements of the king. Forests were pared to make leafy avenues or trimmed to conform to the geometric patterns of the gardens. In spring and summer, groves of orange trees grown in tubs were everywhere; in winter and fall they were housed indoors at great expense. Life-size statues and giant carved urns lined the carefully planned walkways that led to breathtaking views or sheltered grottoes. A cross-shaped artificial canal, more than a mile long, dominated the western end of the park. Italian gondolas skimmed along its surface, carrying visitors to the zoo and aviary on one side or to the king's private chateau on the other.

But that great pile of bricks and stone, of marble and precious metals, expressed the contradictions of its age as well as its grandeur. The seventeenth century was an era when the rich got richer and the poor got poorer. It was a time when the monarchical state expanded its power and prestige even as it faced grave challenges to its very existence. It was an epoch of unrelenting war amid a nearly universal desire for lasting peace. Thus it was fitting that the prodigious monument was uncomfortable to live in, so unpleasant that Louis had a separate chateau built on the grounds as a quiet retreat. His wife and his mistresses complained constantly of accommodations in which all interior comforts had been subordinated to the external facade of the building. Versailles was a seat of state as well as the home of the monarch, and it is revealing that the private was sacrificed to the public.

The duc de Saint-Simon, who passed much of his time at Versailles, was well aware of the contradictions: "The beautiful and the ugly were sown together, the vast and the constricted." Soldiers, artisans, and the merely curious clogged the three great avenues that led from Paris to the palace. When the king dined in public, hordes of Parisians drove out for the spectacle, filing past the monarch as if he were an exhibit at a museum. The site itself was poorly drained. "Its mud is black and stinking with a stench so penetrating that you can smell it for several leagues around." The orange groves and the stone urns filled with flower petals were more practical than beautiful: they masked the stench of sewage that was particularly noxious in the heat and the rain. Even the gardens were too vast to be enjoyed. In the planted areas, the smell of flowers was overpowering while the acres of mown lawn proved unattractive to an aristocracy little given to physical exercise. "The gardens were admired and avoided," Saint-Simon observed acidly. In those contrasts of failure amid achievement, Versailles stands as an apt symbol of its age: a gaudy mask to hide the wrinkles of the royal state.

THE RISE OF THE ROYAL STATE

The religious and dynastic wars that dominated the early part of the seventeenth century had a profound impact upon the western European states. Not only did they cause terrible suffering and deprivation, but they also demanded efficient and better centralized states to conduct them. War was both a product of the European state system and a cause of its continued development. As armies grew in size, the resources necessary to maintain them grew in volume. As the battlefield spread from state to state, defense became government's most important function. More and more power was absorbed by the monarch and his chief advisers; more and more of the traditional privileges of aristocracy and towns were eroded. At the center of the rising states, particularly in western Europe, were the king and his court. In the provinces were tax collectors and military recruiters.

Divine Kings

"There is a divinity that doth hedge a king," wrote Shakespeare. Never was that hedge more luxuriant than in the seventeenth century. In the early sixteenth century, monarchs treated their states and their subjects as personal property. Correspondingly, rulers were praised in personal terms: for their virtue, wisdom, or strength. By the early seventeenth century, the monarchy had been transformed into an office of state. Now rulers embodied their nation and, no matter what their personal characteristics, they were held in awe because they were monarchs.

Thus, as rulers lost direct personal control over their patrimony, they gained indirect symbolic control over their nation. The symbolic power was to be seen everywhere. By the beginning of the seventeenth century, monarchs had set permanent seats of government attended by vast courts of officials, place seekers, and servants. The idea of the capital city emerged, with Madrid, London, Paris, and Vienna as the models. There the grandiose style of the ruler stood proxy for the wealth and glory of the nation. Great display bespoke great pride, and great pride was translated into great strength.

Portraits of rulers in action and repose conveyed the central message. Elizabeth I was depicted bestriding a map of England or clutching a rainbow and wearing a gown woven of eyes and ears to signify her power to see and hear her subjects. The Flemish painter Sir Anthony Van Dyck (1599–1641) created powerful images of three generations of Stuart kings of England. He was court painter to Charles I, whose qualities he portrayed with great sympathy and not a little exaggeration. Diego Velázquez (1599–1660) was court painter to Philip IV of Spain. His series of equestrian portraits of the Habsburgs—kings, queens, princes, and princesses—exude the spirit of the seventeenth-century monarchy, the grandeur and pomp, the power and self-assurance. Peter Paul Rubens (1577–1640) represented 21 separate episodes in the life of Marie de Médicis, queen regent of France.

The themes of writers were no different than those of artists. Monarchy was glorified in a variety of forms of literary representation. National history, particularly of recent events, enjoyed wide popularity. Its avowed purpose was to draw the connection between the past and the present glories of the state. One of the most popular French histories of the period was entitled *On the Excellence of the Kings and the Kingdom of France*. Francis Bacon (1561–1626), who is remembered more as a philosopher and scientist, wrote a laudatory history of Henry VII, founder of the Tudor dynasty.

In England it was a period of renaissance. Poets, playwrights, historians, and philosophers by the dozens gravitated to the English court. One of the most remarkable of them was Ben Jonson (1572–1637). He began life as a bricklayer, fought against the Spanish in Flanders, and then turned to acting and writing. His wit and talent brought him to court, where he made his mark by writing and staging masques, light entertainment that included music, dance, pantomime, and acting. Jonson's masques were distinguished by their lavish productions and exotic costumes and the inventive set designs of the great architect Inigo Jones (1573–1652). They were frequently staged at Christmastime and starred members of the court as players. The masques took the grandeur of England and its rulers for their themes.

Shakespeare and Kingship. The role of William Shakespeare (1564–1616) in the celebration of monarchy was more ambiguous. Like Jonson, Shakespeare came from an ordinary family, had little formal education, and began his astonishing career as an actor and producer of theater. He soon began to write as well as direct his plays and his company, the King's Players, received royal patronage. He set many of his plays at the courts of princes, and even comedies such as *The*

Tempest (1611) and *Measure for Measure* (1604) centered on the power of the ruler to dispense justice and to bring peace to his subjects. Both plays were staged at court. Shakespeare's history plays focused entirely on the character of kings. In *Richard II* (1597) and *Henry VI* (three parts, 1591–1594) Shakespeare exposed the harm that weak rulers inflicted on their states, while in *Henry IV* (two parts, 1598–1600) and *Henry V* (1599) he highlighted the benefits to be derived from strong rulers.

Shakespeare's tragedies made the point in a different way. The tragic flaw in the personality of rulers exposed the world around them to ruin. In *Macbeth* (1606), the flaw was ambition. Macbeth killed to become a king and had to keep on killing to remain one. In *Hamlet* (1602), the tragic flaw was irresolution. The inability of the Prince of Denmark to act decisively and reclaim the crown that was his by right brought his state to the brink of collapse. Shakespeare's plays were viewed in London theaters by members of all social classes, and his concentration on the affairs of rulers helped reinforce their dominating importance in the lives of all of their subjects.

Queen Elizabeth I of England. This portrait was commissioned by Sir Henry Lee to commemorate the queen's visit to his estate at Ditchley. Here the queen is the very image of Gloriana—ageless and indomitable.

Monarchy and Law. The political theory of the divine right of kings further enhanced the importance of monarchs. The theory held that the institution of monarchy had been created by God and that the monarch functioned as God's representative on earth. One clear statement of divine right theory was actually written by a king, James VI of Scotland, who later became James I of England (1603–1625). In *The True Law of Free Monarchies* (1598), James reasoned that God had placed kings on earth to rule and that he would judge them in heaven for their transgressions.

The idea of the divine origin of monarchy was uncontroversial, and it was espoused not only by kings. One of the few things that the French Estates-General actually agreed upon during its meeting in 1614—the last for more than 175 years—was the statement: "The king is sovereign in France and holds his crown from God only." That sentiment echoed the commonplace view of French political theorists. The greatest writer on the subject, Jean Bodin (1530–1596), called the king "God's image on earth." In *The Six Books of the Commonwealth* (1576), Bodin defined the essence of the monarch's power: "The principal mark of sovereign majesty is essentially the right to impose laws on subjects generally without their consent."

Although at first glance the theory of the divine right of kings appears to be a blueprint for arbitrary rule, in fact it was yoked together with a number of principles that restrained the conduct of the monarch. As James I pointed out, God had charged kings with obligations: "to minister justice; to establish good laws; and to procure peace."

Kings were bound by the law of nature and the law of nations. They could not deprive their subjects of their lives, their liberties, or their property without due cause established by law. As one French theorist held, "While the kingdom belongs to the king, the king also belongs to the kingdom." Wherever they turned, kings were instructed in the duties of kingship. In tracts,

A GLIMPSE OF A KING

Louis de Rouvroy, duc de Saint-Simon, spent much of his career at the court of Louis XIV. His Memoires *provide a fascinating study of life at Versailles, as well as poison pen portraits of the king and his courtiers. Here he describes some habits of the king.*

HE ALWAYS TOOK GREAT PAINS to find out what was going on in public places, in society, in private houses, even family secrets, and maintained an immense number of spies and tale-bearers. These were of all sorts; some did not know that their reports were carried to him; others did know it; there were others, again, who used to write to him directly, through channels which he prescribed; others who were admitted by the backstairs and saw him in his private room. Many a man in all ranks of life was ruined by these methods, often very unjustly, without ever being able to discover the reason; and when the King had once take a prejudice against a man, he hardly ever got over it....

No one understood better than Louis XIV the art of enhancing the value of a favour by his manner of bestowing it; he knew how to make the most of a word, a smile, even of a glance. If he addressed any one, were it but to ask a trifling question or make some commonplace remark, all eyes were turned on the person so honored; it was a mark of favour which always gave rise to comment....

He loved splendour, magnificence, and profusion in all things, and encouraged similar tastes in his Court; to spend money freely on equipages and buildings, on feasting and at cards, was a sure way to gain his favour, perhaps to obtain the honour of a word from him. Motives of policy and something to do with this; by making expensive habits the fashion, and, for people in a certain position, a necessity, he compelled his courtiers to live beyond their income, and gradually reduced them to depend on his bounty for the means of subsistence.

From duc de Saint-Simon, *Memoires.*

letters, and literature they were lectured on the obligations of their office. "A true king should be first in government, first in council, and first in all the offices of state."

The Court and the Courtiers

For all of the bravura of divine right theory, far more was expected of kings than they could possibly deliver. The day-to-day affairs of government had grown beyond the capacity of any monarch to handle them. The expansion in the powers of the western states absorbed more officials than ever. At the beginning of the sixteenth century, the French court of Francis I employed 622 officers; at the beginning of the seventeenth century, the court of Henry IV employed more than 1500. Yet the difference was not only in size. Members of the seventeenth-century court were becoming servants of the state as well as of the monarch.

Expanding the court was one way in which monarchs co-opted potential rivals within the aristocracy. In return, those who were favored enhanced their power by royal grants of titles, lands, and income. As the court expanded, so did the political power of courtiers. Royal councils—a small group of leading officeholders who advised the monarch on state business—grew in significance. Not only did the council assume the management of government, it also began to advocate policies for the monarch to adopt.

Yet, like everything else in seventeenth-century government, the court revolved around the monarch. The monarch appointed, promoted, and dismissed officeholders at will. As befit that type of personal government, most monarchs chose a single individual to act as a funnel for private and public business. That person was the "favorite," whose role combined varying proportions of best friend, right-hand man, and hired gun. Some favorites, such as Cardinal Richelieu of France and Spain's Count-Duke Olivares, were able to transform themselves into chief ministers with a political philosophy and a vision of government. Others, like the English duke of Buckingham, simply remained royal companions. Favorites walked a not very tight rope. They could retain their balance only as long as they retained their influence with the monarch. Richelieu claimed that it was "more difficult to dominate the four square feet of the king's study than the affairs of Europe." The parallel careers of Richelieu, Olivares, and Buckingham neatly illustrate the dangers and opportunities of the office.

Cardinal Richelieu (1585–1642) was born into a French noble family of minor importance. A younger son, he trained for the law and then for a position that his family owned in the Church; he was made a cardinal in 1622. After skillful participation in the meeting of the Estates-General of 1614, Richelieu was given a court post through the patronage of Queen Marie de Médicis, mother of Louis XIII. The two men made a good match. Louis XIII hated the work of ruling and Richelieu loved little else.

Although Richelieu received great favor from the king—he became a duke and amassed the largest private fortune in France—his position rested on his managerial abilities. Richelieu never enjoyed a close personal relationship with his monarch, and he never felt that his position was secure. In 1630, Marie de Médicis turned against him and he very nearly was ousted from office. His last years were filled with suppressing plots to undermine his power or to take his life.

Count-Duke Olivares (1587–1645) was a younger son of a lesser branch of a great Spanish noble family. By the time he was 20 he had become a courtier with a title, a large fortune, and, most unusually, a university education. Olivares became the favorite of King Philip IV (1621–1665). He was elevated to the highest

This portrait of Richelieu by Philippe de Champaigne shows the cardinal's intellectual power and controlled determination.

The Spanish master Diego Velázquez painted this portrait of the Count-Duke Olivares.

rank of the nobility and lost no time consolidating his position.

Olivares used his closeness to the monarch to gain court appointments for his relatives and political supporters, but he was more interested in establishing political policy than in building a court faction. His objective was to maintain the greatness of Spain, whose fortunes, like his moods, waxed and waned. Like Richelieu, Olivares attempted to further the process of centralizing royal power, which was not very advanced in Spain. Olivares's plans for a nationally recruited and financed army ended in disaster. His efforts at tax reform went unrewarded. He advocated the aggressive foreign policy that mired Spain in the Thirty Years' War and 80 years of war in the Netherlands. As domestic and foreign crises mounted, Philip IV could not resist the pressure to dismiss his chief minister. In 1643, Olivares was removed from office and two years later, physically exhausted and mentally deranged, he died.

The duke of Buckingham (1592–1628) was also a younger son, but not of the English nobility. He received the aimless education of a country gentleman, spending several years in France learning the graces of fashion and dancing. Reputedly one of the most handsome men in Europe, Buckingham hung about the fringes of the English court until his looks and charm brought him to the attention of Queen Anne, James I's wife. She recommended him for a minor office that gave him frequent access to the king. Buckingham quickly caught the eye of James I, and his rise was meteoric. In less than seven years he went from commoner to duke, the highest rank of the English nobility.

Along with his titles, Buckingham acquired political power. He assumed a large number of royal offices, among them Admiral of the Navy, and placed his relatives and dependents in many others. Buckingham took his obligations seriously. He began a reform of naval administration, for example, but his rise to power had been so sudden that he found enemies at every turn. Those increased dramatically when James I died in 1625. But Buckingham succeeded where so many others had failed by becoming the favorite and chief minister of the new king, Charles I (1625–1649). His accumulation of power and patronage proceeded unabated, as did the enmity he aroused. But Charles I stood firmly behind him. In 1628, a discontented naval officer finally accomplished what the most powerful men in England could not: Buckingham was assassinated. While Charles I wept inconsolably at the news, ordinary Londoners drank to the health of his killer.

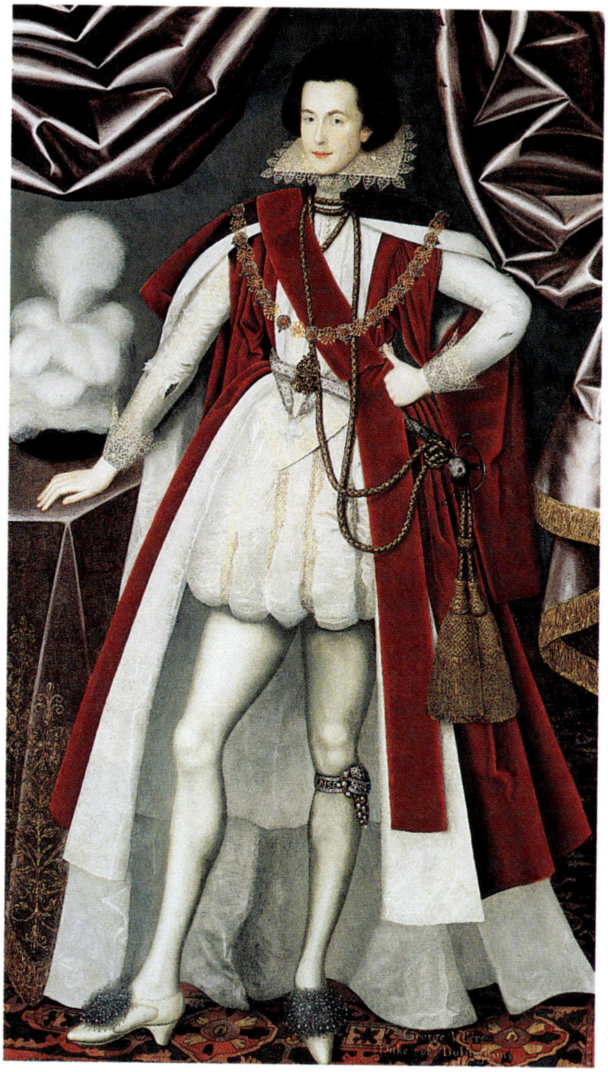

George Villiers, duke of Buckingham. The royal favorite virtually ruled England between 1618 and 1628. The general rejoicing at his death embittered the king and helped bring about the 11 years' rule without Parliament.

The Drive to Centralize Government

Richelieu, Olivares, and Buckingham met very different ends. Yet in their own ways they shared a common goal: to extend the authority of the monarch over his state and to centralize his control over the machinery of governance.

One of the chief means by which kings and councillors attempted to expand the authority of the state was through the legal system. Administering justice was one of the sacred duties of the monarchy. The complexities of ecclesiastical, civil, and customary law gave trained lawyers an essential role in government. As legal experts and the demands for legal services increased, royal law courts multiplied and expanded. In France, the Parlement of Paris, the main law court of the state, became a powerful institution that contested with courtiers for the right to advise the monarch. The number of regional parlements increased, bringing royal justice to the farthest reaches of the realm. Members of the Parlement of Paris and of the expanding provincial parlements were known as nobility of the robe, because of the long gowns lawyers and judges wore.

In Spain, the *letrados*—university-trained lawyers who were normally members of the nobility—were the backbone of royal government. Formal legal training was a requirement for many of the administrative posts in the state. In Castile, members of all social classes frequently used the royal courts to settle personal disputes. The expansion of a centralized system of justice thus joined the interests of subjects and the monarchy.

In England, the legal system expanded differently. Central courts, situated in the royal palace of Westminster, grew and the lawyers and judges who practiced in them became a powerful profession. They were especially active in the House of Commons of the English Parliament, which, along with the House of Lords, had extensive advisory and legislative powers. More important than the rise of the central courts, however, was the rise of the local courts. The English Crown extended royal justice to the counties by granting legal authority to members of the local social elite. The justices of the peace, as they were known, became agents of the Crown in their own localities. Justices were given power to hear and settle minor cases and to imprison those who had committed serious offenses until the assizes, the semiannual sessions of the county court.

Assizes combined the ceremony of rule with its process. Royal authority was displayed in a great procession to the courthouse that was led by the judge and the county justices, followed by the grand and petty juries of local citizens who would hear the cases, and finally by the carts carrying the prisoners to trial. Along with the legal business that was performed, assizes were occasions for edifying sermons, typically on the theme of obedience. Their solemnity—marked by the black robes of the judge, the Latin of the legal proceedings, and the public executions with which assizes invariably ended—all served to instill a sense of the power of the state in the throngs of ordinary people who witnessed them.

Efforts to integrate center and locality extended to more than the exercise of justice. The monarch also needed officials who could enforce royal policy in those localities where the special privileges of groups and individuals remained strong. The best strategy was to appoint local leaders to royal office. But with so much of the aristocracy resident at court, that was not always an effective course. In France, the provincial governors were traditionally members of the ancient nobility who enjoyed wide powers in matters of military recruitment, revenue collection, and judicial administration. But many governors spent far more time in Paris than in the locality that they were to administer and often opposed the exactions demanded by the monarch. By the beginning of the seventeenth century, the French monarchy began to rely on new central officials known as intendants to perform many of the tasks of the provincial governors. Cardinal Richelieu expanded the use of the intendants, and by the middle of the century they had become a vital part of royal government.

The Lords Lieutenant were a parallel institution created in England. Unlike every other European state, England had no national army. Every English county was required to raise, equip, and train its own militia. Lords Lieutenant were in charge of the trained bands. Since the aristocracy was the ancient military class in the state, the lieutenants were chosen from the greatest nobles of the realm. But they delegated their work to members of the gentry, large local landholders who took on their tasks as a matter of prestige rather than profit. Perhaps not surprisingly, the English military was among the weakest in Europe and nearly all its foreign adventures ended in disaster.

Efforts to centralize the affairs of the Spanish monarchy could not proceed so easily. The separate regions over which the king ruled maintained their own laws and privileges. Attempts to apply Castilian rules or implant Castilian officials always drew opposition from other regions. Olivares frequently complained that Philip IV was the king of Castile only and nothing but a thorough plan of unification would make him the king of Spain. He proposed such a plan in 1625 to attempt to solve the dual problems of military manpower and military finance. After 1621, Spain was again deeply involved in European warfare. Fighting in the Netherlands and in Germany demanded large armies and larger sums of money. Olivares launched a plan for a Union of Arms to which all the separate regions of the empire—including Mexico and Peru in the west, Italy in the east, and the separate regions in Iberia—would contribute. He envisioned an army of 140,000 but soon lowered his sights. Not all of the Iberian provinces were persuaded to contribute: Catalonia stood upon its ancient privileges and refused to grant either troops or funds. But Olivares was able to establish at least the principle of unified cooperation.

The Taxing Demands of War

More than anything else, war propelled the consolidation of the state. Whether offensive or defensive, continuous or intermittent, successful or calamitous, war was the irresistible force of the seventeenth-century monarchy. War taxation was its immovable object. Perhaps half of all revenue of the western states went to finance war. To maintain its armies and navies, its fortresses and outposts, the state had to squeeze every penny from its subjects. Old taxes had to be collected more efficiently; new taxes had to be introduced and enforced. As one Spanish jurist observed, in a familiar refrain, "There can be no peace without arms, no arms without money, and no money without taxation." However, the unprecedented demands for money by the state were always resisted. The privileged challenged the legality of levying taxes; the unprivileged did whatever they could to avoid paying them.

The claims and counterclaims of subjects and sovereigns were very strong. Armies had grown bigger and more expensive. In 1625, Philip IV had nearly 300,000 men in arms throughout his empire. The expense of maintaining Spanish fortresses alone had quintupled since the time of Philip II. Not only were there more men to pay, equip, and supply, but the cost of war materials continued to rise with inflation. Similarly, the cost of food and fodder rose. Marauding armies might be able to plunder sufficient grain during the spring and autumn, but they still consumed massive amounts of meat and drink that could not be supplied locally.

The economic hardships caused by the ceaseless military activity touched everyone. Those in the direct path of battle had little left to feed themselves, let alone to provide to the state. The disruption of the

Diego de Velázquez, Surrender of Breda *(1634–1635). Although the incident represented in the painting is fictitious—the leader of the forces of the United Provinces never handed over to the victorious Spanish general the keys to the fortress at Breda—the emotional quality the artist has evoked makes it seem real. Both the victor and the vanquished have been bowed by war, yet meet each other on an almost equal footing in the center of the picture. On either side the faces of the Dutch and Spanish soldiers clearly reflect the fortunes of war.*

delicate cycle of planting and harvesting devastated local communities. Armies plundered ripened grain and trampled seedlings as they moved through fields. The conscription of village men and boys removed vital skills from the community and upset the gender-based division of labor. Peasants were squeezed by the armies for crops, by the lords for rents, and by the state for taxes.

In fact, the inability of the lower orders of European society to finance a century of warfare was clear from the beginning. In Spain and France, the principal problem was that so much of the wealth of the nation was beyond the reach of traditional royal taxation. The nobility and many of the most important towns had long achieved exemption from basic taxes on consumption and wealth. European taxation was regressive, falling most heavily on those least able to pay. Rulers and subjects alike recognized the inequities of the system. Regime after regime began with plans to overhaul the national system of taxation before settling for propping up new emergency levies against the rotting foundations of the old structure. Nevertheless, the fiscal crisis that the European wars provoked did result in an expansion of state taxation.

Fiscal Expedients. In France, for example, royal expenditures rose 60 percent during the first two decades of the seventeenth century, while the yield from the *taille*, the crown's basic commodity tax, remained constant. Thus the crown was forced to search for new revenues, the most important of which was the *paulette*, a tax on officeholding. To raise money, especially in emergencies, the crown had been forced to sell government offices, until by the seventeenth century a majority of offices had been obtained by direct purchase. The sale of an office provided a one-time windfall for the crown, but after that the cost of salaries and benefits was a perpetual drain. Draining, too, were the administrative costs of potentially inefficient officeholders. Many purchased their posts as an investment and treated them as personal property. For an annual payment of one-sixtieth of the value of the office, the paulette allowed the current holder to sell or bequeath it as desired. Henry IV instituted the paulette in 1604, and it became a vital source of royal revenue as well as an acute source of aristocratic and legal complaint. In the early 1620s, revenue from the sale of offices amounted to one-third of the crown's income.

The purchase of office was inherently corrupt, but it was not necessarily inefficient. Sons who were to inherit offices could be trained for their posts, if for no other reason than to operate them profitably. The crown received money from classes in society that were generally beyond the reach of taxation, while members of those classes received power, prestige, and experience in public service. As long as profit and efficiency went hand in hand, both officeholder and monarch might be well served. Unfortunately, it was the king rather than his officers who had the greatest incentive to manipulate the system. The more offices that could be created, the larger the income from the paulette. During fiscal emergencies it was a temptation to which all French monarchs succumbed.

"Fiscal emergency" was just another name for the routine problems of the Spanish monarchy. As the greatest military power in Europe, Spain necessarily had the greatest military budget, and thus the most extensive system of taxation. The crown taxed both domestic and imperial trade and took a healthy share of the gold and silver that continued to be mined in America. But all the revenues fell short of the state's needs. In the 1590s, Philip II established an important new source of internal taxation. In an agreement with the Cortes of Castile, he introduced the *milliones*, a tax on consumption that was to yield millions of ducats a year for war costs. An extremely regressive measure, the milliones taxed the sale of meat, wine, and oil—the basic elements of diet. The tax, which hit urban areas particularly hard, was originally designed to last only six years. But the crises that the crown pleaded in the 1590s were even deeper at the turn of the century. The milliones became a permanent tax and a permanent grievance throughout Castile.

Taxation in England. By contrast, the English crown was never able to persuade Parliament to grant permanent additional revenues. Although uninvolved in European conflicts, England was not immune from military spending. War with Ireland in the 1590s and with Spain between 1588 and 1604 depleted the reserves that the crown had obtained when Henry VIII dissolved the monasteries. Disastrous wars against France and Spain in the 1620s provoked fiscal crisis for a monarchy that had few direct sources of revenue. While the great wealth of the kingdom was in land, the chief sources of revenue for the crown were in trade. In the early seventeenth century, customs duties, or impositions, became a lucrative source of income when the judges ruled that the king could determine which commodities could be taxed and at what rate. Impositions

An equestrian portrait of Charles I by Anthony van Dyck (1599–1641). The antagonism between Charles and Parliament sparked a civil war in England.

fell heavily upon the merchant classes and urban consumers, but unlike the milliones, impositions were placed on luxury import goods rather than on basic commodities.

Because so much of the crown's revenues derived from commerce and because foreign invasion could only come from the sea, the most pressing military need of the English monarchy was for naval defense. Even during the Armada crisis, the largest part of the English fleet had been made up of private merchant ships pressed into service through the emergency tax of Ship Money, which was a tax on each port town to hire a merchant ship and fit it out for war. In the 1630s, Charles I revived Ship Money and extended it to all English localities. His innovation aroused much opposition from the gentry, especially after his refusal to call Parliament into session to have the tax confirmed.

Still, no matter how much new revenue was provided for war finance, more was needed. New taxes and increased rates of traditional taxation created suffering and a sense of grievance throughout the western European states. Opposition to taxation was not based on greed: the state's right to tax was not yet an established principle. Monarchs received certain forms of revenue in return for grants of immunities and privileges to powerful groups in their state. The state's efforts to go beyond the restricted grants were viewed as theft of private property. In the case of Ship Money, challengers argued that the king had no right to what belonged to his subjects except in a case of national emergency. That was a claim that the king accepted, arguing that such an emergency existed in the presence of pirates who were attacking English shipping. But if Charles I did not make a convincing claim for national emergency, the monarchs of France and Spain, the princes of Germany, and the rulers of the states of eastern Europe all did.

Throughout the seventeenth century, monarchy solidified itself as a form of government. The king's authority came from God, but his power came from his people. By administering justice, assembling armies, and extracting resources through taxation, the monarch ruled as well as governed. The richer the king and the more powerful his might, the more potent was his state. Europeans began to identify themselves as citizens of a nation and to see themselves in distinction to other nations.

THE CRISES OF THE ROYAL STATE

The expansion of the functions, duties, and powers of the state in the early seventeenth century was not universally welcomed in European societies. The growth of central government came at the expense of local rights and privileges held by corporate bodies such as the Church and the towns or by individuals such as provincial officials and aristocrats. The state proved a powerful competitor, especially in the contest for the meager surplus produced on the land. As rents and prices stabilized in the early seventeenth century after a long period of inflation, taxation increased, slowly at first and then at a pace with the gathering momentum of the Thirty Years' War. State exactions burdened all segments of society. Peasants lost the small benefit that rising prices had conferred on producers. The surplus that parents had once passed onto children was now taken by the state. Local officials, never altogether popular, came to be seen as parasites and were easy targets for peasant rebellions. Larger landholders, whose prosperity depended on rents and services from an increasingly impoverished peasantry, suffered along with their tenants. Even the great magnates were appalled by the state's insatiable appetite.

Taxation was not the only thing that aroused opposition. Social and economic regulation meant more laws. More laws meant more lawyers and agents of enforcement. State regulation may have been more efficient (though many believed it was more efficient only for the state) but it was certainly disruptive. It was also expensive at a time when the fragile European economy was in a phase of decline. The early seventeenth century was a time of hunger in most of western Europe. Subtle changes in climate reduced the length of growing seasons and the size of crops. Bad harvests in the 1620s and 1640s left disease and starvation in their wake. And the wars ground on. Armies brought misery to those who were forcibly recruited to fight, those who were taxed into destitution, and those who simply had the misfortune to live in the path of destruction.

By the middle of the seventeenth century, a European crisis was taking shape, though its timing and forms differed from place to place. Rural protests, such as grain riots and mob assaults on local institutions, had a long history in all of the European states. Popular revolt was not the product of mindless despair, but rather the natural form of political action for those who fell outside the institutionalized political process. Bread riots and tax revolts became increasingly common in the early seventeenth century. More significantly, as the focus of discontent moved from local institutions to the state, the forms of revolt changed. So, too, did the participants. Members of the political elite began to formulate their own grievances against the expansion of state power. A theory of resistance, first developed in the French wars of religion, came to be applied to political tyranny and posed a direct challenge to the idea of the divine right of kings. By the 1640s, all those forces had converged, and rebellion exploded across the Continent. In Spain, the ancient kingdoms of Catalonia and Portugal asserted their independence from Castilian rule; in France, members of the aristocracy rose against a child monarch and his regent. In Italy, revolts rocked Naples and Sicily. In England, a constitutional crisis gave way to civil war, and then to the first political revolution in European history.

The Need to Resist

Europeans lived more precariously in the seventeenth century than in any period since the Black Death. One benchmark of crisis was population decline. In the Mediterranean, Spain's population fell from 8.5 to 7 million and Italy's population from 13 to 11 million. The ravages of the Thirty Years' War were most clearly felt in central Europe: Germany lost nearly a third of its people, Bohemia nearly half. Northwestern Europe—England, the Netherlands, and France—was hardest hit in the first half of the century and only gradually recovered by 1700. Population decline had many causes and, rather remarkably, direct casualties from warfare was a very small component. The indirect

European Population Data (in millions)

Year	1550	1575	1600	1625	1650	1675	1700
England	3		4	4.5		5.8	5.8
France		20					19.3
Italy	11	13	13	13	12	11.5	12.5
Russia	9		11	8	9.5	13	16
Spain	6.3		7.6		5.2		7
All Europe	85	95	100	100	80	90	100

The Plague in Milan, *a painting by Caspar Crayer of the seventeenth-century Flemish school. The victims of the epidemic are being consoled by a priest.*

effects of war, the disruption of agriculture, and the spread of disease were far more devastating. Spain alone lost a half million people at the turn of the century and another half million between 1647 and 1652. Severe outbreaks of plague in 1625 and in 1665 hit England, while France endured three consecutive years of epidemics, from 1629 to 1631.

All sectors of the European economy, from agriculture to trade, stagnated or declined in the early seventeenth century. Not surprisingly, peasants were hardest hit. The surplus from good harvests did not remain in rural communities to act as a buffer for bad ones. Tens of thousands died during the two great subsistence crises in the late 1620s and the late 1640s. Predictably, acute economic crisis led to rural revolt. As the French peasants reeled from visitations of plague, frost, and floods, the French state was raising the taille, the tax that fell most heavily on the lower orders. A series of French rural revolts in the late 1630s focused on opposition to tax increases. The Nu-Pieds—"the barefooted"—rose against changes in the salt tax; others rose against new levies on wine. The revolts began in the same way: with the murder of a local tax official, the organization of a peasant militia, and the recruitment of local clergy and notables. The rebels forced temporary concessions from local authorities, but they never achieved lasting reforms. Each revolt ended with the reimposition of order by the state. In England, the largest rural protests, like the Midland Revolt of 1607, centered on opposition to the enclosure of grain fields and their conversion to pasture.

The most spectacular popular uprisings occurred in Spanish-occupied Italy. In the spring of 1647, the Sicilian city of Palermo exploded under the pressure of a disastrous harvest, rising food prices, and relentless taxation. A city of 130,000 inhabitants, Palermo imported nearly all of its foodstuffs. As grain prices rose, the city government subsidized the price of bread, running up huge debts in the process. When the town governors could no longer afford the subsidies, they decided to reduce the size of the loaf rather than increase its price. This did not fool the women of the city, who rioted when the first undersized loaves were placed on sale. Soon the entire city was in revolt. "Long live the king and down with taxes!" became the rebel slogan. Commoners who were not part of the urban power structure led the revolt in Palermo. For a time they achieved the abolition of Spanish taxes on basic foodstuffs. Their success provided the model for a similar uprising in Naples, the largest city in Europe. The Neapolitan revolt began in 1647 after the Spanish placed a tax on fruit. A crowd gathered to protest the new imposition, burned the customs house, and murdered several local officials. The protesters were led first by a fisherman and then by a blacksmith, and again the rebels achieved the temporary suspension of Spanish taxation. But neither of the Italian urban revolts could attract support from the local governors or the nobility. Both uprisings were eventually crushed.

The Right to Resist

Rural and urban revolts by members of the lower orders of European society were doomed to failure. Not only did the state control vast military resources, but it could count on the loyalty of the governing classes to suppress local disorder. It was only when local elites rebelled and joined their social and political discontent to the economic grievances of the peasants that the state faced a genuine crisis. Traditionally, aristocratic rebellion focused on the legitimacy rather than the power of the state. Claimants to the throne initiated civil wars for the prize of the crown. By the early seventeenth century, however, hereditary monarchy was too firmly entrenched to be threatened by aristocratic rebellions. When Elizabeth I of England died without an heir, the throne passed to her cousin, James I, without even a murmur of discontent. The assassination of Henry IV in 1610 left a child on the French throne, yet it provoked little more than intrigue over which aristocratic faction would advise him. The principles of hereditary monarchy and the divine right of kings laid an unshakable foundation for royal legitimacy. But if the monarch's right to rule could no longer be challenged, was the method of rule equally unassailable? Were subjects bound to their sovereign in all cases whatsoever?

Luther and Calvin had preached a doctrine of passive obedience. Magistrates ruled by divine will and had to be obeyed in all things, they argued. Both left a tiny crack in the door of absolute submission, however, by recognizing the right of lesser magistrates to resist their superiors if divine law was violated. It was during the French civil wars that a broader theory of resistance began to develop. In attempting to defend themselves from accusations that they were rebels, a number of Huguenot writers responded with an argument that accepted the divine right of kings but limited royal power. They claimed that kings were placed on earth by God to uphold piety and justice. When they failed to do so, lesser magistrates were obliged to resist them. As God would not institute tyranny, oppressive monarchs could not be acting by divine right. Therefore, the king who violated divine law could be punished. In the most influential of such writings, *A Defense of Liberty Against Tyrants* (1579), Philippe Duplessis-Mornay (1549–1623) took the critical next step and argued that the king who violated the law of the land could also be resisted.

In the writings of both Huguenot and Dutch Protestants there remained strict limits to the right to resist. Those authors accepted all the premises of divine right theory and restricted resistance to other divinely ordained magistrates. Obedience tied society together at all levels, and loosening any of the knots might unravel everything. In fact, one crucial binding had already come loose when the arguments used to justify resistance in matters of religion came to be applied to matters of state. Logic soon drove the argument further. If it was the duty of lesser magistrates to resist monarchical tyranny, why was it not the duty of all citizens to do so? That was a question posed not by a Protestant rebel, but by a Jesuit professor, Juan de Mariana (1536–1624). In *The King and the Education of the King* (1598), Mariana described how human government developed from the need of individuals to have leaders to act for their convenience and well-being. The magistrates were established by the people and then legitimated by God. Magistrates were nothing other than the people's representatives, and if it was the duty of magistrates to resist the tyranny of monarchs, then it must also be the duty of every individual citizen. "If the sacred fatherland is falling into ruins, he who tries to kill the tyrant will be acting in no ways unjustly."

Mariana was careful to specify that only the most willful and deliberate lawbreakers were actually tyrants. He also advocated the use of national assemblies rather than individual assassins to make the decision to punish them. But there was no escaping the implications of his argument. If anyone could judge the conduct of kings, then there would be no standards of judgment. As Cardinal Richelieu observed succinctly: "Tyranny is monarchy misliked." In 1605, a Catholic conspiracy to murder James I of England was foiled by government agents at the last moment. In 1610, a religious fanatic assassinated Henry IV of France. The right of individuals to resist tyrants was rapidly developing into the right of subjects to overthrow their monarchs.

In fact, there remained one more vital link in the chain, which was supplied by the great English poet John Milton (1608–1674) in his defense of the English Revolution. Milton built upon traditional resistance theory as it had developed over the previous 50 years. Kings were instituted by the people to uphold piety and justice. Lesser magistrates had the right to resist monarchs. An unjust king forfeited his divine right

The execution of François Ravaillac, the assassin of Henry IV of France.

and was to be punished as any ordinary citizen. In *The Tenure of Kings and Magistrates* (1649), Milton expanded upon the conventional idea that society was formed by a covenant, or contract, between ruler and ruled. The king in his coronation oath promised to uphold the laws of the land and rule for the benefit of his subjects. The subjects promised to obey. Failure by either side to meet obligations broke the contract.

By the middle of the seventeenth century, resistance theory provided the intellectual justification for a number of different attacks on monarchical authority. In 1640, simultaneous rebellions in the ancient kingdoms of Portugal and Catalonia threatened the Spanish monarchy. The Portuguese successfully dissolved the rather artificial bonds that had been created by Philip II and resumed their separate national identity. Catalonia, the easternmost province of Spain, which Ferdinand of Aragon had brought to the union of crowns in the fifteenth century, presented a more serious challenge. Throughout the 1620s, Catalonia, with its rich Mediterranean city of Barcelona, had consistently rebuffed Olivares's attempts to consolidate the Spanish provinces. The Catalonian Cortes—the representative institution of the towns—refused to make even small contributions to the Union of Arms or to successive appeals for emergency tax increases. Catalonian leaders feared that the demands were only the thin edge of the wedge. They did not want their province to go the way of Castile, where taxation was as much an epidemic as plague.

Catalonia relied on its ancient laws to fend off demands for contributions to the Spanish military effort. But soon the province was embroiled in the French war, and Olivares was forced to bring troops into Catalonia. The presence of the soldiers and their conduct inflamed the local population. In the spring of 1640 an unconnected series of peasant uprisings took place. Soldiers and royal officials were slain, and the Spanish viceroy of the province was murdered. But the violence was not directed only against outsiders. Attacks on wealthy citizens raised the specter of social revolt.

At that point a peasant uprising broadened into a provincial rebellion. The political leaders of Barcelona not only decided to approve the rebellion but decided to lead it. They declared that Philip IV had violated the fundamental laws of Catalonia and that as a consequence their allegiance to the crown of Spain was dissolved. They turned to Louis XIII of France, offering him sovereignty if he would preserve their liberties. In fact, the Catalonians simply exchanged a devil they knew for one they did not. The French happily sent troops into Barcelona to repel a Spanish attempt to crush the rebellion, and then two armies occupied

Catalonia. The Catalonian rebellion lasted for 12 years. When the Spanish finally took Barcelona in 1652, both rebels and ruler were exhausted from the struggle.

The revolt of the Catalonians posed a greater external threat to the Spanish monarchy than it did an internal one. In contrast, the French Fronde, an aristocratic rebellion that began in 1648, was more directly a challenge to the underlying authority of the state. It too began in response to fiscal crises brought on by war. Throughout the 1640s the French state had tottered on the edge of bankruptcy. It had used every means of creative financing that its ministers could devise, mortgaging as much of the future as anyone would buy. Still, it was necessary to raise traditional taxes and institute new ones. The first tactic revived peasant revolts, especially in the early years of the decade; the second led to the Fronde.

The Fronde was a rebellion against the regency government of Louis XIV (1643–1715), who was only four years old when he inherited the French throne. His mother, Anne of Austria (1601–1666), ruled as regent with the help of her Italian adviser, Cardinal Mazarin (1602–1661). In the circumstances of war, agricultural crisis, and financial stringency, no regency government was popular, but Anne and Mazarin made the worst of a bad situation. They initiated new taxes on officeholders, Parisian landowners, and the nobility. Soon all three united against them, led by the Parlement of Paris, the highest court in the land, in which new decrees of taxation had to be registered. When the Parlement refused to register a number of the new taxes proposed by the government and soon insisted on the right to control the crown's financial policy, Anne and Mazarin struck back by arresting a number of leading members of the Parlement. But in 1648 barricades went up in Paris, and the court, along with the nine-year-old king, fled the capital. Quickly the Fronde—which took its name from the slingshots that children used to hurl stones at carriages—became an aristocratic revolt aimed not at the king, but at his advisers. Demands for Mazarin's resignation, the removal of the new taxes, and greater participation in government by nobles and Parlement were coupled with profuse statements of loyalty to the king.

The duc de Condé, leader of the Parisian insurgents, courted Spanish aid against Mazarin's forces, and the cardinal was forced to make concessions in order to prevent a Spanish invasion of France. The leaders of the Fronde agreed that the crown must overhaul its finances and recognize the rights of the administrative nobility to participate in formulating royal policy, but they had no concrete proposals to accomplish either aim. Nor could they control the deteriorating political situation in Paris and a number of provincial capitals where urban and rural riots followed the upper-class attack upon the state. The catastrophic winter of 1652,

An episode from the second Fronde, one of two French civil wars that occurred during the minority of Louis XIV.

with its combination of harvest failure, intense cold, and epidemic disease, brought the crisis to a head. Louis XIV was declared old enough to rule and his forces recaptured Paris, where he was welcomed as a savior. Born of frustration, fear, and greed, the Fronde accomplished little. It demonstrated only that the French aristocracy remained an independent force in politics. Like the Catalonian revolt, it revealed the fragility of the absolute state on the one hand, yet its underlying stability on the other.

The English Civil War

On the surface, it is difficult to understand why the most profound challenge to monarchical authority took place in England. Among the nations of Europe, England alone enjoyed peace in the early seventeenth century. Except for a brief period around 1620, the English economy sputtered along. The monarchy itself was stable. James I had succeeded his cousin Elizabeth I without challenge and already had as many children as the Tudors had produced in nearly a century.

James I was not a lovable monarch, but he was capable, astute, and generous. In the eyes of his critics he had two great faults: he succeeded a legend and he was Scottish. There was little he could do about either. Elizabeth I had ruled England successfully for more than 40 years. As the economy soured and the state tilted toward bankruptcy in the 1590s, the queen remained above criticism. She sold off royal lands worth thousands of pounds and ran up huge debts at the turn of the century, yet the gleaming myth of the glorious virgin queen tarnished not the least bit. When she died, the general population wept openly and the governing elite breathed a collective sigh of relief. There was so much to be done to set things right.

At first, James I endeared himself to the English gentry and aristocracy by showering them with the gift of social elevation. On his way to London from Scotland, the first of the Stuart kings knighted thousands of gentlemen who had waited in vain for favor from the queen. He promoted peers and created new titles to meet the pent-up demands of decades of stinginess. But he showered favor equally on his own countrymen, members of his royal Scottish court who accompanied him to England. A strong strain of ethnic prejudice combined with the disappointed hopes of English courtiers to generate immediate hostility to the new regime. If Elizabeth could do no wrong, James could do little right. Although he relied upon Elizabeth's most trusted ministers to guide state business, James was soon plunged into financial and political difficulties. He never escaped from either.

Charles I. James's financial problems resulted directly from the fact that the tax base of the English monarchy was undervalued. For decades the monarchy had staved off a crisis by selling lands that had been confiscated from the Church in the mid-sixteenth century. But that solution reduced the crown's long-term revenues and made it dependent on extraordinary grants of taxation from Parliament. Royal demands for money were met by parliamentary demands for political reform, and the differing objectives provoked unintentional political controversies in the 1620s. The most significant, in 1628, during the reign of Charles I, led to the formulation of the Petition of Right, which restated the traditional English freedoms from arbitrary arrest and imprisonment (habeas corpus), nonparliamentary taxation, and the confiscation of property by martial law.

Religious problems mounted on top of economic and political difficulties. Demands were made for thoroughgoing church reforms by groups and individuals who had little in common apart from the name given to them by their detractors: Puritans. One of the most contentious issues raised by Puritans was the survival in the Anglican church of the Catholic hierarchy of archbishops and bishops. They demanded the abolition of this episcopal form of government and its replacement with a presbyterial system similar to that in Scotland, in which congregations nominated their own representatives to a national assembly. As the king was the supreme head of the English church, an attack upon church structure was an attack upon the monarchy. "No bishop, no king," James I declared as he rejected the first formal attempts at reform. But neither James I nor his son, Charles I, opposed religious reform. They too wanted a better educated clergy, a plain and decorous worship service, and godly citizens. But to achieve their reforms they strengthened episcopal power. In the 1620s, Archbishop William Laud (1573–1645) rose to power in the English church by espousing a Calvinism so moderate that many denied it was Calvinism at all. Laud preached the beauty of holiness and strove to reintroduce decoration in the church and a formal decorum in the service. One of Laud's first projects after he was appointed archbishop of Canterbury was to establish a consistent divine service in England and Scotland by creating new prayer books.

It fell to the unfortunate dean of St. Giles Cathedral in Edinburgh to introduce the new Scottish prayer book in 1637. The reaction was immediate: someone threw a stool at his head and dozens of women screamed that "popery" was being brought to Scotland. There were riots by citizens and resistance to the use of the new prayer book by clergy and the nobility. To Charles I the opposition was rebellion, and he began to raise forces to suppress it. But Scottish soldiers were far more determined to preserve their religious practice than were English soldiers to impose the king's. By the end of 1640, a Scottish army had successfully invaded England.

Now the fiscal and political problems of the Stuart monarchs came into play. For 11 years, Charles I had managed to do what he was in theory supposed to do: live from his own revenues. He had accomplished that by a combination of economy and the revival of ancient feudal rights that struck hard at the governing classes. He levied fines for unheard-of offenses, expanded traditional taxes, and added a brutal efficiency to the collection of revenue. While the expedients sufficed during peacetime, when an army had to be raised and a war fought, Charles I was again dependent upon grants from Parliament, which he reluctantly summoned in 1640.

The Long Parliament. The Long Parliament, which met in November 1640 and sat for 13 years, saw little urgency in levying taxes to repel the Scots. After all, the Scots were resisting Laud's religious innovations, and there were many Englishmen who believed that they should be resisted. More to the point, members of Parliament had a host of political grievances to be redressed before they granted the king his money. Parliament proposed a number of constitutional reforms that Charles I reluctantly accepted. The Long Parliament would not be dismissed without its own consent. In the future, Parliaments would be summoned once every three years. Due process in common law would be observed, and the ancient taxes that the crown had revived would be abolished. To show its seriousness of purpose, Parliament, as the highest court in the land, tried and executed Charles's leading political adviser, the Earl of Strafford, and imprisoned Archbishop Laud.

At first Charles I could do nothing but bide his time and accept the assaults on his power and authority, believing that once he had crushed the Scots he would be able to bargain from a position of strength. But as the months passed, it became clear that Parliament had no intention of providing him with money or forces. Rather, the members sought to negotiate with the Scots themselves and to continue to demand concessions from the king as long as the Scottish threat remained. By the end of 1641, Charles's patience had worn thin. He bungled an attempt to arrest the leaders of the House of Commons, but he successfully spirited his wife and children out of London. Then he too left the capital and headed north where, in the summer of 1642, he raised the royal standard and declared the leaders of Parliament rebels and traitors. England was plunged into civil war.

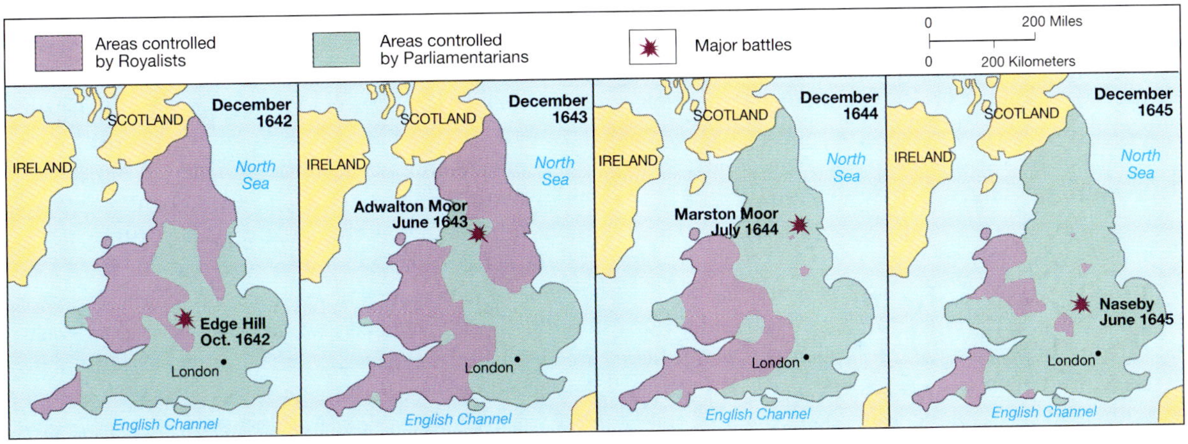

The English Civil War. The maps show the gradual triumph of the parliamentarians whose control of London and the coastal areas gave them a profound logistical advantage during the wars.

Parliament had finally pushed too hard, and its members now found themselves in the unprecedented situation of having to fight a war against their sovereign, a war that few of them wanted and that hardly anyone believed they could win. One of the Parliament's generals summed up the futility of the situation: "If we defeat the king ninety-nine times, yet still he is king. But if he defeat us once we will all be hanged as traitors." Nevertheless, there were strong passions on both sides. Parliamentarians believed that they were fighting to defend their religion, their liberties, and the rule of law. Royalists believed they were fighting to defend their monarch, their church, and social stability. After nearly three years of inconclusive fighting, in June 1645 Parliament won a decisive victory at Naseby and brought the war to an end the following summer. The king was in captivity, bishops had been abolished, a Presbyterian church had been established, and limitations were placed on royal power. All that remained necessary to end three years of civil war was the king's agreement to abide by the judgment of battle.

But Charles I had no intention of surrendering either his religion or his authority. Despite the rebels' successes, they could not rule without him, and he would concede nothing as long as opportunities to maneuver remained. In 1647 there were opportunities galore. The war had proved ruinously expensive to Parliament. It owed enormous sums to the Scots, to its own soldiers, and to the governors of London. Each of those elements had its own objectives in a final settlement of the war, and they were not altogether compatible. London feared the parliamentary army, unpaid and camped dangerously close to the capital. The Scots and the English Presbyterians in Parliament feared that the religious settlement already made would be sacrificed by those known as Independents, who desired a more decentralized church. The Independents feared that they would be persecuted just as harshly by the Presbyterians as they had been by the king. In fact, the war had settled nothing.

The English Revolutions

Charles I happily played both ends against the middle until the army decisively ended the game. In June 1647, soldiers kidnapped the king and demanded that Parliament pay their arrears, protect them from legal retribution, and recognize their service to the nation. Those in Parliament who opposed the army's intervention were impeached, and when London Presbyterians rose up against the army's show of force, troops moved in to occupy the city. The civil war, which had come so close to resolution in 1647, had now become a military revolution. Religious and political radicals flocked to the army and encouraged the soldiers to support their programs and resist disbandment. New fighting broke out in 1648 as Charles encouraged his supporters to resume the war. But forces under the command of Sir Thomas Fairfax (1612–1671) and Oliver Cromwell (1599–1658) easily crushed the royalist uprisings in England and Scotland. The army then demanded that Charles I be brought to justice for his treacherous conduct both before and during the war. When the majority in Parliament refused, still hoping against hope to reach an accommodation with the king, the soldiers again acted decisively. In December 1648, army regiments were sent to London to purge the two houses of Parliament of those who opposed the army's demands. The remaining members, contemptuously called the Rump Parliament, voted to bring the king to trial for his crimes against the liberties of his subjects. On 30 January 1649, Charles I was executed and England was declared to be a commonwealth. (See "'King Charles's Head,'" pp. 560–561.) The monarchy and the House of Lords were abolished, and the nation was to be governed by what was left of the membership of the House of Commons.

Oliver Cromwell. For four years, the members of the Rump Parliament struggled with proposals for a new constitution while balancing the demands of moderate and radical reformers and an increasingly hostile army. It achieved little other than to raise the level of frustration. In 1653, Oliver Cromwell, with the support of the army's senior officers, forcibly dissolved the Rump and became the leader of the revolutionary government. At first he ruled along with a Parliament hand-picked from among the supporters of the commonwealth. When Cromwell's Parliament proved no more capable of governing than had the Rump, a written constitution, The Instrument of Government (1653), established a new polity. Cromwell was given the title Lord Protector, and he was to rule along with a freely elected Parliament and an administrative body known as the Council of State.

Cromwell was able to hold the revolutionary cause together through the force of his own personality. A member of the lesser landed elite who had opposed the arbitrary policies of Charles I, he was a devout

A SHORT, SHARP SHOCK

Charles I was executed at Westminster on a bitter January afternoon in 1649. This excerpt comes from an eyewitness account of his last moments. Charles, who was accompanied on the scaffold by the bishop of London, discovered that the chopping block was very short so that he could be held down if he resisted.

AND TO THE EXECUTIONER HE SAID, "I shall say but very short prayers, and when I thrust out my hands—"

Then he called to the bishop for his cap, and having put it on, asked the executioner, "Does my hair trouble you?" who desired him to put it all under his cap; which, as he was doing by the help of the bishop and the executioner, he turned to the bishop, and said, "I have a good cause, and a gracious God on my side."

The bishop said, "There is but one stage more, which, though turbulent and troublesome, yet is a very short one. You may consider it will soon carry you a very great way; it will carry you from earth to heaven; and there you shall find to your great joy the prize you hasten to, a crown of glory."

The king adjoins, "I go from a corruptible to an incorruptible crown; where no disturbance can be, no disturbance in the world."

The bishop. "You are exchanged from a temporal to an eternal crown—a good exchange."

Then the king asked the executioner, "Is my hair well?" … and looking upon the block, said … "You must set it fast."

The executioner. "It is fast, sir."

King. "It might have been a little higher."

Executioner. "It can be no higher, sir."

King. "When I put out my hands this way, then—"

Then having said a few words to himself, as he stood, with hands and eyes lifted up, immediately stooping down he laid his neck upon the block; and the executioner, again putting his hair under his cap, his Majesty, thinking he had been going to strike, bade him, "Stay for the sign."

Executioner. "Yes, I will, and it please your Majesty."

After a very short pause, his Majesty stretching forth his hands, the executioner at one blow severed his head from his body; which, being held up and showed to the people, was with his body put into a coffin covered with black velvet and carried into his lodging.

His blood was taken up by divers persons for different ends: by some as trophies of their villainy; by others as relics of a martyr; and in some hath had the same effect, by the blessing of God, which was often found in his sacred touch when living.

Puritan who believed in a large measure of religious toleration for Christians. As both a member of Parliament and a senior officer in the army, he had been able to temper the claims of each when they conflicted. Cromwell saw God's hand directing England toward a more glorious future, and he believed that his own actions were divinely ordained: "No man climbs higher than he that knows not whither he goes." Although many urged him to accept the crown of England and begin a new monarchy, Cromwell steadfastly held out for a government in which fundamental authority resided in Parliament. Until his death he defended the achievements of the revolution and held its conflicting constituents together.

But a sense that only a single person could effectively rule a state remained too strong for the reforms of the revolutionary regimes to have much chance of success. When Cromwell died in 1658 it was only natural that his eldest son, Richard, should be proposed as the new Lord Protector despite the fact that Richard had very little experience in either military or civil affairs. Nor did he have the sense of purpose that was his father's greatest source of strength. Without an individual to hold the movement together, the revolution fell apart. In 1659, the army again intervened in civil affairs, dismissing the recently elected Parliament and calling for the restoration of the monarchy to provide stability to the state. After a period of negotiation in

"King Charles's Head"

THEY COULD HAVE KILLED HIM QUIETLY: the executioners slipping away silently in the night, unauthorized, unknown. It was the quickest way, and it would end all doubts. Since June 1647, Charles I had been prisoner of the parliamentary army, and there had been more than one moment in which his elimination would have settled so many vexing problems. They could have let him escape: a small boat, an unlocked door, a guard conveniently asleep. Let him take his chances on the open sea. Let him live out his life in exile. Dangerous, perhaps, but still he would be gone and a new government in the name of the people could get on with creating a new order. They could have done it quietly.

Instead, the leaders of Parliament and the army decided on a trial, a public presentation of charges against the king. A high court of justice, enforcing the laws of England, would try its king for treason against the state. The logic was simple: if Parliament had fought for the preservation of the liberties of all Englishmen, then they could only proceed against the king by law. If they followed any other course, then they were usurpers, ruling by might rather than law. But if the logic was simple, everything else was hopelessly complex. English law was a system of precedents, one case stacked upon another to produce the weighty judgments of what was lawful. Never had there been a treason case like this one. Indeed, how could the king commit treason? How could he violate his own allegiance?

Nor was it clear what court had jurisdiction over the unprecedented case. The royal judges would have no part of it; neither would the House of Lords. The House of Commons was forced to create its own high court of justice, 135 supporters of the parliamentary cause drawn from its own members, from the army, and from among the leading citizens of London. Barely half attended any of the sessions. Judge John Bradshaw, who presided over two provincial royal courts, was chosen to preside at the king's trial after several of his more distinguished colleagues tactfully declined the post. Bradshaw took the precaution of lining his hat with lead against the chance that he would be shot at from the galleries rather than the floor.

The shortcomings did not deter the leaders of the parliamentary cause. The times were unprecedented, and the ossified procedures of lawyers and law courts could not be allowed to detract from the undeniable justice of their cause. Charles I had committed treason against his nation. He had declared war on his people. He had brought Irish and Scottish armies into England to repress Parliament, and when that had failed he had negotiated with French, Danish, and Dutch troops for the same purpose. Even when he had been defeated in battle, when the judgment of God was clear for all to see: even then he plotted and he tricked. His lies were revealed by his own hand, his captured correspondence detailing how he intended to double-cross those to whom he swore he would be faithful. Cromwell called him "a man against whom the Lord had witnessed," and the prosecution needed no better testimony than that. If there were no precedents, then the trial would set one.

Nevertheless, the makeshift nature of the court provided the king with his line of attack. If there was to be a public display, then Charles I was determined to turn it to his advantage. Even as his royal palace was being converted into a courtroom and an execution platform was being hastily erected on one of its balconies, even then the king could not conceive that the nation could be governed without him. Royal government had guided England for a millennium, and for all he could see would do so for another.

About the trial itself, he worried not at all. There could be no court in the land that could try its king, no authority but his own that could determine a charge of treason. When it was read out that he was a tyrant and traitor, he burst out laughing: "Remember, I am your king, your lawful king and what sins you bring upon your heads and the judgment of God upon this land, think well upon it," he told his accusers.

The trial began on Saturday, 20 January 1649. Armed soldiers in battle dress cleared the floor of the large chamber. Curious onlookers packed the galleries. Despite the

fact that all former royalists had been ordered out of the city before the trial began, the king had more than one supporter well placed to heckle the commissioners. The king wore the enormous golden star of the Order of the Garter on his cloak but was allowed no other symbol of royalty to overawe his accusers.

The charge of "treason and high misdemeanors" had carefully been prepared. The king was accused of making war on his people "whereby much innocent blood of the free people of this nation hath been spilt." When the resounding indictment concluded, all eyes turned toward Charles I. He would have to answer the charge, guilty or not guilty, and in answering show the line of his defense. But the king chose a different strategy. Rather than answer the charge, he questioned the authority of the court. "I would know by what power I am called hither, a king cannot be tried by any superior jurisdiction here on earth." That was the weakest point of the parliamentary strategy. Judge Bradshaw could only assert that the court represented the free people of England. But Charles was relentless. He demanded precedents and refused to be silenced by the assertion that his objections were overruled.

The prosecutors had prepared a case against the king and were ready to call their witnesses. They hoped to place the king's evil conduct before the eyes of the nation. But in English law, a defendant who refused to plead was presumed to have pleaded guilty. Thus the king's trial ended as soon as it had begun. After three fruitless sessions and much behind-the-scenes maneuvering, it was decided that the king should be condemned and sentenced to die. On 27 January, Judge Bradshaw appeared in the scarlet robes of justice and issued the sentence. Charles had prepared a statement for maximum effect and waited patiently to deliver it. It was the king's turn to be surprised. After pronouncing sentence, Bradshaw and the commissioners rose from the bench. "Will you not hear me a word, Sir," called a flustered Charles I. "No," replied the judge. "Guards, withdraw your prisoner."

Tuesday, 30 January, dawned cold and clear. It had been a bitter winter. Charles put on two shirts so that if he trembled from the cold it would not be interpreted as fear. In fact, he made a very good end. He spoke briefly and to the point, denying that he had acted against the true interests and rights of his subjects. Then he lay down on the platform, placed his head upon the block, and prayed. As the axe fell, one witness recorded, "such a groan as I never heard before and hope never to hear again" broke forth from the crowd. The English Revolution had begun.

Allegorical view of Cromwell as savior of England. Babylon and Error are trampled under his feet. On the pillar at the right, England, Scotland, and Ireland pay him homage, and the left pillar enumerates the legal bases of his power.

which the king agreed to a general amnesty with only a few exceptions, the Stuarts were restored when Charles II (1649–1685) took the throne in 1660.

Twenty years of civil war and revolution had had their effect. Parliament became a permanent part of civil government and now had to be managed rather than ignored. Royal power over taxation and religion was curtailed, although in fact Parliament proved more vigorous in suppressing religious dissent than the monarchy ever had. England was to be a reformed Protestant state, although there remained much dispute about what constituted reform. Absolute monarchy had become constitutional monarchy, with the threat of revolution behind the power of Parliament and the threat of anarchy behind the power of the crown.

The "Glorious Revolution." The threats of revolution and of anarchy proved potent in 1685 when James II (1685–1688) came to the throne. A declared Catholic, James attempted to use his power of appointment to foil the constraints that Parliament imposed on him. He elevated Catholics to leading posts in the military and in the central government and began a campaign to pack a new Parliament with his supporters. That proved too much for the governing classes, who entered into negotiations with William, Prince of Orange, husband of Mary Stuart, James's eldest daughter. In 1688, William landed in England with a small force. Without support, James II fled to France, the English throne was declared vacant, and William and Mary were proclaimed king and queen of England. There was little bloodshed in England and little threat of social disorder, and the event soon came to be called the Glorious Revolution. Its achievements were set down in the Declaration of Rights (1689), which was presented to William and Mary before they took the throne. The Declaration reasserted the fundamental principles of constitutional monarchy as they had developed over the previous half century. Security of property and the regularity of Parliaments were guaranteed. The Toleration Act (1689) granted religious freedom to nearly all groups of Protestants. The liberties of the subject and the rights of the sovereign were to be in balance.

The events of 1688 in England reversed a trend toward increasing power on the part of the Stuarts and resulted in the development of a unique form of government that a century later would spawn dozens of imitators. John Locke (1632–1704) was the theorist of the Revolution of 1689. He was heir to the century-old debate on resistance, and he carried the doctrine to a new plateau. In *Two Treatises on Civil Government* (1690), Locke developed the contract theory of government. Political society was a compact that individuals entered into freely for their own well-being. It was designed to maintain each person's natural rights—life, liberty, and property. Natural rights were inherent in individuals; they could not be given away. The contract between rulers and subjects was an agreement for the protection of natural rights. "Arbitrary power

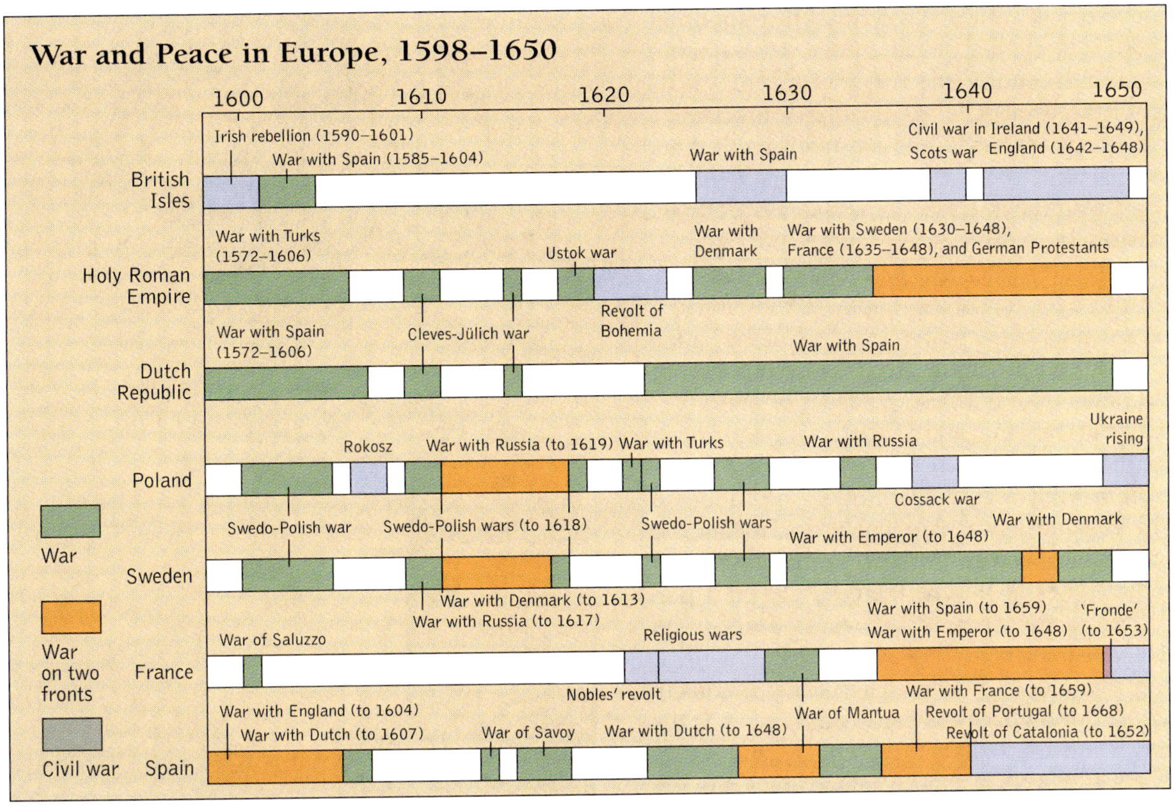

War and Peace in Europe, 1598–1650

cannot consist with the ends of society and government. Men would not quit the freedom of the state of nature were it not to preserve their lives, liberties, and fortunes and by stated rules to secure their peace and happiness." When rulers acted arbitrarily, they were to be deposed by their subjects, preferably in the relatively peaceful manner in which James II had been replaced by William III.

The efforts of European monarchies to centralize their power came at the expense of the Church, the aristocracy, and the localities. It was a struggle that took place over decades and was not accomplished easily. In France, the Fronde was an aristocratic backlash; in Spain, the revolt of the Catalonians pitted the Castilian crown against a proud ethnic province. In England, a civil war fought to prevent the encroachments of the crown against the rights of the community gave way to a bloody revolution that combined religious and constitutional grievances—the excesses of monarchy were succeeded by the excesses of parliamentary rule. But the lesson learned by the English ruling elites was that for a nation to enjoy the benefits of a powerful central authority, it was necessary to restrain that authority. The Glorious Revolution of 1689 helped create a constitutional balance between ruler and ruled.

THE ZENITH OF THE ROYAL STATE

The crises of midcentury tested the mettle of the royal states. Over the long term, the crises had two different consequences. First, they provided a check to the exercise of royal power. Fear of recurring rebellions had a chilling effect upon policy, especially taxation. Reforms of financial administration, long overdue, were one of the themes of the later seventeenth century. Even as royal government strengthened itself, it remained concerned about the impact of its policies. Second, the memory of rebellion served to control the ambitions of factious noblemen and town oligarchs.

If nothing else, the episodes of opposition to the rising royal states made clear the universal desire for stable government, which was seen as the responsibility of both subjects and rulers. By the second half of the seventeenth century, effective government was the byword of the royal state. As Louis XIV proclaimed, rule was a trade that had to be constantly studied and practiced. The natural advantages of monarchy had to be merged with the interests of the state's citizens and their desires for wealth, safety, and honor. After so much chaos and instability, the monarchy had to be elevated above the fray of day-to-day politics; it had to become a symbol of the power and glory of the nation. Control no longer meant the greedy grasp of royal officials but rather their practiced guidance of affairs.

In England, Holland, and Sweden, a form of constitutional monarchy developed in which rulers shared power, in varying degrees, with other institutions of state. In England it was Parliament, in Holland the town oligarchies, and in Sweden the nobility. But in most other states in Europe there developed a pure form of royal government known as absolutism. Absolute monarchy revived the divine right theories of kingship and added to them a cult of the personality of the ruler. Absolutism was practiced in states as dissimilar as Denmark, Brandenburg-Prussia, and Russia. It reached its zenith in France under Louis XIV, the most powerful of the seventeenth-century monarchs.

The title page of the first edition of Thomas Hobbes's Leviathan, *published in 1651. The huge figure, composed of many tiny human beings, symbolizes the surrender of individual human rights to those of the state.*

The Nature of Absolute Monarchy

Locke's theory of contract provided one solution to the central problem of seventeenth-century government: how to balance the monarch's right to command and the subjects' duty to obey. By establishing a constitutional monarchy in which power was shared between the ruler and a representative assembly of subjects, England found one path out of this thicket. But it was not a path that many others could follow. The English solution was most suited to a state that was largely immune from invasion and land war. Constitutional government required a higher level of political participation of citizens than did an absolute monarchical one. Greater participation in turn meant greater freedom of expression, greater toleration of religious minorities, and greater openness in the institutions of government. All were dangerous. The price that England paid was a half century of governmental instability.

The alternative to constitutional monarchy was absolute monarchy. It too found its greatest theorist in England. Thomas Hobbes (1588–1679) was one of many Englishmen who went into exile in France during the course of the English civil wars. In his greatest work, *Leviathan* (1651), Hobbes argued that before civil society had been formed, humans lived in a savage state of nature, "in a war of every man against every man." That was a ghastly condition without morality or law—"the notions of right and wrong, of justice and injustice have there no place." People came together to form a government for the most basic of all purposes: self-preservation. Without government they were condemned to a life that was "solitary, poor, nasty, brutish, and short." To escape the state of nature, indi-

FATHERS KNOW BEST

Sir Robert Filmer's Patriarcha *(1680) is one of the clearest statements of the divine origins of monarchy in human society. Filmer believed that Adam, the first father, was monarch of the universe and that his children owed him absolute obedience.* Patriarcha *was written a half century before it was published in 1680.*

IN ALL KINGDOMS OR COMMONWEALTHS IN THE WORLD, whether the prince be the supreme father of the people or but the true heir of such a father ... there is, and always shall be continued to the end of the world, a natural right of a supreme father over every multitude, although, by the secret will of God, many at first do most unjustly obtain the exercise of it.

To confirm this natural right of regal power, we find in the decalogue that the law which enjoins obedience to kings is delivered in the terms of 'honour thy father' [Exodus, xx, 12] as if all power were originally in the father. If obedience to parents be immediately due by a natural law, and subjection to princes but by the mediation of an human ordinance, what reason is there that the law of nature should give place to the laws of men?...

If we compare the natural duties of a father with those of a king, we find them to be all one, without any difference at all but only in the latitude or extent of them. As the father over one family, so the king, as father over many families, extends his care to preserve, feed, clothe, instruct and defend the whole commonwealth. His wars, his peace, his courts of justice and all his acts of sovereignty tend only to preserve and distribute to every subordinate and inferior father, and to their children, their rights and privileges, so that all the duties of a king are summed up in an universal fatherly care of his people.

From Sir Robert Filmer, *Patriarcha.*

viduals pooled their power and granted it to a ruler. The terms of the Hobbesian contract were simple. Rulers agreed to rule; subjects agreed to obey. When the contract was intact, people ceased to live in a state of nature. When it was broken, they returned to it. With revolts, rebellions, and revolutions erupting in all parts of Europe, Hobbes's state of nature never seemed very far away.

For most states of Europe in the later seventeenth century, absolute monarchy became not only a necessity but an ideal. The consolidation of power in the hands of the divinely ordained monarch who nevertheless ruled according to principles of law and justice was seen as the perfect form of government. Absolutism was an expression of control rather than of power. If the state was sometimes pictured as a horse, the absolute monarch gripped the reins more tightly than the whip. "Many writers have tried to confound absolute government with arbitrary government. But no two things could be more unlike," wrote Bishop Jacques Bossuet (1627–1704), who extolled absolutism in France. The absolute ruler ruled in the interests of his people: "The prince is the public person, the whole state is included in him, the will of all the people is enclosed within his own."

The main features of absolute monarchy were designed to extend royal control. As in the early seventeenth century, the person of the monarch was revered. Courts grew larger and more lavish in an effort to enhance the glory of the monarchy, and thereby of the state. "L'état, c'est moi"—"I am the state"—Louis XIV was supposed to have said. No idea better expresses absolutism's connection between governor and governed. As the king grew in stature, his competitors for power all shrank. Large numbers of nobles were herded together at court under the watchful eye of monarchs who now ruled rather than reigned. The king shed the cloak of his favorites and rolled up his own sleeves to manage state affairs. Representative institutions, especially those that laid claim to control over taxation, were weakened or cast aside for obstructing efficient government and endangering the welfare of the state. Monarchs needed standing armies, permanent forces that could be drilled and trained in the increasingly sophisticated arts of war. Thus the military was expanded and made an integral part of the machinery of government. The military profession developed within nations, gradually replacing mercenary adventurers who had fought for booty rather than for duty.

Yet the absolute state was never as powerful in practice as it was in theory, nor did it ever exist in its ideal shape. Absolutism was always in the making, never quite made. Its success depended upon a strong monarch who knew his own will and could enforce it. It depended upon unity within the state and the absence or ruthless suppression of religious or political minorities. The absolute ruler needed to control information and ideas, to limit criticism of state policy. Ultimately, the absolute state rested upon the will of its citizens to support it. The seventeenth-century state remained a loose confederation of regions, many acquired by conquest, whose loyalty was practical rather than instinctive. There was no state police force to control behavior or attitudes, no newspapers or mass communication to spread propaganda. Censorship might restrict the flow of forbidden books, but it could do little to dam up the current of ideas.

Absolutism in the East

Frederick William, the Great Elector of Brandenburg-Prussia (1640–1688), was one of the European princes who made the most effective use of the techniques of absolutism. In 1640, he inherited a scattered and ungovernable collection of territories that had been devastated by the Thirty Years' War. Brandenburg, the richest of his possessions, had lost nearly half of its population. The war had a lasting impact on Frederick William's character. As a child, he had hidden in the woods to escape bands of marauding soldiers; as a

GENEALOGY

Tsars of Russia

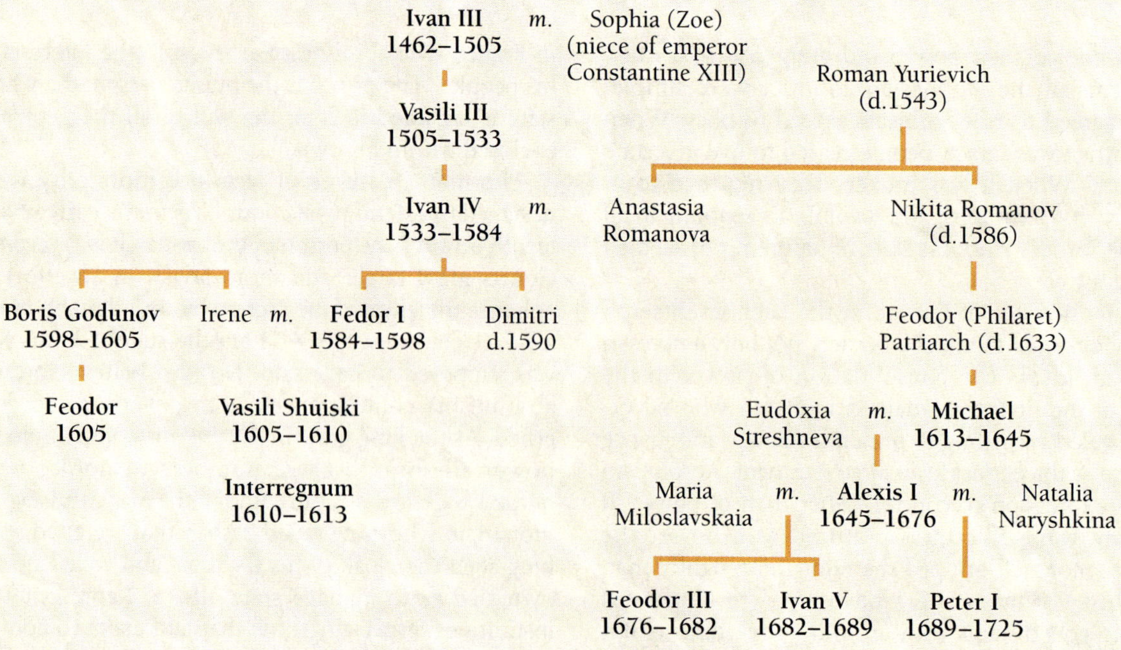

The Expansion of Russia under Peter the Great. Peter added vital territory on the Baltic Sea to the vast Russian empire.

teenager, he had followed to its burial the corpse of Gustavus Adolphus, the man he most admired and wished to emulate. A long stay in Holland during the final stages of the Dutch Revolt impressed on him the importance of a strong army and a strong base of revenue to support it.

Frederick William had neither. In 1640, his forces totaled no more than 2500 men, most of them, including the officers, the dregs of German society. Despite the fact that he was surrounded by powerful neighbors—Sweden and Poland both claimed sovereignty over parts of his inheritance—the territories under his control had no tradition of military taxation. The nobility, known as the Junker, enjoyed immunity from almost all forms of direct taxation, and the towns had no obligation to furnish either men or supplies for military operations beyond their walls. When Frederick William attempted to introduce an excise—the kind of commodity tax on consumption that had so successfully financed the Dutch Revolt and the English Revolution—he was initially rebuffed. But military emergency overcame legal precedents. By the 1650s Frederick William had established the excise in the towns, though not on the land.

With the excise as a steady source of revenue, the Great Elector could now create one of the most capable standing armies of the age. The strictest discipline was maintained in the new army, and the Prussian army developed into a feared and efficient fighting machine. Frederick William organized one of the first departments of war to oversee all of the details of the creation of his army, from housing and supplies to the training of young officer candidates. The department was also responsible for the collection of taxes. By integrating military and civilian government, Frederick William was able to create an efficient state bureaucracy that was particularly responsive in times of crisis. The creation of the Prussian army was the force that led to the creation of the Prussian state.

The same materials that forged the Prussian state led to the transformation of Russia. Soon after the young tsar Peter I (1682–1725) came to the throne, he realized that he could compete with the western states only by learning to play their game. In 1697,

Peter visited the West, ostensibly to build an alliance against the Turks but actually to learn as much as he could about Western military technology. He loved novelty and introduced new agricultural products such as wine and potatoes to his subjects. When he determined that Russians should no longer wear beards, he took a hand in cutting them off. When he was persuaded of the benefits of dentistry, he practiced it himself on his terrified subjects. His campaign to westernize Russia frequently confused the momentous with the inconsequential, but it had an extraordinary impact at all levels of government and society.

Like those of Frederick William, Peter's greatest reforms were military. Peter realized that if Russia were to flourish in a world dominated by war and commerce, it would have to reestablish its hold on the Baltic ports. That meant dislodging the Swedes from the Russian mainland and creating a fleet to protect Russian trade. Neither goal seemed likely. The Swedes were one of the great powers of the age, constant innovators in battlefield tactics and military organization. Peter studied their every campaign. His first wars against the Swedes ended in humiliating defeats, but with each failure came a sharper sense of what was needed to succeed.

First Peter introduced a system of conscription that resulted in the creation of a standing army. Conscripts

In his campaign to modernize Russia, Peter the Great declared that the nobles should shear off their beards, which were a symbol of their status. In this illustration, a clean-shaven Peter wields the scissors himself.

The Battle of Poltava (1709). The defeat of King Charles XII led to the decline of Swedish power in the Baltic.

A CLOSE SHAVE

Peter the Great made many efforts to westernize Russia after his travels in Holland and England. He reformed the navy, built a great seaport at St. Petersburg, and instituted an array of governmental reforms. But nothing was so prominent as or affected ordinary people more than his edicts on beards and clothing.

THE TSAR LABORED AT THE REFORM OF FASHIONS, or, more properly speaking, of dress. Until that time the Russians had always worn long beards, which they cherished and preserved with much care, allowing them to hang down on their bosoms, without even cutting the moustache. With these long beards they wore the hair very short, except the ecclesiastics, who, to distinguish themselves, wore it very long. The tsar, in order to reform that custom, ordered that gentlemen, merchants, and other subjects, except priests and peasants, should each pay a tax of one hundred rubles a year if they wished to keep their beard; the commoners had to pay one kopeck each. Officials were stationed at the gates of the towns to collect that tax, which the Russians regarded as an enormous sin on the part of the tsar and as a thing which tended to the abolition of their religion.

These insinuations, which came from the priests, occasioned the publication of many pamphlets in Moscow, where for that reason alone the tsar was regarded as a tyrant and a pagan; and there were many old Russians who, after having their beards shaved off, saved them preciously, in order to have them placed in their coffins, fearing that they would not be allowed to enter heaven without their beards. As for the young men, they followed the new customs with the more readiness as it made them appear more agreeable to the fair sex.

From the reform in beards we may pass to that of clothes. Their garments, like those of the Orientals, were very long, reaching to the heel. The tsar issued an ordinance abolishing that costume, commanding all the boyars (nobles) and all those who had positions at the court to dress after the French fashion, and likewise to adorn their clothes with gold or silver according to their means....

The same ordinance also provided that in the future women, as well as men, should be invited to entertainments, such as weddings, banquets, and the like, where both sexes should mingle in the same hall, as in Holland and England. It was likewise added that these entertainments should conclude with concerts and dances, but that only those should be admitted who were dressed in English costumes. His Majesty set the example in all these changes.

From "De Missy's Life of Peter."

were branded to inhibit desertion, and a strict discipline was introduced to prepare the soldiers for battle. Peter unified the military command at the top and stratified it in the field. He established promotion based on merit. For the first time, Russian officers were given particular responsibilities to fulfill during both training and battle. Peter created military schools to train cadets for the next generation of officers.

Finally, in 1709, Peter realized his ambitions. At the battle of Poltava, the Russian army routed the Swedes, wounding King Charles XII, annihilating his infantry, and capturing dozens of his leading officers. That night Peter toasted the captured Swedish generals. He claimed that everything he knew about warfare he had learned from them, and he congratulated them on their success as teachers. After the battle of Poltava, Russia gradually replaced Sweden as the dominant power in the Baltic.

Like everything else about him, Peter the Great's absolutism was uniquely his own. But though Peter's power was unlimited, it was not uncontested. He secularized the Russian Orthodox church, subjecting it to the control of state power and confiscating much of its wealth in the process. He broke the old military service class, which attempted a coup d'état when Peter was abroad in the 1690s. By the end of his reign, the Russian monarchy was among the strongest in Europe.

The Origins of French Absolutism

Nowhere was absolutism as successfully implanted as in France. Louis XIII (1610–1643) was only eight years old when he came to the throne, and he grew slowly into his role under the tutelage of Cardinal Richelieu. It was Richelieu's vision that stabilized French government. As chief minister, Richelieu saw clearly that the prosperity and even the survival of France depended upon strengthening royal power. He preached a doctrine of *raison d'état*—reason of state—in which he placed the needs of the nation above the privileges of its most important groups. Richelieu saw three threats to stable royal government: "The Huguenots shared the state, the nobles conducted themselves as if they were not subjects, and the most powerful governors in the provinces acted as if they were sovereign in their office."

Richelieu took measures to control all three. The power of the nobles was the most difficult to attack. The nobles' long tradition of independence from the crown had been enhanced by the wars of religion. Perhaps more importantly, the ancient aristocracy, the nobility of the sword, believed themselves to be in a particularly vulnerable position. Their world was changing and their traditional roles were becoming obsolete. Professional soldiers replaced them at war, professional administrators at government. Mercantile wealth threatened their economic superiority; the growth of the nobility of the robe—lawyers and state officials—threatened their social standing. They were hardly likely to take orders from a royal minister such as Richelieu, especially when he attacked one of the great symbols of their power, the duel.

To limit the power of local officials, Richelieu used intendants to examine their conduct and to reform their administration. He made careful appointments of local governors and brought more regions under direct royal control. Against the Huguenots, Richelieu's policy was more subtle. He was less interested in challenging their religion than their autonomy. In 1627, when the English sent a force to aid the Huguenots against the

Painted by Charles Le Brun between 1679 and 1684, the ceiling of the Hall of Mirrors at Versailles was meant to be an ode to King Louis XIV and his actions.

government, Richelieu and Louis XIII abolished the Huguenots' privileges altogether. They were allowed to maintain their religion, but not their special status. They would have no privileges other than to be subjects of the king of France.

Richelieu's program was a vital prelude to the development of absolute monarchy in France. But the cardinal was not a king. While it is clear that Richelieu did not act without the full support of Louis XIII and clear that the king initiated many reforms for which the cardinal received credit, there can be no doubt that Richelieu was the power behind the throne. Louis XIII hated the business of government and even neglected his principal responsibility of providing the state with an heir. For years he and his wife slept in separate palaces, and only a freak rainstorm in Paris forced him to spend a night with the queen, Anne of Austria, in 1637. It was the night Louis XIV was conceived. Louis XIII and Richelieu died within six months of each other in 1642 and 1643, and the nation again endured the turmoil of a child king. Richelieu's aggressive policy to curb the nobility and his stringent financial program in the 1630s helped precipitate the Fronde. Louis XIV (1643–1715) was never to forget the terror of the aristocratic rebellion in Paris: how he was forced to flee the capital in the dead of night, how he endured the penury of exile, how he suffered the humiliation of being bossed about by the rebels. He would never forget, and he would have a long time to remember.

Louis le Grand

Not quite five years old when he came to the throne, Louis XIV was tutored by Cardinal Jules Mazarin (1602–1661), Richelieu's successor as chief minister. If anything, Mazarin was more ruthless and less popular than his predecessor. An Italian from a modest background, Mazarin won the money to launch his career at the gaming table. Good fortune seemed to follow him everywhere. He gambled with his life and his career, and each time he raked in the stakes. He died with the largest private fortune that had ever been accumulated by a French citizen, easily surpassing the fortune of Richelieu. Like Richelieu, whom he emulated, Mazarin was an excellent administrator who had learned well the lessons of raison d'état. At the conclusion of the Thirty Years' War, for example, Mazarin refused to make peace with Spain, believing that the time was ripe to deliver a knockout blow to the Spanish Habsburgs.

The King and His Ministers. In order to pacify the rebellious nobility of the Fronde, who opposed Mazarin's power, Louis XIV was declared to have reached his majority at the age of 13. But it was not until Mazarin died ten years later in 1661 that the king began to rule. Louis was blessed with able and energetic ministers. The two central props of his state—money and might—were in the hands of dynamic men, Jean-Baptiste Colbert (1619–1683) and the Marquis de Louvois (1639–1691). Colbert—to whom credit belongs for the building of the French navy, the reform of French legal codes, and the establishment of national academies of culture—was Louis's chief minister for finance. Colbert's fiscal reforms were so successful that in less than six years a debt of 22 million French pounds had become a surplus of 29 million. Colbert achieved that astonishing feat not by raising taxes but by increasing the efficiency of their collection. Until Louis embarked on his wars, the French state was solvent.

To Louvois, Louis's minister of war, fell the task of reforming the French army. During the Fronde, royal troops were barely capable of defeating the makeshift forces of the nobility. By the end of the reign, the army had grown to 400,000 and its organization had thoroughly been reformed. Louvois introduced new ranks for the field officers who actually led their men into battle, and promotions were distributed by merit rather than purchase. He also solved one of the most serious logistical problems of the age by establishing storehouses of arms and ammunition throughout the realm. The greatest achievements of the reign were built on the backs of fiscal and military reforms, which were themselves a product of the continuing sophistication of French administration.

Louis XIV furthered the practice of relying on professional administrators to supervise the main departments of state and offer advice on matters of policy. He created a separation between courtiers and officeholders and largely excluded the nobility of the sword from the inner circles of government, which were composed of ministers of departments and small councils that handled routine affairs. The councils were connected to the central advisory body of government, the secret council of the king. Within each department,

This Hyacinthe Rigaud portrait of Louis XIV in his coronation robes shows the splendor of Le Roi Soleil *(the Sun King), who believed himself to be the center of France as the sun is the center of the solar system.*

ministers furthered the process of professionalization that led to the advancement of talented clerks, secretaries, and administrators. Although there still remained a large gulf between the promulgation of policy at Versailles and its enforcement in the provinces, it was now a gulf that could be measured and ultimately bridged. Louis XIV built on the institution of the intendant that Richelieu had developed with so much success. Intendants were now a permanent part of government, and their duties expanded from their early responsibilities as coordinators and mediators into areas of policing and tax collection. It was through the intendants that the wishes of central government were made known in the provinces.

The Court of Versailles. Although Louis XIV was well served, it was the king himself who set the tone for French absolutism. "If he was not the greatest king, he was the best actor of majesty that ever filled the throne," wrote an English observer. The acting of majesty was central to Louis's rule. His residence at Versailles was the most glittering court of Europe, renowned for its beauty and splendor. It was built on a scale never before seen, and Louis took a personal interest in making sure it was fit for a king. When the court and king moved there permanently in 1682, Versailles became the envy of the Continent. But behind the imposing facade of Versailles stood a well-thought-out plan for domestic and international rule.

Louis XIV attempted to tame the French nobles by requiring their attendance at his court. Louis established a system of court etiquette so complex that constant study was necessary to prevent humiliation. While the nobility studied decorum they could not plot rebellion. At Versailles one never knocked on a door; one scratched with a fingernail. That insignificant custom had to be learned and remembered—it was useless anywhere else—and practiced if one hoped for the favor of the king. Leading noblemen of France rose at dawn so that they could watch Louis be awakened and hear him speak his first words. Dozens followed him from hall to gallery and from gallery to chamber as he washed, dressed, prayed, and ate.

That aura of court culture was equally successful in the royal art of diplomacy. During Louis's reign, France replaced Spain as the greatest nation in Europe. Massive royal patronage of art, science, and thought brought French culture to new heights. The French language replaced Latin as the universal European tongue. France was the richest and most populous European state, and Louis's absolute rule finally harnessed the resources to a single purpose. France became a commercial power rivaling the Netherlands, a naval power rivaling England, and a military power without peer. It was not only for effect that Louis took the image of the sun as his own. In court, in the

A symbolic drawing shows how heretics will be driven from France by the Sun King. Such a policy proved shortsighted, however, as thousands of Huguenot émigrés enriched Louis's potential enemies with their valuable skills.

nation, and throughout Europe, everything revolved around him.

France's rise to preeminence in Europe was undoubtedly the greatest accomplishment of the absolute monarchy of Louis XIV. But it did not come without costs. Louis XIV made his share of mistakes, which were magnified by the awe in which his opinions were held. His aggressive foreign policy ultimately bankrupted the crown. But without doubt his greatest error was to persecute the Huguenots. As an absolute ruler, Louis believed that it was necessary to have absolute conformity and obedience. The existence of the Huguenots, with their separate communities and distinct forms of worship, seemed an affront to his authority. Almost from the beginning, Louis allowed the persecution of Protestants, despite the protection provided by the Edict of Nantes. Protestant churches were pulled down, conversions to Catholicism were bought with the lure of immunities from taxation, and children were separated from their families to be brought up in Catholic schools. Finally, in 1685 Louis XIV revoked the Edict of Nantes. All forms of Protestant worship were outlawed, and the ministers

Gian Lorenzo Bernini, The Ecstasy of St. Theresa. *In this work, depicting the ecstatic vision of St. Theresa, the sixteenth-century Spanish Carmelite reformer, the saint floats toward heaven on seemingly weightless marble as an angel is about to pierce her breast with a burning arrow. The artist's creation depicts a mystic vision St. Theresa experienced and described in her writings.*

who were not hunted down and killed were forced into exile. Despite a ban on Protestant emigration, more than 200,000 Huguenots fled the country, many of them carrying irreplaceable skills with them to Holland and England in the west and Brandenburg in the east.

Supporters of the monarchy celebrated the revocation of the Edict of Nantes as an act of piety. Religious toleration in seventeenth-century Europe was still a policy of expediency rather than of principle. Even the English, who prided themselves on developing the concept of toleration, and the Dutch, who welcomed Jews to Amsterdam, would not officially tolerate Catholics. But the persecution of the Huguenots was a social and political disaster for France. Those who fled to other Protestant states spread the stories of atrocities that stiffened European resolve against Louis. Those who remained became an embittered minority who pulled at the fabric of the state at every chance. Nor did the official abolition of Protestantism have much effect upon its existence. Against the policies, the Huguenots held firm to their beliefs. There were well more than a million French Protestants, undoubtedly the largest religious minority in any state. Huguenots simply went underground, practicing their religion secretly and gradually replacing their numbers. No absolutism, however powerful, could succeed in eradicating religious beliefs.

Louis XIV gave his name to the age that he and his nation dominated, but he was not its only towering figure. The Great Elector, Peter the Great, Louis the Great—so they were judged by posterity, kings who had forged nations for a new age. Their style of rule showed the royal state at its height, still revolving around the king but more and more dependent upon permanent institutions of government that followed their own imperatives. The absolute state harnessed the economic and intellectual resources of the nation to the political will of the monarch. It did so to ensure survival in a dangerous world. But while monarchs ruled as well as reigned, they did so by incorporating vital elements of the state into the process of government. In England, the importance of the landholding classes was recognized in the constitutional powers of Parliament. In Prussia, the military power of the Junker was asserted through command in the army, the most important institution of the state. In France, Louis XIV co-opted many nobles at his court while making use of a talented pool of lawyers, clergymen, and administrators in his government. A delicate balance existed between the will of the king and the will of the state, a balance that would soon lead the continental powers into economic competition and military confrontation.

Questions for Review

1. How did war in the seventeenth century contribute to the creation of more powerful monarchical states?
2. What religious and political ideas were developed to justify resistance to monarchical authority?
3. What political and religious problems combined to bring England to civil war, and what results did the conflict produce in English government?
4. How did rulers such as Frederick William of Brandenburg, Peter the Great, or Louis XIV, and theorists such as Hobbes and Bossuet, justify absolute monarchical power?

Suggestions for Further Reading

General Reading

* Thomas Munck, *Seventeenth Century Europe, 1598–1700* (New York: St. Martin's Press, 1990). The most up-to-date survey.

* William Doyle, *The Old European Order* (Oxford: Oxford University Press, 1978). An important synthetic essay, bristling with ideas.

* Geoffrey Parker, *Europe in Crisis, 1598–1648* (London: William Collins and Sons, 1979). The best introduction to the period.

* Euan Cameron, ed., *Early Modern Europe: An Oxford History* (Oxford; New York: Oxford University Press, 1999.) Up-to-date essays by leading historians with well-chosen topics and illustrations.

Perry Anderson, *Lineages of the Absolutist State* (London: NLB Books, 1974). A sociological study of the role of absolutism in the development of the Western world.

* Eric Cochrane, C. M. Gray, and Mark Kishlansky, eds., *Early Modern Europe: Crisis of Authority* (Chicago: University of Chicago Press, 1987). A collection of source materials from the University of Chicago readings in Western Civilization.

The Rise of the Royal State

* Graham Parry, *The Golden Age Restor'd* (New York: St. Martin's Press, 1981). A study of English court culture in the reigns of James I and Charles I.

J. H. Elliott and Jonathan Brown, *A Palace for a King* (New Haven, CT: Yale University Press, 1980). An outstanding work on the building and decorating of a Spanish palace.

Jonathan Brown, *Kings and Connoisseurs: Collecting Art in Seventeenth-Century Europe* (Princeton, N.J.: Princeton University Press, 1995). A synthetic overview of the role of art in expressing royal power.

* J. N. Figgis, *The Divine Right of Kings* (Cambridge: Cambridge University Press, 1914). Still the classic study of this central doctrine of political thought.

* Yves-Marie Bercé, *The Birth of Absolutism* (London: Macmillan, 1996). A history of France from the reign of Louis XIV to the eve of the Revolution by a leading historian of France.

* Kevin Sharpe, *The Personal Rule of Charles I* (New Haven, CT: Yale University Press, 1991). A sympathetic look at the reign of the ill-fated monarch.

* Glenn Burgess, *Absolute Monarchy and the Stuart Constitution* (New Haven, CT: Yale University Press, 1996). The interrelationship of theories of monarchy and absolutism in England.

* J. H. Elliott, *Richelieu and Olivares* (Cambridge: Cambridge University Press, 1984). A brilliant dual portrait.

Park Honan, *Shakespeare: A Life* (Oxford: Oxford University Press, 1998.) Destined to become the standard life of the great playwright.

* Roger Lockyer, *Buckingham* (London: Longman, 1984). A stylish biography of the favorite of two monarchs.

The Crises of the Royal State

* Quentin Skinner, *The Foundations of Modern Political Thought*. 2 vols. (Cambridge: Cambridge University Press, 1978). A seminal work on the history of ideas from Machiavelli to Calvin.

* Perez Zagoin, *Rebels and Rulers*. 2 vols. (Cambridge: Cambridge University Press, 1982). A good survey of revolutions, civil war, and popular protests throughout Europe.

* Trevor Aston, ed., *Crisis in Europe, 1600–1660* (Garden City, NY: Doubleday, 1967). Essays on the theme of a general crisis in Europe by distinguished historians.

G. Parker and L. Smith, eds., *The General Crisis of the Seventeenth Century* (London: Routledge & Kegan Paul, 1978). A collection of essays on the problem of the general crisis.

M. A. Kishlansky, *A Monarchy Transformed* (London: Penguin Books, 1996). The most recent survey of a remarkable era.

* Lawrence Stone, *The Causes of the English Revolution* (New York: Harper & Row, 1972). A vigorously argued explanation of why England experienced a revolution in the mid-seventeenth century.

* Ann Hughes, *The Causes of the English Civil War* (New York: St. Martin's Press, 1991). A lucid introduction to the scholarship of a vast subject.

* D. E. Underdown, *Pride's Purge* (London: Allen & Unwin, 1985). The most important work on the politics of the English Revolution.

Jonathan Israel, ed., *The Anglo-Dutch Moment* (Cambridge: Cambridge University Press, 1991). Essays by an international team of scholars on the European dimensions of the Revolution of 1688.

* W. A. Speck, *The Revolution of 1688* (Oxford: Oxford University Press, 1988). The best single volume on the event that transformed England into a global power.

The Zenith of the Royal State

* Geoffrey Parker, *The Military Revolution* (Cambridge: Cambridge University Press, 1988). A lucid discussion of how power was organized and deployed in the early modern state.

* H. W. Koch, *A History of Prussia* (London: Longman, 1978). A comprehensive study of Prussian history, with an excellent chapter on the Great Elector.

* Paul Dukes, *The Making of Russian Absolutism* (London: Longman, 1982). A thorough survey of Russian history in the seventeenth and eighteenth centuries.

* Vasili Klyuchevsky, *Peter the Great* (London: Random House, 1958). A classic work, still the best study of Peter.

* W. E. Brown, *The First Bourbon Century in France* (London: University of London Press, 1971). A good introduction to French political history.

* William Beik, *Absolutism and Society in Seventeenth Century France* (Cambridge: Cambridge University Press, 1985). The single best study of the government of a French province in the seventeenth century.

Joseph Bergin, *The Rise of Richelieu* (New Haven, CT: Yale University Press, 1991). A fascinating portrait of a consummate politician.

Richard Bonney, *Society and Government in France Under Richelieu and Mazarin, 1624–61* (Basingstoke: Macmillan, 1988). An excellent introduction by a master of the period.

* David Sturdy, *Louis XIV* (London: Macmillan, 1998). A concise survey of the reign organized topically.

Peter Burke, *The Fabrication of Louis XIV* (New Haven, CT: Yale University Press, 1992). A compelling account of a man and a myth.

* Peter R. Campbell, *Louis XIV, 1661–1715* (London: Longman, 1993). A brief account accompanied by source material and an up-to-date bibliography.

* John Wolf, *Louis XIV* (New York: Norton, 1968). An outstanding biography of the Sun King.

* Paperback edition available.

Discovering Western Civilization Online

To further explore the royal state in the seventeenth century, consult the following World Wide Web sites. Since Web resources are constantly being updated, also go to *www.awl.com/Kishlansky* for further suggestions.

The Crisis of the Royal State

www.fordham.edu/halsall/mod/modsbook06.html#
Links to sources relating to the reign of Charles I and the revolution against him.

www.baylor.edu/~BIC/WCIII/Essays/charles.1.html
Excerpts from primary sources describing the execution of Charles I.

www.lawsch.uga.edu/~glorious
A site with links all relating to the Revolution of 1688 in England.

The Zenith of the Royal State

www.kipar.org/
A site on the Golden Age of France in the seventeenth century but with extensive links to England and Dutch materials on a variety of subjects.

www.lcweb.loc.gov/exhibits/bnf/bnf0005.html
The Library of Congress's exhibition on the Age of Absolutism shows manuscripts, medals, and portraits of leading figures at the French court.

CHAPTER

17 SCIENCE AND COMMERCE IN EARLY MODERN EUROPE

- **REMBRANDT'S LESSONS**
- **THE NEW SCIENCE**
  - Heavenly Revolutions
  - The Natural World
  - Science Enthroned
- **EMPIRES OF GOODS**
  - The Marketplace of the World
  - Consumption Choices
  - Dutch Masters
  - Mercantile Organization
- **THE WARS OF COMMERCE**
  - The Mercantile Wars
  - The Wars of Louis XIV
  - The Colonial Wars

Rembrandt's Lessons

BY THE EARLY SEVENTEENTH CENTURY, interest in scientific investigation had spread out from narrow circles of specialists to embrace educated men and women. One of the more spectacular demonstrations of new knowledge was public dissection, by law performed only on the corpses of criminals. There the secrets of the human body were revealed both for those who were training to be physicians and those who had the requisite fee and strong stomach. Curiosity about the human body was becoming a mark of education. New publications, both scientific and popular, spread ancient wisdom as well as the controversial findings of the moderns. Pictures drawn on the basis of dissections filled the new medical texts, such as the one shown in the photo on the stand at the feet of the corpse in *The Anatomy Lesson of Dr. Nicolaes Tulp* (1632) by Rembrandt van Rijn (1606–1669).

Dr. Tulp's anatomy lesson was not meant for the public. In fact, those gathered around him in various poses of concentration were not students at all. They were members of the Amsterdam company of surgeons, the physicians' guild of the early seventeenth century. The sitters had commissioned the picture, which was a celebration of themselves as well as of the noted Professor Tulp. They hired the young

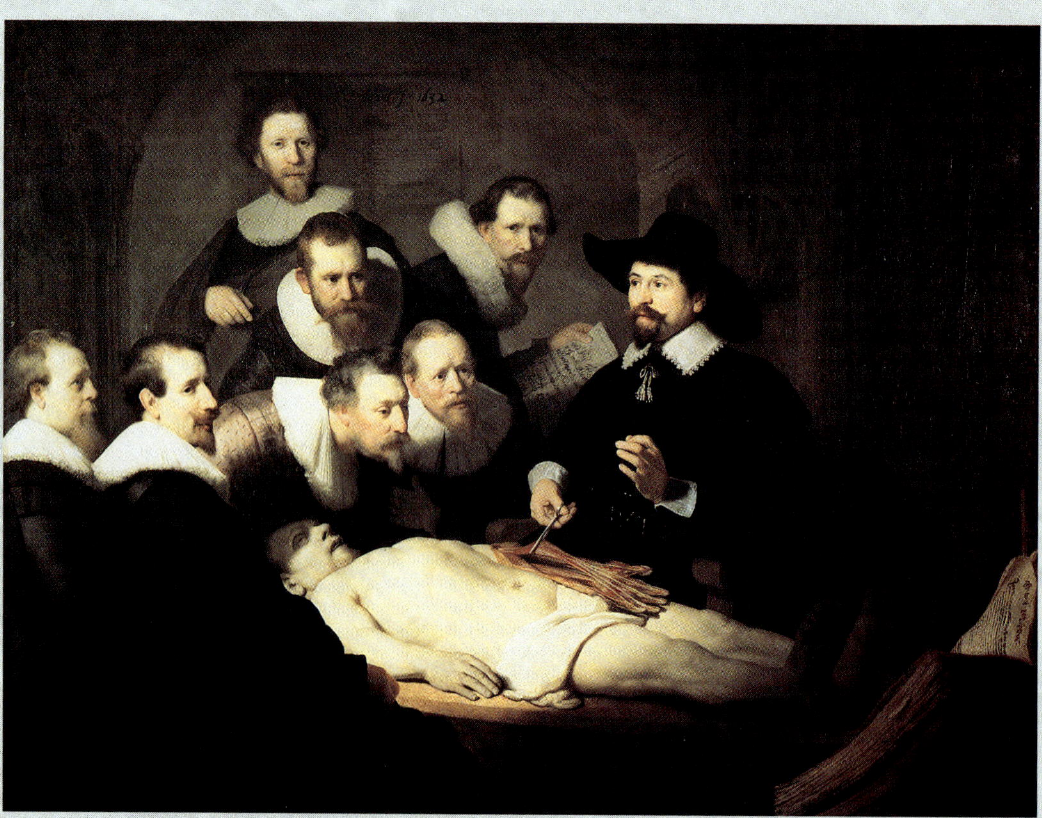

Rembrandt to compose the picture with the assurance that each of the sitters (whose names are written on the paper one of them holds in his hand) would appear as if he alone were the subject of a portrait. Rembrandt succeeded beyond expectation. Each individual was given his due. The expressions on their faces as much as their physical characteristics mark each one out from the group. Yet the portraits were only one part of the painting. The scene that Rembrandt depicted unified them. They became a group by their participation in the anatomy lesson. Rembrandt has chosen a moment of drama to stop the action. Dr. Tulp is demonstrating how the gesture he is making with his left hand would be made by the tendons in the arm of the gruesome cadaver. The central figures of the group are rapt in attention, although only one of them is actually observing the procedure of the dissection. Each listens to Tulp, comparing his own experience and knowledge to that of the professor and the text that stands open.

The *Anatomy Lesson* established the 25-year-old Rembrandt as one of the most gifted and fashionable painters in Amsterdam. If any people could be said to be consumers of art in seventeenth-century Europe, it was the Dutch. Artists flourished and pictures abounded. Travelers were struck by the presence of artwork in both public and private places and in the homes of even moderately prosperous people. The group portrait, which Rembrandt brought to new levels of expression, was becoming a favorite genre. It was used to celebrate the leaders of Dutch society, who—unlike the leaders of most other European states—were not princes and aristocrats, but rather merchants, guild officials, and professionals. Rembrandt captured a spirit of civic pride in his group portraits. Then it was the surgeons' guild; later it would be the leaders of the cloth merchants' guild, another time a militia company.

Like the leaders of the surgeons' guild, who hung their commissioned portraits in their company's hall, the Dutch Republic swelled with pride in the seventeenth century. Its long war with Spain was finally drawing to a close, and it was time to celebrate the birth of a new state. The Dutch were a trading people, and their trade flourished as much in times of war as in times of peace. Their ships traveled to all parts of the globe, and they dominated the great luxury trades of the age. Bankers and merchants were the backbone of the Dutch Republic. Yet that republic of merchants was also one of the great cultural centers of the Continent. Intellectual creativity was cultivated in the same manner as was a trading partner. In the burgeoning port of Amsterdam, the fastest-growing city in Europe, artists, philosophers, and mathematicians lived cheek by jowl. The free exchange of ideas made Amsterdam home to those exiled for their beliefs. The Dutch practiced religious toleration as did no one else. Catholics, Protestants, and Jews all were welcomed to the Dutch Republic and found that they could pursue their own paths without persecution. Freedom of thought and freedom of expression helped develop a new spirit of scientific inquiry, like that portrayed in *The Anatomy Lesson of Dr. Nicolaes Tulp*.

THE NEW SCIENCE

And new Philosophy calls all in doubt,
The element of fire is quite put out;
The sun is lost and the earth, and no man's wit
Can well direct him where to look for it.

So wrote the English poet John Donne (1572–1631) about one of the most astonishing yet perplexing moments in the history of Western thought: the emergence of the new science. It was astonishing because it seemed truly new. The discoveries of the stargazers, like those of the sea explorers, challenged people's most basic assumptions and beliefs. Men dropping balls from towers or peering at the skies through a glass claimed that they had disproved thousands of years of certainty about the nature of the universe: "And new Philosophy calls all in doubt." But the new science was perplexing because it seemed to loosen the moorings of everything that educated people thought they knew about their world. Nothing could be more disorienting than to challenge common sense. People needed to do little more than wake up in the morning to know that the sun moved from east to west while the earth stood still. But mathematics, experimentation, and deduction were needed to understand that the earth was in constant motion and that it revolved around the sun—"And no man's wit/ Can well direct him where to look for it."

The scientific revolution was the opening of a new era in European history. After two centuries of classical revival, European thinkers had finally come against the limits of ancient knowledge. Ancient wisdom had served Europeans well, and it was not to be discarded lightly. But one by one, the certainties of the past were being called into question. The explanations of the universe and the natural world that had been advanced by Aristotle and codified by his followers no longer seemed adequate. There were too many contradictions between theory and observation, too many things that did not fit. Yet breaking the hold of Aristotelianism was no easy task. A full century was to pass before even learned people would accept the proofs that the earth revolved around the sun. Even then, the most famous of them—Galileo—had to recant those views or be condemned as a heretic.

The two essential characteristics of the new science were that it was materialistic and mathematical. Its materialism was contained in the realization that the universe is composed of matter in motion. That meant that the stars and planets were not made of some perfect ethereal substance but of the same matter that was found on earth. They were thus subject to the same rules of motion as were earthly objects. The mathematics of the new science was contained in the realization that calculation had to replace common sense as the basis for understanding the universe. Mathematics itself was transformed with the invention of logarithms, analytic geometry, and calculus. More importantly, scientific experimentation took the form of measuring repeatable phenomena. When Galileo attempted to develop a theory of acceleration, he rolled a brass ball down an inclined plane and recorded the time and distance of its descent 100 times before he was satisfied with his results.

The new science was also a Europewide movement. The spirit of scientific inquiry flourished everywhere. The main contributors to astronomy were a Pole, a Dane, a German, and an Italian. The founder of medical chemistry was Swiss; the best anatomist was Belgian. England contributed most of all—the founders of modern chemistry, biology, and physics. By and large, the scientists operated outside the traditional seats of learning at the universities. Although most were university trained and not a few taught the traditional Aristotelian subjects, theirs was not an academic movement. Rather, it was a public one made possible by the printing press. Once published, findings became building blocks for scientists throughout the Continent and from one generation to the next. Many discoveries were made in the search for practical solutions to ordinary problems, and what was learned fueled advances in technology and the natural sciences. The new science gave seventeenth-century Europeans a sense that they might finally master the forces of nature.

Heavenly Revolutions

There was much to be said for Aristotle's understanding of the world, for his cosmology. For one thing, it was harmonious. It incorporated a view of the physical world that coincided with a view of the spiritual and moral one. The heavens were unchangeable, and therefore they were better than the earth. The sun, moon, and planets were all faultless spheres, unblemished and immune from decay. Their motion was circular because the circle was the perfect form of motion. The earth was at the center of the universe because it was the heaviest planet and because it was at the center of the

This chart of the heavens was engraved by Andreas Cellarius in 1660. It portrays the heliocentric universe described by Nicolaus Copernicus and accepted by Galileo. Earth and Jupiter are shown with moons orbiting them.

Great Chain of Being, between the underworld of spirits and the upper world of gods. The second advantage to the Aristotelian world view was that it was easily incorporated into Christianity. Aristotle's description of the heavens as being composed of a closed system of crystalline rings that held the sun, moon, and planets in their circular orbits around the earth left room for God and the angels to reside just beyond the last ring.

There were, of course, problems with Aristotle's explanation of the universe as it was preserved in the work of Ptolemy, the greatest of the Greek astronomers. For one thing, if the sun revolved in a perfect circle around the earth, then why were the seasons not perfectly equal? If the planets all revolved around the earth in circles, then why did they look nearer or farther, brighter or darker at different times of year? To solve those problems, a host of ingenious hypotheses were advanced. Perhaps the sun revolved around the earth in an eccentric circle, that is, a circle not centered on the earth. That would account for the differing lengths of seasons. Perhaps the planets revolved in circles that rested on a circle around the earth. Then, when the planet revolved within the larger circle, it would seem nearer and brighter, and when it revolved outside it,

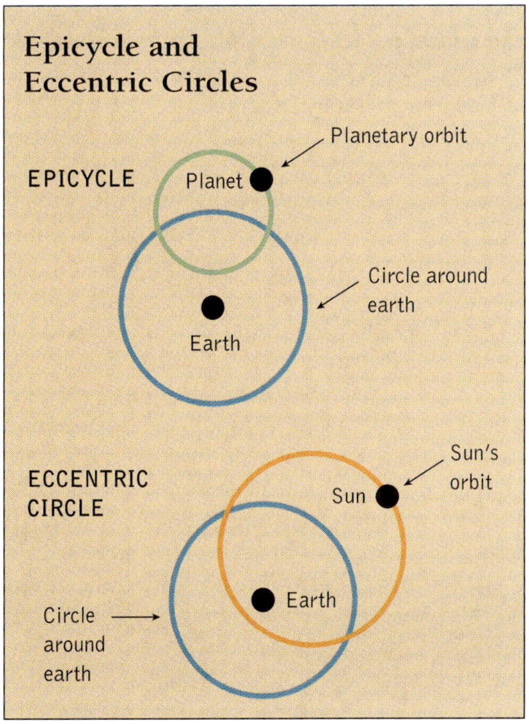

STARGAZING

Nicolaus Copernicus was born in Poland and educated at the University of Krakow, which had one of the greatest mathematics faculties of the age. He prepared for a career in the church, but his abiding interest was the study of astronomy. Through observation and calculation, Copernicus worked out a heliocentric view of the universe in which the earth revolved on an axis and orbited the sun. His pathbreaking work was not published until the year of his death, and he was fully aware of the implications of his discovery.

FOR, FIRST, THE MATHEMATICIANS ARE SO UNSURE of the movements of the Sun and Moon that they cannot even explain or observe the constant length of the seasonal year. Secondly, in determining the motions of these and of the other five planets, they use neither the same principles and hypotheses nor the same demonstrations of the apparent motions and revolutions.... Nor have they been able thereby to discern or deduce the principal thing—namely the shape of the Universe and the unchangeable symmetry of its parts....

Thus assuming motions, which in my work I ascribe to the Earth, by long and frequent observations I have at last discovered that, if the motions of the rest of the planets be brought into relation with the circulation of the Earth and be reckoned in proportion to the circles of each planet, not only do their phenomena presently ensue, but the orders and magnitudes of all stars and spheres, nay the heavens themselves, become so bound together that nothing in any part thereof could be moved from its place without producing confusion of all the other parts of the Universe as a whole.

From Copernicus, *On the Revolutions of Heavenly Spheres* (1543).

it would seem farther away and darker. That was the theory of epicycles. Yet to account for the observable movement of all the known planets, there had to be 55 epicycles. As ingeniously complex as they were, the modifications of Aristotle's views made by the theories of eccentric circles and epicycles had one great virtue: they accurately predicted the movements of the planets. Although they were completely hypothetical, they answered the most troubling questions about the Aristotelian system.

In the 1490s, Nicolaus Copernicus (1473–1543) came to the Polish University of Krakow, which had one of the leading mathematical faculties in Europe. There they taught the latest astronomical theories and vigorously debated the existence of eccentric circles and epicycles. Copernicus came to Krakow for a liberal arts education before pursuing a degree in Church law. He became fascinated by astronomy and puzzled by the debate over planetary motion. Copernicus believed, like Aristotle, that the simplest explanations were the best. If the sun was at the center of the universe and the earth simply another planet in orbit, then many of the most elaborate explanations of planetary motion were unnecessary. "At rest, in the middle of everything is the sun," Copernicus wrote in *On the Revolutions of the Heavenly Spheres* (1543). "For in this most beautiful temple who would place this lamp in another or better position than that from which it can light up the whole thing at the same time?" Because Copernicus accepted most of the rest of the traditional Aristotelian explanation, especially the belief that the planets moved in circles, his sun-centered universe was only slightly better at predicting the position of the planets than the traditional earth-centered one, but Copernicus's idea stimulated other astronomers to make new calculations.

Kepler. Under the patronage of the king of Denmark, Tycho Brahe (1546–1601) built a large observatory to study planetary motion. In 1572, Brahe discovered a nova, a brightly burning star that was previously unknown. The discovery challenged the idea of an immutable universe composed of crystalline rings. In 1577, the appearance of a comet cutting through the supposedly impenetrable rings punched another hole into the old cosmology. Brahe's own views were a hybrid of old and new. He believed that all planets but the earth revolved around the sun and that the sun and the planets revolved around a fixed earth. To demonstrate his theory, Brahe and his students compiled the largest and most accurate mathematical tables of planetary motion yet known. From this research, Brahe's pupil Johannes Kepler (1571–1630), one of the great mathematicians of the age, formulated laws of planetary motion. Kepler discovered that planets orbited the sun in an elliptical rather than a circular path, which accounted for their movements nearer and farther from the earth. More importantly, he demonstrated that there was a precise mathematical relationship between the speed with which a planet revolved and its distance from the sun. Kepler's findings supported the view that the galaxy was heliocentric and that the heavens, like the earth, were made of matter that was subject to physical laws.

Galileo. What Kepler demonstrated mathematically, the Italian astronomer Galileo Galilei (1564–1642) confirmed by observation. Creating a telescope by using magnifying lenses and a long tube, Galileo saw parts of the heavens that had never been dreamed of before. In 1610, he discovered four moons of Jupiter, proving conclusively that all heavenly bodies did not revolve around the earth. He observed the landscape of the earth's moon and described it as full of mountains, valleys, and rivers. It was of the same imperfect form as the earth itself. He even found spots on the sun, which suggested that it, too, was composed of ordinary matter. Through the telescope, Galileo gazed upon an unimaginable universe: "The Galaxy is nothing else but a mass of innumerable stars," he wrote. Galileo's greatest scientific discoveries had to do with motion—he was the first to posit a law of inertia—but his greatest contribution to the new science was his popularization of the Copernican theory. He took the debate over the structure of the universe to the public, popularizing the discoveries of scientists in his vigorous Italian tracts.

As news of his experiments and discoveries spread, Galileo became famous throughout the Continent, and his support for heliocentrism became a celebrated cause. In 1616, the Roman Catholic church cautioned him against promoting his views. In 1633, a year after publishing his *A Dialogue Between the Two Great Systems of the World*, Galileo was tried by the Inquisition and forced specifically to recant the idea that the earth

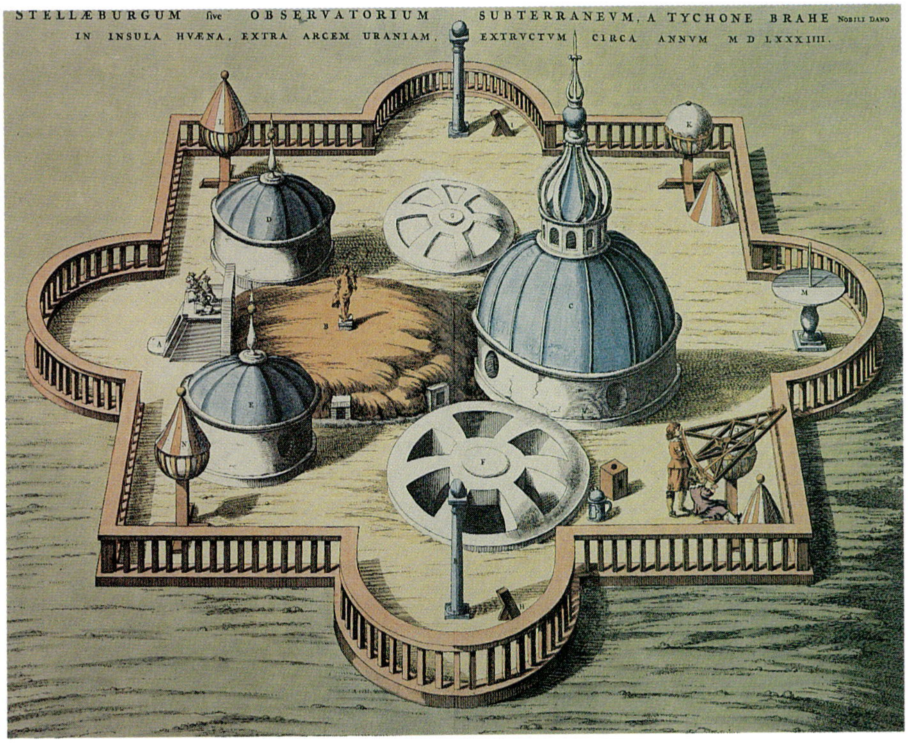

Tycho Brahe designed and built this observatory, much of which was constructed underground. In each of the large cupolas were instruments through which Brahe and his collaborators could make their celestial observations. Astronomers could also view the heavens through apertures in the flat roofs of the underground chambers.

THE TELESCOPE

No single individual is as much associated with the Scientific Revolution as Galileo Galilei. He made formative contributions to mathematics, physics, and astronomy, but he also served as a lightning rod for the dissemination of the newest ideas. He popularized the work of Copernicus and was condemned by the Catholic church for his views and publications. He ended his life under house arrest. Among his other accomplishments, Galileo was the first to use a telescope to make scientific observations.

ABOUT TEN MONTHS AGO a report reached my ears that a certain Fleming had constructed a spyglass by means of which visible objects, though very distant from the eye of the observer, were distinctly seen as if nearby. Of this truly remarkable effect several experiences were related, to which some persons gave credence while others denied them. A few days later the report was confirmed to me in a letter from a noble Frenchman at Paris, Jacques Badovere, which caused me to apply myself wholeheartedly to inquire into the means by which I might arrive at the invention of a similar instrument. This I did shortly afterwards, my basis being the theory of refraction. First I prepared a tube of lead, at the ends of which I fitted two glass lenses, both plane on one side while on the other side one was spherically convex and the other concave. Then placing my eye near the concave lens I perceived objects satisfactorily large and near, for they appeared three times closer and nine times larger than when seen with the naked eye alone. Next I constructed another one, more accurate, which represented objects as enlarged more than sixty times. Finally, sparing neither labor nor expense, I succeeded in constructing for myself so excellent an instrument that objects seen by means of it appeared nearly one thousand times larger and over thirty times closer than when regarded with our natural vision.

It would be superfluous to enumerate the number and importance of the advantages of such an instrument at sea as well as on land. But forsaking terrestrial observations, I turned to celestial ones, and first I saw the moon from as near at hand as if it were scarcely two terrestrial radii....

... Let us speak first of that surface of the moon which faces us. For greater clarity I distinguish two parts of this surface, a lighter and a darker; the lighter part seems to surround and to pervade the whole hemisphere, while the darker part discolors the moon's surface like a kind of cloud, and makes it appear covered with spots.... From observation of these spots repeated many times I have been led to the opinion and conviction that the surface of the moon is not smooth, uniform, and precisely spherical as a great number of philosophers believe it (and the other heavenly bodies) to be, but is uneven, rough, and full of cavities and prominences, being not unlike the face of the earth, relieved by chains of mountains and deep valleys.

From Galileo, *The Starry Messenger* (1610).

moves. He spent the rest of his life under house arrest. Galileo insisted that there was nothing in the new science that was anti-Christian. He rejected the view that his discoveries refuted the Bible, arguing that the words of the Bible were often difficult to interpret and that nature was another way in which God revealed himself. In fact, Galileo feared that the Church's opposition to what he deemed as scientific truth could only bring the Church into disrepute. (See "The Trials of Galileo," pp. 586–587.)

The Natural World

The new science originated from a number of traditions that were anything but scientific. Inquiry into nature and the environment grew out of the discipline of natural philosophy and was nurtured by spiritual and mystical traditions. Much of the most useful medical knowledge had come from the studies of herbalists; the most reliable calculations of planetary motion had come from astrologers. Although the first laboratories and observatories were developed in aid of the new science, practice in them was as much magical as experimental. For those attempting to unlock the mysteries of the universe, there was no separation between magic and science. Some of the most characteristic features of modern science, such as the stress on experimentation and empirical observation, developed only gradually. What was new about the new science was the determination to develop systems of thought that could help humans understand and control their environment. Thus there was a greater openness and spirit of cooperation about discoveries than in the past, when experiments were conducted secretly and results were kept hidden away.

Neoplatonism. Aristotelianism was not the only philosophical system to explain the nature and composition of the universe. During the Renaissance the writings of Plato had attracted a number of Italian humanists, most notably Marsilio Ficino (1433–1499) and Pico della Mirandola (1463–1494). Those Neoplatonic humanists taught Plato's theory that the world was composed of ideas and forms that were hidden by the physical properties of objects. They believed that the architect of the universe possessed the spirit of a geometrician and that the perfect disciplines were music and mathematics. Those elements of Neoplatonism created an impetus for the mathematically based studies of the new scientists. They were especially important among the astronomers, who used both calculation and geometry in exploring the heavens. But they also served to bolster the sciences of alchemy and astrology. Alchemy was the use of fire in the study of metals, an effort to find the essence of things through their purification. While medieval alchemists mostly attempted to find gold and silver as the essence of lead and iron, the new experimentation focused on the properties of metals in general. Astrology was the study of the influence of the stars on human behavior, calculated by planetary motion and the harmony of the heavenly spheres. Astrologers made careful calculations based on the movement of the planets and were deeply involved in the new astronomy. The Neoplatonic emphasis on mathematics also accorded support for a variety of mystical sciences based on numerology. Those were efforts to predict events from the combination of particular numbers.

The most influential of the mystical traditions was that associated with Hermes Trismegistus ("Thrice Greatest"), an Egyptian who was reputed to have lived in the second century C.E. and to have known the secrets of the universe. A body of writings mistakenly attributed to Hermes was discovered during the Renaissance and formed the basis of a Hermetic tradition. The core of Hermetic thinking was belief in a universal spirit that was present in all objects and that spontaneously revealed itself. Kepler was one of many of the new scientists influenced by Hermeticism. His efforts to understand planetary motion derived from his search for a unifying spirit.

A combination of Neoplatonic and Hermetic traditions was central to the work of one of the most curious of the new scientists, the Swiss alchemist Paracelsus (1493–1541). Paracelsus studied with a leading German alchemist before following in his father's footsteps by becoming a physician. Although he worked as a doctor, his true vocation was alchemy, and he conducted innumerable experiments designed to extract the essence of particular metals. Paracelsus taught that all matter was composed of combinations of three principles: salt, sulfur, and mercury. That view replaced the traditional belief in the four elements of earth, water, fire, and air.

Although the Paracelsian system was peculiar, it transformed ideas about chemistry and medicine. Paracelsus rejected the theory that disease was caused by an imbalance in the humors of the body—the standard view of Galen, the great Greek physician of the second century C.E. Instead, Paracelsus argued that each disease had its own cause, which could be diagnosed and remedied. Where traditional doctors treated disease by bloodletting or sweating to correct the patient's imbalance of humors, Paracelsus prescribed the ingestion of particular chemicals—especially distilled metals such as mercury, arsenic, and antimony—and he favored administering them at propitious astrological moments.

Paracelsus's experimentation with metals and his practice of diagnostic medicine gave a practical turn to the study of alchemy. Efforts to cure new diseases such as syphilis led to the continued study of the chemical properties of substances and to a new confidence about medical science. Although established physicians and medical faculties rejected Paracelsian cures and methods, his influence spread among ordinary practitioners. It ultimately had a profound impact on the studies of Robert Boyle (1627–1691), an Englishman who helped establish the basis of the science of chemistry. Boyle devoted his energies to raising the study of medical chemistry above that of merely providing

The Trials of Galileo

For eight years he had held his peace. Since 1616 he had bided his time, waiting for a change in the attitudes of the Catholic authorities—or, as he believed, waiting for reason to prevail. For a time he had even abandoned his astronomical investigations for the supposedly safer fields of motion and physics. Even there, Aristotle had been wrong. No matter what he touched, his reason showed him that the conclusions of Aristotle, the conclusions adopted and supported by the Roman Catholic church, were wrong. Now finally, with the accession of Pope Urban VIII, old Cardinal Barbarini, who was himself a mathematician, Galileo felt confident that he could resume his writing and publishing.

Galileo's rebellion began early, when he decided to study mathematics rather than medicine. Galileo was fascinated with the manipulation of numbers, and by the age of 25 was teaching at the University of Pisa. There he began to conduct experiments to measure rates of motion. Galileo was soon in trouble with his colleagues and was forced to leave Pisa for Padua.

It was in Padua that his real difficulties began. After seeing a small prototype made in Holland, Galileo developed a telescope that could magnify objects to 30 times their size, which made it possible to see clearly the stars and planets that had been only dimly perceptible before. In 1610, Galileo had looked at the moon and discovered that its properties were similar to those of the earth. He had seen four moons of Jupiter, the first conclusive proof that there were heavenly bodies that did not revolve around the earth. Even before he had gazed at the stars, Galileo was persuaded that Copernicus must be right in arguing that the earth revolved around the sun. Now he believed he had irrefutable proof: the proof of his own eyes.

From the publication of *The Starry Messenger* in 1610, Galileo became the most active and best known advocate of the Copernican universe. In 1616, he was called to Rome and warned about his opinions. Belief in the theories of Copernicus was heresy, he was told. If Galileo held or maintained them, he would incur a heavy penalty. The Church accepted unequivocally the Ptolemaic explanations of the structure of the universe and could cite innumerable passages in the Bible to support them. It was willful and stubborn to oppose official doctrine, doctrine that had been frequently and fully examined. At first it seemed that Galileo would be silenced, but the erudite Cardinal Bellarmine, to whom the case had been assigned, wanted only to caution him. Galileo might still examine the Copernican hypotheses; he might still discuss them with his learned colleagues, as long as he did not hold or maintain them to be true.

For eight years Galileo kept his peace. When he decided to write again, it was in the belief that things were changing. He created a dialogue between a Ptolemaist and a Copernican. Let the one challenge the other on the most basic points, just as if they were in formal academic dispute. How did each explain the most difficult things that there were to explain, the existence of spots on the sun or the movement of the tides? Especially the tides.... If the earth stood still and the sun moved, why were there tides in the seas that moved with such regularity that they could be predicted?

Galileo was no heretic. He had no desire to challenge the Church. He would not print his tract anonymously in a Protestant country. Rather, he would create a true dialogue, one with which not even the most narrow-minded censor of the Roman church could find fault. He submitted his book to the official censor in Rome for approval, then to the official censor in Florence. The censors struck out passages, changed some words and deleted others. They demanded a new preface, even a new title: *A Dialogue Between the Two Great Systems of the World.* Finally, in 1632, the book went to press and was an immediate success.

Indeed, it was a success that could not be ignored. The Jesuits, who regarded learning and education as their special mission, demanded that action be taken against Galileo. Their teachings had been held up to ridicule; their official astronomers had been challenged; their doctrines had been repudiated. There was much at stake. Galileo's book had not been the vigorous academic dispute that he promised, and it had not concluded with the triumph of Church doctrine over the speculations of Copernicus. No, it had been advocacy. Anyone could see where the author's true sympathies lay. The character chosen to speak the part of Aristotle was not named Simplicio for nothing. Although this was the name of an ancient Aristotelian, it was also a perfect description of the arguments that the speaker advanced. Especially in the matter of the tides, Galileo had reduced the Aristotelian position to nonsense. The Jesuits brought their case directly to the pope and won an investigation, an investigation that they knew would end with Galileo's condemnation.

Although initially Pope Urban VIII was reluctant to prosecute the 70-year-old astronomer, "the light of Italy," ultimately he had no choice. The great war to stamp out heresy was going badly for the Church. The pope needed the support of the Jesuits in Vienna and in Madrid much more than he needed the support of a scientist who had seen the moons of Jupiter. Nevertheless, when the case was turned over to the Inquisition, it proved weak in law. Galileo had only to present the book itself to show that he had received the official sanction of not one, but two censors of the Roman Catholic church. If there was still anything in his book that offended, could the fault be his alone?

The argument stymied the prosecutors, who were forced to find evidence where none existed. Resurrecting the agreement between Galileo and Bellarmine, they attempted to make it say that Galileo was under an absolute ban from even discussing the Copernican theories. Either Galileo would agree to recant his views, admit his errors, and beg the forgiveness of the Church or he would be tried and burned as a heretic. But though he could be forced to recant his view that the earth orbits the sun, Galileo could not be forced to change his mind.

After his recantation, Galileo was sentenced to live out his days under house arrest. Five years after his death in 1642, his greatest scientific work, *The Two New Sciences,* was smuggled out of Italy and printed anonymously in Holland.

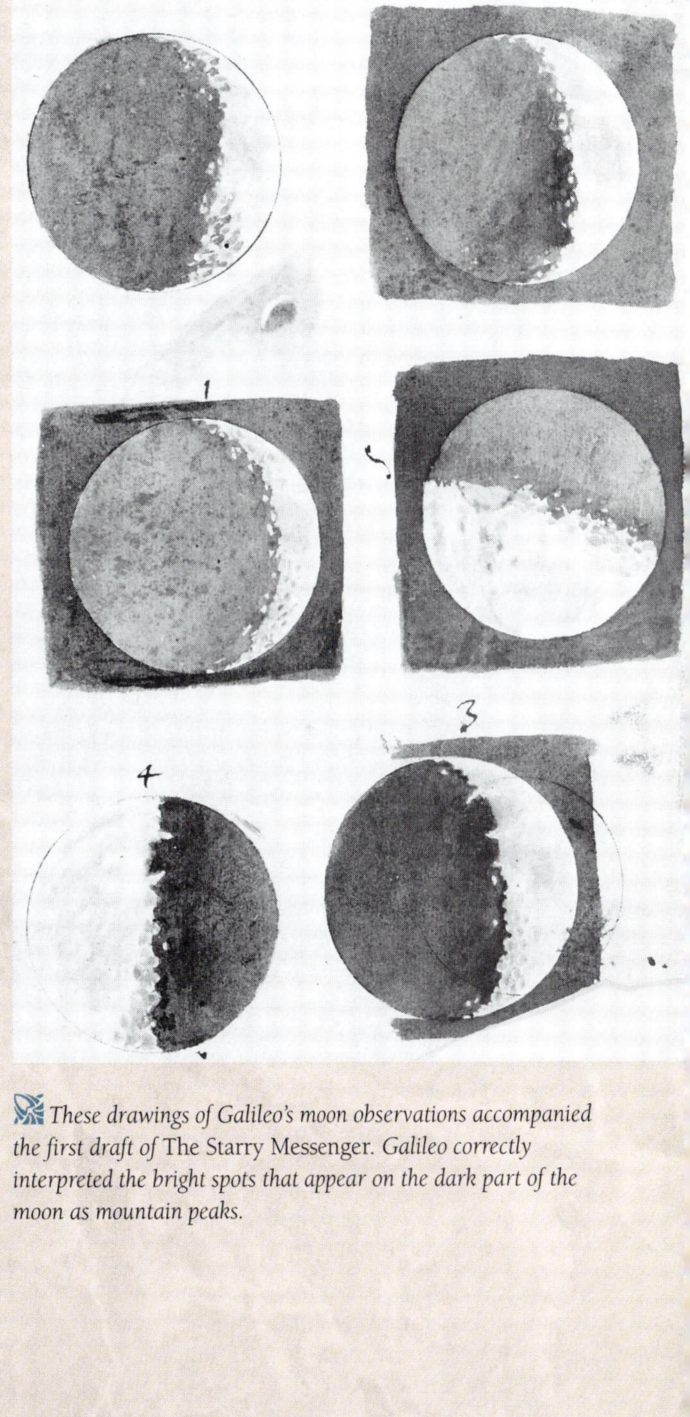

These drawings of Galileo's moon observations accompanied the first draft of The Starry Messenger. *Galileo correctly interpreted the bright spots that appear on the dark part of the moon as mountain peaks.*

Paracelsus was a physician and philosopher who rejected Galen's theory that disease was caused by an imbalance of humors in the body. Instead, he argued that diseases each had their own causes and remedies.

recipes for the cure of disease. He worked carefully and recorded each step in his experiments. Boyle's first important work, *The Sceptical Chymist* (1661), attacked both Aristotelian and Paracelsian views of the basic components of the natural world. Boyle rejected both the four humors and the three principles. Instead he favored an atomic explanation in which matter "consisted of little particles of all sizes and shapes." Changes in the particles, which would later be identified as the chemical elements, resulted in changes in matter. Boyle's most important experiments were with gases—a word invented by Paracelsus. He formulated the relationship between the volume and pressure of a gas (Boyle's law) and invented the air pump.

The new spirit of scientific inquiry also affected medical studies. The study of anatomy through dissection had helped the new scientists reject many of the descriptive errors in Galen's texts. The Belgian doctor Andreas Vesalius (1514–1564), who was physician to the emperor Charles V, published the first modern set of anatomical drawings in 1543, the same year that Copernicus published his work. But accurate knowledge of the composition of the body did not also mean better understanding of its operation. Dead bodies didn't easily yield the secrets of life. Much of what was known about matters as common as reproduction was a combination of ancient wisdom and the practical

Tenth "Muscle Plate" from Andreas Vesalius's De Humani Corporis Fabrica (Concerning the Fabric of the Human Body), *published in 1543. The muscles of the back of the body are laid bare.*

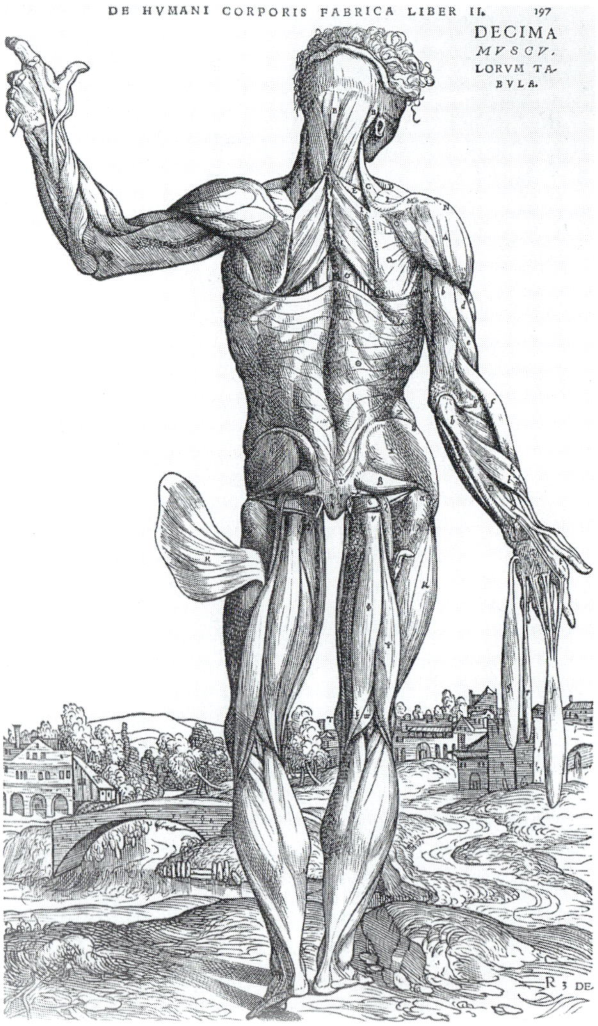

experiences of midwives and doctors. Both were woefully inadequate.

One of the greatest mysteries was the method by which blood moved through the vital organs. It was generally believed that the blood originated in the liver, traveled to the right side of the heart, and then passed to the left side through invisible pores. Anatomical investigation proved beyond doubt that there was blood in both sides of the heart, but no one could discover the pores through which it passed. William Harvey (1578–1657), an Englishman who had received his medical education in Italy, offered an entirely different explanation. Harvey was employed as royal physician to both James I and Charles I and had one of the most lucrative medical practices in Europe. His real interest, however, was in studying the anatomy of the heart. Harvey examined hearts in more than 40 species before concluding that the heart worked like a pump or, as he put it, a water bellows. Harvey observed that the valves of the heart's chambers allowed the blood to flow in only one direction. He thus concluded that the blood was pumped by the heart and circulated throughout the entire body.

Sir Isaac Newton provided a clear and comprehensive explanation of the physical universe in mathematical terms. He established the theory of gravity and invented a new kind of mathematics: calculus.

Sir Isaac Newton. The greatest of all English scientists was the mathematician and physicist Sir Isaac Newton (1642–1727). It was Newton who brought together the various strands of the new science. He merged the materialists and Hermeticists, the astronomers and astrologers, the chemists and alchemists. He made stunning contributions to the sciences of optics, physics, astronomy, and mathematics, and his magnum opus, *Mathematical Principles of Natural Philosophy* (1687), is one of a handful of the most important scientific works ever composed. Most important, Newton solved the single most perplexing problem: If the world was composed of matter in motion, what was motion?

Newton came from a moderately prosperous background and was trained at a local grammar school before entering Cambridge University. There was little in his background or education to suggest his unique talents, and in fact his most important discoveries were not appreciated until years after he had made them. Newton was the first to understand the composition of light, the first to develop a calculus, and the first to build a reflecting telescope. Newton became a professor at Cambridge, but he spent much of his time alone. He made a great study of Hermetic writings and from them revived the mystical notions of attraction and repulsion.

Although Galileo had developed a *theory of inertia,* the idea that a body at rest stays at rest, most materialists believed that motion was inherent in objects. In contrast, Newton believed that motion was the result of the interaction of objects and that it could be calculated mathematically. From his experiments he formulated the concept of force and his famous laws of motion: (1) that objects at rest or of uniform linear motion remain in such a state unless acted upon by an external force; (2) that changes in motion are proportional to force; and (3) that for every action there is an equal and opposite reaction. From the laws of motion, Newton advanced one step further. If the world was no more than matter in motion and if all motion was subject to the same laws, then the movement of the planets could be explained in the same way as the movement of an apple falling from a tree. There was a mathematical relationship between attraction and repulsion—a universal gravitation, as Newton called it—that governed the movement of all objects. Newton's theory of gravity joined together Kepler's astronomy and Galileo's physics. The mathematical, materialistic world of the new science was now complete.

Science Enthroned

By the middle of the seventeenth century, the new science was firmly established throughout Europe. Royal and noble patrons supported the enterprise by paying some of the costs of equipment and experimentation. Royal observatories were created for astronomers, colleges of physicians for doctors, and laboratories for chemists. Both England and France established royal societies of learned scientists to meet together and discuss their discoveries. The French Academie des Sciences (1666) was composed of 20 salaried scientists and an equal number of students, representing the different branches of scientific learning. They met twice weekly throughout the year, and each member worked on a project of his own devising. The English Royal Society (1662) boasted some of the greatest minds of the age. It was there that Newton first made public his most important discoveries. Scientific bodies were also formed outside the traditional universities. Those were the so-called mechanics colleges, such as Gresham College in London, where the practical applications of mathematics and physics were studied and taught. Navigation was a particular concern of the college, and the faculty established close ties with the Royal Navy and with London merchants.

The establishment of learned scientific societies and practical colleges fulfilled part of the program advocated by Sir Francis Bacon (1561–1626), one of the leading supporters of scientific research in England. In *The Advancement of Learning* (1605), Bacon had proposed a scientific method through inductive empirical experimentation. Bacon believed that experiments should be carefully recorded so that results were both reliable and repeatable. He advocated the open world of the scientist over the secret world of the magician. In his numerous writings, he stressed the practical impact of scientific discovery and even wrote a utopian work in which science appeared as the savior of humanity. Although he was not himself a scientific investigator,

Joseph Wright of Derby, An Experiment on a Bird in the Air Pump *(1768). Traveling lecturers fed the growing popular interest in science and often enlivened their talks with demonstrations of the air pump. The demonstration usually involved placing a live animal in a glass receiver attached to a pumping apparatus. Air was pumped out to demonstrate the animal's reaction to the loss of air. If air was readmitted in time, the animal would revive. Usually, the bird used in the experiment would have been a sparrow or some other common species. The artist has taken some liberty—and created a decidedly more dramatic picture—by depicting a white cockatoo as the subject of the demonstration.*

Bacon used his considerable influence to support scientific projects in England.

Bacon's support for the new science contrasts markedly with the stance taken by the Roman Catholic church. Embattled by the Reformation and the wars of religion, the Church had taken the offensive in preserving the core of its heritage. By the early seventeenth century, the missionary work of the Jesuits had won many reconversions and had halted the advance of Protestantism. Now the new science appeared to be another heresy. Not only did it confound ancient wisdom and contradict Church teachings, but it was also a lay movement that was neither directed nor controlled from Rome. The trial of Galileo slowed the momentum of scientific investigation in Catholic countries and starkly posed the conflict between authority and knowledge. But the stand taken by the Church was based on more than narrow self-interest. Ever since Copernicus had published his views, a new skepticism had emerged among European intellectuals. Every year new theories competed with old ones, and dozens of contradictory explanations for the most common phenomena were advanced and debated. The skeptics concluded that nothing was known and nothing was knowable. Their position led inevitably to the most shocking of all possible views: atheism.

There was no necessary link between the new science and an attack upon established religion: so Galileo had argued all along. Few of the leading scientists ever saw a contradiction between their studies and their faith. Sir Robert Boyle endowed a lectureship for the advancement of Christian doctrine and contributed money for the translation of the New Testament into Turkish. Still, by the middle of the century attacks on the Church were increasing, and some blamed the new science for them. Thus it was altogether fitting that one of the leading mathematicians of the day should also provide the method for harmonizing faith and reason.

René Descartes, the seventeenth-century French mathematician, philosopher, and scientist. He remained a faithful Catholic all his life while questioning the very foundations of Catholic philosophy.

René Descartes (1596–1650) was the son of a provincial lawyer and judge. He was trained in one of the best Jesuit schools in France before taking a law degree in 1616. While it was his father's intention that his son practice law, it was René's intention that he become educated in "the school of life." He entered military service in the Dutch Republic, and after the outbreak of the Thirty Years' War served in the Duke of Bavaria's army. Descartes was keenly interested in mathematics, and during his military travels he met and was tutored by a leading Dutch mathematician. For the first time he learned of the new scientific discoveries and of the advances made in mathematics. In 1619, he dreamed that he had discovered the scientific principles of universal knowledge. After the dream, Descartes returned to Holland and began to develop his system. He was on the verge of publishing his views when he learned of the Church's condemnation of Galileo. Reading Galileo's *Dialogue Between the Two Great Systems of the World,* Descartes discovered that he shared many of the same opinions and had worked out mathematical proofs for them. He refrained from publishing until 1637 when he brought out his *Discourse on Method.*

In the *Discourse on Method,* Descartes demonstrated how skepticism could be used to produce certainty. He began by declaring that he would reject everything that could not be clearly proved beyond doubt. Thus he rejected his perception of the material world, the testimony of his senses—all known or imagined opinions. He was left only with doubt. But what was doubt, if not thought, and what was thought, if not the workings of his mind? The only thing of which he could be certain, then, was that he had a mind. Thus his famous formulation: "I think, therefore I am." From this first certainty came another: the knowledge of perfectibility. He knew that he was imperfect and that a perfect being had to have placed that knowledge within him. Therefore, a perfect being—God—existed.

Descartes's philosophy, known as Cartesianism, rested on the dual existence of matter and mind. Matter was the material world, subject to the incontrovertible laws of mathematics. Mind was the spirit of the creator. Descartes was one of the leading mechanistic philosophers, believing that all objects operated in accord with natural laws. He invented analytic geometry and made important contributions to the sciences of optics and physics on which Newton would later build. Yet it was in his proof that the new science could be harmonized with the old religion that Descartes made his greatest contribution to the advancement of learning. Despite the fact that his later work was condemned by the Catholic church and that he preferred the safety of Protestant Holland to the uncertainty of his Catholic homeland, Cartesianism became the basis for the unification of science and religion.

"I shall attempt to make myself intelligible to everyone," Descartes wrote. Like many of the new scientists, he preferred the use of vernacular languages to elite Latin, hoping that his work would reach beyond the narrow bounds of high culture. Descartes was one of many new scientists who saw the practical import of what they had learned and who hoped to bring that knowledge to the aid of the material well-being of their contemporaries. John Dee (1527–1608) translated the Greek geometrician Euclid into English so that ordinary people might "find out and devise new works, strange engines and instruments for sundry purposes in the commonwealth." Although many of the breakthrough discoveries of the new scientists would not find practical use for centuries, the spirit of discovery was to have great impact in an age of commerce and capital. The quest for mathematical certainty and prime movers led directly to improvements in agriculture, mining, navigation, and industrial activity. It also brought with it a sense of control over the material world that provided a new optimism for generations of Europeans.

EMPIRES OF GOODS

Under the watchful eye of the European states, a worldwide marketplace for the exchange of commodities had been created. First the Dutch and then the English had established monopoly companies to engage in exotic trades in the East. First the Spanish and Portuguese, then the English and French, had established colonial dependencies in the Atlantic that they carefully nurtured in hope of economic gain. Protected trade had flourished beyond the wildest dreams of its promoters. Luxury commodities became staples; new commodities became luxuries. Trade enhanced the material life of all Europeans, although it came at great cost to the Asians, Africans, and Latin Americans whose labor and raw materials were converted into the new crazes of consumption.

The Geographer *by Jan Vermeer van Delft, 1669. A Dutch cartographer, holding dividers, is shown surrounded by charts, a globe, and other paraphernalia of his craft. Such cartographers combined the skills of artist and mathematician.*

While long-distance trade was never as important to the European economy as inland and intracontinental trade, its development in the seventeenth and eighteenth centuries had a profound impact on lifestyles, economic policy, and, ultimately, warfare. The Dutch became the first great commercial power. Their achievements were based on innovative techniques, rational management, and a social and cultural environment that supported mercantile activities. Dutch society was freer than any other; it was open to new capital, new ventures, and new ideas. The Dutch improved the organization of trade by developing the concept of the entrepôt, a place where goods were brought for storage before being exchanged. They pioneered in finance by establishing the Bank of Amsterdam. They led in shipbuilding by developing the flyboat, a long, flat-hulled vessel designed specifically to carry bulky cargoes like grain. They traded around the globe with the largest mercantile fleet yet known. It was not until the end of the seventeenth century that England and France surpassed the Dutch. That reversal owed less to new innovations than it did to restrictions on trade. Because the Dutch dominated the European economy, the French and English began to pass laws to eliminate Dutch competition. The English banned imports carried in Dutch ships; the French banned Dutch products. Both policies cut heavily into the Dutch superiority, and both ultimately resulted in commercial warfare.

The Marketplace of the World

By the sixteenth century, all the major trading routes had already been opened. The Spanish moved back and forth across the Atlantic; the Dutch and Portuguese sailed around the tip of Africa to the Indian Ocean. The Baltic trade connected the eastern and western parts of Europe as Danes, Swedes, and Dutch exchanged Polish and Russian raw materials for English and French manufactured goods. The Mediterranean, which had dominated world trade for centuries, was still a vital artery of intercontinental trade, but its role was diminishing. In 1600, almost three-quarters of the Asian trade was still land based, much of it carried through the Middle East to the Mediterranean. A century later, nearly all Asian trade was carried directly to western Europe by Dutch and English vessels. Commercial power was shifting to the northern European states just as dramatically as military and political power.

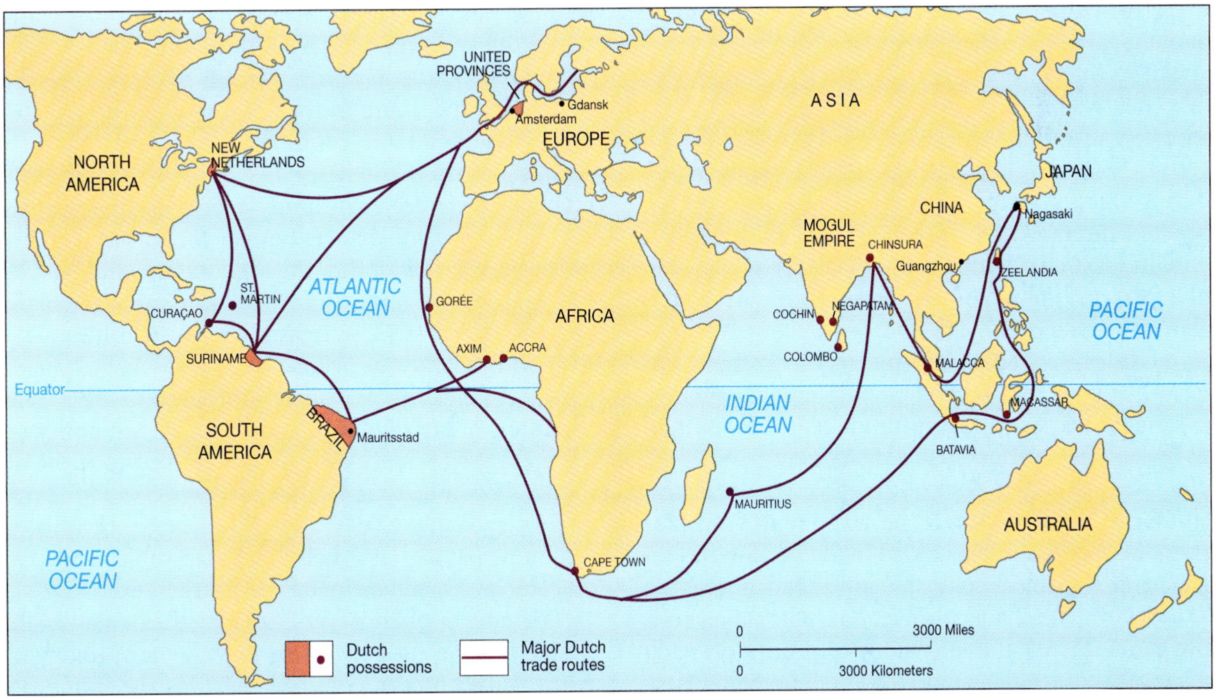

Dutch Trade Routes, ca. 1650. The Dutch were the greatest commercial nation of the seventeenth century.

The Evolution of Long-Distance Travel. The technology associated with commerce achieved no breakthroughs to compare with the great transformations of the fifteenth century, when new techniques of navigation made transatlantic travel possible. It is certainly true that there continued to be improvements. The astronomical findings of the new science were a direct aid to navigation, as were the recorded experiences of so many practiced sea travelers. The materials used to make and maintain ships improved with the importation of pitch and tar from the east and with the greater availability of iron and copper from Scandinavia. It was the Dutch who made the single most important innovation in shipbuilding. To gain maximum profit from their journeys to the Baltic, the Dutch designed the so-called flyboats. Flyboats sacrificed speed and maneuverability, but they were cheap to build and could be manned by small crews. They carried no heavy armaments and were thus well adapted to the serene Baltic trade.

It was unspectacular developments like the flyboat that had such an impact on seventeenth- and eighteenth-century transcontinental trade. Innovation, organization, and efficient management were the principal elements of what historians have called the commercial revolution. Concerted efforts to maximize opportunities and advantages accounted for the phenomenal growth in the volume and value of commercial exchange. One of the least spectacular and most effective breakthroughs was the replacement of bilateral with triangular trade. In bilateral trade, the surplus commodities of one community were exchanged for those of another. The method, of course, restricted the range of trading partners to those with mutually desirable surplus production: England and Italy were unlikely to swap woolens or Sicily and Poland to trade grain. For those with few desirable commodities, bilateral trade meant the exchange of precious metals for goods, and throughout much of the sixteenth and early seventeenth centuries, bullion was by far the most often traded commodity. Triangular trade created a larger pool of desirable goods. British manufactured goods could be traded to Africa for slaves, the slaves could be traded in the West Indies for sugar, and the sugar could be consumed in Britain. Moreover, the merchants involved in shifting the goods from place to place could achieve profits on each exchange. Indeed, their motive in trading could now change from dumping surplus commodities to matching supply and demand.

The New Forms of Banking. Equally important were the changes made in the way trade was financed. As states, cities, and even individuals could stamp their own precious metal, there were hundreds of different European coins with different nominal and metallic values. The influx of American silver further destabilized an already unstable system of exchange. The Bank of Amsterdam was created in 1609 to establish a uniform rate of exchange for the various currencies traded in that city. From that useful function a second developed—transfer, or giro, banking, a system that had been invented in Italy. In giro banking, various merchant firms held money on account and issued bills of transfer from one to another. The transfer system meant that merchants in different cities did not have to transport their precious metals or endure long delays in having their accounts settled.

Giro banking also aided the development of bills of exchange, an early form of checking. Merchants could conclude trades by depositing money in a given bank or merchant house and then having a bill drawn for the sum they owed. Bills of exchange were especially important in international trade, as they made large-scale shipments of precious metals to settle trade deficits unnecessary. By the end of the seventeenth century, bills of exchange had become negotiable; that is, they could pass from one merchant to another without being redeemed. Thus a Dutch merchant could buy French wines in Bordeaux with a bill of exchange drawn on an account in the Bank of Amsterdam. The Bordeaux merchant could then purchase Spanish oranges and use the same bill of exchange as payment. There were two disadvantages to the system: ultimately the bill had to return to Amsterdam for redemption; when it did, the account on which it was drawn might be empty. The establishment of the Bank of England in 1694 overcame such difficulties. The Bank of England was licensed to issue its own bills of exchange, or bank notes, which were backed by the revenue from specific English taxes. That security of payment was widely sought after, and the Bank of England soon became a clearinghouse for all kinds of bills of exchange. The Bank would buy in bills at a discount, paying less than their face value, and pay out precious metal or their own notes in exchange.

The effects of those and many other small-scale changes in business practice helped fuel prolonged growth in European commerce. It was the European merchant who made that growth possible by accepting the risks of each individual transaction and building up small pools of capital from which successive transactions could take place. Most mercantile ventures were conducted by individuals or families and were based on the specialized trade of a single commodity. Trade offered high returns because it entailed high risks. The long delays in moving goods and their uncertain arrival; the unreliability of agents and the unscrupulousness of other traders; and the inefficiencies in transport and communication all weighed heavily against success. Those who succeeded did so less by luck than by hard work. They used family members to receive shipments. They lowered shipping costs by careful packaging. They lowered protection costs by securing their trade routes. Financial publications lowered the costs of information. Ultimately, lower costs meant lower prices. For centuries luxury goods had dominated intercontinental trade. But by the eighteenth century, European merchants had created a world marketplace in which the luxuries of the past were the common fare of the present.

Detail of an Indian textile from the Madras region (ca. 1650). Calicut gave its name to the cotton cloth called calico. This is an example of a "painted Calicut," a wall hanging that shows richly dressed Indian women.

Consumption Choices

As long-distance trade became more sophisticated, merchants became more sensitive to consumer tastes. Low-volume, high-quality goods such as spices and silks could not support the growing merchant communities in the European states. Those goods were the preserve of the largest trading companies and, more importantly, they had reached saturation levels by the early seventeenth century. The price of pepper, the most used of all spices, fell nearly continuously after 1650. Moreover, triangular trade allowed merchants to provide a better match of supplies and demands. The result was the rise to prominence of a vast array of new commodities, which not only continued the expansion of trade but also reshaped diet, lifestyles, and patterns of consumption. New products came from both East and West. Dutch and English incursions into the Asian trade provoked competition with the Portuguese and expanded the range of commodities that were shipped back to Europe. An aggressive Asian triangle was created in which European bullion bought Indonesian spices that were exchanged for Persian silk and Chinese and Japanese finished goods. In the Atlantic, the English were quick to develop both home and export markets for a variety of new or newly available products.

The New Commodities. European trade with Asia had always been designed to satisfy consumer demand rather than to exchange surplus goods. Europeans manufactured little that was desired in Asia, and neither merchants nor governments saw fit to attempt to influence Asian tastes in the way they did those of Europeans. The chief commodity imported to the East was bullion: tons of South American silver, perhaps a third of all that was produced. In return came spices, silk, coffee, jewels, jade, porcelain, dyes, and a wide variety of other exotic goods. By the middle of the seventeenth century, the Dutch dominated the spice trade, obtaining a virtual monopoly over cinnamon, cloves, nutmeg, and mace and carrying the largest share of pepper. Each year, Europeans consumed perhaps a million pounds of the four great spices and seven million pounds of pepper. Both Dutch and English competed for preeminence in the silk trade. The Dutch concentrated on Chinese silk, which they used mostly in trade with Japan. The English established an interest in lower-quality Indian silk spun in

Bengal and even hired Italian silk masters to try to teach European techniques to the Indian spinners.

The most important manufactured articles imported from the East to Europe were the lightweight, brightly colored Indian cottons known as calicoes. The Dutch first realized the potential of the cotton market. Until the middle of the seventeenth century, cotton and cotton blended with silk were used in Europe only for wall hangings and table coverings. Colorful Asian chintz contained floral patterns that Europeans still considered exotic. But the material was also soft and smooth to the touch, and it soon replaced linen for use as underwear and close-fitting garments among the well-to-do. The fashion quickly caught on, and the Dutch began exporting calicoes throughout the Continent. The English and French followed suit, establishing their own trading houses in India and bringing European patterns and designs with them for the Asians to copy. The calico trade was especially lucrative because the piece goods were easy to pack and ship and, unlike consumables, could be stored indefinitely. When the English finally came to dominate the trade in the middle of the eighteenth century, they were shipping more than a million cloths a year into London. The craze for calicoes was so great that both the English and French governments attempted to ban their import to protect their own clothing industries.

Along with the new apparel from the East came new beverages. Coffee, which was first drunk in northern Europe in the early seventeenth century, had become a fashionable drink by the end of the century. Coffeehouses sprang up in the major urban areas of northern Europe. There political and intellectual conversation was as heady as the strong Middle Eastern brew that was served. The Dutch and English both established themselves in the coffee trade, which was centered in the Middle Eastern seaport of Mocha. By the beginning of the eighteenth century, the Dutch had begun to grow their own coffee for export from their island colony of Java, and the two different types of coffee competed for favor.

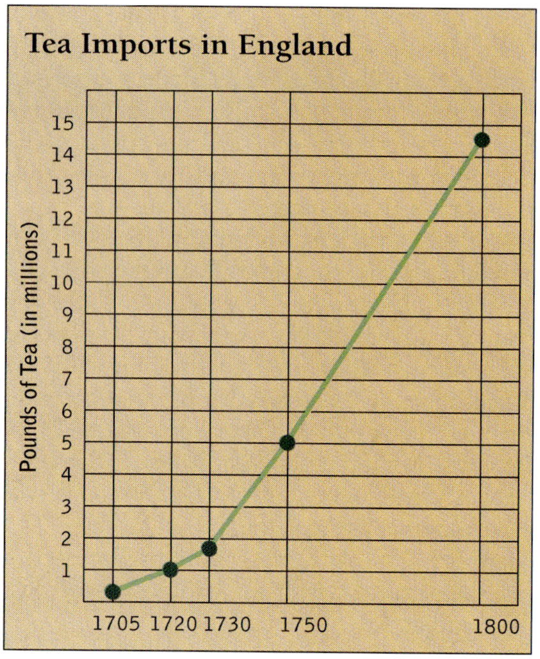

Tea and Sugar. As popular as coffee became among the European elites, it paled in comparison to the importance of tea as both an import commodity and a basic beverage. While coffee drinking remained the preserve of the wealthy, tea consumption spread throughout European society. It was probably most prevalent in England, where the combination of China tea and West Indian sugar created a virtual revolution in nutrition. The growth in tea consumption was phenomenal. In 1706, England imported 100,000 pounds of tea. By the end of the century, the number had risen to more than 15 million pounds. The English imported most of the tea directly from China, where an open port had been established at Canton. Originally just one of a number of commodities that were carried on an Asian voyage, tea soon became the dominant cargo of the large English merchant ships. Some manufactured goods would be brought to India on the outward voyage in order to fill as much cargo space as possible, but once the ships had loaded the green and black teas, they sailed directly home. Almost all tea was purchased with bullion, as the Chinese had even less use for European goods than did other Asians. It was not until the discovery that the Chinese consumed large quantities of opium, which was grown in India and Southeast Asia, that a triangular trade developed.

The success of tea was linked to the explosive growth in the development of sugar in Europe's Atlantic colonies. The Portuguese had attempted to cultivate sugar in the Azores at the end of the fifteenth century, but it was not until the settlement of Brazil, whose hot, humid climate was a natural habitat for the cane plants, that widespread cultivation began. The island of Barbados became the first English sugar colony. Barbados turned to sugar production accidentally, when its first attempts to market tobacco failed.

The planters modeled their methods on those of Brazil, where African slaves were used to plant, tend, and cut the giant canes from which the sugar was extracted. For reasons that will never be fully understood, the English had an insatiable appetite for sugar's sweetness. It was taken plain, like candy; used in small quantities in almost all types of recipes; and diluted in ever-increasing quantities of tea. Hot, sweet tea became a meal for the lower orders of English society, a meal which—unlike beer—provided a quick burst of energy. By 1700, the English were sending home more than 50 million pounds of sugar besides what they were shipping directly to the North American colonies. The quantity doubled by 1730, and still there was no slackening of demand. What might have become a valuable raw material in English trade instead became a staple of consumption.

The triangular trade of manufactures—largely re-exported calicoes—to Africa for slaves, who were exchanged in the West Indies for sugar, became the dominant form of English overseas trade. Colonial production depended upon the enforced labor of hundreds of thousands of Africans. Gold and silver, tobacco, sugar, rice, and indigo were all slave crops. Africans were enslaved by other Africans and then sold to Europeans to be used in the colonies. More than 6 million black slaves were imported into the Americas during the course of the eighteenth century. While rum and calicoes were the main commodities exchanged for slaves, the African tribes that dominated the slave trade organized a highly competitive market. Every colonial power participated in the lucrative trade. More than 3 million slaves were imported into the Portuguese colony of Brazil; by the end of the eighteenth century, there were 500,000 slaves and only 35,000 French inhabitants on the sugar island of Saint Domingue. But it was the English, with their sugar colonies of Barbados and Jamaica and their tobacco colonies of Virginia and Maryland, who ultimately came to control the slave trade. The prosperity of Newport, Rhode Island, in North America and the port of Liverpool in Lancashire were built entirely on the slave trade, as were hundreds of plantation fortunes. The sweet tooth of Europe was fed by the sweat of black Africans.

Sugar was by far the dominant commodity of the colonial trade, but it was not the only one. Furs and fish had first driven Europeans toward North America, and both remained important commodities. Beaver and rabbit skins were the most common materials for making headgear in an age in which everyone wore a hat. The schools of cod in Canadian waters were

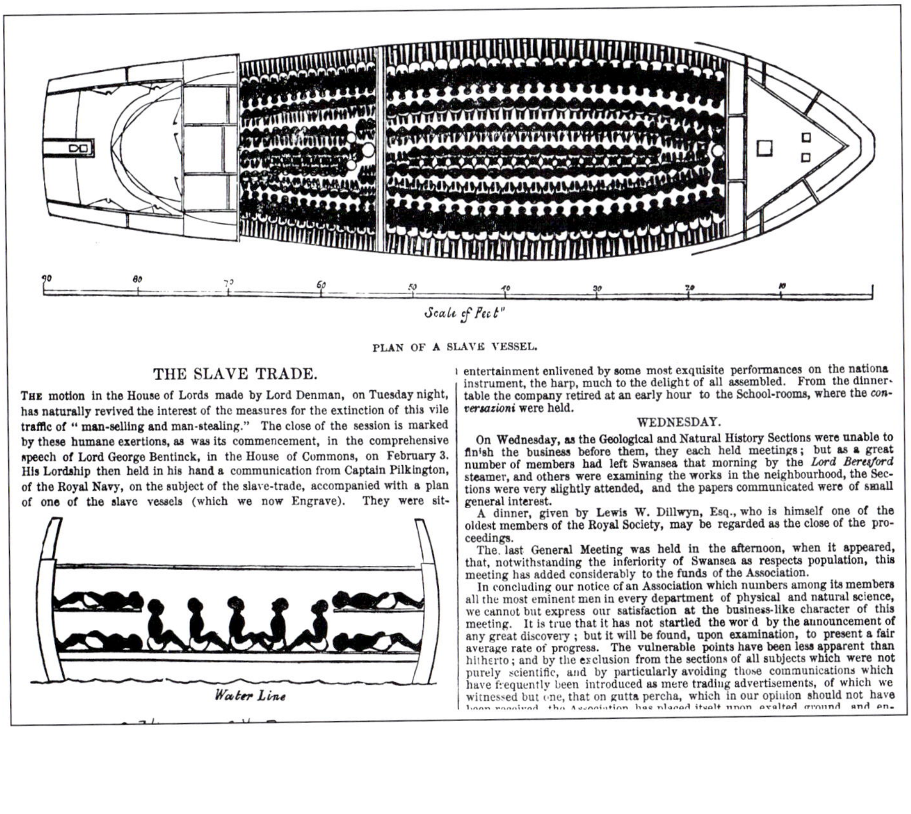

PLAN OF A SLAVE VESSEL.

THE SLAVE TRADE.

THE motion in the House of Lords made by Lord Denman, on Tuesday night, has naturally revived the interest of the measures for the extinction of this vile traffic of "man-selling and man-stealing." The close of the session is marked by these humane exertions, as was its commencement, in the comprehensive speech of Lord George Bentinck, in the House of Commons, on February 3. His Lordship then held in his hand a communication from Captain Pilkington, of the Royal Navy, on the subject of the slave-trade, accompanied with a plan of one of the slave vessels (which we now Engrave). They were sit-

entertainment enlivened by some most exquisite performances on the nationa instrument, the harp, much to the delight of all assembled. From the dinner-table the company retired at an early hour to the School-rooms, where the *conversazioni* were held.

WEDNESDAY.

On Wednesday, as the Geological and Natural History Sections were unable to fin'sh the business before them, they each held meetings; but as a great number of members had left Swansea that morning by the *Lord Beresford* steamer, and others were examining the works in the neighbourhood, the Sections were very slightly attended, and the papers communicated were of small general interest.

A dinner, given by Lewis W. Dillwyn, Esq., who is himself one of the oldest members of the Royal Society, may be regarded as the close of the proceedings.

The last General Meeting was held in the afternoon, when it appeared, that, notwithstanding the inferiority of Swansea as respects population, this meeting has added considerably to the funds of the Association.

In concluding our notice of an Association which numbers among its members all the most eminent men in every department of physical and natural science, we cannot but express our satisfaction at the business-like character of this meeting. It is true that it has not startled the wor d by the announcement of any great discovery; but it will be found, upon examination, to present a fair average rate of progress. The vulnerable points have been less apparent than hitherto; and by the exclusion from the sections of all subjects which were not purely scientific, and by particularly avoiding those communications which have frequently been introduced as mere trading advertisements, of which we witnessed but one, that on gutta percha, which in our opinion should not have

This diagram shows how slaves were packed into cargo holds for the notorious Middle Passage to the Americas. The plan was a model of efficiency, for slave traders sought to maximize profits.

This illustration of a Caribbean tobacco plantation shows an overseer directing the planting of the tobacco shoots while slaves in the drying sheds roll the leaves for export.

among the richest in the world, and the catch was shipped back either salted or dried. The English established what amounted to a manufacturing industry on the Newfoundland coast, where they dried the tons of fish that they caught. In the eighteenth century, rice was grown for export in the southern American colonies, particularly South Carolina. Rice never achieved great popularity in England, though it was in constant demand in the German states. Tobacco was the first new American product to come into widespread use in Europe, and its popularity—despite various official efforts to ban its use as dirty and unhealthy—grew steadily. American tobacco was grown principally in the colonies of Virginia and Maryland and shipped across the ocean, where it was frequently blended with European varieties. Although the English were the principal importers, it was the Dutch who dominated the European tobacco trade, making the most popular blends.

The new commodities flooded into Europe from all parts of the globe. By the middle of the eighteenth century, tea, coffee, cocoa, gin, and rum were among the most popular beverages. All were products that had largely been unknown a century earlier. Among the wealthy, tea was served from porcelain pots imported from China; among all classes it was drunk with sugar imported from America. Beaver hats and Persian silks were fashionable in the upper reaches of society, rabbit caps and calico prints in the lower. New habits were created as new demands were satisfied. Tea and sugar passed from luxury to staple in little more than a generation, and the demand for both products continued to increase. To meet it, the European trading powers needed to create and maintain a powerful and efficient mercantile system.

Dutch Masters

For the nearly 80 years between 1565 and 1648 that the Dutch were at war, they grew ever more prosperous. While the economies of most other European nations were sapped by warfare, the Dutch seemed to draw strength from their interminable conflict with the Spanish empire. They had the advantage of fighting defensively on land and offensively on sea. Land war was terribly costly to the aggressor, who had to raise large armies, transport them to the site of battles or sieges, and feed them while they were there. The defender simply had to fortify strong places, keep its water routes open to secure supplies, and wait for the weather to change. Sea war—or piracy, depending on one's viewpoint—required much smaller outlays for men and material and promised the rewards of captured prizes. The Dutch became expert at attacking the Spanish silver fleets, hunting like a lion against a herd by singling out the slower and smaller vessels for capture. The Dutch also benefited from the massive immigration into their provinces of Protestants who had lived and worked in the southern provinces. The immigrants brought with them vital skills in manufacturing and large reserves of capital for investment in Dutch commerce.

The Dutch grounded their prosperity on commerce. Excellent craftsmen, they took the lead in the skilled occupations necessary for finishing cloth, refining raw materials, and decorating consumer goods. They were also successful farmers, especially given the small amounts of land with which they had to work and the difficult ecological conditions in which they worked it. But their greatest abilities were in trade.

Although the Dutch Republic comprised seven separate political entities, with a total population of about two million, the province of Holland was preeminent among them. Holland contained more than a quarter of that population, and its trading port of Amsterdam was one of the great cities of Europe. The city had risen dramatically in the seventeenth century, growing from a midsized urban community of 65,000 in 1600 to a metropolis of 170,000 fifty years later. The port was one of the busiest in the world, for it was built to be an entrepôt. Vast warehouses and docks lined its canals. Visitors were impressed by the bustle, the cleanliness, and the businesslike appearance of Amsterdam. There were no great public squares and few recognizable monuments. The central buildings were the Bank and the Exchange, testimony to the dominant activities of the residents.

The Dutch dominated all types of European trade. They carried more English coal than England, more French wine than France, more Swedish iron than Sweden. Dutch ships outnumbered all others in every important port of Europe. Goods were brought to Amsterdam to be redistributed throughout the world. Dutch prosperity rested first upon the Baltic trade. Even after it ceased to expand in the middle of the seventeenth century, the Baltic trade composed more than one-quarter of all of Holland's commercial enterprise. The Dutch also were the leaders in the East Indian trade throughout the seventeenth century. They held a virtual monopoly on the sale of exotic spices and the largest share of the pepper trade. Their imports of cottons, and especially of porcelain, began new consumer fads that soon resulted in the development of European industries. Dutch potteries began to produce china, as lower-quality ceramic goods came to be known. Dutch trade in the Atlantic was of less importance, but the Dutch did have a colonial presence in the New World, controlling a number of small islands and the rapidly growing mainland settlement of New Netherland. Yet the Dutch still dominated the secondary market in tobacco and sugar, becoming the largest processor and refiner of those important commodities.

In all of the activities the Dutch acted as merchants rather than as consumers. Unlike most other Europeans, they regarded precious metal as a commodity like any other and took no interest in accumulating it for its own sake. That attitude enabled them to pioneer triangular trading and develop the crucial financial institutions necessary to expand their overseas commerce. The Dutch were not so much inventors as improvers. They saw the practical value in Italian accounting and banking methods and raised them to new levels of efficiency. They made use of marine insurance to help diminish the risks of mercantile activity. Their legal system favored the creation of small trading companies by protecting individual investments. The European stock and commodity markets were centered in Amsterdam. By the 1670s, more than 500 commodities

A prosperous Dutch trader in the East Indies poses with his wife on a hill near the port of Batavia (now Jakarta, Indonesia).

were traded on the Amsterdam exchange, and even a primitive futures market had evolved for those who wanted to speculate.

There were many explanations for the unparalleled growth of the small maritime state into one of the greatest of European trading empires. Geography and climate provided one impetus, the lack of sufficient foodstuffs another. Yet there were cultural characteristics as well. One was the openness of Dutch society. Even before the struggle with Spain, the northern provinces had shown a greater inclination toward religious toleration than had most parts of Europe. Amsterdam became a unique center for religious and intellectual exchange. European Jews flocked there, as did Catholic dissidents like Descartes. Those people brought with them a wide range of skills and knowledge, along with capital that could be invested in trade. There was no real nobility among the Dutch, and certainly no set of values that prized investment in land over investment in trade. The French and Spanish nobility looked with scorn upon their mercantile classes and shunned any form of commercial investment; the English, though more open to industry and trade, sank as much of their capital as possible into landed estates and country houses. The Dutch economic elite invested in trade. By the middle of the seventeenth century, the Dutch Republic enjoyed a reputation for cultural creativity that was the envy of the Continent. A truly extraordinary school of Dutch artists led by Rembrandt celebrated the new state born of commerce with vivid portrayals of its people and its prosperity.

Mercantile Organization

Elsewhere in Europe, trade was the king's business. The wealth of the nation was part of the prestige of the monarch, and its rise or fall part of the crown's power. Power and prestige were far more important to absolute rulers than was the profit of merchants. Indeed, in all European states except the Dutch Republic, the activities of merchants were scorned by

The Old Stock Exchange in Amsterdam was a center of mercantile activity and religious and intellectual interactions.

both the landed elite and the salaried bureaucrats. Leisure was valued by the one and royal service by the other. The pursuit of wealth by buying and selling somehow lacked dignity, yet the activities of the mercantile classes took on increasing importance for the state for two reasons. First, imported goods, especially luxuries, were a noncontroversial target for taxation. Customs duties and excise taxes proliferated all over Europe. Representative assemblies composed of landed elites were usually happy to grant them to the monarch, and merchants could pass them on to consumers in higher prices. Second, the competition for trade was seen as a competition between states rather than individual merchants. Trading privileges involved special arrangements with foreign powers, arrangements that recognized the sovereign power of European monarchs. In this way, trade could bring glory to the state.

Mercantilism. The competition for power and glory derived from the theory of mercantilism, a set of assumptions about economic activity that were commonly held throughout Europe and that guided the policies of almost every government. There were two interrelated ideas. One was that the wealth of a nation resided in its stock of precious metal, and the other was that economic activity was a zero-sum game. There was thought to be a fixed amount of money, a fixed number of commodities, and a fixed amount of consumption. Thus, what one country gained, another lost. If England bought wine from France and paid £100,000 in precious metal for it, then England was £100,000 poorer and France £100,000 richer. If one was to trade profitably, it was absolutely necessary to wind up with a surplus of precious metal. Therefore, it was imperative that governments regulate trade so that the stocks of precious metal were protected from the greed of the merchants. The first and most obvious measure of protection, then, was to prohibit the export of coin except by license, a prohibition that was absolutely unenforceable and was violated more often by government officials than by merchants.

Those ideas about economic activity led to a variety of forms of economic regulation. The most common was the monopoly, a grant of special privileges in return for both financial considerations and an agreement to abide by the rules set out by the state. In the context of the seventeenth-century economy, there were a number of advantages to monopolies. First, of course, were those that accrued to the crown. There were direct and indirect revenues: monopolists usually paid considerable fees for their rights, and their activities were easy to monitor for purposes of taxation. The crown could use the grant of monopoly to reward past favors or to purchase future support from powerful individuals. There were also advantages for the monopolists. They could make capital investments with the expectation of long-term gains. That advantage was especially important in attracting investors for risky and expensive ventures such as long-distance trade. Indeed, there were even benefits for the economy as a whole, as monopolies increased productive investment at a time when most capital was being used to purchase land, luxury goods, or offices.

The East India Companies. Two monopoly companies, the English and the Dutch East India companies, dominated the Asian trade. The English East India Company, founded in 1600 with capital of £30,000, was given the exclusive right to the Asian trade and immediately established itself throughout the Indian Ocean. The Dutch East India Company was formed two years later with ten times the capital of its English counterpart. By the end of the century, the Dutch company employed more than 12,000 people. Both companies were known as joint-stock companies, an innovation in the way in which businesses were organized. Subscribers owned a percentage of the total value of the company, based on the number of shares they bought, and were entitled to a distribution of profits on the same basis. Initially, the English company determined profits on single voyages and was supposed to distribute all of its assets to its shareholders after a given period. But changes in legal practice gave the company an identity separate from the individuals that held the shares. Now shares could be exchanged without the breakup of the company as a whole. Both Amsterdam and London soon developed stock markets to trade the shares of monopoly companies.

Both East India companies were remarkably good investments. The Dutch East India Company paid an average dividend of 18 percent for more than 200 years. The value of English East India Company shares rose fivefold in the second half of the seventeenth century alone. Few other monopoly companies achieved a record comparable to that of the East India companies. The English Royal African Company, founded in 1672 to provide slaves for the Spanish colonies, barely recouped costs and was soon superseded by private trade. Even the French East Indian

EASTERN TRADERS

The Dutch East India Company was the most important of the monopoly trading companies that were founded in the early seventeenth century. It was organized as a stock company and its shares traded on the Amsterdam bourse. Merchants could purchase portions of its ships for both imports and exports, and the company was given total control over the eastern spice trade. It was also given political and diplomatic powers in the areas in which it traded, and its overseas members behaved as much as foreign ambassadors as merchants. This excerpt, from an early history of the company, provides details of its original charter.

After various private merchants joined with others in the 1590s and after the turn of the century to form companies, first in Amsterdam and then in other cities of Holland and Zeeland, to open up and undertake travel and trade with the East Indies, and from time to time equipped and sent out many ships, which returned, on the average, with no small success, the States General came to the conclusion that it would be more useful and profitable not only for the country as a whole but also for its inhabitants individually, especially all those who had undertaken and shared in navigation and trade, that these companies should be combined and this navigation and trade be placed and maintained on a firm footing, with order and political guidance. After much argument and persuasion, this union was worked out by Their High Mightinesses [the government of the United Provinces], in their own words, to advance the prosperity of the United Netherlands, to conserve and increase its industry and to bring profit to the Company and to the people of the country.

... The Company's charter authorized it to make alliances with princes and potentates east of the Cape of Good Hope and beyond the Straits of Magellan, to make contracts, build fortresses and strongholds, name governors, raise troops, appoint officers of justice, and perform other necessary services for the advancement of trade; to dismiss the said governors and officers of justice if their conduct was found to be harmful and disloyal, provided that these governors or officers could not be prevented from returning here to present such grievances or complaints as they think they might have....

The inhabitants of this country were permitted to invest as much or as little as they pleased in shares of the Company.

The subscription had to be made before September 1, 1602....

... When the time for this investment or subscription had expired, various competent persons in different places presented requests in person or by sealed letter to the assembly of the XVII, asking that they be permitted to join the Company with the investment of certain sums of money; it was decided that no one else should be permitted to join in violation of the charter and to the detriment of the shareholders who had paid in their subscriptions before the expiration of the date fixed, and that the subscribed capital should be neither increased nor reduced.

and African companies, which were modeled on the Dutch and English, were forced to abandon their monopolies. The Dutch and English companies were successful not because of their special privileges but because they were able to lower the costs of protecting their ships and cargoes.

Monopolies were not the only form of regulation in which seventeenth-century government engaged. For those states with Atlantic colonies, regulation took the form of restricting markets rather than traders. In the 1660s, the English government, alarmed at the growth of Dutch mercantile activity in the New World, passed a series of Navigation Acts designed to protect English shipping. Colonial goods—primarily tobacco and sugar—could be shipped to and from England only in English boats. If the French wanted to purchase West Indian sugar, they could not simply send a ship to the English colony of Barbados loaded with French goods

Rembrandt, The Syndics of the Cloth Guild *(1662). This work was painted for the Drapers' or Cloth Guild and installed at the Guild's headquarters in Amsterdam. The five hatted Syndics look as though they have been caught in a momentary interruption of business. The bareheaded figure in the background is the valet, who unlike the Syndics, was not required to pay for his portrait.*

and exchange them for sugar. Rather, they had to make their purchases from an English import-export merchant and the goods had to be unloaded in an English port before they could be reloaded to be shipped to France. As a result, the English reexport trade skyrocketed. In the year 1700, reexports amounted to nearly 40 percent of all English commerce. With such a dramatic increase in trading, all moved in English ships, shipbuilding boomed. English coastal towns enjoyed heightened prosperity, as did the great colonial ports of Bristol and Liverpool. For a time, colonial protection proved effective.

French protectionism was as much internal as colonial. The French entered the intercontinental trade later than their North Atlantic rivals, and they were less dependent on trade for their subsistence. Of all the states of Europe, only France could satisfy its needs from its own resources. But to achieve such self-sufficiency required coordination and leadership. In the 1670s, Louis XIV's finance minister, Jean-Baptiste Colbert (1619–1683), developed a plan to bolster the French economy by protecting it against European imports. First Colbert followed the English example of restricting the reexport trade by requiring that imports come to France either in French ships or in the ships of the country from which the goods originated. In addition, he used tariffs to make imported goods unattractive in France. He sponsored a drive to increase French manufacturing, especially of textiles, tapestries, linens, glass, and furniture. To protect the investments in French manufacturing, enormous duties were placed on the import of similar goods manufactured elsewhere. The Venetian glass industry, for example, suffered a serious blow from Colbert's tariffs. English woolen manufacturers were also damaged, and the English sought retaliatory measures. But in fact, the English had already begun to imitate that form of protection. In the early eighteenth century, England attempted to limit the importation of cotton goods from India to prevent the collapse of the domestic clothing industry.

The Navigation Acts and Colbert's program of protective tariffs were directed specifically against Dutch reexporters. The Dutch were the acknowledged leaders in all branches of commerce in the seventeenth century. There were many summers when there were more Dutch vessels in London Harbor than there were English ships. In the 1670s, the Dutch merchant fleet was probably larger than the English, French, Spanish, Portuguese, and German fleets combined! Restrictive navigation practices were one way to combat an advantage that the Dutch had built through heavy capital investment and by breaking away from the prevailing theories about the relationship between wealth and precious metals. The English and French Navigation Acts cut heavily into the Dutch trade, and ultimately both the English and French overtook them. But protectionism had its price. Just as the dynastic wars were succeeded by the wars of religion, so the wars of religion were succeeded by the wars of commerce.

"The discovery of America and that of a passage to the East Indies by the Cape of Good Hope are the two greatest and most important events in the history of mankind." So wrote the great Scottish economist Adam Smith (1723–1790) in *The Wealth of Nations* (1776). For Smith and his generation, the first great age of commerce was coming to an end. The innovations of the Dutch had given way to a settled pattern of international long-distance trade. States now viewed commerce as a part of their national self-interest. They developed overseas empires, which they protected as markets for their goods and sources for their raw materials. The empires were justified by the theory of mercantilism and the demands of a generation of consumers who saw the luxuries of the past as the necessities of the present.

THE WARS OF COMMERCE

The belief that there was a fixed amount of trade in the world was still strong in the late seventeenth century. One country's gains in trade were another's losses. There was not more than enough to go around, and it could not be easily understood how the expansion of one country's trade could benefit all countries. Competition for trade was the same as competition for territory or subjects, part of the struggle by which the state grew powerful. It was not inevitable that economic competition would lead to warfare, only that restrictive competition would.

Thus the scramble for colonies in the seventeenth century led to commercial warfare in the eighteenth. As the English gradually replaced the Dutch as the leading commercial nation, so the French replaced the English as the leading competitor. Hostility between the English and the French had existed for centuries, and it was not without cause that the commercial wars of the eighteenth century should be likened to the territorial wars of the Middle Ages. The greed of merchants and the glory of princes fueled a struggle for the dominance of world markets that brought European warfare to every corner of the globe.

Painter Jan Peter depicts an incident in the naval warfare caused by trade rivalry between the Dutch and the English. The Dutch fleet sailed up the Medway River and destroyed many English vessels, towing away a battleship.

DEFINING COMMERCE

Adam Smith was a Scottish political theorist whose work The Wealth of Nations *(1776) was the first great work of economic analysis in European history. Smith had wide-ranging interests and wrote with equal authority about manufacturing, population, and trade. He was the first to develop the doctrine of free trade, which he called laissez-faire. Smith argued that the government that governed least governed best, and he was an early critic of protective tariffs and monopolies.*

EVERY INDIVIDUAL NECESSARILY LABOURS to render the annual revenue of the society as great as he can. He generally, indeed, neither intends to promote the public interest, nor knows how much he is promoting it. By preferring the support of domestic to that of foreign industry, he intends only his own security; and by directing that industry in such a manner as its produce may be of the greatest value, he intends only his own gain, and he is in this, as in many other cases, led by an invisible hand to promote an end which was no part of his intention. Nor is it always the worse for the society that it was no part of it. By pursuing his own interest he frequently promotes that of the society more effectually than when he really intends to promote it. I have never known much good done by those who affected to trade for the public good....

... Each nation has been made to look with an invidious eye upon the prosperity of all the nations with which it trades, and to consider their gain as its own loss. Commerce, which ought naturally to be, among nations as among individuals, a bond of union and friendship, has become the most fertile source of discord and animosity. The capricious ambition of kings and ministers has not, during the present and the preceding century, been more fatal to the repose of Europe, than the impertinent jealousy of merchants and manufacturers. The violence and injustice of the rulers of mankind is an ancient evil, for which, I am afraid, the nature of human affairs can scarce admit of a remedy. But the mean rapacity, the monopolizing spirit of merchants and manufacturers, who neither are, nor ought to be, the rulers of mankind, though it cannot perhaps be corrected, may very easily be prevented from disturbing the tranquillity of anybody but themselves....

The natural advantages which one country has over another in producing particular commodities are sometimes so great, that it is acknowledged by all the world to be in vain to struggle with them.... Very good grapes can be raised in Scotland, and very good wine too can be made of them at about thirty times the expense for which at least equally good can be brought from foreign countries. Would it be a reasonable law to prohibit the importation of all foreign wines merely to encourage the making of claret and burgundy in Scotland?

From Adam Smith, *The Wealth of Nations* (1776).

The Mercantile Wars

Commercial warfare in Europe began between the English and the Dutch in the middle of the seventeenth century. Both had established aggressive overseas trading companies in the Atlantic and in Asia. In the early seventeenth century, the Dutch were the undisputed leaders, their carrying capacity and trade monopolies the greatest in the world. But the English were rising quickly. Their Atlantic colonies began to produce valuable new commodities such as tobacco and sugar, and their Asian trade was expanding decade after decade. Conflict was inevitable, and the result was a series of three naval wars fought between 1652 and 1674.

The Dutch had little choice but to strike out against English policy, but they also had little chance of overall success. Their spectacular naval victory in 1667, when the Dutch fleet surprised many English warships at port and burned both ships and docks at Chatham, obscured the fact that Dutch commercial superiority was slipping. In 1664, the English conquered New Netherland on the North American mainland and renamed it New York. With that defeat, the Dutch lost their largest colonial possession. The wars were costly to both states, nearly bankrupting the English Crown in 1672. Anglo-Dutch rivalry was finally laid to rest after 1688, when William of Orange, stadtholder of Holland, became William III (1689–1702), king of England.

The Anglo-Dutch commercial wars were just one part of a larger European conflict. Dutch commerce was as threatening to France as it was to England, though in a different way. Under Colbert, France pursued a policy of economic independence. The state supported internal industrial activity through the financing of large workshops and the encouragement of new manufacturing techniques. To protect French products, Colbert levied a series of punitive tariffs on Dutch imports, which severely depressed both trade and manufacture in Holland. Although the Dutch retaliated with restrictive tariffs of their own—in 1672 they banned the import of all French goods for an entire year—the Dutch economy depended on free trade. The Dutch had much more to lose than did France in a battle of protective tariffs.

But the battle that Louis XIV had in mind was to be more deadly than one of tariffs. Greedily he eyed the Spanish Netherlands—to which he had a weak claim through his Habsburg wife—believing that the Dutch stood in the way of his plans. The Dutch had entered into an alliance with the English and Swedes in 1668 to counter French policy, and Louis was determined to crush them in retaliation. He successfully bought off both of Holland's supposed allies, providing cash pensions to the kings of England and Sweden in return for England's active participation and Sweden's passive neutrality in the impending war. In 1672, Louis's army, more than 100,000 strong, invaded the Low Countries and swept all before them. Only the opening of the dikes prevented the French from entering the province of Holland itself.

The French invasion coincided with the third Anglo-Dutch war, and the United Provinces found themselves besieged on land and sea. Their international trade was disrupted, their manufacturing industries were in ruins, and their military budget skyrocketed. Only able diplomacy and skillful military leadership prevented total Dutch demise. A separate peace was made with England, and Spain, whose sovereign territory had been invaded, entered the war on the side of the Dutch, as did a number of German states. Louis's hope for a lightning victory faded, and the war settled into a series of interminable sieges and reliefs of fortified towns. The Dutch finally persuaded France to come to terms in the Treaty of Nijmegen (1678–1679). While Louis XIV retained a number of the territories he had taken from Spain, his armies withdrew from the United Provinces and he agreed to lift most of the commercial sanctions against Dutch goods. The first phase of mercantile warfare was over.

The Wars of Louis XIV

It was Louis XIV's ambition to restore the ancient Burgundian territories to the French crown and to provide secure northern and eastern borders for his state. Pursuit of those aims involved him in conflicts with nearly every other European state. Spain had fought for 80 years to preserve the Burgundian inheritance in the Low Countries. By the Peace of Westphalia (1648), the northern portion of the territory became the United Provinces, while the southern portion remained loyal to the crown and became the Spanish Netherlands. That

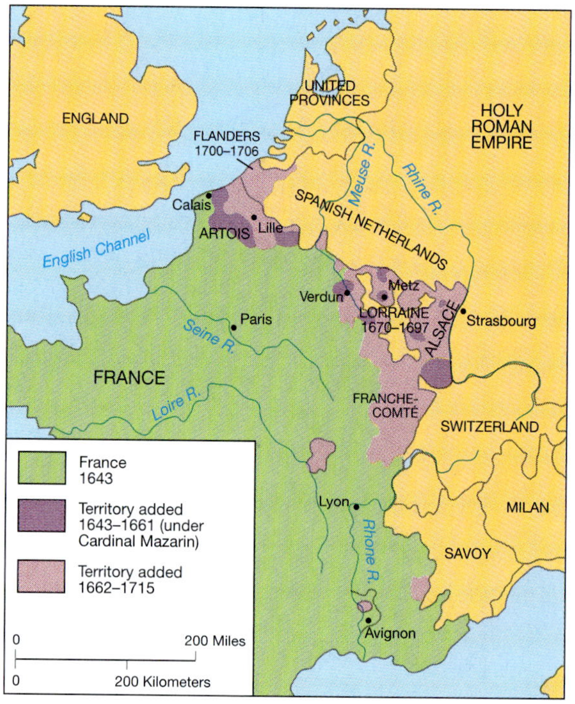

France Under Louis XIV. France gained vital territories in the north and east including Alsace and Lorraine which would become a source of friction for centuries.

The ratification of the Treaty of Münster (1648). Under the treaty, Spain finally recognized Dutch independence.

territory provided a barrier between Holland and France that both states attempted to strengthen by establishing fortresses and bridgeheads at strategic places. In the east, Louis eyed the duchies of Lorraine and Alsace and the large swath of territory farther south known as Franche-Comté. The Peace of Westphalia had granted France control of a number of imperial cities in the duchies, and Louis aimed to link them together. All the territories were ruled by Habsburgs: Alsace and Lorraine by the Austrian Holy Roman Emperor, Franche-Comté by the Spanish king.

The Balance of Power. In the late seventeenth century, ambassadors and ministers of state began to develop the theory of a balance of power in Europe. It was a belief that no state or combination of states should be allowed to become so powerful that its existence threatened the peace of the others. Behind the purely political idea of the balance of power lay a theory of collective security that knit together the European state system. French expansion in either direction not only threatened the other states directly involved but also posed a threat to European security in general.

Louis showed his hand clearly enough in the Franco-Dutch war that had ended in 1679. Although he withdrew his forces from the United Provinces and evacuated most of the territories he had conquered, France absorbed Franche-Comté by the Treaty of Nijmegen, as well as portions of the Spanish Netherlands. Louis began plotting his next adventure almost as soon as the treaty was signed. During the next several years, French troops advanced steadily into Alsace, ultimately forcing the city of Strasbourg, a vital bridgehead on the Rhine, to recognize French sovereignty. Expansion into northern Italy was similarly calculated. Everywhere Louis looked, French engineers rushed to construct fortresses and magazines in preparation for another war.

War finally came in 1688 when French troops poured across the Rhine to seize Cologne. A united German empire led by Leopold I, archduke of Austria, combined with the maritime powers of England and Holland, led by William III, to form the Grand Alliance, the first of the great balance-of-power coalitions. In fact, the two sides proved so evenly matched that the Nine Years' War (1688–1697) settled very little, but it demonstrated that a successful European

GENEALOGY

The Spanish Succession

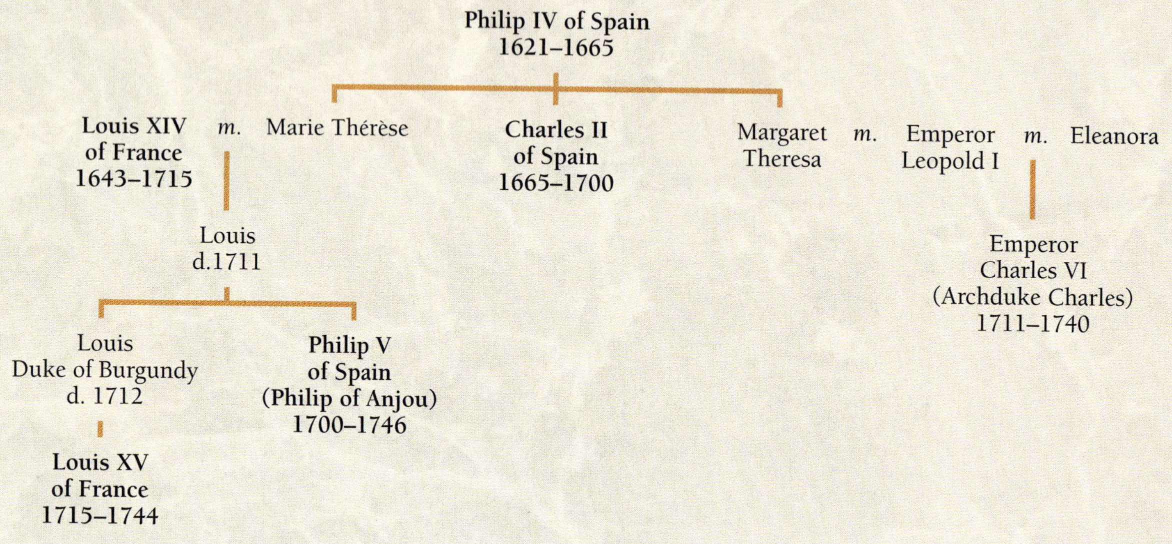

coalition could be formed against France. It also signified the permanent shift in alliances that resulted from the Revolution of 1688 in England. Although the English had allied with France against the Dutch in 1672, after William became king he persuaded the English Parliament that the real enemy was France. Louis's greatest objective, to secure the borders of his state, had withstood its greatest test. He might have rested satisfied but for the vagaries of births, marriages, and deaths.

Like his father, Louis XIV had married a daughter of the king of Spain. Philip IV had married his eldest daughter to Louis XIV and a younger one to Leopold I of Austria, who subsequently became the Holy Roman Emperor (1658–1705). Before he died, Philip finally fathered a son, Charles II (1665–1700), who attained the Spanish crown at the age of four but was mentally and physically incapable of ruling his vast empire. For decades it was apparent that there would be no direct Habsburg successor to an empire that, despite its recent losses, still contained Spain, South America, the Spanish Netherlands, and most of Italy. Louis XIV and Leopold I both had legitimate claims to an inheritance that would have irreversibly tipped the European balance of power.

The War of the Spanish Succession. As Charles II grew increasingly feeble, efforts to find a suitable compromise to the problem of the Spanish succession were led by William III, who, as stadtholder of Holland, was vitally interested in the fate of the Spanish Netherlands and, as king of England, in the fate of the Spanish American colonies. In the 1690s, two treaties of partition were drawn up. The first achieved near universal agreement but was nullified by the death of the German prince who was to inherit the Spanish crown. The second, which would have given Italy to Louis's son and everything else to Leopold's son, was opposed by Leopold, who had neither naval nor commercial interests and who claimed most of the Italian territories as imperial fiefs.

All the plans had been made without consulting the Spanish. If it was the aim of the European powers to partition the Spanish empire in order to prevent any one state from inheriting too much of it, it was the aim of the Spanish to maintain their empire intact. To this end, they devised a brilliant plan. Charles II bequeathed his entire empire to Philip of Anjou, the younger grandson of Louis XIV, with two stipulations: first, that Philip renounce his claim to the French throne; and second, that he accept the empire intact, without par-

War of the Spanish Succession. The great British victories in this war were in the Spanish Netherlands and the Holy Roman Empire and they established Britain as a great power.

tition. If he—or more to the point, if his grandfather Louis XIV—did not accept the conditions, then the empire would pass to Archduke Charles, the younger son of Leopold I. Such provisions virtually assured war between France and the empire unless compromise between the two powers could be reached. But before terms could even be suggested, Charles II died and Philip V (1700–1746) was proclaimed king of Spain and its empire.

Thus the eighteenth century opened with the War of the Spanish Succession (1702–1714). Emperor Leopold rejected the provisions of Charles's will and sent his troops to occupy Italy. Louis XIV confirmed the worst fears of William III when he provided his grandson with French troops to "defend" the Spanish Netherlands. William III revived the Grand Alliance and initiated a massive land war against the combined might of France and Spain. The allied objectives were twofold: to prevent the unification of the French and Spanish thrones and to partition the Spanish empire so that both Italy and the Netherlands were ceded to Austria. The objective of Louis XIV was simply to preserve as much as possible of the Spanish inheritance for the house of Bourbon.

William III died in 1702 and was succeeded by Anne (1702–1714). John Churchill (1650–1722), duke of Marlborough and commander in chief of the army, continued William's policy. England and Holland again provided most of the finance and sea power, but, in addition, the English also provided a land army nearly 70,000 strong. Prussia joined the Grand Alliance, and disciplined Prussian troops helped offset the addition of the Spanish army to Louis's forces. In 1704, Churchill defeated French forces at Blenheim in Germany, and in 1706 at Ramillies in the Spanish Netherlands. France's military ascendancy was over.

Efforts to negotiate a peace settlement took longer than the war itself. The Austrians had taken control of Italy, the English and Dutch had secured the Spanish

An eighteenth-century English playing card showing Philip of Anjou, the grandson of Louis XIV, stealing the Spanish crown.

Netherlands, and the French had been driven back beyond the Rhine. The Allies believed that they could now enforce any treaty they pleased on Louis XIV and, along with concessions from France, attempted to oust his grandson, Philip V, from the Spanish throne. That proved impossible to achieve, though it took more than five years to learn the lesson. By then the European situation had taken another strange twist. Both Emperor Leopold and his eldest son had died. Now Leopold's younger son, Archduke Charles, inherited the empire as Charles VI (1711–1740) and raised the prospect of an equally dangerous combined Austrian-Spanish state.

English artist Sir James Thornhill paid tribute to the new English rulers William and Mary in this extravagant depiction, which adorns the ceiling of the Painted Hall in the naval hospital at Greenwich.

Between 1713 and 1714, a series of treaties at Utrecht settled the War of the Spanish Succession. Spanish possessions in Italy and the Netherlands were ceded to Austria; France abandoned all its territorial gains east of the Rhine and ceded its North American territories of Nova Scotia and Newfoundland to England. England also acquired from Spain Gibraltar, on the southern coast of Spain, and the island of Minorca in the Mediterranean. Both were strategically important to English commercial interests. English intervention in the Nine Years' War and the War of the Spanish Succession did not result in large territorial gains, but it did result in an enormous increase in English power and prestige. During the next 30 years England would assert its own imperial claims.

The Colonial Wars

The Treaty of Utrecht (1713–1714) ushered in almost a quarter century of peace in western Europe. Austrian rule in the Netherlands and Italy remained a major irritant to the Spanish, but Spain was too weak to do more than sulk and snarl. The death of Louis XIV in 1715 quelled French ambitions for a time and even led to an Anglo-French accord that guaranteed the preservation of the settlement reached at Utrecht. Peace allowed Europe to rebuild its shattered economy and resume the international trade that had been so severely disrupted during the last 40 years. The Treaty of Utrecht had resolved a number of important trading issues, all in favor of Great Britain (as England was known after its union with Scotland in 1707). In addition to receiving Gibraltar and Minorca from Spain, Britain was also granted the monopoly to provide slaves to the Spanish American colonies and the right to send one trading ship a year to them. In east and west, Britain was becoming the dominant commercial power in the world.

At least some of the reason for Britain's preeminence was the remarkable growth of the Atlantic colonies. The colonial economy was booming, and consumer goods that were in demand in London, Paris, and Amsterdam were also in demand in Boston, Philadelphia, and New York. Like every other colonial power, the British held a monopoly on their colonial trade. They were far less successful than the Spanish and French in enforcing the notion that colonies existed only for the benefit of the parent country, but the English Parliament continued to pass legislation aimed at restricting colonial trade with other nations and other nations' colonies.

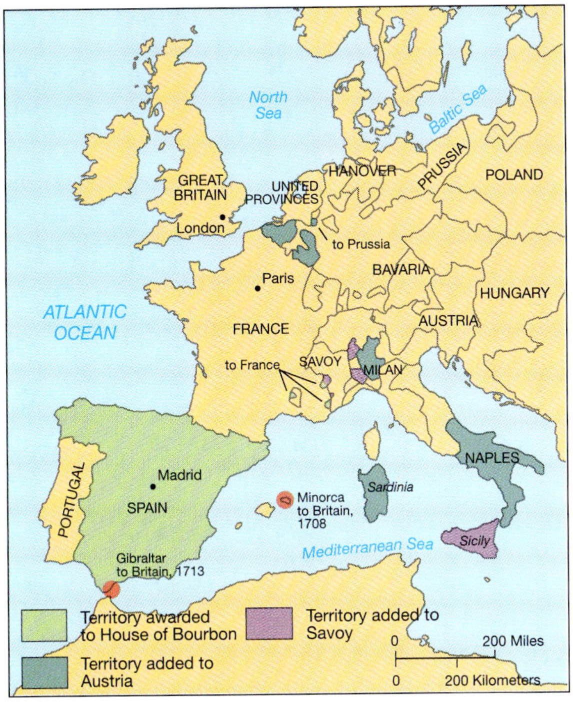

The Treaty of Utrecht, Europe 1714. The treaty redistributed European possessions to create a balance of power.

Like almost all other mercantile restrictions, the efforts were stronger in theory than in practice. Tariffs on imports and customs duties on British goods provided a double incentive for smuggling.

France emerged as Britain's true colonial rival. In the Caribbean, the French had the largest and most profitable of the West Indian sugar islands, Saint Domingue (modern-day Haiti). In North America, France not only held Canada but laid claim to the entire continent west of the Ohio River. The French did not so much settle their colonial territory as occupy it. They surveyed the land, established trading relations with the Native Americans, and built forts at strategic locations. The English, in contrast, had developed fixed communities, which grew larger and more prosperous by the decade. France determined to defend its colonies by establishing an overseas military presence. Regular French troops were shipped to Canada and installed in Louisbourg, Montreal, and Quebec. The British responded with troops of their own and sent an expeditionary force to clear the French from the Ohio River Valley. That action was the immediate cause of the Seven Years' War (1756–1763).

Although the Seven Years' War had a bitter Continental phase, it was essentially a war for empire between the English and the French. There were three main theaters: the North American mainland, the West Indian sugar plantations, and the eastern coast of India. All over the globe, the British won smashing victories. The British navy blockaded the water route to Canada, inflicting severe hardship on French settlers in Montreal and Quebec. British forces ultimately captured both towns. After some initial successes, the French were driven back west across the Mississippi River, and their line of fortresses in the Ohio Valley fell into English hands. The English also succeeded in taking all the French sugar islands except Saint Domingue. British

Portrait of John Churchill, Duke of Marlborough, by Sir Godfrey Kneller (ca. 1706). Justice smiles down from the clouds at the triumphant duke as Victory reaches down to crown him with laurel. Trampled under the horse's hooves is the disheveled figure of Discord.

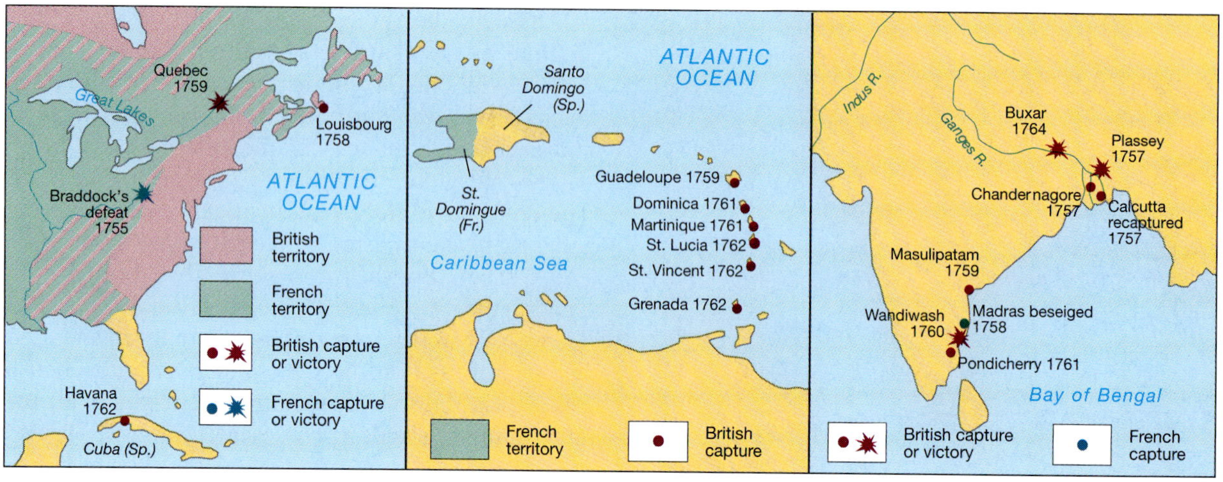

The Seven Years' War. This war was fought all around the globe between Britain and France for imperial supremacy. In North America it was called the French and Indian War.

success in India was equally complete. The French were chased from their major trading zone and English dominance was secured.

By the end of the Seven Years' War, Britain had become a global imperial power. In the Peace of Paris (1763), France ceded all of Canada in exchange for the return of its West Indian islands. British dominion in the East Indian trade was recognized and led ultimately to British dominion of India itself. In less than a century, the ascendancy of France was broken and Europe's first modern imperial power had been created.

European commercial expansion was the first step in a long process that would ultimately transform the material life of all human beings. The quest for new commodities led to increased sophistication in transportation, marketing, and distribution—all vital developments for agricultural changes in the future. The ability to move large quantities of goods from place to place and to exchange them between different parts of the globe laid the foundation for organized manufacturing. The practical impact of scientific discovery, as yet only dimly glimpsed, would soon spur the transformation of handicrafts into industries. In the eighteenth century, the material world was still being conquered, and the most unattractive features of that conquest were all too plainly visible. Luxuries for the rich were won by the labors of the poor. The pleasures of sugar and tobacco were purchased at the price of slavery for millions of Africans. The greed of merchants and the glory of princes was an unholy alliance that resulted in warfare around the globe. But it was a shrinking globe, one whose peoples were becoming increasingly interdependent, tied together by the goods and services that they could provide to each other.

Questions for Review

1. What was new about the methods and ideas of Copernicus, Brahe, Kepler, and Galileo, and why were they threatening to Catholic doctrine?
2. In what ways did the new science build upon traditional ideas associated with alchemy, astrology, and Hermetic thinking? In what ways was it a departure?
3. What new technologies, trading practices, and financial devices assisted the expansion of long-distance trading?
4. Why were the Dutch especially well suited to participate in the worldwide expansion of European commerce?
5. How did the governments of the various European nations promote their own commercial interests?

Suggestions for Further Reading

General Reading

* A. Rupert Hall, *The Revolution in Science, 1500–1750* (London: Longman, 1983). The best introduction to the varieties of scientific thought in the early modern period. Detailed and complex.

* Jan de Vries, *The European Economy in an Age of Crisis* (Cambridge: Cambridge University Press, 1976). A comprehensive study of economic development, including long-distance trade and commercial change.

* K. H. D. Haley, *The Dutch in the Seventeenth Century* (London: Thames and Hudson, 1972). A well-written and well-illustrated history of the golden age of Holland.

* Derek McKay and H. M. Scott, *The Rise of the Great Powers, 1648–1815* (London: Longman, 1983). An outstanding survey of diplomacy and warfare.

* Jeremy Black, *The Rise of the European Powers, 1679–1793* (New York: Edward Arnold, 1990). A new look at diplomatic history from an English point of view.

The New Science

* Margaret C. Jacob, *The Cultural Meaning of the Scientific Revolution* (New York: Alfred A. Knopf, 1988). Scientific thought portrayed in its social context.

* Steven Shapin, *The Scientific Revolution* (Chicago, IL: University of Chicago Press, 1996). An excellent brief introduction.

* H. F. Cohen, *The Scientific Revolution* (Chicago: University of Chicago Press, 1994). The history of the idea of the scientific revolution and of the events that comprised it.

* Stillman Drake, *Galileo* (New York: Hill and Wang, 1980). A short but engaging study of the great Italian scientist.

* Mario Biagioli, *Galileo, Courtier* (Chicago: University of Chicago Press, 1993). A remarkable study of Galileo that sets his science within the context of the culture of absolutism.

* Londa Schiebinger, *The Mind Has No Sex? Women in the Origins of Modern Science* (Cambridge, MA: Harvard University Press, 1990). The role of women in the scientific revolution.

* Allen Debus, *Man and Nature in the Renaissance* (Cambridge: Cambridge University Press, 1978). An especially good account of the intellectual roots of scientific thought.

* Richard Westfall, *The Construction of Modern Science: Mechanisms and Mechanics* (Cambridge: Cambridge University Press, 1977). A survey of scientific developments from Kepler to Newton. A good introduction to both mechanics and mathematics.

Charles Webster, *The Great Instauration: Science, Medicine, and Reform* (London: Duckworth, 1975). A complicated but rewarding analysis of experimental science and the origins of scientific medicine.

* David Lindberg and Robert Westman, eds., *Reappraisals of the Scientific Revolution* (Cambridge: Cambridge University Press, 1990). A collection of essays that survey recent scholarship on the scientific revolution.

* Frank E. Manuel, *Sir Isaac Newton: A Portrait* (Cambridge, MA: Harvard University Press, 1968). A readable account of one of the most complex intellects in European history, from a psychoanalytic point of view.

* Richard Westfall, *The Life of Isaac Newton* (Cambridge: Cambridge University Press, 1993). The best short biography.

Empires of Goods

* Ralph Davis, *The Rise of the Atlantic Economies* (Ithaca, NY: Cornell University Press, 1973). A nation-by-nation survey of the colonial powers.

J. N. Ball, *Merchants and Merchandise: The Expansion of Trade in Europe* (London: Croom Helm, 1977). A good overview of European overseas economies.

* James D. Tracy, *The Rise of Merchant Empires: Long-Distance Trade in the Early Modern World, 1350–1750* (Cambridge: Cambridge University Press, 1993). An outstanding collection of essays by internationally recognized scholars.

John J. McCusker, *Essays in the Economic History of the Atlantic World* (London; New York: Routledge, 1997). A collection of studies by one of the leading economic historians of the British colonial empire.

* K. N. Chaudhuri, *The Trading World of Asia and the English East India Company* (Cambridge: Cambridge University Press, 1978). A brilliant account of the impact of the Indian trade on both Europeans and Asians.

* Sidney Mintz, *Sweetness and Power* (New York: Viking Press, 1985). An anthropologist explores the lure of sugar and its impact on Western society.

* Philip Curtin, *The Atlantic Slave Trade* (Madison: University of Wisconsin Press, 1969). A study of the importation of African slaves into the New World, with the best estimates of the numbers of slaves and their destinations.

* Joseph Miller, *Way of Death: Merchant Capitalism and the Angolan Slave Trade, 1730–1830* (Madison: University of Wisconsin Press, 1988). An illuminating portrait of the eighteenth-century slave trade, with an unforgettable account of the slave voyages.

* Jonathan Israel, *Dutch Primacy in World Trade, 1585–1740* (Oxford: Oxford University Press, 1989). The triumph of Dutch traders and techniques written by the leading authority.

* Simon Schama, *The Embarrassment of Riches* (New York: Alfred A. Knopf, 1987). A social history of the Dutch Republic that explores the meaning of commerce in Dutch society.

Jonathan Israel, *The Dutch Republic* (Oxford: Oxford University Press, 1995). A comprehensive history of the Dutch rise to world prominence and its subsequent decline.

* Holden Furber, *Rival Empires of Trade in the Orient, 1600–1800* (Minneapolis: University of Minnesota Press, 1976). A comprehensive survey of the battle for control of the Asian trade in the seventeenth and eighteenth centuries.

The Wars of Commerce

A. C. Carter, *Neutrality or Commitment: The Evolution of Dutch Foreign Policy, 1667–1795* (London: Edward Arnold, 1975). A tightly written study of the objectives and course of Dutch diplomacy.

Charles Wilson, *Profit and Power* (London: Longman, 1957). Still the best study of the Anglo-Dutch wars of the mid-seventeenth century.

* Jeremy Black, *A System of Ambition? British Foreign Policy, 1660–1793* (London: Longman, 1991). The best survey of Britain's international relations during the long eighteenth century.

* Jeremy Black, *America or Europe?* (London: UCL Press, 1998). A useful survey of British diplomacy and warfare in the mid-eighteenth century.

Herbert Rowan, *The Princes of Orange* (Cambridge: Cambridge University Press, 1988). An engrossing history of the family that ruled the Dutch Republic.

Paul Langford, *The Eighteenth Century, 1688–1815* (New York: St. Martin's Press, 1976). A reliable guide to the growth of British power.

Ragnhild Hatton, ed., *Louis XIV and Europe* (London: Macmillan, 1976). An important collection of essays on French foreign policy in its most aggressive posture.

Richard Pares, *War and Trade in the West Indies, 1739–1763* (Oxford: Oxford University Press, 1936). A blow-by-blow account of the struggle for colonial supremacy in the sugar islands.

* Paperback edition available.

Discovering Western Civilization Online

To further explore science and commerce in early modern Europe, consult the following World Wide Web sites. Since Web resources are constantly being updated, also go to *www.awl.com/Kishlansky* for further suggestions.

The New Science

www.fordham.edu/halsall/mod/modsbook09.html
Links to sources and other sites dealing with the Scientific Revolution.

www.es.rice.edu/ES/humsoc/Galileo//
A site devoted to Galileo that contains pictures of his instruments and guides to his experiments.

Empires of Goods

www.bell.lib.umn.edu/Products/Products.html
A site describing the new products introduced to Europe during the period of global expansion.

www.historyhouse.com/stories/tulip.htm
The story of Tulipmania in seventeenth-century Holland.

CHAPTER

18 THE BALANCE OF POWER IN EIGHTEENTH-CENTURY EUROPE

- CALLING THE TUNE

GEOGRAPHICAL TOUR
EUROPE IN 1714
Expansion in the West
Realignment in the East

- THE RISE OF RUSSIA

The Reforms of Peter the Great
Life in Rural Russia
The Enlightened Empress Catherine

- THE TWO GERMANIES

The Rise of Prussia
Austria Survives
The Politics of Power

- THE GREATNESS OF GREAT BRITAIN

The British Constitution
Parties and Ministers
America Revolts

Calling the Tune

FREDERICK THE GREAT LOVED MUSIC. During his youth it was one of his private passions that infuriated his father. Mathematics, political economy, modern languages—even the dreaded French—those were the subjects that a future king of Prussia should learn. But music, never. Rather, the boy should be at the hunt watching the dogs tear apart a stag, or on maneuvers with the Potsdam guards, a troop of soldiers all nearly seven feet tall. That was the regimen King Frederick William I prescribed for his son. It was no longer enough to reign over one's subjects; to be a successful monarch in the power politics of the eighteenth century, a king had to be a soldier.

But Frederick the Great loved music. He secretly collected all the books and manuscripts he could find on the subject, outspending his tiny allowance in the process. He had Johann Quantz (1697–1773), the greatest flutist of the day, placed on his staff to teach him and to conspire with him against his father. At night, while the old king drank himself into a stupor—an activity he warmly recommended to his son—Frederick powdered his hair, put on a jacket of the latest French style, and regaled his friends with his newest compositions. A lookout guarded the door in case the king wandered by unexpectedly. Once the musicians were almost discovered and Frederick's fine new jacket was tossed on the fire, but the flutes and musical scores remained safely hidden.

After he became king, Frederick the Great could indulge his passion more openly. Yet he preferred to hold his concerts, usually small gatherings, at the Palace of San Souci, which he built in Potsdam. A special music room was designed for the king's use, and he lavished attention on it. The great chandelier, lit by a circle of candles, illuminated the center of the room and highlighted the soloist. The entire palace reflected Frederick's personal taste. Unlike most great palaces of state, it was small, functional, and beautiful. There Frederick could escape the mounting cares of governing one of the most powerful states in Europe by reading, corresponding with eminent French intellectuals, and playing the flute. In the picture, *Das Flötenkonzert* (The Flute Concert), Frederick is portrayed performing in his great music room. Before a small audience of courtiers and intimates, he plays to the accompaniment of cello, violins, and piano.

Frederick's talent was real enough. A British visitor to Sans Souci, who had little reason to flatter the king, reported: "I was much pleased and surprised with the neatness of his execution. His performance surpassed anything I had ever heard among the dilettanti or even professors." That judgment is reinforced when the expressions of the three men in the left corner of the painting are studied. They are taking genuine pleasure in the music they are hearing (all the more genuine in that the king's back is to them). So, too, are the musicians who are accompanying the king. There is as much joy as concentration upon their faces.

Frederick's musical accomplishment was not unique among eighteenth-century monarchs; Joseph II of Austria was also a skilled flutist. But it was not so much music as accomplishment that was coming to be valued among the monarchs of the new European powers. Catherine the Great of Russia corresponded with philosophers; Frederick the Great brought the great French intellectual Voltaire (1698–1778) to his court—although they quickly took a dislike to each other. The acquisition of culture seemed to matter more and more as the century wore on. Museums, opera houses, and great art collections were established all over the Continent. The Hermitage in Saint Petersburg was stocked with the works of Dutch and English masters. The British Museum was founded in London with the support of King George II, who deposited his great library there. Whether the veneer of culture did anything to lessen the brutality of warfare and power politics is a matter of opinion. But as a veneer it was as highly polished as the flute that Frederick the Great is so delicately pressing to his mouth.

GEOGRAPHICAL TOUR
EUROPE IN 1714

Within a relatively short span of time at the beginning of the eighteenth century, two treaties brought about a considerable reorganization of the political geography of Europe. The Treaty of Utrecht (1713–1714) created a new Europe in the west. The Treaty of Nystad (1721) created a new Europe in the east. Both agreements reflected the dynamics of change that had taken place over the previous century. The rise of France on the Continent and Britain's colonial empire around the globe were facts that could no longer be ignored. The decline of Sweden and Poland and the emergence of Russia as a great power were the beginning of a long-term process that would continue to dominate European history.

All of that could be seen on a map of Europe in the early eighteenth century. France's absorption of Alsace and encroachments into Lorraine would be bones of contention between the French and the Germans for two centuries and would ultimately contribute to the outbreak of World Wars I and II. The political footballs of the Spanish Netherlands and Spanish Italy, now temporarily Austrian, continued to be kicked about until the nationalist movements of the nineteenth century gave birth to Belgium, Luxembourg, and a united Italy. The emergence of Brandenburg-Prussia on the north German coast and the gradual decline of the Holy Roman Emperor's power were both

Europe in 1714. Europe as established by the Treaty of Utrecht.

vital to the process that created a unified Germany and a separate Austria. In the southeast, the slow but steady reconquest of the Balkans from Ottoman dominion restored the historic southern border of the Continent. The inexorable expansion of Russia was also already apparent.

Expansion in the West

Perhaps the most obvious transformation in the political geography of western Europe was the expansion of European power around the globe. In the Atlantic, Spain remained the largest colonial power. Through its vice-royalty system it controlled all of Mexico and Central America; the largest and most numerous of the Caribbean islands; North America from Colorado to California (as well as Florida); and most of South America. The other major colonial power in the region was Portugal, which shared dominion over the South American continent. In the Portuguese colony of Brazil, production of sugar, dyestuffs, timbers, and exotic commodities amply repaid the meager investment the Portuguese had made.

In North America, the French and British shared the eastern half of the continent. The French controlled most of it. They had landed first in Canada and then slowly made their way down the Saint Lawrence River. New France, as their colonial empire was called, was a trading territory, and it expanded along the greatest of the waterways: the Great Lakes and the Ohio, Missouri, and Mississippi rivers. French settlements had sprung up as far south as the Gulf of Mexico. France also claimed the territory of Louisiana, named for Louis XIV, which stretched from New Orleans to Montana. The British settlements were all coastal, stretching from Maine to Georgia on the Atlantic seaboard. Unlike the French, the British settled their territory and were only interested in expansion when their population, which was doubling every 25 years, outgrew its resources. By the early eighteenth century, the ports of Boston, New York, Philadelphia, and Charleston were thriving commercial centers.

Europeans managed their eastern colonial territories differently than they did those in the Atlantic. Initially, the Portuguese and the Dutch had been satisfied with establishing trading factories—coastal fortresses in Africa and Asia that could be used as warehouses and defended against attack. But in the seventeenth century, the European states began to take control of vital ports and lucrative islands. There the Dutch were the acknowledged leaders, replacing the Portuguese, who had begun the process at the end of the sixteenth century. Holland held by force or in conjunction with local leaders all the Spice Islands in the Pacific. The Dutch also occupied both sides of the Malay Peninsula and nearly all the coastal areas of the islands in the Java Sea. Dutch control of Ceylon was strategically important for its Indian trade. Compared to the Dutch Republic, all other European states had only a minor territorial presence in the East, with the exception of Spain, which still controlled the Philippines. The British had limited their eastern outposts to trading establishments, and through those they maintained a significant presence in India. During the eighteenth century, the British began to colonize the Indian subcontinent directly.

Imperial expansion was the most obvious change in the geopolitical boundaries of Europe, but it was not the only one. A brief tour of the western states after the Treaty of Utrecht reveals some others. In 1707,

The Americas. Much of the American continents were still uncharted with most settlements in the coastal areas.

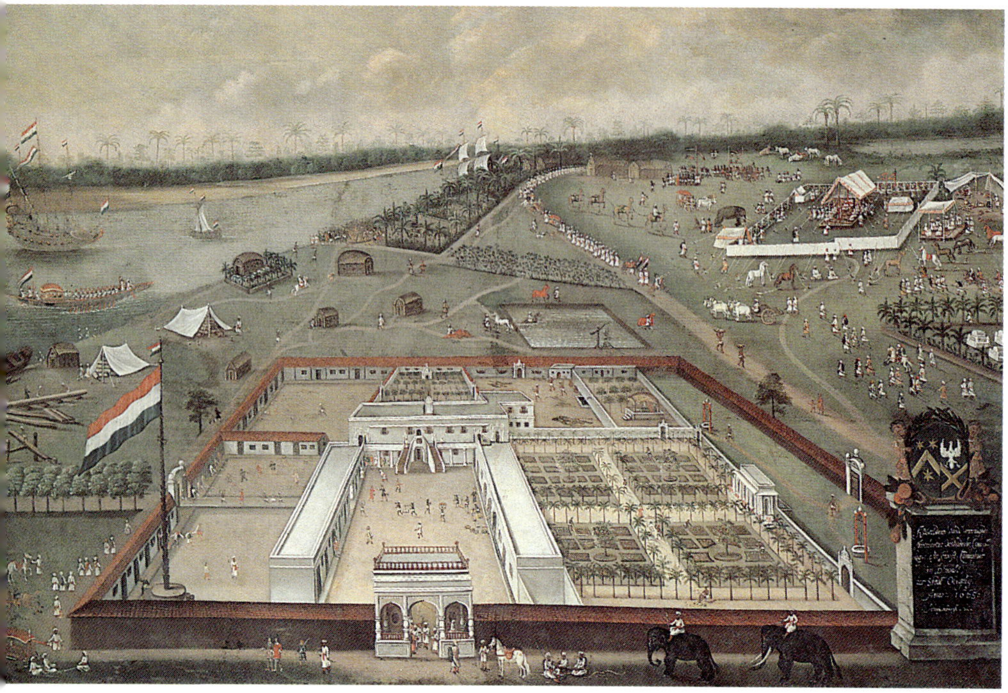

The Dutch East India Company's trading station on the Hooghly River in Bengal, 1665. The station was one of a network of bases the company established throughout its eastern trading empire.

England and Scotland formally joined together to form Great Britain. In addition to its eastern and western colonies, Britain had also gained control of Gibraltar at the foot of Spain and the island of Minorca in the Mediterranean. Both territories were strategically important to British commerce.

Across the English Channel were the Low Countries, now permanently divided between the United Provinces in the north, led by Holland, and those provinces in the south that had remained loyal to the Spanish crown in the sixteenth century. By 1714 the golden age of the Dutch was over. Although the Dutch continued as a colonial and maritime power, their small numbers and meager natural resources eventually outweighed their abilities as innovators and managers. They lost their eastern empire to Britain and their predominance in European trade to France. What the Dutch gained at Utrecht was the right to maintain their forces in the towns along the border between France and the old Spanish Netherlands. The Spanish Netherlands, the original Burgundian inheritance, were now being slowly dismembered. Since the accession of Louis XIV, France had plucked small pieces from the territories that had been contested between France and Spain since the fifteenth century. Between French aggression and the Dutch occupation of such important places as Ghent and Ypres, the ability of the southern provinces to maintain a separate identity suffered a grave blow. But the blow was not as grave as that delivered at Utrecht, when sovereignty over the territory was assigned to Austria, ostensibly because the emperor was a Habsburg, but really because the balance of power in western Europe demanded it.

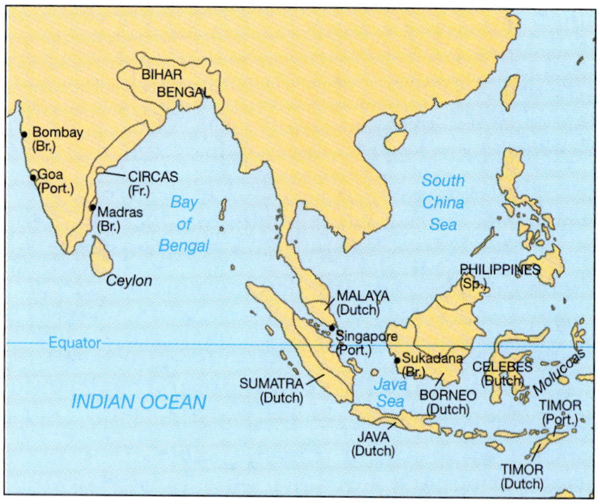

India and the East Indies. The famous spice islands were still controlled by the Dutch while the British gained footholds on both coasts of India.

Great Britain and the Low Countries. Great Britain and the Low Countries were the two leading European commercial nations.

France and Spain. The War of the Spanish Succession permanently separated France and Spain.

France. To the south lay France, still the most powerful nation in Europe despite its losses in the War of the Spanish Succession. By 1714, Louis XIV had broken forever the danger of Spanish encirclement that had been the worry of every French king since Francis I in the early sixteenth century. Louis had methodically set out to occupy those territories that were strategically necessary to defend his state from invasion by the Dutch, the Spanish, the British, or the emperor. In the northeast, he absorbed the Duchy of Bar. In the north, he absorbed a healthy portion of Flanders, including Dunkirk on the English Channel and the prosperous clothing town of Lille. He pushed the eastern boundary of his state to the Rhine by overrunning Alsace and parts of Lorraine. Strasbourg remained French under the settlement of 1714, testimony to the fact that it was possible to hold France only at the western banks of the Rhine. Finally, farther to the south, Louis had won and held Franche-Comté, once the center of Burgundy. In 1714, France was larger, stronger, and better able to defend its borders than ever before. It was also exhausted.

As France expanded, so Spain contracted. Less than two centuries earlier, a Spanish king had dreamed of being monarch of all of Europe. Instead, a French Bourbon sat on the great Habsburg throne and Spain was slowly being sliced to pieces. By 1714 the European territories of the Spanish empire had been reduced to Iberia itself. But the loss of its European empire was to prove a blessing in disguise for Spain, which now entered a new and unexpected phase of growth and influence.

The Empire. The center of Europe remained occupied by the agglomeration of cities, bishoprics, principalities, and small states known collectively as the Holy Roman Empire, but now more accurately called the German empire. There were still more than 300 separate jurisdictions, most of them vulnerable to preying neighbors such as Louis XIV. Bavaria in the south and Saxony, Brandenburg, and Hanover in the north were among the most important of the large states, with the added twist that Hanover was now ruled by the king of Great Britain. The emperor, now officially prohibited from interference in the internal administration of the large states, was less dominant in German affairs than he had been before the Thirty Years' War.

The Holy Roman Empire. It was still a conglomeration of towns, principalities, and bishoprics, but increasingly the empire was losing political and administrative control over its lands.

Increasingly, Habsburg power centered on Austria, Bohemia, and Hungary. That was especially true during the reign of Leopold I (1655–1705). Withstanding threats on all sides, Leopold was able to expand his state both to the west and to the south and to bring Austria into the ranks of the great European powers. Such an outcome could hardly have been foreseen in the middle of the seventeenth century, when the Ottomans made their last great thrust into the interior of Europe. In 1683, the Ottomans besieged Vienna itself, and only the arrival of 70,000 Polish-led troops saved it from falling. But from that time forward, Austrian forces scored stunning victories. By 1699 almost all of Hungary had been retaken by Austria; with the Treaty of Passarowitz in 1718 Austria gained the rest of Hungary and Serbia. When the Treaty of Utrecht granted Austria control of the Netherlands, Lombardy, and Naples, the Austrian Habsburgs became rulers of a European empire.

Austria's Italian possessions included the vast southern territories of Naples (including Sicily after 1720) and the rich industrial area surrounding Milan in the north. Alongside the Austrian territories, a number of independent city-states continued to flourish on the Italian peninsula. Both Venice and Genoa remained prosperous and independent. The Grand Duchy of Tuscany, with its great city of Florence, and the Papal States had both expanded over the course of the seventeenth century, absorbing their smaller neighbors until both were large consolidated territories. To the west of the Italian states was the Duchy of Savoy. Savoy had pursued a flexible foreign policy, pleasing whichever of its powerful neighbors was most dangerous and accepting the patronage of whichever seemed most friendly. As a client of the Spanish, French, and

The siege of Vienna, 1683. The invading Turks were repelled in this, their last great advance in Europe.

Austrians, Savoy grew and prospered. After the War of the Spanish Succession, Savoy was counted among the victors, though it had fought on both sides. Duke Victor Amadeus II became a king when he received the island of Sicily, which he exchanged with Austria for Sardinia in 1720.

Thus the Treaty of Utrecht signaled a new configuration of political power. England, France, Prussia, and Austria were the ascending powers, Holland and Spain the declining ones. Italy and the southern Netherlands were the bones over which the biggest dogs fought, sometimes playfully, sometimes in deadly earnest.

Realignment in the East

In western Europe, the Treaty of Nystad (1721) ended the Great Northern War (1700–1721), and fixed the political geography in the east. There the emerging powers were Russia and Prussia, while those in decline were Sweden and Poland. The critical factor in eastern European politics remained access to the sea. Outlets to the Baltic Sea in the north and the Black Sea in the south were the vital lifeline for that part of the Continent, and control of those outlets was the central motivation for the long years of war fought among the eastern states.

The expansion of Russia is one of the central events in European history, and the early eighteenth century is its pivotal period. During the long years of social and economic recovery after the death of Ivan the Terrible in 1584, Russia had been easy prey for its powerful neighbors Sweden and Poland. Through a series of wars and political pacts, Russia had ceded most of its Baltic territories to Sweden, while it had relinquished land and population in the west to Poland. Peter the Great (1682–1725) set out to reclaim what had been lost. As a result of the Great Northern War, Russia regained the eastern Baltic coastline from the southeastern end of Finland to Riga in the west. Russia now controlled all of the vital Baltic ports in the east. Peter built a new capital on the Gulf of Finland. In the new city, named Saint Petersburg, he laid the foundation for the Russian navy.

What Russia gained, Sweden lost. At the height of its power in the middle of the seventeenth century, Sweden had dominated the Baltic. It occupied all of Finland, controlled the important eastern coast of Norway, and had gained a foothold in Germany. Most importantly, Sweden had captured the southern tip of its own peninsula from the Danes, making the mainland portion of its state whole. But Sweden's century-

Russia and Sweden. Sweden's age of territorial expansion was over by the beginning of the eighteenth century.

long rise to power was followed by a rapid period of decline. The small and relatively poor population could not long succeed in governing an empire. The Great Northern War ended whatever pretensions Sweden still had. It lost all of its German territories: those on the North Sea went to Hanover, those on the Baltic to Prussia. Livonia, Estonia, and the eastern provinces were returned to Russia, but Sweden was able to hold on to its vital gains from the Danes. Sweden had built its own window to the west at Göteborg on the North Sea, and from there it could carry on a direct trade with Britain and the Netherlands.

Since the end of the Thirty Years' War, Brandenburg-Prussia had been growing steadily. A strange configuration of a state, with its geographical heart in Brandenburg, it was one of the domains of the Holy Roman Empire. From the capital at Berlin the princes of Brandenburg directed the accumulation of small neighboring German lands: Magdeburg and Halle to the southwest, a piece of Pomerania to the northeast. But while Brandenburg expanded in every direction, it could do little to join itself to the kingdom of Prussia. A huge swath of Poland, cutting between the two, stood in the way. That division of Brandenburg-Prussia was its most important geopolitical feature. In the eighteenth century, the determination to join together dominated Prussian history.

That aim, of course, meant eventual conflict with Poland. Despite its political weakness, Poland was one of the largest landmasses in Europe. On its southern border it held back Ottoman expansion; on its eastern border it held back the Russians. Its great port of Gdansk on the Baltic dominated the grain and timber trade with northern Europe as well as local Baltic commerce between Scandinavia and the mainland. Sweden and Russia, the eastern powers, controlled Poland politically, helping nominate its elected kings and ensuring that its decentralized form of aristocratic government kept Poland weak. Poland served as a useful counterweight in the balance of power in eastern Europe. Except for its Baltic territories, Poland was not yet seen as a great prize to be fought over. But by the beginning of the eighteenth century it was a helpless giant ready to be toppled.

Thus a potent Prussia and Russia and a prostrate Poland characterized the realignment of the eastern portion of Europe. Most importantly, the separation between east and west was narrowing. Prussia's German orientation and the westernization of Russia led to closer ties with the west.

This portrait of Peter the Great by his court painter Louis Caravaque pays homage to Peter's intense interest in naval matters. Ships flying English, Dutch, Danish, and Russian flags prepare for maneuvers under his command.

THE RISE OF RUSSIA

At the beginning of the eighteenth century, Russia was scarcely known or cared about in the rest of Europe. Peter the Great changed that. The Treaty of Nystad had confirmed the magnitude of his victory over the Swedes in the Great Northern War, both in territory and prestige. The change created consternation in the courts of Europe. Just a quarter century before, no one had cared very much what the king of Russia called himself. In fact, little was known for sure about the Russian ruler or his state. What little mercantile contact there was between Russia and the West was conducted entirely by westerners. Foreign merchants were allowed to live in Moscow in a separate ghetto called "Germantown." Their letters were the main source of western knowledge about the vast Muscovite empire.

Peter the Great brought Europe to Russia and Russia to Europe. Twice he visited Europe to discover the secrets of western prosperity and might. He arranged marriages between the closest heirs to his throne, including his son Alexis, and the sons and daughters of German princes and dukes. By 1721 he had established 21 separate foreign embassies. The sons of the Russian gentry and nobility were sent west—sometimes forcibly—to further their education and to learn to adapt to western outlooks. Peter recruited Europeans to fill the most important skilled positions in the state: foreign engineers and gunners to serve in the army; foreign architects to build the new capital at Saint Petersburg; foreign scholars to head the new state schools; foreign administrators to oversee the new departments of state. Peter borrowed freely and adapted sensibly. If necessary, he would drag his countrymen kicking and screaming into the modern world.

By 1721, Russia was recognized all over Europe as an emerging power. The military defeat of the seemingly invincible Swedes had made monarchs from Louis XIV to William III sit up and take notice. And the great Russian victory over Sweden at Poltava in 1709 was no fluke. Peter's forces followed it up with several strong campaigns, which proved that Russia could organize, equip, finance, and train an up-to-date military force. Moreover, Peter's absorption of Sweden's Baltic territories made Russia a power in the north. The Russian navy, built mostly by foreigners, was now capable of protecting Russian interests and defending important ports such as Riga and Saint Petersburg. Even the Dutch, who had long plotted the decline of Swedish might, now became nervous. Thus it was unsettling that Peter wanted to be recognized as emperor.

The Reforms of Peter the Great

Peter the Great was not the first Russian tsar to attempt to borrow from western developments. The process had been under way for decades. The opening of the northern port of Archangel in 1584 led to direct contact with British and Dutch traders, who brought with them new ideas and useful products, which were then adapted to Russian needs and conditions. Russia was a vast state, and Europe was only one of its neighbors. Its religion had come from Byzantium rather than Rome, thus giving Russian Christianity an eastern flavor. Its Asian territories mixed the influence of Mongols and Ottomans; its southern borders met Tartars and Cossacks. While most European states were racially and ethnically homogeneous, Russia was a loose confederation of diverse peoples. Yet it was the western states that posed the greatest threat to Russia in the seventeenth century, and it was to the west that Peter, like his father before him, turned his attention.

It would be wrong to see Peter's westernizing innovation as a systematic program. More to the point, nearly all of his reforms—economic, educational, administrative, social, military—were done to enhance military efficiency rather than civil progress. In his 30 years of active rule there was only one year—1724—during which he was not at war. Vital reforms such as the poll tax (1724), which changed the basis of taxation from the household to the individual adult male, had enormous social consequences. The new policy of taxing individuals officially erased whole social classes. A strict census taken (and retaken) to inhibit tax evasion became the basis for further governmental encroachments on the tsar's subjects. Yet the poll tax was not designed for any of those purposes. It was instituted to increase tax revenue for war. Similarly, compulsory lifetime military service required of the landowning classes (the nobility and gentry) was established to provide officers and state servants for an expanding military machine.

Yet if Peter's reforms were not systematic and developed from little other than military necessity, nevertheless they constituted a fundamental transformation in the life of all Russian people. The creation of a gigantic standing army and an entirely new navy meant conscription of the Russian peasantry on a grand scale. In a ten-year period of the Great Northern War, the army

Peter the Great was a precocious child. He began his education at the age of two, using a book similar to the illustrated Russian speller whose "Z" page is shown here.

absorbed 330,000 conscripts, most of whom never returned to their homes. Military service was not confined to the peasantry. Traditionally, the rural gentry raised and equipped the local conscript forces and gave them what training they could. Most gentry lived on estates that had been granted to them, along with the resident peasants, as a reward for their military contributions. Peter the Great intensified the obligations of the gentry. Not only were they to serve the state for life, but they were to accompany their regiments to the field and lead them in battle. When too old for active military service, they were to perform administrative service in the new departments of state.

The expansion of military forces necessitated an expansion of military administration as well. Peter's first innovation was the creation of the Senate, a group of nine senior administrators who were to oversee all aspects of military and civil government. The Senate became a permanent institution of government led by an entirely new official, the Procurator-General, who presided over its sessions and could propose legislation as well as oversee administration. From the Senate emanated 500 officials known as the fiscals, who traveled throughout the state looking for irregularities in tax assessment and collection. They quickly developed into a hated and feared internal police force.

Peter's efforts to reorganize his government went a step further in 1722, when he issued the Table of Ranks, an official hierarchy of the state that established the social position or rank of individuals. It was divided into three categories—military service, civil service, and owners of landed estates. Each category contained 14 ranks, and it was decreed that every person who entered the hierarchy did so at the bottom and worked his way up. The creation of the Table of Ranks was significant in a number of ways. It demonstrated Peter's continued commitment to merit as a criterion for advancement. The standard had been shown in the military, where officers were promoted on the basis of service and experience rather than birth or background. Equally important was Peter's decision to make the military service the highest of the three categories, which reversed the centuries-old position of the landed aristocracy and the military service class. Although the old nobility also served in the military and continued to dominate state service, the Table of Ranks opened the way for the infusion of new elements into the Russian elite.

Many of those who were able to advance in the Table of Ranks did so through attendance at the new institutions of higher learning that Peter founded. His initial educational establishments were created to further the military might of the state. The Colleges of Mathematics, Engineering, and Artillery, which became the training grounds for his army officers, were all founded during the Great Northern War. But Peter was interested in liberal education as well. He had scores of western books translated into Russian. He had a press established in Moscow to print original works, including the first Russian newspaper. He decreed that a new, more westernized alphabet replace the one used by the Russian Orthodox church and that books be written in the language that the people spoke rather than in the formal literary language of religious writers. He also introduced Arabic numerals into official accounting records.

Peter's reforms of government and society were matched by his efforts to energize the economy. No state in Europe had as many natural resources as did Russia, yet manufacturing barely existed there. As with everything else he did, Peter took a direct hand in establishing factories for the production of textiles, glass, leather, and, most importantly, iron and copper. The state directly owned about half of the establishments, most of them on a larger scale than any known in the west. By 1726, more than half of all Russian exports were manufactured goods and Russia had become the largest producer of iron and copper in the world.

In all those ways and more, Peter the Great transformed Russia. But the changes Peter wrought did not come without cost. The traditions of centuries were not easily broken. Intrigue against Peter led first to confrontation with the old military elite, and later to conflict with his only son, Alexis. It remains unclear whether the plot with which Alexis was connected actually existed or whether it was a figment of Peter's imagination, but it is abundantly clear that Alexis's death from torture plunged the state into a succession crisis in 1725. Finally, the great costs of westernization were paid by the masses of people, who benefited little from the improvement in Russia's international standing or from the social and economic changes that affected the elites.

Life in Rural Russia

At the beginning of the eighteenth century, nearly 97 percent of the Russian people lived on the land and practiced agriculture. Farming techniques and agrarian lifestyles had changed little for centuries. Most of the country's soil was poor. Harsh climate and low yields characterized Russian agriculture. Thirty-four of the 100 Russian harvests during the eighteenth century can be termed poor or disastrous, yet throughout the century state taxation was making larger and larger demands upon the peasantry. During Peter's reign alone, direct taxation increased by 500 percent.

The theory of the Russian state was one of service, and the role of Russian peasants was to serve their master. Beginning in the mid-seventeenth century, the peasantry had undergone a change in status. The law code of 1649 formalized a process that had been under way for more than a century whereby peasants were turned into the property of their landlords. During the next century, laws curtailed the ability of peasants to move freely from one place to another, eliminated their right to hold private property, and abolished their freedom to petition the tsar against their masters. At the same time that landlords increased their hold over peasants, the state increased its hold over landlords. They were made responsible for the payment of taxes owed by their peasants and for the military service due from them. By the middle of the eighteenth century, more than half of all peasants—6.7 million adult males by 1782—had thus become serfs, the property of their masters, without any significant rights or legal protection.

Private landlords reckoned their wealth in the number of serfs they owned, but in fact most owned only a small number—fewer than 50—in the middle of the eighteenth century. The small number resulted from the common practice whereby a father divided his estate among all of his surviving sons. Most gentry were small landholders, constantly in debt and rarely able to meet their financial and service obligations to the state. The life of poverty at the top was, of course, magnified at the bottom. The vast majority of serfs lived in small villages where they divided up their meager surplus to pay their taxes and drew lots to see who would be sent for military service. When the debts of their lords became too heavy, it was the serfs who were foreclosed upon.

If serfs made up the bottom half of the Russian peasantry, there were few advantages to being in the top half, among the state peasants. State peasants lived on lands owned by the monarchy itself. Like the serfs, they were subject to the needs of the state for soldiers and workers. The use of forced labor was a feature of each of Peter's grandiose projects. Saint Petersburg was built by the backbreaking labor of peasant conscripts. From 1709, when the project began, perhaps as many as 40,000 laborers a year were forced to work on the various sites. The unhealthy conditions of the swampy environment from which the new capital rose claimed the lives of thousands of the workers, as did the appalling conditions of overwork and undernourishment in which they lived.

Many Russian peasants developed a philosophy of submission and a rich folk culture that valued a stubborn determination to endure. For those who would no longer bend to the knout—the heavy leather whip that was the omnipresent enforcer of obedience—there was only flight or rebellion. Hundreds of thousands of serfs fled to state-owned lands in hope of escaping the cruelties of individual landlords. Although severe penalties were imposed for aiding runaway serfs, in fact most state overseers and many private landlords encouraged runaways to settle on their lands. In their social and economic conditions, eighteenth-century Russian peasants were hardly distinguishable from medieval European serfs.

The Enlightened Empress Catherine

Of all the legacies of Peter the Great, perhaps the one of most immediate consequence was that government could go on without him. During the next 37 years, six tsars ruled Russia, "three women, a boy of twelve, an infant, and a mental weakling," as one commentator acidly observed. More to the point, each succession was contested, as there were no direct male heirs to the throne in this period. Nevertheless, despite turmoil at the top, government continued to function smoothly and Peter's territorial conquests were largely maintained. Russia also experienced a remarkable increase in numbers during this period. Between 1725 and 1762, the population increased from 13 to 19 million, a jump of nearly one-half in a single generation. The explosion of people dramatically increased the wealth of the landholding class, who reckoned their status by the number of serfs they owned.

The expansion of the economic resources of the nobility was matched by a rise in legal status and political power. This was the period sarcastically dubbed "the emancipation of the nobility," a phrase that captures not only the irony of the growing gap between rich and poor but also the contrast between the social structures of Russia and those of western Europe. In return for their privileges and status, Peter the Great

Catherine before She Was Great

CATHERINE THE GREAT wasn't always called the Empress of All the Russias. In fact, she wasn't always called Catherine. Sophie of Anhalt-Zerbst was the daughter of a petty German prince whose estates were too poor to provide for his family. He hired out as a military officer to the kings of Prussia and became governor of the dreary Baltic port of Stettin. There Sophie passed her childhood. The family lived comfortably, and Sophie was provided with a French governess, Babette Cardel. From Babette she learned not only the language of the French but their ways. Sophie was no easy child to handle. Her natural curiosity led to some narrow escapes, and she was nearly killed at the age of three when she pulled a cupboard down. To curiosity was added spirit, and the shouting matches in which she and Babette engaged were long remembered. Indeed, Babette took to bribing young Sophie with sweets, which in the long run did less to soften her temper than to ruin her teeth.

By far the most significant event of Sophie's childhood was the sudden sickness that overtook her at the age of seven. She was seized by coughing, fevers, and fits that incapacitated her for weeks. For a time her life was in danger. It was not unusual in those days for unexplained illness to appear and disappear with bewildering suddenness, and that is what happened to Sophie. One morning she awoke without fever and without the racking cough that had seared her body. But in its place had come a physical change. Weeks of lying on her side had deformed her physique: "I had assumed the shape of a letter Z. My right shoulder was much higher than the left, the backbone running in a zigzag and the left side falling in," she later recalled. Such a result was as mysterious as the illness that occasioned it. Doctors were sought for advice. None could help until at last a veterinarian who practiced on the limbs of horses and cows was found. He prescribed a useless concoction of medicines but also built a body frame for Sophie that was designed to reshape her deformity. She wore the frame for four years until she regained her former posture.

Sophie's father was a strict Lutheran who prescribed a regimen for the education of his children that was to be followed precisely. Just after her recovery, Sophie was told that she could no longer play with her toys but must behave as an adult. Tutors were brought to teach her history and geography, and a Lutheran minister was deputed to train her in religion. Sophie took delight in confounding her religion instructor and in general showed the same high spirits as she had in childhood.

Although Sophie did not have a close relationship with her mother—in later years they quarreled incessantly—it was her mother who showed her the world outside Stettin. Joanna of Holstein-Gottorp had grown up surrounded by courtly pomp. While her family, too, came from the ranks of the minor princes of the Holy Roman Empire, marriages and inclination had brought them into the circle of German aristocratic life. That was a world for which Joanna longed, and every year she visited her relations in Brunswick. Sophie began to accompany her mother on the trips, and they became for her the means to escape the boredom of Stettin. On one visit to Berlin she was introduced to Frederick William I, king of Prussia. Her relatives included a future king of Sweden and a future queen of Britain. The trips to Brunswick and Berlin opened Sophie's eyes to the possibility of a different life, the possibility of life with one of the crown princes of Europe.

As it happened, Sophie had little need to wish. By a twist of fate, another of her mother's innumerable cousins had recently been declared heir to the throne of Russia. He was Peter, soon to be duke of Holstein-Gottorp and ultimately Peter III of Russia. Empress Elizabeth of Russia was childless, and Peter was her nearest relative. She determined to have him married to an eligible German princess, and after much casting about, the choice fell on Sophie. In 1744, Sophie was summoned to Russia. Joanna was thrilled with the prospect, not only because of the possibility of a successful marriage for her daughter, but also because she was to have a role in the affair. No one asked Sophie what she thought, since her opinion hardly mattered.

The journey to Russia was a trip that Sophie would never forget. Stettin was no tropical paradise, but the climate there had little prepared Sophie and her mother for the rigors of the east. Carriages gave way to sleighs, and her heavy cloth clothing to sable.

Sophie and Joanna huddled together for warmth, covering their faces and hands from the bitter arctic winds. It took nearly four weeks to reach Saint Petersburg, and when they arrived they were informed that they must hurry to join the royal court at Moscow. There they were received with unusual warmth, as it was the sixteenth birthday of the new heir to the throne and all of Russian society was eager to see his bride-to-be.

Sophie's earliest meetings with her fiancé were not entirely satisfactory. In a strange land she might have expected strange customs, but Peter was a German like herself. Thus she was unprepared for their first interview, in which Peter professed his passionate love for one of the ladies of the court. Sophie was only 15 and, by her own account at least, innocent in sexual matters. Peter's frank confession, which was accompanied by assurances that he would marry Sophie anyhow, caused her as much confusion as it did anger and resentment. She resolved to keep her own counsel and to attempt to please the empress, if not the heir. Sophie spent the days before her marriage learning both the Russian language and the Eastern Orthodox religion. She would have to convert to the old faith before she could be betrothed. As part of her conversion, she had to take a Russian name, and thus she came to be called Catherine. Whether her change of religion was sincere or not, it was required. Sophie was shrewd enough to realize the importance of the Church, and she won many admirers at court when, after being taken suddenly ill, she asked for an Orthodox priest rather than a Lutheran minister or a doctor.

Sophie's marriage took place in 1745 in one of the most magnificent ceremonies anyone could recall. By then she knew that she was alone in the world. She had fought bitterly with her mother. Sophie shared nothing with her new husband—including the marriage bed. The household set up for her was composed entirely of spies for the empress, and even her correspondence was monitored. She spent the next 15 years supplementing the education that she had received as a child. She read everything she could get hold of. Her Russian improved dramatically as she read Russian and French or German versions of the same works. She devoured the classics, especially history and philosophy, and for the first time became acquainted with the works of the new European writers whose reputations had reached as far as Russia. Sophie indulged her enthusiasm for riding, an exercise not usually taken by women. She also developed a passion for the handsome guardsmen who inhabited the palace. Perhaps in revenge for her husband's conduct, perhaps in return for his neglect, she took the first of more than 20 lovers. When she became pregnant in 1754, it was almost certainly not with Peter's child. Eight years later, Empress Elizabeth died and the private life of Sophie of Anhalt-Zerbst ended. The half-mad Peter III acceded to the throne, and Sophie, now known to the world as Catherine, began her remarkable public career.

CHILDHOOD TRAUMAS

Catherine the Great left a fascinating account of her early years, which is in sharp contrast to her reputation for ruthlessness as a ruler.

MY FATHER, WHOM I SAW VERY SELDOM, considered me to be an angel, my mother did not bother much about me. She had had, eighteen months after my birth, a son whom she passionately loved, whereas I was merely tolerated and often repulsed with violence and temper, not always with justice. I was aware of all this, but not always able to understand what I really felt about it.

At the age of seven I was suddenly seized with a violent cough. It was the custom that we should kneel every night and every morning to say our prayers. One night as I knelt and prayed I began to cough so violently that the strain caused me to fall on my left side, and I had such sharp pains in my chest that they almost took my breath away.

Finally, after much suffering, I was well enough to get up and it was discovered, as they started to put on my clothes, that I had in the meantime assumed the shape of the letter *Z*: my right shoulder was much higher than the left, the backbone running in a zigzag and the left side falling in.

From Catherine the Great, *Memoirs* (1755).

extended the duties the landowning classes owed to the state. By granting unique rights, such as the ownership of serfs, to the descendants of the old military service class, Peter had forged a Russian nobility. Lifetime service, however, was the price of nobility.

In order to gain and hold the throne, each succeeding tsar had to make concessions to the nobility to gain their loyalty. At first it was a few simple adjustments. The sons of wealthy landowners who completed a course of education at one of the state academies were allowed to enter the Table of Ranks in the middle of the hierarchy rather than at the bottom. Then life service was commuted to a term of 25 years, still a long time in a world of short lives and sudden deaths. But the concessions were not enough.

Twenty-five years of service did not solve the problem of estate management, especially as the tasks of management grew along with the population of serfs. Thus the next capitulation was that a single son could remain on the estate and escape service altogether. The births of younger sons were concealed; owners of multiple estates claimed the exemption of one son for each. Most decisively, the talented remained at home to serve the family while the wastrels were sent to serve the state. Finally, in 1762, the obligation for state service by the nobility was abolished entirely.

Catherine's Accession. The abolition of compulsory service was not the same as the abolition of service itself. In fact, the end of compulsory service enabled Catherine II, "the Great" (1762–1796), to enact some of the most important reforms of her reign. (See "Catherine Before She Was Great," pp. 628–629.) At first, Catherine's accession seemed nothing more than a continuation of monarchical instability—her first two acts were to have her husband, Peter III, murdered and to lower the salt tax. Each brought her a measure of security.

Catherine was a dynamic personality who alternately captivated and terrified those with whom she came into contact. Her policies were as complex as her personality, influenced on the one hand by the new French ideas of social justice and the nobility of the human race, and on the other hand by the traditional Russian ideas of absolute rule over an enserfed and subhuman population. Catherine handled the contrasting dimensions of her rule masterfully, gaining abroad the reputation as the most enlightened of European monarchs and at home the sincere devotion of her people.

The most important event in the early years of Catherine's reign was the establishment of a legislative commission to review the laws of Russia. Catherine herself wrote the *Instruction* (1767), by which the elected commissioners were to operate. She borrowed her theory of law from the French jurist Baron de Montesquieu (1689–1755) and her theory of punishment from the Italian reformer Cesare Beccaria (1738–1794). Among other things, Catherine advocated the abolition of capital punishment, torture, serf auctions, and the breakup of serf families by sale. Few of the radical reforms were ever put into practice.

But in 1775 Catherine did restructure local government. Russia was divided into 50 provincial districts, each with a population of between 300,000 and 400,000 inhabitants. Each district was to be governed by both a central official and elected local noblemen. The reform was modeled upon the English system of justices of the peace. Previous local reforms had failed because of the absence of a resident local nobility. The abolition of compulsory service finally made possible the establishment of local institutions. In 1785, Catherine issued the Charter of the Nobility, a formal statement of the rights and privileges of the noble class. The Charter incorporated all the gains the nobility had made since the death of Peter the Great, but it also instituted the requirements for local service that had been the basis of Catherine's reforms. District councils with the right to petition directly to the tsar became the centerpiece of Russian provincial government.

In order to train the local nobility for government service, Catherine introduced educational reforms. Peter had established military schools for the nobility and had staffed them with foreigners. The University of Moscow had been founded in 1755, and its faculty too was dominated by European emigrants. Catherine saw the need to broaden the educational system. Borrowing from the Austrian system, she established provincial elementary schools to train the sons and daughters of the local nobility. To staff the schools, Catherine created teachers' colleges so that the state would have its own educators. Although the program called for the equal education of women, except in Saint Petersburg and Moscow few females attended either elementary or high schools.

Catherine's reforms did little to enhance the lives of the vast majority of her people. Although she often spoke in the terms of the French philosophers who saw the enserfment of fellow humans as a blot on civilization, Catherine took no effective action either to end serfdom or to soften its rigors. In fact, by grants of state land Catherine gave away 800,000 state peasants, who became serfs. So, too, did millions of Poles who became her subjects after the partition of Poland in 1793 and 1795.

Pugachev's Revolt. The most significant uprising of the century, Pugachev's revolt (1773–1775), took place during Catherine's reign. Emelyan Pugachev (1726–1775) was a Cossack who in his youth had been a military adventurer. Disappointed in his career, he made his way to the Ural mountains, where he recruited Asian tribesmen and laborers forced to work in the mines. By promising freedom and land ownership, he drew peasants to his cause. In 1773, Pugachev declared himself to be Tsar Peter III, the murdered husband of Catherine II. He began with small raiding parties against local landlords and military outposts

Chained but undaunted, Emelyan Pugachev awaits punishment for leading a peasant rebellion in the southern Urals.

and soon had gained the allegiance of tens of thousands of peasants. In 1774, with an army of nearly 20,000, Pugachev took the city of Kazan and threatened to advance on Moscow. It was another year before state forces could effectively control the rebellion. Finally, Pugachev was betrayed by his own followers and sent to Moscow, where he was executed.

During the reigns of Peter and Catherine the Great, Russia was transformed into an international power. Saint Petersburg, a window to the west, was a capital worthy of a potent monarch, and during the course of the eighteenth century it attracted many of Europe's leading luminaries. At court French was spoken, the latest fashions were worn, and the newest ideas for economic and educational reform were aired. The Russian nobility mingled comfortably with its European counterparts, while the military service class developed into bureaucrats and administrators. But if life glittered at court, it remained the same dull regimen in the country. Millions of peasants were owned either by the state or by private landlords, and their quality of life was no different at the end of the campaign of westernization than it had been at the beginning.

THE TWO GERMANIES

The Thirty Years' War, which ended in 1648, initiated a profound transformation of the Holy Roman Empire. Warfare had devastated imperial territory. It was decades before the rich imperial lands recovered, and then the political consequences of the war had taken effect. There were now two empires, a German and an Austrian, though both were ruled by the same person. In the German territories, whether Catholic or Protestant, the Holy Roman Emperor was more a constitutional monarch than the absolute ruler he was in Austria. The larger states such as Saxony, Bavaria, and Hanover made their own political alliances despite the jurisdictional control that the emperor claimed to exercise. Most decisively, so did Brandenburg-Prussia. By the beginning of the eighteenth century, the electors of Brandenburg had become the kings of Prussia, and Prussia's military power and efficient administrative structure became the envy of its German neighbors.

The Austrian empire was composed of Austria and Bohemia, the Habsburg hereditary lands, and as much

The Expansion of Prussia. This was the most important geopolitical event of the eighteenth century, creating a great power to balance Russia and Austria.

of Hungary as could be controlled. In Austria, the Habsburgs clung tightly to their power. For decades, Austria was the center of the still-flourishing Counter-Reformation, and the power and influence of the Jesuits was as strong there as it was in Spain. The War of the Spanish Succession, which gave the Habsburgs control of the southern Netherlands and parts of Italy, brought Austria an enhanced role in European affairs. Austria remained one of the great powers of Europe and the leading power in the Holy Roman Empire despite the rise of Prussia. Indeed, from the middle of the eighteenth century, the conflict between Prussia and Austria was the defining characteristic of central European politics.

The Rise of Prussia

The transformation of Brandenburg-Prussia from a petty German principality to a great European power was one of the most significant and least expected developments of the eighteenth century. Frederick William, the Great Elector (1640–1688), had begun the process of forging Brandenburg-Prussia into a power in its own right by building a large and efficient military machine. At the beginning of the eighteenth century, Prussia was on the winning side in both the War of the Spanish Succession and the Great Northern War. When the battlefield dust had settled, Prussia found itself in possession of Pomerania and the Baltic port of Stettin. It was now a recognized power in eastern Europe.

Frederick William I. Frederick William I (1713–1740) and his son Frederick II, "the Great" (1740–1786), turned the promising beginning into an astounding success. A devout Calvinist, Frederick William I deplored waste and display as much on moral as on fiscal grounds. The reforms he initiated were intended to subordinate both aristocracy and peasantry to the needs of the state and to subordinate the needs of the state to the demands of the military.

Because of its geographical position, Prussia's major problem was to maintain an efficient and well-trained army during peacetime. Defense of its exposed territories required a constant state of military preparedness, yet the relaxation of military discipline and the desertion of troops to their homes inevitably followed the cessation of hostilities. Frederick William I solved the problem by integrating the economic and military structures of his state. First he appointed only German officers to command his troops, eliminating the mercenaries who sold their services to the highest bidders. Then he placed the noblemen at the head of locally recruited regiments. Each adult male in every district was required to register for military service in the regiment of the local landlord. The reforms dramatically increased the effectiveness of the army by shifting the burden of recruitment and training to the localities.

Yet despite all the attention that Frederick William I lavished on the military—by the end of his reign nearly 70 percent of state expenditures went to the army—his foreign policy was largely pacific. In fact, his greatest achievements were in civil affairs, reforming the bureaucracy, establishing a sound economy, and raising state revenues. Through generous settlement schemes and by welcoming Protestant and Jewish refugees, Frederick William was able to expand the economic potential of the eastern territories. Frederick William I pursued an aggressive policy of land purchase to expand the royal domain, and the addition of so many new inhabitants in Prussia further increased his wealth. While the major western European powers were discovering deficit financing and the national debt, Prussia was running a surplus.

Frederick the Great. Financial security was vital to the success of Frederick the Great. Father and son had quarreled bitterly throughout Frederick's youth—not only about music—and most observers expected that out of spite Frederick would tear down all that his father had built up. In fact, father and son were cast in the same mold, with the unexpected difference that the son was more ruthless and ambitious. With his throne, Frederick II inherited the fourth largest army in Europe and the richest treasury. He wasted no time in putting both to use. His two objectives were to acquire the Polish corridor of West Prussia that separated his German and Prussian territories and to acquire the agriculturally and industrially rich Austrian province of Silesia to the southeast of Berlin. Just months after his coronation, Frederick conquered Silesia, increasing the size of Prussia by nearly a quarter. Within a decade, the province dominated the Prussian economy, outproducing and outconsuming all other areas of Frederick's state.

It was Frederick's military prowess that earned him the title "the Great." But that was only a part of his achievement. More than his father, Frederick II forged

A KING'S-EYE VIEW

Frederick the Great wrote philosophical and military tracts as well as composing dozens of compositions for the flute. Here is his definition of the enlightened despot.

THE SOVEREIGN IS ATTACHED BY INDISSOLUBLE TIES to the body of the state; hence it follows that he, by repercussion, is sensible to all the ills which afflict his subjects; and the people, in like manner, suffer from the misfortunes which affect their sovereign. There is but one general good, which is that of the state.... The sovereign represents the state; he and his people form but one body, which can only be happy as far as united by concord. The prince is to the nation he governs what the head is to the man; it is his duty to see, to think, and act for the whole community, so that he may procure it every advantage of which it is capable.... Such are in general the duties imposed upon a prince, from which, in order that he may never depart, he ought often to recollect that he himself is but a man, like the least of his subjects. If he be the first general, the first minister of the realm, it is not so that he should shelter in the shadow of authority, but that he should fulfill the duties of such titles. He is only the first servant of the state, who is obliged to act with probity and prudence; and to remain as totally disinterested as if he were each moment liable to render an account of his administration to his fellow citizens.

From Frederick the Great, *An Essay on Forms of Government.*

an alliance with the Prussian nobility, integrating them into a unified state. A tightly organized central administration, which depended upon the cooperation of the local nobility, directed both military and bureaucratic affairs. At the center, Frederick worked tirelessly to oversee his government. Where Louis XIV had proclaimed, "I am the state," Frederick the Great announced, "I am the first servant of the state." He codified the laws of Prussia, abolished torture and capital punishment, and instituted agricultural techniques imported from the states of western Europe. By the end of Frederick's reign, Prussia had become a model for bureaucratic organization, military reform, and enlightened rule.

Austria Survives

Austria was the great territorial victor in the War of the Spanish Succession, acquiring both the Netherlands and parts of Italy. Austrian forces recaptured a large part of Hungary from the Turks, thereby expanding their territory to the south and the east. As hereditary ruler of Austria and Bohemia, king of Hungary, and Holy Roman Emperor of the German nation, Charles VI (1711–1740) was recognized as one of Europe's most potent rulers. But appearances were deceptive. The apex of Austrian power and prestige had already passed. Austria had benefited from balance-of-power politics, not so much from its own strength as from the leverage it could give to others. With the rise of Russia and Prussia, there was now more than one fulcrum to power in eastern Europe.

Decentralized Rule. The difficulties facing Austria ran deep. The Thirty Years' War had made the emperor more an Austrian monarch than an imperial German ruler. On the Austrian hereditary estates, the Catholic Counter-Reformation continued unabated, bringing with it the benefits of Jesuit education, cultural revival, and the religious unity necessary to motivate warfare against the Ottomans. But the benefits came at a price. Perhaps as many as 200,000 Protestants fled Austria and Bohemia, taking with them their skills and capital. For centuries, the vision of empire had dominated Habsburg rule. That meant that the Austrian monarchy was a multiethnic confederation of lands loosely tied together by loyalty to a single head. The components preserved a high degree of autonomy: Hungary elected the Habsburg emperor its king in a separate ceremony. Local autonomy continually restricted the imposition of central policy, and never were the localities more

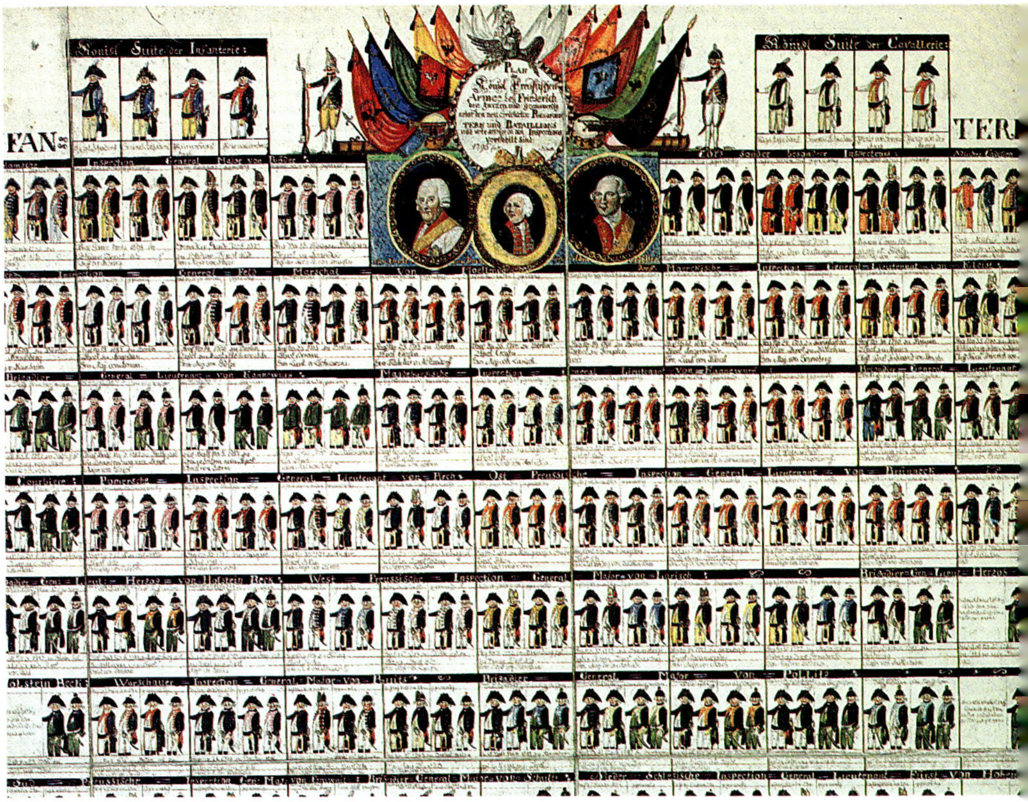

Prussian infantry officers display their uniforms in this painting from the late eighteenth century. Distinctive, colorful, and elaborate uniforms, different for each regiment, were common in European armies before the field-gray and khaki era of the twentieth century.

autonomous than in the matter of taxation. Thus it was hard for Austria to centralize in the same way as had Prussia.

Austria was predominantly rural and agricultural. Less than 5 percent of the population lived in towns of 10,000 or more; less than 15 percent lived in towns at all. On the land, the local aristocracy, whether nobility or gentry, exploited serfs to the maximum. Not only were serfs required to give labor service three days a week (and up to six during planting and harvest times), but the nobility maintained a full array of feudal privileges, including the right to mill all grain and brew all beer. When serfs married, when they transferred property, even when they died, they paid taxes to their lord. As a result, they had little left to give the state. In consequence, the Austrian army was among the smallest and the poorest of the major powers despite the fact that it had the most active enemies along its borders.

Lack of finance, human resources, and governmental control were the underlying problems of Austria, but they were not the most immediate difficulties facing Charles VI. With no sons to succeed him, Charles feared that his hereditary and elective states would go their separate ways after his death and that the great Habsburg monarchy would end. For 20 years, his abiding ambition was to gain recognition for the principle that his empire would pass intact to his daughter, Maria Theresa. He expressed the principle in a document known as the Pragmatic Sanction, which stated that all Habsburg lands would pass intact to the eldest heir, male or female. Charles VI made concession after concession to gain acceptance of the Pragmatic Sanction. But the leaders of Europe licked their lips at the prospect of a dismembered Austrian empire.

Maria Theresa. Maria Theresa (1740–1780) inherited the imperial throne in 1740 and quickly discovered what it was like to be a woman in a man's world. In 1740, Frederick of Prussia invaded the rich Austrian province of Silesia and attracted allies for an assault upon Vienna. Faced with Bavarian, Saxon, and Prussian armies, Maria Theresa might well have lost her inheritance had she not shown her remarkable

MILITARY DISCIPLINE

Herman Maurice de Saxe was the illegitimate son of the king of Poland. He had extensive military experience in both eastern and western Europe. He ultimately achieved the office of Marshal of France, where he was celebrated as a military reformer. He modeled many of his reforms on the Prussian army.

WOULD IT NOT BE MUCH BETTER to establish a law obliging men of all conditions of life to serve their king and country for the space of five years? A law, which could not reasonably be objected against, as it is both natural and just for people to be engaged in the defense of that state of which they constitute a part, and in choosing them between the years of twenty and thirty, no manner of inconvenience can possibly be the result; for those are years devoted, as it were, to libertinism; which are spent in adventures and travels, and, in general, productive of but small comfort to parents. An expedient of this kind could not come under the denomination of a public calamity, because every man, at the expiration of his five years service, would be discharged. It would also create an inexhaustible fund of good recruits, and such as would not be subject to desertion. In course of time, everyone would regard it as an honor rather than a duty to perform his task; but to produce this effect upon a people, it is necessary that no sort of distinction should be admitted, no rank or degree whatsoever excluded, and the nobles and rich rendered, in a principal manner, subservient to it. This would effectually prevent all murmur and repining, for those who had served their time, would look upon such, as betrayed any reluctance, or dissatisfaction at it, with contempt; by which means, the grievance would vanish insensibly, and every man at length esteem it an honor to serve his term. The poor would be comforted by the example of the rich; and the rich could not with decency complain, seeing themselves on a footing with the nobles.

From Marshal de Saxe, *Memoirs on the Art of War* (1757).

capacities so early in her reign. She appeared before the Hungarian estates, accepted their crown, and persuaded them to provide her with an army capable of halting the allied advance. Although she was unable to reconquer Silesia, Hungarian aid helped her hold the line against her enemies.

The loss of Silesia, the most prosperous part of the Austrian domains, signaled the need for fundamental reform. The new eighteenth-century idea of building a state replaced the traditional Habsburg concern with maintaining an empire. Maria Theresa and her son Joseph II (1780–1790) began the process of transformation. For Austria, state building meant first the reorganization of the military and civil bureaucracy to clear the way for fiscal reform. As in Prussia, a central directory was created to oversee the collection of taxes and the disbursement of funds. Maria Theresa personally persuaded her provincial estates both to increase taxation and to extend it to the nobles and the clergy. While her success was limited, she finally established royal control over the raising and collection of taxes.

The second element in Maria Theresa's reform program involved the condition of the Austrian peasantry. Maria Theresa established the doctrine that "the peasant must be able to support himself and his family and pay his taxes in time of peace and war." She limited labor service to two days per week and abolished the most burdensome feudal dues. Joseph II ended serfdom altogether. The new Austrian law codes guaranteed peasants' legal rights and established their ability to seek redress through the law. Joseph II hoped to extend reform even further. In the last years of his life, he abolished obligatory labor service and ensured that all peasants kept one-half of their income before paying local and state taxes. Such a radical reform met a storm of opposition and was ultimately abandoned at the end of the reign.

Maria Theresa and her family. Eleven of Maria Theresa's 16 children are posed with the empress and her husband, Francis of Lorraine. Standing next to his mother is the future emperor Joseph II.

The reorganization of the bureaucracy, the increase in taxation, and the social reforms that created a more productive peasantry revitalized the Austrian state. The efforts of Maria Theresa and Joseph II to overcome provincial autonomy worked better in Austria and Bohemia than in Hungary. The Hungarians declined to contribute at all to state revenues, and Joseph II took the unusual step of refusing to be crowned king of Hungary so that he would not have to make any concessions to Hungarian autonomy. He even imposed a tariff on Hungarian goods sold in Austria. More seriously, parts of the empire already had been lost before the process of reform could begin. Prussia's seizure of Silesia was the hardest blow of all. Yet in 1740, when Frederick the Great and his allies swept down from the north, few would have predicted that Austria would survive.

The Politics of Power

Frederick the Great's invasion of Silesia in 1740 was callous and cynical. Since the Pragmatic Sanction bound him to recognize Maria Theresa's succession, Frederick cynically offered her a defensive alliance in return for which she would simply hand over Silesia. It was an offer she should not have refused. Although Frederick's action initiated the War of the Austrian Succession, he was not alone in his desire to shake loose parts of Austria's territory. Soon nearly the entire Continent became embroiled in the conflict.

The War of the Austrian Succession. The War of the Austrian Succession (1740–1748) resembled a pack of wolves stalking its injured prey. It quickly became a major international conflict, involving Prussia, France, and Spain on one side and Austria, Britain, and Holland on the other. Spain joined the fighting to recover its Italian possessions, Saxony claimed Moravia, France entered Bohemia, and the Bavarians moved into Austria from the south. With France and Prussia allied, it was vital that Britain join with Austria to maintain the balance of power. Initially, the British did little more than subsidize Maria Theresa's forces, but once France renewed its efforts to conquer the Netherlands, both Britain and the Dutch Republic joined in the fray.

That the British cared little about the fate of the Habsburg empire was clear from the terms of the treaty that they dictated at Aix-la-Chapelle (Aachen) in 1748. Austria recognized Frederick's conquest of Silesia, as well as the loss of parts of its Italian territories to Spain. France, which the British had always regarded as the real enemy, withdrew from the Netherlands in return for the restoration of a number of colonial possessions. The War of the Austrian Succession made Austria and Prussia permanent enemies and gave Maria Theresa a crash course in international diplomacy. She learned firsthand that self-interest rather than loyalty underlay power politics.

That lesson was reinforced in 1756 when Britain and Prussia entered into a military accord at the beginning of the Seven Years' War (1756–1763). Prussian expansion and duplicity had already alarmed both Russia and France, and Frederick II feared that he would be squeezed from east and west. He could hardly expect help from Maria Theresa, so he extended overtures to the British, whose interests in protecting Hanover, the hereditary estates of their German-born king, outweighed their prior commitments to Austria. Frederick's actions drove France into the arms of both the Austrians and the Russians, and an alliance that included the German state of Saxony was formed in defense. Thus was initiated a diplomatic revolution in which France and Austria became allies after 300 years as enemies.

Once again Frederick the Great took the offensive, and once again he won his risk against the odds. His attack on Saxony and Austria in 1756 brought a vigorous response from the Russians, who interceded on Austria's behalf with a massive army. Three years later, at the battle of Kunersdorf, Frederick suffered the worst military defeat of his career when the Russians shattered his armies. In 1760, his forces were barely a third of the size of those massed by his opponents, and it was only a matter of time before he was fighting defensively from within Prussia.

In 1762 Empress Elizabeth died. She was succeeded by her nephew, the childlike Peter III, a German by birth who worshipped Frederick the Great. When Peter came to the throne, he immediately negotiated peace with Frederick, abandoning not only his allies but also the substantial territorial gains that the Russian forces had made within Prussia. It was small wonder that the Russian military leadership joined in the coup d'état that brought Peter's wife, Catherine, to the throne in 1762. With Russia out of the war, Frederick was able to fend off further Austrian offensives and to emerge with his state, including Silesia, intact.

The Seven Years' War did little to change the boundaries of the German states, but it had two important political results. The first was to establish beyond doubt the status of Prussia as a major power and a counterbalance to Austria in central Europe. The existence of the dual Germanies, one led by Prussia and the other by Austria, was to have serious consequences for German unification in the nineteenth century and for the two world wars in the twentieth century. The second result of the Seven Years' War was to initiate a long period of peace in eastern Europe. Both Prussia and Austria were financially exhausted from two decades of fighting. Both states needed a breathing spell to initiate administrative and economic improvements, and the period following the Seven Years' War witnessed the sustained programs of internal reforms for which Frederick the Great, Maria Theresa, and Joseph II were famous in the decades following 1763.

The Partitions of Poland. Peace among the eastern European powers did not mean that they abandoned their territorial ambitions. All over Europe, absolute rulers reformed their bureaucracies, streamlined their administrations, increased their sources of revenue, and built enormous standing armies. All over Europe, except in Poland. There the autonomous power of the nobility remained as strong as ever. No monarchical

This engraving by Le Mire is called "The Cake of the Kings: First Partition of Poland, 1773." The monarchs of Russia, Austria, and Prussia join in carving up Poland. The Polish king is clutching his tottering crown.

dynasty was ever established, and each elected ruler not only confirmed the privileges of the nobility but usually was forced to extend them. In the Diet, the Polish representative assembly, small special-interest groups could bring legislative business to a halt by exercising their veto power. Given the size of Poland's borders, its army was pathetically inadequate for the task it had to face. The Polish monarchy was helpless to defend its subjects from the destruction on all sides.

In 1764, Catherine the Great and Frederick the Great joined to place one of Catherine's former lovers on the Polish throne and to turn Poland into a weak dependent. Russia and Prussia had different interests in Poland's fate. For Russia, Poland represented a vast

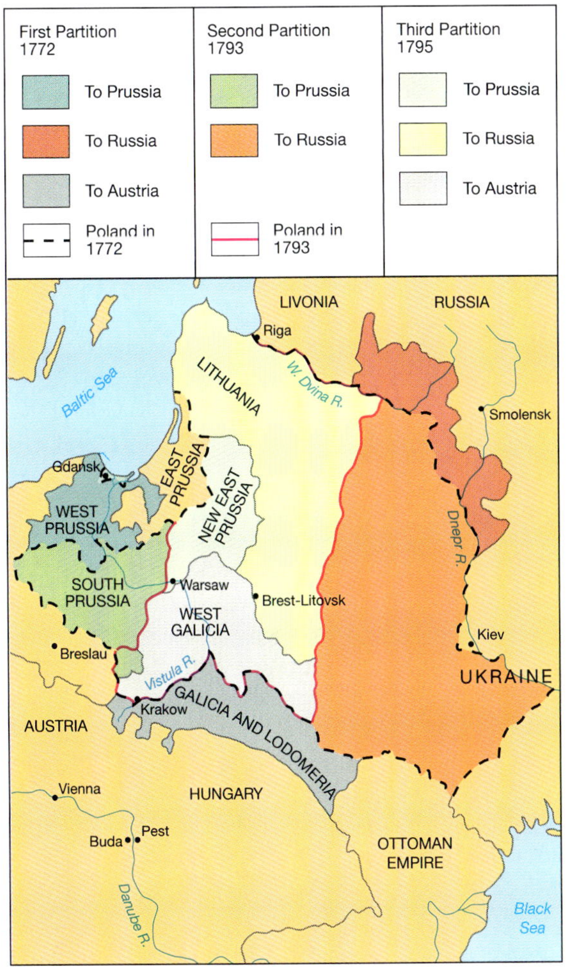

The Partitions of Poland. Poland had once been one of the largest of the states of Europe but three successive partitions left it weak and dismembered.

Jan Sobieski III, King of Poland (1629–1696). Persuaded by Pope Innocent III, Sobieski joined Emperor Leopold I in his war against the Turks. His troops were instrumental in lifting the siege of Vienna.

buffer state that kept the German powers at a distance from Russia's borders. It was more in Russia's interest to dominate Polish foreign policy than to conquer its territory. For Prussia, Poland looked like another helpless flower, "to be picked off leaf by leaf," as Frederick observed. Poland seemed especially appealing because Polish territory, including the Baltic port of Gdansk, separated the Prussian and Brandenburg portions of Frederick's state.

By the 1770s the idea of carving up Poland was being actively discussed in Berlin, Saint Petersburg, and Vienna. Austria, too, had an interest in a Polish partition, especially to maintain its power and status with the other two states, and perhaps to use Polish territory as a potential bargaining chip for the return of Silesia. Finally, in 1772, the three great eastern powers struck a deal. Russia would take a large swath of the grain fields of northeast Poland, which included more than one million people, while Frederick would unite his lands by seizing West Prussia. Austria gained both the largest territories, including Galicia, and the greatest number of people, nearly two million Polish subjects.

In a half century, the balance of power in central Europe had shifted decisively. Prussia's absorption of Silesia and parts of Poland made it a single geographical entity, as well as a great economic and military power. Austria, despite its lost territory, proved capable of surviving the accession of a female ruler and of fighting off an attempt to dismember its empire. Its participation in the partition of Poland strengthened its role in the politics of the eastern powers, while its alliance with France fortified its role in the west. From one empire there were now two states, and the relationship between Prussia and Austria would dominate central Europe for the next century.

THE GREATNESS OF GREAT BRITAIN

By the middle of the eighteenth century, Great Britain had become the leading power of Europe. It had won its spurs in Continental and colonial wars. Britain was unsurpassed as a naval power, able to protect its far-flung trading empire and to make a show of force in almost any part of the world. Perhaps more impressively for a nation that did not support a large standing army, British soldiers had won decisive victories in the European land wars. Until the American Revolution, Britain came up a winner in every military venture it undertook. But might was only one part of British success. Economic preeminence was every bit as important. British colonial possessions in the Atlantic and Indian oceans poured consumer products into Britain for export to the European marketplaces. Growth in overseas trade was matched by growth in home production. British advances in agricultural technique had transformed Britain from an importer to an exporter of grain. The manufacturing industries that other European states attempted to create with huge government subsidies flourished in Britain through private enterprise.

British military and economic power was supported by a unique system of government. In Britain, the nobility served the state through government. The British constitutional system, devised in the seventeenth century and refined in the eighteenth, shared power between the monarchy and the ruling elite through the institution of Parliament. Central government integrated monarch and ministers with chosen representatives from the localities. Such integration not only provided the Crown with the vital information necessary to formulate national policy, but it eased acceptance and enforcement of government decisions. Government was seen as the rule of law that, however imperfect, was believed to operate for the benefit of all.

The parliamentary system gave Britain some of its particular strengths, but they came at a cost. Politics was a national pastime rather than the business of an elite of administrators and state servants. Decentralization of decision making led to half-measures designed to placate competing interests. Appeals to public opinion, especially by candidates for Parliament, often played upon fears and prejudices that divided rather than united the nation. Moreover, the relative openness of the British system hindered diplomatic and colonial affairs, in which secrecy and rapid changes of direction were often the monarch's most potent weapons. The weaknesses came to light most dramatically during the struggle for independence waged by Britain's North American colonists. There the clash of principle and power was most extreme and the strengths and weaknesses of parliamentary rule were ruthlessly exposed.

The British Constitution

The British Constitution was a patchwork of laws and customs that was gradually sewn together to form a workable system of government. Many of its greatest innovations came about through circumstance rather than design, and circumstance continued to play an essential role in its development in the eighteenth century. At the apex of the government stood the king, not an absolute monarch like his European counterparts, but not necessarily less powerful for having less arbitrary power. The British people revered monarchy and the monarch. The theory of mixed government depended upon the balance of interests represented by the monarchy in the Crown, the aristocracy in the House of Lords, and the people in the House of Commons. Less abstractly, the monarch was still regarded as divinely ordained and a special gift to the nation. The monarch was the actual and symbolic leader of the nation as well as the Supreme Head of the Church of England. Allegiance to the Anglican church, whether as a political creed among the elite or as a simple matter of devotion among the populace, intensified allegiance to the king.

The partnership between Crown and representative body was best expressed in the idea that the British government was composed of King-in-Parliament. Parliament consisted of three separate organs: monarch, lords, and commons. Although each existed separately as a check upon the potential excesses of the others, it was only when the three functioned together that parliamentary government could operate. The king was charged with selecting ministers, initiating policy, and supervising administration. The two houses of Parliament were charged with raising revenue, making laws, and presenting the grievances of subjects to the Crown.

There were 558 members of the House of Commons after the union with Scotland in 1707. Most members of the lower house were nominated to their seats. The largest number of seats were located in small towns where a local oligarchy, or neighboring patron, had a customary right to make nominations that were invariably accepted by the electorate. Even in the largest cities, influential citizens made arrangements for nominating members in order to avoid the cost and confusion of an actual election. Campaigns were ruinously expensive for the candidates—an election in 1754 cost the losing candidates £40,000—and potentially dangerous to the local community, where bitter social and political divisions boiled just below the surface.

The British gentry dominated the Commons, occupying more than 80 percent of the seats in any session. Most of the members also served as unpaid local officials in the counties, as justices of the peace, captains of the local militias, or collectors of local taxes. They came to Parliament not only as representatives of the interests of their class, but as experienced local governors who understood the needs of both Crown and subject.

Nevertheless, the Crown had to develop methods to coordinate the work of the two houses of Parliament and facilitate the passage of governmental programs. The king and his ministers began to use the deep royal pockets of offices and favors to bolster their friends in Parliament. Not only were those employed by the Crown encouraged to find a place in the House of Commons, but those who had a place in Parliament were encouraged to take employment from the Crown. Despite its potential for abuse, it was a political process that integrated center and locality, and at first it worked rather well. Those with local standing were brought into central offices, where they could influence central policy making while protecting their local constituents. The officeholders, who came to be called placemen, never constituted a majority of the members of Parliament. They formed the core around

William Pitt addressing the House of Commons on the French declaration of war, 1793.

which eighteenth-century governments operated, but it was a core that needed direction and cohesion. It was such leadership and organization that was the essential contribution of eighteenth-century politics to the British Constitution.

Parties and Ministers

Although parliamentary management was vital to the British Crown, it was not the Crown that developed the basic tools of management. Rather, those techniques originated within the political community itself, and their usefulness was only slowly grasped by the monarchy. The first and, in the long term, most important tool was the party system.

Political parties initially developed in the late seventeenth century around the issue of the Protestant succession. Those who opposed James II because he was a Catholic attempted to exclude him from inheriting the crown. They came to be called by their opponents *Whigs,* which had come to mean "horse thieves" (the term originally derived from *Wiggamore,* a name for Western Isle Scots who cried "Whig, whig!" to spur their horses on). Those who supported James's hereditary rights but who also supported the Anglican church came to be called by their opponents *Tories,* which in Gaelic meant "cattle rustlers."

The Tories cooperated in the Revolution of 1688 that placed William and Mary on the throne because James had threatened the Anglican church by tolerating Catholics and because Mary had a legitimate hereditary right to be queen. After the death of Queen Anne in 1714, the Tories supported the succession of James III, James II's Catholic son, who had been raised in France, rather than of George I (1714–1727), prince of Hanover and Protestant great-grandson of James I. An unsuccessful rebellion to place James III on the throne in 1715 discredited the leadership of the Tory party but did not weaken its importance in both local and parliamentary politics.

The Whigs supported the Protestant succession and a broad-based Protestantism. They attracted the allegiance of large numbers of dissenters, heirs to the Puritans of the seventeenth century who practiced forms of Protestantism different from that of the Anglican church. The struggle between Whigs and Tories was less a struggle for power than it was for loyalty to their opposing viewpoints. As the Tories opposed the Hanoverian succession and the Whigs supported it, it was no mystery which party would find favor with George I. Moreover, as long as there was a pretender to the British throne—another rebellion took place in Scotland in 1745 led by the grandson of James II—the Tories continued to be tarred with the brush of disloyalty.

The division of political sympathies between Whigs and Tories helped create a set of groupings to which parliamentary leadership could be applied. A national rather than a local or regional outlook could be used to organize support for royal policy as long as royal policy conformed to that national outlook. The ascendancy of the Whigs enabled George I and his son George II (1727–1760) to govern effectively through Parliament, but at the price of dependence upon the Whig leaders. Although the monarch had the constitutional freedom to choose his ministers, realistically he could choose only Whigs, and practically none but the Whig leaders of the House of Commons. Happily for the first two Georges, they found Sir Robert Walpole, who was able to manage Parliament but desired only to serve the Crown.

Sir Robert Walpole (1676–1745) came from a long-established gentry family in Norfolk. Walpole was an early supporter of the Hanoverian succession and an early victim of party warfare. But once George I was securely on the throne, Walpole became an indispensable leader of the House of Commons. His success rested upon his extraordinary abilities: he was an excellent public speaker, he relished long working days and the details of government, and he understood better than anyone else the intricacies of state finance. Walpole became First Lord of the Treasury, a post that he transformed into first minister of state. From his treasury post, Walpole assiduously built a Whig parliamentary party. He carefully dispensed jobs and offices, using them as bait to lure parliamentary supporters. Walpole's organization paid off both in the passage of legislation desired by the Crown and at the polls, where Whigs were returned to Parliament time and again.

From 1721 to 1742, Walpole was the most powerful man in the British government. He refused an offer of a peerage so that he could continue to lead the House of Commons. Walpole's long tenure in office was as much a result of his policies as of his methods of governing. He brought a measure of fiscal responsibility to government by establishing a fund to pay off the national debt. In foreign policy he pursued peace with the same fervor that both his predecessors and successors pursued war. The long years of peace brought prosperity to both the landed and merchant classes, but they also brought criticism of Walpole's methods. The way in which he used government patronage to build his parliamentary party was attacked as corruption. So, too, were the ways in which the pockets of Whig office-holders were lined. During his last decade in office, Walpole struggled to survive. His attempt to extend the excise tax on colonial goods nearly led to his loss of office in 1733. His refusal to respond to the clamor for continued war with Spain in 1741 finally led to his downfall.

Walpole's 20-year rule established the pattern of parliamentary government. The Crown needed a "prime" minister who was able to steer legislation through the House of Commons. It also needed a patronage broker who could take control of the treasury and dispense its largess in return for parliamentary backing. Walpole's personality and talents had combined the two roles. Thereafter they were divided. Those who had grown up under Walpole had learned their lessons well. The Whig monopoly of power continued unchallenged for nearly another 20 years. The patronage network Walpole had created was vastly extended by his Whig successors. Even minor posts in the customs or the excise offices were now exchanged for political favor, and only those approved by the Whig leadership could claim them. The cries of corruption grew louder not only in the country houses of the long-disenfranchised Tories, but in the streets of London, where a popular radicalism developed in opposition to the Whig oligarchy. They were taken up as well in the North American colonies, where two million British subjects champed at the bit of imperial rule.

America Revolts

Britain's triumph in the Seven Years' War (1756–1763) had come at great financial cost to the nation. At the beginning of the eighteenth century, the national debt stood at £14 million; by 1763, it had risen to £130 million, despite the fact that Walpole's government had been paying off some of it. Then, as now, the cost of world domination was staggering. George III (1760–1820) came to the throne with a taste for reform and a desire to break the Whig stranglehold on government. He was to have limited success on both counts, though not for want of trying. In 1763, the king and his ministers agreed that reform of colonial administration was long overdue. Such reform would have the twin benefit of shifting part of the burden of taxation from Britain to North America and of making the commercial side of colonization pay.

That was sound thinking all around, and in due course Parliament passed a series of duties on goods imported into the colonies, including glass, wine, coffee, tea, and, most notably, sugar. The so-called Sugar Act (1764) was followed by the Stamp Act (1765), a tax on printed papers such as newspapers, deeds, and court documents. Both acts imposed taxes in the colonies similar to those that already existed in Britain. Accompanying the acts were administrative orders designed to cut into the lucrative black market trade. The government instituted new rules for searching ships and transferred authority over smuggling from the local colonial courts to Britain's Admiralty courts. Although British officials could only guess at the value of the new duties imposed, it was believed that with effective enforcement £150,000 would be raised. All that would go to pay the vastly greater costs of colonial administration and security.

British officials were more than perplexed when the mild measures met with a ferocious response. Assemblies of nearly every colony officially protested the Sugar Act. They sent petitions to Parliament begging for repeal and warning of dire economic and political consequences. Riots followed passage of the Stamp Act. Tax collectors were hounded out of office, their resignations precipitated by threats and acts of physical violence. In Massachusetts, mobs that included political leaders in the colony razed the homes of the collector and the lieutenant-governor. However much the colonists might have regretted the violence that was done, they believed that an essential political principle was at stake. It was a principle of the freedom of an Englishman.

At their core, the protests of the American colonists underscored the vitality of the British political system. The Americans argued that they could not be taxed without their consent and that their consent could come only through representation in Parliament. Since there were no colonists in Parliament, Parliament had no jurisdiction over the property of the colonists. Taxation without representation was tyranny. There were a number of subtleties to the argument that were quickly lost as political rhetoric and political action heated up. In the first place, the colonists did tax themselves through their own legislatures and much of that money paid the costs of administration and defense. Second, as a number of pamphleteers pointed

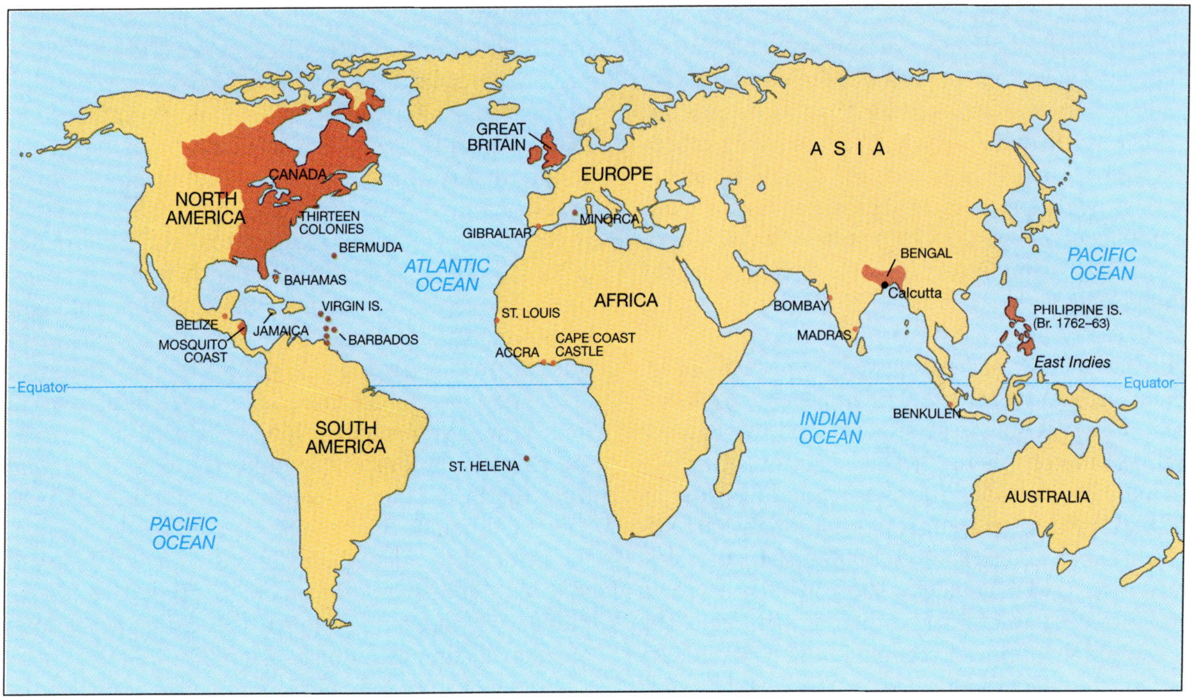

The First British Empire (ca. 1763). The empire was the result of commercial enterprise and Britain's military successes.

out, no one in the colonies had asked the British government to send regiments of the army into North America. The colonists had little reason to put their faith in British protection. Hard-fought colonial victories were tossed away at European negotiating tables, while the British policy of defending Indian rights in the Ohio Valley ran counter to the interests of the settlers. When defense was necessary, the colonists had proved themselves both able and cooperative in providing it. A permanent tax meant a permanent army, and a standing army was as loathed in Britain as it was in the colonies.

In opposing the Stamp Act, colonists also tried to draw a distinction between internal and external taxation. They deemed regulation of overseas commerce a legitimate power of Parliament but argued that the regulation of internal exchange was not. But that distinction was lost once the issue of parliamentary representation was raised. If the colonists had not consented to British taxation, then it made no difference whether taxation was internal or external. The passion generated in the colonies was probably no greater than that generated in Britain. The British government also saw the confrontation as a matter of principle, but for Britain the principle was parliamentary sovereignty. That, above all, was the rock upon which the British constitution had been built over the last century. Parliament had entered into a partnership with the Crown. The Crown had surrendered—willingly or not—many of its prerogatives. In return, Parliament had bound the people to obedience. There were well-established means by which British subjects could petition Parliament for redress of grievances against the monarch, but there were no channels by which they could question the sovereignty of Parliament.

Once the terms of debate had been so defined, it was difficult for either side to find a middle ground. Parliamentary moderates managed repeal of the Stamp Act and most of the clauses of the Sugar Act, but they also joined in passing the Declaratory Act (1766), which stated unequivocally that Parliament held sovereign jurisdiction over the colonies "in all cases whatsoever." That was a claim that became more and more difficult to sustain as colonial leaders began to cite the elements of resistance theory that had justified the Revolution of 1688. Then the protest had been against

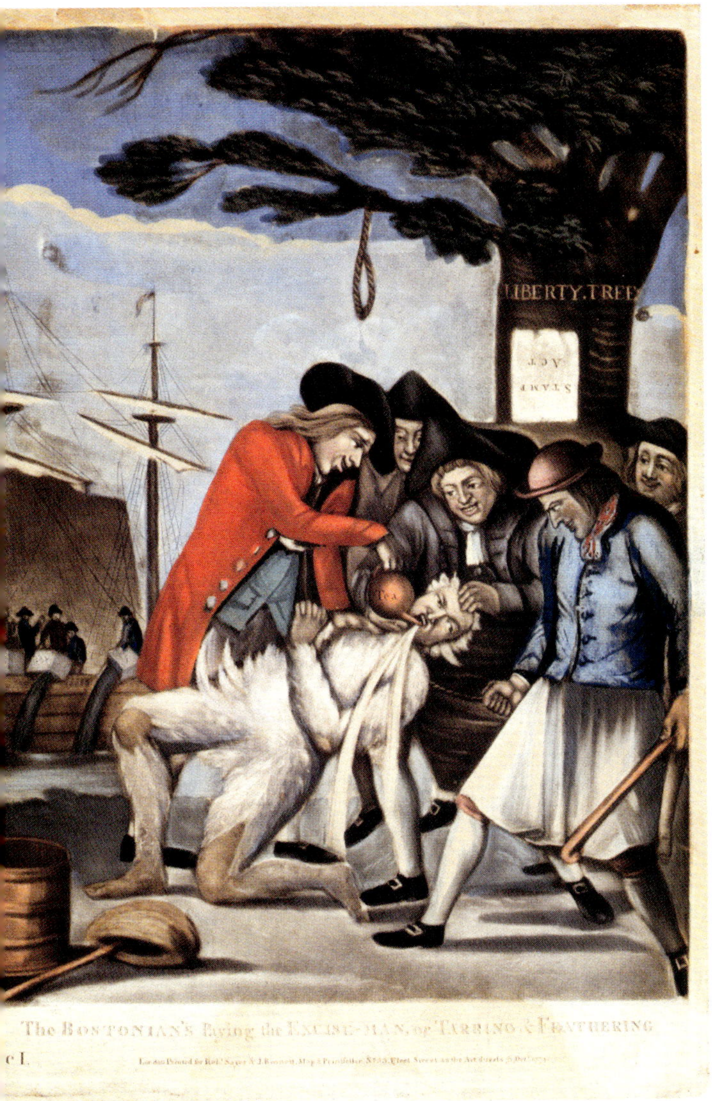

In Britain's North American colonies, public sentiment against the importation of tea and other British goods often found expression in a coat of tar and feathers applied to the bare skin of the offending importer. Note the symbols in The Bostonians Paying the Excise-Man: *the Liberty Tree from which dangles a hangman's noose and the overturned copy of the Stamp Act. In the background, Bostonians dump chests of tea into the harbor.*

the tyranny of the king; the new protest was against the tyranny of Parliament. American propagandists claimed that a conspiracy existed to deprive the colonists of their property and rights and to enslave them for the benefit of special interests and corrupt politicians.

The techniques of London radicals who opposed parliamentary policy were imported into the colonies. Newspapers were used to whip up public support; boycotts brought ordinary people into the political arena; public demonstrations such as the Boston Tea Party (1774) were carefully designed to intimidate; mobs were occasionally given free rein. Although the government had faced down those tactics when they were used in London to support John Wilkes (1725–1797), an ardent critic of royal policy, they were less successful when the crisis lay an ocean away. When, in 1770, British troops fired on a Boston mob, American propagandists were provided with empirical evidence that Britain intended to enslave the colonies. Violence was met by violence, passion by passion. In 1775, full-scale fighting was under way. Eight years later, Britain withdrew from a war it could not win, and the American colonies were left to govern themselves.

CHRONOLOGY

The New European Powers

1707	England and Scotland unite to form Great Britain
1713–1714	Peace of Utrecht ends War of the Spanish Succession (1702–1714)
1714	British crown passes to House of Hanover
1721	Treaty of Nystad ends Great Northern War (1700–1721)
1721–1742	Sir Robert Walpole leads British House of Commons
1722	Peter the Great of Russia creates Table of Ranks
1740	Frederick the Great of Prussia invades Austrian province of Silesia
1748	Treaty of Aix-la-Chapelle ends War of the Austrian Succession (1740–1748)
1756–1763	Seven Years' War pits Prussia and Britain against Austria, France, and Russia
1773–1775	Pugachev's revolt in Russia
1774	Boston Tea Party
1775	American Revolution begins
1785	Catherine the Great of Russia issues Charter of the Nobility

UNALIENABLE RIGHTS

The Declaration of Independence, written by Thomas Jefferson (1776), succinctly summarized the principles on which the American Colonists were to build a new form of democratic government.

WE HOLD THESE TRUTHS TO BE SELF-EVIDENT, that all men are created equal, that they are endowed by their Creator with certain unalienable Rights, that among these are Life, Liberty and the pursuit of Happiness. That to secure these rights, Governments are instituted among Men, deriving their just powers from the consent of the governed. That whenever any Form of Government becomes destructive of these ends, it is the Right of the People to alter or to abolish it, and to institute new Government, laying its foundation on such principles and organizing its powers in such form, as to them shall seem most likely to effect their Safety and Happiness. Prudence, indeed, will dictate that Governments long established should not be changed for light and transient causes; and accordingly all experience hath shown, that mankind are more disposed to suffer, while evils are sufferable, than to right themselves by abolishing the forms to which they are accustomed. But when a long train of abuses and usurpations, pursuing invariably the same Object, evinces a design to reduce them under absolute Despotism, it is their right, it is their duty, to throw off such Government, and to provide new Guards for their future security.

From the Declaration of Independence.

By the end of the third quarter of the eighteenth century, Europe had a new political configuration. A continent once dominated by a single power—Spain in the sixteenth century and France in the seventeenth—was now dominated by a state system in which alliances among several great powers held the balance. Despite the loss of its American colonies, Great Britain had proved the most potent of the states. Its victories over the French in the Seven Years' War and over France and Prussia in the War of the Austrian Succession secured its position. But it was a position that could be maintained only through alliances with the German states, with either Prussia or Austria. The rise of Prussia provided a counterweight to French domination of the Continent. Although those two states became allies in the middle of the century, the ambitions of their rulers made them natural enemies, and it would not be long before French and Prussian armies were again pitted against each other. France, still the wealthiest and most populous of European states, had slumbered through the eighteenth-century reorganization. The legacies of Louis XIV took a long time to reach fruition. He had claimed glory for his state, giving the French people a sense of national identity and national destiny, but making them pay an enormous price in social and economic dislocation. Thus the mid-eighteenth century was to be an age of the greatest literary and philosophical achievement for France, but the late eighteenth century was to be an age of the greatest social upheaval that Europe had ever known.

Questions for Review

1. What were the great powers of Europe in the eighteenth century and in what ways was there a "balance of power" among them?
2. What did Peter I and Catherine II of Russia accomplish during their reigns that justifies the title "the great"?
3. How was the tiny state of Brandenburg-Prussia able to make itself into one of Europe's major powers and what did that mean for the Austrian empire?
4. How did Britain's theory of mixed government and its parliamentary party system assist its rise to become Europe's great imperial power?
5. How and why did the "balance of power" shift during the eighteenth century?

Suggestions for Further Reading

General Reading

* Olwen Hufton, *Europe: Privilege and Protest, 1730–1789* (Ithaca, NY: Cornell University Press, 1980). An excellent survey of the political and social history of the mid-eighteenth century.

* Leonard Krieger, *Kings and Philosophers, 1689–1789* (New York: Norton, 1970). A brilliant depiction of the personalities and ideas of eighteenth-century Europe.

* Jeremy Black, *Eighteenth Century Europe* (London: Macmillan, 1990). The eighteenth century arranged thematically by society, culture, and economy.

M.S. Anderson, *War and Society in Europe of the Old Regime, 1618–1789,* 2d ed. (Montreal: McGill-Queen's University Press, 1998). A brief survey of the military history of the period.

* M. S. Anderson, *Europe in the Eighteenth Century, 1713–1783,* 3d ed. (London: Longman, 1987). A country-by-country survey of political developments.

Nicholas Riasanovsky, *A History of Russia* (New York: Oxford University Press, 1993). The best one-volume history of Russia.

* David Kirby, *Northern Europe in the Early Modern Period* (London: Longman, 1991). Political history from a Baltic perspective, with excellent chapters on Sweden and Russia.

Geographical Tour: Europe in 1714

* Derek McKay and H. M. Scott, *The Rise of the Great Powers* (London: Longman, 1983). An outstanding survey of diplomacy and warfare.

The Rise of Russia

* Paul Dukes, *The Making of Russian Absolutism, 1613–1801* (London: Longman, 1982). An extensive survey of the Russian monarchy in its greatest period.

* B. H. Sumner, *Peter the Great and the Emergence of Russia* (New York: Collier Books, 1962). A short and readable study; the best introduction.

* M. S. Anderson, *Peter the Great* (London: Thames and Hudson, 1978). A well-constructed, comprehensive biography.

John P. LeDonne, *Absolutism and Ruling Class: The Formation of the Russian Political Order, 1700–1825* (New York: Oxford University Press, 1991).

* Jerome Blum, *Lord and Peasant in Russia* (New York: Columbia University Press, 1961). The best work on the social life of Russians.

* John T. Alexander, *Catherine the Great: Life and Legend* (Oxford: Oxford University Press, 1989). A lively account of the public and private life of the Russian Empress.

* Isabel de Madariaga, *Catherine the Great, a Short History* (New Haven, CT: Yale University Press, 1990). The best brief life.

The Two Germanies

* H. W. Koch, *A History of Prussia* (London: Longman, 1978). The most recent study of the factors that led to Prussian dominance of Germany.

* Rudolf Vierhaus, *Germany in the Age of Absolutism* (Cambridge: Cambridge University Press, 1989). A synoptic survey of society, culture, and politics.

* Charles Ingrao, *The Habsburg Monarchy, 1618–1815* (Cambridge: Cambridge University Press, 1994). Divided evenly between foreign and domestic affairs; rewarding for readers of all levels.

* J. Gagliardo, *Germany Under the Old Regime* (London: Longman, 1991). The best single-volume history.

* Gerhard Ritter, *Frederick the Great* (Berkeley: University of California Press, 1974). A classic biography, short and readable.

* Walther Hubatsch, *Frederick the Great of Prussia* (London: Thames and Hudson, 1975). A full account of the reign of Prussia's greatest leader.

* Ernst Wangermann, *The Austrian Achievement* (New York: Harcourt Brace Jovanovich, 1973). The most readable study of Austrian politics, culture, and society in the eighteenth century.

* T. C. W. Blanning, *Joseph II and Enlightened Despotism* (London: Longman, 1970). Displays the relationship between new ideas, reform policies, and the practical necessities of government.

C. A. Macartney, *Maria Theresa and the House of Austria* (Mystic, CT: Verry Inc., 1969). Still the best introductory study.

* Reed S. Browning, *The War of Austrian Succession* (London: Macmillan, 1995). A comprehensive history of a complicated event.

John Stoye, *Marsigli's Europe* (New Haven, CT: Yale University Press, 1994). European civilization seen through the eyes of a virtuoso statesman and soldier.

The Greatness of Great Britain

* J. C. D. Clark, *English Society, 1688–1832* (Cambridge: Cambridge University Press, 1985). A bold reinterpretation of the most important features of English society.

* J. H. Plumb, *The Origins of Political Stability, England 1675–1725* (Boston: Houghton Mifflin, 1967). The fullest of the contributions of Walpole to the establishment of the British constitution.

* Jeremy Black, *Britain as a Military Power* (London: UCL Press, 1999). A reliable survey of military developments in Britain.

* Linda Colley, *Britons* (New Haven, CT: Yale University Press, 1992). A lively account of how a nation was forged from Welsh, Scots, and English and how unity and diversity intermixed.

* H. V. Bowen, *War and British Society, 1688–1815* (Cambridge: Cambridge University Press, 1998). An important study of the impact of war on Britain during its great military expansion.

Ragnhild Hatton, *George I Elector and King* (Cambridge, MA: Harvard University Press, 1978). An outstanding biography that shows the German side of a British monarch.

* John Brewer, *Party Ideology and Popular Politics at the Accession of George III* (Cambridge: Cambridge University Press, 1976). An important book about the pressures on the political system in the late eighteenth century.

* Paul Langford, *A Polite and Commercial People: England 1727–1783* (Oxford: Oxford University Press, 1989). The standard survey in the Oxford history series.

* D. Hay and N. Rogers, *Eighteenth-Century English Society* (Oxford: Oxford University Press, 1997). An up-to-date survey of social life in Britain.

* Gordon Wood, *The Radicalism of the American Revolution* (New York: Alfred A. Knopf, 1992). How the ideals of the American Revolution shaped an emerging nation.

* Ian Christie and Benjamin W. Labaree, *Empire or Independence, 1760–1777* (New York: Norton, 1977). The American troubles from the British point of view.

* Bernard Bailyn, *The Ideological Origins of the American Revolution* (Cambridge, MA: Harvard University Press, 1967). A brilliant interpretation of the underlying causes of the break between Britain and the North American colonies.

* Robert Middlekauff, *The Glorious Cause: The American Revolution, 1763–1789* (New York: Oxford University Press, 1982). A lively narrative account from the American perspective.

* Paperback edition available.

Discovering Western Civilization Online

To further explore the balance of power in eighteenth-century Europe, consult the following World Wide Web sites. Since Web resources are constantly being updated, also go to *www.awl.com/Kishlansky* for further suggestions.

The Rise of Russia

www.english.upenn.edu/~jlynch/FrankDemo/Places/russia.html
A site detailing the history of Russia from the time of Peter the Great. Links to the building of St. Petersburg.

www.fordham.edu/halsall/mod/18catherine.html
Sources from the reign of Catherine the Great.

The Two Germanies

www.members.tripod.com/~Nevermore/king.html
A site devoted to the history of the reign of Frederick the Great.

The Greatness of Great Britain

www.revolution.h-net.msu.edu/
A site with extensive links to all aspects of the American Revolution.

CHAPTER

19 CULTURE AND SOCIETY IN EIGHTEENTH-CENTURY EUROPE

- HAPPY FAMILIES
- EIGHTEENTH-CENTURY CULTURE

  The Enlightenment

  The Spirit of the Enlightenment

  The Impact of the Enlightenment
- EIGHTEENTH-CENTURY SOCIETY

  The Nobility

  The Bourgeoisie

  The Masses

Happy Families

"HAPPY FAMILIES ARE ALL ALIKE," wrote Lev Tolstoy in the nineteenth century when the idea of a happy family was already a cliché. Such an idea would never have occurred to his eighteenth-century forebears. For them the happy family was new. Personal happiness was an invention of the Enlightenment, the result of novel attitudes about human aspirations and human capabilities. "Happiness is a new idea in Europe," wrote Louis de Saint-Just (1767–1794). It emerged in response to the belief that what was good brought pleasure and what was evil brought pain. Happiness, both individual and collective, became the yardstick by which life was measured. That meant a reorientation in personal conduct and, most of all, a reorientation of family life. Especially for those with an economic cushion, a pleasurable family life became essential. Husbands and wives were to be companions, filled with romantic love for each other and devoted to domestic bliss. Children, the product of their affection, were to be doted on, treated not as miniature adults to be lectured and beaten, but as unfilled vessels into which was poured all that was good.

Were ever a couple more in love than the husband and wife depicted in *A Visit to the Wet Nurse* by Jean-Honoré Fragonard (1732–1806)? In the painting, the man clasps his wife's arm to his cheek, she lays her hand on his shoulder. Their sighs are almost audible! Together they admire the fruit of their love, the baby asleep in the cradle. It is hard to guess which parent dotes more, the mother with her rapturous expression or the father with his intensity as he kneels on a cushion in almost religious devotion, his hands folded as if in prayer. Who would doubt their companionship or their love for their babe? They have come together to see how the wet nurse is caring for their child.

At the beginning of the eighteenth century, the use of a wet nurse was still common among the families of the French bourgeoisie, the class to which the couple pictured belonged. As time passed, however, more and more families began to keep their children at home and more mothers began to nurse their babies themselves. In part this change was a response to the higher mortality rate among infants sent out to wet nurses. But a wet nurse who could be supervised, that is, one who lived near enough to be visited, but far enough away from the town to enjoy wholesome air, might be the best of both worlds. That is just what the couple here found, and in the picture they come, with their other child (the boy in the hat), to see their baby sleeping peacefully, the wet nurse sitting attentively at the infant's side.

But there are two families in this picture, and they are hardly alike. At first glance, the wet nurse looks like an old woman, perhaps even an aging nanny. She sits with her distaff in her hand, for the arrival of her clients has interrupted her spinning. It is shocking to realize that she cannot be much older than 30, an age beyond which wealthy families would not hire her for fear either that she would not have much

milk or that it would be sour. The two younger children on the far right are undoubtedly hers, the youngest probably just weaned so that all of the milk would go to the baby. No adoring husband sits beside the wet nurse. Her husband, if he is still alive, is hard at work with no leisure time for visits to the country. Not only does the wet nurse have to sell her milk, but she also spins, to keep her family clothed and to earn a little extra to put away for hard times.

The newest fads of the age have passed her family by. While the child in the cradle will be spoiled by toys manufactured especially for children—puzzles, games, rocking horses, and balls—the children of the wet nurse must make do with household objects and their own imaginations. A ball of yarn thrown to the cat helps the elder child while away the hours. Like much else in the eighteenth century, the world of the family was divided between high and low.

EIGHTEENTH-CENTURY CULTURE

The eighteenth century spawned a rich and costly culture. Decorative architecture, especially interior design, reflected the increasing sociability of the aristocracy. Entertainment became a central part of aristocratic life, losing its previous formality. Music became a cultural passion. The string quartet made its first appearance in the eighteenth century, and chamber music enjoyed unparalleled popularity. Only the wealthiest could afford to stage private operas, the other musical passion of the age. The Esterhazys of Hungary employed 22 musicians and a conductor, who for most of the late eighteenth century was Joseph Haydn (1732–1809), the father of the modern symphony. Haydn's post was not an honorary one. In addition to hiring and managing the orchestra, he was expected to direct two operas and two concerts a week, as well as the music for Sunday services. An aristocratic patron was essential for the aspiring composer. If he could not find one or if, like Wolfgang Amadeus Mozart (1756–1791), he could not bend his will to one, he could not flourish. While Haydn lived comfortably in a palace, Mozart, probably the greatest musical genius in Western history, lived impoverished in a garret and died at age 35 from lack of medical attention.

Musical entertainments in European country houses were matched by the literary and philosophical entertainments of the urban salons. Papers on scientific and literary subjects were read at gala dinner parties and discussed with great seriousness in drawing rooms. In the salons, most of which were organized by the wives and daughters of the nobility, were to be found the most influential thinkers of the day presenting the ideas of the Enlightenment, a new European outlook on religion, society, and politics.

The seven-year-old musical prodigy Wolfgang Amadeus Mozart plays the harpsichord while his father Leopold plays the violin and his sister Nannerl sings. The boy won great ovations on concert tours throughout Europe.

The Enlightenment

The Enlightenment was less a set of ideas than it was a set of attitudes. At its core was criticism, a questioning of traditional institutions, customs, and morals. In 1762, the French philosopher Jean-Jacques Rousseau (1712–1778) published one of the most important works on social theory, *The Social Contract,* which opened with the gripping maxim, "Man is born free and everywhere he is in chains." But most of the great thinkers of the Enlightenment were not so much philosophers as savants, knowledgeable popularizers whose skills were in simplifying and publicizing a hodgepodge of new views.

In France, Enlightenment intellectuals were called *philosophes* and claimed all the arts and sciences as their purview. The *Encyclopedia* (35 volumes, 1751–1780), edited by Denis Diderot (1713–1784), was one of the greatest achievements of the age. Titled *Systematic Dictionary of the Sciences, Arts, and Crafts,* it attempted to summarize all acquired knowledge and to dispel all imposed superstitions. There was no better definition of a philosophe than that given them by one of their enemies: "Just what is a philosophe? A kind of mon-

THE ALL-KNOWING

The Encyclopedia *was one of the great collaborative ventures of the new spirit of reason that so characterized the Enlightenment. Following is the* Encyclopedia's *entry on itself, the purpose of compiling human knowledge in book form.*

ENCYCLOPEDIA ... IN TRUTH, the aim of an *encyclopedia* is to collect all the knowledge scattered over the face of the earth, to present its general outlines and structure to the men with whom we live, and to transmit this to those who will come after us, so that the work of past centuries may be useful to the following centuries, that our children, by becoming more educated, may at the same time become more virtuous and happier, and that we may not die without having deserved well of the human race....

I have said that it could only belong to a philosophical age to attempt an *encyclopedia;* and I have said this because such a work constantly demands more intellectual daring than is commonly found in [less courageous periods]. All things must be examined, debated, investigated without exception and without regard for anyone's feelings.... We must ride roughshod over all these ancient puerilities, overturn the barriers that reason never erected, give back to the arts and sciences the liberty that is so precious to them.... We have for quite some time needed a reasoning age when men would no longer seek the rules in classical authors but in nature....

From Denis Diderot, *Encyclopedia* (1751–72).

ster in society who feels under no obligation towards its manners and morals, its proprieties, its politics, or its religion. One may expect anything from men of their ilk."

The influence of French counterculture on enlightened thought was great, but the Enlightenment was by no means a strictly French phenomenon. Its greatest figures included the Scottish economist Adam Smith (1723–1790), the Italian legal reformer Cesare Beccaria (1738–1794), and the German philosopher Immanuel Kant (1724–1804). In France, it began among anti-establishment critics; in Scotland and the German states, it flourished in the universities; in Prussia, Austria, and Russia, it was propagated by the monarchy. The Enlightenment began in the 1730s and was still going strong a half century later when its attitudes had been absorbed into the mainstream of European thought.

No brief summary can do justice to the diversity of enlightened thought in eighteenth-century Europe. Because it was an attitude of mind rather than a set of shared beliefs, there are many contradictory strains to follow. In his famous essay *What Is Enlightenment?* (1784), Immanuel Kant described it simply as freedom to use one's own intelligence. "I hear people clamor on all sides: Don't argue! The officer says: Don't argue, drill! The tax collector says: Don't argue, pay. The pastor says: Don't argue, believe." To all of them Kant replied: "Dare to know! Have the courage to use your own intelligence."

The Spirit of the Enlightenment

In 1734, there appeared in France a small book titled *Philosophical Letters Concerning the English Nation.* Its author, Voltaire (1694–1778), had spent two years in Britain, and while there he had made it his business to study the differences between the peoples of the two nations. In a simple but forceful style, Voltaire demonstrated time and again the superiority of the British. They practiced religious toleration and were not held under the sway of a venal clergy. They valued people for their merits rather than their birth. Their political constitution was a marvel: "The English nation is the only one on earth that has succeeded in controlling the power of kings by resisting them." They made national heroes of their scientists, poets, and philosophers. In all of this, Voltaire contrasted British virtue with French vice. He attacked the French clergy and nobility directly, the French monarchy implicitly. Not only did he praise the genius and accomplishments of Sir Isaac Newton above those of René Descartes, but he also graphically contrasted the Catholic church's persecution of Descartes with the British state's celebration of Newton. "England, where men think free and noble thoughts," Voltaire enthused.

The most famous of the philosophes, Voltaire sought to reinvent the universe of knowledge.

Voltaire. It is difficult to recapture the psychological impact that the *Philosophical Letters* had on the generation of educated Frenchmen who first read them. The book was officially banned and publicly burned, and a warrant was issued for Voltaire's arrest. The *Letters* dropped like a bombshell upon the moribund intellectual culture of the Church and the universities and burst open the complacent, self-satisfied Cartesian worldview. The book ignited in France a movement that would soon be found in nearly every corner of Europe.

Born in Paris in 1694 into a bourgeois family with court office, François-Marie Arouet, who later took the pen name Voltaire, was educated by the Jesuits, who encouraged his poetic talents and instilled in him an enduring love of literature. He was a difficult student, especially as he had already rejected the core of the Jesuits' religious doctrine. He was no less difficult as he grew older and began a career as a poet and playwright. It was not long before he was imprisoned in the Bastille for penning verses that maligned the honor of the regent of France. Released from prison, he insulted a nobleman, who retaliated by having his servants publicly beat Voltaire. Voltaire issued a challenge for a duel, a greater insult than the first, given his low birth. Again he was sent to the Bastille and was only released on the promise that he would leave the country immediately.

Thus Voltaire found himself in Britain, where he spent two years learning English, writing plays, and enjoying his celebrity free from the dangers that celebrity entailed in France. When he returned to Paris in 1728, it was with the intention of popularizing Britain to Frenchmen. He wrote and produced a number of plays and began writing the *Philosophical Letters,* a work that not only secured his reputation but also forced him into exile at the village of Cirey, where he moved in with the Marquise du Châtelet (1706–1749).

The Marquise du Châtelet, though only 27 at the time of her liaison with Voltaire, was one of the leading advocates of Newtonian science in France. She built a laboratory in her home and introduced Voltaire to experimental science. While she undertook the immense challenge of translating Newton into French, Voltaire worked on innumerable projects: poems, plays, philosophical and antireligious tracts (which she wisely kept him from publishing), and histories. It was one of the most productive periods of his life, and when the Marquise du Châtelet died in 1749, Voltaire was crushed.

Then older than 50, Voltaire began his travels. He was invited to Berlin by Frederick the Great, who admired him most of all the intellectuals of the age. The relationship between the two great egotists was predictably stormy and resulted in Voltaire's arrest in Frankfurt. Finally allowed to leave Prussia, Voltaire eventually settled in Geneva, where he quickly became embroiled in local politics and was none too politely asked to leave. He was tired of wandering and tired of being chased. His youthful gaiety and high spirits,

THE HUMAN CONDITION

More than anyone else, Voltaire symbolized the new thinking of the Enlightenment. Witty, ironic, irreverent, and penetrating, his writings provoked howls of protest and squeals of delight. Among the most widely read was his philosophical dictionary, from which this definition of evil is drawn.

PEOPLE CLAMOR THAT HUMAN NATURE IS ESSENTIALLY PERVERSE, that man is born the child of the devil, and of evil. Nothing is more ill-advised; for, my friend, in preaching at me that everybody is born perverse, you warn me that you were born that way, that I must distrust you as I would a fox or a crocodile.... It would be much more reasonable, much nobler, to say to me: "You were all born good; see how frightful it would be to corrupt the purity of your being." We should treat mankind as we should treat all men individually....

Man is not born evil; he becomes evil, as he becomes sick.... Gather together all the children of the universe; you will see in them nothing but innocence, gentleness, and fear....

If men were essentially evil, if they were all born the subjects of a being as malevolent as it is unhappy, who inspired them with all this frenzy to avenge his own torment, we would see husbands murdered by their wives, and fathers by their children every morning....

From Voltaire, *The Philosophical Dictionary* (1764).

which remained in Voltaire long past youth, were dealt a serious blow by the tragic earthquake in Lisbon in 1755, when thousands of people attending church services were killed.

Optimism in the face of such a senseless tragedy was no longer possible. His black mood was revealed in *Candide* (1759), which was to become his enduring legacy. *Candide* introduced the ivory-tower intellectual Dr. Pangloss, the overly optimistic Candide, and the very practical philosophy, "We must cultivate our own garden." It was Voltaire's capacity to challenge all authority that was probably his greatest contribution to Enlightenment attitudes. He held nothing sacred. He questioned his own paternity and the morals of his

During the Enlightenment, salons showcased the most influential thinkers of the day. Here, a lecture is being given at the house of Madame Geoffrin.

mother; he lived openly with the Marquise du Châtelet and her husband; and he spoke as slightingly of kings and aristocrats as he did of his numerous critics. At the height of the French Revolution, Voltaire's body was removed from its resting place in Champagne and taken in great pomp to Paris, where it was interred in the Panthéon, where the heroes of the nation were put to rest. "Voltaire taught us to be free" was the slogan that the Parisian masses chanted during the funeral procession. It was an ending perhaps too solemn and conventional for one as irreverent as Voltaire. When the monarchy was restored after 1815, his bones were unceremoniously dumped in a lime pit.

Hume and Montesquieu. Some enlightened thinkers based their critical outlook on skepticism, the belief that nothing could be known for certain. When the Scottish philosopher David Hume (1711–1776) was accused of being an atheist, he countered the charge by saying he was too skeptical to be certain that God did not exist. Hume's first major philosophical work, *A Treatise of Human Nature* (1739), made absolutely no impression upon his contemporaries. For a time he took a post as a merchant's clerk, then he served as a tutor, and finally he found a position as a private secretary. During the course of his various employments he continued to write, publishing a series of essays on the subject of morality and rewriting his treatise into *An Enquiry Concerning Human Understanding* (1748), his greatest philosophical work.

Scottish philosopher David Hume argued that neither matter nor mind could be proved to exist with any certainty.

Hume made two seminal contributions to Enlightenment thought. He exploded the synthesis of Descartes by arguing that neither matter nor mind could be proved to exist with any certainty. He believed that only perceptions existed, either as impressions of material objects or as ideas and if human understanding was based on sensory perception rather than on reason, then there could be no certainty in the universe. Hume's second point launched a frontal attack upon established religion: if there could be no certainty, then the revealed truths of Christian religion could have no basis. In his historical analysis of the origins of religion, Hume argued that "religion grows out of hope or fear." He attacked the core of Christian explanations based on either Providence or miracles by arguing that to anyone who understood the basis of human perception it would take a miracle to believe in miracles.

In 1749, Hume received in the mail a work from an admiring Frenchman, titled *The Spirit of the Laws*. The sender was Charles-Louis de Secondat, Baron Montesquieu (1689–1755). Born in Bordeaux, he ultimately inherited both a large landed estate and the office of president of the Parlement of Bordeaux. His novel *Persian Letters* (1721) was a brilliant satire of Parisian morals, French society, and European religion all bound together by the story of a Persian despot who leaves his harem to learn about the ways of the world. The use of the Persian outsider allowed Montesquieu to comment on the absurdity of European customs in general and French practices in particular. The device of the harem allowed him to titillate his audience with exotic sexuality.

After that success, Montesquieu decided to sell his office and make the grand tour. He spent nearly two years in England, for which, like Voltaire, he came to have the greatest admiration. Back in Bordeaux, Montesquieu began to assemble his thoughts for what

OF THE PEOPLE

Baron de Montesquieu's The Spirit of the Laws *(1750) was one of the most important political works of the Enlightenment. It analyzed the various forms of government and estimated their strengths and weaknesses. Montesquieu provided inspiration for the American Declaration of Independence and the Constitution.*

IN A DEMOCRACY THE PEOPLE ARE IN SOME RESPECTS THE SOVEREIGN, and in others the subject. There can be no exercise of sovereignty but by their suffrages, which are ... fundamental to this government. And indeed it is as important to regulate in a republic, in what manner, by whom, to whom, and concerning what suffrages are to be given, as it is in a monarchy to know who is the prince, and after what manner he ought to govern....

The people are extremely well qualified for choosing those whom they are to intrust with part of their authority.... They can tell when a person has fought many battles, and been crowned with success; ... They can tell when a judge is assiduous in his office, gives general satisfaction, and has never been charged with bribery.... But are they capable of conducting an intricate affair, of seizing and improving the opportunity and critical moment of action? No; this surpasses their abilities....

As most citizens have sufficient ability to choose, though unqualified to be chosen, so the people, though capable of calling others to an account for their administration, are incapable of conducting the administration themselves....

Again, there is no liberty if the judiciary power be not separated from the legislative and executive. Were it joined with the legislative, the life and liberty of the subject would be exposed to arbitrary control; for the judge would be then the legislator. Were it joined to the executive power the judge might behave with violence and oppression.

From Montesquieu, *The Spirit of the Laws.*

he believed would be a great work of political theory. The two societies that he most admired were ancient Rome and the then present-day Britain, and he studied the forms of their government and the principles that animated them. *The Spirit of the Laws* was published in 1748, and despite its gargantuan size and densely packed examples, it was immediately recognized as a masterpiece. Catherine the Great of Russia kept it at her bedside, and it was the single most influential work for the framers of the United States Constitution.

In both *Persian Letters* and *The Spirit of the Laws* Montesquieu explored how liberty could be achieved and despotism avoided. He divided all forms of government into republics, monarchies, and despotisms. Each form had its own peculiar spirit: virtue and moderation in republics, honor in monarchies, and fear in despotisms. Like each form, each spirit was prone to abuse and had to be restrained if republics were not to give way to vice and excess, monarchies to corruption, and despotisms to repression. Montesquieu classified regimes as either moderate or immoderate, and through the use of extensive historical examples attempted to demonstrate how moderation could be maintained through rules and restraints, through the spirit of the law.

For Montesquieu, a successful government was one in which powers were separated and checks and balances existed within the institutions of the state. As befit a provincial magistrate, he insisted on the absolute separation of the judiciary from all other branches of government. The law needed to be independent and impartial, and it needed to be just. Montesquieu advocated that law codes be reformed and reduced mainly to regulate crimes against persons and property. Punishment should fit the crime but should be humane. Montesquieu was one of the first to advocate the abolition of torture. Like most Europeans of his age, he saw monarchy as the only realistic form of government, but he argued that for a monarchy to be successful, it needed a strong and independent aristocracy to restrain its tendency toward corruption and despotism. He based his arguments on what he believed was the case in Britain, which he praised as the only state in Europe in which liberty resided.

Enlightened thinkers attacked established institutions, above all the Church. Most were deists who believed in the existence of God on rational grounds only. Following the materialistic ideas of the new science, deists believed that nature conformed to its own material laws and operated without divine intervention. God, in a popular Enlightenment image, was like a clockmaker who constructed the elaborate mechanism, wound it, and gave the pendulum its first swing. After that the clock worked by itself. Deists were accused of being anti-Christian, and they certainly opposed the ritual forms of both Catholic and Protestant worship. They also opposed the role of the Church in education, for education was the key to an enlightened view of the future. That meant, above all, conflict with the Jesuits. "Let's eat a Jesuit," was Voltaire's half-facetious comment.

The frontispiece from Montesquieu's The Spirit of the Laws *has a medallion of the author surrounded by allegorical figures, including the blind Justice. In the lower left corner are copies of the author's works.*

Rousseau and Locke. Jean-Jacques Rousseau attacked the educational system. His tract on education, disguised as the romantic novel *Émile* (1762), argued that children should be taught by appealing to their interests rather than with strict discipline. Education was crucial because the Enlightenment was dominated by the idea of the British philosopher John Locke (1632–1704) that the mind was blank at birth, a *tabula rasa*—"white paper void of all characters"—and that it was filled up by experience. Contrary to the arguments of Descartes, Locke wrote in *An Essay Concerning Human Understanding* (1690) that there were no innate ideas and no good or evil that was not conditioned by experience. For Locke, as for a host of thinkers after him, good and evil were defined as pleasure and pain: people did good because it was pleasurable and avoided evil because it was painful. Morality was a sense experience rather than a theological experience. It was also relative rather than absolute, an observation that derived from increased interest in non-European cultures. The *Persian Letters* of Baron Montesquieu was the most popular of a genre describing non-European societies that knew nothing of Christian morality.

By the middle of the eighteenth century, the pleasure/pain principle enunciated by Locke had come to be applied to the foundations of social organization. If personal good was pleasure, then social good was happiness. The object of government, in the words of the Scottish moral philosopher Francis Hutcheson (1694–1746), was "the greatest happiness of the greatest number." The principle was at the core of *Crimes and Punishments* (1764), Cesare Beccaria's pioneering work of legal reform. Laws were instituted to promote happiness within society. They had to be formulated equitably for both criminal and victim. Punishment was to act as a deterrent to crime rather than as retribution. Therefore, Beccaria advocated the abolition of torture to gain confessions, the end of capital punishment, and the rehabilitation of criminals through the improvement of penal institutions. By 1776, happiness was established as one of the basic rights of man, enshrined in the American Declaration of Independence as "life, liberty, and the pursuit of happiness."

It was in refashioning the world through education and social reform that the Enlightenment revealed its orientation toward the future. *Optimism* was a word invented in the eighteenth century to express the feel-

THE GOOD OF ALL

The Social Contract (1762) was one of the greatest visionary tracts of the eighteenth century. In it Jean-Jacques Rousseau envisioned a harmonious society capable of eliminating want and controlling evil. Here he discusses his famous idea of the general will.

AS LONG AS MEN UNITED TOGETHER look upon themselves as a single body, they have but one will relating to the common preservation and general welfare. Then all the energies of the state are vigorous and simple: its maxims are clear and luminous; there are no mixed contradictory interests; the common prosperity shows itself everywhere, and requires only good sense to be appreciated. Peace, union, and equality are enemies of political subtleties. Upright, honest men are difficult to deceive, because of their simplicity: decoys and pretexts do not impose upon them, they are not cunning enough to be dupes. When we see among the happiest people in the world troops of peasants regulating the affairs of state under an oak, and conducting themselves wisely, can we help despising the refinements of other nations, who make themselves illustrious and miserable with so much art and mystery?

From Jean-Jacques Rousseau, *The Social Contract.*

Jean-Jacques Rousseau produced one of the greatest works of the Enlightenment, The Social Contract *(1762) in which he envisioned a society capable of controlling evil.*

ing of liberation from the weight of centuries of traditions. "This is the best of all possible worlds and all things turn out for the best," was the satirical slogan of Voltaire's *Candide*. But if Voltaire believed that enlightened thinkers had taken optimism too far, others believed that it had to be taken further still.

Progress, an idea that not all enlightened thinkers shared, was another invention of the age. It was expressed most cogently by the French philosopher the Marquis de Condorcet (1743–1794) in *The Progress of the Human Mind* (1795), in which he developed an almost evolutionary view of human development from a savage state of nature to a future of harmony and international peace.

The Impact of the Enlightenment

As there was no single set of Enlightenment beliefs, so there was no single impact of the Enlightenment. Its general influence was felt everywhere, even seeping to the lowest strata of society. Its specific influence is harder to gauge. Paradoxically, enlightened political reform took firmer root in eastern Europe, where the ideas were imported, than in western Europe, where they originated. It was absolute rulers who were most successful in borrowing Enlightenment reforms.

It is impossible to determine what part enlightened ideas and what part practical necessities played in the eastern European reform movement that began around midcentury. In at least three areas, the coincidence between ideas and actions was especially strong: law, education, and the extension of religious toleration. Law was the basis of Enlightenment views of social interaction, and the influence of Montesquieu and Beccaria spread quickly. In Prussia and Russia, the movement to codify and simplify the legal system did not reach fruition in the eighteenth century, but in both places it was well under way. The Prussian jurist Samuel von Cocceji (1679–1755) initiated the reform of Prussian law and legal administration. Cocceji's project was to make the enforcement of law uniform throughout the realm, to prevent judicial corruption, and to produce a single code of Prussian law. The code, finally completed in the 1790s, reflected the principles of criminal justice articulated by Beccaria. In Russia, the Law Commission summoned by Catherine the Great in 1767 never completed its work. Nevertheless, profoundly influenced by Montesquieu, Catherine attempted to abolish torture and to introduce the Beccarian principle that the accused was innocent until proved guilty. In Austria, Joseph II presided over a wholesale reorganization of the legal system. Courts were centralized, laws codified, and torture and capital punishment abolished.

Enlightenment ideas also underlay the efforts to improve education in eastern Europe. The religious orders, especially the Jesuits, were the most influential educators of the age, and the Enlightenment attack upon them created a void that had to be filled by the state. Efforts at compulsory education were first undertaken in Russia under Peter the Great, but those were aimed at the compulsory education of the nobility. It was Catherine who extended the effort to the provinces, attempting to educate a generation of Russian teachers. She was especially eager that women receive primary schooling, although the prejudice against educating women was too strong to overcome. Austrian and Prussian reforms were more successful in extending the reach of primary education, even if its content remained weak.

Religious toleration was the area in which the Enlightenment had its greatest impact in Europe, though again it was in the eastern countries that it was most visible. Freedom of worship for Catholics was barely whispered about in Britain, while neither France nor Spain were moved to tolerate Protestants. Nevertheless, within those parameters there were some important changes in the religious makeup of the western European states. In Britain, Protestant dissenters were no longer persecuted for their beliefs. By the end of the eighteenth century, the number of Protestants outside the Church of England was growing; and by the early nineteenth century discrimination against Protestants was all but eliminated. In France and Spain, relations between the national church and the papacy were undergoing a reorientation. Both states were asserting more independence—both theologically and financially—from Rome. The shift was symbolized by disputes over the role of the Jesuits, who were finally expelled from France in 1764 and from Spain in 1767.

In eastern Europe, enlightened ideas about religious toleration did take effect. Catherine the Great abandoned persecution of a Russian Orthodox sect known as the Old Believers. Prussia had always tolerated various Protestant groups, and with the conquest of Silesia it acquired a large Catholic population. Catholics were guaranteed freedom of worship, and Frederick the Great even built a Catholic church in Berlin to symbolize the policy. Austria extended enlightened ideas about toleration the furthest. Maria Theresa was a devout Catholic and had actually increased religious persecution in her realm, but Joseph II rejected his mother's dogmatic position. In 1781, he issued the Patent of Toleration, which granted freedom of worship to Protestants and members of the Eastern Orthodox church. The following year he extended the toleration to Jews. Joseph's attitude toward toleration was as practical as it was enlightened. He believed that the revocation of the Edict of Nantes—which had granted limited toleration to Protestants—at the end of the seventeenth century had been an economic disaster for France, and he encouraged religious toleration as a means to economic progress.

A science of economics was first articulated during the Enlightenment. A group of French thinkers known as the Physiocrats subscribed to the view that land was wealth and thus argued that agricultural activity, especially improved means of farming and livestock breeding, should take first priority in state reforms. As wealth came from land, taxation should be based only on land ownership, a principle that was coming into increased prominence despite the opposition of the landowning class. Physiocratic ideas combined a belief in the sanctity of private property with the need for the state to increase agricultural output. Ultimately the Physiocrats, like the great Scottish economic theorist Adam Smith, came to believe that government should cease to interfere with private economic activity. They articulated the doctrine *Laissez faire, laissez passer*—"Let it be, let it go." The ideas of Adam Smith and the Physiocrats ultimately formed the basis for nineteenth-century economic reform.

CHRONOLOGY

Major Works of the Enlightenment

1690	*An Essay Concerning Human Understanding* (Locke)
1721	*Persian Letters* (Baron Montesquieu)
1734	*Philosophical Letters Concerning the English Nation* (Voltaire)
1739	*A Treatise of Human Nature* (Hume)
1740	*Pamela* (Richardson)
1748	*An Enquiry Concerning Human Understanding* (Hume); *The Spirit of the Laws* (Baron Montesquieu)
1751–1780	*Encyclopedia* (Diderot)
1759	*Candide* (Voltaire)
1762	*Émile; The Social Contract* (Rousseau)
1764	*Crimes and Punishments* (Beccaria)
1784	*What Is Enlightenment?* (Kant)
1795	*The Progress of the Human Mind* (Marquis de Condorcet)
1798	*An Essay on the Principles of Population* (Malthus)

If the Enlightenment did not initiate a new era, it did offer a new vision, whether in Hume's psychology, Montesquieu's political science, Rousseau's sociology, or Smith's economic theory. All of the subjects, which have such a powerful impact on contemporary life, had their modern origins in the Enlightenment. As the British poet Alexander Pope (1688–1744) put it: "Know then thyself, presume not God to scan/ The proper study of mankind is man." Enlightened thinkers challenged existing ideas and existing institutions. A new emphasis on self and on pleasure led to a new emphasis on happiness. All three fed into the distinctively Enlightenment idea of self-interest. Happiness and self-interest were values that would inevitably corrode the old social order, which was based upon principles of self-sacrifice and corporate identity. It was only a matter of time.

EIGHTEENTH-CENTURY SOCIETY

Eighteenth-century society was a hybrid of old and new. It remained highly stratified socially, politically, and economically. Birth and occupation determined wealth, privilege, and quality of life as much as they had in the past. But in the eighteenth century the gulf between top and bottom was being filled by a thriving middle class, a *bourgeoisie*, as they were called in France. There were now more paths toward the middle and upper classes, more wealth to be distributed among those above the level of subsistence. It was bourgeois culture and bourgeois values that were new in the eighteenth century. At the bottom of society, poverty still gripped the mass of European people. Changes in agriculture allowed more to survive than ever before, but their survival was still perilous, dependent upon chance rather than effort.

The Nobility

Nobles were defined by their legal rights. They had the right to bear arms, the right to special judicial treatment, the right to tax exemptions. In Russia, only nobles could own serfs; in Poland, only nobles could hold government office. In France and Britain, the highest court positions were always reserved for noblemen. Nobles dominated the Prussian army. In 1786, out of nearly 700 senior officers only 22 were not noblemen. The Spanish nobility claimed the right to live idly. Rich or poor, they shunned all labor as a right of their heritage. Swedish and Hungarian noblemen had their own legislative chambers, just as the British had the House of Lords. Noble privilege was as vibrant as ever.

Although all who enjoyed the special rights were noble, not all nobles were equal. In many states, the noble order was subdivided into easily identifiable groups. The Spanish grandees, the upper nobility, numbered in the thousands; the Spanish hidalgos, the lower nobility, in the hundreds of thousands. In Hungary, out of 400,000 noblemen only about 15,000 belonged to the landed nobility, who held titles and were exempt from taxes. The landed nobility were personally members of the upper chamber of the Hungarian Diet, while the lesser nobility sent representatives to the lower chamber.

The situation was similar in England, where the elite class was divided between the peerage and the gentry. The peerage held titles, were members of the House of Lords, and had a limited range of judicial and fiscal privileges. In the mid-eighteenth century, there were only 190 British peers. The gentry, which numbered more than 20,000, dominated the House of Commons and local legal offices but were not strictly members of the nobility. The French nobility was informally distinguished among the small group of

European artists often created allegorical paintings contrasting "civilized" Europe with "savage" America. In this work, by Italian artist Giovanni Battista Tiepolo, the figure of America is adorned with gold and feathers and riding on the back of an alligator. She receives tributes of stags, bundles of brazil wood, and ripe fruit. In the right foreground, a pile of severed heads pierced with arrows recalls America's savage heritage.

peers known as the Grandes, whose ancient lineage, wealth, and power set them apart from all others; a rather larger service nobility whose privileges derived in one way or another from municipal or judicial service; and what might be called the country nobility, whose small estates and local outlook made their fiscal immunities vital to their survival.

The distinctions among the nobilities of the European states masked a more important one: wealth. As the saying went, "All who were truly noble were not wealthy, but all who were truly wealthy were noble." In the eighteenth century, despite the phenomenal increase in mercantile activity, wealth was still calculated in profits from the ownership of land, and it was the wealthy landed nobility who set the tone of elite life in Europe.

Eighteenth-century Europe was a society of orders gradually transforming itself into a society of classes. At the top, as vigorous as ever, was the nobility, the privileged order in every European state. In different parts of Europe the nobility used different methods to maintain their land-based wealth. In places such as Britain, Spain, Austria, and Hungary, forms of entail were the rule. In simple terms, an entail was a restriction prohibiting the breakup of a landed estate either through sale or inheritance. The owner of the estate was merely a caretaker for his heir, and while he could add land, he could not easily subtract any. Entailed estates grew larger and larger and, like magnets, attracted other entailed estates through marriage. In Britain, where primogeniture—inheritance by the eldest son—accompanied entail, 400 families owned one-quarter of the entire country. Yet the concentration of landed wealth paled into insignificance when compared to the situation in Spain, where just four families owned one-third of all the cultivable land. In the east, where land was plentiful, the Esterhazys of Hungary and the Radziwills of Poland owned millions of acres.

The second method by which the European nobility ensured that the wealthy would be noble was by absorption. There were several avenues to upward mobility, but by the eighteenth century the holding of state offices was the most common. In France, for example, a large number of offices were reserved for the nobility. Many of those were owned by their holders and passed on to their children, but occasionally an office was sold on the market and the new holder was automatically ennobled. The office of royal secretary was one of the most common routes to noble status. The number of secretaries increased from 300 to 900 during the course of the eighteenth century, yet despite the dilution the value of the offices continued to skyrocket. An office that was worth 70,000 French pounds at the beginning of the century was worth 300,000 by the 1780s. In fact, in most European societies there was more room for new nobles than there were aspiring candidates because of the costs that maintaining the new status imposed. In Britain, anyone who could live like a gentleman was accounted one. But the practice of entail made it very difficult for a newcomer to purchase the requisite amount of land. Philip V increased the number of Spanish grandees in an effort to dilute their power, yet when he placed a tax on entrance into the lower nobility, the number of hidalgos dropped precipitously.

For the wealthy, aristocracy was becoming an international status. The influence of Louis XIV and the court of Versailles lasted for more than a century and spread to town and country life. Most nobles maintained multiple residences. The new style of aristocratic entertainment required more public space on the first floor, while the increasing demand for personal and familial privacy necessitated more space in the upper stories. The result was larger and more opulent homes. There the British elite led all others. More than 150 country houses were built in the early eighteenth century alone, including Blenheim Palace, which was built for John Churchill, duke of Marlborough, at a cost of £300,000. To the expense of architecture was added the expense of decoration. New materials such as West Indian mahogany occasioned new styles, and both drove up costs. The high-quality woodwork and plastering made fashionable by the English Adam brothers was quickly imitated on the Continent. Only the Spanish nobility shunned country estates, preferring to reside permanently in towns.

The building of country houses was only one part of the conspicuous consumption of the privileged orders. Improvements in travel, both in transport and roads, permitted increased contact between members of the national elites. The stagecoach linked towns, and canals linked waterways. Both made travel quicker and more enjoyable. The grand tour of historical sites continued to be used as a substitute for formal education. Young men would pass from country house to country house buying up antiquities, paintings, and books along the way. The grand tour was a means of introducing the European aristocracies to each other, and also a means of communicating taste and fashion among them. Whether it was a Russian noble in Germany, a Swede in Italy, or a Briton in Prussia, all spoke French and shared a cultural outlook.

Much of that outlook was cultivated in the salons, a social institution begun in the seventeenth century by French women that gradually spread throughout the Continent. In the salons, especially those in Paris, the aristocracy and bourgeoisie mingled with the leading intellectuals of the age. There wit and insight replaced polite conversation. At formal meetings, papers on scientific or philosophical topics were read and discussed. At informal gatherings, new ideas were examined and exchanged. The British ambassador to Spain was appalled to discover that men and women were still kept separate in the salons of Madrid and that there was no serious conversation during evenings out. It was in the salons that the impact of the Enlightenment, the great European intellectual movement of the eighteenth century, first made itself felt.

The Bourgeoisie

Bourgeois is a French word, and it carried the same tone of derision in the eighteenth century that it does today. The bourgeois was a man on the make, scrambling after money or office or title. He was neither wellborn nor well-bred, or so said the nobility. Yet the bourgeoisie served vital functions in all European societies. They dominated trade, both nationally and internationally. They made their homes in cities and did much to improve the quality of urban life. They were the civilizing influence in urban culture, for unlike the nobility, they were the city's permanent denizens. Perhaps most importantly, the bourgeoisie provided the safety valve between the nobility and those who were acquiring wealth and power but lacked the advantages of birth and position. By developing their own culture and class identity, the bourgeoisie provided successful individuals with their own sense of pride and achievement and eased the explosive buildup of social resentments.

During the eighteenth century, the bourgeoisie grew both in numbers and importance. An active commercial and urban life gave many members of the group new social and political opportunities, and many of them passed into the nobility through the purchase of land or office. But for those whose aspirations or abilities were different, the social group began to define its own values, which centered on the family and the home. A new interest in domestic affairs touched both men and women of the European bourgeoisie. Their homes became social centers for kin and neighbors, and their outlook on family life reflected new personal relationships. Marriages were made for companionship as much as for economic advantage. Romantic love between husbands and wives was newly valued. So were children, whose futures came to dominate familial concern. Childhood was recognized as a separate stage of life and the education of children as one of the most important of all parental responsibilities. The image of the affectionate father replaced that of the hard-bitten businessman; the image of the doting mother replaced that of the domestic drudge.

Urban Elites. In the society of orders, nobility was the acid test. The world was divided into the small number of those who had it and the large number of those who did not. At the apex of the non-noble pyramid was the bourgeoisie, the elites of urban Europe whose place in the society of orders was ambiguous. *Bourgeois,* or *burgher,* simply meant "town dweller," but as a social group it had come to mean wealthy town dweller. The bourgeoisie was strongest where towns were strongest: in western rather than in eastern Europe and in northern rather than southern Europe, with the notable exception of Italy. Holland was the exemplar of a bourgeois republic. More than half of the Dutch population lived in towns, and there was no significant aristocratic class to compete for power. The Regents of Amsterdam were the equivalent of a European court nobility in wealth, power, and prestige, though not in the way in which they had accumulated their fortunes. The size of the bourgeoisie in various European states cannot be determined absolutely. At the end of the eighteenth century, the British middle classes probably constituted around 15 percent of the population, the French bourgeoisie less than 10 percent. By contrast, the Russian or Hungarian urban elites were less than 2 percent of the population in those states.

Like the nobility, the bourgeoisie constituted a diverse group. At the top were great commercial families engaged in the expanding international marketplace and reaping the profits of trade. In wealth and power they were barely distinguishable from the nobility. At the bottom were the so-called petite bourgeoisie: shopkeepers, artisans, and small manufacturers. The solid core of the bourgeoisie was employed in trade, exchange, and service. Most were engaged in local or national commerce. Trade was the lifeblood of the city, for by itself the city could neither feed nor clothe its inhabitants. Most bourgeois fortunes were first acquired in trade. Finance was the natural outgrowth

This dining room from Landsdowne House in London is one of the finest examples of Robert Adam's style. Characteristic of Adam's style are the vases, trophies of arms, leaf garlands, sprays, rosettes, scrolls, and fan-shaped motifs cast in plaster adorning the room.

of commerce, and another segment of the bourgeoisie accumulated or preserved their capital through the sophisticated financial instruments of the eighteenth century. While the very wealthy loaned directly to the central government or bought shares in overseas trading companies, most bourgeois participated in government credit markets. They purchased state bonds or lifetime annuities and lived on the interest. The costs of war flooded the urban credit markets with high-yielding and generally stable financial instruments. Finally, the bourgeoisie were members of the burgeoning professions that provided services for the rich. Medicine, law, education, and the bureaucracy were all bourgeois professions, for the cost of acquiring the necessary skills could be borne only by those already wealthy.

During the course of the eighteenth century, the combination of occupational groups was expanding, both in numbers and in importance, all over Europe. So was the bourgeois habitat. The urbanization of Europe continued steadily throughout the eighteenth century. A greater percentage of the European population were living in towns, and a greater percentage were living in large towns of more than 10,000 inhabitants, which, of necessity, were developing complex socioeconomic structures. In France alone there were probably more than a hundred such towns, each requiring the services of the bourgeoisie and providing opportunities for their expansion. And the larger the metropolis, the greater the need. In 1600, only 20 European cities contained as many as 50,000 people; in 1700, that number had risen to 32, and by 1800 it reached 48. During the course of the eighteenth century, the number of cities with 75,000 inhabitants doubled. London, the largest city, had grown to 865,000, a remarkable feat considering that in 1665 more than one-quarter of the London population had died in the Great Plague. In such cities the demand for lawyers, doctors, merchants, and shopkeepers was almost insatiable.

Besides wealth, the urban bourgeoisie shared another characteristic: mobility. The aspiration of the bourgeoisie was to become noble, either through office or by acquiring rural estates. In Britain, a gentleman

The Dutton Family *by John Zoffany. This eighteenth-century painting shows the comforts enjoyed by the British upper middle class.*

was still defined by lifestyle: "All are accounted gentlemen in England who maintain themselves without manual labor." Many trading families left their wharves and countinghouses to acquire rural estates, live off rents, and practice the openhanded hospitality of gentlemen. In France and Spain, nobility could still be purchased, though the price was constantly going up. For the greater bourgeoisie, the transition was easy; for the lesser, the failure to move up was all the more frustrating for being just beyond their grasp. The bourgeoisie did not only imagine their discomfort, they were made to feel it at every turn. They were the butt of jokes, theater, and popular songs. They were the first victims in the shady financial dealings of crown and court, the first casualties in urban riots. Despised from above and envied from below, the bourgeoisie were uncomfortable with their present yet profoundly conservative about their future. The one consolation to their perpetual misery was that as a group they became richer and richer. And as a group they began to develop a distinctive culture that reflected their qualities and aspirations.

Bourgeois Values. Many bourgeoisie viewed their condition as temporary and accepted the pejorative connotations of the word *bourgeois*. They had little desire to defend a social group out of which they fervently longed to pass. Others, whose aspirations were lower, were nevertheless uncomfortable with the status that they had already achieved. They had no ambition to wear the silks and furs reserved for the nobility or to attend the opening night at the opera decked in jewels and finery. In fact, such ostentation was alien to their existence and to the success that they had achieved. There was a real tension between the values of noble and bourgeois. The ideal noble was idle, wasteful, and ostentatious; the ideal bourgeois was industrious, frugal, and sober. Voltaire, who made his fortune as a financial speculator rather than as a man of letters, aped the lifestyle of the nobility. But he could never allow himself to be cheated by a tradesman, a mark of his origins. When Louis XVI tried to make household economies in the wake of a financial crisis, critics said that he acted "like a bourgeois."

Even if the bourgeoisie did not constitute a class, they did share certain attitudes that constituted a culture. The wealthy among them participated in the new world of consumption, whether they did so lavishly or frugally. For those who aspired to more than their birth allowed, there was a loosening of the strict codes of dress that reserved certain fabrics, decorative materials, and styles to the nobility. Merchants and bankers could now be seen in colored suits or with piping made of cloth of gold; their wives could be seen in furs and silks. They might acquire silverware, even if they did not go so far as the nobility and have a coat of arms engraved upon it. Coaches and carriages were also becoming common among the bourgeoisie, to take them on the Sunday rides through the town gardens or to their weekend retreats in the suburbs. Parisian merchants, even master craftsmen such as clockmakers, were acquiring suburban homes, although they could not afford to retire to them for the summer months.

But more and more, the bourgeoisie was beginning to travel. In Britain, whole towns were established to cater to leisure travelers. The southwestern town of Bath, which was rebuilt in the eighteenth century, was the most popular of all European resort towns, famous since Roman times for the soothing qualities of its waters. Bath was soon a social center as notable for its marriage market as for its recreations. Brighton, a seaside resort on the south coast, quadrupled in size in the second half of the eighteenth century. Bathing—what we would call swimming—either for health or recreation, became a middle-class fad, displacing traditional fear of the sea.

Leisure and Entertainment. The leisure that wealth bestowed on the bourgeoisie, in good bourgeois fashion, quickly became commercialized. Theater and music halls for both light and serious productions proliferated. By the 1760s, an actual theater district had arisen in London and was attracting audiences of more than 20,000 a week. London was unusual, both for its size and for the number of well-to-do visitors who patronized its cultural events. The size of the London audiences enabled the German-born composer Georg Friedrich Handel (1685–1759) to earn a handsome living by performing and directing concerts. He was one of the few musicians in the eighteenth century to live without noble patronage. But it was not only in Britain that theater and music flourished. Voltaire's plays were performed before packed houses in Paris, with the author himself frequently in attendance to bask in the adulation of the largely bourgeois audiences who attended them. In Venice, it was estimated that more than 1200 operas were produced in the eighteenth century. Rome and Milan were even better known, and Naples was the center for Italian opera. Public concerts were a mark of bourgeois culture, for

L'Amour au Théâtre Français (Love in the French Theater) *(ca. 1716), by Antoine Watteau. The painting is thought to portray a scene from* Les Fêtes de l'Amour et de Bacchus, *a comic opera composed in 1672.*

the court nobility was entertained at the royal palaces or great country houses. Public concerts began in Hamburg in the 1720s, and Frederick the Great helped establish the Berlin Opera House some decades later.

Theater and concert going were part of the new attitude toward socializing that was one of the greatest contributions of the Enlightenment. Enlightened thinkers spread their views in the salons, and the salons soon spawned the academies, local scientific societies that, though led and patronized by provincial nobles, included large numbers of bourgeois members. The academies sponsored essay competitions, built up libraries, and became the local centers for intellectual interchange. A less structured form of sociability took place in the coffeehouses and tearooms that came to be a feature of even small provincial towns. In the early eighteenth century, there were more than 2000 London coffee shops where men—for the coffeehouse was largely a male preserve—could talk politics, read the latest newspapers and magazines, and indulge their taste for this still-exotic beverage. More exclusive clubs were also a form of middle-class sociability, some centering on political issues, some (such as the chambers of commerce) centering on professional interests. Parisian clubs, called *sociétés,* covered a multitude of diverse interests. Literary sociétés were the most popular, maintaining their purpose by forbidding drinking, eating, and gambling on their premises.

Above all, bourgeois culture was literate culture. Wealth and leisure led to mental pursuits—if not always to intellectual ones. The proliferation of relatively cheap printed material had an enormous impact on the lives of those who were able to afford it. Holland and Britain were the most literate European societies and also, because of the absence of censorship, the centers of European printing.

It was the first great period of the newspaper and the magazine. The first daily newspaper appeared in London in 1702; 80 years later, 37 provincial towns had their own newspapers, while the London papers were read all over Britain. Then as now, the newspaper was as much a vehicle for advertisement as for news. News reports tended to be bland, avoiding controversy and concentrating on general national and international events. Advertising, on the other hand, tended to be lurid, promising cures for incurable ills and the most exquisite commodities at the most reasonable prices.

For entertainment and serious political commentary, the British reading public turned to magazines, of which there were more than 150 separate titles by the 1780s. The most famous were *The Spectator,* which ran in the early part of the century and did much to set the tone for a cultured middle-class life, and *The Gentleman's Magazine,* which ran in midcentury and was said to have had a circulation of nearly 15,000. The longest-lived of all British magazines was *The Ladies' Diary,* which continued in existence from 1704 to 1871 and doled out self-improvement, practical advice, and fictional romances in equal proportion.

The Ladies' Diary was not the only literature aimed at the growing number of leisured and lettered bourgeois women. Although enlightened thinkers could be ambivalent about the place of women in the new social order, they generally stressed the importance of female education and welcomed women's participation in intellectual pursuits. Whether it was new ideas about women or simply the fact that more women had leisure, a growing body of both domestic literature and light entertainment was available to them. The literature included a vast number of teach-yourself books aimed at instructing women how best to organize domestic life and how to navigate the perils of polite society. Moral instruction, particularly on the themes of obedience and sexual fidelity, was also popular. But the greatest output directed toward women was in the form of fanciful romances, from which a new genre emerged. The novel first appeared in its modern form in the 1740s. Samuel Richardson (1689–1761) wrote *Pamela* (1740), the story of a servant girl who successfully resisted the advances of her master until he finally married her. It was composed in long episodes, or chapters, that developed Pamela's character and told her story at the expense of the overt moral message that was Richardson's original intention. Richardson's novels were printed in installments and helped to drive up the circulation of national magazines.

Family Life. While the public life of the bourgeoisie can be measured in the sociability of the coffeehouse and the academy, private life must be measured in the home. There a remarkable transformation was under way, one that the bourgeoisie shared with the nobility. In the pursuit of happiness encouraged by the Enlightenment, one of the newest joys was domesticity. The image—and sometimes the reality—of the happy home, where love was the bond between husband and wife and care the bond between parents and children, came to dominate both the literary and visual arts. Only those wealthy enough to afford to dispense with women's work could partake of the new domesticity; only those touched by Enlightenment ideas could attempt to make the change. But where it occurred, the transformation in the nature of family life was one of the most profound alterations in eighteenth-century culture.

The first step toward the transformation of family relationships was in centering the conjugal family in the home. In the past, the family was a less important structure for most people than the social groups to which they belonged or the neighborhood in which they lived. Marriage was an economic partnership and a means to carry on lineage. Individual fulfillment was not an object of marriage, and that attitude could be seen among the elites in the great number of arranged marriages, the speed with which surviving spouses remarried, and the formal and often brutal personal relationships between husbands and wives.

Patriarchy was the dominant value within the family. Husbands ruled over wives and children, making all of the crucial decisions that affected both the quality of their lives and their futures. As late as the middle of the eighteenth century, a British judge established the "rule of thumb," which asserted that a husband had a legal right to beat his wife with a stick, but the stick should be no thicker than a man's thumb. It was believed that children were stained with the sin of Adam at birth and that only the severest upbringing could clean some of it away. In nearly 200 child-rearing advice books published in England before the middle of the eighteenth century, only three did not advise the beating of children. John Wesley (1703–1791), the founder of Methodism, remembered his own mother's dictum that "children should learn to fear the rod and cry softly." Children were sent out first for wet-nursing; then at around the age of seven for boarding, either at school or in a trade; and finally into their own marriages.

There can be no doubt that the profile of family life began to change, especially in western Europe, during the second half of the eighteenth century. Although the economic elements of marriage remained strong—newspapers actually advertised the availability of partners and the dowries or annual income that they would bring to the marriage—other elements appeared. Fed

This writing desk, designed by Jean-Francois Oeben, who was appointed cabinetmaker to Louis XV of France in 1754, features the intricate pictorial marquetry and elaborate ormolu (a brass imitation of gold) that are characteristic of French Rococo style.

by an unending stream of stories and novels and a new desire for individual happiness, romantic and sexual attraction developed into a factor in marriage. Potential marriage partners were no longer kept away from each other or smothered by chaperons. The social season of polite society, in which prospective partners could dance, dine, and converse with each other to determine compatibility, gave greater latitude to courtship. Perhaps more importantly, the role of potential spouses in choosing a partner appears to have increased. That was a subtle matter, for even in earlier centuries parents did not simply assign a spouse to their children. But by the eighteenth century, adolescents themselves searched for their own marriage partners and exercised a strong negative voice in identifying unsuitable ones.

Companionate Marriage. The quest for compatibility, no less than the quest for romantic love, led to a change in personal relationships between spouses. The extreme formality of the past was gradually breaking down. Husbands and wives began spending more time with each other, developing common interests and pastimes. Their personal life began to change. For the first time, houses were built to afford a couple privacy from their children, servants, and guests. Rooms were designed for specific functions and were set off by hallways. Corridors were an important innovation in creating privacy. In earlier architecture, one walked through a room to the next one behind it. In new design, rooms were separated and doors could be closed, which allowed for an intimate life that earlier generations did not find necessary and that they could not, in any case, have put into practice.

Couples had more time for each other because they were beginning to limit the size of their families. There were a number of reasons for that development, which again pertained only to the upper classes. For one thing, child mortality rates were declining among wealthy social groups. Virulent epidemic diseases such as the plague, which knew no class lines, were gradually disappearing. Moreover, though there were few medical breakthroughs in the period, sanitation was improving. Bearing fewer children had an enormous impact on the lives of women, reducing the danger of death and disablement in childbirth and giving them leisure time to pursue domestic tasks. However, that did not mean that the early part of a woman's marriage was not dominated by children; in fact, because of new attitudes toward child-rearing it may have been dominated more than ever by children. Many couples appear to have made a conscious decision to space births, though success was limited by the fact that the most common technique of birth control was coitus interruptus, or withdrawal.

The transformation in the quality of relationships between spouses was mirrored by an even greater transformation in attitudes toward children. There were many reasons why childhood now took on a new importance. Decline in mortality rates had a profound psychological impact. Parents could feel that their emotional investment in their children had a greater chance of fulfillment. But equally important were the new ideas about education, especially Locke's belief that the child enters the world a blank slate whose personality is created through early education. That view not only placed a new responsibility on parents but also gave them the concept of childhood as a stage through which individuals passed. The idea could be seen in the commercial sphere as well as in any other. In 1700, there was not a single shop in London that sold children's toys exclusively; by the 1780s, there were toy shops everywhere, three of which sold nothing but rocking horses. Children's toys abounded: soldiers and forts, dolls and dollhouses. The jigsaw puzzle was invented in the 1760s as a way to teach children geography. There were also shops that sold nothing but clothes specifically designed for children, no longer simply adult clothes in miniature.

Most important of all was the development of materials for the education of children, which took place in two stages. At first, so-called children's books were books whose purpose was to help adults teach children. Later came books directed at children themselves, with large print, entertaining illustrations, and nonsensical characters, usually animals who taught moral lessons. In Britain, the Little Pretty Pocket Book series, created by John Newbery (1713–1767), not only encompassed educational primers but also included books for the entertainment of the child. Newbery published a Mother Goose book of nursery rhymes and created the immortal character of Miss Goody Two-Shoes. Instruction and entertainment also lay behind the development of children's playing cards, in which the French specialized. Dice games, such as one in which a child made a journey across Europe, combined geographical instruction with the amusement of competition.

The commercialization of childhood was, of course, directed at adults. The new books and games that were designed to enhance a child's education not only had to be purchased by parents but had to be used by them as well. More and more mothers were devoting their time

The Snatched Kiss, *or* The Stolen Kiss *(1750s), by Jean-Honoré Fragonard, was one of the "series paintings" popular in the late eighteenth century. A later canvas entitled* The Marriage Contract *shows the next step in the lives of the lovers.*

to their children. Among the upper classes, the practice of wet-nursing began to decline. Mothers wanted to nurture their infants—both literally, by breast-feeding, and figuratively, by teaching them. Children became companions to be taken on outings to the increasing number of museums or shows of curiosities, which began to discount children's tickets by the middle of the century.

The preconditions of the transformation of family life could not be shared by the population at large. Working women could afford neither the cost of instructional materials for their children nor the time to use them. Ironically, they now began using wet nurses, once the privilege of the wealthy, for increasingly a working woman's labor was the margin of survival for her family. Working women enjoyed no privacy in the hovels in which they lived, with large families in single rooms. Wives and children were still beaten by husbands and fathers and were unacquainted with enlightened ideas of the worth of the individual and the innocence of the child. By the end of the eighteenth century, two distinct family cultures coexisted in Europe: one based on companionate marriage and the affective bonds of parents and children; the other based on patriarchal dominance and the family as an economic unit.

The Masses

The paradox of the eighteenth century was that for the masses, life was getting better by getting worse. More Europeans were surviving than ever before, and more food was available to feed them; there was more housing, better sanitation, and even better charities. Yet for all of this, there was more misery. Those who would have succumbed to disease or starvation a century before now survived from day to day, beneficiaries—or victims—of increased farm production and improved agricultural marketing. The market economy organized a more effective use of land, but it created a widespread social problem. The landless agrarian laborer of the eighteenth century was the counterpart of the sturdy sixteenth-century beggar, capable of working but incapable of finding work. In the cities, the plight of the poor was as desperate as ever. Men and women sold their labor or their bodies for a pittance, while beggars slept at every doorway. Even the most openhearted charitable institutions were unable to cope with the massive increase in the poor. By the thousands, mothers abandoned their children to the foundling hospitals, where it was believed they would have a better chance of survival, even though hospital death rates were nearly 80 percent.

Jean Baptiste Greuze (1725–1805), Broken Eggs. *French artist Greuze studied in Lyon and Paris but was deeply influenced by Dutch genre painting. Greuze's depictions of village life are in marked contrast to the extravagant Rococo style of his contemporaries.*

Giving Birth in the Eighteenth Century

"IN SORROW THOU SHALT BRING FORTH CHILDREN." Such was Eve's punishment for eating of the forbidden tree, and that sorrow continued for numberless generations. Childbirth was painful, dangerous, and all too often deadly. Although successful childbirth needed no outside intervention, without the accumulated wisdom of the ages, babies and mothers routinely perished. The wisdom was passed from mother to daughter and finally was collected by skilled women who practiced the craft of midwifery. Every village, no matter how small, had women who were capable of assisting others in childbirth. Midwives' skills ranged widely, from the use of herbal potions and strong drink to ease the pain of labor to a rudimentary understanding of how to assist a complicated delivery when the fetus was not in the proper position.

Midwives, who until the late seventeenth century were always women, were part of the support group that attended a woman during her labor. Typically, childbirth was a social occasion. Along with the midwife would be a wet nurse and female kin and neighbors, who would offer encouragement, bring refreshments, and tend to the chores that the pregnant woman would have performed herself. Without chemicals to induce contractions and without the ability to intervene in the delivery, labor was usually long. Ordinarily, it did not take place in bed, but rather in a room or a part of a room that had been set aside for the occasion. By the eighteenth century, at least in larger urban areas, poor women who had no separate space for labor could give birth in lying-in hospitals. Within the birthing room, the conclave of women was much like a social gathering. The pregnant woman was advised to adopt any position that made her feel comfortable; standing and walking were favored in the belief that the effects of gravity helped the baby move downward. The woman might sit on a neighbor's lap or on a birthing stool, a chair open at the bottom, during contractions and delivery.

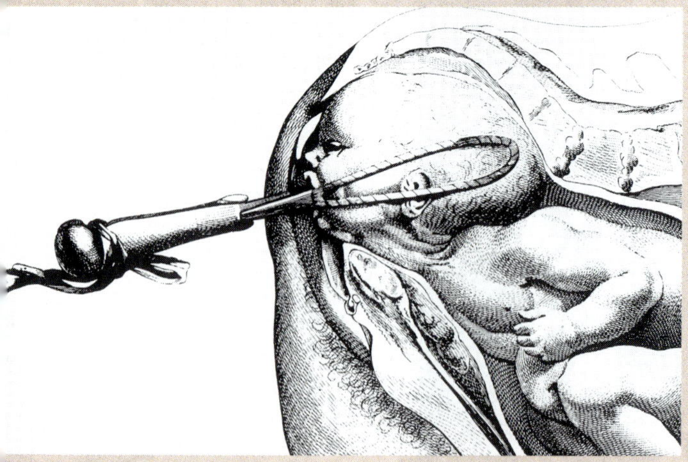

Most midwives subscribed to the philosophy of letting nature take its course. Because the difficulties and length of labor differed markedly from woman to woman, the midwife's most important contribution was to offer comfort and reassurance based on her long experience. By the seventeenth century, manuals for midwives were being published, some of them written by women, but most by male doctors with surgical experience. Midwives and doctors were always at daggers drawn. Trained physicians increasingly saw childbirth as a process that could be improved by the application of new medical knowledge, but as childbirth was a female experience, midwives jealously guarded their role in it. No matter how skilled they were, they were denied access to medical training that might have enabled them to develop lucrative practices on their own. Thus they had no intention of letting male doctors into their trade. For a time, the compromise was the handbooks, which contained guides to anatomy, descriptions of the most common complications, and the direst warnings to call trained physicians when serious problems arose.

By the beginning of the eighteenth century, the "man-midwife" had made his appearance in western Europe. Medically trained and usually experienced in other forms of surgery, the emergence of the man-midwife led to a number of breakthroughs in increasing the safety of childbirth. There can be no question that more mothers and children survived as a result of the man-midwives' knowledge and skills. But at the same time, the social experience of childbirth changed dramatically. What had been a female rite of passage, experienced by and with other women, now became a private event experienced by an individual woman and her male doctor. As female midwives were still excluded from medical training and licensing, their ability to practice their trade eroded in the face of new techniques and information to which they were denied access.

Although most man-midwives trained in hospitals where the poor came to give birth, they practiced among the rich. New attitudes toward marriage and children made the pain and danger of childbirth less acceptable to husbands, who sought every remedy they could afford. British and French man-midwives made fortunes practicing their trade. Their first task was to ascertain that the fetus was in the proper position to descend. In order to do this, however, they had to make an examination that was socially objectionable. Although advanced thinkers could face their man-midwife with the attitude that shame was better than death—"I considered that through modesty I was not to give up my life," as one English noblewoman reasoned—many women and more husbands were unprepared for the actual practice of a man. Thus students were taught as much about bedside manner as about medicine. They were not to examine the patient unless there was another person present in the room, they were not to ask direct questions, and they were not to face the patient during any of their procedures. They were taught to keep a linen cloth on top of the woman's abdomen and to make the examination only by touch—incredulous students were reminded that the most famous French man-midwife was blind! If the fetus was in the correct position, nothing further would be done until the delivery itself. It was only when the fetus was in what was labeled an "unnatural" position that the skill of the physician came into play.

For the most part, a child that could not be delivered head first, face down was in serious risk of being stillborn and the mother in serious risk of dying in labor. That was the problem to which the physicians addressed themselves in the eighteenth century and for which they found remarkable solutions. Most answers came from better understanding of female anatomy and a better visualization of the way in which the fetus moved during labor. The first advance was the realization that the fetus could be turned while still in the womb. Pressure applied on the outside of the stomach, especially in early stages of labor, could help the fetus drop down correctly. A baby who emerged feet first had to be turned face down before it was pulled through the birth canal.

For babies who could not be manually manipulated, the greatest advance of the eighteenth century was the invention of the forceps, or the *tire-tête,* as the French called them. With forceps, the physician could pull the baby by force when the mother was incapable of delivery. Forceps were used mostly in breech births but were also a vital tool when the baby was too large to pass through the cervix by contraction. The forceps were invented in Britain in the middle of the seventeenth century but were kept secret for more than 50 years. During that time they were used by three generations of a single family of man-midwives. In the eighteenth century, they came into general use when the Scotsman William Smellie (1697–1765) developed a short, leather-covered instrument that enabled the physician to do as little damage as possible to either mother or child. Obstetrics now emerged as a specialized branch of medical practice. If neither the pain nor the sorrow of childbirth could be eliminated, its dangers could be lessened.

Not all members of the lower orders succumbed to poverty or despair. In fact, many were able to benefit from existing conditions and lead a more fulfilling life than ever before. The richness of popular culture, signified by a spread of literacy into the lower reaches of European society, was one indication of the change. So, too, were the reforms urged by enlightened thinkers to improve basic education and the quality of life in the cities. For the segment of the lower orders that could keep its head above water, the eighteenth century offered new opportunities and new challenges.

Breaking the Cycle. Of all the legacies of the eighteenth century, none was more fundamental than the steady increase in European population that began around 1740. It was not the first time that Europe had experienced sustained population growth, but it was the first time that such growth was not checked by a demographic crisis. Breaking the cycle of population growth and crisis was a momentous event in European history, despite the fact that it went unrecorded at the time and unappreciated for centuries after.

The figures tell one part of the story. In 1700, European population is estimated to have been 120 million. By 1800, it had grown 50 percent, to more than 180 million. And the aggregate hides significant regional variations. While populations in France, Spain, and Italy expanded between 30 and 40 percent, the population of Prussia doubled and those of Russia and Hungary may have tripled in number. Britain's population increased by 80 percent, from about 5 to 9 million, but the rate of growth was accelerating. In 1695, the English population stood at 5 million. It took 62 years to add the next million and 24 years to add the million after that. In 1781, the population was 7 million, but it took only 13 years to reach 8 million and only 10 more years to reach 9 million. Steady population growth had continued without significant checks for more than a half century.

Ironically, the traditional pattern of European population found its theorist at the very moment that it was about to disappear. In 1798, Thomas Malthus (1766–1834) published *An Essay on the Principles of Population*. Reflecting on the history of European population, Malthus observed the cyclical pattern by which growth over one or two generations was checked by a crisis that significantly reduced population. From the lower levels new growth began until it was checked and the cycle repeated itself. Because people increased more quickly than did food supplies, the land could only sustain a certain level of population. When that level was near, population became prone to a demographic check. Malthus divided population checks into two categories: positive and preventive. Positive checks were famine, war, and disease, all of which Malthus believed were natural, although brutal, means of population control. Famine was the obvious result of the failure of food supplies to keep pace with demand; war was the competition for scarce resources; disease often accompanied both. It was preventive checks that most interested Malthus. Those were the means by which societies could limit their growth to avoid the devastating consequences of positive checks. Celibacy, late marriages, and sexual abstinence were among the choices that Malthus approved, although abortion, infanticide, and contraception were also commonly practiced.

Patterns of Population. In the sixteenth and seventeenth centuries, the dominant pattern of the life cycle was high infant and child mortality, late marriages, and early death. All controlled population growth. Infant and child mortality rates were staggering: only half of all those born reached the age of ten. Late marriage was the only effective form of birth control—given the strong social taboos against sexual relations outside marriage—for a late marriage reduced a woman's childbearing years. Women in western Europe generally married between the ages of 24 and 26; they normally ceased bearing children at the age of 40. But not all marriages lasted that 14- or 16-year span, as one or the other partner died. On average, the childbearing period for most women was between 10 and 12 years, long enough to endure six pregnancies, which would result in three surviving children. (See "Giving Birth in the Eighteenth Century," pp. 672–673.)

Three surviving children for every two adults would, of course, have resulted in a 50 percent rise in population in every generation. Celibacy was one limiting factor; cities were another. Perhaps as much as 15 percent of the population in western Europe remained celibate, either by entering religious orders that imposed celibacy or by lacking the personal or financial attributes necessary to make a match. Religious orders that enforced celibacy were still central features of Catholic societies, and spinsters, as unmarried women were labeled, were increasing everywhere. Cities were like sticky webs, trapping the surplus rural population for the spiders of disease, famine, and exposure to devour. Throughout the early modern period, urban areas grew through migration. Settled town dwellers might have been able to sustain their own numbers despite the unsanitary conditions of cities, but it was migrants who brought about the cities' explosive growth. Rural migrants accounted for the appallingly high urban death rates. The largest European cities were continuously growing—London from 200,000 in 1600 to 675,000 in 1750; Paris from 220,000 to 576,000; Rome from 105,000 to 156,000; Madrid from 49,000 to 109,000; Vienna from 50,000 to 175,000—and many countless thousands of immigrants perished before marriage. If urban perils were not enough, there were still the so-called positive checks. Plagues carried away hundreds of thousands, wars halved populations of places in their path, and famine overwhelmed the weak and the poor. The worst famine in European history came as late as 1697, when one-third of the population of Finland starved to death.

The late seventeenth and early eighteenth centuries was a period of population stagnation, if not actual decline. It was not until the third or fourth decade of the eighteenth century that another growth cycle began. It rapidly gained momentum throughout the Continent and showed no signs of abating after two full generations. More important, the upward cycle revealed unusual characteristics. In the first place, fertility was increasing, for several reasons. In a few areas, most notably in Britain, women were marrying younger, thereby increasing their childbearing years. That pattern was also true in eastern Europe, where women traditionally married younger. In the late eighteenth century, the average age at marriage for Hungarian women had dropped to 18.6 years. Elsewhere, most notably in France, the practice of wet-nursing was becoming more common among the masses. As working women increasingly took jobs outside the house, they were less able to nurse their own children. Finally, sexual activity outside marriage was rising. Illegitimacy rates, especially in the last decades of the century, were spurting everywhere. Over the course of the century, they rose by 60 percent in France, more than doubled in England, and nearly quadrupled in Germany. So, too, were the rates of premarital pregnancy on the rise. The number of couples rushed to the altar in 1800 was nearly double that before 1750 in most of western Europe.

But increasing fertility was only part of the picture. More significant was decreasing mortality. The positive checks of the past were no longer as potent. European warfare not only diminished in scale after the middle of the century, it changed location as well. Rivalry for colonial empires removed the theater of conflict from European communities. So did the increase in naval warfare. The damage caused by war had always been more by aftershock than by actual fighting. The destruction and pillage of crops and the wholesale slaughter of livestock created food shortages that weakened local populations for the diseases that came in train with the armies. As the virulence of warfare abated, so did that of epidemic disease. The plague had all but disappeared from western Europe by the middle of the eighteenth century. The widespread practice of quarantine—especially in Hungary, which had been the crucial bridge between eastern and western epidemics—went far to eradicate the scourge of centuries.

Without severe demographic crises to maintain the cyclical pattern, the European population began a gentle but continuous rise. Urban sanitation, at least for permanent city dwellers, was becoming more effective. Clean water supplies, organized waste and sewage disposal, and strict quarantines were increasingly part of urban regulations. The use of doctors and trained

The poverty of eighteenth-century London slums was a favorite subject of the English artist William Hogarth. Gin Lane *depicts the London poor in alcoholic delirium, their only escape from the misery of their daily lives.*

midwives helped lower the incidence of stillbirth and decreased the number of women who died in childbirth. Almost everywhere levels of infant and child mortality were decreasing. More people were being born, more were surviving the first ten dangerous years, and thus more were marrying and reproducing. Increased fertility and decreased mortality could have only one result: renewed population growth. No wonder Malthus was worried.

Agricultural Improvements. In the past, if warfare or epidemic diseases failed to check population growth, famine would have done the job. How the European economy conquered famine in the eighteenth century is a complicated story. There was no single breakthrough that accounts for the ability to feed the tens of millions of additional people who inhabited the continent. Holland and Britain, at the cutting edge of agricultural improvement, employed dynamic new techniques that would ultimately provide the means to support continued growth, but most European agriculture was still mired in the time-honored practices that had endured for centuries. Still, not everyone could be fed or fed adequately. Widespread famine might have disappeared, but slow starvation and chronic undernourishment had not. Hunger was more common at the end of the eighteenth century than at the beginning and the nutritional content of a typical diet might have reached its lowest point in European history.

Nevertheless, the capacity to sustain rising levels of population can only be explained in terms of agricultural improvement. Quite simply, European farmers were now producing more food and marketing it better. In the most advanced societies, that was a result of conscious efforts to make agriculture more efficient. In traditional open-field agriculture, communities quickly ran up against insurmountable obstacles to growth. The three-field crop rotation system left a significant proportion of land fallow each year, while the concentration on subsistence cereal crops progressively eroded the land that was in production. Common farming was only as strong as the weakest member of the community. There was little incentive for successful individuals to plow profits back into the land, either through the purchase of equipment or the increase of livestock. Livestock was a crucial variable in agricultural improvement. As long as there was only enough food for humans to eat, only essential livestock could be kept alive over the winter. Oxen, which were still

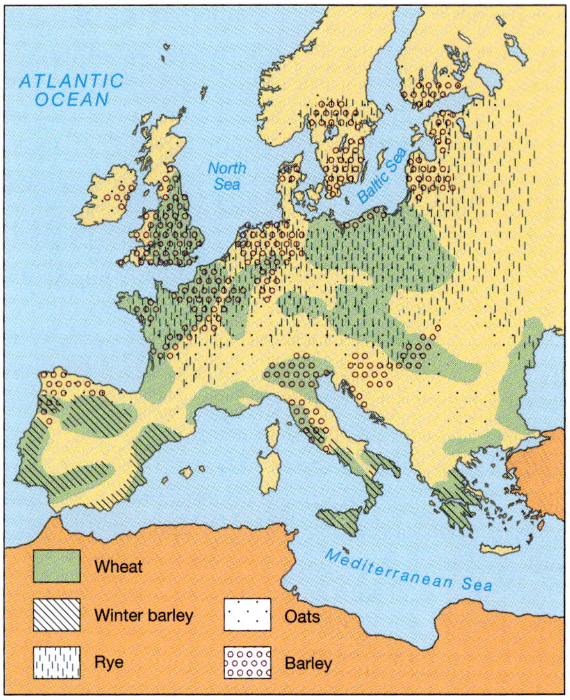

Cereal crops in Europe. Soil, climate, and agricultural techniques all combined to determine the diet of Europeans in different parts of the continent. Wheat was the most prized grain, but barley could be baked or brewed.

the ordinary beasts of burden, and pigs and poultry, which required only minimal feed, were the most commonly kept livestock. But few animals meant little manure, and without manure the soil could not easily be regenerated.

It was not until the middle of the seventeenth century that solutions to those problems began to appear. The first change was consolidation of landholdings so that traditional crop rotations could be abandoned. A second innovation was the introduction of fodder crops, some of which—such as clover—added nutrients to the soil, while others—such as turnips—were used to feed livestock. Better grazing and better winter feed increased the size of herds, while new techniques of animal husbandry, particularly crossbreeding, produced hardier strains. It was quite clear that the key to increased production lay in better fertilization, and by the eighteenth century some European farmers had broken through the "manure barrier." Larger herds, the introduction of clover crops, the use of human waste from towns, and even the first experiments with lime as an artificial fertilizer were all part of the new agricultural methods. The impact of new farming techniques was readily apparent. In Britain and Holland, where they were used most extensively, grain yields exceeded ten kernels harvested for each one planted, while in eastern Europe, where the techniques were hardly known, yields were less than five to one.

The New Staples. Along with the new crops that helped nourish both soil and animals came new crops that helped nourish people. Indian corn, or maize, was a staple crop for Native Americans and gradually came to be grown in most parts of western Europe. Maize not only had higher nutritional value than most other cereals, it also yielded more food per acre than traditional grains, reaching levels as high as 40 to 1. So, too, did the potato, which also entered the European diet from the New World. The potato grew in poor soil, required less labor, and yielded an abundant and nutritious harvest. It rapidly took hold in Ireland and parts of Prussia, from where it spread into eastern Europe. French and Spanish peasants reluctantly introduced it into their diet. Wherever it took root, the potato quickly established itself as survival food. It allowed families to subsist on smaller amounts of land and with less capital outlay. As a result, potato cultivation enabled people in some parts of Europe to marry younger, and thus to produce more children.

However, the new developments involved only a very narrow range of producers. The new techniques were expensive, and knowledge of the new crops spread slowly. Change had to overcome both inertia and intransigence. With more mouths to feed, profits from agriculture soared without landowners having to lift a finger. Only the most ambitious were interested in improvement. At the other end, peasant farmers were more concerned with failure than success. An experiment that did not work could devastate a community; one that did work only meant higher taxes. Thus the most important improvements in agricultural production were more traditional ones. Basically, there was an increase in the amount of land that was utilized for growing. In most of western Europe there was little room for agricultural expansion, but in the east there remained great tracts of uncultivated land. In Russia, Prussia, and Hungary, hundreds of thousands of new acres came under the plow, although some of it simply went to replace land that had been wastefully exhausted in previous generations. In one German province, nearly 75 percent more land was in cultivation at the end of the eighteenth century than had been at the beginning. Even in the west, drainage schemes and forest clearance expanded productive capacity.

Agricultural techniques are illustrated in this plate from Diderot's Encyclopedia. *In the foreground, a man steers a high-wheeled horse-drawn plow while a woman operates a hopper device to sow seeds.*

There was also an upswing in the efficiency with which agricultural products were marketed. From the seventeenth century onward, market agriculture was gradually replacing subsistence agriculture in most parts of Europe. Market agriculture had the advantage of allowing specialization on farms. Single-crop farming enabled farmers to benefit from the peculiarities of their own soil and climate. They could then exchange their surplus for the range of crops they needed to subsist. Market exchange was facilitated by improved transportation and communication, and above all by the increase in the population of towns, which provided demand. On a larger scale, market agriculture was able to respond to regional harvest failures in a way that subsistence agriculture could not. The most hated figure in the eighteenth century was the grain engrosser, a middleman who bought up local surplus and shipped it away. Engrossers were accused of driving up prices—which they did—and of creating famines—which they did not. In fact, the national and international trade in large quantities of grain evened out regional variations in harvests and went a long way toward reducing local grain shortages. The upkeep of roads, the building of canals, and the clearing of waterways created a national lifeline for the movement of grain.

Finally, the increase in agricultural productivity may have owed something to a change in climate that took place in the late eighteenth century. It is thought that the annual ring of growth inside tree trunks is an indicator of changes in climate. Hot years produce markedly different rings than cold ones; wet years are etched differently than dry ones. Examination of trees that are centuries old seems to indicate that the European climate was unusually cold and wet during the seventeenth century—some have even called it a little ice age—and that it gradually warmed during the eighteenth century. Even moderate climatic change, when combined with new techniques, new crops, expanded cultivation, and improved marketing, would go a long way toward explaining how so many more people were being fed at the end of the eighteenth century.

The Plight of the Poor. "Of every ten men one is a beggar, five are too poor to give him alms, three more are ill at ease, embarrassed by debts and lawsuits, and the tenth does not represent a hundred thousand families." So observed an eighteenth-century Frenchman about the distribution of wealth in his country. There can be no doubt that the most serious social problem of the eighteenth century was the explosion of poor people throughout Europe. There was grim irony in the fact that advances in the production and distribution of food and the retreat of war and plague allowed more people to survive hand-to-mouth than ever before. Where their ancestors had succumbed to quick death from disease or starvation, they eked out a miserable existence of constant hunger and chronic pain, with death at the end of a seemingly endless corridor.

It is impossible to gauge the number of European poor or to separate them into categories of greater and greatest misery. The truly indigent, the starving poor, probably composed 10 to 15 percent of most societies, perhaps as many as 20 million people throughout the Continent. They were most prevalent in towns but were an increasing burden on the countryside, where

Der Pesthof (The Plague Ward), *1746, illustrates the conditions in eighteenth-century medical facilities. The centerpiece is a gruesome amputation.*

they wandered in search of agricultural employment. The wandering poor had no counterpart in the east, where serfdom kept everyone tied to the land, but the hungry and unsheltered certainly did. Yet the problem of poverty was not only to be seen among the destitute. In fact, the uniqueness of the poor in the eighteenth century was that they were drawn from social groups that even in the hungry times of the early seventeenth century had been successful subsistence producers. Perhaps another 40 percent of the population in western Europe was described by contemporaries as those without a fixed interest: in the country, those without land; in the towns, those without steady jobs.

It was easy to see why poverty was increasing. The relentless advance of population drove up the price of food and drove down the price of wages. In the second half of the eighteenth century, the cost of living in France rose by more than 60 percent while wages rose only by 25 percent. In Spain, the cost of living increased by 100 percent while wages rose only 20 percent. Only in Britain did wages nearly keep pace with prices. Rising prices made land more valuable. At the beginning of the eighteenth century, as the first wave of population expansion hit western Europe, small holdings began to decrease in size. The custom of partible inheritance, by which each son received a share of land, shrank the average size of a peasant holding below that necessary to sustain an average-size family, much less one that was growing larger. In one part of France it was estimated that 30 acres was a survival plot of land in good times. At the end of the seventeenth century, 80 percent of the peasants there owned less than 25 acres.

As holdings contracted, the portion of the family income derived from wage labor expanded. In such circumstances, males were more valuable than females, both as farmers and laborers, and there is incontrovertible evidence that European rural communities practiced female infanticide. In the end, however, it became increasingly difficult for the peasant family to remain on the land. Mediterranean sharecroppers fell further and further into debt until they finally lost their land entirely. Small freeholders were forced to borrow against future crops until a bad harvest led to foreclosure. Many were allowed to lease back their own lands, on short terms and at high rents, but most swelled the ranks of agricultural laborers, migrating during the planting and harvest seasons and suffering cruelly during winter and summer. In Britain, the rural landless outnumbered the landed by two to one. In France, there were as many as 8 million peasants who no longer owned their own land.

Emigration was the first logical consequence of poverty. In places where rural misery was greatest, such as Ireland, whole communities pulled up stakes and moved to America. Frederick the Great attracted hundreds of thousands of emigrants to Prussia by offering them land. But most rural migrants did not move to new rural environments. Rather, they followed the well-trodden paths to the cities. Many traditional domestic crafts were evolving into industrial activities. In the past, peasants had supplemented their family income by processing raw materials in the home. Spinning, weaving, and sewing were common cottage industries in which the workers took in the work, supplied their own equipment, and were paid by the piece. Now, especially in the cloth trades, a new form of industrial activity was being organized. Factories, usually located in towns or larger villages, assembled workers together, set them at larger and more efficient machines, and paid them for their time rather than for their output. Families unable to support themselves from the land had no choice but to follow the movement of jobs.

Caring for the Poor. Urban poverty seemed more extreme to observers because there were more poor to observe. They crowded into towns in search of work or charity, though they were unlikely to find much of either. Urban areas were better equipped to assist the poor than were the rural communities from which they came, but the likelihood of finding aid only attracted more and more poor, straining and finally breaking the capacities of urban institutions. The death rate of the migrants and their children was staggering. It is perhaps best typified by the dramatic increase in the numbers of abandoned babies throughout western European cities. The existence of foundling hospitals in cities meant that unwed or poor mothers could leave their children in the hope that they would receive better care than the mother herself could provide. In fact, that was rarely the case. In the largest foundling hospital in Paris, only 15 percent of the children survived their first year of "care." But that did little to deter abandonment. In 1772, more than 7500 babies were left at that charnel house, representing 40 percent of all the children born in Paris that year. The normal rates of abandonment of between 10 and 15 percent of all children born in cities as diverse as Madrid and Brussels were little better.

Neither state nor private charities could cope with the flood of poor immigrants. Although the English pundit Samuel Johnson (1709–1784) opined that "a decent provision for the poor is the true test of civilization," what he meant was provision for the deserving poor, those unfortunates who were physically or mentally unable to support themselves. The distinction between the worthy and unworthy poor was one involved with changing definitions of charity itself. In earlier times, charity was believed to benefit the soul of the giver as much as the body of the recipient. Thus the poor were socially useful, providing the rich with the opportunity to do good works. But the poor were coming to be viewed as a problem of social administration. Hospitals, workhouses, and, more ominously, prisons were established or expanded to deal with them.

Hospitals were residential asylums rather than places for health care. They took in the old, the incapacitated, and, increasingly, the orphaned young. Those in France were aptly named "Hotels of God," considering their staggering death rates. "There children dwell who know no parents' care/Parents who know no children's care dwell there," one poet lamented. Workhouses existed for those who were capable of work but incapable of finding it. They were supposed to improve the values of the idle by keeping them busy, though in most places they served only to improve the profits of the industrialists, who rented out workhouse inmates at below-market wages. Prisons grew with crime. There were spectacular increases in crimes against property in all eighteenth-century cities, and despite severe penalties that could include hanging for petty theft, more criminals were incarcerated than executed. Enlightened arguments for the reform of prisons and punishment tacitly acknowledged the social basis of most crime. As always, the victims of crime were mostly drawn from the same social backgrounds as the perpetrators. Along with all of their other troubles, it was the poor who were most commonly robbed, beaten, and abused.

A 1781 colored mezzotint by J. R. Smith shows a lady leaving a lending library with a book.

Popular Culture. However depressing the story of the unrelieved misery of the poor is, the masses of eighteenth-century society were not only the downtrodden victims of social and economic forces beyond their control. For the peasant farmer about to lose his land or the urban artisan without a job, security was an overwhelming concern. But while many were to endure such fates, many others lived comfortably by the standards of the age, and almost everyone believed that things were better than they had ever been before. Popular culture was a rich mixture of family and community activities that provided outlets from the pressures of work and the vagaries of fortune. It was no less sustaining to the population at large than was the purely literate culture of the elite, no less vital as a means of explanation for everyday events than the theories of the philosophers or the programs of the philosophes.

In fact, the line between elite and popular culture in the eighteenth century is a thin one. For one thing, there was still much mixing of social classes in both rural and urban environments. Occasions of display such as festivals, village fairs, and religious holidays brought entire communities together and reinforced their collective identities. Moreover, there were many shared elements between the two cultures. All over Europe, literacy was increasing, the result of primary education, of new business techniques, and of the millions of books that were available in editions tailored to even the most modest purse. Nearly half of the inhabitants of France were literate by the end of the eighteenth century, perhaps 60 percent of those in Britain. Men were more likely to have learned to read than women, as were those who lived in urban areas. More than a quarter of French women could read, a number that had doubled over the century. As the rates of female literacy rose, so did overall rates, for women took the lead in teaching children.

Popular literacy spawned popular literature in remarkable variety. Religious works remained the most important, but they were followed by almanacs, romances, and (perhaps surprisingly) chivalric fiction. Religious tracts aimed at the populace were found throughout Europe. They contained stories of the saints in Catholic countries and of the martyrs in Protestant ones, proverbs intended to increase spirituality, and prayers to be offered for all occasions. Almanacs combined prophecies, home remedies, astrological tables, predictions about the weather, and advice on all varieties of agricultural and industrial activities. In the middle of the century, just one of the dozens of British almanacs was selling more than 80,000 copies a year. Romances were the staple of lending libraries, which were also becoming a common feature of even small towns. The books were usually published in inexpensive installments spaced according to the time working families needed to save the pennies to purchase them. Written by middle-class authors, popular romances had a strong moral streak, promoting chastity for women and sobriety for men. Yet the best-selling popular fiction, at least in western Europe, was melodramatic tales of knights and ladies from the age of chivalry. The themes had seeped into popular consciousness after having fallen out of favor among the elites. But cultural tastes did not only trickle down. The masses kept the chivalric tradition alive during the eighteenth century; it would percolate up into elite culture in the nineteenth.

Nevertheless, literate culture was not the dominant form of popular culture. Traditional social activities continued to reflect the violent and even brutal nature of day-to-day existence. Village festivals were still the safety valve of youth gangs who enforced sexual morals by shaming husbands whose wives were unfaithful or women whose reputations were sullied.

William Hogarth, The Cockpit *(ca. 1759). The central figure is a blind nobleman who was said never to have missed an important cockfight. The steel spurs on the birds' legs enabled them to inflict serious damage in the heat of battle.*

Many holidays were celebrated by sporting events that pitted the inhabitants of one village against those of another. The events almost always turned into free-for-alls in which broken bones were common and deaths not unknown. In fact, the frequent breakdown of sporting activities into gang wars was the principal cause for the development of rules for soccer, as well as more esoteric games such as cricket in Britain. Well-organized matches soon became forms of popular entertainment. More than 20,000 spectators attended one eighteenth-century cricket match, and soccer and cricket soon became as popular for gambling as horse racing was among the wealthy.

Even more popular were the so-called blood sports, which continued to be the most common form of popular recreation. Those were brutal competitions in which, in one way or another, animals were maimed or slaughtered. Dog- and cockfighting were among those that survive today. Less attractive to the modern mind were blood sports such as bearbaiting or bull running, in which the object was the slaughter of a large beast over a prolonged period of time. Blood sports were certainly not confined to the masses—fox-hunting and bullfighting were pastimes for the very rich—but they formed a significant part of local social activity.

The local tavern or alehouse also became a significant part of social activity, and in town or country was the site for local communication and recreation. There women and men gossiped and gambled to while away the hours between sundown and bedtime. Discussions and games became animated as the evening wore on, for staggering amounts of alcohol were consumed. "Drunk for a penny, dead drunk for two pennies, straw for nothing," advertised one of the thousands of British gin mills that dominated the poorer quarters of towns. The increased use of spirits—gin, brandy, rum, and vodka—changed the nature of alcohol consumption in Europe. Wine and beer had always been drunk in quantities that we would find astounding, but those beverages were also an important part of diet. The nutritional content of spirits was negligible. People drank spirits to get drunk. The British reformer Francis Place (1771–1854), who grew up in a working-class family, commented that the British masses had only two pleasures, "sex and drinking. And drunkenness is by far the most desired." The level to which it rose in the eighteenth century speaks volumes about the changes in social and economic life that the masses of European society were then experiencing.

Eighteenth-century society was a hybrid of old and new. It remained highly stratified. Birth and occupation determined wealth, privilege, and quality of life as much as they had in the past, but there were now more paths toward the middle and upper classes, more wealth to be distributed among those above the level of subsistence. Opulence and poverty increased in step as the fruits of commerce and land enriched the upper orders while rising population impoverished the lower ones. Enlightenment ideas highlighted the contradictions. The attack on traditional authority, especially the Roman Catholic church, was an attack on a conservative, static world view. Enlightenment thinkers looked to the future, to a new world shaped by reason and knowledge, a world ruled benevolently for the benefit of all human beings. Government, society, the individual—all could be improved if only the rubble of the past was cleared away. Those thinkers could hardly imagine how potent their vision would become.

Questions for Review

1. What were the main elements of Enlightenment thought?
2. What social, moral, and religious traditions were challenged by the ideas of thinkers such as Voltaire, Hume, Montesquieu, and Rousseau?
3. How did the European nobility maintain its social eminence in the face of a new bourgeois culture created by an expanding middle class?
4. Why did Europe's population begin to grow so dramatically in the eighteenth century and how did society respond to the challenges that posed?

Suggestions for Further Reading

General Reading

* Olwen Hufton, *Europe: Privilege and Protest, 1730–1789* (Ithaca, NY: Cornell University Press, 1980). An excellent survey of the political and social history of the mid-eighteenth century.

* Leonard Krieger, *Kings and Philosophers, 1689–1789* (New York: Norton, 1970). A brilliant depiction of the personalities and ideas of eighteenth-century Europe.

* Isser Woloch, *Eighteenth Century Europe, Tradition and Progress, 1715–89* (New York: Norton, 1982). Especially strong on social movements and popular culture.

* William Doyle, *The Old European Order, 1660–1800,* 2d ed. (Oxford: Oxford University Press, 1992). An important

essay on the structure of European societies and the ways in which they held together.

Raymond Birn, *Crisis, Absolutism, Revolution: Europe, 1648–91* (New York: Holt, Rinehart and Winston, 1977). A reliable survey with especially good chapters on the Enlightenment.

Eighteenth-Century Culture

* Norman Hampson, *The Enlightenment* (London: Penguin Books, 1982). The best one-volume survey.

* Peter Gay, *The Enlightenment: An Interpretation,* 2 vols. (New York: Alfred A. Knopf, 1966–1969). A difficult but rewarding study by one of the leading historians of the subject.

Ulrich Im Hof, *The Enlightenment* (Oxford: Blackwell, 1994). A wide-ranging survey from a German perspective.

Carolyn Lougee, *Le Paradis des Femmes: Women, Salons, and Social Stratification* (Princeton, NJ: Princeton University Press, 1976). A study of the foundation of the French salons and the role of women in it.

* Judith Sklar, *Montesquieu* (Oxford: Oxford University Press, 1987). A concise, readable study of the man and his work.

Theodore Besterman, *Voltaire* (Chicago: University of Chicago Press, 1976). The best of many biographies of an all-too-full life.

A. J. Ayer, *Voltaire* (New York: Random House, 1986). A brief and vibrant study.

* Dorinda Outram, *The Enlightenment* (Cambridge: Cambridge University Press, 1995). A survey of the different theories on the Enlightenment.

Daniel Roche, *France in the Enlightenment* (Cambridge, MA: Harvard University Press, 1998). A wide-ranging survey of everything from politics to popular culture.

* Peter Gay, *The Enlightenment: A Comprehensive Anthology* (New York: Simon & Schuster, 1985). The best single volume for selections of the major works of the Enlightenment.

* John G. Gagliardo, *Enlightened Despotism* (New York: Thomas Y. Crowell, 1967). A sound exploration of the impact of Enlightenment ideas on the rulers of Europe, with emphasis on the east.

* John W. Yolton, ed., *The Blackwell Companion to the Enlightenment* (Cambridge, MA: Blackwell, 1995). A comprehensive dictionary that identifies major people, works, and events.

Eighteenth-Century Society: The Nobility

Michael Bush, *Noble Privilege* (New York: Holmes & Meier, 1983). A good analytic survey of the rights of European nobles.

J. V. Beckett, *The Aristocracy in England* (London: Basil Blackwell, 1986). A comprehensive study of a tightly knit national aristocracy.

* Jonathan Dewald, *The European Nobility 1400–1800* (Cambridge: Cambridge University Press, 1996). An insightful survey.

* H. M. Scott, *The European Nobilities in the Seventeenth and Eighteenth Centuries* (London: Longman, 1995). An exploration of the wealth and power of Europe's dominant social class.

* Albert Goodwin, ed., *The European Nobility in the Eighteenth Century* (New York: Harper & Row, 1967). Separate essays on national nobilities, including those of Sweden, Poland, and Spain.

Eighteenth-Century Society: The Bourgeoisie

Jan de Vries, *European Urbanization, 1500–1800* (Cambridge, MA: Harvard University Press, 1984). An important, though difficult, study of the transformation of towns into cities, with the most reliable estimates of size and rates of growth.

* P. J. Corfield, *The Impact of English Towns 1700–1800* (Oxford: Oxford University Press, 1982). A thorough survey of the role of towns in English social and economic life.

* John Brewer, *The Pleasures of the Imagination: English Culture in the Eighteenth Century* (London : HarperCollins, 1997). A fascinating study of the making of high culture in England.

Peter Earle, *The Making of the English Middle Class* (London: Methuen, 1989). The manners, mores, and mindset of the group that would come to dominate nineteenth-century Britain.

* Elinor Barber, *The Bourgeoisie in Eighteenth-Century France* (Princeton, NJ: Princeton University Press, 1955). Still the best study of the French bourgeoisie.

* Simon Shama, *The Embarrassment of Riches* (Berkeley: University of California Press, 1987). The social life of Dutch burghers, richly portrayed.

* Olwen Hufton, *The Prospect Before Her: A History of Women in Western Europe* (New York: Alfred Knopf, 1996). A survey of women's history that is particularly strong for the eighteenth century.

* Ian Watt, *The Rise of the Novel* (Berkeley: University of California Press, 1957). An important essay on the relationship between literature and society in the eighteenth century.

David Garrioch, *Neighborhood and Community in Paris, 1740–90* (Cambridge: Cambridge University Press, 1986). A good microstudy of Parisian neighborhoods and the people who inhabited them.

George Sussman, *Selling Mothers' Milk: The Wet-Nursing Business* (Bloomington: Indiana University Press, 1982). A study of buyers and sellers in this important social marketplace.

* Samia Spencer, *French Women and the Age of Enlightenment* (Bloomington: Indiana University Press, 1992). A survey of the role of women in French high culture.

* Lawrence Stone, *The Family, Sex and Marriage in England, 1500–1800* (New York: Harper & Row, 1979). A controversial but extremely important argument about the changing nature of family life.

* Jean-Louis Flandrin, *Families in Former Times* (Cambridge: Cambridge University Press, 1979). Strong on family and household organization.

Eighteenth-Century Society: The Masses

* Michael W. Flinn, *The European Demographic System* (Baltimore, MD: Johns Hopkins University Press, 1981). The best single-volume study especially for the non-specialist.

E. A. Wrigley and R. S. Schofield, *The Population History of England* (Cambridge, MA: Harvard University Press, 1981). The most important reconstruction of a national population, by a team of researchers.

Olwen Hufton, *The Poor in Eighteenth-Century France* (Oxford: Oxford University Press, 1974). A compelling study of the life of the poor.

* Roy Porter, *English Society in the Eighteenth Century* (London: Penguin Books, 1982). A breezy, entertaining survey of English social life.

* J. M. Beattie, *Crime and the Courts in England* (Princeton, NJ: Princeton University Press, 1986). A difficult but sensitive analysis of crime and criminal justice.

* Peter Linebaugh, *The London Hanged: Crime and Civil Society in the Eighteenth Century* (Cambridge: Cambridge University Press, 1993). A controversial study of capital punishment and its uses in the war between the classes.

* Peter Burke, *Popular Culture in Early Modern Europe* (New York: Harper & Row, 1978). A wide survey of practices throughout the continent.

* Robert Muchembled, *Popular Culture and Elite Culture in France, 1400–1750* (Baton Rouge: Louisiana State University Press, 1985). A complex but richly textured argument about the relationship between two cultures.

* Robert Malcolmson, *Popular Recreation in English Society, 1700–1850* (Cambridge: Cambridge University Press, 1973). Sport and its role in society.

* Paperback edition available.

Discovering Western Civilization Online

To further explore culture and society in eighteenth-century Europe, consult the following World Wide Web sites. Since Web resources are constantly being updated, also go to *www.awl.com/Kishlansky* for further suggestions.

Eighteenth-Century Culture

www.history.evansville.net/enlighte.html
The best starting point for the culture and history of the age of Enlightenment.

www.fordham.edu/halsall/mod/modsbook10.html
An outstanding collection of texts of Enlightenment writers.

Eighteenth-Century Society

www.uampfa.berkeley.edu/exhibits/newchild/
A site devoted to the nature of childhood in eighteenth-century Britain.

www.vos.ucsb.edu/shuttle/eng-18th.html
An inclusive site for the study of English literature in the eighteenth century.

CHAPTER

20 THE FRENCH REVOLUTION AND THE NAPOLEONIC ERA, 1789–1815

- ADMIRING THE AMERICAN REVOLUTION
- THE CRISIS OF THE OLD REGIME IN FRANCE, 1715–1788
  - Louis XV's France
  - Louis XVI and the National Debt
  - The Three Estates
- THE FIRST STAGE OF THE FRENCH REVOLUTION, 1789–1792
  - Taking Politics to the People
  - Convening the Estates-General
  - The Storming of the Bastille
  - The Revolution of the Peasantry
  - Women on the March
  - The Revolution Threatened
- EXPERIMENTING WITH DEMOCRACY: THE REVOLUTION'S SECOND STAGE, 1792–1799
  - Declaring Political Rights
  - The Second Revolution: The Revolution of the People
  - "Terror Is the Order of the Day"
  - The End of the Revolution
- THE REIGN OF NAPOLEON, 1799–1815
  - Bonaparte Seizes Power
  - Napoleon at War with the European Powers
  - The First Empire and Domestic Reforms
  - Decline and Fall

Admiring the American Revolution

IN THE SECOND HALF OF THE EIGHTEENTH CENTURY, two separate revolutions toppled regimes on both sides of the Atlantic. In the first of the two great upheavals, the American Revolution, which lasted from 1775 to 1783, the thirteen British colonies located along the Atlantic seaboard secured their independence from Great Britain. They formed themselves into the United States, a democratic republic with its own Declaration of Independence and Constitution. While the American Revolution was challenging British hegemony in the New World, France appeared to be ruled by a stable and powerful monarchy, one so secure in its reign that it was able to lend a helping hand to those colonists opposing England's king George III.

In the image shown here, entitled "Independence of the United States," the unknown artist is glorifying both the king of France, Louis XVI (1774 –1791) and the American Revolution. More dramatically still, the inscription on the base of the pedestal acknowledges Louis as the "Liberator" of America and the seas, an assertion that would have come as a surprise to the

colonists struggling to cast off the British yoke. Louis XVI, the king who would be guillotined by radical revolutionaries in 1793, is commemorated in the painting as a great man of revolution, more important by virtue of his position on the monument than even George Washington and Benjamin Franklin, whose medallions surrounded by laurels serve as a base for Louis's image. Washington, whose name is misspelled under his likeness as "Waginston," is not memorialized as father of his country. Instead, it is Louis XVI who is described as America's savior. The memorial column itself is topped by images of the French monarchy including a globe with three *fleurs de lys* and the rooster of the French nation.

Next to the monument and commanding equal interest is the figure of America. America is not symbolized by a minuteman, a colonial militiaman, or a farmer typical of those who fought the American Revolution. Instead, America appears half naked as a "noble savage" draped in animal skins and feathers. In his right hand America holds the scepter of power and in his left hand a pole surmounted by Phrygian cap of ancient Roman origins, which became popular in the French Revolution as the symbol of liberty. Under his left foot, America is trampling the British lion, a sorry sight lying next to the broken British trident symbolizing British failure both as a land and sea power.

The landscape of the scene is not a New England scene at all, but a tropical one with palm trees swaying. One of the trees is wrapped in a banner proclaiming, "In raising myself up, I make myself beautiful." The aura of the New World as an uncharted territory as different from Europe and the French countryside as could be imagined served both to idealize the American continent and to distance its revolution from the political experience of the French. In an exotic terrain, Louis XVI could appear as a "liberator," as unearned as the designation might be.

The American Revolution was popular in France and attracted supporters among whom was the French aristocrat and military man, the Marquis de Lafayette. Lafayette was so enthusiastic about the American Revolution that he packed his bags in 1777 and embarked for the New World to fight for the cause. He stood beside General Washington at Valley Forge, was appointed a major general in the American revolutionary army, and was given his own command. It was Lafayette who persuaded the French government to provide financial aid to the American cause. Lafayette was so enamored of the American Revolution and respectful of its leader that he named his first son George Washington.

The French Revolution began six years after the American War of Independence ended, and lasted for a decade. The French revolutionaries of 1789 shared many elements in common with their American counterparts, including an awareness of the writings of the same philosophers and intellectuals on both sides of the Atlantic whose works questioned existing institutions and traditions in favor of democracy, liberty, and equality. Members of the educated classes in France were familiar with the writings of the American Tom Paine, just as Benjamin Franklin had read the works of the French Enlightenment thinkers. Yet to understand the Revolution in France, which, like its American predecessor, also embodied new ideas about government and citizenship, one must understand the distinctive nature of French society, economy, and politics in the 50 years or so preceding 1789 and the crisis in the Old Regime that was hidden from the artist who depicted Louis XVI, Franklin, and Washington as brothers in revolution.

The Crisis of the Old Regime in France, 1715–1788

France in the eighteenth century, the age of the Enlightenment, was a state invigorated by new ideas, but it was also dominated by tradition. The traditional institutions of monarchy, Church, and aristocracy defined power and status. Talk of reform, progress, and perfectibility coexisted with the social realities of privileges and obligations determined by birth. The eighteenth century was a time when old ways prevailed even as a new view of the world was taking shape.

At the end of the eighteenth century, a number of foreign visitors to France commented on the disparities that characterized French social and political life. One English visitor in particular—Arthur Young (1741–1820), an agronomist writing on his travels in France in the 1780s—observed that although a prosperous land, France was pocked with extreme poverty; that although a land of high culture and great art, it was riddled with ignorance, illiteracy, and superstition; and that although a land with a centralized bureaucracy, it was also saddled with local pettiness and obsolete practices.

The tensions generated by the clash of continuity and change made it an exciting and complex period in France. Reformers talked of progress while peasants still used wooden plows. The *philosophes* glorified reason in a world of violence, superstition, and fear. The great crisis of eighteenth-century France, the French Revolution, destroyed the *ancien régime* (old regime). But the revolution was as much a product of continuities and traditions as it was a product of change and the challenge of new ideas.

Louis XV's France

Louis XV, like his great-grandfather Louis XIV, laid claim to rule as an absolute monarch. He insisted that "the rights and interests of the nation ... are of necessity one with my own, and lie in my hands only." Such claims failed to mask the weaknesses of royal rule. Louis XV lacked a sufficiently developed bureaucracy to administer and tax the nation in an evenhanded fashion. By the beginning of the eighteenth century, the absolute monarchy had extended royal influence into the new areas of policing, administration, lawmaking, and taxation. But none of the changes proved sufficient to meet the growing needs of the state.

The heightened tensions between the monarch and the aristocracy found expression in various institutions, especially the parlements, which were the 13 sovereign courts in the French judicial system, with their seats in Paris and a dozen provincial centers. The magistrates of each parlement were members of the aristocracy, some of them nobles of recent origin and others of long standing, depending on the locale. The king needed the parlements to record royal decrees before they could become law. The recording process conferred real political power on the parlements, which could withhold approval for the king's policies by refusing to register his decrees. When decrees involved taxation, the magistrates often refused to endorse them. By successfully challenging the king, the parlements became a battleground between the elite, who claimed that they represented the nation, and the king, who said the nation was himself.

The king repeatedly attempted to neutralize the power of the parlements by relying instead on his own state bureaucracy. His agents in the provinces, called intendants, were accountable directly to the central government. The intendants, as the king's men, and the magistrates who presided in the parlements represented contradictory claims to power. As the king's needs increased in the second half of the eighteenth century, the situation was becoming intolerable for those exercising power and those aspiring to rule in the name and for the good of the nation.

The Financial Crisis. The nadir of Louis XV's reign came in 1763, with the French defeat in the Seven Years' War both on the Continent and in the colonies. In the Treaty of Paris, France ceded territory, including its Canadian holdings, to Great Britain. France lost more than lands: it lost its footing in the competition with its chief rival, Great Britain, which had been pulling ahead of France in international affairs since the mid-eighteenth century. The war was also a financial debacle, paid for by loans secured against the guarantee of victory. The defeat not only left France barren of funds, it also promoted further expenditures for strengthening the French navy against the superior British fleet. New taxation was the way out of the financial trap in which the king now found himself.

Louis XV's revenue problem was not easily solved. In order to raise taxes, the king had to turn to the recording function of the parlements. Following the costly Seven Years' War, the parlements chose to exercise the power of refusal by blocking a proportional tax to be imposed on nobles and commoners alike. The magistrates resisted taxation, arguing that the king was attacking the liberty of his subjects by attempting to tax those who were exempt by virtue of their privileged status.

A Failed Solution. René Nicolas Charles Augustin de Maupeou (1714–1792), Louis XV's chancellor from 1768 to 1774, decided that the political power of the parlements had to be curbed. In 1770, in an attempt to coerce the magistrates into compliance with the king's wishes, he engineered the overthrow of the Parlement of Paris, the most important of the high courts. The magistrates who remained obdurate were sent into exile. New courts, whose membership was based on appointment instead of the sale of offices, took their place amid much public criticism. Ultimately, Maupeou's attempt failed. His action did nothing to improve the monarch's image, and it did even less to solve the fiscal problems of the regime. The conflict between Louis XV and the parlements revealed the dependent nature of the monarchy that claimed to be absolute and accountable only to God.

This cartoon from 1789 depicts Necker (at left) showing the king how to conceal the size of the deficit from the Estates. On the wall, a list of royal loans is headed "New ways to revive France"—but the total is "Deficit."

When Louis XV (1715–1774) died, he was a hated man. In his 59-year reign, he managed to turn the public against him. He was denounced as a tyrant who was trying to starve his people, a slave to the mistresses who ruled his court, and an indecisive sybarite dominated by evil ministers. The declining fortunes and the damaged prestige of the monarchy, however, reflected more than the personality traits of an ineffectual king: they reflected structural challenges to fiscal solvency and absolutist rule that the monarchy was unable to meet.

The dignity and prestige of the monarchy were seriously damaged in the course of Louis XV's long reign. His legacy was well captured in the expression erroneously attributed to him, *Après moi le deluge* ("After me, the flood"). Continuing to live the good life at the court, he failed dismally to offset rising state expenditures—caused primarily by military needs—with new sources of revenue. In 1774, Louis XV died suddenly of smallpox. His unprepared 20-year-old grandson, Louis XVI (1774–1792), a young man who amused himself by hunting and pursuing his hobby as an amateur locksmith, was left to try to stanch the flood.

Louis XVI and the National Debt

Louis XV left to his heir Louis XVI the legacy of a disastrous deficit. From the beginning of his reign, Louis XVI was caught in the vicious circle of excessive state spending—above all, military spending—followed by bouts of heavy borrowing. Borrowing at high rates required the government to pay out huge sums in interest and service fees on the loans that were keeping it afloat. The outlays in turn piled the state's indebtedness ever higher, requiring more loans, and threatening to topple the whole financial structure of the state and the regime itself.

In inheriting the trouble-ridden fiscal structure, Louis XVI made his own contribution to it. Following in the footsteps of his grandfather, he involved France in a costly war, the War of American Independence (1775–1783), by supporting the 13 colonies in their revolt against Great Britain. The involvement brought the French monarchy to the brink of bankruptcy. Contrary to public opinion, most of the state's expenditures did not go toward lavishing luxuries on the royal court and the royal family at Versailles. They went to pay off loans. More than half of the state budget in the 1780s represented interest on loans taken to pay for foreign military ventures.

The king needed money, and he needed it fast. To those who could afford to purchase them, the king continued to sell offices that carried with them titles, revenues, and privileges. He also relied on the sale of annuities that paid high interest rates and that attracted speculators, large and small. The crown had leased out its rights to collect the salt tax in return for large lump-sum advances from the Royal General Farms, a syndicate of about 100 wealthy financier families. The Royal General Farms reaped healthy profits on their annual transactions at the state's expense. The combined revenues collected by the king through the various stratagems were little more than a drop in the vast ocean of debt that threatened to engulf the state.

The Problem with Tax Revenues. The existing tax structure proved hopelessly inadequate to meet the state's needs. The *taille,* a direct tax, was levied, either on persons or on land, according to region. Except for those locales where the taille was attached to land, the nobility was always exempt from direct taxation. Members of the bourgeoisie could also avoid the direct tax as citizens of towns enjoying exemption. That meant that the wealthy, those best able to pay, were often exempt. Indirect taxes, such as those on salt (the *gabelle*) and on food and drink (the *aide*), and internal and external customs taxes were regressive taxes that weighed heavily on those least able to pay. The peasantry bore the brunt of the nation's tax burden, and Louis XVI knew all too well that he could not squeeze blood from a stone by increasing indirect taxes. A peasantry too weighted down would collapse—or rebel.

The privileged elite persisted in rejecting the crown's attempts to tax them. As one of the first acts of his reign, in 1775 Louis XVI had restored the magistrates to their posts in the parlements, treating their offices as a form of property of which they had been deprived. In his conciliatory act, Louis XVI nevertheless stressed that the self-interest of the aristocracy was at odds with the common good of the nation and urged the approval of his programs. Nevertheless, by 1776 the Parlement of Paris was again obstructing royal decrees.

Louis XVI appointed Anne Robert Jacques Turgot (1727–1781) as his first controller-general. Turgot's reformist economic ideas were influenced by Enlightenment philosophes. In order to generate revenues, Turgot reasoned, France needed to prosper economically. The government was in a position to stimulate economic growth by eliminating regulations, economizing at court, and improving the network of roads through a tax on landowners. Each of Turgot's reforms offended established interests, thereby ensuring his early defeat. Emphasis on a laissez-faire economy outraged the guilds; doing away with the forced labor of peasants on the roads (the *corvée*) threatened privileged groups who had never before been taxed.

Necker's Reforms. As he floundered about for a solution to his economic difficulties, the king turned to a new adviser, Jacques Necker (1732–1804), a Swiss-born Protestant banker. The king and the public expected great things from Necker, whose international business experience was counted on to save the day. Necker, a prudent man, applied his accounting skills to measuring—for the first time—the total income and expenditures of the French state. The budget he produced and widely circulated allayed everyone's fears of certain doom and assured the nation that no new taxes were necessary—an assurance based on disastrous miscalculations. Instead of raising taxes, Necker committed his ministry to eliminating costly inefficiencies. He set his sights on contracts of the farmers-general, collectors of the indirect salt taxes, whom he likened to weeds sprouting in a swamp. Necker's aim was to reduce ordinary expenses of the realm in order to be ready for the extraordinary ones associated with waging a war. Such policies made him enemies in high places and numbered his days in office.

Necker and those who preceded him in controlling and directing the finances of the state under Louis XV and Louis XVI were committed to reforming the system. All the advisers recognized that the state's fiscal problems were structural and required enlightened solutions, but no two of them agreed on the same program of reforms. Necker had somehow captivated popular opinion, and there was widespread regret expressed over his forced resignation.

Charles Alexandre de Calonne (1734–1802), appointed controller-general in 1783, had his own ideas of how to bail out the ship of state. He authored a program of reforms that would have shifted the tax burden off those least able to pay and onto those best able to support the state. Specifically, he proposed a tax on land proportional to land values, a measure that would have most seriously affected the land-rich nobility. In addition, taxes that affected the peasantry were to be lightened or eliminated. Finally, Calonne proposed the sale of Church lands for revenues. In an attempt to bypass the recalcitrant parlements, Calonne advised the crown in 1787 to convene an Assembly of Notables made up of 150 individuals from the magistracy, the Church hierarchy, the titled nobility, and municipal bodies, for the purpose of enlisting their support for reforms. Louis listened to Calonne, who was denounced by the Assembly of Notables for attacking the rights of the privileged. He too was forced to resign. All of Louis XVI's attempts to persuade the nobility to agree to tax reforms had failed.

A new controller-general, Archbishop Loménie de Brienne (1727–1794), recommended emergency loans. The crown once again disbanded the Paris Parlement, which was now threatening to block loans as well as taxes. Aristocratic magistrates now insisted on a constitution, in which their own right to govern would be safeguarded and the accountability of the king would be defined. In opposing the royal reforms, nobles spoke of the "rights of man" and used the term *citizen*. They had no sympathy for tax programs that threatened their privileges.

The Three Estates

Louis XVI was a desperate man in 1788, so desperate that he yielded to the condition placed on him by the Paris Parlement: he agreed to convene the Estates-General, a medieval body that had not met since 1614 and that had been considered obsolete with the rise of a centralized bureaucratic government.

The Estates-General. Eighteenth-century French society continued to be divided by law and custom into a pyramid of three tiers called orders or estates. At the top were those who prayed (the clergy), followed by those who fought (the nobility). The base of the pyramid was formed by the largest of the three estates, those who worked—the bourgeoisie, the peasantry, and urban and rural workers. The Estates-General included equal representation from the three estates of the clergy, nobility, and commoners. Yet only about 200,000 subjects belonged to the first two estates. The Third Estate was composed of all those members of the realm who enjoyed a common identity only in their lack of privilege—more than 23 million French people. Traditionally, each of the three orders was equally weighted. The arrangement favored the nobility, who controlled the first two estates. The nobility, therefore, was understandably not worried about the prospect of having the Estates-General decide the tax-reform program.

In the second half of the eighteenth century, the traditional groups no longer reflected social realities—a situation that proved to be a source of serious problems for the Estates-General. The piety of the first order had been called into doubt as religious leaders were criticized for using the vast wealth of the Church for personal benefit instead of public worship. The protective military function of the second order had ceased to

This cartoon depicts the plight of the French peasants. An old farmer is bowed down under the weight of the privileged aristocracy and clergy while birds and rabbits, protected by unfair game laws, eat his crops.

exist with the rise of the state and the changing nature of war. Some members of the bourgeoisie—those who worked with their heads, not their hands—shared privileges with the nobility and aspired to a noble lifestyle, in spite of their legal and customary presence in the ranks of the Third Estate alongside peasants and urban workers.

The vast majority of French subjects who constituted the Third Estate certainly were identified by work, but the array of mental and physical labor—and lack of work—splintered the estate into a myriad of occupations, aspirations, and identities. All power flowed upward in the arrangement, with the First and Second Estates dominating the social and political universe. Women and men accepted the hierarchy as the natural organization of society in eighteenth-century France.

The king continued to stand at the pinnacle of the eighteenth-century social pyramid. Traditionally revered as the "father" of his subjects, he claimed to be divinely appointed by God. Kingship in the era had a dual nature. The king was both supreme overlord (a legacy from feudal times) and absolute monarch. As supreme overlord, he stood dominant over the aristocracy and the court. As absolute monarch, he stood at the head of the state and society. When the king equated himself with the state—*"L'état, c'est moi,"* as Louis XIV boasted—all problems—economic, social, and political—also came to be identified with the king. Absolutism required a weakened nobility and a bureaucracy strong enough to help the monarchy to adjust to changes. After the death of Louis XIV in 1715, Louis XV and Louis XVI faced a resurgent aristocracy without the support of a state bureaucracy capable of successfully challenging aristocratic privilege or of solving fiscal problems.

Aristocratic Power and Noble Values. "To live nobly," that is, to live as a noble, was the social ideal to which one could aspire in the eighteenth century. While the system of orders set clear boundaries of social status, distinctions within estates created new hierarchies. The clergy, a privileged order, contained both commoners and nobles, but leadership in the Church depended on social rank. The aristocracy retained control of the bishoprics even as an activist element among the lower clergy agitated for reforms and better salaries. In a state in which the king claimed to rule by God's will, Catholicism, virtually the state religion, was important in legitimizing the divine claims of the monarchy.

There were two kinds of nobility: the older nobility of the sword, who claimed descent from medieval times, and the more recent nobility of the robe, who had acquired their position through the purchase of offices that conferred noble status. By increasing the numbers of the nobility of the robe, Louis XIV had hoped to undermine the power of the aristocracy as a whole and to decrease its political influence. But aristocrats rallied and closed ranks against the dilution of their power. As a result, both Louis XV and Louis XVI faced a reviving rather than a declining aristocracy. One in four nobles had moved from the bourgeoisie to the aristocratic ranks in the eighteenth century; two out of every three had been ennobled during the seventeenth or eighteenth centuries. Nobles had succeeded in restoring their economic and social power. Furthermore, a growing segment of the aristocracy, influenced by Enlightenment ideas and the example of English institutions, was intent on increasing the political dominance of the aristocracy.

Nobles strengthened their powers in two ways. First, they monopolized high offices and closed access to non-nobles, thereby controlling posts in ministries, the Church, and the army. Second, the nobility benefited greatly from the doubling in land values brought on by the increase in the value of crops. Nobles enjoyed privileges, the greatest being, in most cases, exemption from taxes. Seeking ever higher returns from the land, some members of the aristocracy adopted new agricultural techniques to achieve greater crop yields. There were poor aristocrats who lacked the lands to benefit from the trend, but those who did control sizable holdings profited greatly from higher dues paid to them and reaped increased incomes from crops. In addition, many aristocrats revived their feudal claims to ancient seigneurial, or lordly, privileges. They hired lawyers to unearth old claims and hired agents to collect dues.

A spirit of innovation characterized the values of certain members of the nobility. Although technically prevented from participating in trade by virtue of their titles and privileges, an active group among the nobility succeeded in making fortunes in metallurgy, glassmaking, and mining. Others participated in trade. Those nobles were an economically dynamic and innovative segment of the aristocracy. In spite of the obsolete aspect of their privileges, aristocrats were often responsible for the introduction of modern ideas and techniques in the management of estates and in the bookkeeping involved with collection of rents.

Capitalist techniques were not unknown to nobles adapting to the marketplace. Those nobles formed an elite partnership with forward-looking members of the bourgeoisie.

The Third Estate. The Third Estate was composed of the vast majority of the French state, those individuals who had no claim to aristocratic status. Commoners—that is, those who did not enjoy the privileges of the nobility—constituted a broad range of the French populace. The peasantry was by far the largest group of commoners. Most French peasants were free, no longer attached to the soil as serfs were in a feudal system. Yet all peasants endured common obligations placed on them by the crown and the privileged classes. A bewildering array of taxes afflicted peasants: they owed the tithe to the Church, land taxes to the state, and seigneurial dues and rents to the landlord. In some areas, peasants repaired roads and drew lots for military service. Dues affected almost every aspect of rural life, including harvests and the sale of property. In addition, indirect taxes like that on salt were a serious burden for the peasantry. As if all that were not enough, peasants who were forced to take loans to survive from one harvest to another paid exorbitant interest rates. No matter how bad conditions were, peasants had to be sure to save the seed for next year's crop.

The peasants who staggered and collapsed under all their obligations were forced to work as itinerants or leave the land. The precariousness of rural life and the increase in population in the countryside contributed to the permanent displacement and destitution of a growing sector of rural society. Without savings and destroyed by poor harvests, impoverished rural inhabitants wandered the countryside looking for odd jobs and eventually begging to survive. The labor of women was essential to the survival of the rural family. Peasant women sought employment in towns and cities as seamstresses and servants in order to send money back home to struggling relatives. Children, too, added their earnings to the family pot. In spite of various strategies for survival, more and more peasant families were disrupted by the end of the eighteenth century.

Another group of commoners in the Third Estate, the bourgeoisie, embraced within it a variety of professions, from bankers and financiers to businessmen, merchants, entrepreneurs, lawyers, shopkeepers, and artisans. Along with the nobility, wealthy bourgeois formed the urban elites that administered cities and towns. Prestigious service to the state or the purchase of offices that carried with them noble status enabled the wealthiest members of the bourgeoisie to move into the ranks of the nobility. Many bourgeois served as middlemen for the nobility by running estates and collecting dues.

No longer tied to the land as serfs, peasants were nevertheless bound to rural life for their survival.

Like the rest of the social universe, the world of artisans and workers was shaded with various gradations of wealth and status. Those who owned their own shops and perhaps employed other workers stood as an elite among the working class. In spite of their physical proximity, there was a vast difference between those who owned their own shops and those who earned wages or were paid by the piece. Wage earners represented about 30 percent of the population of cities and towns, and their numbers were swelling as artisans were pushed out of their guilds and peasants were pushed off their land.

Those who worked in crafts were a labor elite, and guilds were intended to protect the corporations of masters, journeymen, and apprentices through monopolistic measures. But the emphasis on free trade and the expansion of markets in the eighteenth century weakened the hold of the guilds. Merchants often took guilds over and paid workers by the piece. The effect was a reduction in the wages of skilled workers. By the 1780s, most journeymen who hoped to be masters knew that their dream would never be realized.

So, when Louis XVI announced in August 1788 that the Estates-General would meet at Versailles in May 1789, people from all walks of life hoped for some redress of the miseries. The king hoped that the clergy, nobility, and commoners would somehow solve his fiscal problems. Yet every social group, from the nobles to the poorest laborers, had its own agenda and its own ideas about justice, social status, and economic well-being.

THE FIRST STAGE OF THE FRENCH REVOLUTION, 1789–1792

Those who lived through it were sure that there had never been a time like it before. The French Revolution, or the Great Revolution, as it was known to contemporaries, was a time of creation and discovery. The ten years from 1789 to 1799 were punctuated by genuine euphoria and democratic transformations. From the privileged elites who initiated the overthrow of the existing order to the peasants and workers, men and women, who railed against tyranny, the revolution touched every segment of society.

The revolution achieved most in the area of politics. The overthrow of absolutist monarchy brought with it new social theories, new symbols, and new behavior. The excitement of anarchy was matched by the terror of repression. Revolutionary France had to contend with war throughout Europe. The revolution had its dark side of violence and instability: in its wake came internal discord, civil war, and violent repression. In the search for a new order, political forms followed one after the other in rapid succession: constitutional monarchy, republic, oligarchy. The creation of Napoleon's dictatorship at the end of the century signified that the revolution had come to an end.

Revolutionary incidents flared up throughout Europe in the second half of the eighteenth century in the Netherlands, Belgium, and Ireland. Absolute authority was challenged and sometimes modified. Across the Atlantic, American colonists concerned with the principle of self-rule had thrown off the yoke of the British in the War of Independence. But none of the events, including the American Revolution, was so violent in breaking with the old order, so extensive in involving millions of men and women in political action, and so consequential for the political futures of other European states as was the French Revolution. The triumphs and contradictions of the revolutionary experiment in democracy mark the end of the old order and the beginning of modern history. Politics would never be the same again.

Taking Politics to the People

Choosing representatives for the Estates-General in March and April 1789 stirred up hope and excitement in every corner of France. From the very beginning, there were warning signs that a more astute monarch might have noticed. The call for national elections set in motion a politicizing process the king could not control.

Rising Expectations. Members of the Third Estate, traditionally excluded from political and social power, were presented with the opportunity of expressing their opinions on the state of government and society. In an increasingly literate age, pamphlets, broadsides, and political tracts representing every political persuasion blanketed France. Those who could not read stood in marketplaces and city squares or sat around evening fires and had the political literature read to them. Farmhands and urban laborers realized that they were participating in the same process as their social betters, and they believed they had a right to speak and be heard.

It was a time of great hope, especially for people who had been buffeted by the rise in prices, decline in real wages, and the hunger that followed crop failures and poor harvests. There was new promise of a respite and a solution. Taxes could be discussed and changed, the state bureaucracy could be reformed—or better, abolished. Intellectuals discussed political alternatives in the salons of the wealthy. Nobles and bourgeois met in philosophical societies dedicated to enlightened thought. Commoners gathered in cafes to drink and debate. Although the poor often fell outside of the network of communication, they were not immune to the ideas that emerged. In the end, people of all classes had opinions and were more certain than ever of their right to express their ideas. Absolutism was in trouble, though Louis XVI did not know it, as people began to forge a collectively shared idea of politics. People now had a forum—the Estates-General—and a focus—the politics of taxation. But most important, they had the elections.

In competing for power, some members of the Third Estate were well aware of their vast numerical superiority over the nobility. Because of it, they demanded greater representation than the 300 members per estate defined according to the practices of 1614. At the very least, they argued, the number of representatives of the Third Estate should be doubled to 600 members, giving commoners equality in numbers with nobles and priests together. Necker, recalled as director-general of finance in August 1788, agreed to the doubling in the size of the Third Estate as a compromise but left unresolved the additional demand of vote by head rather than by order. If voting was to be left as it was, in accordance with the procedures of 1614, the nobility who controlled the First and Second Estates would determine all outcomes. With a voting procedure by head instead of by order, however, the deputies of the Third Estate could easily dominate the Estates-General, confident that they could count on parish priests and liberal nobles such as the French hero of the American Revolution, the Marquis de Lafayette, to defect from voting with the First and Second Estates and join their cause.

Revolutionary France. The Revolution was not merely a Parisian phenomenon, as this map shows. The forces of the Revolution and the Counterrevolution spread across France. The French borders in 1793 were the result of two years of military expansion in Europe.

"If Only the King Knew." In conjunction with the political activity and in scheduled meetings, members of all three estates drew up statements of their problems. It took place in a variety of forums, including guilds and village and town meetings. The people of France set down their grievances in notebooks—known as *cahiers de doléances*—that were then carried to Versailles by the deputies elected to the Estates-General. The cahiers expressed the particular grievances of each estate. The notebooks contained a collective outpouring of problems and are important for two major reasons. First, they made clear the similarity of grievances shared throughout France. Second, they indicated the extent to which a common political culture, based on a concern with political reform, had permeated different levels of French society. Both the privileged and the nonprivileged identified a common enemy in the system of state bureaucracy to which the monarch was so strongly tied. Although the king was still addressed with respect, new concerns with liberty, equality, property, and the rule of law were voiced.

"If only the king knew!" In that phrase, French men and women had for generations expressed their belief in the inevitability of their fate and the benevolence of their king. They saw the king as a loving and wise father who would not tolerate the injustices visited on his subjects if only he knew what was really happening. In 1789, peasants and workers were questioning why their lives could not be better, but they continued to express their trust in the king. Combined with their old faith was a new hope. The peasants in the little town of Saintes recorded their newly formed expectations in their cahier:

> Our king, the best of kings and father of a great and wise family, will soon know everything. All vices will be destroyed. All the great virtues of industriousness, honesty, modesty, honor, patriotism, meekness, friendliness, equality, concord, pity, and thrift will prevail and wisdom will rule supreme.

Those who opposed the revolution later alleged that the notebooks proved the existence of a highly coordinated plot on the part of secret societies out to destroy the regime. They were wrong. Similarities in complaints, demands, and language proved the forging of a new political consciousness, not a conspiracy. Societies and clubs circulated "model" cahiers among themselves, resulting in the use of similar forms and vocabulary. People were questioning their traditional roles and now had elected deputies who would represent them before the king. In the spring of 1789, a severe economic crisis that heightened political uncertainty swept through France. For a king expected to save the situation, time was running out.

Convening the Estates-General

The elected deputies arrived at Versailles at the beginning of May 1789 carrying in their valises and trunks the grievances of their estates. The opening session of the Estates-General took place in a great hall especially constructed for the event. The 1248 deputies presented a grand spectacle as they filed to their assigned places to hear speeches by the king and his ministers. Contrasts among the participants were immediately apparent. Seated on a raised throne under a canopy at one end of the hall, Louis XVI was vested in full kingly regalia. On his right sat the archbishops and cardinals of the First Estate, strikingly clad in the pinks and purples of their offices. On his left were the richly and decorously attired nobility. Facing the stage sat the 648 deputies of the Third Estate, dressed in plain black suits, stark against the colorful and costly costumes of the privileged. It was clear, in the most visual terms, that "clothes make the man." Members of the Third Estate had announced beforehand that they would not follow the ancient custom for commoners of kneeling at the king's entrance. Fired by the hope of equal treatment and an equal share of power, they had come to Versailles to make a constitution. The opening ceremony degenerated into a moment of confusion over whether members of the Third Estate should be able to wear their hats in the presence of the king. Many saw in the politics of clothing a tense beginning to their task.

The Crisis in Voting by Estate. The tension between commoners and privileged was further aggravated by the unresolved issue of how the voting was to proceed. The Third Estate was adamant in its demand for vote by head. The privileged orders were equally firm in insisting on vote by order. Paralysis set in, as days dragged into weeks and the Estates were unable to act. The body that was to save France from fiscal collapse was hopelessly deadlocked.

Two men whose backgrounds made them unlikely heroes emerged as leaders of the Third Estate. One, Abbé Emmanuel Joseph Sieyès (1748–1836), was a member of the clergy who frequented Parisian salons. The other, the comte Honoré Gabriel Victor de Mirabeau (1749–1791), a black sheep among the nobility, had spent time in prison because of his father's charges that he was a defiant son who led a misspent, debauched, and profligate youth. In spite of his nobility, Mirabeau appeared at Versailles as a deputy for Aix and Marseilles to the Third Estate. His oratory and presence commanded attention from the start. As a consummate politician, Mirabeau combined forces with Sieyès, who had already established his reputation as a firebrand reformer with his eloquent pamphlet, "What Is the Third Estate?" published in January 1789.

Sieyès and Mirabeau reminded members of the Third Estate of the reformist consensus that characterized their ranks. Under their influence, the Third Estate decided to proceed with its own meetings. On 17 June 1789, the Third Estate, joined by some sympathetic clergy, changed its name to the National Assembly as

"WHAT IS THE THIRD ESTATE?"

As an ambitious clergyman from Chartres, Abbé Emmanuel Joseph Sieyès was a member of the First Estate. Yet Sieyès was elected deputy to the Estates-General for the Third Estate on the basis of his attacks on aristocratic privilege. He participated in the writing and editing of the great documents of the early revolution: the Oath of the Tennis Court and the Declaration of the Rights of Man and Citizen. The pamphlet for which he is immortalized in revolutionary lore was his daring, "What Is the Third Estate?" Written in January 1789, it boldly confronted the bankruptcy of the system of privilege of the Old Regime and threw down the gauntlet to those who ruled France. In this document the revolution found its rallying point.

1st. What is the third estate? Everything.

2nd. What has it been heretofore in the political order? Nothing.

3rd. What does it demand? To become something therein....

Who, then, would dare to say that the third estate has not within itself all that is necessary to constitute a complete nation? It is the strong and robust man whose one arm remains enchained. If the privileged order were abolished, the nation would not be something less but something more. Thus, what is the third estate? Everything; but an everything shackled and oppressed. What would it be without the privileged order? Everything; but an everything free and flourishing. Nothing can progress without it; everything would proceed infinitely better without the others. It is not sufficient to have demonstrated that the privileged classes, far from being useful to the nation, can only enfeeble and injure it; it is necessary, moreover, to prove that the nobility does not belong to the social organization at all; that, indeed, it may be a *burden* upon the nation, but that it would not know how to constitute a part thereof.

The third estate, then, comprises everything appertaining to the nation; and whatever is not the third estate may not be regarded as being of the nation. What is the third estate? Everything!

an assertion of its true representation of the French nation. Three days later, members of the new National Assembly found themselves locked out of their regular meeting room by the king's guard. Outraged by the insult, they moved to a nearby indoor tennis court, where they vowed to stay together for the purpose of writing a constitution. The event, known as the Oath of the Tennis Court, marked the end of the absolutist monarchy and the beginning of a new concept of the state that power resided in the people. The revolution had begun.

The Importance of Public Opinion. The drama of Versailles, a staged play of gestures, manners, oaths, and attire, also marked the beginning of a far-reaching political revolution. Although it was a drama that took place behind closed doors, it was not one unknown to the general public. Throughout May and June 1789, Parisians trekked to Versailles to watch the deliberations and then they brought the news back to the capital. Deputies wrote home to their constituents to keep them abreast of events. Newspapers that reported daily on the wranglings and pamphleteers who analyzed them spread the news throughout the nation. Information, often conflicting, stirred up anxiety; news of conflict encouraged action.

The frustration and stalemate of the Estates-General threatened to put the spark to the kindling of urban unrest. The people of Paris had suffered through a harsh winter and spring under the burdens of high prices (especially of bread), limited supplies, and relentless tax demands. The rioting of the spring had for the moment ceased as people waited for their problems to be solved by the deputies of the Estates-General. The suffering of the urban poor was not new, but their ability to connect economic hardships with the politics at Versailles and to blame the government was. As hopes began to dim with the news of political stalemate, news broke of the creation of the National Assembly. It was greeted with new anticipation.

The Storming of the Bastille

The king, who had temporarily withdrawn from sight following the death of his son at the beginning of June, reemerged to meet with the representatives of each of the three estates and propose reforms, including a constitutional monarchy. But Louis XVI refused to accept the now popularly supported National Assembly as a legitimate body, insisting instead that he must rely on the three estates for advice. He simply did not understand that the choice was no longer his to make. He summoned troops to Versailles and began concentrating soldiers in Paris. Civilians continually clashed with members of the military, whom they jostled and jeered. The urban crowds recognized the threat of repression that the troops represented. People decided to meet force with force. To do so, they needed arms themselves—and they knew where to get them.

On 14 July 1789, the irate citizens of Paris stormed the Bastille, a royal armory that also served as a prison for a handful of debtors. The storming of the Bastille became the great symbol in the revolutionary legend of the overthrow of the tyranny and oppression of the old regime. But it is significant for another reason. It was an expression of the power of the people to take politics into their own hands. Parisians were following the lead of their deputies in Versailles. They had formed a citizen militia known as the National Guard, and they were prepared to defend their concept of justice and law.

The people who stormed the Bastille were not the poor, the unemployed, the criminals, or the urban rabble, as their detractors portrayed them. They were bourgeois and petit-bourgeois: shopkeepers, guild members, family men and women who considered it their right to seize arms in order to protect their interests. The Marquis de Lafayette (1757–1834), a noble beloved of the people because of his participation in the American Revolution, helped organize the National Guard. Under his direction, the militia adopted the tricolor flag as its standard. The tricolor combined the red and blue colors of the city of Paris with the white of the Bourbon royal family. It became the flag of the revolution, replacing the fleur-de-lis of the Bourbons. It is the national flag of France today.

The king could no longer dictate the terms of the constitution. By their actions, the people in arms had ratified the National Assembly. Louis XVI was forced to yield. The events in Paris set off similar uprisings in cities and towns throughout France. National guards in provincial cities modeled themselves after the Parisian militia. Government officials fled their posts and abandoned their responsibilities. Commoners stood ready to fill the power vacuum. But the revolution was not just an urban phenomenon: the peasantry had their own grievances and their own way of making a revolution.

The Revolution of the Peasantry

In the spring and early summer of 1789, food shortages drove bands of armed peasants to attack manor houses throughout France. In the areas surrounding Paris and Versailles, peasants destroyed game and devastated the forests where the king and his nobles hunted. The anger reflected in the seemingly isolated events was suspended as the hope grew that the proceedings at Versailles would produce results. Remote as peasant involvement in the drawing up of the cahiers might have been, peasants everywhere expected that aid was at hand.

The Fear of An Aristocratic Plot. News of the events of Versailles and then of the revolutionary action in Paris did not reassure rural inhabitants. By the end of June the hope of deliverance from crippling taxes and dues was rapidly fading. The news of the Oath of the Tennis Court and the storming of the Bastille terrified country folk, who saw the actions as evidence of an aristocratic plot that threatened sorely needed reforms. As information moved along postal routes in letters from delegates to their supporters, or news was repeated in the Sunday market gatherings, distortions and exaggerations crept in. It seemed to rural inhabitants that their world was falling apart. Some peasants believed that Paris was in the hands of brigands and that the king and the Estates-General were victims of an aristocratic plot. Rural vision, fueled by empty stomachs, was apocalyptic.

That state of affairs was aggravated as increasing numbers of peasants were pushed off the land to seek employment as transient farm laborers, moving from one area to another with the cycles of sowing and harvesting. Throughout the 1780s, the number of peasants without land was increasing steadily. Starving men, women, and children, filthy and poorly dressed, were frightening figures to villagers who feared that the same fate would befall them with the next bad harvest. As one landowner lamented, "We cannot lie down without

This lively amateur painting of the fall of the Bastille is by Claude Cholat, one of the attackers. Tradition has it that Cholat is manning the cannon in the background. The inscription proclaims that the painting is by one of the "conquerors of the Bastille."

fear, the nighttime paupers have tormented us greatly, to say nothing of the daytime ones, whose numbers are considerable."

Most peasants had lived in the same place for generations and knew only the confines of their own villages. They were uneasy about what existed beyond the horizon. Transients, often speaking strange dialects, disrupted and threatened the social universe of the village. In order to survive, wanderers often resorted to petty theft, stealing fruit from trees or food from unwatched hearths. Often traveling in groups, hordes of vagabonds struck fear into the hearts of farm workers, trampling crops and sleeping in open fields. Peasants were sure that the unfortunate souls were brigands paid by the local aristocracy to persecute a peasantry already stretched to the breaking point.

The Peasant Revolt. Hope gave way to fear. Beginning on 20 July 1789, peasants in different areas of France reacted collectively throughout France, spreading false rumors of a great conspiracy. Fear gripped whole villages and in some areas spawned revolt. Just as urban workers had connected their economic hardships to politics, so too did desperate peasants see their plight in political terms. They banded together and marched to the residences of the local nobility, breaking into châteaus with a single mission in mind: to destroy all legal documents by which nobles claimed payments, dues, and services from local peasants. They drove out the lords and in some cases burned their châteaus, putting an end to the tyranny of the privileged over the countryside. The peasants had taken matters into their own hands. They intended to consign the last vestiges of aristocratic privilege to the bonfires of aristocratic documents.

The overthrow of privileges rooted in a feudal past was not as easy as that. Members of the National Assembly were aghast at the eruption of rural violence. They knew that to stay in power they had to maintain peace. They also knew that to be credible they had to protect property. Peasant destruction of seigneurial claims posed a real dilemma for the bourgeois deputies

Caricature of the nobility and clergy crushing laborers with taxes. (Musee de la Ville de Paris, Musee Carnavalet, Paris, France.)

directing the revolution. If they gave in to peasant demands, they risked losing aristocratic support and undermining their own ability to control events. If they gave in to the aristocracy, they risked a social revolution in the countryside, which they could not police or repress. Liberal members of the aristocracy cooperated with the bourgeois leaders in finding a solution.

In a dramatic meeting that lasted through the night of 4 August 1789, the National Assembly agreed to abolish the principle of privilege. The peasants had won—or thought they had. In the weeks and months ahead, rural people learned that they had lost their own prerogatives—the rights to common grazing and gathering—and were expected to buy their way out of their feudal services. In the meantime, parliamentary action had saved the day: the deputies stabilized the situation through legislating compromise.

Women on the March

Women participated with men in both urban and rural revolutionary actions. Acting on their own, women were responsible for the most dramatic event of the early years of the revolution: in October 1789 they forced the king and the royal family to leave Versailles for Paris to deal in person with the problems of bread supply, high prices, and starvation. Women milling about in the marketplaces of Paris on the morning of 5 October were complaining bitterly about the high cost and shortages of bread. The National Assembly was in session, and the National Guards were patrolling the streets of Paris. But the trappings of political change had no impact on the brutal realities of the marketplace.

Women were in charge of buying the food for their families. Every morning they stood in lines with their neighbors reenacting the familiar ritual. Some mornings they were turned away, told by the baker or his assistants that there was no bread. On other days they

A contemporary print of the women of Paris advancing on Versailles. The determined marchers are shown waving pikes and dragging an artillery piece. The women were hailed as heroines of the revolution.

did not have enough coins in their purses to buy the staple of their diet. Women responsible for managing the consumption of the household were most directly in touch with the state of provisioning the capital. When they were unable to feed their families, the situation became intolerable.

So it was, on the morning of 5 October 1789, that 6000 Parisian women marched out of the city and toward Versailles. They were taking their problem to the king with the demand that he solve it. Later in the day, Lafayette, sympathetic to the women's cause, led the Parisian National Guard to Versailles to mediate events. The women were armed with pikes, the simple weapon available to the poorest defender of the revolution, and they were prepared to use them. The battle came early the next morning, when the women, tired and cold from waiting all night at the gates of the palace, invaded the royal apartments and chased Marie Antoinette from her bedroom. Several members of the royal guards, hated by the people of Paris for alleged insults against the tricolor cockade, were killed by the angry women, who decapitated them and mounted their heads on pikes. A shocked Louis XVI agreed to return with the crowd to Paris. The crowd cheered Louis's decision, which briefly reestablished his personal popularity. But as monarch, he had been humiliated at the hands of women of the capital. Reduced to the roles of "the baker, the baker's wife, and the baker's son" by jeering crowds, the royal family was forced to return to Paris that very day. Louis XVI was now captive to the revolution, whose efforts to form a constitutional monarchy he purported to support.

The Revolution Threatened

The disciplined deliberations of committees intent on fashioning a constitutional monarchy replaced the passion and fervor of revolutionary oratory. The National, or Constituent, Assembly divided France into new administrative units—*départements*—for the purpose of establishing better control over municipal governments. Along with new administrative trappings, the government promoted its own rituals. On 14 July 1790, militias from each of the newly created 83 départements of France came together in Paris to celebrate the first anniversary of the storming of the Bastille. A new national holiday was born and with it a sense of devotion and patriotism for the new France liberated by the revolution. In spite of the unifying elements, however, the newly achieved revolutionary consensus began to show signs of breaking down.

The Church Stripped of Its Power. In February 1790, legislation dissolved all monasteries and convents, except for those that provided aid to the poor or that served as educational institutions. As the French church was stripped of its lands, Pope Pius VI (1775–1799) denounced the principles of the revolution. In July 1790, the government approved the Civil Constitution of the Clergy: priests now became the equivalent of paid agents of the state. By requiring an oath of loyalty to the state from all practicing priests, the National Assembly created a new arena for dissent. Catholics were forced to choose to embrace or reject the revolution. Many "nonjuring" priests who refused to take the oath went into hiding. The wedge driven between the Catholic church and revolutionary France allowed a mass-based counterrevolution to emerge. Aristocratic émigrés who had fled the country because of their opposition to the revolution were languishing for lack of a popular base. From his headquarters in Turin, the king's younger brother, the comte d'Artois, was attempting to incite a civil war in France. When the revolutionaries decided to attack the Church not just as a landed and privileged institution but also as a religious one, the counterrevolution rapidly expanded.

Constitutional Monarchy. The Constitution of 1791, completed after more than two years of deliberations, established a constitutional monarchy with a ministerial executive power answerable to a legislative assembly. Louis XVI, formerly the divinely anointed ruler of France, was now "Louis, by the grace of God and the constitutional law of the state, King of the French." In proclaiming his acceptance of the constitution, Louis expressed the sentiments of many when he said, "The end of the revolution is come. It is time that order be reestablished so that the constitution may receive the support now most necessary to it; it is time to settle the opinion of Europe concerning the destiny of France, and to show that French men are worthy of being free." Louis, who had been wrong often enough in the past, could not have been more mistaken when he declared that the end of the revolution was at hand.

The Constitution of 1791 marked the triumph of the principles of the revolution. But it was at best a precarious political compromise. Months before the ink was dry on the final document, the actions of the

The fleeing Louis XVI and his family were apprehended at Varennes in June 1791.

king doomed the new constitution to failure. To be successful, constitutional monarchy required a king worthy of honor and respect. Louis XVI seemed to be giving the revolutionaries what they wanted by cooperating with the framers of the constitution. Yet late one night in June 1791, Louis XVI, Marie Antoinette, and their children disguised themselves as commoners, crept out of the royal apartments in the Tuileries Palace, and fled Paris. Louis intended to leave France to join foreign forces opposing the revolution at Metz. He got as far as Varennes, where he was captured by soldiers of the National Guards and brought back to a shocked Paris. The king had abandoned the revolution. Although he was not put to death for another year and a half, he was more than ever a prisoner of the revolution. The monarchy was effectively finished as part of a political solution; with its demise went liberal hopes for a constitutional settlement.

The Revolution's Fiscal Crisis. The defection of the king was certainly serious, but it was not the only problem facing the revolutionaries. Other problems plagued the revolutionary government, notably foreign war and the fiscal crisis, coupled with inflation. In order to establish its seriousness and legitimacy, the National Assembly had been willing in 1789 to absorb the debts of the old regime. The new government could not sell titles and offices, as the king had done to deal with financial problems, but it did confiscate Church property. In addition, it issued treasury bonds in the form of assignats in order to raise money. The assignats soon assumed the status of bank notes, and by the spring of 1790 they had become compulsory legal tender. Initially they were to be backed by land confiscated from the Church and sold by the state. But the need for money soon outran the value of the land available, and the government continued to print assignats according to its needs. Depreciation of French currency in international markets and inflation at home resulted. The revolutionary government found itself in a situation which in certain respects was worse than that experienced by Louis XVI before the calling of the Estates-General. Assignat-induced inflation produced a sharp decline in fortunes of bourgeois investors living on fixed incomes. Rising prices meant increased misery for workers and peasants.

New counterrevolutionary groups were becoming frustrated with revolutionary policies. Throughout the winter and spring of 1791–1792, people rioted and demanded that prices be fixed, while the assignat dropped to less than half its face value. Peasants refused to sell crops for the worthless paper. Hoarding further drove up prices. Angry crowds turned to pillaging, rioting, and murder, which became more frequent as the value of the currency declined and prices rose.

Foreign war beginning in the fall of 1791 also challenged stability. Some moderate political leaders welcomed war as a blessing in disguise, since it could divert the attention of the masses away from problems at home and promote loyalty to the revolution. Others envisioned war as a great crusade to bring revolutionary principles to oppressed peoples throughout Europe. The king and queen, trapped by the revolution, saw war as their only hope of liberation. Louis XVI could be rightfully restored as the leader of a France defeated by the sovereigns of Europe. Some who opposed the war believed it would destabilize the revolution. France must solve its problems at home, they argued, before fighting a foreign enemy. Louis, however, encouraged those ministers and advisers eager for battle. In April 1792, France declared war against Austria.

Individuals, events, economic realities, and the nature of politics conspired against the success of the first constitutional experiment. The king's attempt to flee France in the summer of 1791 seriously wounded the attempt at compromise. Many feared that the goals of the revolution could not be preserved in a country at war and with a king of dubious loyalties.

EXPERIMENTING WITH DEMOCRACY: THE REVOLUTION'S SECOND STAGE, 1792–1799

The Revolution was a school for the French nation. A political universe populated by individual citizens replaced the eighteenth-century world of subjects loyal to their king. The new construction of politics, in which all individuals were equal, ran counter to prevailing ideas about collective identities defined in guilds and orders. People on all levels of society learned politics by doing it. In the beginning, experience helped. The elites, both noble and bourgeois, had served in government and administration. But the rules of the game under the old regime had been very different, with birth determining power.

After 1789, all men were declared free and equal, in opportunity if not in rights. Men of ability and talent, who had served as middlemen for the privileged elite under the old regime, now claimed power as their due. Many of them were lawyers, educated in the rules and regulations of the society of orders. They experienced firsthand the problems of the exercise of power in the old regime, and they had their own ideas about reform. But the school of the revolution did not remain the domain of a special class. Women demanded their places but continued to be excluded from the political arena, though the importance of their participation in the revolution was indisputable. Workers talked of seizing their rights, but because of the inherent contradictions of representation and participation, experimenting with democracy led to outcomes that did not look very democratic at all.

Declaring Political Rights

"Liberty consists in the ability to do whatever does not harm another." So wrote the revolutionary deputies of 1789. Sounding a refrain similar to that of the American Declaration of Independence, the Declaration of the Rights of Man and Citizen appeared on 26 August 1789. The document amalgamated a variety of Enlightenment ideas drawn from the works of political philosophy, including those of Locke and Montesquieu. "Men are born and remain free and equal in rights. Social distinctions may be based only on common utility." Perhaps most significant of all was the attention given to property, which was declared a "sacred and inviolable," "natural," and "imprescriptible" right of man.

In the year of tranquility that followed the violent summer of 1789, the new politicians set themselves the task of creating institutions based on the principle of liberty and others embodied in the Declaration of the Rights of Man and Citizen. The result was the Constitution of 1791, a statement of faith in a progressive constitutional monarchy. A king accountable to an elected parliamentary body would lead France into a prosperous and just age. The constitution acknowledged the people's sovereignty as the source of political power. It also enshrined the principle of property by making voting rights dependent on property ownership. All men might be equal before the law, but by the Constitution of 1791 only wealthy men had the right to vote for representatives and hold office.

Civil Liberties. All titles of nobility were abolished. In the early period of the revolution, civil liberties were extended to Protestants and Jews, who had been persecuted under the old regime. Previously excluded groups were granted freedom of thought, worship, and full civil liberties. More reluctantly, deputies outlawed slavery in the colonies in 1794. Slave unrest in Saint Domingue (modern-day Haiti) had coincided with the political conflicts of the revolution and exploded in rebellion in 1791, driving the revolutionaries in Paris to support black independence although it was at odds with French colonial interests. Led by Toussaint L'Ouverture (1743–1803), black rebels worked to found an independent Haitian state, which

Slaves revolting against the French in Saint Domingue in 1791. Napoleon sent an army to restore colonial rule in 1799, but yellow fever decimated the French soldiers, and the rebels defeated the weakened French army in 1803.

was declared in 1804. But the concept of equality with regard to race remained incompletely integrated with revolutionary principles, and slavery was reestablished in the French colonies in 1802.

Women's Rights. Men were the subject of the newly defined rights. No references to women or their rights appear in the constitutions or the official Declarations of Rights. Women's organizations agitated for an equitable divorce law, and divorce was legalized in September 1792. Women were critical actors in the revolution from its very inception, and their presence shaped and directed the outcome of events, as the women's march to Versailles in 1789 made clear. The Marquis de Condorcet (1743–1794), elected to the Legislative Assembly in 1791, was one of the first to chastise the revolutionaries for overlooking the political rights of women who, he pointedly observed, were half of the human race. "Either no individual of the human race has genuine rights, or else all have the same; and he who votes against the right of another, whatever the religion, color, or sex of that other, has henceforth abjured his own." Condorcet argued forcefully but unsuccessfully for the right of women to be educated.

The revolutionaries had declared that liberty was a natural and inalienable right, a universal right that was extended to all with the overthrow of a despotic monarch and a privileged elite. The principle triumphed in religious toleration. Yet the revolutionary concept of liberty foundered on the divergent claims of excluded groups—workers, women, and slaves—who demanded full participation in the world of politics. In 1792, revolutionaries confronted the contradictions inherent in their political beliefs of liberty and equality that were being challenged in the midst of social upheaval and foreign war. In response, the revolution turned to more radical measures to survive.

The Second Revolution: The Revolution of the People

The first revolution, from 1789 through the beginning of 1792, was based on liberty—the liberty to compete, to own, and to succeed. The second revolution, which began in 1792, took equality as its rallying cry. It was the revolution of the working people of French cities. The popular movement that spearheaded political action in 1792 was committed to equality of rights in a way not characteristic of the leaders of the revolution of 1789. Urban workers were not benefiting from the revolution, but they had come to believe in their own power as political beings. Organized on the local level into sections, artisans in cities identified themselves as *sans-culottes*—literally, those trousered citizens who did not wear knee breeches (*culottes*)—to distinguish themselves from the privileged elite.

On 10 August 1792, the people of Paris stormed the Tuileries, chanting their demands for "Equality!" and "Nation!" The people tramped across the silk sheets of the king's bed and broke his fine furniture, reveling in the private chambers of the royal family. Love and respect for the king had vanished. What the people of Paris demanded was universal manhood suffrage and participation in a popular democracy. Working people were acting independently of other factions, and the bourgeois political leadership became quickly aware of the need to scramble to maintain order.

Who constituted the popular movement? The self-designated sans-culottes were the working men and women of Paris. Some were wealthier than others, some were wage earners, but all shared a common identity as consumers in the marketplace. They hated the privileged (*les gros*), who appeared to be profiting at the expense of the people. The sans-culottes wanted government power to be decentralized, with neighborhoods ruling themselves through sectional organizations. As the have-nots, they were increasingly intent on pulling down the haves, and they translated the sense of vengeance into a new revolutionary justice. When they invaded the Tuileries Palace on the morning of 10 August, the sans-culottes did so in the name of the people. They saw themselves as patriots whose duty it was to brush the monarchy aside. The people were now a force to be reckoned with and feared.

"Terror Is the Order of the Day"

Political factions characterized revolutionary politics from the start. The terms *Left* and *Right,* which came to represent opposite ends of the political spectrum, originated in a description of where people sat in the Assembly in relation to the podium. Political designations were refined in successive parliamentary bodies. The Convention was the legislative body elected in September 1792 that succeeded the Legislative Assembly and had as its charge determining the best form of government after the collapse of the monarchy. On 21 September 1792, the monarchy was abolished in France; on the following day the Republic, France's first, came into being. Members of the Convention conducted the trial of Louis XVI for treason and pronounced his sentence: execution by the guillotine in January 1793.

The various political factions of the Convention were described in terms borrowed from geography. The Mountain, sitting on the upper benches on the left, was made up of members of the Jacobin Club (named for its meeting place in an abandoned monastery). The Jacobins were the most radical element in the National Convention, supporting democratic solutions and speaking in favor of the cause of people in the streets. The Plain held the moderates, who were concerned with maintaining public order against popular unrest. Many members of the Plain came to be called Girondins in the mistaken belief that they originated in the département of the Gironde.

Jacobin Ascendancy. Both Girondins and Jacobins were from the middle ranks of the bourgeoisie, and both groups were dedicated to the principles of the revolution. Although they controlled the ministries, the Girondins began to lose their hold on the revolution and the war. The renewed European war fragmented the democratic movement, and the Girondins, unable to control violence at home, saw political control slipping away. They became prisoners of the revolution when 80,000 armed Parisians surrounded the National Convention in June 1793.

Girondin power had been eroding in the critical months between August 1792 and June 1793. A new leader was working quietly and effectively behind the scenes to weld a partnership between the popular movement of sans-culottes and the Jacobins. He was Maximilien Robespierre (1758–1794), leader of the Mountain and the Jacobin Club. Robespierre was typical of the new breed of revolutionary politician. Only 31 years old in 1789, he wrote mediocre poems and attended the local provincial academy to discuss the new ideas when he was not practicing law in his hometown of Arras. Elected to the Estates-General, he joined the Jacobin Club and quickly rose to become its leader. He was willing to take controversial stands on issues: unlike most of his fellow members of the Mountain—including his rival, the popular orator Georges-Jacques Danton (1759–1794)—he opposed the war in 1792. Although neither an original thinker

The Guillotine and Revolutionary Justice

In the sultry summer days of 1792, Parisians found a new way to entertain themselves. They attended executions. French men, women, and children were long accustomed to watching criminals being tortured and put to death in public view. During the old regime, spectators could enjoy the variety of a number of methods: drawing and quartering, strangling, or hanging. Decapitation, reputedly a less painful death, was a privilege reserved for nobles sentenced for capital crimes. The French Revolution extended that formerly aristocratic privilege to all criminals condemned to death. What especially attracted people to public squares in the third year of the revolution was the introduction of a novel method of decapitation. In 1792, the new instrument of death, the guillotine, became the center of the spectacle of revolutionary justice.

The guillotine promised to eliminate the suffering of its victims. Axes, swords, and sabers—the traditional tools of decapitation and dismemberment—were messy and undependable, producing slow and bloody ordeals when inept or drunken executioners missed their mark or victims flinched at the fatal moment. The design of the guillotine took all of that into account. On its easel-like wooden structure, victims, lying on their stomachs, were held in place with straps and a pillory. Heavy pulleys guaranteed that the sharp blade would fall efficiently from its great height. A basket was placed at the base of the blade to catch the severed head; another was used to slide the headless body through the base of the scaffolding for removal. In place of unintended torture and gore, the guillotine was devised as a humanitarian instrument to guarantee swift and painless death.

It should have been called the Louisette, after its inventor, Dr. Antoine Louis. In what now seems a dubious honor, the new machine was named instead after its greatest supporter, Dr. Joseph Ignace Guillotin, a delegate to the National Assembly. Both Guillotin and Louis were medical doctors, men of science influenced by Enlightenment ideas and committed to the revolution's elimination of the cruelty of older forms of punishment. In the spirit of scientific experimentation, Louis's invention was tested on sheep, cadavers, and then convicted thieves. In 1792, it was used for the first time against another class of offenders: political prisoners.

Early in the revolution, the Marquis de Condorcet, philosophe and mathematician, had opposed capital punishment with the argument that the state did not have the right to take life. Ironically, Maximilien Robespierre, future

architect of the Reign of Terror, was one of the few revolutionaries who agreed with Condorcet. Those who favored justice by execution of the state's enemies prevailed. The revolutionary hero and associate of the radical Jacobins Jean-Paul Marat (1743–1793), who was himself stabbed to death in his bathtub, advocated the state's use of violence against its enemies: "In order to ensure public tranquility, 200,000 heads must be cut off." By the end of 1792, as revolution and civil war swept over France, 83 identical guillotines were constructed and installed in each of the départements of France. For the next two years, the guillotine's great blade was rhythmically raised and lowered daily in public squares all over France. In the name of the revolution, the "axe of the people" dispatched over 50,000 victims.

Although intended as a humanitarian instrument, the guillotine became the symbol of all that was arbitrary and repressive about a revolution run amok. Day and night, the Revolutionary Tribunal in Paris delivered the death sentence to the "enemies of the people." Most of those executed were members of what had been the Third Estate: members of the bourgeoisie, workers, and peasants. Only 15 percent of the condemned were nobles and priests. During the Terror, the guillotine could be used to settle old scores. Sans-culottes turned in their neighbors, sometimes over long-standing grievances that owed more to spite than politics. The most fanatical revolutionaries had fantasies that guillotines were about to be erected on every street corner to dispense with hoarders and traitors. Others suggested that guillotines be made portable so that by putting justice on wheels, it could be taken directly to the people.

As usual, Paris set the style. The most famous of the guillotines stood on the Place du Carrousel, deliberately placed in front of the royal palace of the Tuileries. It was eventually moved to the larger Place de la Révolution in order to accommodate the growing numbers of spectators. Famous victims drew especially large crowds. The revolutionary drama took on the trappings of a spectacle as hawkers sold toy guillotines, miniature pikes, and liberty caps as souvenirs, along with the usual food and drink. Troops attended the events, but not to control the crowd. Members of the National Guard in formation, their backs to the people, faced the stage of the scaffold. They, like the citizenry, were there to witness the birth of a new nation and, by their presence, to give legitimacy to the event. The crowd entered into the ritual, cheering the victim's last words and demanding that the executioner hold high the severed head. In the new political culture, death was a festival.

For two centuries, Western societies have debated the legitimacy of the death sentence and have periodically considered the relative merits of the guillotine, the gas chamber, and the electric chair. For the French, the controversy temporarily ceased in 1794, when people were convinced that justice had gotten out of hand and that they had had enough. For the time being, the government put an end to capital punishment. The guillotine would return. But at the height of its use, between 1792 and 1794, it had played a unique role in forging a new system of justice: the guillotine had been the great leveler. In the ideology of democracy, people were equal—in death as well as in life. The guillotine came to be popularly known as the "scythe of equality." It killed king and commoner alike.

French towns and villages set up "Liberty Trees" to show their revolutionary fervor. The trees were hung with cockades and topped with red caps. This drawing shows a tree near the captured Bastille. In the background, sans-culottes rout an Austrian army.

These women are Jacobin tricoteuses, *women knitting, who met to applaud radical motions in the Jacobin Club. Militant women of the Revolution failed to achieve their major goal—political equality with men.*

nor a compelling orator, Robespierre discovered with the revolution that he was an adroit political tactician. He gained a following and learned how to manipulate it. It was he who engineered the Jacobins' replacement of the Girondins as leaders of the government.

Robespierre and the Reign of Terror. Robespierre's chance for real power came when he assumed leadership of the Committee of Public Safety in July 1793. Faced with the threat of internal anarchy and external war, the elected body, the National Convention, yielded political control to the 12-man Committee of Public Safety that ruled dictatorially under Robespierre's direction. The Great Committee, as it was known at the time, orchestrated the Reign of Terror (1793–1794), a period of systematic state repression that meted out justice in the people's name. Summary trials by specially created revolutionary tribunals were followed by the swift execution of the guilty under the blade of the guillotine.

Influenced by *The Social Contract* (1762) and other writings of Jean-Jacques Rousseau, Robespierre believed that sovereignty resided with the people. For

ON REVOLUTIONARY GOVERNMENT

As the leader of the Jacobins, Maximilien Robespierre oversaw the Reign of Terror as a necessary expedient to save the hard-won republican gains of the Revolution. Speaking before the National Convention in December 1793, Robespierre made clear how the enemies of the Revolution should be treated—in the harshest manner possible. Robespierre considered it acceptable to suspend the rights of citizens in the name of revolutionary justice.

THE THEORY OF REVOLUTIONARY GOVERNMENT is as new as the Revolution that created it. It is as pointless to seek its origins in the books of the political theorists, who failed to foresee this revolution, as in the laws of the tyrants, who are happy enough to abuse their exercise of authority without seeking out its legal justification. As so this phrase is for the aristocracy a mere subject of terror or a term of slander, for tyrants an outrage and for many an enigma. It behooves us to explain it all that we may rally good citizens, at least, in support of the principles governing the public interest.

It is the function of government to guide the moral and physical energies of the nation toward the purposes for which it was established.

The object of constitutional government is to preserve the Republic; the object of revolutionary government is to establish it.

Revolution is the war waged by liberty against its enemies; a constitution is that which crowns the edifice of freedom once victory has been won and the nation is at peace.

The revolutionary government has to summon extraordinary activity to its aid precisely because it is at war. It is subjected to less binding and less uniform regulations because the circumstances in which it finds itself are tempestuous and shifting, above all because it is compelled to deploy, swiftly and incessantly, new resources to meet new and pressing dangers.

The principal concern of constitutional government is civil liberty; that of revolutionary government, public liberty. Under a constitutional government little more is required than to protect the individual against abuses by the state, whereas revolutionary government is obliged to defend the state itself against the factions that assail it from every quarter.

To good citizens revolutionary government owes the full protection of the state; to the enemies of the people it owes only death.

him, individual wills and even individual rights did not matter when weighed against the will of the nation. The king was dead; the people were the new source of political power. Robespierre saw himself in the all-important role of interpreting and shaping the people's will. His own task was to guide the people "to the summit of its destinies." As he explained to his critics, "I am defending not my own cause but the public cause." As head of the Great Committee, Robespierre oversaw a revolutionary machinery dedicated to economic regulation, massive military mobilization, and a punitive system of revolutionary justice characterized by the slogan, "Terror Is the Order of the Day." Militant revolutionary committees and revolutionary tribunals were established throughout France to identify traitors and to mete out the harsh justice that struck hardest against those members of the bourgeoisie perceived as opponents of the government.

The guillotine became the symbol of revolutionary justice, but it was not the only means of execution. In Lyon, officials of the Reign of Terror had prisoners tied to stakes in open fields and fired on with cannons. In Nantes, a Parisian administrator of the new justice had enemies of the revolution chained to barges and drowned in the estuary of the Loire. The civil war, which raged most violently in the Vendée in the west of France, consisted often of primitive massacres that sent an estimated quarter of a million people to their deaths. The bureaucratized Reign of Terror was responsible for about 40,000 executions in a nine-month period, resulting in the image of the republicans as "drinkers of blood." (See "The Guillotine and Revolutionary Justice," pp. 706–707.)

The Cult of the Supreme Being, a civic religion without priests or churches and influenced by Rousseau's ideas about nature, followed de-Christianization. The cathedral of Notre Dame de Paris was turned into the Temple of Reason, and the new religion established its own festivals to undermine the persistence of Catholicism. The cult was one indication of the Reign of Terror's attempt to create a new moral universe of revolutionary values.

Women Excluded. Women remained conspicuously absent from the summit of political power. After 1793, Jacobin revolutionaries, who had been willing to empower the popular movement of workers, turned against women's participation and denounced it. Women's associations were outlawed and the Society of Revolutionary Republican Women was disbanded. Olympe de Gouges, revolutionary author of the Declaration of the Rights of Woman and Citizen, was guillotined. Women were declared unfit for political participation, according to the Jacobins, because of their biological functions of reproduction and child-rearing. Rousseau's ideas about family policy were probably more influential than his political doctrines. His best-selling books, *La Nouvelle Héloïse* (1761) and *Émile* (1762), which combined went into 72 editions before 1789, were moral works that transformed people's ideas about family life. Under his influence, the reading public came to value a separate and private sphere of domestic and conjugal values. Following Rousseau's lead, Robespierre and the Jacobins insisted that the role of women as mothers was incompatible with women's participation in the political realm.

The Thermidorian Reaction. By attacking his critics on both the Left and the Right, Robespierre undermined the support he needed to stay in power. He abandoned the alliance with the popular movement that had been so important in bringing him to power. Robespierre's enemies—and he had many—were able to break the identification between political power and the will of the people that Robespierre had established. As a result, he was branded a traitor by the same process that he had used against many of his own enemies. He saved France from foreign occupation and internal collapse, but he could not save democracy through terror. In the summer of 1794, Robespierre was guillotined. The Reign of Terror ceased with his death in the revolutionary month of Thermidor 1794.

The revolution did not end with the Thermidorian Reaction, as the fall of Robespierre came to be known, but his execution initiated a new phase. For some, democracy lost its legitimacy. The popular movement was reviled, and sans-culotte became a term of derision. Jacobins were forced underground. Price controls were abolished, resulting in extreme hardship for most urban residents. Out of desperation, in April 1795 the Jacobins and the sans-culottes renewed their alliance and united to demand "bread and the Constitution of 1793." The politics of bread had never been more accurately captured in slogan. Those who took to the streets in 1795 saw the universal manhood suffrage of the unimplemented 1793 constitution as the way to solve their economic problems. But their demands went unheeded; the popular revolution had failed.

The End of the Revolution

In the four years after Robespierre's fall, a new government by committee, called the Directory, appeared to offer mediocrity, caution, and opportunism in place of the idealism and action of the early years of the revolution. No successor to Robespierre stepped forward to command center stage. There were no heroes like Lafayette or the great Jacobin orator Georges-Jacques Danton to inspire patriotic fervor. Nor were there women like Olympe de Gouges to demand in the public arena equal rights for women. Most people, numbed after years of change, barely noticed that the revolution was over. Ordinary men in parliamentary institutions effectively did the day-to-day job of running the government. They tried to steer a middle path between royalist resurgence and popular insurrection. That nearly forgotten period in the history of the French Revolution was the fulfillment of the liberal hopes of 1789 for a stable constitutional rule.

The Directory, however, continued to be dogged by European war. A mass army of conscripts and volunteers had successfully extended France's power and frontiers. France expelled foreign invaders and annexed territories, including Belgium, while increasing its control in Holland, Switzerland, and Italy. But the expansion of revolutionary France was expensive and increasingly unpopular. Military defeats and the corruption of the Directory undermined government control. The Directory might have succeeded in the slow accretion of a parliamentary tradition, but reinstate-

CHRONOLOGY

The French Revolution

August 1788	Louis XVI announces meeting of Estates-General to be held May 1789
5 May 1789	Estates-General convenes
17 June 1789	Third Estate declares itself the National Assembly
20 June 1789	Oath of the Tennis Court
14 July 1789	Storming of the Bastille
20 July 1789	Revolution of peasantry begins
26 August 1789	Declaration of the Rights of Man and Citizen
5 October 1789	Parisian women march to Versailles; force Louis XVI to return to Paris
February 1790	Monasteries, convents dissolved
July 1790	Civil Constitution of the Clergy
June 1791	Louis XVI and family attempt to flee Paris; are captured and returned
April 1792	France declares war on Austria
10 August 1792	Storming of the Tuileries
22 September 1792	Revolutionary calendar implemented
January 1793	Louis XVI executed
July 1793	Robespierre assumes leadership of Committee of Public Safety
1793–1794	Reign of Terror
1794	Robespierre guillotined
1799	Napoleon overthrows the Directory and seizes power

ment of conscription in 1798 met with widespread protest and resistance. No matter what their political leanings, people were weary. They turned to those who promised stability and peace.

In the democratic experiment at the heart of the second stage of the French Revolution, the sovereign will of the people permanently replaced the monarch's claim to divine right to rule. Yet with democracy came tyranny. The severe repression of the terror revealed the pressures that external war and civil unrest created for the new Republic. The Thermidorian Reaction and the elimination of Robespierre as the legitimate interpreter of the people's will ushered in a period of conciliation, opportunism, and a search for stability. Ironically, the savior that France found to answer its needs for peace and a just government was a man of war and a dictator.

THE REIGN OF NAPOLEON, 1799–1815

The great debate that rages to this day about Napoleon revolves around the question of whether he fulfilled the aims of the revolution or perverted them. In his return to a monarchical model, Napoleon resembled the enlightened despots of eighteenth-century Europe. In a modern sense, he was also a dictator, manipulating the French population through a highly centralized administrative apparatus. He locked French society into a program of military expansion that depleted its human and material resources. Yet, in spite of destruction and war, he dedicated his reign to building a French state according to the principles of the Revolution. Napoleon is one of those individuals about whom one can say that if he had not lived, history would have been different. He left his mark on an age and a continent.

Bonaparte Seizes Power

In Paris in 1795 a young, penniless, and unknown military officer moved among the wealthy and the beautiful of Parisian society and longed for fame. Already nicknamed at school "the Little Corporal" on account of his short stature, he was snubbed because of his background and ridiculed for his foreign accent. His story is typical of all stories of thwarted ambition. Yet the outcome of his story is unique: within four years, that young man would become ruler of France. The story of his ascent to power is also a story of the demise of the revolution.

Napoleon's Training and Experience. Napoleon Bonaparte (1769–1821) was a true child of the eighteenth century. He shared the philosophes' belief in a rational and progressive world. Born in Corsica, which until a few months before his birth was part of the Republic of Genoa, he received his training in French military schools. As a youth, he was arrogant and ambitious. But he could have never aspired to a position of leadership in the army during the old regime because he lacked the noble birth necessary for advancement. The highest rank Napoleon could hope to achieve was that of captain or major.

The revolution changed everything for him. First, it opened up careers previously restricted by birth, including those in the military, to talent. Second, the revolution made new posts available when aristocratic generals defected and crossed over to the enemy side, both before and after the execution of the king. Finally, the revolution created great opportunities for military men to test their mettle.

Foreign war and civil war required military leaders devoted to the revolution. Forced to flee Corsica because he had sided with the Jacobins, Napoleon and his troops were given the task of crushing Parisian protesters who rioted against the Directory in 1795. His victories in the Italian campaign in 1796–1797 launched his political career. As he extended French rule into central Italy, he became the embodiment of revolutionary values and energy.

The revolutionary wars had begun as wars to liberate humanity in the name of liberty, equality, and fraternity. Yet concerns for power, territory, and riches soon replaced earlier concerns with defense of the nation and of the revolution. The aggrandizement was nowhere more evident than in the Egyptian campaign of 1798, in which Napoleon Bonaparte headed an expedition whose goal was to enrich France by hastening the collapse of the Turkish empire, crippling British trade routes, and handicapping Russian interests in the region. With Napoleon's highly publicized campaigns in Egypt and Syria, the war left the European theater and moved to the East, leaving behind its original revolutionary ideals. The Egyptian campaign, which was in reality a disaster, made Napoleon a hero at home.

Napoleon as First Consul. In 1799, Napoleon Bonaparte readily joined a conspiracy that pulled down the Directory, the government he had earlier preserved, and became the First Consul of a triumvirate of consuls.

Napoleon set out to secure his position of power by eliminating his enemies on the Left and weakening those on the Right. He guaranteed the security of property acquired in the revolution, a move that undercut royalists who wanted to return property to its original owners. Through policing forces and special criminal courts, law and order prevailed and civil war subsided. The First Consul promised a balanced budget and appeared to deliver it. Bonaparte spoke of healing the nation's wounds, especially those opened by de-Christianization during the revolution. Realizing the importance of religion in maintaining domestic peace, Napoleon reestablished relations with the pope in 1801 by the Concordat, which recognized Catholicism as the religion of the French and restored the Roman Catholic hierarchy.

Napoleon's popularity as First Consul flowed from his military and political successes and his religious reconciliation. He had come to power in 1799 by appealing for the support of the army. In 1802, Napoleon decided to extend his power by calling for a plebiscite in which he asked the electorate to vote him First Consul for life. Public support was overwhelming. An electoral landslide gave Napoleon greater political power than any of his Bourbon predecessors. Using revolutionary mechanisms, Napoleon laid the foundation for a new dynasty.

Napoleon at War with the European Powers

Napoleon was either at war or preparing for war during his entire reign. He certainly seemed up to the task of defeating the European powers. His military successes before 1799, real and apparent, had been crucial in his bid for political power. By 1802, he had signed favorable treaties with both Austria and Great Britain. He appeared to deliver a lasting peace and to establish France as the dominant power in Europe. But the peace was short-lived. In 1803, France embarked on an 11-year period of continuous war. Under Napoleon's command, the French army delivered defeat after defeat to the European powers. Austria fell in 1805, Prussia in 1806, and the Russian armies of Alexander I were defeated at Friedland in 1807. In 1808, Napoleon invaded Spain to drive out British expeditionary forces intent on invading France. The great painter of the Spanish court, Francisco Goya (1746–1828), produced a series of etchings, *The Disasters of War,* that depicted the atrocities accompanying the Napoleonic invasion. Spain became a satellite kingdom of France, though the conflict continued.

Britain was the one exception to the string of Napoleonic victories. Napoleon initially considered sending a French fleet to invade the island nation. Lacking the strength necessary to achieve that, he turned to economic warfare, blockading European ports against British trade. Beginning in 1806, the Continental System, as the blockade was known,

This engraving, from the series Disasters of War *by Francisco Goya, depicts the horrors of war. The series was inspired by Napoleon's invasion and occupation of Spain from 1808 to 1813.*

erected a structure of protection for French manufactures in all continental European markets. The British responded to the tariff walls and boycotts with a naval blockade that succeeded in cutting French commerce off from its Atlantic markets. The Continental System did not prove to be the decisive policy that Napoleon had planned: the British economy was not broken and the French economy did not flourish when faced with restricted resources and the persistence of a black market in smuggled goods.

Still, by 1810 the French leader was master of the Continent. French armies had extended revolutionary reforms and legal codes outside France and brought with them civil equality and religious toleration. They had also drained defeated countries of their resources and had inflicted the horrors of war with armies of occupation, forced billeting, and pillage. Napoleon's empire extended across Europe, with only a diminished Austria, Prussia, and Russia remaining independent. He placed his relatives and friends on the thrones of the new satellite kingdoms of Italy, Naples, Westphalia, Holland, and Spain. It was a fine empire, Napoleon later recalled in the loneliness of exile. Napoleon's empire did not endure, but at its acme, it seemed as though it would never fall.

Napoleon's Empire. By 1812, Napoleon directly ruled or controlled most of Europe.

German caricature of Napoleon (1814). The anonymous artist who created this caricature depicted on the French general's face the victims of Napoleon's doomed Russian campaign.

The First Empire and Domestic Reforms

Napoleon measured domestic prosperity in terms of the stability of his reign. Through the 1802 plebiscite that voted him First Consul for life, he maintained the charade of constitutional rule while he ruled as virtual dictator. In 1804, he abandoned all pretense and had himself proclaimed emperor of the French. Mimicking the rituals of kingship, he staged his own coronation and that of his wife Josephine at the cathedral of Notre Dame de Paris. Breaking the tradition set by Charlemagne, Napoleon took the crown from the hands of Pope Pius VII (1800–1823) and placed it on his own head.

The Importance of Science and Economic Reforms. Secure in his regime, surrounded by a new nobility that he created based on military achievement and talent and that he rewarded with honors, Napoleon set about implementing sweeping reforms in every area of government. Like many of the men of the revolutionary assemblies who had received scientific educations in their youth, he recognized the importance of science for both industry and war. The revolution had removed an impediment to the development of a national market by creating a uniform system of weights and measures. The metric system was established by 1799. But Napoleon felt the need to go further: France must be first in scientific research and application. To assure French predominance, Napoleon became a patron of science, supporting important work in the areas of physics and chemistry. Building for the future, Napoleon made science a pillar in the new structure of higher education.

The Directory had restored French prosperity through stabilization of the currency, fiscal reform, and support of industry. Napoleon's contribution to the French economy was the much needed reform of the tax system. He authorized the creation of a central banking system. French industries flourished under the protection of the state. The blockade forced the development of new domestic crops such as sugar beets and indigo, which became substitutes for colonial products. Napoleon extended the infrastructure of roads necessary for the expansion of national and European markets.

The New Legal System. Perhaps his greatest achievement was the codification of law, a task begun under the revolution. Many of the new articles of the Napoleonic Code were hammered out in Napoleon's presence, as he presided regularly over meetings with legal reformers. Combined with economic reforms, the Napoleonic Code facilitated trade and the development of commerce by regularizing contractual relations and protecting property rights and equality before the law.

The civil laws of the new code carved out a family policy characterized by hierarchy and subordination. Married women were neither independent nor equal to men in ownership of property, custody of children, or access to divorce. Women also lacked political rights. In the Napoleonic Code, women, like children, were

THE CIVIL CODE OF THE *CODE NAPOLÉON* (1804)

While still First Consul, Bonaparte assembled a group of the country's leading legal specialists to replace the vast agglomeration of feudal, customary, and canon laws, all with their own courts and procedures, with a unified system based on Roman law. The Civil Code, *along with the* Criminal Code, *made up the* Code Napoléon, *and consisted of 2281 articles intended to cover all aspects of civil life from birth to death, all civic aspects relating to family and property, contractual responsibilities, and civil liberties. A unified legal system became the basis for economic development and was arguably Napoleon's greatest achievement as ruler of France. The* Civil Code *replaced the Roman Catholic Church as having authority over marriage, and although divorce was permitted in the* Code, *it was outlawed in 1816 and not permitted again until 1884.*

Of the Respective Rights and Duties of Parent and Children

212. HUSBAND AND WIFE owe each other fidelity, support, and assistance.
213. A husband owes protection to his wife; a wife owes obedience to her husband.
214. A wife is bound to live with her husband and to follow him wherever he deems proper to reside. The husband is bound to receive her, and to supply her with whatever is necessary for the wants of life, according to his means and condition.
215. A wife cannot sue in court without the consent of her husband, even if she is a public tradeswoman or if there is no community or she is separated as to property.
216. The husband's consent is not necessary when the wife is prosecuted criminally or in a police matter.
217. A wife, even when there is no community, or when she is separated as to property, cannot give, convey, mortgage, or acquire property, with or without consideration, without the husband joining in the instrument or giving his written consent.
218. If a husband refuses to allow his wife to sue in court, the Judge may grant the authorization.
219. If a husband refuses to allow his wife to execute and instrument, the wife can cause her husband to be summoned directly before the Tribunal of the First Instance of the common domicile, and such Tribunal shall grant or refuse its consent in the Judges' room after the husband has been heard or has been duly summoned.
220. A wife may, if she is a public tradeswoman, bind herself without the husband's consent with respect to what relates to her trade, and in that case she also binds her husband if there is a community of property between them. She is not considered a public tradeswoman if she merely retails the goods of her husband's business, but only when she has a separate business.
221. When a sentence has been passed upon a husband which carries with it a degrading corporal punishment, even if it has been passed by default, a wife, even of full age, cannot, during the continuance of the punishment, sue in court nor bind herself, unless she has been authorized by the Judge, who may in such cases grant the consent without the husband having been heard or summoned.
222. If a husband has been interdicted or is absent, the Judge may with proper knowledge of the case, authorize the wife to sue in court or to bind herself.
223. Any general authorization, even given by marriage contract, is only valid as to the management of the wife's property.
224. If the husband is a minor, the authorization of the Judge is necessary to the wife, either to sue in court or to bind herself.
225. A nullity based on the want of authorization can only be set up by the wife, the husband, or the heirs.
226. A wife can make a will without her husband's consent.

subjected to paternal authority. The Napoleonic philosophy of woman's place is well captured in an anecdote told by Madame Germaine de Staël (1766–1817), a leading intellectual of her day. As the daughter of Jacques Necker, the Swiss financier and adviser to Louis XVI at the time of the revolution, she had been taught Enlightenment ideas from an early age. On finding herself seated next to Napoleon at a dinner party, she asked him what was very likely a self-interested question: Whom did he consider the greatest woman, alive or dead? Napoleon had no name to give her but responded, without pausing: "The one who has had the most children."

Napoleon turned his prodigious energies to every aspect of French life. He encouraged the arts while creating a police force. He had monuments built but did not forget about sewers. He organized French administrative life in a fashion that has endured. In place of the popular democratic movement, he offered his own singular authority. In place of elections, clubs, and free associations, he gave France plebiscites and army service. To be sure, Napoleon believed in constitutions, but he thought they should be "short and obscure." For Napoleon, the great problem of democracy was its unpredictability. His regime solved that problem by eliminating choices.

Decline and Fall

Militarily, Napoleon went too far. The first cracks in the French facade began to show in the Peninsular War (1808–1814) with Spain, in which Spanish guerrilla tactics proved costly for French troops. Napoleon's biggest mistake, the one that shattered the myth of his invincibility, occurred when he decided to invade Russia in June 1812.

The Invasion of Russia and the Battle of Nations. Having decisively defeated Russian forces in 1807, Napoleon had entered into a peace treaty with Tsar Alexander I that guaranteed Russian allegiance to French policies. Alexander repudiated the Continental System in 1810 and appeared to be preparing for his own war against France. Napoleon seized the initiative, sure that he could defeat Russian forces once again. With an army of 500,000 men, Napoleon moved deep into Russia in the summer of 1812. The tsar's troops fell back in retreat. It was a strange war, one that pulled the French army to Moscow like a bird following bread crumbs. When Napoleon and his men entered Moscow in September, they found a city in flames. The people of Moscow had destroyed their own city to deprive the French troops of winter quarters.

Winter came early in Moscow, Napoleon's men discovered. They had left France basking in the warmth of summer and sure of certain and early victory. They then found themselves facing a severe Russian winter without overcoats, supplies, or food. Russia's strategy has become legendary. The Russians destroyed grain and shelter that might be of use to the French. Napoleon and his starving and frostbitten troops were forced into retreat. The horses of the French cavalry died because they were not properly shod for cold weather. The French army was decimated. Fewer than 100,000 men made it back to France.

Britain, unbowed by the Continental System, remained Napoleon's sworn enemy. Prussia joined Great Britain, Sweden, Russia, and Austria in opposing France anew. In the Battle of Nations at Leipzig in October 1813, France was forced to retreat. Napoleon refused a

CHRONOLOGY

The Reign of Napoleon

1799	Napoleon establishes consulate, becomes First Consul
1801	Napoleon reestablishes relations with pope, restores Roman Catholic hierarchy
1802	Plebiscite declares Napoleon First Consul for life
1804	Napoleon proclaims himself Emperor of the French
1806	Continental System implemented
1808–1814	France engaged in Peninsular War with Spain
June 1812	Napoleon invades Russia
September 1812	French army reaches Moscow, is trapped by Russian winter
1813	Napoleon defeated at Battle of Nations at Leipzig
March 1814	Napoleon abdicates and goes into exile on island of Elba
March 1815	Napoleon escapes Elba and attempts to reclaim power
15 June 1815	Napoleon is defeated at Waterloo and exiled to island of Saint Helena

This 1835 painting by De Boisdenier depicts the suffering of Napoleon's Grand Army on the retreat from Moscow. The Germans were to meet a similar fate more than 100 years later when they invaded Russia without adequate supplies for the harsh winter.

negotiated peace and fought on until the following March, when the victorious allies marched down the streets of Paris and occupied the French capital. Only then did Napoleon abdicate in favor of his young son, François, the titular king of Rome (1811–1832). Napoleon was exiled to the Mediterranean island of Elba.

The allies refused to accept the young "Napoleon II" and supported instead the Bourbon claimant to the throne, the brother of the guillotined Louis XVI. Naming himself Louis XVIII (skipping "XVII" in deference to his nephew dead at the hands of the Revolution), the new king claimed to rule over a "restored" France.

Napoleon's Final Defeat: Waterloo. Still it was not quite the end for Napoleon. While the European heads of state sat in Vienna trying to determine the future of Europe and France's place in it, Napoleon returned from his exile on the Mediterranean island of Elba to reclaim leadership of France. On 15 June 1815, Napoleon once again, and for the final time, confronted the European powers in one of the most famous military campaigns in history. With 125,000 loyal French forces, Napoleon seemed within hours of reestablishing the French empire in Europe.

But he had underestimated his opponents. The defeat of Napoleon's forces at Waterloo was decisive. Napoleon later explained, "Everything failed me just when everything had succeeded!" He had met his Waterloo, and with his defeat a new expression entered the language to describe devastating, permanent, irreversible downfall. Napoleon's return proved brief—it lasted only 100 days. An era had come to an end. Napoleon was exiled to the inhospitable island of Saint Helena in the South Atlantic. For the next six years, Napoleon wrote his memoirs under the watchful eyes of his British jailers. He died a painful death from cancer on 5 May 1821.

The period of revolution and empire from 1789 to 1815 radically changed the face of France. A new, more cohesive elite of bourgeois and nobles emerged, sharing power based on wealth and status. Ownership of land remained a defining characteristic of both old and new elites. A new state bureaucracy, built on the foundations of the old, expanded and centralized state power.

The people as sovereign now legitimated political power. Napoleon at his most imperial never doubted that he owed his existence to the people. In this sense, Napoleon was the king of the revolution—an apparently contradictory fusion of old forms and new ideology. Napoleon channeled democratic forces into enthusiasm for empire. He learned his lessons from the failure of the Bourbon monarchy and the politicians of the revolution. For 16 years, Napoleon successfully reconciled the old regime with the new France. Yet he could not resolve the essential problem of democracy: the relationship between the will of the people and the exercise of political power. The picture in 1815 was not dramatically different from the situation in 1789. The revolution might have been over, but changes fueled by the revolutionary tradition were just beginning. The struggle for a workable democratic government continued in France for another century, and elsewhere in Europe throughout the twentieth century.

Questions for Review

1. To what extent was the French nobility responsible for the crisis that destroyed the *ancien régime?*
2. How did commoners, men and women, transform a crisis of government into a revolution?
3. Why did the leaders of the Revolution resort to a "reign of terror" and what effect did that have on the Revolution?
4. What problems in France and beyond contributed to the rise of Napoleon?
5. What did Napoleon accomplish in France, and what brought about his fall?

Suggestions for Further Reading

The Crisis of the Old Regime in France, 1715–1788

* Keith Michael Baker, *Inventing the French Revolution* (Cambridge: Cambridge University Press, 1992). In a set of essays, Keith Baker views the French Revolution as a basically political event that can only be understood in the context of the changing political culture of the eighteenth century. In examining the political dynamic of the Old Regime, Baker pays special attention to the use of language and the role of public opinion as a political invention.

C. B. A. Behrens, *Society, Government, and the Enlightenment* (New York: Harper & Row, 1985). A comparative study of eighteenth-century France and Prussia, focusing on the relationship between government and the ruling classes, that explains how pressures for change in both countries led to different outcomes: revolution in France and reform in Prussia.

* Roger Chartier, *The Cultural Origins of the French Revolution,* tr. Lydia G. Cochrane (Durham, NC: Duke University Press, 1991). Argues for the importance of the rise of critical modes of thinking in the public sphere in the eighteenth century and of long-term de-Christianization in shaping the desire for change in French society and politics.

Olwen Hufton, *The Poor in Eighteenth-Century France, 1750–1789* (Oxford: Clarendon, 1974). Examines the lives of the poor before the revolution and the institutions that attempted to deal with the problem of poverty.

Olwen Hufton, *Europe: Privilege and Protest, 1730–1789* (Sussex, England: Harvester Press, 1980). An overview of the impact of rapid social, ideological, and economic changes on the concept and exercise of privilege.

* Daniel Roche, *The People of Paris* (Berkeley: University of California Press, 1987). An essay on popular culture in the eighteenth century in which the author surveys the lives of the Parisian popular classes—servants, laborers, and artisans—and examines their housing, furnishing, dress, and leisure activities.

Isser Woloch, *Eighteenth-Century Europe: Tradition and Progress, 1715–1789* (New York: Norton, 1982). A discussion of eighteenth-century Europe comparing social, economic, political, and intellectual developments elsewhere on the Continent to the French experience, with special attention to cultural aspects such as popular beliefs and religion.

The First Stage of the French Revolution, 1789–1792

François Furet and Denis Richet, *The French Revolution* (New York: Macmillan, 1970). Two experts on the French Revolution present a detailed overview of the period from 1789 to 1798, when Bonaparte returned to Paris.

* Georges Lefebvre, *The Great Fear of 1789* (New York: Pantheon Books, 1973). This classic study analyzes the rural panic that swept through parts of France in the summer of 1789. The Great Fear is presented as a distinct episode in the opening months of the revolution, with its own internal logic.

Colin Lucas, ed., *Rewriting the French Revolution* (Oxford: Clarendon Press, 1991). Responding to the historiographic challenge of the bicentenary of the French Revolution, eight scholars present new interpretations in the areas of social development, ideas, politics, and religion.

* D. M. G. Sutherland, *France, 1789–1815: Revolution and Counter-Revolution* (New York: Oxford University Press, 1986). An interpretation of the revolutionary period that stresses the struggle against counterrevolution and presents the revolution as a complex and contradictory process of social and political conflict over incompatible rights and privileges enjoyed by significant portions of the population.

Timothy Tackett, *Becoming a Revolutionary: The Deputies of the French National Assembly and the Emergence of a Revolutionary Culture* (Princeton: Princeton University Press, 1996). This thoroughly researched collective biography of the cohort of deputies to the National Assembly demonstrates that their practical experience was distinct from that of the nobility. The revolutionary politics of the cohort was forged in their service as deputies in the first year of the Revolution.

* Michel Vovelle, *The Fall of the French Monarchy* (Cambridge: Cambridge University Press, 1984). A social history of the origins and early years of the revolution, beginning with a brief examination of the old regime and paying special attention to social and economic changes initiated by the revolution, the role of the popular classes, and the creation of revolutionary culture.

Experimenting with Democracy: The Revolution's Second Stage, 1792–1799

* François Furet, *Interpreting the French Revolution* (Cambridge: Cambridge University Press, 1981). A series of essays challenging many of the assumptions about the causes and outcome of the revolution and reviewing its historiography. The author argues that political crisis, not class conflict, was the revolution's primary cause and that revolutionary ideas concerning democracy are central to an understanding of the Reign of Terror.

* Dominique Godineau, *The Women of Paris and Their French Revolution* (Berkeley: University of California Press, 1998). A compelling account on the lives of women revolutionaries. Godineau presents women's protests as a mass movement within the Revolution.

* Lynn Hunt, *Politics, Culture, and Class in the French Revolution* (Berkeley: University of California Press, 1984). A study of the revolution as the locus of the creation of modern political culture. The second half of the book examines the social composition and cultural experiences of the new political class that emerged during the revolution.

Lynn Hunt, *The Family Romance of the French Revolution* (Berkeley: University of California Press, 1992). Studies recurrent images of the family in French revolutionary politics in order to understand the gendered nature of the revolution and republicanism.

* Joan B. Landes, *Women and the Public Sphere in the Age of the French Revolution* (Ithaca, NY: Cornell University Press, 1988). Landes examines the genesis of the modern notion of the public sphere from a feminist perspective and argues that within the revolutionary process women were relegated to the private sphere of the domestic world.

* Sara E. Melzer and Leslie Rabine, eds., *Rebel Daughters: Women and the French Revolution* (New York: Oxford University Press, 1992). Contributors from a variety of disciplines examine the importance of women in the French Revolution, with special attention to the exclusion of women from the new politics.

Dorinda Outram, *The Body of the French Revolution: Sex, Class and Political Culture* (New Haven, CT: Yale University Press, 1989). Examines how images of the body in the late eighteenth century differed from class to class and how bourgeois attitudes toward physicality resulted in a gendered political discourse in which the hero replaced the king.

* Albert Soboul, *The Sans-Culottes* (New York: Anchor, 1972). An exhaustive study of the artisans who composed the core of popular political activism in revolutionary Paris. Soboul examines the political demands and ideology of the sans-culottes, as well as the composition, culture, and actions of the popular movement during the revolution.

The Reign of Napoleon, 1799–1815

* Louis Bergeron, *France Under Napoleon* (Princeton, NJ: Princeton University Press, 1981). An analysis of the structure of Napoleon's regime, its social bases of support, and its opponents.

* Felix Markham, *Napoleon* (New York: New American Library, 1963). This classic study treats both Napoleon's life and legend while giving a balanced account of the social and intellectual life of the period and the impact of the Napoleonic Empire on Europe.

Jean Tulard, *Napoleon: The Myth of the Saviour* (London: Weidenfeld and Nicolson, 1984). This biography of Napoleon situates his rise to power within the crisis of legitimacy created by the destruction of the monarchy during the revolution. The Napoleonic Empire is presented as a creation of the bourgeoisie, who desired to end the revolution and consolidate their gains and control over the lower classes.

Isser Woloch, *The New Regime: Transformations of the French Civic Order* (New York: Norton, 1994). Woloch's study emphasizes the break of the new regime from the old, placing the institutions created or revamped after 1789 in the context of a new civic order and citizenship.

* Paperback edition available.

Discovering Western Civilization Online

To further explore the French Revolution and the Napoleonic Era, consult the following World Wide Web sites. Since Web resources are constantly being updated, also go to *www.awl.com/Kishlansky* for further suggestions.

The Crisis of the Old Regime in France, 1715–1788

www.fordham.edu/halsall/mod/modsbook05.html
Part of the Modern History Sourcebook sponsored by Fordham University with the goal to direct students to historical documents, this site is devoted to resources discussing absolutism with a subsection on France during the *ancien régime.*

www.loc.gov/exhibits/bnf/bnf0001.html
Different aspects of French culture as a form of elite power from Charlemagne to Charles de Gaulle are presented by the Library of Congress. Most of the material is from the collections of the Bibliothèque Nationale de France.

www.chateauversailles.fr/en/
Devoted to the history and images of Versailles, this site provides brief essays about the people and events significant to court culture during the seventeenth and eighteenth centuries. It also explores the role of Versailles in French culture after the French Revolution.

The First Stage of the French Revolution, 1789–1792

www.campus.northpark.edu/history/WebChron/WestEurope/AgeRevs.html
A collection of links to chronologies for the "Age of Revolution."

www.history.hanover.edu/modern/frenchrv.htm
A site devoted to the French Revolution with several links to primary source documents, essays, and bibliographies.

Experimenting with Democracy: The Revolution's Second Stage, 1792–1799

www.history.hanover.edu/texts/stjust.html
Texts by St. Just, a close colleague of Robespierre, and a member of the Committee of Public Safety, which orchestrated the Reign of Terror.

www.fordham.edu/halsall/mod/robespierre-supreme.html
This site contains Robespierre's words on "The Cult of Supreme Being," and links to other sites.

The Reign of Napoleon, 1799–1815

www.fordham.edu/halsall/mod/modsbook13.html
This site will direct students to the Modern History Sourcebook section of documents on the French Revolution, Napoleon, and the Napoleonic Wars.

www.napoleon.org
Sponsored by the Foundation Napoleon for "the furtherance of study and research into the civil and military achievements of the First and Second Empires," this site is aimed at a nonacademic audience, but provides chronologies, essays, images and videos, and links to other sites on Napoleon.

www.home.earthlink.net/~womenwhist/lesson7.html
This site is part of a teaching unit on Women in World History that provides further pages on all aspects of women's history. It provides testimonies from women working in three different industries: textile workers, miners, and seamstresses.

CHAPTER

21 INDUSTRIAL EUROPE

- **PORTRAIT OF AN AGE**
- **THE TRADITIONAL ECONOMY**
  - Farming Families
  - Rural Manufacture
  - The Agricultural Revolution
- **THE INDUSTRIAL REVOLUTION IN BRITAIN**
  - Britain First
  - Minerals and Metals
  - Cotton Is King
  - The Iron Horse
  - Entrepreneurs and Managers
  - The Wages of Progress
- **THE INDUSTRIALIZATION OF THE CONTINENT**
  - Industrialization Without Revolution
  - Industrialization and Union
  - The Lands That Time Forgot

Portrait of an Age

THE NORMANDY TRAIN HAS REACHED PARIS. The coast and the capital are once again connected. Passengers in their city finery disembark and are greeted by others who have awaited their scheduled arrival. Workmen stand ready to unload freight, porters to carry luggage. Steam billows forth from the resting engine, which is the object of all human activity. The engine stares as enigmatically as any character in a Renaissance portrait. Yet the train that has arrived in *La Gare Saint-Lazarre* by Claude Monet (1840–1926) is as much the central character in this portrait of the industrial age as was any individual in portraits of ages past.

The train's iron bulk dwarfs the people around it. Indeed, iron dominates; tons of it are in view. The rails, the lampposts, the massive frame of the station, no less than the train itself, are all formed from iron—pliable, durable, inexpensive iron—the miracle product of industrialization. The iron station with its glass panels became as central a feature of nineteenth-century cities as stone cathedrals were in the Middle Ages. Railway stations changed the shape of urban settings, just as railway travel changed the lives of millions of people.

There had never been anything like it before. Ancient Romans had hitched four horses to their chariots; nineteenth-century Europeans hitched four horses to their stagecoaches. The technology of overland transportation had hardly changed in 2000 years. Coach journeys were long, uncomfortable, and expensive, and were governed by the elements and muddy, rutted roads that caused injuries to humans and horses with alarming regularity. First-class passengers rode inside, where they were jostled against one another and breathed the dust that the horses kicked up in front of them.

Second-class passengers rode on top, braving the elements and risking life and limb in an accident.

Railway travel was a quantum leap forward. It was faster, cheaper, and safer. Overnight it changed conceptions of time, space, and, above all, speed. People could journey to what once were distant places in a single day. Voyages became trips, and the travel holiday was born. Commerce was transformed, as was the way in which it was conducted. Large quantities of goods could be shipped quickly from place to place; orders could instantly be filled. The whole notion of locality changed, as salesmen could board a morning train for what only recently had been an unreachable market. Branch offices could be overseen by regional directors, services and products could be standardized, and the gap between great and small cities and between town and countryside could be narrowed.

Wherever they went, the railroads created links that had never been forged before. In Britain, the railroad schedule became the source of the creation of official time. Trains that left London were scheduled to arrive at their destinations according to London time, which came to be kept at the royal observatory in Greenwich. Trains carried fresh fish inland from the coasts and fresh vegetables from rural farms to city tables. Mail moved farther and more quickly; news spread more evenly. Fashionable ideas from the capital cities of Europe circulated everywhere, as did new knowledge and discoveries. The railroads brought both diversity and uniformity.

They also brought wonderment. The engine seemed to propel itself with unimaginable power and at breathtaking speed. The English actress Fanny Kemble (1809–1893) captured the sensation memorably: "You can't imagine how strange it seemed to be journeying on thus, without any visible cause of progress other than the magical machine, with its flying white breath and rhythmical, unvarying pace. I felt no fairy tale was ever half so wonderful as what I saw." For many, the railroad symbolized the genius of the age in which they were living, an age in which invention, novelty, and progress were everywhere to be seen. It combined the great innovations of steam, coal, and iron that were transforming nearly every aspect of ordinary life. But for others, the railway was just as centrally a symbol of disquiet, of the passing of a way of life that was easier to understand and to control. "Seated in the old mail-coach we needed no evidence out of ourselves to indicate the velocity," wrote the English author Thomas De Quincey (1785–1859) in his obituary for the passing of horse travel. "We heard our speed, we saw it, we felt it. This speed was not the product of blind, insensate agencies, that had no sympathy to give, but was incarnated in the fiery eyeballs of the noblest among brutes."

The fruits of the railways, like the fruits of industrialization, were not all sweet. As the nineteenth century progressed, there could be no doubt that, year by year, one way of life was being replaced by another. More and more laborers were leaving the farms for the factories; more and more products were being made by machines. Everywhere there was change, but it was not always or everywhere for the better. Millions of people poured into cities that mushroomed up without plan or intention. Population growth, factory labor, and ultimately the grinding poverty that they produced overwhelmed traditional means of social control. Families and communities split apart; the expectations of ordinary people were no longer predictable. Life was spinning out of control for individuals, groups, and even whole societies. It was an engine racing down a track that only occasionally ended as placidly as did the Normandy train at the Gare Saint-Lazarre.

THE TRADITIONAL ECONOMY

The curse of Adam and Eve was that they would earn their daily bread by the sweat of their brows. For generation after generation, age after age, economic life was dominated by toil. Man, woman, and child labored to secure their supply of food against the caprice of nature. There was nothing even vaguely romantic about the backbreaking exertion needed to crack open the hard ground, plant seeds in it, and protect the crops from the ravages of insects, birds, and animals long enough to be harvested. Every activity was labor-intensive. Wood for shelter or fuel was chopped with thick, blunt axes. Water was drawn from deep wells by the long, slow turn of a crank or dragged in buckets from the nearest stream. Everything that was consumed was pulled or pushed or lifted. French women carried soil and water up steep terraces in journeys that could take as long as seven hours. "The women seemed from their persons and features to be harder worked than horses," Arthur Young (1741–1820), the English agricultural expert, observed with a combination of admiration and disgust. The capital that was invested in the traditional economy was human capital, and by the middle of the eighteenth century nearly eight out of every ten Europeans still tilled the soil, earning their bread by the sweat of their brow.

Although the traditional economy was dominated by agriculture, an increasing amount of labor was devoted to manufacture. The development of a secure and expanding overseas trade created a worldwide demand for consumer goods. In the countryside, small domestic textile industries grew up. Families would take in wool for spinning and weaving to supplement their income from agriculture. When times were good, they would expend proportionately less effort in manufacturing; when times were bad, they would expend more. Their tasks were set by an entrepreneur who provided raw materials and paid the workers by the piece. Wages paid to rural workers were lower than those paid to urban laborers because they were not subject to guild restrictions and because the wages supplemented farm income. Thus entrepreneurs could profit from lower costs, although they had to bear the risk that the goods produced in that fashion would be of lesser quality or that markets would dry up in the interval. Although domestic industry increased the supply of manufactured commodities, it demanded even more labor from an already overworked sector of the traditional economy.

Throughout the traditional economy, the limits on progress were set by nature. Good harvests brought prosperity, bad harvests despair. Over the long run, the traditional economy ran in all-too-predictable cycles. Sadly, the adage, "Eat, drink, and be merry, for tomorrow we may die," was good advice. Prosperity was sure to bring misery in its train. The good fortune of one generation was the hard luck of the next, as more people competed for a relatively fixed quantity of food. No amount of sweat and muscle and, as yet, ingenuity could rescue the traditional economy from its pendulum swings of boom and bust.

By the eighteenth century, the process that would ultimately transform the traditional economy was already under way. It began with the agricultural revolution, one of the great turning points in human history. Before it occurred, the life of every community and of every citizen was always held hostage to nature. The struggle to secure an adequate food supply was the dominant fact of life to which nearly all productive labor was dedicated. After the agricultural revolution, an inadequate food supply was a political rather than an economic fact of life. Fewer and fewer farmers were required to feed more and more people. In Britain, where nearly 70 percent of the population was engaged in agriculture at the end of the seventeenth century, fewer than 2 percent today work on farms. By the middle of the nineteenth century, the most advanced economies were capable of producing vast surpluses of basic commodities. The agricultural revolution was not an event, and it did not happen suddenly. It would not deserve the label "revolution" at all were it not for its momentous consequences: Europe's escape from the shackles of the traditional economy.

Farming Families

Over most of Europe, agricultural activity in the eighteenth century followed methods of crop rotation that had been in place for more than a thousand years. Fields were divided into strips of land, and each family "owned" a certain number of strips, which they cultivated for their livelihood. Between one-half and one-third of village land lay fallow each year so that its nutrients could be restored. Open-field farming, as the system was called, was communal rather than individual. Decisions about which crops to grow in the productive fields, where animals would be pastured, or how much wood could be cut from the common wastes affected everyone. Moreover, many activities, such as plowing, gleaning, and manuring, could not conveniently observe the distinctions of ownership of separate strips. Nor, given the realities of nature, could individual families be self-sustaining without the services of a village tanner or milkmaid or hog minder drawn from the closely intertwined group of kin and neighbors that constituted the community. Communal agriculture was effective, but it also limited the number of people that could survive on the produce from a given amount of land.

There were a number of reasons why the pattern of agricultural production remained unchanged century after century, including that there was little incentive for the peasantry to change it. Although they worked hard to ensure their subsistence, they had little desire to create a surplus. For one thing, almost every commodity produced in the village was perishable, and unless it could be consumed or converted at market into durable goods or cash it was largely worthless. For another thing, peasants owed much of their productivity—in one form or another—to their lords. In eastern Europe, serfdom tied the peasantry to the land, where they were used as laborers for the production of foodstuffs for export. Peasants in central Europe were still obligated to perform labor service for their lords, though in parts of Germany in the eighteenth century the obligation was being commuted to money rents. In France and Scandinavia, peasants "owned" much of their land in the sense that within the constraints imposed by the village, they could cultivate it as they saw fit and bequeath it to their heirs. But they paid dearly for those rights. Manorial taxes, in both money and kind, could take as much as half of each year's output, while demands from the state and the Church might absorb another quarter. The surplus wealth produced by the European peasantry, whether free or unfree, was extracted by their lords.

That is not to say that European peasants were uninterested in bettering their immediate economic circumstances or that they obstructed agricultural change. Agriculture was a profoundly conservative occupation, for the risk of experimentation was nothing less than survival. Lords and peasants both practiced defensive innovation, introducing change only after its practical benefits were easily demonstrable. For example, in the mid-seventeenth century two French provincial parlements banned the cultivation of potatoes in the mistaken belief that they caused leprosy. Yet both potatoes and corn became peasant crops and spread rapidly throughout southern Europe, not least because as new commodities they were untaxed. Peasants bartered their surplus, hoarded their profits, and took what few advantages they could out of a system in which the deck was stacked against them.

As the European population entered a new cycle of growth in the second quarter of the eighteenth century, the traditional economy began to increase agricultural productivity in traditional ways. In the east, new lands were colonized and slowly brought under cultivation. Frederick the Great welcomed immigrants to Prussia, where land was plentiful, if not very fertile. In settled communities, less productive land, which had provided fodder for animals at the end of the seventeenth century, now had to provide food for humans. Scrubland was cleared and hillsides terraced. Dry ground was irrigated manually by women and children working in bucket brigades. As always, an increase in population initially meant an increase in productivity. For a time, more able-bodied workers produced more food.

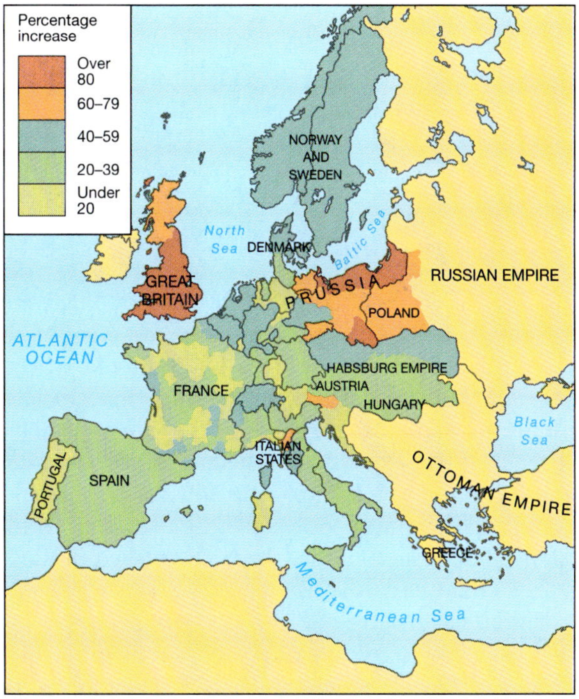

Population Growth in Europe, 1800–1850. While the populations of Britain and Prussia exploded, those of France and Spain grew slowly, leaving them behind as industrialization took shape.

In the half century that ended in the 1770s, French peasants increased agricultural production by nearly 60 percent. The intensification of traditional methods rather than innovation accounted for the increase. The number of strips held by each family declined, but each strip was more carefully cultivated.

By the end of the eighteenth century, the European population was reaching the point at which another check on its growth might be expected. Between 1700 and 1800, total European population had increased by nearly 50 percent, and the rate of growth was continuing to accelerate. The vast expansion of rural population placed a grave strain on agricultural production. Decade by decade, more families attempted to eke out an existence from the same amount of land. The gains made by intensive cultivation were now lost to overpopulation. In areas that practiced partible inheritance, farms were subdivided into units too small to provide subsistence. Competition for the "morsels" of land, as the French called them, was intense. Older sons bought out younger brothers; better-off families purchased whatever came on the market to prevent their children from slipping into poverty. Even in areas in which primogeniture was the rule, portions for younger sons and daughters ate into the meager inheritance of the eldest son. Over much of Europe, it was becoming increasingly difficult to live by bread alone.

Rural Manufacture

The crisis of overpopulation meant that not only were there more mouths to feed, there were more bodies to clothe. That increased the need for spun and woven cloth, and thus for spinners and weavers. Traditionally, commercial cloth production was the work of urban artisans, but the expansion of the marketplace and the introduction of new fabrics, especially cotton and silk, had eroded the monopoly of most of the clothing guilds. Merchants could sell as much finished product as they could find, and the teeming rural population provided a tempting pool of inexpensive labor for anyone willing to risk the capital to purchase raw materials. Initially, farming families took manufacturing work into their homes to supplement their income. Spinning and weaving were the most common occupations, and they were treated as occasional work, reserved for the slow times in the agricultural cycle. It was known as cottage industry. It was supplementary employment, less important and less valuable than the vital agricultural labor that all members of the family undertook.

But by the middle of the eighteenth century, cottage industry was developing in a new direction. As landholdings grew smaller, even good harvests did not promise subsistence to many families. The oversupply of labor was soon organized into the putting-out system, which mobilized the resources of the rural labor force for commercial production of large quantities of manufactured goods. The characteristics of the putting-out system were similar throughout Europe, whether it was undertaken by individual entrepreneurs or lords of the manor, or even sponsored by the state. The process began with the capital of the entrepreneur, which was used to purchase raw materials. The materials were "put out" to the homes of workers where the manufacture, most commonly spinning or weaving, took place. The finished goods were returned to the entrepreneur, who sold them at a profit, with which he bought raw materials to begin the process anew.

The simplicity of the putting-out system was one of its most valuable features. All of its essential elements were already present in rural communities. The small nest egg of a prosperous farmer or small trader was all the money needed to make the first purchase of raw materials. The raw materials could be put out to his kin or closest neighbors and the finished goods then delivered to market along with surplus crops. Not only could a small amount of cash begin the cycle of putting-out, but that capital continued to circulate to keep the process in motion.

The small scale of the initial enterprise can be seen in the fact that many entrepreneurs had themselves begun as workers. In Bohemia, for example, some of the largest putting-out operations were run by serfs who paid their lords fees for the right to engage in trade. At the end of the eighteenth century, there were more than one-quarter million spinners in the Bohemian linen industry alone, most of them organized into small groups around a single entrepreneur, though one monastery employed more than 650 women spinners. Putting-out also required only a low level of skill and common, inexpensive tools. Rural families did their own spinning and rural villages their own weaving. Thus, putting-out demanded little investment, either in plant, equipment, or education. Nor did it inevitably disrupt traditional gender-based tasks in the family economy. In most places spinning was women's work, weaving was done by men, and

Linen production is the subject of an engraving from Nuremberg by Franz Philipp Florin, 1705. The flax stems were soaked to soften the tough outer fibers, which were then removed by beating. The inner fibers were spun into linen on hand looms.

children helped at whichever task was under way. In fact, certain occupations, such as lacemaking in France, were so gender-based that men would not even act as entrepreneurs. In Austria, lacemaking was considered less honorable than other forms of clothmaking because of its association with women and household-based production. Performed at home, rural manufacture remained a traditional family-oriented occupation.

Because that form of manufacturing began as supplementary work, rural laborers were willing to accept low wages. In urban areas, guild restrictions regulated the number of laborers and ensured that they were paid a living wage. Lower labor costs were probably a necessary condition for the success of domestic-based manufacturing. It was vital that the finished goods could readily be sold at market, for it was that sale that allowed the purchase of more raw material. If the entrepreneur could not dispose of his product, his network of workers collapsed. On the other hand, piecework provided farmers with the cushion they needed to survive too-small harvests or too-small plots of land. In the Swiss highlands during the late eighteenth century, farmers prospered on farms one-eighth the size of those tilled by their grandfathers. But more of their time was occupied in cloth production than in agriculture. As long as rural manufacture supplemented agricultural income, it was seen as a benefit for everyone involved—the entrepreneur, the individual worker, and the village community.

Gradually, the putting-out system came to dominate the lives of many rural families. From small networks of isolated villages, domestic manufacture grew to cover entire regions. Perhaps as many as one-quarter of the inhabitants of the Irish province of Ulster were engaged in manufacturing linen by the end of the eighteenth century. Spinning and weaving became full-time occupations for families that kept no more than a small garden. But without agricultural earnings, piecework rates became starvation wages, and families unable to purchase their subsistence were forced to rely upon loans from the entrepreneurs who set them at work. Long hours in dank cottages performing endlessly repetitive tasks became the lot of millions of rural inhabitants, and their numbers increased annually. While the sons of farmers waited to inherit land before they formed their families, the sons of cottage weavers needed only a loom to begin theirs. They could afford to marry younger and to have more children, for children could contribute to manufacturing from an early age.

Consequently, the expansion of the putting-out system, like the expansion of traditional agriculture,

This 1791 engraving by William Hincks shows women engaged in typical tasks of eighteenth-century cottage industry: spinning, reeling with the clock reel, and boiling the yarn.

fueled the continued growth of population. Like traditional agriculture, putting-out contained a number of structural inefficiencies. Both entrepreneur and worker were potential victims of unscrupulousness. Embezzlement of raw materials was a problem for the entrepreneur, arbitrary wage cuts for the laborers. Because the tasks were performed at home, the entrepreneur could not supervise the work. Most disputes in domestic manufacturing arose over specifications of quality. Workers would not receive full pay for poorly produced goods that could not be sold for full value. Inexperienced, aged, or infirm workers could easily spoil costly raw materials. One Bohemian nobleman created village spinning rooms on his estates so that young girls could be given four weeks of training before they set up on their own. Finally, the putting-out system was labor- rather than capital-intensive. As long as there were ready hands to employ, there was little incentive to seek better methods or more efficient techniques.

The Agricultural Revolution

The continued growth of Europe's population necessitated an expansion of agricultural output. In most places that was achieved by intensifying traditional practices, bringing more land into production and more labor to work the land. But in the most advanced European economies, first in Holland and then in England, traditional agriculture underwent a long but dynamic transformation, an agricultural revolution. It was a revolution of technique rather than technology. Humans were not replaced by machines nor were new forms of energy substituted for human and animal muscle. Indeed, many of the methods that were to increase crop yields had been known for centuries and practiced during periods of population pressure. But they had never been practiced as systematically as they came to be from the seventeenth century onward, and they were never combined with a commercial attitude toward farming. It was the willingness and ability of owners to invest capital in their land that transformed subsistence farming into commercial agriculture.

Enclosures. As long as farming was practiced in open fields, there was little incentive for individual landowners to invest in improvements to their scattered strips. While the community as a whole could enclose a small field or plant some fodder crops for the animals, its ability to change traditional practice was limited. In farming villages, even the smallest landholder had rights in common lands, which were jealously guarded.

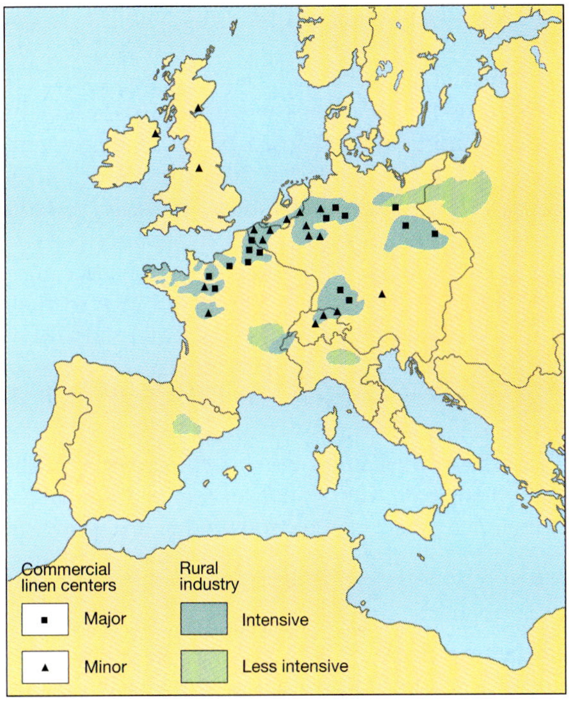

The European Linen Industry. By the eighteenth century, linen production was dominated by the Low Countries and the north German principalities where skilled labor could still be found for the complicated process of linen weaving.

Rights in commons meant a place in the community itself. Commercial agriculture was more suited to large rather than small estates and was more successful when the land could be utilized in response to market conditions rather than the necessities of subsistence.

The consolidation of estates along with the enclosure of fields was thus the initial step toward change. It was a long-term process that took many forms. In England, where it was to become most advanced, enclosure was already under way in the sixteenth century. Prosperous families had long been consolidating their strips in the open fields, and at some point the lord of the manor and the members of the community agreed to carve up the common fields and make the necessary exchanges to consolidate everyone's lands. Perhaps as much as three-quarters of the arable land in England was enclosed by agreement before 1760. Enclosure by agreement did not mean that the breakup of the open-field community was necessarily a harmonious process. Riots preceding or following agreed enclosures were not uncommon.

Paradoxically, it was the middling rather than the poorest villagers who had the most to lose. The breakup of the commons initially gave the poor more arable land from which to eke out their subsistence, and few of them could afford to sacrifice present gain for future loss. The smallholders were quickly bought out. It was the middle-size holders who were squeezed hardest. Although prosperous in communal farming, those families did not have access to the capital necessary to make agricultural improvements such as converting grass to grain land or purchasing large amounts of fertilizer. They could not compete in producing for the market, and gradually they, too, disappeared from the enclosed village. Their opposition to enclosure by agreement led, in the eighteenth century, to enclosure by act of Parliament. Parliamentary enclosure was legislated by government, a government composed for the most part of large landowners. A commission would view the community's lands and divide them, usually by a prescribed formula. Between 1760 and 1815, more than 1.5 million acres of farmland were enclosed by act of Parliament. During the late eighteenth century, the Prussian and French governments emulated the practice by ordering large tracts of land enclosed.

The enclosure of millions of acres of land was one of the largest expenses of the new commercial agriculture. Hedging or fencing off the land and plowing up the commons required extra labor beyond that necessary for basic agrarian activities. Thus many who sold the small estates that they received on the breakup of the commons remained in villages as agricultural laborers or leaseholders. But they practiced a different form of farming. More and more agricultural activity became market-oriented. Single crops were sown in large enclosed fields and exchanged at market for the mixture of goods that previously had been grown in the village. Market production turned attention from producing a balance of commodities to increasing the yield of a single one.

Fodder Crops. The first innovation was the widespread cultivation of fodder crops such as clover and turnips. Crops like clover restore nutrients to the soil as they grow, shortening the period in which land has to lie fallow. Moreover, farm animals grazing on clover or feeding on turnips return more manure to the land, further increasing its productivity. Turnip cultivation had begun in Holland and was brought to England in the sixteenth century. But it was not until the late seventeenth century that Viscount Charles "Turnip" Townsend (1675–1738) made turnip cultivation popular. Townsend and other large Norfolk landowners developed a new system of planting known as the four-crop rotation, in which wheat, turnips, barley, and clover succeeded one another. The method kept the land in productive use, and both the turnip and clover crops were used to feed larger herds of animals.

The ability of farmers to increase their livestock was as important as their ability to grow more grain. Not only were horses and oxen more productive than humans—a horse could perform seven times the labor of a man while consuming only five times the food—but the animals also refertilized the land as they worked. Light fertilization of a single acre of arable land required an average of 25,000 pounds of manure. But animals competed with humans for food, especially during the winter months when little grazing was possible. To conserve grain for human consumption, lambs were led to the slaughter and the fatted calf was killed in the autumn. Thus the development of the technique of meadow floating was a remarkable breakthrough. By flooding low-lying land near streams in the winter, English and Dutch farmers could prevent the ground from freezing during their generally mild winters. When the water was drained, the land beneath it would produce an early grass crop on which the beasts could graze. That meant that more animals could be kept alive during the winter.

The relationship between animal husbandry and grain growing became another feature of commercial agriculture. In many areas farmers could choose between growing grain and pasturing animals. When prices for wool or meat were relatively higher than those for grain, fields could be left in grass for grazing. When grain prices rose, the same fields could be plowed. Consolidated enclosed estates made convertible husbandry possible. The decision to hire fieldworkers or shepherds could be taken only by large agricultural employers. Whatever the relative price of grain, the open-field village continued to produce grain as its primary crop. Farmers who could convert their production in tune to the market not only could maximize their profits but also could prevent shortages of raw materials for domestic manufacturers or of foodstuffs for urban and rural workers.

Convertible husbandry was but the first step in the development of a true system of regional specialization in agriculture. Different soils and climates favored different use of the land. In southern and eastern England the soil was thin and easily depleted by grain growing. Traditionally, the light soil areas had been used almost exclusively for sheep rearing. On the other hand, the clay soils of central England, though poorly drained and hard to work, were more suited to grain growing. The new agricultural techniques reversed the pattern. The introduction of fodder crops and increased fertilization rejuvenated thin soils, and southeastern England became the nation's breadbasket. Large enclosed estates provided a surplus of grain throughout the eighteenth century. By the 1760s, England was exporting enough grain to feed more than a half million people. Similarly, the midland clays became the location of great sheep runs and cattle herds.

Surveyors measure a field for land enclosure. The enclosure movement eliminated large areas of what had formerly been communal land.

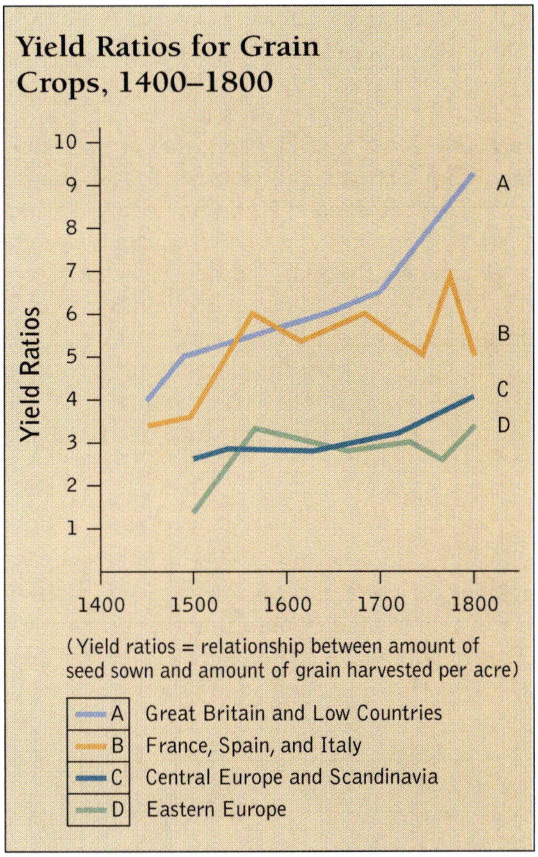

Experiments in herd management, crossbreeding, and fattening all resulted in increased production of wool, milk, meat, leather, soap, and tallow for candles.

There can be no doubt about the benefits of the transformation of agricultural practices that began in Holland and England in the seventeenth century and spread slowly to all corners of the Continent over the next 200 years. Millions more mouths were fed at lower cost than ever before. In 1700, each person engaged in farming in England produced enough food for 1.7 people; in 1800, each produced enough for 2.5 people. Cheaper food allowed more discretionary spending, which fueled the demand for consumer goods, which in turn employed more rural manufacturers. But there also were costs. The transformation of agriculture was also a transformation in a way of life. The open-field village was a community; the enclosed estate was a business. The plight of the rural poor was tragic enough in villages of kin and neighbors, where face-to-face charity might be returned from one generation to the next. With their scrap of land and their common rights, even the poorest villagers laid claim to a place of their own. But as landless laborers, either on farms or in rural manufacturing, they could no longer make that claim and many soon became fodder for the factories, the "dark satanic mills" that came to disfigure the land once tilled in open-field villages. For the destitute, charity was now visited upon them in anonymous parish workhouses or in the good works of the comfortable middle class. In all of those ways the agricultural revolution changed the face of Europe.

THE INDUSTRIAL REVOLUTION IN BRITAIN

Like the changes in agriculture, the changes in manufacturing that began in Britain during the eighteenth century were more revolutionary in consequence than in development. But their consequences were revolutionary indeed. A work force that was predominantly agricultural in 1750 had become predominantly industrial a century later. A population that for centuries had centered on the south and east was now concentrated in the north and west. Liverpool, Manchester, Glasgow, and Birmingham mushroomed into giant cities. While the population of England grew by 100 percent between 1801 and 1851, from about 8.5 million people to more than 17 million, the populations of Liverpool and Manchester grew by more than 1000 percent.

It was the replacement of animal muscle by hydraulic and mineral energy that made the continued population growth possible. Water and coal drove machinery that dramatically increased human productivity. In 1812, one woman could spin as much thread as 200 women had in 1770. What was most revolutionary about the Industrial Revolution was the wave after wave of technological innovation, a constant tinkering and improving of the ways in which things were made, which could have the simultaneous effects of cutting costs and improving quality. It was not just the great breakthrough inventions such as the steam engine, the smelting of iron with coke, and the spinning jenny that were important, but also the hundreds of adjustments in technique that applied new ideas in one industry to another, opened bottlenecks, and solved problems. Ingenuity rather than genius was at the root of the Industrial Revolution in Britain.

The Industrial Revolution was a sustained period of economic growth and change brought about by the application of mineral energy and technological innovations to the process of manufacturing. It took place during the century between 1750 and 1850, though different industries moved at different paces and sustained economic growth continued in Britain until the First World War. It is difficult to define the timing of the Industrial Revolution with any great precision because, unlike a political event, an economic transformation does not happen all at once. Nor are new systems and inventions ever really new. Coal miners had been using rails and wheeled carriages to move ore since the seventeenth century. In the sixteenth century, "Jack of Newbury" had housed his cloth workers in a large shed. The one was the precursor of the railroad and the other the precursor of the factory, but each preceded the Industrial Revolution by more than a century. Before 1750, innovations made their way slowly into general use, and after 1850 the pace of growth slowed appreciably. By then, Britain had a manufacturing economy: fewer than one-quarter of its labor force engaged in agriculture and nearly 60 percent were involved in industry, trade, and transport.

Britain First

The Industrial Revolution occurred first in Britain, but even in Britain industrialization was a regional rather than a national phenomenon. There were many areas of Britain that remained untouched by innovations in manufacturing methods and agricultural techniques, although no one remained unaffected by the prosperity that industrialization brought. That was the result of both national conditions and historical developments. When industrialization spread to the Continent, it took hold—as it had in Britain—in regions where mineral resources were abundant or where domestic manufacturing was a traditional activity. There was no single model for European industrialization, however often contemporaries looked toward Britain for the key to unlock the power of economic growth. There was as much technological innovation in France, as much capital for investment in Holland. Belgium was rich in coal, while eastern Europe enjoyed an agricultural surplus that sustained an increase in population. The finest cotton in the world was made in India; the best iron was made in Sweden. Each of those factors was in some way a precondition for industrialization, but none by itself proved sufficient. Only in Britain did those circumstances meld together.

Water and Coal. Among Britain's blessings, water was foremost. Water was its best defense, protecting the island from foreign invasion and making it unnecessary to invest in a costly standing army. Rather, Britain invested heavily in its navy to maintain its commercial preeminence around the globe. The navy protected British interests in times of war and transported British wares in times of peace. Britain's position in the Asian trade made it the leading importer of cottons, ceramics, and teas. Its colonies, especially in North America, not only provided sugar and tobacco but also formed a rich market for British manufacturing.

But the commercial advantages that water brought were not confined to oceanic trade. Britain was favored by an internal water system that tied inland communities together. In the eighteenth century, no place in Britain was more than 70 miles from the sea or more than 30 miles from a navigable river. Water transport was far cheaper than hauling goods overland; a pack-

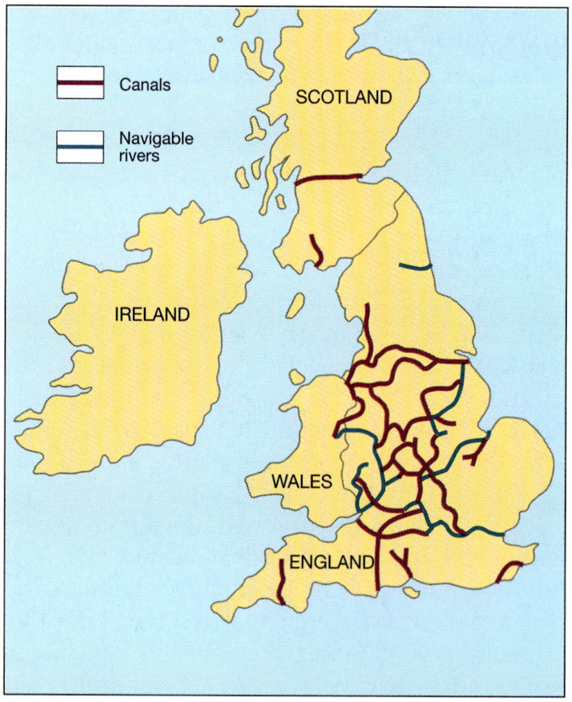

Great Britain: Canals and Navigable Rivers. These were concentrated in the Midlands and south of England, joining the centers of natural resources of those of largest population.

horse could carry 250 pounds of goods on its back but could move 100,000 pounds by walking alongside a river and pulling a barge. Small wonder that river transport was one of the principal interests of merchants and traders. Beginning in the 1760s, private concerns began to invest in the construction of canals, first to move coal from inland locations to major arteries and then to connect the great rivers themselves. Over the next 50 years several hundred miles of canals were built by authority of Navigation Acts, which allowed for the sale of shares to raise capital. In 1760, the Duke of Bridgewater (1736–1803) lived up to his name by completing the first great canal. It brought coal to Manchester and ultimately to Liverpool. It cost more than £250,000 and took 14 years of labor to build, but it repaid the duke and his investors many times over by bringing an uneconomical coal field into production. Not the least of the beneficiaries were the people of Manchester, where the price of coal was halved.

Coal was the second of Britain's natural blessings on which it improved. Britain's reserves of wood were nearly depleted by the eighteenth century, especially those near centers of population. Coal had been in use as a fuel for several centuries, and the coal trade between London and the northern coal pits had been essential to the growth of the capital. Coal was abundant, much of it almost at surface level along the northeastern coast and easily transported on water. The location of large coalfields along waterways was a vital condition of its early use. As canals and roadways improved, more inland coal was brought into production for domestic use. Yet it was in industry rather than in the home that coal was put to its greatest use. There again Britain was favored, for large seams of coal were also located near large seams of iron. At first, the coincidence was of little consequence, since iron was smelted by charcoal made from wood and iron foundries were located deep in forests. But ultimately ironmakers learned to use coal for fuel, and then the natural economies of having mineral, fuel, and transport in the same vicinity were given full play.

Economic Infrastructure. The factors that contributed to Britain's early industrialization were not only those of natural advantage. Over the course of years, Britain had developed an infrastructure for economic advancement. The transformation of domestic handicrafts to industrial production depended as much on the abilities of merchants as on those of manufacturers. The markets for domestic manufacturing had largely been overseas, where British merchants built up relationships over generations. Export markets were vital to the success of industrialization as production grew dynamically and most ventures needed a quick turnaround of sales to reinvest the profits in continued growth. The flexibility of English trading houses would be seen in their ability to shift from

The Worsley-Manchester Canal, as shown in Arthur Young's Six Months' Tour Through the North of England, *1770. This view shows the mouth of the subterranean tunnel at Worsley, where the canal was driven underground to a coal mine. The crane was used to hoist blocks of stone onto canal boats.*

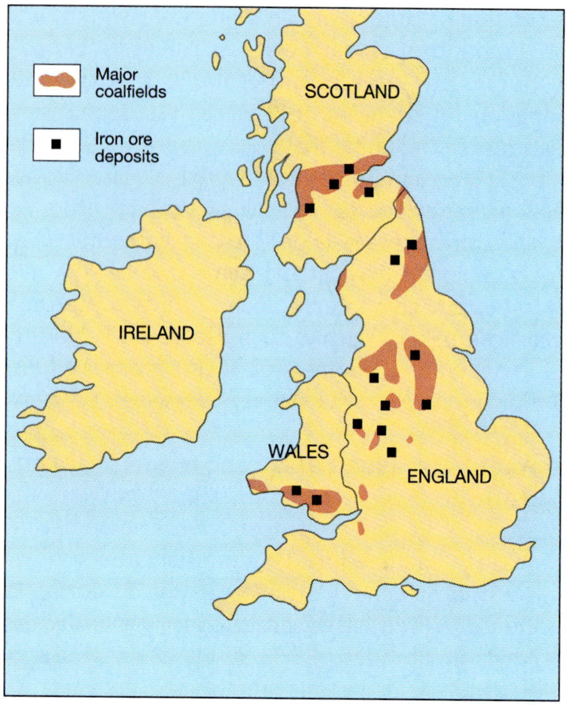

Great Britain: Coal and Iron Ore Deposits. Coal and iron were located away from large concentrations of population. This was a spur to railroad building in the mid-nineteenth century.

reexporting Eastern and North American goods to exporting British manufactures. Equally important, increased production meant increased demand for raw materials: Swedish bar iron for casting, Egyptian and American cotton for textiles, and Oriental silk for luxuries. The expansion of shipping mirrored the expansion of the economy, tripling during the eighteenth century to more than one million tons of cargo capacity.

The expansion of shipping, agriculture, and investment in machines, plant, and raw material all required capital. Not only did capital have to exist, but it had to be made productive. Profits in agriculture, especially in the south and east, somehow had to be shifted to investment in industry in the north and west. The wealth of merchants, which flowed into London, had to be redistributed throughout the economy. More importantly, short-term investments had to give way to long-term financing. At the end of the seventeenth century, the creation of the Bank of England had begun the process of constructing a reliable banking system. The Bank of England dealt almost entirely with government securities, but it also served as a bill broker. It bought the debts of reputable merchants at a discount in exchange for Bank of England notes; Bank of England notes could then be exchanged between merchants, which increased the liquidity of the English economy, especially in London. It also became the model for provincial banking by the middle of the eighteenth century.

Private family banks also grew in importance in London, handling the accounts of merchants and buying shares in profitable enterprises, of which the canals were a favorite. Regional banks, smaller and less capitalized, began to use the private London banks as correspondents, that is, as extensions of their own banks in the city. That allowed local manufacturers and city merchants to do business with one another. The connections between the regional banks and London facilitated the flow of capital from one section of the nation to the other. In 1700, there were just 12 provincial banks; by 1790, there were nearly 300. Banks remained reluctant to invest for the long term, preferring to discount bills for a few months, but after they developed a relationship with a particular firm, they were usually willing to continue to roll the debt over. Although the banking system was vital to large enterprises, in fact the capital for most industry was raised locally, from kin and neighbors, and grew by plowing back profits into the business. At least at the beginning, manufacturers were willing to take risks and to work for small returns to ensure the survival and growth of their business.

Minerals and Metals

There could have been no Industrial Revolution without coal. It was the black gold of the eighteenth century, the fuel that fed the furnaces and turned the engines of industrial expansion. The coal produced by one miner generated as much energy as 20 horses. Coal was the first capital-intensive industry in Britain, already well developed by the seventeenth century. Owners paid the costs of sinking shafts, building roads, and erecting winding machines. Miners were brought to a pit and paid piecework for their labor. Only the very wealthy could afford to invest in coal mining, and it was by chance that British law vested mineral rights in owners rather than users of the land, as was the case on the Continent. That meant that the largest English coalfields were owned by landed families of means who were able to invest agricultural profits in mining. Britain's traditional elites thus played a crucial role in the industrial transformation of the agrarian economy from which their wealth and social standing had derived.

Early Coal Mining. The technical problems of coal mining grew with demand. As surface seams were exhausted it became necessary to dig deeper shafts, to lower miners farther underground, and to raise the coal greater heights to the surface. Men loosened the coal from the seam; women and children hauled it to the shaft. They also cleared the tons of debris that came loose with the coal. Underground mining was extremely dangerous. In addition to all-too-frequent cave-ins, miners struggled against inadequate ventilation and light. Better ventilation was achieved by the expensive method of sinking second and third shafts into the same seam, allowing for cross breezes. Candles and sparks created by flint wheels addressed the problem of light, though both methods suffered from the disadvantage that most pits contained combustible gases. Even after a fireman walked through the mine exploding gas with a long lighted stick, many miners preferred to work in total darkness, feeling the edges of the seam.

But by far the most difficult mining problem was water. As pits were sunk deeper they reached pools of groundwater, which enlarged as the coal was stripped away from the earth. Dripping water increased the difficulty of hewing, standing water the difficulty of hauling. The pit acted like a riverbed and filled quickly. Water drainage presented the greatest obstacle to deep-shaft mining. Women and children could carry the water out in large skin-lined baskets, which were attached to a winding wheel and pulled up by horses. Primitive pumps, also horse-powered, had been devised for the same purpose. Neither method was efficient or effective when shafts sank deeper. In 1709, Thomas Newcomen (1663–1729) introduced a steam-driven pump that enabled water to be sucked through a pipe directly from the pit bottom to the surface. Although the engine was expensive to build and needed tons of coal to create the steam, it could raise the same amount of water in a day as 2500 humans. Such economies of labor were enormous, and within 20 years of its introduction there were 78 engines draining coal and metal mines in England.

Innovations such as Newcomen's engine helped increase output of coal at just the time that it became needed as an industrial fuel. Between 1700 and 1830, coal production increased tenfold despite the fact that deeper and more difficult seams were being worked. Eventually, the largest demand for coal came from the iron industry. In 1793, just two ironworks consumed as much coal as the entire population of Edinburgh. Like mining coal, making iron was both capital- and labor-intensive, requiring expensive furnaces, water-powered bellows, and mills in which forged iron could be slit into rods or rolled into sheets. Ironmaking depended upon an abundance of wood, for it took the charcoal derived from 10 acres of trees to refine 1 ton of iron ore. After the ore was mined, it was smelted into pig iron, a low-grade, brittle metal. Pig iron was converted to higher-quality bar iron in charcoal-powered forges that burned off some of its impurities. From bar

Joseph Wright of Derby, A Blacksmith's Shop (1771). Many of Wright's paintings are associated with the industrial revolution of the eighteenth century, but his principal artistic interest was in the dramatic rendering of light and shade. Nevertheless the three men at the anvil shown here wear typical working clothes and strike realistic poses. The two boys on the right react differently to the scene. The boy in front turns away from the noise and the heat, while behind him the other, whose attire suggests that he is an apprentice, looks on steadily.

Women and children often labored in horrible conditions that were cramped, lacked fresh air, and offered little sunlight.

iron came the rods and sheets used in casting household items such as pots and nails or in making finer wrought iron products such as plows and armaments. Because each process in the making of iron was separate, furnaces, forges, and mills were located near their own supplies of wood. The shipping of the bulky ore, pig iron, and bar iron added substantially to its cost, and it was cheaper to import bars from Sweden than to carry them 20 miles overland.

The great innovations in the production of iron came with the development of techniques that allowed for the use of coal rather than wood charcoal in smelting and forging. As early as 1709, Abraham Darby (ca. 1678–1717), a Quaker nail maker, experimented with smelting iron ore with coke, coal from which most of the gas has been burned off. Iron coking greatly reduced the cost of fuel in the first stages of production, but because most ironworks were located in woodlands rather than near coal pits, the method was not widely adopted. Moreover, although coke made from coal was cheaper than charcoal made from wood, coke added its own impurities to the iron ore. Nor could it provide the intense heat needed for smelting without a large bellows. The cost of the bellows offset the savings from the coke until James Watt (1736–1819) invented a new form of steam engine in 1775.

The Steam Engine. Like most innovations of the Industrial Revolution, James Watt's steam engine was an adaptation of existing technology made possible by the sophistication of techniques in a variety of fields. Although Watt is credited with the invention of the condensing steam engine, one of the seminal creations in human history, the success of his work depended upon the achievements of numerous others. Watt's introduction to the steam engine was accidental. An instrument maker in Glasgow, he was asked to repair a model of a Newcomen engine and immediately realized that it would work more efficiently if there were a separate chamber for the condensation of the steam. Although his idea was sound, Watt spent years attempting to implement it. He was continually frustrated that poor-quality valves and cylinders never fit well enough together to prevent steam from escaping from the engine.

Watt was unable to translate his idea into a practical invention until he became partners with the Birmingham ironmaker and manufacturer Matthew Boulton (1728–1809). At Boulton's works, Watt found craftsmen who could make precision engine valves, and at the foundries of John Wilkinson (1728–1808) he found workers who could bore the cylinders of his engine to exact specifications. Watt's partnership with Boulton and Wilkinson was vital to the success of the steam engine. But Watt himself possessed the qualities necessary to ensure that his ideas were transformed into reality. He persevered through years of unsuccessful experimentation and searched out partners to provide capital and expertise. He saw beyond bare mechanics, realizing the practical utility of his invention long before it was perfected. Watt designed the mechanism to convert the traditional up-and-down motion of the pumping engine into rotary motion, which could be used for machines and ultimately for locomotion.

Watt's engine received its first practical application in the iron industry. Wilkinson became one of the largest customers for steam engines, using them for pumping, moving wheels, and ultimately increasing the power of the blast of air in the forge. Increasing the heat provided by coke in the smelting and forging of iron led to the transformation of the industry. In the 1780s, Henry Cort (1740–1800), a naval contractor,

An engraving of the Soho Engineering Works at Birmingham, England. Here James Watt and his partner Matthew Boulton manufactured steam engines from 1775 to 1810.

experimented with a technique for using coke as fuel in removing the impurities from pig iron. The iron was melted into puddles and stirred with rods. The gaseous carbon that was brought to the surface burned off, leaving a purer and more malleable iron than even charcoal could produce. Because the iron had been purified in a molten state, Cort reasoned that it could be rolled directly into sheets rather than first made into bars. He erected a rolling mill adjacent to his forge and combined two separate processes into one.

Puddling and rolling had an immediate impact upon iron production. There was no longer any need to use charcoal in the stages of forging and rolling. From mineral to workable sheets, iron could be made entirely with coke. Ironworks moved to the coalfields, where the economies of transporting fuel and finished product were great. Moreover, the distinct stages of production were eliminated. Rather than separate smelting, forging, and finishing industries, one consolidated manufacturing process had been created. Forges, furnaces, and rolling machines were brought together and powered by steam engines. Cort's rolling technique alone increased output 15 times. By 1808, output of pig iron had grown from 68,000 to 250,000 tons and of bar iron from 32,000 to 100,000 tons.

Cotton Is King

Traditionally, British commerce had been dominated by the woolen cloth trade, in which techniques of production had not changed for hundreds of years. Running water was used for cleaning and separating fleece; crude wooden wheels spun the thread; simple handlooms wove together the long warp threads and the short weft ones. It took nearly four female spinners to provide the materials for one male weaver, the tasks having long been gender-specific. During the course of the seventeenth century, new fabrics appeared on the domestic market, particularly linen, silk, and cotton. It was cotton that captured the imagination of the eighteenth-century consumer, especially brightly colored, finely spun Indian cotton.

Domestic Industries. Spinning and weaving were organized as domestic industries. Work was done in the home on small, inexpensive machines to supple-

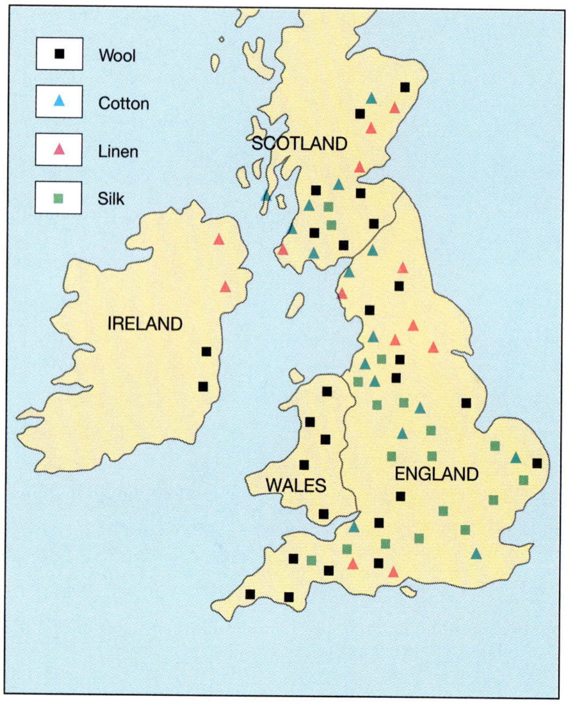

Great Britain: Textile Centers. Textiles had been the traditional industrial activity in Britain and almost every part of the state had organized textile production.

ment the income from farming. Putters-out were especially frustrated by the difficulty in obtaining yarn for weaving in the autumn, when female laborers were needed for the harvest. Even the widespread development of full-time domestic manufacturers did not satisfy the increased demand for cloth. Limited output and variable quality characterized British textile production throughout the early part of the eighteenth century. The breakthrough came with technological innovation. Beginning in the mid-eighteenth century, a series of new machines dramatically increased output and, for the first time, allowed English textiles to compete with Indian imports.

The first innovation was the flying shuttle, invented by John Kay (1704–1764) in the 1730s. A series of hammers drove the shuttle, which held the weft, through the stretched warp on the loom. The flying shuttle allowed weavers to work alone rather than in pairs, but it was adopted slowly because it increased the demand for spun thread, which was already in short supply. The spinning bottleneck was opened by James Hargreaves (d. 1778), who devised a machine known as the jenny. The jenny was a wooden frame containing a number of spindles around which thread was drawn by means of a hand-turned wheel. The first jennies allowed for the spinning of eight threads at once, and improvements brought the number to more than 100. Jennies replaced spinning wheels by the tens of thousands. The jenny was a crucial breakthrough in redressing the balance between spinning and weaving, though it did not solve all problems. Jenny-spun thread was not strong enough to be used as warp, which continued to be wheel spun. But the jenny could spin cotton in unimaginable quantities.

As is often the case with technological change, one innovation followed another. The problem set by improvements in weaving gave rise to solutions for increasing the output of spinners. The need to provide stronger warp threads posed by the introduction of the jenny was ultimately solved by the development of the water frame. It was created in 1769 by Richard Arkwright (1732–1792), whose name was also to be associated with the founding of the modern factory system. Arkwright's frame consisted of a series of water-power-driven rollers that stretched the cotton before spinning. The stronger fibers could be spun into threads suitable for warp, and English manufacturers could finally produce an all-cotton fabric. It was not long before another innovator realized that the water frame and the jenny could be combined into a single machine, one that would produce an even finer cotton yarn than that made in India. The mule, so named because it was a cross between a frame and a jenny, was invented by Samuel Crompton (1753–1827), who sold its rights for only £60. It was the decisive innovation in cotton production. By 1811, ten times as many threads were being spun on mules as on water frames and jennies combined.

The original mules were small machines that, like the jennies, could be used for domestic manufactures. But increasingly the mule followed the water frame into purposely built factories, where it became larger and more expensive. The need for large rooms to house the equipment and for a ready source of running water to power it provided an incentive for the creation of factories, but secrecy provided a greater one. The original factories were called "safe-boxes," and whether they were established for the manufacture of silk or cotton, their purpose was to protect trade secrets. Innovators took out patents to prevent their inventions from being copied and fought long lawsuits to prevent their machines from being used. Workers were sworn to secrecy about the techniques they were taught. Imitators practiced industrial espionage as sophisticated as the age would allow: enticing knowledgeable workers; employing spies; copying inventions. Although the factory was designed to protect secrets, its other benefits were quickly realized. Manufacturers could maintain control over the quality of products through strict supervision of the work force. Moreover, workers in shifts could keep the costly machines in continuous use.

Cotton Factories. Richard Arkwright constructed the first cotton factories in Britain, all of which were designed to house water frames. The first was established in 1769 at Cromford near Nottingham, which was the center of stocking manufacture. The site was chosen for its isolation, since stockings were an article of fashion in which secrecy was most important. The Cromford mill was a four-story building that ultimately employed more than 800 workers. During the next quarter century, Arkwright built more than a dozen other mills, most in partnership with wealthy manufacturers. Arkwright's genius lay in industrial management rather than mechanical innovation. As others switched from frames to mules, Arkwright stubbornly stuck to his own invention. When steam power began to replace water, he failed to make the shift. But his methods of constructing and financing factories were undeniably successful. From a modest beginning as a traveling salesman of wigs, Sir Richard Arkwright died in possession of a fortune worth more than £500,000.

The organization of the cotton industry into factories was one of the pivotal transformations in economic life. Domestic spinning and weaving took place in agricultural villages; factory production took place in mill towns. The location of the factory determined movements of population, and from the first quarter of the eighteenth century onward a great shift toward northeast England was under way. Moreover, the character of the work itself changed. The operation of heavy machinery reversed the traditional gender-based tasks. Mule spinning became men's work, while handloom weaving was taken over by women. The mechanization of weaving took longer than that of spinning, both because of difficulties in perfecting a power loom and because of opposition to its introduction by workers known as Luddites, who organized machine-breaking riots in the 1810s. The Luddites attempted

This hand-colored engraving shows the interior of a German weaver's shop around 1850. Two men are weaving at looms and two women are winding bobbins. The scene is bordered with details of tools such as shuttles and quills.

THE WEALTH OF BRITAIN

Cotton was the first of the new industries that led to British economic domination in the nineteenth century. In producing cotton, new inventions such as the spinning jenny and the water frame revolutionized manufacture and the factory system was born. Britain's domination of cotton production impressed contemporaries. In this excerpt, a contemporary tries to explain why Britain took the lead in industrialization.

IN COMPARING THE ADVANTAGES OF ENGLAND for manufactures with those of other countries, we can by no means overlook the excellent commercial position of the country—intermediate between the north and south of Europe; and its insular situation, which, combined with the command of the seas, secures our territory from invasion or annoyance. The German ocean, the Baltic, and the Mediterranean are the regular highways for our ships; and our western ports command an unobstructed passage to the Atlantic, and to every quarter of the world.

A temperate climate, and a hardy race of men, have also greatly contributed to promote the manufacturing industry of England.

The political and moral advantages of this country, as a seat of manufactures, are not less remarkable than its physical advantages. The arts are the daughters of peace and liberty. In no country have these blessings been enjoyed in so high a degree, or for so long a continuance, as in England. Under the reign of just laws, personal liberty and property have been secure; mercantile enterprise has been allowed to reap its reward; capital has accumulated in safety; the workman has "gone forth to his work and to his labour until the evening"; and, thus protected and favoured, the manufacturing prosperity of the country has struck its roots deep, and spread forth its branches to the ends of the earth.

England has also gained by the calamities of other countries, and the intolerance of other governments. At different periods, the Flemish and French protestants, expelled from their native lands, have taken refuge in England, and have repaid the protection given them by practising and teaching branches of industry, in which the English were then less expert than their neighbours.

From Edward Baines, *The History of the Cotton Manufacture in Great Britain* (1835).

to maintain the traditional organization of their industry and the independence of their labor. For a time, handloom weavers managed to survive by accepting lower and lower piece rates. But their competition was like that of a horse against an automobile. In 1820, there were more than 250,000 handloom weavers in Britain; by 1850, the number was less than 50,000. Weaving as well as spinning became factory work.

The transformation of cotton manufacture had a profound effect on the overall growth of the British economy. It increased shipping because the raw material had to be imported, first from the Mediterranean and then from America. American cotton—especially after 1794, when American inventor Eli Whitney (1765–1825) patented his cotton gin—fed a nearly insatiable demand. In 1750, Britain imported less than 5 million pounds of raw cotton; a century later the volume had grown to 588 million pounds. And to each pound of raw cotton, British manufacturers added the value of their technology and their labor. By the mid-nineteenth century, nearly a half million people earned their living from cotton, which alone accounted for more than 40 percent of the value of all British exports. Cotton was undeniably the king of manufactured goods.

The Iron Horse

The first stage of the Industrial Revolution in Britain was driven by the production of consumer goods. Pottery, cast-iron tools, clocks, toys, and textiles, especially cottons—all were manufactured in quantities unknown in the early eighteenth century. The products fed a ravenous market at home and abroad. The greatest complaint of industrialists was that they could not get enough raw materials or fuel, nor could they ship their finished products fast enough to keep up with demand. Transportation was becoming a serious stumbling block to continued economic growth. Even with the completion of the canal network that linked the major rivers and improvement in highways and tollways, raw materials and finished goods moved slowly and uncertainly. It was said that it took as long to ship goods from Manchester to Liverpool on the Duke of Bridgewater's canal as it did to sail from New York to Liverpool on the Atlantic Ocean. Furthermore, once the canals had a monopoly on bulk cargo, transportation costs began to rise.

It was the need to ship increasing amounts of coal to foundries and factories that provided the spur for the development of a new form of transportation. Ever since the seventeenth century, coal had been moved from the seam to the pit on rails, first constructed of wood and later of iron. Broad-wheeled carts hitched to horses were as much dragged as rolled, but that still represented the most efficient form of hauling, and those railways ultimately ran from the seam to the dock. By 1800, there was perhaps as much as 300 miles of iron rail in British mines.

In the same year, Watt's patent on the steam engine expired, and inventors began to apply the engine to a variety of mechanical tasks. Richard Trevithick (1771–1833), whose father managed a tin mine in Cornwall, was the first to experiment with a steam-driven carriage. George Stephenson (1781–1848), who is generally recognized as the father of the modern railroad, made two crucial improvements. In mine railways the wheels of the cart were smooth and the rail was grooved. Stephenson reversed the construction to provide better traction and less wear. Perhaps more importantly, Stephenson made the vital improvement in engine power by increasing the steam pressure in the boiler and exhausting the smoke through a chimney. In 1829, he won a £500 prize with his engine "The Rocket," which pulled a load three times its own weight at a speed of 30 miles per hour and could actually outrun a horse.

The First Railways. In 1830 the first modern railway, the Manchester-to-Liverpool line, was opened. Like the Duke of Bridgewater's canal, it was designed to move coal and bulk goods, but surprisingly its most important function came to be moving people. In its first year, the Manchester–Liverpool line carried more than 400,000 passengers, which generated double the revenue derived from freight. The railway was quicker,

In the eighteenth century, a number of British inventors patented new machines that transformed the British textile industry and marked the beginning of the Industrial Revolution. Among the inventions was the spinning jenny, invented by James Hargreaves in 1764, and named for his daughter. The jenny, which permitted the spinning of a number of threads at the same time, made possible the automatic production of cotton thread.

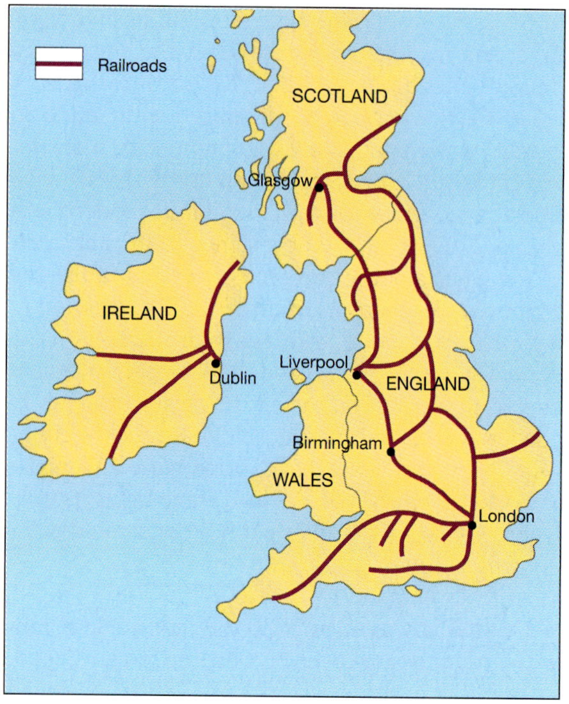

Great Britain: Railroads (ca. 1850). All rails led to London as the major lines were built to transport passengers as well as goods.

more comfortable, and ultimately cheaper than the coach. Investors in the Manchester–Liverpool line, who pocketed a comfortable 9.5 percent when government securities were paying 3.5 percent, learned quickly that links between population centers were as important as those between industrial sites. The London–Birmingham and London–Bristol lines were both designed with passenger traffic in mind.

Railway building was one of the great boom activities of British industrialization. Since it came toward the end of the mechanization of factories, investors and industrialists were psychologically prepared for the benefits of technological innovation. By 1835, Parliament had passed 54 separate acts to establish more than 750 miles of railways. Ten years later, more than 6000 miles had been sanctioned and more than 2500 miles built; by 1852, more than 7500 miles of track were in use. The railways were built on the model of the canals. Private bills passed through Parliament, which allowed a company to raise money through the sale of stock. Most railways were trunk lines, connecting one town to another or joining two longer lines together. They were run by small companies, and few ultimately proved profitable. Only because of the dominant influence of George Stephenson and his son Robert (1803–1859) was there an attempt to establish a standard gauge for tracks and engines. Britain was the only country in which the government did not take a leading role in building the railways. Hundreds of millions of pounds were raised privately, and in the end it is calculated that the railroads cost £40,000 a mile to build, more than three times the cost per mile of railroads on the Continent and in the United States.

From Goods to Passengers. Nevertheless, the investment paid huge dividends. By the 1850s, the original purpose of the railways was being realized as freight revenues finally surpassed passenger revenues. Coal was the dominant cargo shipped by rail, and the speedy, efficient service continued to drive down prices. The iron and steel industries were modernized on the back of demand for rails, engines, and cast-iron seats and fittings. In peak periods—and railway building was a boom-and-bust affair—as much as a quarter of the output of the rolling mills went into domestic railroads, and much more into Continental systems. The railways were also a massive consumer of bricks for beddings, sidings, and especially bridges, tunnels, and stations. Finally, the railways were a leading employer of labor, surpassing the textile mills in peak periods. Hundreds of thousands worked in tasks as varied as engineering and ditch digging, for even in that most advanced industry, sophisticated mechanized production went hand in hand with traditional drudgery. More than 60,000 workers were permanently engaged in the industry to run trains, mind stations, and repair track. Countless others were employed in manufacturing engines, carriages, boxcars, and the thousands of components that went into making them.

Most of all, the railroads changed the nature of people's lives. Whole new concepts of time, space, and speed emerged to govern daily activities. As Henry Booth, an early railroad official, observed, "Notions which we have received from our ancestors and verified by our own experience are overthrown in a day. What was slow is now quick; what was distant is now near." Coach travel had ordinarily been limited to those with means, not only because it was expensive, but also because it was time-consuming. Ordinary people could not take off the days necessary to complete relatively short round-trip journeys. When passenger rail service began, there was even a debate over whether provision should be made for third-class passengers, a class unknown on the coaches, where the only choices

Honore Daumier (1808–1879), The Third-Class Carriage. *Daumier captured a human condition peculiar to the modern era: "the lonely crowd."*

were riding inside for comfort or outside for savings. Third-class passengers quickly became the staple of railroad service. The cheap excursion was born to provide short holidays or even day trips. The career of Thomas Cook (1808–1892), who became the world's first travel agent, began after he took a short excursion. More than six million people visited London by train to view the Crystal Palace exhibition in 1851, a number equivalent to one-third of the population of England and Wales. The railways did more than link

This representation of travel on the Liverpool and Manchester railway illustrates the great difference between first-class (top) and second-class (bottom) travel conditions.

places; they brought people together and helped develop a sense of national identity by speeding all forms of communication.

Entrepreneurs and Managers

The Industrial Revolution in Britain was not simply invented. Too much credit is given to a few breakthroughs and too little to the ways in which they were improved and dispersed. The Industrial Revolution was an age of gadgets when people believed that new was better than old and that there was always room for improvement. "The age is running mad after innovation," the English moralist Dr. Johnson wrote. "All the business of the world is done in a new way; men are hanged in a new way." Societies for the advancement of knowledge sprang up all over Britain. Journals and magazines promoted new ideas and techniques. Competitions were held for the best invention of the year; prizes were awarded for agricultural achievements. Practical rather than pure science was the hallmark of industrial development.

Yet technological innovation was not the same as industrialization. A vital change in economic activity took place in the organization of industry. Putters-out with their circulating capital and hired laborers could never make the economies necessary to increase output and quality while simultaneously lowering costs. That was the achievement of industrialists, producers who owned workplace, machinery, and raw materials and invested fixed capital by plowing back their profits. Industrial enterprises came in all sizes and shapes. A cotton mill could be started with as little as £300 or as much as £10,000. As late as 1840, fewer than 10 percent of the mills employed more than 500 workers. Most were family concerns with less than 100 employees, and many of them failed. For every story with a happy ending, there was another with a sad one. When Major Edmund Cartwright (1740–1824) erected a cotton mill, he was offered a Watt steam engine built for a distiller who had gone bankrupt. He acquired his machinery at the auction of another bankrupt mill. Cartwright's mill, engine, and machinery ended on the auction block less than three years later. There were more than 30,000 bankruptcies in the eighteenth century, testimony both to the risks of business and to the willingness of entrepreneurs to take them.

To survive against the odds, successful industrialists had to be both entrepreneur and manager. As entrepreneurs, they raised capital, almost always locally from relatives, friends, or members of their church. Quakers were especially active in financing each other's enterprises. The industrial entrepreneur also had to understand the latest methods for building and powering machinery and the most up-to-date techniques for performing the work. One early manufacturer claimed "a practical knowledge of every process from the cotton-bag to the piece of cloth." Finally, entrepreneurs had to know how to market their goods. In those functions, industrial entrepreneurs developed logically from putters-out.

But industrialists also had to be managers. The most difficult task was organization of the workplace. Most gains in productivity were achieved through the specialization of function. The processes of production were divided and subdivided until workers performed a basic task over and over. The education of the work force was the industrial manager's greatest challenge. Workers had to be taught how to use and maintain their machines and disciplined to apply themselves continuously. At least at the beginning, it was difficult to staff the factories. Many employed children as young as seven from workhouses or orphanages, who, though cheap to pay, were difficult to train and discipline. It was the task of the manager to break old habits of intermittent work, indifference to quality, and petty theft of materials. Families were preferred to individuals, for then parents could instruct and supervise their children. There is no reason to believe that industrial managers were more brutal masters than farmers or that children were treated better in workhouses than in mills. Labor was a business asset, what was sometimes called "living machinery," and its control with carrots and sticks was the chief concern of the industrial manager.

Who were the industrialists who transformed the traditional economy? Because British society was relatively open, they came from every conceivable background: dukes and orphans, merchants and salesmen, inventors and improvers. Although some went from rags to riches—such as Richard Arkwright, who was the thirteenth child of a poor barber—it was extremely difficult for a laborer to acquire the capital necessary to set up a business. Wealthy landowners were prominent in capital-intensive aspects of industries—for example, owning ironworks and mines—but few established factories. Most industrialists came from the middle classes, which, while comprising one-third of the British population, provided as much as two-thirds

Jasperware copy of the Portland vase by Josiah Wedgwood. The Portland vase is one of the most famous ancient vases. It was found near Rome in the seventeenth century in a tomb believed to be that of Alexander Severus.

of the first generation of industrialists. That first generation included lawyers, bankers, merchants, and those already engaged in manufacturing, as well as tradesmen, shopkeepers, and self-employed artisans. The career of every industrialist was different, as a look at two—Josiah Wedgwood and Robert Owen—will show.

Josiah Wedgwood. Josiah Wedgwood (1730–1795) was the thirteenth child of a long-established English potting family. He worked in the potteries from childhood, but a deformed leg made it difficult for him to turn the wheel. Instead he studied the structure of the business. His head teemed with ideas for improving ceramic manufacturing, but it was not until he was 30 that he could set up on his own and introduce his innovations, which encompassed both technique and organization, the entrepreneurial and managerial sides of his business.

Wedgwood developed new mixtures of clays that took brilliant colors in the kiln and new glazes for both useful and ornamental ware. His technical innovations were all the more remarkable in that he had little education in mineral chemistry and made his discoveries by simple trial and error. But there was nothing of either luck or good fortune in Wedgwood's managerial innovations. He was repelled by the disorder of the traditional pottery, with its waste of materials, uneven quality, and slow output. When he began his first works, he divided the making of pottery into distinct tasks and assigned separate workers to them. One group did nothing but throw the pots on the wheel; another painted designs; a third glazed. To achieve the division of function, Wedgwood had to train his own workers almost from childhood. Traditional potters performed every task from molding to glazing and prized the fact that no two pieces were ever alike. Wedgwood wanted each piece to replicate another, and he stalked the works breaking defective wares on his wooden leg. He invested in schools to help train young artists, in canals to transport his products, and

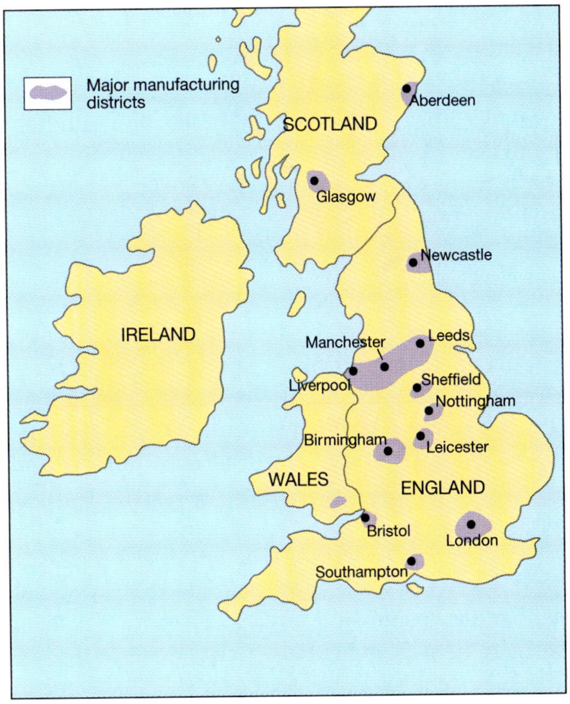

Great Britain: Manufacturing Centers. The growth of manufacturers in the midlands led to a massive population shift and the development of major urban areas such as Manchester.

THE SIN OF WAGES

Robert Owen was both a successful manufacturer and a leading philanthropist. He believed that economic advance had to take place in step with the improvement of the moral and physical well-being of the workers. He organized schools, company shops, and ultimately utopian communities in an effort to improve the lives of industrial laborers. Owen was one of the first social commentators to argue that industrialism threatened the fabric of family and community life.

THE ACQUISITION OF WEALTH, and the desire which it naturally creates for a continued increase, have introduced a fondness for essentially injurious luxuries among a numerous class of individuals who formerly never thought of them, and they have also generated a disposition which strongly impels its possessors to sacrifice the best feelings of human nature to this love of accumulation. To succeed in this career, the industry of the lower orders, from whose labour this wealth is now drawn, has been carried by new competitors striving against those of longer standing, to a point of real oppression, reducing them by successive changes, as the spirit of competition increased and the ease of acquiring wealth diminished, to a state more wretched than can be imagined by those who have not attentively observed the changes as they have gradually occurred. In consequence, they are at present in a situation infinitely more degraded and miserable than they were before the introduction of these manufactories, upon the success of which their bare subsistence now depends....

The inhabitants of every country are trained and formed by its great leading existing circumstances, and the character of the lower orders in Britain is now formed chiefly by circumstances arising from trade, manufactures, and commerce; and the governing principle of trade, manufactures, and commerce is immediate pecuniary gain, to which on the great scale every other is made to give way. All are sedulously trained to buy cheap and to sell dear; and to succeed in this art, the parties must be taught to acquire strong powers of deception; and thus a spirit is generated through every class of traders, destructive of that open, honest sincerity, without which man cannot make others happy, nor enjoy happiness himself.

From Robert Owen, *Observations on the Effect of the Manufacturing System* (1815).

in London shops to sell them. Wedgwood was a marketing genius. He named his famed cream-colored pottery Queen's Ware and made special coffee and tea services for leading aristocratic families. He would then sell replicas by the thousands. In less than 20 years, Wedgwood pottery was prized all over Europe and Wedgwood's potting works were the standard of the industry.

Robert Owen. Robert Owen (1771–1858) did not have a family business to develop. The son of a small tradesman, he was apprenticed to a clothier at the age of 10. As a teenager he worked as a shop assistant in Manchester, where he audaciously applied for a job as a manager of a cotton mill. At 19, he was supervising 500 workers and learning the cotton trade. Owen was immediately successful, increasing the output of his workers and introducing new materials to the mill. In 1816, he entered a partnership to purchase the New Lanark mill in Scotland. Owen found conditions in Scotland much worse than those in Manchester. More than 500 workhouse children were employed at New Lanark, where drunkenness and theft were endemic. Owen believed that to improve the quality of work one had to improve the quality of the workplace. He replaced old machinery with new, reduced working hours, and instituted a monitoring system to check theft. To enhance life outside the factory, he established a high-quality company-run store, which plowed its profits into a school for village children.

Owen was struck by the irony that in the mills, machines were better cared for than were humans. He thought that with the same attention to detail that had so improved the quality of commodities he could make even greater improvements in the quality of life. He prohibited children under 10 from mill work and instituted a 10-hour day for child labor. His local school took infants from one year old, freeing women to work and ensuring each child an education. Owen instituted old-age and disability pensions, funded by mandatory contributions from workers' wages. Taverns were closed and workers were fined for drunkenness and sexual offenses. In the factory and the village, Owen established a principle of communal regulation to improve both the work and the character of his employees. New Lanark became the model of the world of the future, and each year thousands made an industrial pilgrimage to visit it.

The Wages of Progress

Robert Owen ended his life as a social reformer. His efforts to improve the lot of his workers at New Lanark led to experiments to create ideal industrial communities throughout the world. He founded cooperative societies, in which all members shared in the profits of the business, and supported trade unions in which workers could better their lives. His followers planted colonies where goods were held in common and the fruits of labor belonged to the laborers. Owen's agitation for social reform was part of a movement that produced results of lasting consequence. The Factory Act (1833) prohibited factory work by children under nine, provided two hours of daily education, and effectively created a 12-hour day in the mills until the Ten Hours Act (1847). The Mines Act (1842) prohibited women and children from working underground.

Nor was Owen alone in dedicating time and money to the improvement of workers' lives. The rapid growth of unplanned cities exacerbated the plight of those too poor and overworked to help themselves. Conditions of housing and sanitation were appalling even by nineteenth-century standards. The *Report on the Sanitary Condition of the Laboring Population in Britain* (1842), written by Edwin Chadwick (1800–1890), so shocked Parliament and the nation that it helped to shift the burden of social reform to government. The Public Health Act (1848) established boards of health and the office of medical examiner, while the Vaccination Act (1853) and the Contagious Diseases Act (1864) attempted to control epidemics. (See "Industry and the Environment," pp. 748–749.)

The movement for social reform began almost as soon as industrialization. The Industrial Revolution initiated profound changes in the organization of British society. Cities sprang up from grain fields almost overnight. The lure of steady work and high wages prompted an exodus from rural Britain and spurred an unremitting boom in population. In the first half of the nineteenth century, the population of England doubled from 9 to 18 million, with growth most rapid in the newly urban north and west. In 1750, about 15 percent of the population lived in urban areas; by 1850, about 60 percent did. Industrial workers married younger and produced more children than their agricultural counterparts. For centuries, women had married in their middle twenties, but by 1800, age at first marriage had dropped to 23 for the female population as a whole and to nearly 20 in the industrial areas. That was in part because factory hands did not have to wait until they inherited land or money, and in part because they did not have to serve an apprenticeship. But early marriage and large families were also a bet on the future, a belief that things were better now and would be even better soon, that the new mouths would be fed and the new bodies clothed. It was an investment on the part of ordinary people similar to that made by bankers and entrepreneurs when they risked their capital in new businesses. Was it an investment that paid off?

It is difficult to calculate the benefits of the Industrial Revolution or to weigh them against the costs. What is certain is that there was a vast expansion of wealth as well as a vast expansion of people to share it. Agricultural and industrial change made it possible to support comfortably a population more than three times larger than that of the seventeenth century, when it was widely believed that England had reached the limits of expansion. Despite the fact that population doubled between 1801 and 1851, per capita income rose by 75 percent. Had the population remained stable, per capita income would have increased by a staggering 350 percent. At the same time, untold millions of pounds had been sunk into canals, roads, railways, factories, mines, and mills.

But the expansion of wealth is not the same as the improvement in the quality of life, for wealth is not equally distributed. An increase in the level of wealth may mean only that the rich are getting richer more quickly than the poor are getting poorer. Similarly, economic growth over a century involved the lives of several generations, each of which experienced different standards of living. One set of parents may have sacrificed for the future of their children; another may have

Industry and the Environment

The Industrial Revolution changed the landscape of Britain. Small villages grew into vast metropolises seemingly overnight. The rates of growth were absolutely staggering: in 1801, there were 75,000 people in Manchester; by 1851, the number had more than quadrupled. The unremitting boom in population did more than strain the resources of local authorities: it broke them apart. It was not that the new industrial cities were unplanned; they were beyond the capacity of planning. Every essential requirement for human survival became scarce and expensive. Shortages of food, water, and basic accommodation were commonplace.

Shantytowns sprang up wherever space would allow, making the flimsily built habitations of construction profiteers seem like palaces. There was loud complaint about those nineteenth-century rip-off artists, but in truth the need for housing was so desperate that people willingly lived anywhere that provided shelter. Houses were built back to back and side by side, with only narrow alleyways to provide sunlight and air. In Edinburgh, one could step through the window of one house into the window of the adjoining one. Whole families occupied single rooms where members slept as they worked, in shifts. In Liverpool, more than 38,000 people were estimated to be living in cellars—windowless underground accommodations that flooded with the rains and the tides.

Most cities lacked both running water and toilet facilities. Districts were provided with either pumps or capped pipes through which private companies ran water for a few hours each day. The water was collected in buckets and brought to the home, where it would stand for the rest of the day and serve indifferently for washing, drinking, and cooking. Outhouse toilets were an extravagant luxury; in one Manchester district, 33 outhouses had to accommodate 7095 people. They were a mixed blessing even in the middle-class districts where they were more plentiful, as there was no system of drainage to flush away the waste. It simply accumulated in cesspools, which were emptied manually about every two years. The thing that most impressed visitors as they approached an industrial city was the smoke; what impressed them most when they arrived was the smell.

The quality of life experienced by most of the urban poor who lived in the squalid conditions has been recorded by a number of contemporary observers. Friedrich Engels was a German socialist who was sent to England to learn the cotton trade. He

lived in Manchester for two years and spent much of his time exploring the working-class areas of the city. "In this district I found a man, apparently about sixty years old, living in a cow stable," Engels recounted from one of his walking tours in *The Condition of the Working Class in England in 1844*. "He had constructed a sort of chimney for his square pen, which had neither windows, floor, nor ceiling, had obtained a bedstead and lived there, though the rain dripped through his rotten roof. This man was too old and weak for regular work, and supported himself by removing manure with a hand-cart; the dung-heaps lay next door to his palace!" From his own observations Engels concluded that "in such dwellings only a physically degenerate race, robbed of all humanity, degraded, reduced morally and physically to bestiality, could feel comfortable and at home." And as he was quick to point out, his own observations were no different from those of parliamentary commissioners, medical officers, or civic authorities who had seen conditions firsthand.

Among the observers, the most influential by far was Sir Edwin Chadwick, who began his government career as a commissioner for the poor law and ended it as the founder of a national system of public health. Chadwick wrote the report of a parliamentary commission, *The Sanitary Condition of the Laboring Population of Britain* (1842), which caused a sensation among the governing classes. Building on the work of physicians, overseers of the poor, and the most technical scholarship available, Chadwick not only painted the same grim picture of urban life as Engels did, he proposed a comprehensive solution to one of its greatest problems, waste management.

Chadwick was a civil servant, and he believed that problems were solved by government on the basis of conclusions of experts. He had heard doctors argue their theories about the causes of disease, some believing in fluxes that resulted from combinations of foul air, water, and refuse; others believing disease was spread by the diseased, in this case Irish immigrants who settled in the poorest parts of English industrial towns. Although medical research had not yet detected the existence of germs, it was widely held that lack of ventilation, stagnant pools of water, and the accumulation of human and animal waste in proximity to people's dwellings all contributed to the increasing incidence of disease. Chadwick fixed upon the last element as crucial. Not even in middle-class districts was there any effective system for the removal of waste. Chamber pots and primitive toilets were emptied into ditches, which were used to drain rain off into local waterways. The few underground sewers that existed were square containers without outlets that were simply emptied once filled. Chadwick's vision was for a sanitation system, one that would carry waste out of the city quickly and deposit it in outlying fields where it could be used as fertilizer.

Chadwick realized that the key to disposing of waste was a constant supply of running water piped through the system. Traditionally, only heavy rainstorms cleared the waste ditches in most cities, and those were too infrequent to be effective. The river had to be the beginning of the sewerage system as well as its end. River water had to be pumped through an underground construction of sewage pits that were built to facilitate the water's flow. Civil engineers had already demonstrated that pits with rounded rather than angular edges were far more effective, and Chadwick advocated the construction of a system of oval-shaped tunnels, built on an incline beneath the city. Water pumped from one part of the river would rush through the tunnels, which would empty into pipes that would carry the waste to nearby farms.

Chadwick's vision took years to implement. He had all of the zeal of a reformer and none of the tact of a politician. He offended nearly everyone with whom he came into contact, because he believed that his program was the only workable one and because he believed that it must be implemented whatever the price. He was uninterested in who was to pay the enormous costs of laying underground tunnel and building pumping stations and insisted only that the work begin immediately. In the end, he won his point. Sanitation systems became one of the first great public-works projects of the industrial age.

Dudley Street, Seven Dials, London, *by Gustave Doré, depicts life in the London slums of the early nineteenth century.*

mortgaged it. Moreover, economic activity is cyclical. Trade depressions, such as those induced by the War of 1812 and the American Civil War, which interrupted cotton supplies, could have disastrous short-term effects. The "Great Hunger" of the 1840s was a time of agrarian crisis and industrial slump. The downturn of 1842 threw 60 percent of the factory workers in the town of Bolton out of work at a time when there was neither unemployment insurance nor a welfare system. Finally, quality of life cannot be measured simply in economic terms. People with more money to spend may still be worse off than their ancestors, who may have preferred leisure to wealth or independence to the discipline of the clock.

Thus there are no easy answers to the quality-of-life question. In the first stages of industrialization, it seems clear that only the wealthy benefited economically, though much of their increased wealth was reinvested in expansion. Under the impact of population growth, the Napoleonic wars, and regional harvest failure, real wages seem to have fallen from the levels reached in the 1730s. Industrial workers were not substantially better off than agricultural laborers when the high cost of food and rent is considered. But beginning around 1820, there is a convincing evidence that the real wages of industrial workers were rising despite the fact that more and more work was semi- and unskilled machine-minding and more of it was being done by women, who were generally paid only two-thirds the wages of men. Although the increase in real wages was still subject to trade cycles, such as the Great Hunger of the 1840s, it continued nearly unabated for the rest of the nineteenth century. Thus, in the second half of the Industrial Revolution, both employers and workers saw a bettering of their economic situation, which was one reason why rural workers flocked to the cities and Irish peasants emigrated in the hundreds of thousands to work the lowest paid and least desirable jobs in the factories.

EXPLOITING THE YOUNG

The condition of child laborers was a concern of English legislators and social reformers from the beginning of industrialization. Most of the attention was given to factory workers, and most legislation attempted to regulate the age at which children could begin work, the number of hours they could be made to work, and the provision of schooling and religious education during their leisure. It was not until the mid-1840s that a parliamentary commission was formed to investigate the condition of child labor in the mines. In this extract, the testimony of the child is confirmed by the observations of one of the commissioners.

ELLISON JACK, 11-YEARS-OLD GIRL COAL-BEARER AT LOANHEAD COLLIERY, SCOTLAND: I have been working below three years on my father's account; he takes me down at two in the morning, and I come up at one and two next afternoon. I go to bed at six at night to be ready for work next morning: the part of the pit I bear in the seams are much on the edge. I have to bear my burthen up four traps, or ladders, before I get to the main road which leads to the pit bottom. My task is four or five tubs: each tub holds 4G cwt. I fill five tubs in twenty journeys.

I have had the strap when I did not do my bidding. Am very glad when my task is wrought, as it sore fatigues. I can read, and was learning the writing; can do a little; not been at school for two years; go to kirk occasionally, over to Lasswade: don't know much about the Bible, so long since read.

R. H. Franks, Esq., the sub-commissioner: A brief description of this child's place of work will illustrate her evidence. She has first to descend a nine-ladder pit to the first rest, even to which a shaft is sunk, to draw up the baskets or tubs of coals filled by the bearers; she then takes her creel (a basket formed to the back, not unlike a cockle-shell flattened towards the neck, so as to allow lumps of coal to rest on the back of the neck and shoulders), and pursues her journey to the wall-face, or as it is called here, the room of work. She then lays down her basket, into which the coal is rolled, and it is frequently more than one man can do to lift the burden on her back. The tugs or straps are placed over the forehead, and the body bent in a semicircular form, in order to stiffen the arch.

"Child Labor in the Coal Mines," Testimony to the Parliamentary Investigative Committee (1842).

But economic gain had social costs. The first was the decline of the family as a labor unit. In both agricultural and early industrial activity, families labored together. Workers would not move to mill towns without the guarantee of a job for all members of their family, and initially they could drive a hard bargain. The early factories preferred family labor to workhouse conscripts, and it was traditional for children to work beside their parents, cleaning, fetching, or assisting in minding the machines. Children provided an essential part of family income, and youngest children were the agency of care for infirm parents. Paradoxically, it was agitation for improvement in the conditions of child labor that spelled the end of the family work unit. At first, young children were barred from the factories and older ones allowed to work only a partial adult shift. Although reformers intended that schooling and leisure be substituted for work, the separation of children from parents in the workplace ultimately made possible the substitution of teenagers for adults, especially as machines replaced skilled human labor. The individual worker now became the unit of labor, and during economic downturns it was adult males with their higher salaries who were laid off first.

The decline of the family as a labor unit was matched by other changes in living conditions when rural dwellers migrated to cities. Many rural habits were unsuited to both factory work and urban living. The tradition of "Saint Monday," for example, was one that was deeply rooted in the pattern of agricultural life. Little effort was expended at the beginning of the work week and progressively more at the end. Sunday leisure was followed by Monday recovery, a slow start to renewed labor. The factory demanded constant application six days a week. Strict rules were enforced to keep workers at their stations and their minds on their jobs. More than efficiency was at stake. Early machines were not only crude, they were dangerous, with no safety features to cover moving parts. Maiming accidents were common in the early factories, and they were the fault of both workers and machines. Similarly, industrial workers entered a world of the cash economy. Most agricultural workers were used to being paid in kind and to barter exchange. Money was an unusual luxury that was associated with binges of food, drink, and frivolities, which made adjustment to the wage packet as difficult as adjustment to the clock. Cash had to be set aside for provisions, rent, and clothing. On the farm, the time of a bountiful harvest was the time to buy durable goods; in the factory, "harvest time" was always the same.

Such adjustments were not easy, and during the course of the nineteenth century a way of life passed forever from England. For some, its departure caused profound sorrow; for others, it was a matter of rejoicing. A vertically integrated society in which lord of the manor, village worthies, independent farmers, workers, and servants lived together interdependently was replaced by a society of segregated social classes. By the middle decades of the nineteenth century, a class of capitalists and a class of workers had begun to form and had begun to clash. The middle classes abandoned the city centers, building exclusive suburban communities in which to raise their children and insulate their families. Conditions in the cities deteriorated under the pressure of overcrowding, lack of sanitation, and the absence of private investment. The loss of interaction between the different segments of society had profound consequences for the struggle to improve the quality of life for everyone. Leaders of labor saw themselves fighting against profits, greed, and apathy; leaders of capital against drunkenness, sloth, and ignorance. Between the two stereotypes there was little middle ground.

THE INDUSTRIALIZATION OF THE CONTINENT

Although Britain took the first steps along the road to an industrial economy, it was not long before other European nations followed. There was intense interest in "the British miracle," as it was dubbed by contemporaries. European ministers, entrepreneurs, even heads of state visited British factories and mines in hope of learning the key industrial secrets that would unlock the prosperity of a new age. The Crystal Palace exhibition of manufacturing and industry held in London in 1851 was the occasion for a Continentwide celebration of the benefits of technology and a chance for ambitious Europeans to measure themselves against the mighty British. By then many European nations had begun the transformation of their own economies and had entered a period of sustained growth.

There was no single model for the industrialization of the Continental states. Contemporaries continually made comparisons with Britain, but in truth the process of British industrialization was not well suited to any but the coal-rich regions in Belgium and the Rhineland. Nevertheless, all of Europe benefited from the British experience. No one else had to invent the jenny, the mule, or the steam engine. Although the British government banned the export of technology, none of the path-breaking inventions remained a secret for long. Britain had demonstrated a way to make cheap, durable goods in factories, and every other state in Europe was able to skip the long stages of discovery and improvement. Thus, while industrialization began later on the Continent, it could progress more quickly. France and Germany were building a railroad system within years of Britain despite the fact that they had to import most of the technology, raw materials, and engineers.

Britain shaped European industrialization in another way. Its head start made it very difficult for follower nations to compete against British commodities in the world market, which meant that European industrialization would be directed first and foremost to home markets, where tariffs and import quotas could protect fledgling industries. Although European states were willing to import vital British products, they placed high duties on British-made consumer goods and encouraged higher-cost domestic production. Britain's competitive advantage demanded that European governments become involved in the industrialization of their countries, financing capital-intensive industries, backing the railroads, and favoring the establishment of factories.

European industrialization was therefore not the thunderclap it was in Britain. In France, it was a slow, accretive development that took advantage of traditional skills and occupations and gradually modernized the marketplace. In Germany, industrialization had to overcome the political divisions of the empire, the economic isolation of the petty states, and the wide dispersion of vital resources. Regions rather than states industrialized in the early nineteenth century, and parts of Austria, Italy, and Spain imported machinery and techniques and modernized their traditional crafts. But most of the states and most of the eastern part of Europe remained tied to a traditional agrarian-based economy that provided neither labor for industrial production nor purchasing power for industrial goods. The areas quickly became sources for raw materials and primary products for their industrial neighbors.

Industrialization Without Revolution

The experience of France in the nineteenth century demonstrates that there was no single path to industrialization. Each state blended together its natural resources, historical experiences, and forms of economic organization in unique combinations. While some mixtures resulted in explosive growth, as in Britain, others made for steady development, as in France.

Industrialization in France. French industrialization was keyed to domestic rather than export markets and to the application of new technology to a vast array of traditional crafts. The French profited, as did all of the Continental states, from British inventions, but they also benefited from the distinct features of their own economy. France possessed a pool of highly skilled and highly productive labor, a manufacturing tradition oriented toward the creation of high-quality goods, and consumers who valued taste and fashion over cost and function. Thus while the British dominated the new mass market for inexpensive cottons and cast-iron goods, a market with high sales but low profit margins, the French were producing luxury items whose very scarcity kept both prices and profits high.

Two decisive factors determined the nature of French industrialization: population growth and the French Revolution. From the early eighteenth to the mid-nineteenth centuries, France grew slowly. In 1700, the French population stood at just less than 20 million; in 1850, it was just less than 36 million, a growth rate of 80 percent. In contrast, Germany grew 135 percent, from 15 to 34 million, and England 300 percent, from 5 to 20 million, during the same period.

The Industrial Revolution on the Continent. The major developments took place in Germany and in the coastal areas along the English Channel where there were better natural resources or pools of labor.

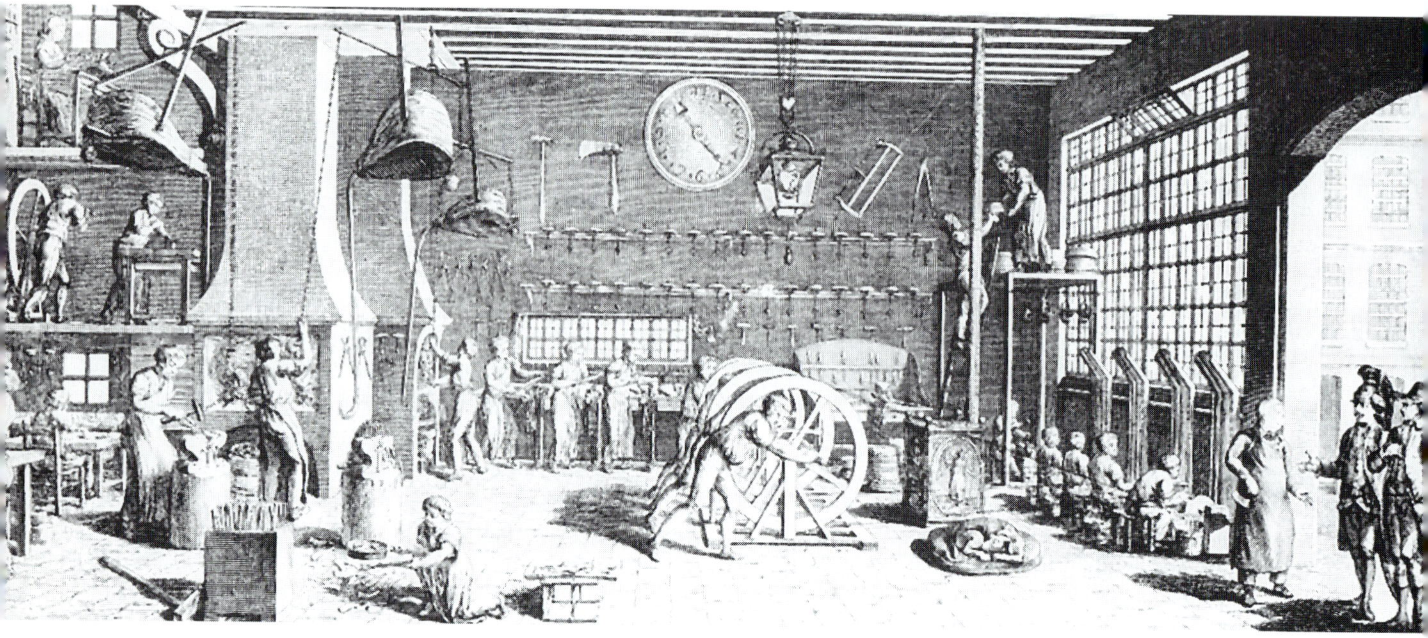

This engraving shows a French steelworks, Manufacture Nationale, in Paris, 1800. At that time, it was the only French steelworks that compared with those in Sheffield, England.

Nevertheless, France remained the most populous nation in western Europe, second on the Continent only to Russia. There is no simple explanation for France's relatively sluggish population growth. The French had been hit particularly hard by subsistence crises in the seventeenth century, and there is reliable evidence that the rural population consciously attempted to limit family size by methods of birth control as well as by delaying marriages. Moreover, France urbanized slowly at a time when city dwellers were marrying younger and producing larger families. As late as the 1860s, a majority of French workers were farmers. Whatever the cause of the moderate population growth, its consequences were clear. France was not pressured by the force of numbers to abandon its traditional agricultural methods, nor did it face a shortage of traditional supplies of energy. Except during crop failures, French agriculture could produce to meet French needs, and there remained more than enough wood for domestic and industrial use.

Slow Growth. The consequences of the French Revolution are less clear. Throughout the eighteenth century, the French economy performed at least as well as the British, and in many areas better. French overseas trade had grown spectacularly until checked by military defeat in the Seven Years' War (1756–1763). French agriculture steadily increased output, while French rural manufactures flourished. A strong guild tradition still dominated urban industries, and although it restricted competition and limited growth, it also helped maintain the standards for the production of high-quality goods that made French commodities highly prized throughout the world. The Revolution disrupted every aspect of economic life. Some of its outcomes were unforeseen and unwelcome. For example, Napoleon's Continental System, which attempted to close European markets to Britain, resulted in a shipping war, which the British won decisively and which eliminated France as a competitor for overseas trade in the mid-nineteenth century. But other outcomes were the result of direct policies, even if their impact could not have been entirely predicted. Urban guilds and corporations were abolished, opening trades to newcomers but destroying the close-knit groups that trained skilled artisans and introduced innovative products. Similarly, the breakup of both feudal and common lands to satisfy the hunger of the peasantry had the effect of maintaining a large rural population for decades.

Despite the efforts of the central government, there had been little change in the techniques used by French farmers over the course of the eighteenth century. French peasants clung tenaciously to traditional rights that gave even the smallest landholder a vital say in community agriculture. Landlords were predominantly absentees, less interested in the organization of their estates than in the dues and taxes that could be extracted from them. Thus the policies of successive revolutionary governments strengthened the hold of small peasants on the land. With the abolition of many feudal dues and with careful family planning, smallholders could survive and pass a meager inheritance onto their children. Even prosperous farmers could not grow into the large-scale proprietors that had enclosed English fields, for little land came on the market, and many parts of France practiced partible inheritance, which, over time, tended to even out the size of holdings. French agriculture continued to be organized in its centuries-old patterns. While it was able to supply the nation's need for food, it could not release large numbers of workers for purely industrial activity.

Thus French industrial growth was constrained on the one hand by the relatively small numbers of workers who could engage in manufacturing and on the other by the fact that a large portion of the population remained subsistence producers, cash-poor, and linked only to small rural markets. Throughout the eighteenth century, the French economy continued to be regionally segregated rather than nationally integrated. The size of the state inhibited a highly organized internal trade, and there was little improvement of the infrastructure of transportation. Although some British-style canals were built, canals in Britain were built to move coal rather than staple goods and France did not have much coal to move. Manufacturing concerns were still predominantly family businesses whose primary markets were regional rather than international. Roads that connected the short distances between producers and consumers were of greater importance to the producers than arterial routes that served the markets of others. Similarly, there was no national capital market until the mid-nineteenth century, and precious few regional ones. French producers were as thrifty and profit-oriented as any others, but they found it more difficult to raise the large amounts of capital necessary to purchase the most expensive new machinery and build the most up-to-date factories. Ironworks, coal mines, and railroads, the three capital-intensive ventures of industrialization, were financed either by government subsidy or by foreign investment.

All those factors determined the slow, steady pace of French industrialization. Recovery after 1815 came in fits and starts. British inventors, manufacturers, and entrepreneurs were enticed to France to demonstrate new machinery and industrial techniques, but in most places the real engine of growth was skilled workers' steady application of traditional methods. By 1820, only 65 French factories were powered by steam engines, and even water-powered machinery was uncommon. Industrial firms remained small and were frequently a combination of putting-out and factory production. It was not until midcentury that sustained industrial growth became evident. This was largely the result of the construction of railroads on a national plan, financed in large part by the central government. Whereas in Britain the railways took advantage of a national market, in France they created one. They also gave the essential stimulation to the modernization of the iron industry, in which much refining was still done with charcoal rather than coke; of machine making; and of the capital markets. Imported steel and foreign investment were vital ingredients in a process that took several decades to reach fruition.

The disadvantages of being on the trailing edge of economic change were mitigated for a time by conventional practices of protectionism. Except in specialty goods, agricultural produce, and luxury products, French manufactures could not compete with either British or German commodities. Had France maintained its position as a world trader, the comparative disadvantage would have been devastating. But defeat in the wars of commerce had led to a drawing inward of French economic effort. Marseille and Bordeaux, once bustling centers of European trade, became provincial backwaters in the nineteenth century. But the internal market was still strong enough to support industrial growth, and domestic commodities could be protected by prohibitive tariffs, especially against British textiles, iron, and, ironically, coal. Despite the fact that France had to import more than 40 percent of its meager requirements of coal, it still insisted upon slapping high import duties on British supplies. That was in part to protect French mine owners, who had never integrated their operations with iron production and therefore had no interest in keeping fuel costs low. Moreover, the slow pace of French industrialization allowed for the skipping of intermediate stages of development. France had hardly entered the canal age when it began to build its railways. Ultimately, industry moved from hand power to steam power in one long step.

While France achieved industrialization without an industrial revolution, it also achieved economic growth within the context of its traditional values. Agriculture may not have modernized, but the ancient village communities escaped the devastation modernization would bring. The orderly progression of generations of farming families characterized rural France until the shattering experiences of the Franco-Prussian War (1870) and the First World War (1914–1918). Nor did France experience the mushroom growth of new cities with all of their problems of poverty, squalor, and homelessness. Slow population growth ameliorated the worst of the social diseases of industrialization while traditional rural manufacturing softened the transformation of a way of life. If France did not reap the windfall profits of the Industrial Revolution, neither did it harvest the bitter crop of social, economic, and spiritual impoverishment that was pulled in its train.

Industrialization and Union

The process of industrialization in Germany was dominated by the historic divisions of the empire of the German peoples. Before 1815, there were more than 300 separate jurisdictional units within the empire, and after 1815 there were still more than 30.. Those included large advanced states such as Prussia, Austria, and Saxony as well as small free cities and the personal enclaves of petty nobles who had guessed right during the Napoleonic wars. Political divisions had more than political impact. Each state clung tenaciously to its local laws and customs, which favored its citizens over outsiders. Merchants who lived near the intersection of separate jurisdictions could find themselves liable for several sets of tolls to move their goods and several sets of customs duties for importing and exporting them. The tolls and duties would have to be paid in different currencies at different rates of exchange according to the different regulations of each state. Small wonder that German merchants exhibited an intense localism, preferring to trade with members of their own state and supporting trade barriers against others. Such obstacles had a depressing effect on the economies of all German states but pushed with greatest weight against the manufacturing regions of Saxony, Silesia, and the Rhineland.

German Agriculture. Most of imperial Germany was agricultural land suited to a diversity of uses. The mountainous regions of Bavaria and the Austrian alpine communities practiced animal husbandry; there was a grain belt in Prussia, where the soil was poor but the land plentiful, and one in central Germany in which the soil was fertile and the land densely occupied. The Rhine Valley was one of the richest in all of Europe and was the center of German wine production. The introduction of the potato was the chief innovation of the eighteenth century. While English farmers were turning farms into commercial estates, German peasants were learning how to make do with less land.

Agricultural estates were organized differently in different parts of Germany. In the east, serfdom still prevailed. Peasants were tied to the land and its lord and were responsible for labor service during much of the week. Methods of cultivation were traditional, and neither peasants nor lords had much incentive to adopt new techniques. The vast agricultural domains of the Prussian Junkers, as those landlords were called, were built on the backs of cheap serf labor, and the harvest was destined for the Baltic export trade, where world grain prices rather than local production costs would determine profits. In central Germany, the long process of commuting labor service into rents was nearly completed by the end of the eighteenth century. The peasantry was not yet free, as a series of manorial relationships still tied them to the land, but they were no longer mere serfs. Moreover, western Germany was dominated by free farmers who either owned or leased their lands and who had a purely economic relationship with their landlords. The restriction of peasant mobility in much of Germany posed difficulties for the creation of an industrial work force. As late as 1800, more than 80 percent of the German population was engaged in agriculture, a proportion that would drop slowly over the next half century.

Although Germany was well endowed with natural resources and skilled labor in a number of trades, it had not taken part in the expansion of world trade during the seventeenth century, and the once bustling Hanseatic ports had been far outdistanced by the rise of the Atlantic economies. The principal exported manufacture was linen, which was expertly spun and woven in Saxony and the Prussian province of Silesia. The linen industry was organized traditionally, with a mixture of domestic production managed on the putting-out system and some factory spinning, especially after the introduction of British mechanical innovations. But even the most advanced factories were still being powered by water, and thus they were located in mountainous regions where rapidly running streams could turn the wheels. In the 1840s there were only 22 steam-driven spinning mills in Germany, several of them established by the Prussian government, which imported British machines and technicians to run them. Neither linens nor traditional German metal crafts could compete on the international markets, but they could find a wider market within Germany if only the problems of political division could be resolved.

The German Zollverein. The problems of political division were especially acute for Prussia after the reorganization of European boundaries in 1815 (see Chapter 22). Prussian territory included the coal- and iron-rich Rhineland provinces, but a number of smaller states separated those areas from Prussia's eastern domain. Each small state exacted its own tolls and customs duties whenever Prussian merchants wanted to move goods from one part of Prussia to the other. Such movement became more common in the nineteenth century as German manufacturing began to grow in step with its rising population. Between 1815 and 1865, the population of Germany grew by 60 percent to more than 36 million people. It was an enormous internal market, nearly as large as the population of France, and the Prussians resolved to make it a unified trading zone by creating a series of alliances with smaller states known as the Zollverein (1834). The Zollverein was not a free-trade zone, as was the British empire, but rather a customs union in which member states adopted the liberal Prussian customs regulations. Every state was paid an annual portion of receipts based upon its population, and every state—except Prussia—increased its revenues as a result. The crucial advantage the Prussians received was the ability to move goods and materials from east to west, but Prussia reaped political profits as well. It forced Hanover and Saxony into the Zollverein and kept its powerful rival Austria out. Prussia's economic union soon proved to be the basis for the union of the German states.

The creation of the Zollverein was vital to German industrialization. It permitted the exploitation of natural advantages, such as plentiful supplies of coal and iron, and it provided a basis for the building of railroads. Germany was a follower nation in the process of industrialization. It started late and it self-consciously modeled its success on the British experience. British equipment and engineers were brought to Germany to attempt to plant the seeds of an industrial economy. German manufacturers sent their children to England to learn the latest techniques in industrial management. Friedrich Engels (1820–1895) worked in a Manchester cotton factory, where he observed the appalling conditions of the industrial labor force and wrote *The Condition of the Working Class in England* (1845). Steam engines were installed in coal mines, if not in factories, and the process of puddling revolutionized ironmaking, though most iron was still smelted with charcoal rather than coke. Although coal was plentiful in Prussia, it was found at the eastern and western extremities of Germany. Even with the lowering of tolls and duties, it was still too expensive to move over rudimentary roads and an uncompleted system of canals.

Thus the railroads were the key to tapping the industrial potential of Germany. There they were a cause rather than a result of industrialization. The agreements hammered out in the creation of the Zollverein made possible the planning necessary to build single lines across the boundaries of numerous states. Initially, German railroads were financed privately, with much foreign investment. But ultimately governments saw the practical advantages of rail transport and took an active part in both planning and financing the system. More than a quarter of the track constructed in Prussia before 1870 was owned directly by the government, and most of the rest had been indirectly financed by the government, which purchased land and guaranteed interest on stock issues.

Germany imported most of its engines directly from Britain and thus adopted standard British gauge for its system. As early as 1850 there were more than 3500 miles of rail in Germany, with important roads linking the manufacturing districts of Saxony and the coal and iron deposits of the Ruhr. Twenty years later, Germany was second only to Britain in the amount of track that had been laid and opened. By then it was no longer simply a follower. German engineers and machinists, trained in Europe's best schools of technology, were turning out engines and rolling stock second to none. And the railroads transported a host of high-quality manufactures, especially durable metal goods that came to carry the most prestigious trademark of the late nineteenth century: "Made in Germany."

THE SLAVERY OF LABOR

Although born in Germany, Friedrich Engels witnessed industrialization in England firsthand. His father owned a factory in Manchester of which Engels was put in charge. By day he oversaw industrial production, and by night he wandered the city streets overwhelmed by the suffering of the working classes. His analysis of industrialization developed from his own observations. He became first a socialist and then, with Karl Marx, a founder of the Communist party.

CAPITAL IS THE ALL-IMPORTANT WEAPON IN THE CLASS WAR. Power lies in the hands of those who own, directly or indirectly, foodstuffs and the means of production. The poor, having no capital, inevitably bear the consequences of defeat in the struggle. Nobody troubles about the poor as they struggle helplessly in the whirlpool of modern industrial life. The working man may be lucky enough to find employment, if by his labour he can enrich some member of the middle classes. But his wages are so low that they hardly keep body and soul together. If he cannot find work, he can steal, unless he is afraid of the police; or he can go hungry and then the police will see to it that he will die of hunger in such a way as not to disturb the equanimity of the middle classes....

The only difference between the old-fashioned slavery and the new is that while the former was openly acknowledged the latter is disguised. The worker *appears* to be free, because he is not bought and sold outright. He is sold piecemeal by the day, the week, or the year. Moreover he is not sold by one owner to another, but he is forced to sell himself in this fashion. He is not the slave of a single individual, but of the whole capitalist class. As far as the worker is concerned, however, there can be no doubt as to his servile status. It is true that the apparent liberty which the worker enjoys does give him some *real* freedom. Even this genuine freedom has the disadvantage that no one is responsible for providing him with food and shelter. His real masters, the middle-class capitalists, can discard him at any moment and leave him to starve, if they have no further use for his services and no further interest in his survival....

From Friedrich Engels, *The Condition of the Working Class in England in 1844* (1845).

The Lands That Time Forgot

Nothing better demonstrates the point that industrialization was a regional rather than a national process than a survey of those states that did not develop industrial economies by the middle of the nineteenth century. The states ranged from the Netherlands, which was still one of the richest areas in Europe, to Spain and Russia, which were the poorest. Also included were Austria-Hungary, the states of the Italian peninsula, and Poland. In all those nations there was some industrial progress. The Bohemian lands of Austria contained a highly developed spinning industry; the Spanish province of Catalonia produced more cotton than did Belgium, and the Basque region was rich in iron and coal. Northern Italy mechanized its textile production, particularly silk spinning, while in the regions around both Moscow and Saint Petersburg, factories were run on serf labor. Nevertheless, the economies of all the states remained nonindustrial and, with the exception of the Netherlands, dominated by subsistence agriculture.

There were many reasons why the states were unable to develop their industrial potential. Some, such as Naples and Poland, were simply underendowed with resources; others, such as Austria-Hungary and Spain, faced difficulties of transport and communications that could not easily be overcome. Spain's modest resources were located on its northern and eastern edges, while a vast, arid plain dominated the center. To move raw materials and finished products from one end of the country to the other was a daunting task, made more difficult by lack of waterways and the rudimentary condition of Spanish roads. Two-thirds of

Austria-Hungary was either mountains or hills, a geographic feature that presented obstacles not even the railroads could easily solve. But there was far more than natural disadvantage behind the failure of those parts of Europe to move in step with the industrializing states. Their social structure, agricultural organization, and commercial policies all hindered the adoption of new methods, machines, and modes of production.

Despite the fact that industrialization created new and largely unmanageable social problems, the follower states were eager for its benefits. All imported the latest products of technology, and the ruling elites in even the most traditional economies lived a material life similar to those in the most advanced. British entrepreneurs and artisans were courted by heads of state and their ministers and were offered riches in exchange for their precious knowledge. British industrialists set up textile factories in Moscow, built spinning machines in Bohemia, and taught Spanish miners how to puddle iron. Railroad pioneer George Stephenson himself surveyed the prospect of creating a passenger rail system in Spain, though he concluded pessimistically, "I have not seen enough people of the right sort to fill a single train." In the later part of the nineteenth century, French, Belgian, and German industrialists served similar roles. There were no traditional economies by choice. Industrialization was seen as a miracle, and the latecomers worshiped avidly at its shrine.

It was work rather than faith that would produce economic salvation. The most common characteristic of the latecomers was a traditional agrarian structure that consumed the lion's share of labor and capital while producing little surplus for any but a small dominant class. In areas as dissimilar as Spain, Italy, and Russia, agriculture was organized in vast estates, which kept the mass of peasants perpetually poor. Sharecropping systems in the west and serfdom in the east differed only in formal organization. Both conditions made it impossible for peasants to accumulate the land necessary to invest in capital improvements or to send their children to towns to engage in industrial occupations. In Hungary, Poland, and Russia, it was illegal for people to change occupations, and serfs who engaged in industrial activity paid their lords for the privilege. Although a number of serfs amassed considerable fortunes in organizing domestic or factory spinning, legal constraints restricted the efforts of potential entrepreneurs.

Similarly, the leaders of traditional economies maintained tariff systems that insulated their own producers from competition. Austrian tariffs were not only artificially high, they were accompanied by import quotas to keep all but the smallest fraction of foreign products from Austrian consumers. The Spanish government prohibited the importation of grain, forcing its eastern provinces to pay huge transport costs for domestic grain despite the fact that cheaper Italian grain was readily available. Such policies sapped much-needed capital from industrial investment. There were many reasons for so-called protective tariffs, and it was not only the follower states that imposed them. France and the Zollverein protected domestic industry while Britain was converted to free trade only in the 1840s. But protection was sensible only when it protected rather than isolated. Inefficiently produced goods of inferior quality were the chief results of the protectionist policies of the follower nations. Failure to adopt steam-powered machines made traditionally produced linens and silks so expensive that smuggling occurred on an international scale. Although the goods might find buyers in domestic markets, they could not compete in international trade, and one by one the industries of the follower nations atrophied. Such nations became exporters of raw materials and foodstuffs. The export of Russian linen was replaced by the export of Russian flax. Spain, once the largest exporter of woolen cloth in Europe, exported mainly wines and fruits. Those economies that remained traditionally organized came to be exploited for their resources by those that had industrialized.

The international situation was not all that different from the dual system that came into effect within the nonindustrialized states. In Austria-Hungary, for example, it was Hungary that was kept from industrializing, first by the continuation of serf-based agriculture, then by the high internal tariffs that favored Austrian over Hungarian manufactures. In Italy, the division was between north and south. In Lombardy and Tuscany, machine-based manufacturing took hold alongside mining and metallurgy; in 1860, northern Italy contained 98 percent of the railways and 87 percent of the roads that existed on the entire peninsula. In Naples and Sicily, half-starved peasants eked out a miserable existence on once-rich soil that had become depleted from overuse. It was estimated that of the 400,000 people living in Naples, more than 100,000 were destitute beggars. In Spain, Catalonia modernized while Castile stagnated. Until the loss of its Latin American empire in the first half of the nineteenth century, Spain had a ready market for Catalonian textiles and

A Russian peasant tills a field with a primitive horse-drawn wooden plow. Russian fields produced low yields, partly because of the use of such crude farming methods.

handicrafts. But since Castile remained the cultural and administrative center of the state, it did little to encourage change, and much government policy was actually counterproductive. The chief problem faced by the dual economies was that neither part could sustain the other. Traditional agriculture could not produce the necessary surplus of either labor or capital to support industry, and industry could not economize sufficiently to make manufactured goods cheap enough for a poor peasantry.

Thus the advantages of being a follower were all missed. Technology could not be borrowed or stages skipped because the ground was not prepared for widespread industrial activity to be cultivated. Even by standing still, followers fell behind. While over the course of the nineteenth century male illiteracy dropped dramatically in the industrialized states—to 30 percent in Britain and France and 10 percent in Prussia—it remained at 75 to 80 percent in Spain and Italy and more than 90 percent in Russia. There was more than irony in the fact that one of the first railroads built on the Continent was built in Austria but was built to be powered by horses rather than engines. The first railways in Italy linked royal palaces to capital cities. Those in Spain radiated from Madrid and bypassed most centers of natural resources. In those states, the railroads were built to move the military rather than passengers or goods. They were state-financed, occasionally state-owned, and almost always lost money. They were symbols of the industrial age, but in those states they were symbols without substance.

The industrialization of Europe in the eighteenth century was an epochal event in human history. The constraints on daily life imposed by nature were loosened for the first time. No longer did population growth in one generation mean famine in the next; no longer was it necessary for the great majority of people to toil in the fields to earn their daily bread. Manufacture replaced agriculture as humanity's primary activity, though the change was longer and slower than the burst of industrialization that took place in the first half of the nineteenth century. For the leaders, Britain especially, industrialization brought international eminence. British achievements were envied, British inventors celebrated, Britain's constitutional and social organization lauded. A comparatively small island nation had become the greatest economic power in Europe. Industrialization had profound consequences for economic life, but its effects ran deeper than that.

The search for new markets would result in the conquest of continents; the power of productivity unleashed by coal and iron would result in the first great arms race. Both would reach fruition in World War I, the first industrial war. For better or worse, the industrial era that began in Britain in the middle of the eighteenth century continues today.

Questions for Review

1. Why did early manufacturing develop in the countryside, and what effect did that have on manufacturing practices and social relations?
2. In what ways were the ideas about organization of manufacturers such as Josiah Wedgwood and Robert Owen as significant as new technology in the development of industry in Britain?
3. How did British society address some of the changes in peoples' lives that were brought about by industrialization?
4. How did industrialization on the Continent differ from industrialization in England?
5. Why did some nations develop little industry at all?

Suggestions for Further Reading

General Reading

* Carlo Cipolla, ed., *The Fontana Economic History of Europe: The Emergence of Industrial Societies,* 2 vols. (London: Fontana Books, 1973). A country-by-country survey of Continental European industrialization.

* David Landes, *The Unbound Prometheus* (Cambridge: Cambridge University Press, 1969). A vigorously argued study of the impact of technology on British and European society from the eighteenth to the twentieth century.

* Jordan Goodman and Katrina Honeyman, *Gainful Pursuits: The Making of Industrial Europe, 1600–1914* (London: Edward Arnold, 1988). A brief overview of the entire process of industrialization.

* E. L. Jones, *The European Miracle,* 2d ed. (Cambridge: Cambridge University Press, 1987). A comparative study of the acquisition of technology in Europe and Asia and the impact that industrialization had upon the two continents.

* T. S. Ashton, *The Industrial Revolution* (Oxford: Oxford University Press, 1997). A compelling brief account of the traditional view of industrialization.

The Traditional Economy

* E. A. Wrigley, *Continuity, Chance and Change* (Cambridge: Cambridge University Press, 1988). Explores the nature of the traditional economy and the way in which Britain escaped from it.

* L. A. Clarkson, *Proto-Industrialization: The First Phase of Industrialization?* (London: Macmillan, 1985). A study of domestic manufacturing and its connection to the process of industrialization.

* Richard Brown, *Society and Economy in Modern Britain, 1700–1850* (London: Routledge, 1991). A comprehensive survey.

J. D. Chambers and G. E. Mingay, *The Agricultural Revolution* (London: Batsford, 1966). The classic survey of the changes in British agriculture.

E. L. Jones, *Agriculture and the Industrial Revolution* (New York: John Wiley & Sons, 1974). A detailed study of the relationship between agricultural innovations and the coming of industrialization in Britain.

The Industrial Revolution in Britain

* Peter Mathias, *The First Industrial Nation,* 2d ed. (London: Methuen, 1983). An up-to-date general survey of British industrialization.

* Phyllis Deane, *The First Industrial Revolution,* 2d ed. (Cambridge: Cambridge University Press, 1979). The best introduction to the technological changes in Britain.

* Kenneth Morgan, *The Birth of Industrial Britain: Economic Change, 1750–1850* (London; New York: Longman, 1999). A brief synthesis with selections of sources and an up-to-date bibliography.

* Martin Daunton, *Progress and Poverty: An Economic and Scoial History of Britain, 1700–1850* (Oxford: Oxford University Press, 1995). The best single volume survey on the Industrial Revolution and its effects on British society.

A. E. Musson, *The Growth of British Industry* (New York: Holmes & Meier, 1978). An in-depth survey of British industrialization that is especially strong on technology.

* John Rule, *The Vital Century: England's Developing Economy, 1714–1815* (London: Longman, 1992). The most up-to-date survey on the British economy.

* N. F. R. Crafts, *British Economic Growth During the Industrial Revolution* (Oxford: Oxford University Press, 1986). A highly quantitative study by a new economic historian arguing the case that economic growth was slow in the early nineteenth century.

T. S. Ashton, *Iron and Steel in the Industrial Revolution* (Manchester: Manchester University Press, 1963). A lucid account of the transformation of ironmaking, including the story of James Watt.

Eric Hopkins, *Birmingham: The First Manufacturing Town in the World, 1760–1840* (London: Weidenfeld & Nicolson, 1989). An intimate portrait of one of the greatest of all boom towns.

Philip Bagwell, *The Transport Revolution from 1770* (London: Batsford, 1974). A thorough survey of the development of canals, highways, and railroads in Britain.

* François Crouzet, *The First Industrialists* (Cambridge: Cambridge University Press, 1985). An analysis of the social background of the first generation of British entrepreneurs.

* Joel Mokyr, *The Lever of Riches: Technological Creativity and Economic Progress* (New York: Oxford University Press, 1992). A compelling argument concerning the role of technology by a leading econometrician.

* Harold Perkin, *The Origins of Modern English Society, 1780–1880* (London: Routledge & Kegan Paul, 1969). An outstanding survey of British social history in the industrial era.

* E. P. Thompson, *The Making of the English Working Class* (New York: Random House, 1966). A brilliant and passionate study of the ways laborers responded to the changes brought about by the industrial economy.

Friedrich Engels, *The Condition of the Working Class in England in 1844* (London: Allen and Unwin, 1952). The classic eyewitness account of the horrors of the industrial city.

The Industrialization of the Continent

* Tom Kemp, *Industrialization in Nineteenth-Century Europe*, 2d ed. (London: Longman, 1985). Survey of the process of industrialization in the major European states.

* Clive Trebilcock, *The Industrialization of the Continental Powers, 1780–1914* (London: Longman, 1981). A complex study of Germany, France, and Russia.

* Sidney Pollard, *Peaceful Conquest* (Oxford: Oxford University Press, 1981). Argues the regional nature of industrialization throughout western Europe.

Roger Price, *The Economic Transformation of France* (London: Croom Helm, 1975). A study of French society before and during the process of industrialization.

Alain Corbin, *The Lure of the Sea: The Discovery of the Seaside in the Western World, 1750–1840* (Cambridge: Polity Press, 1993). One dimension of European cultural responses to industrialization.

* Richard Sylla and Gianni Toniolo, eds., *Patterns of European Industrialization* (London: Routledge, 1993). A strong collection of essays that presents case studies from both east and west.

W. O. Henderson, *The Rise of German Industrial Power* (Berkeley: University of California Press, 1975). A chronological study of German industrialization that centers on Prussia.

Herbert Kisch, *From Domestic Manufacture to Industrial Revolution: The Case of the Rhineland Textile Districts* (New York: Oxford University Press, 1989). A scholarly study of the slow pace of industrialization in Germany.

* Wolfgang Schivelbusch, *The Railway Journey* (Berkeley: University of California Press, 1986). A social history of the impact of railways, drawn from French and German sources.

* Paperback edition available.

Discovering Western Civilization Online

To further explore industrial Europe, consult the following World Wide Web sites. Since Web resources are constantly being updated, also go to *www.awl.com/Kishlansky* for further suggestions.

The Industrial Revolution in Britain

www.history.rochester.edu/steam/hart/
A nineteenth-century account of the life of James Watt and his role as inventor of the steam engine with links to the history of the steam engine.

www.home.earthlink.net/~womenwhist/lesson7.html
Sponsored by Women in World History Curriculum, this site details the plight of women's work in industrial England.

www.spartacus.schoolnet.co.uk/IRchild.main.htm
This site chronicles child labor in Britain, including life in the factory and first-hand experiences.

The Industrialization of the Continent

www.fordham.edu/halsall/mod/indrevtabs1.html
Charts and statistics about industrialization in Europe.

www.fordham.edu/halsall/mod/modsbook14.html
An outstanding collection of documents on the Industrial Age with links.

The search for new markets would result in the conquest of continents; the power of productivity unleashed by coal and iron would result in the first great arms race. Both would reach fruition in World War I, the first industrial war. For better or worse, the industrial era that began in Britain in the middle of the eighteenth century continues today.

Questions for Review

1. Why did early manufacturing develop in the countryside, and what effect did that have on manufacturing practices and social relations?
2. In what ways were the ideas about organization of manufacturers such as Josiah Wedgwood and Robert Owen as significant as new technology in the development of industry in Britain?
3. How did British society address some of the changes in peoples' lives that were brought about by industrialization?
4. How did industrialization on the Continent differ from industrialization in England?
5. Why did some nations develop little industry at all?

Suggestions for Further Reading

General Reading

* Carlo Cipolla, ed., *The Fontana Economic History of Europe: The Emergence of Industrial Societies*, 2 vols. (London: Fontana Books, 1973). A country-by-country survey of Continental European industrialization.

* David Landes, *The Unbound Prometheus* (Cambridge: Cambridge University Press, 1969). A vigorously argued study of the impact of technology on British and European society from the eighteenth to the twentieth century.

* Jordan Goodman and Katrina Honeyman, *Gainful Pursuits: The Making of Industrial Europe, 1600–1914* (London: Edward Arnold, 1988). A brief overview of the entire process of industrialization.

* E. L. Jones, *The European Miracle*, 2d ed. (Cambridge: Cambridge University Press, 1987). A comparative study of the acquisition of technology in Europe and Asia and the impact that industrialization had upon the two continents.

* T. S. Ashton, *The Industrial Revolution* (Oxford: Oxford University Press, 1997). A compelling brief account of the traditional view of industrialization.

The Traditional Economy

* E. A. Wrigley, *Continuity, Chance and Change* (Cambridge: Cambridge University Press, 1988). Explores the nature of the traditional economy and the way in which Britain escaped from it.

* L. A. Clarkson, *Proto-Industrialization: The First Phase of Industrialization?* (London: Macmillan, 1985). A study of domestic manufacturing and its connection to the process of industrialization.

* Richard Brown, *Society and Economy in Modern Britain, 1700–1850* (London: Routledge, 1991). A comprehensive survey.

J. D. Chambers and G. E. Mingay, *The Agricultural Revolution* (London: Batsford, 1966). The classic survey of the changes in British agriculture.

E. L. Jones, *Agriculture and the Industrial Revolution* (New York: John Wiley & Sons, 1974). A detailed study of the relationship between agricultural innovations and the coming of industrialization in Britain.

The Industrial Revolution in Britain

* Peter Mathias, *The First Industrial Nation*, 2d ed. (London: Methuen, 1983). An up-to-date general survey of British industrialization.

* Phyllis Deane, *The First Industrial Revolution*, 2d ed. (Cambridge: Cambridge University Press, 1979). The best introduction to the technological changes in Britain.

* Kenneth Morgan, *The Birth of Industrial Britain: Economic Change, 1750–1850* (London; New York: Longman, 1999). A brief synthesis with selections of sources and an up-to-date bibliography.

* Martin Daunton, *Progress and Poverty: An Economic and Scoial History of Britain, 1700–1850* (Oxford: Oxford University Press, 1995). The best single volume survey on the Industrial Revolution and its effects on British society.

A. E. Musson, *The Growth of British Industry* (New York: Holmes & Meier, 1978). An in-depth survey of British industrialization that is especially strong on technology.

* John Rule, *The Vital Century: England's Developing Economy, 1714–1815* (London: Longman, 1992). The most up-to-date survey on the British economy.

* N. F. R. Crafts, *British Economic Growth During the Industrial Revolution* (Oxford: Oxford University Press, 1986). A highly quantitative study by a new economic historian arguing the case that economic growth was slow in the early nineteenth century.

T. S. Ashton, *Iron and Steel in the Industrial Revolution* (Manchester: Manchester University Press, 1963). A lucid account of the transformation of ironmaking, including the story of James Watt.

Eric Hopkins, *Birmingham: The First Manufacturing Town in the World, 1760–1840* (London: Weidenfeld & Nicolson, 1989). An intimate portrait of one of the greatest of all boom towns.

Philip Bagwell, *The Transport Revolution from 1770* (London: Batsford, 1974). A thorough survey of the development of canals, highways, and railroads in Britain.

* François Crouzet, *The First Industrialists* (Cambridge: Cambridge University Press, 1985). An analysis of the social background of the first generation of British entrepreneurs.

* Joel Mokyr, *The Lever of Riches: Technological Creativity and Economic Progress* (New York: Oxford University Press, 1992). A compelling argument concerning the role of technology by a leading econometrician.

* Harold Perkin, *The Origins of Modern English Society, 1780–1880* (London: Routledge & Kegan Paul, 1969). An outstanding survey of British social history in the industrial era.

* E. P. Thompson, *The Making of the English Working Class* (New York: Random House, 1966). A brilliant and passionate study of the ways laborers responded to the changes brought about by the industrial economy.

Friedrich Engels, *The Condition of the Working Class in England in 1844* (London: Allen and Unwin, 1952). The classic eyewitness account of the horrors of the industrial city.

The Industrialization of the Continent

* Tom Kemp, *Industrialization in Nineteenth-Century Europe*, 2d ed. (London: Longman, 1985). Survey of the process of industrialization in the major European states.

* Clive Trebilcock, *The Industrialization of the Continental Powers, 1780–1914* (London: Longman, 1981). A complex study of Germany, France, and Russia.

* Sidney Pollard, *Peaceful Conquest* (Oxford: Oxford University Press, 1981). Argues the regional nature of industrialization throughout western Europe.

Roger Price, *The Economic Transformation of France* (London: Croom Helm, 1975). A study of French society before and during the process of industrialization.

Alain Corbin, *The Lure of the Sea: The Discovery of the Seaside in the Western World, 1750–1840* (Cambridge: Polity Press, 1993). One dimension of European cultural responses to industrialization.

* Richard Sylla and Gianni Toniolo, eds., *Patterns of European Industrialization* (London: Routledge, 1993). A strong collection of essays that presents case studies from both east and west.

W. O. Henderson, *The Rise of German Industrial Power* (Berkeley: University of California Press, 1975). A chronological study of German industrialization that centers on Prussia.

Herbert Kisch, *From Domestic Manufacture to Industrial Revolution: The Case of the Rhineland Textile Districts* (New York: Oxford University Press, 1989). A scholarly study of the slow pace of industrialization in Germany.

* Wolfgang Schivelbusch, *The Railway Journey* (Berkeley: University of California Press, 1986). A social history of the impact of railways, drawn from French and German sources.

* Paperback edition available.

Discovering Western Civilization Online

To further explore industrial Europe, consult the following World Wide Web sites. Since Web resources are constantly being updated, also go to *www.awl.com/Kishlansky* for further suggestions.

The Industrial Revolution in Britain

www.history.rochester.edu/steam/hart/
A nineteenth-century account of the life of James Watt and his role as inventor of the steam engine with links to the history of the steam engine.

www.home.earthlink.net/~womenwhist/lesson7.html
Sponsored by Women in World History Curriculum, this site details the plight of women's work in industrial England.

www.spartacus.schoolnet.co.uk/IRchild.main.htm
This site chronicles child labor in Britain, including life in the factory and first-hand experiences.

The Industrialization of the Continent

www.fordham.edu/halsall/mod/indrevtabs1.html
Charts and statistics about industrialization in Europe.

www.fordham.edu/halsall/mod/modsbook14.html
An outstanding collection of documents on the Industrial Age with links.

CHAPTER

22 POLITICAL UPHEAVALS AND SOCIAL TRANSFORMATIONS, 1815–1850

- POTATO POLITICS
- GEOGRAPHICAL TOUR
  EUROPE IN 1815
  - The Congress of Vienna
  - The Alliance System
- THE NEW IDEOLOGIES
  - The New Politics of Preserving Order
  - Romanticism and Change
  - Reshaping State and Society
- PROTEST AND REVOLUTION
  - Causes of Social Instability
  - The Revolutions of 1830
  - Reform in Great Britain
  - Workers Unite
  - Revolutions Across Europe, 1848–1850

Potato Politics

VEGETABLES HAVE HISTORIES TOO. But none has a more interesting history in the West than the humble potato. First introduced to northern Europe from the Andean highlands in South America at the end of the sixteenth century, it rapidly became a staple of peasant diets from Ireland to Russia. The potato's vitamins, minerals, and high carbohydrate content provided a rich source of energy to Europe's rural poor. It was simple to plant, required little or no cultivation, and did well in damp, cool climates. Best of all, it could be grown successfully on the smallest plots of land. One acre could support a peasant family of four for a year. Potato peelings helped sustain the family cow and pig, further supplementing family income.

The French painter Jean-François Millet (1814–1875) provided a view of the peasant labor involved in *Planting Potatoes*. Millet, the son of a wealthy peasant family, understood well the importance of the potato crop in the peasant diet. The man and woman in the painting plant their potatoes as a reverent act, bowing as field laborers might in prayer (laborers actually do pray in Millet's more sentimental work *The*

Angelus). The primitive nature of the process is striking: the man uses a short hoe to scrape at what seems to be unyielding soil. The peasants seem part of the nature that surrounds them, patient as the beast that waits in the shade, bent and gnarled and lovely as the tree that arches in the background.

The fleshy root not only guaranteed health, it also affected social relations. Traditionally, peasants delayed marrying and starting families because of the unavailability of land. The potato changed that behavior. Now the potato allowed peasants with only a little land to marry and have children earlier. Millet's depiction of the man and woman working together in the field resonates with the simple fact that potato cultivation aided in the formation of the couple. Millet's couple are parents whose baby sleeps swaddled in a basket and shaded by the tree. In those peasant homes where family members did putting-out work for local entrepreneurs, potato cultivation drew little labor away from the spinning wheel and loom. It permitted prosperous farmers to devote more land to cash crops, since only a small portion of land was required to feed a family. As the sole item of diet, it provided life-sustaining nutrients and a significant amount of the protein so necessary for heavy labor. The Irish adult male ate an average of 12 to 14 pounds of potatoes a day—a figure that may seem preposterous to us today.

Proverbs warned peasants against putting all their eggs in one basket, but no folk wisdom prepared the Irish, many of whom relied on the potato as a single crop, for the potato disaster that struck them. In 1845, a fungus from America destroyed the new potato crop. Although peasants were certainly accustomed to bad harvests and crop failures, they had no precedent for the years of blight that followed. From 1846 to 1850, famine and the diseases resulting from it—scurvy, dysentery, cholera, and typhus fever—killed more than a million people in what became known as the Great Hunger. Another million people emigrated, many to the United States. Total dependence on the potato reaped its grim harvest, devastating all levels of Irish society. Within five years, the Irish population was reduced by almost 25 percent.

The Irish potato famine has been called the "last great European *natural* disaster," to distinguish it from the man-made horrors of war and revolution. But it was as much a social and political disaster as a natural one. As the wealth of European societies expanded in the nineteenth century, so did the number of those who lived on the edge, poised between unemployment and starvation. The Irish Great Hunger was the most striking example of the problem that plagued all Western societies in the first half of the nineteenth century: what to do with the poor.

GEOGRAPHICAL TOUR
EUROPE IN 1815

In his quest for empire, Napoleon had given Europe a geography lesson. Because no one state had been able to defeat him, Napoleon had made clear the territorial and political interdependence of the European powers. The lesson was not lost on the leaders of Russia, Austria, Prussia, and France as they sat down to redraw the map of Europe in 1815. They shared the vision of Europe as a machine that must be kept in running order. Those victorious in defeating Napoleon's Empire looked on the whole of Europe as one entity and conceived of peace in terms of a general European security.

The primary goal of European leaders was to devise the most stable territorial arrangement possible. That goal entailed redrawing the map of Europe. During the negotiations, traditional claims of the right to rule came head to head with new ideas about stabilization. The equilibrium established in 1815 made possible a century-long European peace. Conflicts erupted, to be sure, but they took on the characteristics of the new system that was constructed at Vienna in 1815.

The Congress of Vienna

In 1814, representatives of the victorious Allies agreed to convene in the Austrian capital of Vienna for the purposes of mopping up the mess created in Europe by French rule and restoring order to European monarchies.

Europe 1815. In a series of treaties following Napoleon's defeat, the European powers redrew the map of Europe to create the most stable territorial arrangement and ensure European security. At the center of Europe stood the German confederation, outlined here in red.

France, 1815. *In determining the borders of France, European heads of state were torn between the need to punish and control France and the importance of reconciliation with France for a stable Europe. The Second Peace of Paris of November 1815 permitted France to return to the borders of 1790 and to resume its role as one of the Great Powers.*

Settling with France. Because of the concern with establishing harmony at the time of Napoleon's defeat, the peace enforced against France was not a punitive one. After Napoleon's abdication in 1814, the victorious powers of Great Britain, Russia, Prussia, and Austria decided that leniency was the best way to support the restored Bourbon monarchy. After 1793, royalist émigrés referred to the young son of the executed Louis XVI as Louis XVII, although the child died in captivity and never reigned. In 1814, the four powers designated the elder of the two surviving brothers of Louis XVI as the appropriate candidate for the restored monarchy. Because of the circumstances of his restoration, the new king, Louis XVIII (1814–1815; 1815 –1824), bore the ignominious image of returning "in the baggage car of the Allies." Every effort was made not to weigh down Louis XVIII with a harsh settlement. The First Peace of Paris, signed by the Allies with France in May 1814, had reestablished the French frontiers at the 1792 boundaries, which included Avignon, Venaissin, parts of Savoy, and German and Flemish territories—none of which had belonged to France in 1789.

Even after the hundred-day return of Napoleon, the "Usurper," the Second Peace of Paris of November 1815 declared French frontiers restricted to the boundaries of 1790 and exacted from France an indemnity of 700 million francs. An army of occupation consisting of 150,000 troops was also placed on French soil at French expense but was removed ahead of schedule in 1818. Contrary to the terms of the first treaty, the second treaty also required France to return plundered art treasures to their countries of origin.

On the surface, the Congress of Vienna, which began its deliberations in September 1814, seemed to be no more than an excuse for endless partying among Europe's royalty. Glittering balls as costly as battles gave critics the impression that statesmen were waltzing their way through treaty arrangements. The survival of

Kingdom of the Netherlands. *As a buffer on France's northernmost border, the new Kingdom of the Netherlands was a forced union of two regions with different languages and religions. The union lasted only until 1831 when the southern provinces revolted to form Belgium.*

Italian Peninsula, 1815. Austria gained major territorial concessions on the Italian peninsula. The Austrian Empire now included Lombardy and Venetia. Austria was also influential throughout the peninsula in the Papal States, the three small duchies (Tuscany, Parma, Modena), and the Kingdom of the Two Sicilies.

an old system of precedence and etiquette hobbled negotiations. Issues of who should sign a treaty first and who should have the preferred places at the dinner table were the subjects of endless debates and fatal duels. But the image of bewigged men arguing over how to determine who would enter a room first belied the reality of the diplomats' serious negotiations as they sought to fashion a lasting peace by redrawing the map of Europe.

The central actors whose personalities dominated the Congress were Austrian minister of foreign affairs Prince Klemens von Metternich (1809–1848), British foreign secretary Viscount Castlereagh (1812–1822), French minister of foreign affairs Charles Maurice de Talleyrand (1814–1815), the Russian tsar Alexander I (1801–1825), and the Prussian king Frederick William III (1797–1840). In spite of personal eccentricities, animosities, and occasionally outright hostilities among Europe's leaders, all shared a common concern with reestablishing harmony in Europe.

New Territorial Arrangements. The dominant partnership of Austria and Britain at the Congress of Vienna resulted in treaty arrangements that served to restrain the ambitions of Russia and Prussia. No country was to receive territory without giving up something in return, and no one country was to receive enough territory to make it a present or future threat to the peace of Europe. To contain France, some steps taken prior to the Congress were ratified or expanded. In June 1814, the Low Countries had been set up as a unitary state to serve as a buffer against future French expansion on the Continent and a block to the revival of French sea power. The new Kingdom of the Netherlands, created out of the former Dutch Republic and the Austrian Netherlands, was placed under the rule of William I (1815–1840). The Catholic southern provinces were thus uneasily reunited with the Protestant northern provinces, regions that had been separated since the Peace of Westphalia in 1648. Lest there be any doubt about the intended purpose of the new kingdom, Great Britain gave William I of the Netherlands £2 million to fortify his frontier against France.

A reestablished monarchy that united the island kingdom of Sardinia with Piedmont and included Savoy, Nice, and part of Genoa contained France on its southeast border. To the east, Prussia was given control of the left bank of the Rhine. Switzerland was reestablished as an independent confederation of cantons. Finally, Bourbon rule was restored in Spain on France's southwestern border.

Austria's power was firmly established in Italy, either through outright territorial control or influence over independent states. The Papal States were returned to Pope Pius VII (1800–1823), along with territories that had been Napoleon's Cisalpine Republic and the Kingdom of Italy. The Republic of Venice was absorbed into the Austrian empire. Lombardy and the Illyrian provinces on the Dalmatian coast were likewise restored to Austria. The Italian duchies of Tuscany, Parma, and Modena were placed under the rule of Habsburg princes.

After the fall of Napoleon, the Allies made no attempt to restore the Holy Roman Empire. Napoleon's Confederation of the Rhine, which organized the majority of German territory under French auspices in 1806, was dissolved. In its place, the lands once divided into 300 petty states in central Europe were reorganized into 38 states in the German Confederation. The 38 states, along with Austria as the thirty-ninth, were represented in a new Federal Diet at Frankfurt, dominated by Austria. The German Confederation was intended as a bulwark against France, not to serve any nationalist or parliamentary function.

All of the changes were the result of carefully discussed but fairly uncontroversial negotiations. The question of Poland was another matter indeed. Successive partitions by Russia, Austria, and Prussia in 1772, 1793, and 1795 had completely dismembered the land that had been Poland. Napoleon had reconstituted a small portion of Poland as the Grand Duchy of Warsaw. The Congress faced the dilemma of what to do with the Napoleonic creation and with Polish territory in general. Fierce debate over Poland threatened to shatter congressional harmony.

Tsar Alexander I of Russia argued for a large Poland that he intended to be fully under his influence, thus extending Russian-controlled territories to the banks of the Oder. He also envisioned extending Russian dominance farther into central and eastern Europe. He based his claim on the significant contribution the Russian army had made to Napoleon's defeat. But such thinking conflicted with the Austrian minister Metternich's pursuit of equilibrium. Frederick William III of Prussia contended that if a large Poland was to be created, Prussia would expect compensation by absorbing Saxony. Both Great Britain and France distrusted Russian and Prussian territorial aims.

German Confederation. The league of German states created in 1815 replaced the Holy Roman Empire. The 39 states, of which 35 were monarchies and 4 were free cities, existed to ensure the independence of its member states and support in case of external attack. The member states of Austria and Prussia lay partially outside of the Confederation.

In this French cartoon satirizing the Congress of Vienna, left to right, Talleyrand is watching and waiting as Castlereagh balks, Metternich leads the "dancing," the king of Saxony clutches his crown in fear, and Genoa jumps up and down on the sidelines.

Saxony. In 1806, Saxony had sided with France against Prussia, and remained allies with the French for the remainder of the wars. With Napoleon's defeat in 1815, about 40 percent of Saxony became part of Prussia.

Negotiating for the French, Talleyrand was a man who knew something about survival and taking advantage of opportunities. A bishop under the old regime, a revolutionary who managed to keep his head, an exile in America during the Terror, Napoleon's chief minister, and then the representative of the restored Bourbon monarchy at the Congress, he was a shrewd and experienced diplomat who managed to convince the Allies to accept France, their defeated enemy, as an equal partner in negotiations. In the midst of the crisis over Poland, he persuaded Britain and Austria to sign a secret treaty with France in order to preserve an independent Polish territory. He then deliberately leaked news of the secret agreement of those powers to go to war, if necessary, to block Russian and Prussian aims. Alexander I and Frederick William III immediately backed down. Talleyrand's private opinion of the other four powers was acidic: "Too frightened to fight each other, too stupid to agree."

But under Talleyrand's manipulation, agree they did. In the final arrangement, Prussia retained the Polish territory of Posen and Austria kept the Polish province of Galicia. Krakow, with its population of 95,000, was declared a free city. Finally, a kingdom of Poland, nominally independent but in fact under the tutelage of Russia, emerged from what remained of the Grand Duchy of Warsaw. It was a solution that benefited no one in particular and disregarded Polish wishes.

In addition to receiving Polish territories, Prussia gained two-fifths of the kingdom of Saxony. Prussia also received territory on the left bank of the Rhine, the Duchy of Westphalia, and Swedish Pomerania. With the acquisitions, Prussia doubled its population to around 11 million people. The Junkers, the landed class of east Prussia, reversed many of the reforms of the Napoleonic period. The new territories that Prussia gained were rich in waterways and resources but geographically fragmented. The dispersal of holdings that was intended to contain Prussian power in central Europe spurred Prussia to find new ways of uniting its markets. In the endeavor, Prussia constituted a future threat to Austrian power over the German Confederation.

In Scandinavia, the members of the Congress acknowledged Russia's conquest of Finland, and in

Poland, 1815. An independent kingdom in name only, Poland was under the influence of Russia. Prussia carved off Posen, and Austria maintained control of Galicia. Krakow was defined by treaty as an independent republic.

return Sweden acquired Norway from Denmark. Unlike Austria, Prussia, and Russia, Great Britain made no claim to territories at the Congress. Having achieved its aim of containing France, its greatest rival for dominance on the seas, Britain returned the French colonies it had seized in war. For the time being, the redrawing of the territorial map of Europe had achieved its pragmatic aim of guaranteeing the peace. It was now left to a system of alliances to preserve that peace.

The Alliance System

Only by joining forces had the European powers been able to defeat Napoleon, and a system of alliances continued to be needed even after the battles were over. Two alliance pacts dominated the post-Napoleonic era: the renewed Quadruple Alliance and the Holy Alliance.

The Quadruple Alliance, signed by the victorious powers of Great Britain, Austria, Russia, and Prussia in November 1815, was intended to protect Europe against future French aggression and to preserve the status quo.

Holy Alliance. Under the influence of the religious mysticism of the Russian Tsar Alexander I, Emperor Francis I of Austria and King Frederick William III of Prussia entered an accord to treat each other according to the precepts of the Christian religion. As a counterweight to the Quadruple Alliance, it served as a justification for repression against dissent.

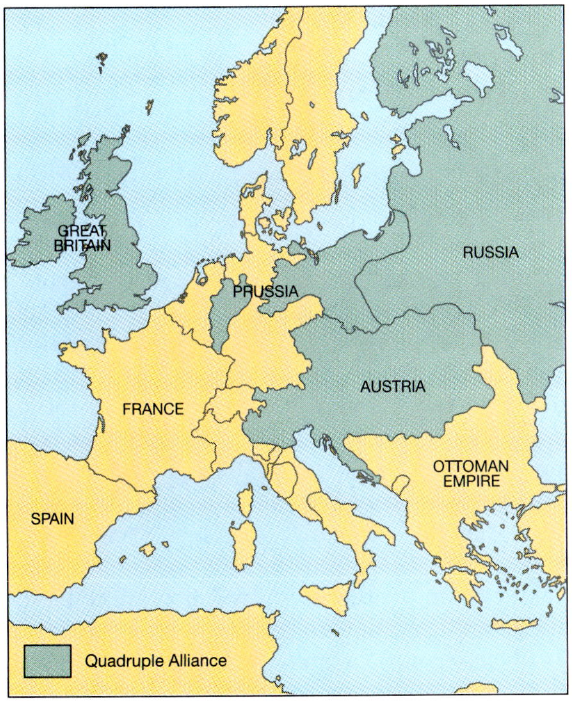

Quadruple Alliance. This Alliance grew out of the need of the Great Powers to create a stable Europe, and had as its initial impulse the creation of a buffer against a future French threat. Austria, Great Britain, Prussia, and Russia entered into the agreement as the basis for defining the balance of power in Europe.

In 1818, France, having completed its payment of war indemnities, joined the pact, which now became the Quintuple Alliance. The five powers promised to meet periodically over the following 20 years to discuss common problems and to ensure the peace.

The Holy Alliance, very different in tone and intent, was the brainchild of Alexander I and was heavily influenced by his mystical and romantic view of international politics. In the pact, the monarchs of Prussia, Austria, and Russia agreed to renounce war and to protect the Christian religion. The Holy Alliance spoke of "the bonds of a true and indissoluble brotherhood ... to protect religion, peace, and justice." Russia was able to give some credibility to the alliance with the sheer size of its army. Career diplomats were aware of its hollowness as a treaty arrangement, but it did indicate the willingness of Europe's three eastern autocracies to intervene in the affairs of other states.

The concept of Europe acting as a whole, through a system of periodic conferences, marked the emergence

CHRONOLOGY

The Alliance System

May 1814	First Peace of Paris
23 September 1814–9 June 1815	Congress of Vienna
26 September 1815	Formation of the Holy Alliance
20 November 1815	Second Peace of Paris; Formation of the Quadruple Alliance
November 1818	Quadruple Alliance expands to include France in Quintuple Alliance
1823	French restoration of Bourbon Monarchy in Spain

of a new diplomatic era. Conflict, however, was inherent in the tension between the commitment of parliamentary governments to open consultation and the need for secrecy in diplomacy. Dynastic regimes sought to intervene in smaller states to buoy up despots, as was the case in 1822, when European powers met to consider restoring the Bourbon monarchy in Spain. The British acted as a counterbalance to interventionist tendencies, refused to cooperate, and blocked united action by the Alliance. France took military action on its own in 1823, restored King Ferdinand VII, and abolished the Spanish constitution.

Both in the Congress of Vienna and the system of alliances that succeeded it, European nations aimed to establish a balance of power that recognized legitimate rulers and preserved the peace. The upheaval of the French Revolution and the revolutionary and Napoleonic wars had made clear the interdependence of one nation on another as a guarantee of survival. By maintaining an international equilibrium, Europe's statesmen hoped—erroneously, as it turned out—that by keeping the peace abroad, domestic peace would follow.

THE NEW IDEOLOGIES

After 1815, the world was changing in many ways. As national boundaries were being redefined, the ways in which Europeans regarded their world was also being transformed. Steam-driven mechanical power in production and transportation steadily replaced human and animal power. In deference to what it was replacing, the new mechanical force was measured in units of horsepower. The new technology combined with political changes to challenge old values; new definitions of worth emerged from the increasingly mechanized world of work. The fixed, castelike distinctions of the old aristocratic world were under attack or in disarray. Western intellectuals struggled with the changes as they sought to make sense of the way in which Europeans lived, looked at the world, and defined their place in it.

The political and economic upheavals of the first half of the nineteenth century encouraged a new breed of thinkers to search for ways to explain the transformations of the period. During that period, Europeans witnessed one of the most intellectually fertile periods in the history of the West. The search for understanding during this era gave birth to new ideologies—liberalism, nationalism, romanticism, conservatism, and socialism—that continue to shape the ideas and institutions of the present day.

The New Politics of Preserving Order

European states had been dealing with war for more than two decades. Now they faced the challenge of peace. The Revolution and Napoleon had not only meant military engagements; they had also brought the force of revolutionary ideas to the political arena, and those ideas did not retire from the field after Waterloo. Nor did treaties restore an old order, in spite of claims to doing so. Governments throughout Europe had to find new ways to deal with the tension between state authority and individual liberty. Conservative and liberal thinkers took very different paths in the pursuit of political stability.

Conservatism. Conservatism was not a rejection of political, economic, or social change. Early nineteenth-century conservatism represented a dynamic adaptation to a social system in transition. In place of individualism, conservatives stressed the corporate nature of European society; in place of reason and progress, conservatives saw organic growth and tradition. Liberty, argued British statesman Edmund Burke (1729–1797) in *Reflections on the Revolution in France* (1790), must emerge out of the gradual development of the old order, and not its destruction. On the

Continent, conservatives Louis de Bonald (1754–1840) and Joseph de Maistre (1753–1821) defended the monarchical principle of authority against the onslaught of revolutionary events.

Conservatism took a reactionary turn in the hands of the Austrian statesman Metternich. The Carlsbad decrees of 1819 are a good example of the "Metternich system" of espionage, censorship, and repression in central Europe, which sought to eliminate any constitutional or nationalist sentiments that had arisen during the Napoleonic period. The German Confederation approved decrees against free speech and civil liberties and set up mechanisms to root out "subversive" university students. Students who had taken up arms in the Wars of Liberation (1813–1815) against France had done so in hopes of instituting liberal and national reforms. Metternich's system aimed at uprooting those goals. Student fraternities were closed, and police became a regular fixture in the university. Political expression in central Europe was driven underground for at least a decade. Metternich set out to crush any form of democratic government, constitutionalism, and parliamentarianism in central Europe.

This cameo, made by Josiah Wedgwood for the Society for the Abolition of Slavery, shows a chained and manacled slave and bears the inscription, "Am I Not a Man and a Brother?" Wedgwood sent a batch of the cameos to Benjamin Franklin for distribution among American abolitionists.

Liberalism. The term *liberal* was first used in a narrow political sense to indicate the Spanish party of reform that supported the constitution modeled on the French document of 1791. But the term assumed much broader connotations in the first half of the nineteenth century as its appeal spread among the European middle classes. The two main tenets of belief that underlay liberalism were the freedom of the individual and the corruptibility of authority. As a political doctrine, liberalism built on Enlightenment rationalism and embraced the right to vote, civil liberties, legal equality, constitutional government, parliamentary sovereignty, and a free-market economy. Liberals firmly believed that less government was better government and that noninterference would produce a harmonious and well-ordered world. They also believed that human beings were basically good and reasonable and needed freedom in which to flourish. The sole end of government should be to promote that freedom.

No single representative thinker embodied all the tenets of liberal thought, but many shared similar ideas and beliefs. Liberal thinkers tried to make sense of the political conflicts of the revolutionary period and the economic disruptions brought on by industrialization. The Great Revolution at the end of the eighteenth century spawned a vast array of liberal thought in France. Republicans, Bonapartists, and constitutional monarchists cooperated as self-styled "liberals" who shared a desire to preserve the gains of the revolution while ensuring orderly rule.

By the mid-nineteenth century, liberal thinking constituted a dominant strain in British politics. Jeremy Bentham (1748–1832), trained in British law, fashioned himself into a social philosopher. He founded utilitarianism, a fundamentally liberal doctrine that argued for "the greatest happiness of the greatest number" in such works as *Introduction to the Principles of Morals and Legislation.* Bentham believed that government could achieve positive ends through limited and "scientific" intervention. Only the pursuit of social harmony justified interference with individual liberty. He found the best testing grounds for his theories in prisons, among convicted criminals. By supporting the reform of penal codes and prison regulations in *Rationale of Punishments and Rewards* (1825), he hoped that rewards and punishments could be meted out to convicts in a measurable "geometry" of pain and pleasure. He was sure that behavior could be improved and that prisoners could be rehabilitated and returned as honest citizens to society. (See "The Birth of the Prison," pp. 774–775.)

The Birth of the Prison

THERE WAS ONCE A TIME when modern prisons, what we call penitentiaries, did not exist. Prisons, like modern hospitals and schools, were one of the great achievements of the age of reform in the first half of the nineteenth century. Thanks to the efforts of humanitarians and social reformers, a new rationale for punishment emerged, one that claimed modern prisons were capable of rehabilitating criminals. Reformers argued that the controlled environment of a new prison system would be able to fashion wrongdoers into upstanding citizens through moral instruction, hard work, constant surveillance, and, in some cases, isolation from human contact.

The principles of the new penal arrangement were silence and separation—total or partial, in order to rehabilitate prisoners through supervised activities, including productive work. In French penitentiaries, prisoners were given an occupation and produced goods for the prison system itself—shoes or mattresses, for example—or for sale on the open market. The belief was that through productive labor, prisoners could be taught to be good workers and good citizens. Idle hands were the devil's workshop, so no moment of the prisoner's day was unoccupied or, in theory, unsupervised.

Some of the "new" prisons were built in the shells of ancient military garrisons, seminaries, convents, and retreat houses. Before the beginning of the nineteenth century, prisons existed but they served as waystations, holding areas for those who were about to face their "real" punishments, which could be death, mutilation, forced labor in prison ships, or banishment. After 1820, however, incarceration became a punishment in itself throughout western Europe, with the goal to deprive prisoners of liberty and freedom of movement.

A typical prisoner in the new penitentiaries was a man convicted of theft serving a sentence of from five to seven years. He entered a prison world where every aspect of his life was prescribed and supervised. The experience of the prison was intended to transform the behavior of the prisoner. Prisoners for the first time were required to wear uniforms. In addition to the regimented routine of work, meals, and sleep, the prisoner now also received moral and religious instruction behind bars.

Although populations in the old prisons of the eighteenth century were mixed with women and men, adults and children confined in the same spaces, by contrast, in the nineteenth century convicted women and children were systematically separated from male prisoners and subject to separate rules of confinement. Religious orders and philanthropic groups supervised women and children in prisons and continued to watch them in their lives after prison. Reformers now spoke of the punishment being made to fit the criminal—not the crime.

The most controversial aspect of the new punishment was solitary confinement. Women were usually exempted from the initial isolation experiments, deemed as too "social" or too weak to support total separation. Young boys on the other hand were targeted for the special experimental punishment of solitary isolation, something French observers such as historian and political philosopher Alexis de Tocqueville greatly admired on his travels in the United States. In one particularly brutal period of experimentation, beginning in 1838 French prison officials confined boys between the ages of six and sixteen to their cells day and night where they were expected to follow a strict regime of silence, discipline, religious instruction, and constant occupation. Most of the children were court custody cases committed by their fathers because of unruly behavior. The results were dire. There was no accurate way to measure recidivism, and, worse, the children's mortality rates increased sharply. Children in solitary confinement may have been protected from the "moral depravity" of other inmates, but they became sick and died more frequently than their counterparts in free society and than other kinds of prisoners. What began as a humanitarian advance was soon denounced as a form of torture for juvenile offenders.

Why did penitentiaries come into being in the first half of the nineteenth century? The new punishment was considered attractive because, in an age confronted with industrial and political transformations and revolutionary upheavals, it seemed to be a way of controlling criminal disruptions and social unrest. The middle classes, whether in London or Paris, grew increasingly fearful about potential threats to their property and well-being. Industrial workers crowded into substandard urban housing could face long periods of unemployment, when it was feared that desperate men and women would commit crimes to feed themselves and their families. The fear of the poor as dangerous influenced many of the prison reforms of the early nineteenth century. Great Britain and France created growing bureaucracies of penal, policing, and judicial institutions to guarantee the safety of honest citizens. At the same time that new prisons opened their doors, policemen started walking their neighborhood beats in European capitals.

Almost from the beginning prisons were deemed a failure. Specialists concluded that prisons did not correct criminals but instead served as schools for crime. Statistics—a new scientific practice in itself—proved them right. Recidivism rates rose dramatically, as penal authorities devised new ways—eventually fingerprinting and photography—to follow the activities of released prisoners. It is very likely that what was increasing in this era was not criminality but the ability of the state to track it.

The science of the new punishment evolved directly in relation to political and social changes in the first half of the nineteenth century. The three major spurts of prison reform in France, for example, coincided with the revolutionary upheavals of 1789, 1830, and 1848. Social reformers and legislators turned to the prison system as a crucial mechanism in the regulation of civil society. The new prisons were part of the network of institutions created to maintain an orderly working class in the new democratic age.

Vincent Van Gogh, The Prison Courtyard (1890). *The painting is copied after a wood engraving by Gustave Doré representing Newgate-the Exercise Yard in* London, a Pilgrimage (1872).

The Scottish philosopher, economist, and historian James Mill (1773–1836) met Jeremy Bentham in 1808 and dedicated the rest of his life to promulgating Bentham's utilitarian philosophy. James Mill's son John Stuart Mill (1806–1873) reacted to his early and intense education in Benthamite ideas by rejecting the tenets of utilitarianism. Forging his own brand of classical liberalism in his treatise *On Liberty* (1859), the younger Mill became the greatest liberal thinker of the age. John Stuart Mill criticized Bentham for ignoring human emotions and for the mass tyranny implicit in his ideas. Mill went beyond existing political analyses by applying economic doctrines to social conditions in *Principles of Political Economy* (1848). With his wife and collaborator Harriet Taylor (d. 1858), he espoused social reform for the poor and championed the equality of women and the necessity of birth control. By 1848, his writings on liberty and equality were questioning the sacredness of private property. In later life, John Stuart Mill came to believe that a more equitable distribution of wealth was both necessary and possible.

David Ricardo (1772–1823) was a stockbroker prodigy who by the age of 20 had made his fortune. In *Principles of Political Economy and Taxation* (1817), Ricardo outlined his opposition to government intervention in foreign trade and elaborated his "iron law of wages," which contended that wages would stabilize at the subsistence level. Increased wages would cause the working classes to grow, and the resulting competition in the labor market would drive wages down to the level of subsistence. Other liberals, more concerned with social welfare than Ricardo, argued that state intervention was unavoidable but could be limited.

Romanticism and Change

Unlike liberalism and conservatism, which were fundamentally political ideologies, romanticism designated a variety of literary and artistic movements throughout Europe that spanned the period from the late eighteenth century to the mid-nineteenth century. One could be a liberal and a romantic just as easily as one could be a conservative and a romantic.

The Romantic World View. Above all, and in spite of variations, romantics shared similar beliefs and a common view of the world. Among the first romantics were the English poets William Wordsworth (1770–1850) and Samuel Taylor Coleridge (1772–1834), whose collaborative *Lyrical Ballads* (1798) exemplified the iconoclastic romantic idea that poetry was the result of "the spontaneous overflow of powerful feelings" rather than a formal and highly disciplined intellectual exercise. Romantics, in general, rebelled against the confinement of classical forms and refused to accept the supremacy of reason over emotions.

The English gardens designed at the end of the eighteenth century provide one of the best visual examples of the new romanticism. The formal gardens that surrounded the castles and manor houses of Europe's wealthy elite throughout the eighteenth century relied on carefully drawn geometric patterns, minutely trimmed hedges and lawns, and symmetrically arranged flowers planted in rows by size and color to achieve the effect of total mastery of nature. The gardens at the great palace of Versailles are a good example of the formal landscaping chosen by France's kings and emulated by the wealthy everywhere in Europe. The romantic or English garden was, by contrast, a rebellious profusion of color in which the landscaper rejected the carefully drawn geometric patterns then in vogue and set out instead, deliberately and somewhat paradoxically, to imitate nature. The romantic aesthetic, whether in landscape gardening or in literature, recognized the beauty of untamed nature and the inspiration produced by the release of human emotions.

Intellectuals, Artists, and Freedom. By rooting artistic vision in spontaneity, romantics endorsed a concept of creativity based on the supremacy of human freedom. The artist was valued in a new way as a genius through whose insight and intuition great art was created. Intuition, as opposed to scientific learning, was endorsed as a valid means of knowing. Building on the work of the eighteenth-century philosopher Immanuel Kant (1724–1804), romanticism embraced subjective knowledge. Inspiration and intuition took the place of reason and science in the romantic pantheon of values.

Germaine de Staël (1766–1817), often hailed as the founder of French romanticism, was an extraordinary woman whose writings influenced French liberal political theory after 1815. Madame de Staël's mother had followed the principles of education spelled out by Jean Jacques Rousseau in *Émile* (1762), according to which the child was allowed to follow his or her own path of intellectual development. De Staël authored histories, novels, literary criticism, and political tracts that opposed what she judged to be the tyranny of Napoleonic rule. She, like many other romantics, was greatly influenced by the writings of Rousseau, and through him she discovered that "the soul's elevation is born of self-consciousness." The recognition of the subjective meant for de Staël that women's vision was as essential as men's for the flowering of European culture.

"It is within oneself that one must look at what lies outside." Following de Staël's lead, Victor Hugo (1802–1885), one of the great French writers of the nineteenth century, identified another essential ingredient in romanticism. The turning "within oneself" so apparent in Hugo's poetry was profoundly influenced by the political events of the French Revolution and its principles of liberty and equality. His greatest novels, including *Notre-Dame de Paris* (1831) and *Les Misérables* (1862), offer bold panoramic sweeps of the social universe of Paris across the ages. Whether in words or in music or on canvas, romanticism conveyed a new way of understanding the world. The supremacy of the emotions over reason found its way into the works of the great romantic composers of the age. Liberation from the forms that dominated the classical era could be heard in the works of French composer Louis Hector Berlioz (1803–1869), who set Faust's damnation to music; Polish virtuoso Frédéric Chopin (1810–1849), who created lyric compositions for the piano; and Hungarian concert pianist Franz Liszt (1811–1886), who composed symphonic poems and Hungarian rhapsodies.

Artists as different as J. M. W. Turner (1775–1851), the English landscape painter, and Eugène Delacroix (1798–1863), the leader of the French romantic school in painting, shared a commitment to their iconoclastic art. Turner's intense and increasingly abstract vision of an often turbulent natural world and Delacroix's epic historical and political masterpieces shared a rebellious experimentation with color and a rejection of classical conventions and forms. Characteristic of a particular strain within romanticism was the political message of Delacroix's art. In the magnificent painting *Liberty Leading the People* (1831), for example, Delacroix immortalized the revolutionary events that swept Paris in 1830 in his moving portrayal of valiant revolutionaries of different social classes led into battle by a female Liberty.

In the postrevolutionary years between 1815 and 1850, romanticism claimed to be no more than an aesthetic stance in art, letters, and music, a posture that had no particular political intent. Yet its validation of the individual as opposed to the caste or the estate was the most revolutionary of doctrines, just as its justification of subjective knowledge threatened to erode the authority of classical learning. Artists did not make revolutions, but they supported them. Some stood by on the sidelines; others mounted the barricades; but all

Liberty Leading the People *(1831) by Eugène Dalacroix captures the spirit of the French romantics, who looked upon revolutionary action as a way to achieve union with the spirit of history.*

YOUNG ITALY (1832)

Giuseppe Mazzini, an Italian patriot and revolutionary, was the principal theorist of national revolution in Europe in the first half of the nineteenth century. He claimed that his strong commitment to equality and democratic principles stemmed from his readings on the French Revolution of 1789 and his study of the Latin classics. As a young man, he resolved to dress always in black as a sign of mourning for his country, disunited and under foreign oppressors. In 1832 he founded the secret society Young Italy. *The goal of the revolutionary group was the unification of Italy under a republican form of government through direct popular action.*

WE HAVE BEHELD ITALY—Italy, the purpose, the soul, the consolation of our thoughts, the country chosen of God and oppressed by men, twice queen of the world and twice fallen through the infamy of foreigners and the guilt of her citizens, yet lovely still though she be dust, unmatched by any other nation whatever fortune has decreed; and Genius returns to seek in this dust the word of eternal life, and the spark that creates the future....

Young Italy: but we chose this term because the one term seems to marshal before the youth of Italy the magnitude of its duties and the solemnity of the mission that circumstances have entrusted to it, so that it will be ready when the hour has struck to arise from its slumber to a new life of action and regeneration. And we chose it because we wanted to show ourselves, writing it, as what we are, to do battle with raised visors, to bear our faith before us, as the knights of medieval times bore their faith on their shields. For while we pity men who do not know the truth, we despise men who, though they know the truth, do not dare to speak it.

romantics, no matter how political or apolitical, helped shape a new way of looking at the world and helped define a new political consciousness.

Reshaping State and Society

As another legacy of the French Revolution, the concept of the *nation* as a source of collective identity and political allegiance became a political force after 1815. Just as nationalism put the needs of the people at the heart of its political doctrine, so did socialism focus on the needs of society and especially of the poor.

Nationalism. In its most basic sense, nationalism between 1815 and 1850 was the political doctrine that glorified the people united against the absolutism of kings and the tyranny of foreign oppressors. The success of the French Revolution and the spread of Napoleonic reforms boosted nationalist doctrines. In Germany, Johann Gottfried von Herder (1744–1803) rooted national identity in German folk culture. The *Fairy Tales* (1812–1814) of the brothers Jacob Ludwig Grimm (1785–1863) and Wilhelm Carl Grimm (1786–1859) had a similar national purpose. The brothers painstakingly captured in print the German oral tradition of peasant folklore. The philosophers Johann Fichte (1762–1814) and Georg Wilhelm Friedrich Hegel (1770–1831) emphasized the importance of the state.

Nationalism gave birth to a search for new symbols, just as the tricolor flag replaced the fleur-de-lis and the image of Marianne replaced the monarch as a result of the Great Revolution in France. There was a new concern with history as nationalists sought to revive a common cultural past.

The nationalist yearning for liberation sometimes meshed with the liberal political program of overthrowing tyrannical rule. Giuseppe Mazzini (1805–1872) represented the new breed of liberal nationalist. A less-than-liberal nationalist was political economist Georg Friedrich List (1789–1846), who formulated a statement of economic nationalism to counter the liberal doctrines of David Ricardo. Arguing that free trade worked only for the wealthy and powerful, List advocated a program of protective tariffs for developing German industries. He perceived British free trade as merely economic imperialism in disguise. List was one of the few nationalists who did not wholeheartedly embrace liberal economic doctrines. Beyond ideology and political practices, nationalism began to capture the imagination of groups who resented foreign domination. Expanding state bureaucracies did little to tame the centrifugal forces of nationalist feeling and probably exacerbated a desire for independence in eastern and central Europe, especially in the Habsburg-ruled lands.

Nationalists valued the authenticity of the vernacular and folklore over the language and customs imposed by a foreign ruler. Herder and the brothers Grimm were German examples of the romantic appreciation of the roots of German culture. While French romantics emphasized the glories of their revolutionary heritage, German romantics stressed the importance of history as the source of one's identity. By searching for the self in a historic past, and especially in the Middle Ages, they glorified their collective cultural identity and national origins.

Socialism. Socialists rejected the world as it was. Socialism, like other ideologies of the first half of the nineteenth century, grew out of changes in the structure of daily life and the structure of power. There were as many stripes of socialists as there were liberals, nationalists, and conservatives. Socialists as a group shared a concern with "alienation," though they may not all have used the term.

Henri de Saint-Simon (1760–1825) rejected liberal individualism in favor of social organization and, for this reason, has been called the father of French socialism. To Saint-Simon, the accomplishments and potential of industrial development represented the highest stage in history. In a perfect and just society, productive work would be the basis of all prestige and power. The elite of society would be organized according to the hierarchy of its productive members, with industrial leaders at the top. Work was a social duty. The new industrial society that Saint-Simon foresaw would be both efficient and ethical, based on a religion similar to Christianity.

Like Saint-Simon, the French social theorist Pierre-Joseph Proudhon (1809–1865) recognized the social value of work. But unlike Saint-Simon, Proudhon refused to accept the dominance of industrial society. A self-educated typesetter of peasant origin, Proudhon gained national prominence with his ideas about a just society, free credit, and equitable exchange. In his famous pamphlet *What Is Property?* (1840), Proudhon

Proudhon and His Children *(1865) by Gustave Courbet. Proudon's literary and political activities often led to trouble with the authorities. He spent a number of years in prison or in exile.*

THE COMMUNIST MANIFESTO

The Communist Manifesto *is one of the most important documents in world history. Translated into many languages in countless editions, it inspired worker organizations throughout Europe in the second half of the nineteenth century and fired the imagination of Communist leaders in Asia, Latin America, Africa, and Europe well into the twentieth century.*

The pamphlet, which in its entirety consists of no more than 12,000 words, was written at the beginning of 1848 by Karl Marx, founder of modern communism, and his collaborator and friend, Friedrich Engels. Their intention was to urge exploited workers throughout Europe to prepare themselves for the coming revolution by uniting across national boundaries. The Communist Manifesto *is a concise statement of the basic tenets of Marxism. Although mistaken in most of its predictions about the future development of capitalism, it accurately distilled some of the most salient inequities of industrial economies whose remedies, Marx and Engels asserted, could only be found through the revolutionary overthrow of the capitalist system.*

Bourgeois and Proletarians*

THE HISTORY OF ALL HITHERTO EXISTING SOCIETY is the history of class struggles.

Freeman and slave, patrician and plebeian, lord and serf, guild-master and journeyman, in a word, oppressor and oppressed, stood in constant opposition to one another, carried on an uninterrupted, now hidden, now open fight, a fight that each time ended, either in a revolutionary reconstitution of society at large, or in the common ruin of the contending classes....

The modern bourgeois society that has sprouted from the ruins of feudal society has not done away with class antagonisms. It has but established new classes, new conditions of oppression, new forms of struggle in place of the old ones.

Our epoch, the epoch of the bourgeoisie, possesses, however, this distinctive feature: it has simplified the class antagonisms. Society as a whole is more and more splitting up into two great hostile camps, into two great classes directly facing each other: Bourgeoisie and Proletariat....

The bourgeoisie cannot exist without constantly revolutionizing the instruments of production, and thereby the relations of production, and with them the whole relations of society. Conservation of the old modes of production in unaltered form, was, on the contrary, the first condition of existence for all earlier industrial classes. Constant revolutionizing of production, uninterrupted disturbance of all social conditions, everlasting uncertainty and agitation distinguish the bourgeois epoch from all earlier ones. All fixed, fast-frozen relations, with their train of ancient and venerable prejudices and opinions are swept away, all new-formed ones become antiquated before they can ossify. All that is solid melts

answered, "Property is theft." That statement was not, however, an argument for the abolition of private ownership. Proudhon reasoned that industrialization had destroyed workers' rights, which included the right to the profits of their own labor. In attacking "property" in the form of profits amassed from the labor of others, Proudhon was arguing for a socialist concept of limited possession—people had the right to own only what they had earned from their own labor. Proudhon, who did not himself participate in political agitation, held a profoundly anarchistic view of society, hated government, and favored instead small self-ruling communities of producers. Proudhon's ideal world would be one of comfort but not great wealth.

At least one socialist believed in luxury. Charles Fourier (1772–1837), an unsuccessful traveling salesman, devoted himself to the study and improvement of society and formulated one of the most trenchant criticisms of industrial capitalism. In numerous writings between 1808 and his death, the eccentric, solitary man put forth his vision of a utopian world organized into units called phalanxes that took into account the social, sexual, and economic needs of their members. With a proper mix of duties, everyone in the phalanx into air, all that is holy is profaned, and man is at last compelled to face with sober senses, his real conditions of life, and his relations with his kind.

The need of a constantly expanding market for its products chases the bourgeoisie over the whole surface of the globe. It must nestle everywhere, settle everywhere, establish connections everywhere....

The proletariat goes through various stages of development. With its birth begins its struggle with the bourgeoisie. At first the contest is carried on by individual labourers, then by the workpeople of a factory, then by the operatives of one trade, in one locality, against the individual bourgeois who directly exploits them. They direct their attacks not against the bourgeois conditions of production, but against the instruments of production themselves; they destroy imported wares that compete with their labour, they smash to pieces machinery, they set factories ablaze, they seek to restore by force the vanished status of the workman of the Middle Ages.

Proletarians and Communists

In what relation do the Communists stand to the proletarians as a whole?

The Communists do not form a separate part opposed to other working-class parties. They have no interests separate and apart from those of the proletariat as a whole....

You are horrified at our [Communists'] intending to do away with private property. But in your existing society, private property is already done away with for nine-tenths of the population; its existence for the few is solely due to its non-existence in the hands of those nine-tenths. You reproach us, therefore, with intending to do away with a form of property the necessary condition for whose existence is the non-existence of any property for the immense majority of society....

In short, the Communists everywhere support every revolutionary movement against the existing social and political order of things.

In all these movements they bring to the front, as the leading question in each, the property question, no matter what its degree of development at the time.

Finally, they labour everywhere for the union and agreement of the democratic parties of all countries.

The Communists disdain to conceal their views and aims. They openly declare that their ends can be attained only by the forcible overthrow of all existing social conditions. Let the ruling classes tremble at a Communistic revolution. The proletarians have nothing to lose but their chains. They have a world to win.

WORKING MEN OF ALL COUNTRIES, UNITE!

*By bourgeoisie is meant the class of modern Capitalists, owners of the means of social production and employers of wage labour. By proletariat, the class of modern wage-labourers who, having no means of production of their own, are reduced to selling their labour power in order to live. [*Note by Engels to the English edition of 1888.*]

would work only a few hours a day. In Fourier's scheme, work was not naturally abhorrent, but care had to be taken to match temperaments with tasks. Women and men fulfilled themselves and found pleasure and gratification through work. People would be paid according to their contributions in work, capital, and talent. In his vision of a better world, Fourier's phalanxes were always rural and were organized communally, though neither poverty nor property would be eliminated. Education would help alleviate discord, and rich and poor would learn to live together in perfect harmony.

Charles Fourier's work, along with that of Saint-Simon and Proudhon, became part of the tradition of utopian thinking that can be traced back to Thomas More in the sixteenth century. Because he believed in the ability of individuals to shape themselves and their world, Fourier intended his critique of society to be a blueprint for living. Fourier's followers set up communities in his lifetime—40 phalanxes were established in the United States alone—but because of financial problems and petty squabbling, all of them failed.

Women, who were active in demanding their own emancipation, were often joined by men who espoused utopian socialist and liberal views. The issue of increased civil liberties for women, tied as it often was to talk of freeing the slaves, was both a moral and political question for social reformers and utopian thinkers, including Fourier, who put the issue of women's freedom at the center of their plans to redesign society. Saint-Simonians argued for woman's social elevation and searched for a female messiah. Other social reformers joined with conservative thinkers in arguing that women must be kept in their place and that their place was in the home. Proudhon, for example, saw women's only choices as working at home as housewives or working in the streets as prostitutes.

Socialists, along with other ideologues in the decades before the middle of the nineteenth century, were aware of how rapidly their world was changing. Many believed that a revolution that would eliminate poverty and the sufferings of the working class was at hand. Followers of Saint-Simon, Fourier, and Proudhon all hoped that their proposals and ideas would change the world and prevent violent upheaval. Not all social critics were so sanguine.

In January 1848, two young men, one a philosopher living in exile and the other a businessman working for his father, began a collaboration that would last a lifetime with the publication of a short tract entitled *The Communist Manifesto*. Karl Marx (1818–1883) and Friedrich Engels (1820–1895) described the dire situation of the European working classes throughout the 1840s. The growing poverty and alienation of the proletariat, the authors promised, would bring to industrialized Europe a class war against the capitalists. Exploited workers were to prepare themselves for the moment of revolution by joining with each other across national boundaries: "Workers of the world unite. You have nothing to lose but your chains." In light of subsequent events, the *Manifesto* appears to be a work of great predictive value. But neither Marx nor Engels realized that the hour of revolution was at hand.

Intellectuals and reformers hoped to reshape the world in which they lived with the force of their ideas. Yet the new ideologies were themselves the consequence of the changing role of government and the changing practices of daily life. The technology of industrial production influenced people's values and required a new way of looking at the world. Liberals, nationalists, romantics, conservatives, and socialists addressed the challenges of a changing economy in a political universe buffeted by democratic ideas. The new ideologies did not provide easy answers, but they did serve to incite their followers to take up arms in protests and revolutions throughout Europe.

PROTEST AND REVOLUTION

For European societies that had remained stable, if not stagnant, for centuries, the changes in the first half of the nineteenth century were undoubtedly startling and disruptive. New factories created the arena for exploitation and misery. More people than ever before lived in cities, and national populations faced the prospect of becoming urban. Urban congestion brought crime and disease; patterns of consumption demonstrated beyond dispute that people were not created equal. A new European society that challenged existing political ideas and demanded new political formulations was in the process of emerging.

Causes of Social Instability

The fabric of stability began unraveling throughout Europe in the 1820s. The forces of order reacted to protest with repression everywhere in Europe. Yet armed force proved inadequate to contain the demands for political participation and the increased political awareness of whole segments of the population. Workers, the middle class, and women's political organizations now demanded, through the vote, the right to govern themselves.

Urban Miseries. In 1800, two of every 100 Europeans lived in a city. By 1850, the number of urban dwellers per hundred had jumped to five and was rising rapidly. In England, the shift was more concentrated than the general European pattern. With one of every two people living in a city, England had become an urban society by mid-century. London was the fastest-growing city in Europe, followed at some distance by Paris and Berlin. The numbers of smaller urban centers were also multiplying.

Massive internal migrations caused most urban growth. People from the same rural areas often lived together in the same urban neighborhoods, and even in the same boardinghouses. Irish emigrants crowded together in the "Little Dublin" section of London. Similarly, districts in other cities were set off by regional accents and native provincial dress. Workers from the same hometowns gravitated to their favorite cafes. The social networks helped make the transition from rural to urban life bearable for the tens of thousands of people who poured into Europe's cities in search of jobs and opportunity. Until mid-century, many migrants returned to their rural homes for the winter when work, especially in the building trades, was scarce in the city. Young migrant women who came to the city to work as servants sent money home to support rural relatives, or worked to save a nest egg—or dowry—with the plan of returning to the village permanently. Before 1850, 20 percent of the workers in London were domestics, and most of them were women.

Despite the support networks that migrants constructed for themselves, the city was not always a hospitable place. Workers were poorly paid, and women workers were more poorly paid than men. When working women were cut free of the support of home and family, uncounted numbers were forced into part-time prostitution to supplement meager incomes. It is conservatively estimated that in 1850 there were 34,000 prostitutes in Paris and 50,000 in London. The phenomenon of prostitution indicated changing mores about sexuality in the first half of the nineteenth century. The "angel" of middle-class households and the "whore" of the streets were subjects of fascination in fiction and nonfiction. Increased prostitution created a veritable epidemic of venereal diseases, especially syphilis, for which there was no known cure until the twentieth century.

Urban crime also grew astronomically, with thefts accounting for the greatest number of crimes. Social reformers identified poverty and urban crowding as causes of the increase in criminal behavior. In 1829, both Paris and London began to create modern urban police forces to deal with the challenges to law and order. Crime assumed the character of disease in the minds of middle-class reformers. Statisticians and social scientists, themselves a new urban phenomenon, produced massive theses on social hygiene, lower-class immorality, and the unworthiness of the poor. The pathology of the city was widely discussed. Always at the center of the issue was the growing problem of what to do with the poor.

The "Social Question." State-sponsored work relief expanded after 1830 for the deserving poor: the old, the sick, and children. Able-bodied workers who were idle were regarded as undeserving and dangerous, regardless of the causes of their unemployment. Performance of work became an indicator of moral worth as urban and rural workers succumbed to downturns in the economic cycle. Those unable to

European urbanization often meant squalid living conditions and pollution.

work sought relief from the state as a last resort. What has been called a "revolution in government" took place in the 1830s and 1840s as legislative bodies increased regulation of everything from factories and mines to prisons and schools.

Poverty was not just an urban problem, although it was both more conspicuous and more feared in urban areas. Politicians, social reformers, religious thinkers, and revolutionaries all had different solutions that followed one of two general orientations. There were those who argued, as in the case of the Irish famine, that the government must do nothing to intervene because the problem would correct itself, as Thomas Malthus had predicted 40 years earlier. Malthus had argued that the "positive" means of famine and death would keep population from outgrowing available resources and food supplies. The Irish population, one of the poorest in Europe, had indeed doubled between 1781 and 1841, and for Malthusians the Irish famine was the fulfillment of their vision that famine was the only way to correct overpopulation. Some insisted that poverty was a social necessity; by interfering with it, governments could only make matters worse.

Child labor in the textile factories. The meager wages of children were often necessary for the survival of their families.

Others contended that poverty was society's problem, and perhaps society's creation, and not a law of nature. Thus it was the social responsibility of the state to take care of its members. The question of how to treat poverty—or the "social question," as it came to be known among contemporaries—underlay many of the protests and reforms of the two decades before 1850 and fueled the revolutionary movements of 1848. Parliamentary legislation attempted to improve the situation of the poor, especially the working class, during the 1830s and 1840s. In 1833, British reformers turned their attention to the question of child labor. Against the opposition of those who argued for a free market for labor, Parliament passed the Factory Act of 1833, which prohibited the employment of children under nine years of age and restricted the workweek of children aged nine to thirteen to 48 hours. No child in this age group could work more than nine hours a day. Teenagers between 13 and 18 years could work no more than 69 hours a week. By modern standards, the "reformed" workloads present a shocking picture of the heavy reliance on child labor. The British Parliament commissioned investigations, compiled in the "Blue Books," that reported the abusive treatment of men, women, and children in factories. Similar studies existed for French and Belgian industry.

British legislation marked an initial step in state intervention in the workplace. Additional legislation over the next three decades further restricted children's and women's labor in factories and concerned itself with improving conditions in the workplace. Fundamentally, the "social question" was the question of what the state's role and responsibility were in caring for its citizens.

The Revolutions of 1830

Few Europeans alive in 1830 remembered the age of revolution that spanned the period from 1789 to 1799. Yet the legends were kept alive from one generation to the next. Secret political organizations perpetuated Jacobin republicanism. Mutual aid societies and artisans' associations preserved the rituals of democratic culture. A new generation of radicals seemed to be budding in the student riots in Germany and in the revolutionary waves that swept across southern and central Europe in the early 1820s. In August 1819, a crowd of 80,000 people gathered outside Manchester, England, in St. Peter's Field to hear speeches for parliamentary reform and universal male suffrage. The cav-

A savage satire of the Peterloo Massacre by cartoonist George Cruikshank. One soldier urges the others on by telling them that the more poor people they kill, the fewer taxes they will have to pay for poor relief.

alry swept down on them in a bloody slaughter that came to be known as the "Peterloo" massacre, a bitter reference to the Waterloo victory four years before.

Poor harvests in 1829 followed by a harsh winter left people cold, hungry, and bitter. Misery fueled social protest, and political issues of participation and representation commanded a new attention. The convergence of social unrest with long-standing political demands touched off apparently simultaneous revolutions all over Europe. Governmental failure to respond to local grievances sparked the revolutions of 1830. Highly diverse groups of workers, students, lawyers, professionals, and peasants rose up spontaneously to demand a voice in the affairs of government.

The French Revolution of 1830. In France, the late 1820s were a period of increasing political friction. Charles X (1824–1830), the former comte d'Artois, had never resigned himself to the constitutional monarchy accepted by his brother and predecessor, Louis XVIII. When Charles assumed the throne in 1824, he dedicated himself to a true restoration of kingship as it had existed before the revolution. To this end, he realigned the monarchy with the Catholic church and undertook several unpopular measures, including approval of the death penalty for those found guilty of sacrilege. The king's bourgeois critics, heavily influenced by liberal ideas about political economy and constitutional rights, sought increased political power through their activities in secret organizations and in public elections. The king responded to his critics by relying on his ultraroyalist supporters to run the government. In May 1830, the king dissolved the Chamber of Deputies and ordered new elections. The elections returned a liberal majority unfavorable to the king. Charles X retaliated with what proved to be his last political act, the Four Ordinances, in which he censored the press, changed the electoral law to favor his own candidates, dissolved the newly elected Chamber, and ordered new elections.

Opposition to Charles X might have remained at the level of political wrangling and journalistic protest, if it had not been for the problems plaguing the people of Paris. A severe winter in France had driven up food prices by 75 percent. Most urban dwellers were barely subsisting. The king had erred in hoping that France's recent conquest of Algeria in North Africa would keep the populace quiet. He underestimated the extent of hardship and the political volatility of the population. Throughout the spring of 1830, prices continued to rise and Charles continued to blunder. In a spontaneous uprising in the last days of July 1830, workers took to the streets of Paris. The revolution they initiated spread rapidly to towns and the countryside as people throughout France protested the cost of living, hoarding by grain merchants, tax collection, and wage cuts. In "three glorious days," the restored Bourbon regime was pulled down and Charles X fled to England.

The people fighting in the streets demanded a republic, but they lacked organization and political experience. Liberal bourgeois politicians quickly filled the power vacuum. They presented Charles's cousin Louis-Philippe, formerly the duc d'Orléans, as the savior of France and the new constitutional monarch. The July Monarchy, born of a revolution, put an end to the Bourbon Restoration. Louis-Philippe became "king of the French." The charter that he brought with him was, like its predecessor, based on restricted suffrage, with property ownership a requisite for voting. The voting age was lowered from 30 to 25, and the tax requirement was also lowered. The electorate nearly doubled, from 90,000 to 170,000, but nevertheless voting remained restricted to a small fraction of the population.

Unrest in Europe. Popular disturbances did not always result in revolution. In Britain, rural and town riots erupted over grain prices and distribution, but no revolution followed. German workers broke their machines to protest low wages and loss of control of the workplace, but no prince was displaced. In Switzerland, reformers found strength in the French revolutionary example. Ten Swiss cantons granted liberal constitutions and established universal manhood suffrage, freedom of expression, and legal equality.

In southern Europe, Greece had languished as a subjugated country for centuries. Turkish overlords ruled Greece as part of the Ottoman Empire. The longing for independence smoldered in Greece throughout the 1820s as public pressure to support the Greeks mounted in Europe. Greek insurrections were answered by Turkish retaliations throughout the Ottoman Empire. In 1822, a Turkish fleet captured the island of Chios in the Aegean Sea off the west coast of Turkey and massacred or enslaved the population. The atrocities committed by the Turks against Greeks in Constantinople provoked international reaction in the form of a Philhellenic (literally, "lover of Greece") movement supported by two of Britain's great romantic poets, Lord Byron (1788–1824) and Percy Bysshe Shelley (1792–1822). Byron sailed to the besieged Greek city of Missolonghi in 1824 to help coordinate the military effort, and there he contracted malaria and died. The sultan of Turkey had been able to call upon his vassal, the pasha of Egypt, to subdue Greece. In response, Great Britain, France, and Russia signed the Treaty of London in 1827, pledging intervention on behalf of Greece. In a joint effort, the three powers defeated the Egyptian fleet. Russia declared war on Turkey the following year, seeking territorial concessions from the Ottoman Empire. Following the Russian victory, Great Britain and France joined Russia in declaring Greek independence.

The concerted action of the three powers in favor of Greek independence was neither an endorsement of liberal ideals nor a support of Greek nationalism. The British, French, and Russians were reasserting their commitment made at the Congress of Vienna to territorial stability. Yet beneath the veneer of their commitment, the Russians intervened, hoping for territorial gains in the Ottoman Empire. The British favored Ottoman stability while distrusting Russian ambitions in the area. The Turks had been unable to maintain stability on their own. Finally, the three powers abandoned their policy of propping up the Ottoman Empire and supported instead the movement for Greek independence. But they did so on their own terms by creating a monarchy in Greece and placing a German-born prince on the new throne.

Belgian Independence. The overthrow of the Bourbon monarch in France served as a model for revolution in other parts of Europe. Following the French lead, in the midst of the Greek crisis the Belgian provinces revolted against the Netherlands. The Belgians' desire for their own nation struck at the heart of the Vienna settlement. Provoked by a food crisis similar to that in France, Belgian revolutionaries took to the streets in August 1830. As a symbol of their solidarity with the successful French Revolution, they flew the tricolor in defiance of their Dutch rulers. Belgians protested the deterioration of their economic situation and made demands for their own Catholic religion, their own language, and constitutional rights. Bitter fighting on the barricades in Brussels ensued, and the movement for freedom and independence spread to the countryside.

The Great Powers disagreed on what to do. Russia, Austria, and Prussia were all eager to see the revolution crushed. France, having just established the new regime of the July Monarchy, and Great Britain, fearing the involvement of the central and eastern European powers in an area where Britain had traditionally had interests, were reluctant to intervene. A provisional government in Belgium set about the task of writing a constitution. All five great powers recognized Belgian independence, with the proviso that Belgium was to maintain the status of a neutral state.

Russia, Prussia, and Austria were convinced to accept Belgian independence because they were having their own problems in eastern and southern Europe. Revolution erupted to the east in Warsaw, Poland. Driven by a desire for national independence, Polish army cadets and university students revolted in November 1830, demanding a constitution. Landed aristocrats and gentry helped establish a provisional government but soon split over how radical reforms should be. Polish peasants refused to support either landowning group. Within the year, Russia brought in 180,000 troops to crush the revolution and reassert its rule over Poland. All pretext of constitutional rule ended. Thousands of Poles were executed; others fled to exile in western Europe, including the 5000 who settled in France. Inspired by the poetry of Adam Mickiewicz (1798–1855) and the music of Frédéric Chopin, many of them dedicated themselves to the cause of Polish nationalism and to resurrecting an independent Polish kingdom. The Poles remained a captive people of the Habsburg, Hohenzollern, and Romanov empires until 1918–1919.

In February 1831, the Italian states of Modena and Parma rose up to throw off Austrian domination of northern Italy. The revolutionaries were ineffective against Austrian troops. Revolution in the Papal States resulted in French occupation that lasted until 1838 without serious reforms. Nationalist and republican yearnings were driven underground, kept alive there in the Young Italy movement under the leadership of Giuseppe Mazzini.

Although the revolutions of 1830 are called "the forgotten revolutions" of the nineteenth century, they are important for several reasons. First, they made clear to European states how closely tied together were their fates. The events of 1830 were a test of the Great Powers' commitment to stability and a balance of power in Europe. True to the principles of the Vienna settlements of 1815, European leaders preserved the status quo. Revolutions in Poland and Italy were contained by Russia and Austria without interference from the other powers. Where adaptation was necessary, as in Greece and Belgium, the Great Powers were able to compromise on settlements, though the solutions ran counter to previous policies. Heads of state were willing to use the forces of repression to stamp out protest. Although each revolution followed its own pattern of development, all shared origins in domestic crises unsuccessfully addressed by those in power.

The international significance of the revolutions reveals a second important aspect of the events of 1830: the vulnerability of international politics to domestic instability. No state could practice diplomacy in a vacuum. Grain prices and demands for democratic participation had direct impact on the balance of power of European states. The five Great Powers broke down into two ideological camps. On the one hand were the liberal constitutional states of Great Britain and France, on the other stood the autocratic monarchies of Russia, Austria, and Prussia. Yet ideological differences were always less important than the shared desire for internal stability as a prerequisite for international peace.

This English cartoon of 1832 is titled "The Clemency of the Russian Monster." It shows Nicholas I in the guise of a bear with menacing teeth and claws addressing the Poles after crushing their rebellion against Russian rule.

Finally, the 1830 revolutions exposed a growing awareness of politics at all levels of European society. If policies in 1830 revealed a shared consciousness of events and shared values among ruling elites, the revolutions disclosed a growing awareness among the lower classes of the importance of politics in their daily lives. The cry for "liberty, equality, and fraternity" transcended national borders and the French language. The demands for constitutions, national identity, and civic equality resounded from the Atlantic to the Urals. In a dangerous combination of circumstances, workers and the lower classes throughout Europe were politicized, yet they continued to be excluded from political power.

Reform in Great Britain

The right to vote had been an issue of contention in the revolutions of 1830 in western Europe. Only the Swiss cantons enforced the principle of "one man, one vote." The July Revolution in France had doubled the electorate, but still only a tiny minority of the population (less than 1 percent) enjoyed the vote. Universal male suffrage had been mandated in 1793 during the Great Revolution but not implemented. The exclusion of the mass of the population from participation in electoral politics was no oversight. Those in power believed that the wealthiest property owners were best qualified to govern, in part because they had the greatest stake in politics and society. One also needed to own property to hold office. Because those who served in parliaments received no salary, only the wealthy had the resources and the leisure to represent the electorate. When confronted by his critics, François Guizot (1787–1874), French prime minister and chief spokesman for the July Monarchy, offered this glib advice to an aspiring electorate: "Get rich!"

The Rule of the Landed. Landowners also ruled Britain. There the dominance of a wealthy elite was strengthened by the geographic redistribution of population resulting from industrialization. Migration to cities had depleted the population of rural areas. Yet the electoral system did not adjust to the changes: large towns had no parliamentary representation, while dwindling county electorates maintained their parliamentary strength. Areas that continued to enjoy representation greater than that justified by their population were dubbed "rotten" or "pocket" boroughs to indicate a corrupt and antiquated electoral system. In general, urban areas were grossly underrepresented and the wealthy few controlled county seats.

Liberal reformers attempted to rectify the electoral inequalities by reassigning parliamentary seats on the basis of density of population, but vested interests balked at attempted reforms and members of Parliament wrangled bitterly. Popular agitation by the lower classes provoked the fear of civil war, which helped break the parliamentary deadlock. The Great Reform Bill of 1832 proposed a compromise. Although the vast majority of the population still did not have the vote, the new legislation strengthened the industrial and commercial elite in the towns, enfranchised most of the middle class, opened the way to social reforms, and encouraged the formation of political parties.

Years of bad harvests, unemployment, and depression, coupled with growing dissatisfaction with the government's weak efforts to address social problems, put the spur to a new national reform movement in the 1830s. Radical reformers, disillusioned with the 1832 Reform Bill because it strengthened the power of a wealthy capitalist class, argued that democracy was the only answer to the problems plaguing British society.

The Chartist Movement. In 1838, a small group of labor leaders, including representatives of the London Working Men's Association, an organization of craft workers, drew up a document known as the People's Charter. The single most important demand of the charter was that all men must have the vote. In addition, Chartists petitioned for a secret ballot, salaries for parliamentary service, elimination of the requirement that a person must own property in order to run for office, equal electoral districts, and annual elections. The proposal favored direct democracy, guaranteed by frequent elections that would ensure maximum accountability of officials to their constituents.

Chartist appeal was greatest in periods of economic hardship. A violent mood swept through the movement in 1839. The Irish Chartist leader Feargus O'Connor (1794–1855) and the Irish journalist and orator James Bronterre O'Brien (1805–1864) urged an unskilled and poorly organized working class to protest inequities through strikes that on occasion became violent. O'Brien thrilled his working-class listeners by haranguing "the big-bellied, little-brained, numbskull aristocracy." Chartism blossomed as a communal phenomenon in working-class towns and appeared to involve all members of the family: "Every kitchen is now a political meeting house; the little children are members of the unions and the good mother is the political teacher," one Chartist organizer boasted. Chartist babies were christened with the names of Chartist heroes. When Mrs. King of Manchester, England, attempted to register the birth of her son, James Feargus O'Connor King, her choice of names was challenged. The registrar demanded, "Is your husband a Chartist?" Mrs. King replied, "I don't know, but his wife is." Women organized Chartist schools and Sunday schools in radical defiance of local church organizations. Many middle-class observers were sure that the moment for class war and revolutionary upheaval had arrived. The government responded with force to the perceived threat of armed rebellion and imprisoned a number of Chartist leaders.

Throughout the 1840s, bad harvests and economic hardships continued to fan the flames of discontent. National petitions signed by millions were submitted to the House of Commons, which stubbornly resisted the idea of universal manhood suffrage. Strikes and attacks on factories spread throughout England, Scotland, and Wales in 1842. Increased violence served to make the Parliament intransigent and caused the movement to splinter and weaken as moderates formed their own factions. The final moment for Chartism occurred in April 1848 when 25,000 Chartist workers, inspired by revolutionary events on the Continent, assembled in London to march on the House of Commons. They carried with them a newly signed petition demanding the enactment of the terms of the People's Charter. In response, the government deputized nearly 200,000 "special" constables in the streets. The deputized private citizens were London property owners and skilled workers intent on holding back a revolutionary rabble. Tired, cold, and rain-soaked, the Chartist demonstrators disbanded. No social revolution took place in Great Britain, and the dilemma of democratic representation was deferred.

Workers Unite

The word *proletariat* entered European languages before the mid-nineteenth century to describe those workers afloat in the labor pool who owned nothing, not even the tools of their labor, and who were becoming "appendages" to the new machines that dominated production. To workers, machines could mean the elimination of jobs or the de-skilling of tasks; almost always machines meant a drop in wages.

The Reform Bill of 1832 is praised by a contemporary cartoonist. "Rotten boroughs" and political corruption are put through a meat grinder by Whig leaders, and a triumphant Britannia emerges.

Luddism. Mechanization deprived skilled craft workers of control of the workplace. In Great Britain, France, and Germany, groups of textile workers destroyed machines in protest. Workers demanding a fair wage smashed cotton power looms, knitting machines, and wool carding machines. Sometimes the machines were a bargaining point for workers who used violence against them as a last resort. Machine-breakers tyrannized parts of Great Britain from 1811 to 1816 in an attempt to frighten masters. The movement was known as Luddism after its mythical leader, Ned Ludd. Workers damaged and destroyed property for more control over the work process, but such destruction met with severe repression. From the 1820s to the 1850s, sporadic but intense outbursts of machine-breaking occurred in continental Europe. Suffering weavers in Silesia and Bohemia resorted to destroying their looms in 1844.

Craft production continued to deteriorate with the rise in industrial competition. Skilled workers, fearing that they would be pulled down into the new proletariat because of mechanization and the increased scale of production, began organizing in new ways after 1830 by forming associations to assert their control over the workplace and to demand a voice in politics.

In Britain, skilled craft workers built on a tradition of citizenship. They resisted the encroachments of factory production, and some channeled their political fervor into the Chartist movement. Skilled workers in France also built on a cultural heritage of shared language and values to create a consciousness of themselves as an exploited class. Uprisings and strikes in France, favoring the destruction of the monarchy and the creation of a democratic republic, increased dramatically from 1831 to 1834. Many French craft workers grew conscious of themselves as a class and embraced a socialism heavily influenced by their own traditions and contemporary socialist writings. Republican socialism spread throughout France by means of a network of traveling journeymen and tapped into growing economic hardship and political discontent with the July Monarchy. Government repression drove worker organizations underground in the late 1830s, but secret societies proliferated. Increasingly, workers saw the validity of the slogan of the silk workers of Lyon: "Live Working or Die Fighting!"

Women in the Work Force. Women were an important part of the work force in the industrializing societies. Working men were keenly aware of the competition with cheaper female labor in the factories. Women formed a salaried work force in the home, too. In order to turn out products cheaply and in large quantities, some manufacturers turned to subcontractors to perform the simpler tasks in the work process. The new middlemen contracted out work such as cutting and sewing to needy women who were often responsible for caring for family members in their homes. That kind of subcontracting, called "sweated labor" because of the exertion and long hours involved in working in one's own home, was always poorly paid.

Cheap female labor paid by the piece allowed employers to profit by keeping overhead costs low and by driving down the wages of skilled workers. Trade unions opposed women's work, both in the home and

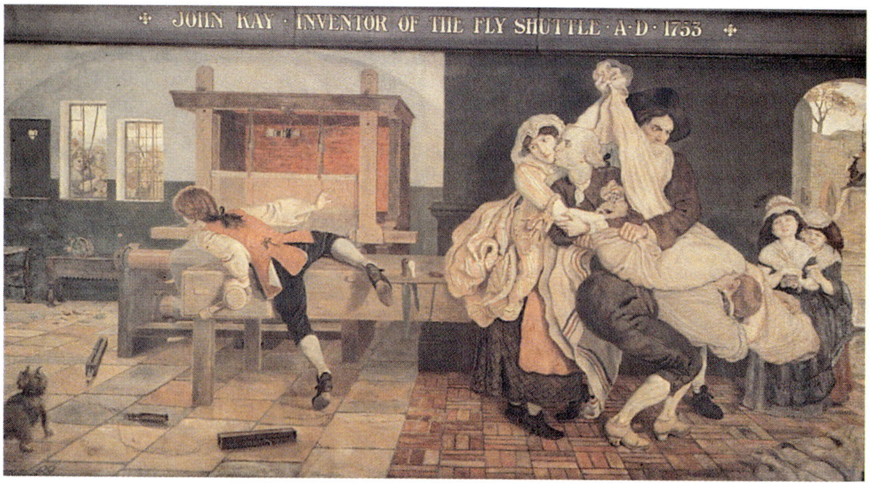

Workers known as Luddites felt threatened by the mechanization of weaving and often organized machine-breaking riots in England. In this illustration, John Kay, inventor of the flying shuttle, is carried off while his loom is being destroyed.

FLORA TRISTAN AND THE RIGHTS OF WORKING WOMEN

Flora Tristan (1803–1844) was a feminist and socialist who in the 1830s was actively involved in efforts to reintroduce divorce and to abolish the death penalty. She made her greatest political efforts for the creation of an international union of workers. The education of women was, Tristan asserted, essential for the success and prosperity of the working class. She toured slums in England and traveled across France on lecture tours to promote workers' unions and the education of women. The excerpt below is taken from her important book, L'Union Ouvrière, *1843. Tristan's argument for women's education is based not only on the claims of women to basic human rights, but on her assertion that educated women held the key to the betterment of families, the working class, and the whole society.*

... [I]T IS IMPERATIVE, in order to improve the intellectual, moral, and material condition of the working class, that women of the lower classes be given a rational and solid education, conducive to the development of their good inclinations, so that they may become skillful workers, good mothers, capable of raising and guiding their children, and of tutoring them in their school work, and so that they may act as moralizing agents in the life of the men on whom they exert an influence from the cradle to the grave.

Do you begin to understand, you, men, who cry shame before even looking into the question, why I demand rights for woman? Why I should like her to be placed on a footing of absolute equality with man in society, and that she should be so by virtue of the legal right every human being brings at birth?

I demand rights for women because I am convinced that all the misfortunes in the world result from the neglect and contempt in which woman's natural and inalienable rights have so far been held. I demand rights for woman because it is the only way she will get an education, and because the education of man in general and man of the lower classes in particular depends on the education of woman. I demand rights for woman because it is the only way to obtain her rehabilitation in the Church, the law, and society, and because this preliminary rehabilitation is necessary to achieve the rehabilitation of the workers themselves. All the woes of the working class can be summed up in these two words: poverty and ignorance, ignorance and poverty. Now, I see only one way out of this labyrinth: begin by educating women, because women have the responsibility of educating male and female children....

As soon as the dangerous consequences of the development of the moral and physical faculties of women—dangerous because of women's current slave status—are no longer feared, woman can be taught with great care so as to make the best possible use of her intelligence and work. Then, you, men of the lower classes, will have as mothers skillful workers who earn a decent salary, are educated, well brought up, and quite capable of raising you, of educating you, the workers, as is proper for free men. You will have well brought up and well educated sisters, lovers, wives, friends, with whom daily contacts will be most pleasant for you. Nothing is sweeter or more agreeable to a man's heart than the sensible and gracious conversation of good and well educated women.

in the factories. Women's talents, union leaders explained, were more properly devoted to domestic chores. Unions argued that their members should earn a family wage "sufficient to support a wife and children." Unions consistently excluded women workers from their ranks.

French labor leader Flora Tristan, speaking not only as a worker but also as a wife and mother, had a very different answer for those who wanted to remove women from the workplace and assign them to their "proper place" in the home. She recognized that working women needed to work in order to support themselves and their families. Tristan told audiences in Europe and Latin America that the emancipation of women from their "slave status" was essential if the working class as a whole was to enjoy a better future.

She deplored the economic competition between working men and women and denounced the degradation of women in both the home and the workplace. A working woman earned one-third or less of the average working man's wages, and women's working conditions were often deplorable. In the 1840s, British parliamentary commissions heard the horrifying testimony of one young London dressmaker from the country who was forced to work grueling hours—often 20 hours a day—under unhealthy working conditions that had destroyed her health. She concluded that "no men could endure the work enforced from the dressmakers."

Working women's only hope, according to Tristan, lay in education and unionization. She urged working men and women to join together to lay claim to their natural and inalienable rights. In some cases, working women formed their own organizations, like that of the Parisian seamstresses who joined together to demand improved working conditions. On the whole, however, domestic workers in the home remained isolated from other working women, and many women in factories feared the loss of their jobs if they engaged in political activism. The wages of Europe's working women remained low, often below the level of subsistence. In the absence of a man's income, working women and their children were the poorest of the poor in European society in the middle of the nineteenth century.

For some men and women of the working class, the 1840s were a time of mounting unrest, increased organization, and growing protest. Workers used their unity in associations, unions, and mutual aid societies to press for full political participation and government action in times of economic distress.

Revolutions Across Europe, 1848–1850

Europeans had never experienced a year like 1848. Beginning soon after the ringing in of the New Year, revolutionary fervor swept through nearly every European country. By year's end, regimes had been created and destroyed. France, Italy, the German states, Austria, Hungary, and Bohemia were shaken to their foundations. Switzerland, Denmark, and Romania experienced lesser upheavals. Great Britain had survived reformist agitation, and famine-crippled Ireland had endured a failed insurrection. No one was sure what had happened. Each country's conflict was based on a unique mix of issues, but all were connected in their conscious emulation of a revolutionary tradition.

Hindsight reveals warning signs in the two years before the 1848 cataclysm. Beginning in 1846, a severe famine—the last serious food crisis Europe would experience—racked Europe. Lack of grain drove up prices. An increasing percentage of disposable income was spent on food for survival. Lack of spending power severely damaged markets and forced thousands of industrial workers out of their jobs. The famine hurt everyone—the poor, workers, employers, and investors—as recession paralyzed the economy.

The food crisis took place in a heavily charged political atmosphere. Throughout Europe during the 1840s, the middle and lower classes had intensified their agitation for democracy. Chartists in Great Britain argued for a wider electorate. Bourgeois reformers in France campaigned for universal manhood suffrage. Known as the "banquet" campaign because its leaders attempted to raise money by giving speeches at subscribed dinners, the movement for the vote appeared to be developing a mass following by taking its cause directly to the people. In making demands for political participation, those agitating for suffrage necessarily criticized those in power. Freedom of speech and freedom of assembly were demanded as inalienable rights. The food crisis and political activism provided the ingredients for an incendiary situation.

In addition to a burgeoning democratic culture, growing demands for national autonomy based on linguistic and cultural claims spread through central, southern, and eastern Europe. The revolts in Poland in 1846, though failures, encouraged similar movements for national liberation among Italians and Germans. Even in the relatively homogeneous nation of France, concerns with national mission and national glory grew among the regime's critics. National unity was primarily a middle-class ideal. Liberal lawyers, teachers, and businessmen from Dublin to Budapest to Prague agitated for separation from foreign rule. Austria, with an empire formed of numerous ethnic minorities, had the most to lose. Since 1815, Metternich had been ruthless in stamping out nationalist dissent. However, by the 1840s, national claims were assuming a cultural legitimacy that was difficult to dismiss or ignore.

France Leads the Way. The events in France in the cold February of 1848 ignited the conflagration that swept Europe. Bourgeois reformers had arranged for their largest banquet to date in support of extension of the vote, to take place in Paris on 22 February. City officials became nervous at the prospect of thousands of workers assembling for political purposes and can-

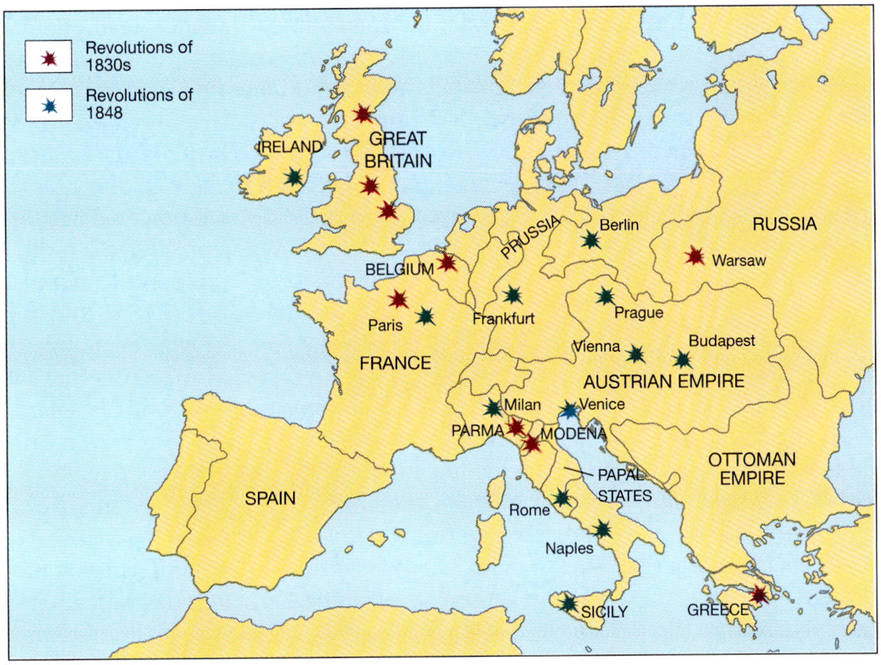

Revolutions of 1830 and 1848. In less than a generation, Europe saw two major revolutions sweep across it from west to east. France experienced the full force of both events, which pulled down successive regimes.

celed the scheduled banquet. That was the spark that touched off the powder keg. In a spontaneous uprising, Parisians demonstrated against the government's repressive measures. Skilled workers took to the streets, not only in favor of the banned banquet but also with the hope that the government would recognize the importance of labor to the social order. Shots were fired; a demonstrator was killed. The French Revolution of 1848 had begun.

Events moved quickly. The National Guard, a citizen militia of bourgeois Parisians, defected from Louis-Philippe. Many army troops garrisoned in Paris crossed the barricades to join revolutionary workers. The king attempted some reform, but it was too little and too late. Louis-Philippe fled. The Second Republic was proclaimed at the insistence of the revolutionary crowds on the barricades. The Provisional Government, led by the poet Alphonse de Lamartine (1790–1869), included members of both factions of political reformers of the July Monarchy: moderates who sought constitutional reforms and an extension of the suffrage, and radicals who favored universal manhood suffrage and social programs to deal with poverty and work. Only the threat of popular violence held together the uneasy alliance.

The people fighting in the streets had little in common with the bourgeois reformers who assumed power on 24 February. Workers made a social revolution out of a commitment to their "right to work," which would replace the right to property as the organizing principle of the new society. Only one member of the new Provisional Government was a worker, and he was included as a token symbol of the intentions of the new government. He was known as "Albert, the worker," and was not addressed by his surname, Martin. The government acknowledged the demand of the "right to work" and set up two mechanisms to guarantee workers' relief. First, a commission of workers and employers was created to act as a grievance and bargaining board and settle questions of common concern in the workplace. Headed by the socialist Louis Blanc (1811–1882) and known as the Luxembourg Commission, the worker-employer parliament was an important innovation, but accomplished little other than deflecting workers' attention away from the problems of the Provisional Government. The second measure was the creation of "national workshops" to deal with the problems of unemployment in Paris. Although the name was taken from Blanc's plan for worker control of production, the national workshops were no more than an inefficient charity program that paid men minimal wages. The national workshops quickly proved disastrous. Workers from all over France poured into Paris with the hope of finding jobs. However, the workshops had a residency requirement that even Parisians had difficulty meeting. As a result, unemployment skyrocketed. Furthermore, the government was going bankrupt trying to support the program. The need to raise taxes upset peasants in the provinces. National pressure mounted to repudiate the programs of the revolution.

French workers were too weak to dominate the revolution. The government dissolved the workshops and recalled General Louis Cavaignac (1802–1857) from service in Algeria to maintain order. In a wave of armed insurrection, Parisian workers rebelled in June. Using provincial troops having no identification with the urban population and employing guerrilla techniques he had mastered in Algeria, Cavaignac put down the uprising. The June fighting was the bloodiest that Paris had ever seen. The Second Republic was placed under the military dictatorship of Cavaignac until December, when presidential elections were scheduled.

Revolutions in Central and Eastern Europe. The overthrow of the July Monarchy at the end of February set off shock waves of protest in central and eastern Europe. Long-suppressed desires for civil liberties and constitutional reforms erupted in widespread popular disturbances throughout Prussia and the German states. Fearing a war with France and unable to count on Austria or Russia for support, the princes who ruled Baden, Württemberg, Hesse-Darmstadt, Bavaria, Saxony, and Hanover followed the advice of moderate liberals and acceded quickly to revolutionary demands. In Prussia, Kaiser Friedrich Wilhelm IV (1840–1861) preferred to use military force to respond to popular demonstrations. Only in mid-March 1848 did the Prussian king yield to the force of the revolutionary crowds building barricades in Berlin by ordering his troops to leave the city and by promising to create a national Prussian assembly. The king was now a prisoner of the revolution.

Meanwhile, the collapse of absolute monarchy in Prussia gave further impetus to a constitutional movement among the liberal leaders of the German states. The governments of all the German states were invited to elect delegates to a national parliament in Frankfurt. The Frankfurt Assembly, which was convened in May 1848, had as its dual charge the framing of a constitution and the unification of Germany. It was composed for the most part of members of the middle class, with civil servants, lawyers, and intellectuals predominating. In spite of the principle of universal manhood suffrage, no members of the working class served among the 800 men elected. To most of the delegates, who

Club-wielding police break up a radical demonstration in Berlin, the capital of Prussia, in 1848. In March, King Frederick William of Prussia acceded to the demands of liberal reformers. But in November, after uprisings against conservative regimes elsewhere in Europe had been put down, the monarch allowed the Prussian army to regain control of Berlin.

had been trained in universities and shared a social and cultural identity, nationalism and constitutionalism were inextricably related.

As straightforward as the desire for a German nation appeared to be, it was complicated by two important facts. First, there were non-German minorities living in German states. What was to be done with the Poles, Czechs, Slovenes, Italians, and Dutch in a newly constituted and autonomous German nation? Second, there were Germans living outside the German states under Habsburg rule in Austria, in Danish Schleswig and Holstein, in Posen (Poznan), in Russian Poland, and in European Russia. How were they to be included within the linguistically and ethnically constituted German nation? No matter how small the circle was drawn, it included non-Germans; no matter how wide, it excluded Germans. After much wrangling over a "small" Germany that excluded Austrian Germans and a "large" Germany that included them, the Frankfurt Assembly opted for the small-Germany solution in March 1849. The crown of the new nation was offered to the unpredictable Friedrich Wilhelm IV of Prussia, head of the largest and most powerful of the German states. Unhappy with his capitulation to the revolutionary crowd in March 1848, the Prussian king refused to accept a "crown from the gutter." He had his own plans to rule over a middle-European bloc, but not at the behest of a liberal parliament. The attempt to create a German nation crumbled with his unwillingness to lead.

Revolution in Austrian-dominated central Europe was concentrated in three places: Vienna, where German-speaking students, workers, and middle-class liberals were agitating for constitutional reform and political participation; Budapest, where the Magyars, the dominant ethnic group in Hungary, led a movement for national autonomy; and Prague, where Czechs were attempting self-rule. By April 1848, Metternich had fallen from power and the Viennese revolutionaries had set up a constituent assembly. In Budapest, the initial steps of the patriot Lajos Kossuth (1802–1894) toward establishing a separate Hungarian state seemed equally solid as the Magyars defeated Habsburg troops. Habsburg armies were more successful in Prague, where they crushed the revolution in June 1848.

In December 1848, Emperor Ferdinand I (1835–1848), whose authority had been weakened irreparably by the overthrow of Metternich, abdicated in favor of his 18-year-old nephew, Franz Josef I (1848–1916).

Italian Nationalism. The Habsburg empire was also under siege on the Italian Peninsula, where the Kingdom of the Two Sicilies, Tuscany, and Piedmont declared new constitutions in March 1848. Championed by Charles Albert of Piedmont, Venice and Lombardy rose up against Austria. Italian middle-class intellectuals and professionals championed the idea of national unification and the expulsion of the hated Austrian overlords. Nationalist sentiments had percolated underground in the Young Italy movement, founded in 1831 by Giuseppe Mazzini. A tireless and idealistic patriot, Mazzini favored a democratic revolution. In spite of his reputation as a liberal, Pope Pius IX (1846–1878) lost control of Rome and was forced to flee the city. Mazzini became head of the Republic of Rome, created in February 1849.

The French government decided to intervene to protect the pope's interests and sent in troops to defeat the republicans. One of Mazzini's disciples, Giuseppe Garibaldi (1807–1882), returned from exile in South America to undertake the defense of Rome. Garibaldi was a capable soldier who had learned the tactics of guerrilla warfare by joining independence struggles in

Pope Pius IX (1846–1878) expressed sympathy for Italian unification but failed to support the revolution in Italy.

CHRONOLOGY

Protest and Revolution

August 1819	Peterloo Massacre
1824	Charles X assumes French throne
1827	Treaty of London to support liberation of Greece
July 1830	Revolution in Paris; creation of July Monarchy under Louis-Philippe
August 1830	Revolution in Belgium
November 1830	Revolution in Poland
1831–1838	Revolutions in Italian states
1831–1834	Labor protests in France
1832	Britain's Great Reform Bill
1838	Drawing up the first People's Charter in Britain
1846	Beginning of food crisis in Europe; revolts in Poland
1846–1848	Europewide movements for national liberation
February 1848	Revolution in France; overthrow of the July Monarchy; proclamation of the French Second Republic and creation of Provisional Government
March 1848	Uprisings in some German states; granting of a constitution in Prussia
March 1848–June 1849	Revolutions in Italy
April 1848	Revolutions in Vienna, Budapest, Prague
May 1848	Frankfurt Assembly
June 1848	Second revolution in Paris, severely repressed by army troops under General Cavaignac
December 1848	Presidential elections in France; Louis Napoleon wins

Brazil and Argentina. Although his legion of poorly armed patriots and soldiers of fortune, known from their attire as the Red Shirts, waged a valiant effort to defend the city from April to June 1849, they were no match for the highly trained French army. French troops restored Pius IX as ruler of the Papal States.

Meanwhile, from August 1848 to the following spring, the Habsburg armies fought and finally defeated each of the revolutions. Austrian success can be explained in part because the various Italian groups of Piedmontese, Tuscans, Venetians, Romans, and Neapolitans continued to identify with their local concerns and lacked coordination and central organization. Both Mazzini and Pius IX had failed to provide the focal point of leadership necessary for a successful national movement. By the fall of 1849, Austria had solved the problems in its own capital and with Italy and Hungary by military repression.

Europe in 1850. In 1850, Austrians threatened the Prussians with war if they did not give up their plans for a unified Germany. In November of that year, Prussian ministers signed an agreement with their Austrian counterparts in the Moravian city of Olmütz. The convention became known as "the humiliation of Olmütz" because Prussia was forced to accept Austrian dominance or go to war. In every case, military force and diplomatic measures prevailed to defeat the national and liberal movements within the German states and the Austrian Empire.

By 1850, a veneer of calm had spread over central Europe. In Prussia, the peasantry were emancipated from feudal dues, and a constitution, albeit conservative and based on a three-class system, was established. Yet beneath the surface, there was the deeper reality of Austrian decline and Prussian challenge. The great Habsburg empire needed to call on outside help from Russia to defeat its enemies within. The imperial giant was again on its feet, but for how long? In international relations, Austria's dominance in the German Confederation had diminished, while Prussia assumed greater political and economic power.

The 1848 revolutions spelled the end to the concert of Europe as it had been defined in the peace settlement of 1815. The European powers were incapable of united action to defend established territorial interests.

The revolutions of 1848 failed in part because of the irreconcilable split between moderate liberals and radical democrats. The participation of the masses had frightened members of the middle classes, who were committed to moderate reforms that did not threaten property. In France, working-class revolutionaries had attempted to replace property with labor as the highest social value. Property triumphed. In the face of more extreme solutions, members of the middle class were willing to accept the increased authority of existing rule as a bulwark against anarchy. In December 1848,

Prince Louis Napoleon, nephew of the former emperor, was elected president of the Second Republic by a wide margin. The first truly modern French politician, Louis Napoleon managed to appeal to everyone—workers, bourgeois, royalists, and peasants—by making promises that he did not keep. Severe repression forced radical protest into hiding. The new Bonaparte bided his time, apparently as an ineffectual ruler, until the moment in 1851 when he seized absolute power.

Similar patterns emerged elsewhere in Europe. In Germany, the bourgeoisie accepted the dominance of the old feudal aristocracy as a guarantee of law and order. Repressive government, businessmen were sure, would restore a strong economy. The attempts in 1848 to create new nations based on ethnic identities were in shambles by 1850.

Nearly everywhere throughout Europe, constitutions had been systematically withdrawn with the recovery of the forces of reaction. With the French and Swiss exceptions, the bid for the extension of the franchise failed. The propertied classes remained in control of political institutions. Radicals willing to use violence to press electoral reforms were arrested, killed, or exiled. The leadership of the revolutionary movements had been decapitated, and there seemed no effective opposition to the rise and consolidation of state power. The 1848 revolutions have been called a turning point at which modern history failed to turn. Contemporaries wondered how so much action could have produced so few lasting results.

The perception that nothing had changed was wrong. The revolutions of 1848 and subsequent events galvanized whole societies to political action. Conservatives and radicals alike turned toward a new realism in politics. Everywhere governments were forced to adapt to new social realities. No longer could the state ignore economic upheavals and social dislocations if it wanted to survive. Revolutionaries also learned the lesson of repression. The state wielded powerful forces of violence against which nationalists, socialists, republicans, and liberals had all been proved helpless. Organizing, campaigning, and lobbying were newly learned political skills, as was outreach across class lines—from bourgeoisie to peasantry—around common political causes. In these ways, 1848 was a turning point in the formation of a modern political culture.

Questions for Review

1. What problems did European peacemakers confront at the Congress of Vienna and how did they attempt to resolve the problems?
2. How did industrialization change European families?
3. In what ways were liberalism and nationalism compatible with each other; how were they in conflict?
4. What are the connections between various ideologies—for instance, liberalism, romanticism, or socialism—and the revolutions of 1830 and 1848?

Suggestions for Further Reading

Geographical Tour: Europe in 1815

* Robert Gildea, *Barricades and Borders, Europe 1800–1914* (Oxford: Oxford University Press, 1987). A synthetic overview of economic, demographic, political, and international trends in European society.

* Harold Nicolson, *The Congress of Vienna: A Study in Allied Unity, 1812–1822* (New York: Viking Press, 1965). Dissects the maneuverings of the Allied diplomats and analyzes their cooperation in reconstructing Europe.

* Alan Sked, *The Decline and Fall of the Habsburg Empire, 1815–1918* (London: Longman, 1989). A revisionist interpretation that demonstrates the strength and viability of Europe's greatest dynasty throughout the nineteenth century.

The New Ideologies

* Jonathan Beecher, *Charles Fourier: The Visionary and His World* (Berkeley: University of California Press, 1986). An intellectual biography that traces the development of Fourier's theoretical perspective and roots it firmly in the social context of nineteenth-century France.

* Craig Calhoun, *The Question of Class Struggle: Social Foundations of Popular Radicalism During the Industrial Revolution* (Chicago: University of Chicago Press, 1982). Presents popular protest of eighteenth- and early nineteenth-century England as the reaction of communities of artisans defending their traditions against encroaching industrialization.

* William H. Sewell, Jr., *Work and Revolution in France: The Language of Labor from the Old Regime to 1848* (Cambridge: Cambridge University Press, 1980). Traces nineteenth-century working-class socialism to the corporate culture of Old Regime guilds through traditional values, norms, language, and artisan organizations.

Gareth Stedman Jones, *Languages of Class: Studies in English Working Class History, 1832–1982* (Cambridge: Cambridge University Press, 1983). A series of essays, on topics such as working-class culture and Chartism, that examine the development of class consciousness.

Denis Mack Smith, *Mazzini* (New Haven, CT: Yale University Press, 1994). Mazzini is presented as an important force in legitimizing Italian nationalism by associating it with republicanism and the interests of humanity.

* Edward P. Thompson, *The Making of the English Working Class* (New York: Pantheon Books, 1963). Spans the late eighteenth to mid-nineteenth centuries in examining the social, political, and cultural contexts in which workers created their own identity and put forward their own demands.

Protest and Revolution

* Maurice Agulhon, *The Republican Experiment, 1848–1852* (Cambridge: Cambridge University Press, 1983). Traces the Revolution of 1848 from its roots to its ultimate failure in 1852 through an analysis of the republican ideologies of workers, peasants, and the bourgeoisie.

Clive Church, *Europe in 1830: Revolution and Political Change* (London: Allen & Unwin, 1983). Considers the origins of the 1830 revolutions within a wider European crisis through a comparative analysis of European regions.

* Gertrude Himmelfarb, *The Idea of Poverty: England in the Early Industrial Age* (New York: Vintage Books, 1983). Traces the concept of poverty in Britain from the mid-eighteenth to the mid-nineteenth century through a discussion of inadequate solutions, changing material conditions of industrialism, and new modes of thought and sensibility.

Catherine J. Kudlick, *Cholera in Post-Revolutionary Paris: A Cultural History* (Berkeley: University of California Press, 1996). Examines the cultural values of ruling elites and demonstrates the role disease played in shaping political life and class identity in nineteenth-century France.

* Joel Mokyr, *Why Ireland Starved: A Quantitative and Analytical History of the Irish Economy, 1800–1850* (London: Allen & Unwin, 1983). An analysis of the structural factors that produced poverty in pre-famine Ireland and a thorough examination of the impact of the famine.

Patricia O'Brien, *The Promise of Punishment: Prisons in Nineteenth-Century France* (Princeton: Princeton University Press, 1982). An overview of the creation of the penitentiary system in nineteenth-century France and the rise of the new science of punishment, criminology, and the eventual appearance of alternatives to the penitentiary system.

* Redcliffe N. Salaman, *The History and Social Influence of the Potato,* revised impression edited by J. G. Hawkes (Cambridge: Cambridge University Press, 1985). The classic study of the potato. A major portion of the work is devoted to the potato famine.

* Peter N. Stearns, *1848: The Revolutionary Tide in Europe* (New York: Norton, 1974). Surveys the causes, impact, and legacy of the revolutions in France, Germany, the Habsburg Empire, and Italy, which shattered the diplomatic framework established at the Congress of Vienna and served as a transition to a new society.

* Dorothy Thompson, *The Chartists: Popular Politics in the Industrial Revolution* (New York: Pantheon Books, 1984). Thompson demonstrates that Chartism was an extraordinary coalition of women, laborers, artisans, and alehouse keepers whose goals were transforming public life and forging a new political culture.

* Paperback edition available.

Discovering Western Civilization Online

To further explore social transformations and political upheavals between 1815 and 1850, consult the following World Wide Web sites. Since Web resources are constantly being updated, also go to *www.awl.com/Kishlansky* for further suggestions.

Geographical Tour: Europe in 1815

www.fordham.edu/halsall/mod/modsbook16.html
The site provides documents, discussions, and bibliographies on the Congress of Vienna and charts the development of conservative thought.

The New Ideologies

www.history.hanover.edu/modern/modecon.html
A collection of links to electronic texts in modern economic theory, including Adam Smith, Thomas Malthus, John Stuart Mill, and Karl Marx.

www.fordham.edu/halsall/mod/modsbook18.html
A collections of links to primary documents and bibliographies on liberalism.

www.history.hanover.edu/modern/national.htm and *www.fordham/edu/halsall/mod/modsbook17.html*
Both sites provide links to primary documents and bibliographies of nationalism.

www.history.hanover.edu/modern/romant.htm and *www.fordham.edu/halsall/mod/modsbook15.html*
Both sites provide links to primary texts on romantic philosophy and literature.

www.csf.colorado.edu/mirrors/marxists.org
The site provides translated texts of Marx and Engels as well as other prominent Social Democrats and Communists.

Protest and Revolution

www.spartacus.schoolnet.co.uk/IRchild.htm
A collection of biographies of reformers and promoters of child labor, electronic texts of major child labor legislation, and excerpts from primary sources concerning child labor in nineteenth-century Britain.

www.spartacus.schoolnet.co.uk/women.htm
The site contains links to biographies of major figures, essays on the major organizations and societies, and electronic texts of the women's movement in Britain.

www.fordham/edu/halsall/mod/modsbook19.html
The site provides documents, discussions, bibliographies and other links to the revolutions of 1848.

CREDITS

Document Credits

CHAPTER 11

"On the Family": From Leon Battista Alberti, "On the Family" in *The Family in Renaissance Florence* by Renee Watkins. Reprinted by permission of Renee Watkins.

"The Renaissance Man": From Giorgio Vasari, "Life of Leonardo da Vinci," in *Lives of the Most Eminent Painters, Sculptors, and Architects,* translated by Gaston du C. de Vere. (London: Warner, 1912–14).

"The Lion and the Fox": From *The Prince* (1513) by Niccolo Machiavelli, translated and edited by Robert M. Adams. (New York: Norton, 1977).

"The Siege of Constantinople": From Kritovoulos, *The History of Mehmed the Conqueror,* pp. 324–325.

CHAPTER 12

"A Momentous Discovery": From Christopher Columbus, *Letter from the First Voyage* (1493), in *Letters of Christopher Columbus,* translated by R. H. Major. (London: Hakluyt Society, 1947).

"The Halls of Montezuma": From Bernal Diaz, *The True History of the Conquest of New Spain,* in *The Bernal Diaz Chronicles,* translated and edited by Albert Idell, pp. 169–171.

"Last Words": From Anne Boleyn, "Scaffold Speech," 1536.

"The Kingdom of France": From Claude de Seyssel, *The Monarchy of France,* translated by J. H. Hexter and edited by Donald R. Kelley. Copyright © 1981 by Yale University Press. All rights reserved. Reprinted by permission.

CHAPTER 13

"A Dutch Wit": From Desiderius Erasmus, *In Praise of Folly.* (London: Reeves & Turner, 1876).

"Luther on Marriage": From Martin Luther, *On Good Works,* translated and edited by William Hazlitt (London: George Bell and Sons, 1895).

"The Eternal Decree": From John Calvin, *Institutes of the Christian Religion,* in *John Calvin, Selections from His Writings,* edited and with an introduction by John Dillenberger.

"Heavenly Vision": From The Life of St. Teresa of Avila (1611), translated by David Lewis.

CHAPTER 14

"Catholics and Huguenots": From the "Edict of Nantes," translated by James Harvey Robinson, in *Readings in European History, Volume II: From the Opening of the Protestant Revolt to the Present Day.* (Boston: Ginn & Company, 1906).

"Cannibals": Excerpted from *The Complete Essays of Montaigne,* translated by Donald M. Frame, with the permission of the publishers, Stanford University Press. © 1958 by the Board of Trustees of the Leland Stanford Junior University.

"War is Hell": From Hans Jacob Cristoph Von Grimmelshausen, *The Adventurous Simplicissmus,* translated by A. T. S. Goodrick (1912).

"Fire and Sword": From *The Destruction of Magdeburg.*

CHAPTER 15

"Living By One's Wits": From *The Life of Lazarillo des Tormes,* translated and edited by Louis How, with an introduction by Charles Philip Wagner. (New York: Mitchell Kennerly, 1917).

"The Peasants' Revolt": From "The Twelve Articles of the Peasants of Swabia" in *Readings in European History, Volume II: From the Opening of the Protestant Revolt to the Present Day,* edited by James Harvey Robinson. (Boston: Ginn & Company, 1906).

"A Feminine Perspective": From Arcangela Tarabotti, "Innocence Undone," translated by Brendan Dooley. Reprinted by permission of Brendan Dooley.

"The Devil's Due": From "Medieval Witchcraft" in *Translations and Reprints from the Original Sources of European History, Volume III.* Reprinted by permission of The University of Pennsylvania Press.

CHAPTER 16

"A Glimpse of a King": From *Memoirs of the Duke of Saint-Simon,* translated by Bayle St. John. (London: Swan Sonnonschein & Co., 1900).

"A Short, Sharp Shock": From an eyewitness account of the execution of Charles I, 1649, excerpted from *The Execution of Charles I.*

"Fathers Know Best": From Sir Robert Filmer, *Patriarcha,* 1680.

"A Close Shave": From "DeMissy's Life of Peter" in *Readings in European History, Volume II: From the Opening of the Protestant Revolt to the Present Day,* edited by James Harvey Robinson. (Boston: Ginn & Company, 1906).

CHAPTER 17

"Stargazing": From Copernicus, *On the Revolutions of Heavenly Spheres* (1543), in Movement of the Earth by Thomas S. Kuhn.

"The Telescope": From *Discoveries and Opinions of Galileo* by Galileo Galilei, translated by Stillman Drake. Copyright © 1957 by Stillman Drake. Used by permission of Doubleday, a Division of Random House, Inc.

"Eastern Traders": Excerpt, p. 353 from *The Low Countries in Early Modern Times: A Documentary History* by Herbert H. Rowen. Copyright © 1972 by Herbert H. Rowen. Reprinted by permission of HarperCollins Publishers, Inc.

"Defining Commerce": From Adam Smith, *The Wealth of Nations,* edited by James E. Thorold Rogers, Volume I, 2nd ed. (Oxford: Clarendon Press, 1880).

CHAPTER 18

"Childhood Traumas": From *The Memoirs of Catherine the Great,* edited by Dominique Maroger.

"A King's-Eye View": From Frederick the Great, *An Essay on Forms of Government,* translated by T. Holcroft.

"Military Discipline": Excerpt from Marshal de Saxe, *Memoirs on the Art of War* (1757), in *War, Diplomacy, and Imperialism, 1618–1763,* edited by Geoffrey Symcox. Copyright © 1974 by Geoffrey Symcox. Reprinted by permission of the author.

"Unalienable Rights": From *The Declaration of Independence,* 1776.

CHAPTER 19

"The All-Knowing": From Denis Diderot, *Encyclopedia* (1751–1752).

"The Human Condition": From *Voltaire's Philosophical Dictionary,* Volume One, by Peter Gay, 1962. Reprinted by permission of the author, Peter Gay.

"Of the People": From Baron de Montesquieu, "Of the Republican Government...," in *The Spirit of the Laws,* by Montesquieu, translated by Thomas Nugent, 1900.

"The Good of All": From Jean-Jacques Rousseau, *The Social Contract,* translated by Rose M. Harrington, 1906.

CHAPTER 20

"What is the Third Estate": From *A Documentary Survey of the French Revolution* by John Hall Stewart. Copyright © 1951. Reprinted by permission of Prentice-Hall, Inc., Upper Saddle River, NJ.

"On Revolutionary Government": From *A Documentary Survey of the French Revolution* by John Hall Stewart. Copyright © 1951. Reprinted by permission of Prentice-Hall, Inc., Upper Saddle River, NJ.

"The Civil Code of the Code Napoleon (1804)": From Henry Cachard, *The French Civil Code.* (London: Stevens and Sons, 1895).

CHAPTER 21

"The Wealth of Britain": From Edward Baines, *The History of the Cotton Manufactures in Great Britain* (1835).

"The Sin of Wages": From Robert Owen, *Observations on the Effect of the Manufacturing System* (1815).

"Exploiting the Young": From "Child Labor in the Coal Mines," Testimony to the Parliamentary Investigative Committee (1842).

"The Slavery of Labor": From Friedrich Engels, *The Condition of the Working Class in England in 1844,* translated by Florence Kelley Wischnewetsky, (London: Allen and Unwin, 1892).

CHAPTER 22

"Flora Tristan": From "Flora Tristan" in *L'Union Ouvriere,* 3rd ed., (Paris and Lyons, 1843) as translated by Giselle Pincetl in *Harvest Quarterly,* 7 (Fall 1977). Reprinted by permission of Giselle Pincetl.

"Young Italy (1832)": From *Young Italy* by Giuseppe Mazinni in *Metternich's Europe,* edited and translated by Mack Walker, 1968.

"The Communist Manifesto": From Karl Marx and Friedrich Engels, *Manifesto of the Communist Party* (1848).

Photo Credits

Unless otherwise acknowledged, all photographs are the property of Addison Wesley Educational Publishers, Inc. Page abbreviations are as follows: (T) top, (B) bottom, (L) left, (R) right.

Prints appearing on the following pages were hand-colored for Addison Wesley Educational Publishers, Inc. by Cheryl Kucharzak: 392, 431, 436, 449, 452, 485, 486, 487, 489, 521, 532, 564, 568, 598, 625, 638, 658, 659, 675, 689, 727, 733, 750, 787

CHAPTER 11

354 Scala/Art Resource, NY **358** Scala/Art Resource, NY **360** Scala/Art Resource, NY **362** Erich Lessing/Art Resource, NY **363** The Bridgeman Art Library **365** Scala/Art Resource, NY **366(L)** Scala/Art Resource, NY **366(R)** Erich Lessing/Art Resource, NY **367** Scala/Art Resource, NY **368** Scala/Art Resource, NY **369** Scala/Art Resource, NY **370** Scala/Art Resource, NY **372** Biblioteca Nazionale Marciana, Venice **373(L)** Scala/Art Resource, NY **373(B)** Scala/Art Resource, NY **376** Scala/Art Resource, NY **378** Scala/Art Resource, NY **379** Samuel H. Kress Collection, © Board of Trustees, National Gallery of Art, Washington, D.C. **380** Scala/Art Resource, NY **381** Erich Lessing/Art Resource, NY **383** Bibliothèque Nationale de France, Paris

CHAPTER 12

389 Michael Holford **392** Corbis **393** Giraudon/Art Resource, NY **394** Arxiu Mas **398(T)** Laurie Platt Winfrey, Inc. **398** Bodleian Library, University of Oxford **401** Bibliothèque Nationale de France, Paris **402** Reproduced by courtesy of the Trustees, © The National Gallery, London **409** Michael Holford **410** Czartotsky Collection, Krakow **411** Thyssen Bornemisza Collection **416** The Art Archive **417** Reproduced by courtesy of the Trustees, © The National Gallery, London **420** Scala/Art Resource, NY **421** © SuperStock, Inc. **422** Royal Collection; Her Majesty Queen Elizabeth II **423** Sonia Halliday Photographs

CHAPTER 13

428 Library of Congress **429** Library of Congress **433** The Saint Louis Art Museum, Museum Purchase **436** Lutherhalle/Melanchthonhaus Wittenburg, Germany **437** Courtesy of the Fogg Art Museum, Harvard University, Cambridge, MA; Gift of Meta and Paul J. Sachs **439** Erich Lessing/Art Resource, NY **441** Giraudon/Art Resource, NY **445** François Martin, Geneva/Document BPU **447** National Portrait Gallery, London **451** The Granger Collection, NY **454** Scala/Art Resource, NY **456** Erich Lessing/Art Resource, NY **457** Erich Lessing/Art Resource, NY **458** Camption Hall, Oxford **460** Giraudon/Art Resource, NY

CHAPTER 14

467 Giraudon/Art Resource, NY **469** Art Resource, NY **470** National Portrait Gallery, London **473** Musée Cantonal des Beaus Arts, Lausanne **475** Giraudon/Art Resource, NY **477** National Gallery, London **478** National Maritime Museum, London **481** Scala/Art Resource, NY **483** © British Museum **487** © British Museum **489** Mansell Collection **492** Musée de Strasbourg **494** The British Library

CHAPTER 15

501 Roudnice Lobkowicz Collection **504** Scala/Art Resource, NY **506** The British Library **508** Musées Royaux des Beaus Artes de Belgiques, Brussels **509** Erich Lessing/Art Resource, NY **512** Bridgeman/Art Resource, NY **513** Giraudon/Art Resource, NY **514** Bibliothèque Nationale de France, Paris **516** Metropolitan Museum of Art, Rogers Fund, 1960 (60.30) **517** Reproduced by courtesy of the Trustees, © The National Gallery, London **519** Rijkmuseum Foundation, Amsterdam

526 Scala/Art Resource, NY **527** Victoria & Albert Museum, London/Art Resource, NY **528** Reproduced by courtesy of the Trustees, © The National Gallery, London **529** Bridgeman/Art Resource, NY **534** By permission of the Astronomer Royal of Scotland, Crawford Collection, Royal Observatory, Edinburgh **535** Erich Lessing/Art Resource, NY

CHAPTER 16

540 © Photo R. M. N. **543** National Portrait Gallery, London **545(L)** Reproduced by courtesy of the Trustees, © The National Gallery, London **545(R)** Hispanic Society of America, New York **546** National Portrait Gallery, London **548** Scala/Art Resource, NY **550** Reproduced by courtesy of the Trustees, © The National Gallery, London **552** Corbis **554** Corbis **555** © Photo R. M. N. **561** By permission of the Earl of Rosebury, on loan to the Scottish National Portrait Gallery **568** Modadori Photo Archives **570** Châteaux de Versailles et de Trianon, © Photo R. M. N, Gérard Blot **572** Scala/Art Resource, NY **573(T)** Scala/Art Resource, NY **573(B)** Scala/Art Resource, NY

CHAPTER 17

578 Photograph © Maritshuis, The Hague **581** The British Library **583** Newberry Library **587** Biblioteca Nazionale, Florence **588(L)** Erich Lessing/Art Resource, NY **588(R)** National Library of Medecine **589** Giraudon/Art Resource, NY **590** Reproduced by courtesy of the Trustees, © The National Gallery, London **591** Erich Lessing/Art Resource, NY **592** Städelsches Kunstistitut, Frankfurt **595** The Metropolitan Museum of Art, Gift of Mrs. Albert Blum, 1920 (20.79) **598** Bibliothèque Nationale de France, Paris **599** Rijksmuseum Foundation, Amsterdam **600** Museum Boijmans Van Beuningen, Rotterdam **603** Rijksmuseum Foundation, Amsterdam **604** National Maritime Museum, London **607** Reproduced by courtesy of the Trustees, © The National Gallery, London **609** © British Museum **610** A. F. Kersting **611** National Portrait Gallery, London

CHAPTER 18

617 © bpk, Berlin **620** Rijksmuseum Foundation, Amsterdam **622** Sonia Halliday Photos **624** Central Naval Museum, St. Petersburg **625** Slavonic Division, The New York Public Library, Astor, Lenox and Tilden Foundations **629** Kunstsammlungen zu Weimar **637** Kunsthistoriches Museum, Vienna **639** Erich Lessing/Art Resource, NY **641** National Portrait Gallery, London **645** Library of Congress

CHAPTER 19

651 Sameul H. Kress Collection, © Board of Trustees, National Gallery of Art, Washington, D.C. **652** © British Museum **654** V & A Picture Library **655** Giraudon/Art Resource, NY **656** Scottish National Portrait Gallery **659** Brown Brothers **662** Erich Lessing/Art Resource, NY **664** The Metropolitan Museum of Art, Rogers Fund, 1932 (32.12) **665** Private Collection **667** © bpk, Berlin **669** © SuperStock, Inc. **670** Scala/Art Resource, NY **671** The Metropolitan Museum of Art, Bequest of William K. Vanderbilt, 1920 (20.155.8) **675** Metropolitan Museum of Art, Harris Brisbane Dick Fund, 1932 **678** Germanisches Nationalmuseum, Nuremberg **680** © British Museum **681** Mary Evans Picture Library

CHAPTER 20

686 Spencer Collection, The New York Public Library, Astor, Lenox and Tilden Foundations **691** Bulloz **693** Roger-Viollet **699** Bulloz **700(T)** Musée de la Ville de Paris, Musee Carnavalet, Paris, France/Giraudon/Art Resource, NY **700(B)** Bulloz **702** Mansell Collection **704** Library of Congress **706** Giraudon/Art Resource, NY **708(T)** Bibliothèque Nationale de France, Paris **708(B)** Giraudon/Art Resource, NY **714** Giraudon/Art Resource, NY **717** Musée de Beaux-Arts, Rouen

CHAPTER 21

722 Claude Monet, French, 1840–1926, Arrival of the Normandy Train, Gare Saint-Lazare, oil on canvas, 1877, 59.6 × 80.2 cm, Mr. and Mrs. Martin A. Ryerson Collection, 1933. 1158, photograph © 1994 The Art Institute of Chicago. All Rights Reserved. **728** © SuperStock, Inc. **730** Reproduced from the original in Bedfordshire Record Office **733** British Library **735** Yale Center for British Art, Paul Mellon Collection **736** AKG London **737** The Granger Collection, New York **739** Museum of American Textile History **741** The Granger Collection, New York **743(B)** Mansell Collection **745** Victoria & Albert Museum, London/Art Resource, NY **748** John R. Freeman/Fotomas, London **750** Mansell Collection **754** Bulloz **760** Courtesy of the Print and Picture Department, Free Library of Philadelphia

CHAPTER 22

764 Gift of Quincy Adams Shaw through Quincy A. Shaw, Jr. and Mrs. Marian Shaw Haughton. Courtesy, Museum of Fine Arts, Boston **773** Trustees of the Wedgwood Museum, Barlaston, Staffordshire **775** AKG London **777** Giraudon/Art Resource, NY **779** Giraudon/Art Resource, NY **783** Gustave Dore and Blanchard Jerrold, London: A Pilgrimage, Grant & Co. London, 1872 **784** The British Library **785** © British Museum **790** The Art Archive **794** © bpk, Berlin **795** The Art Archive

INDEX

Aachen, 435
Absolutism, 553, 564–574. *See also* French Revolution
  in Brandenburg-Prussia, 566–567
  French, 570–574, 697
  nature of, 564–566
  in Russia, 567–570
Academie des Sciences, 590
Adam brothers, 663, 664
Address to the Christian Nobility of the German Nation (Luther), 439
Administration. *See* Government(s)
Adoration of the Name of Jesus, The (El Greco), 477
Adriatic region, 378
Advancement of Learning, The (Bacon), 590–591
Adventurous Simplicissimus, The (Von Grimmelshausen), 490
Advertising, 668
Africa. *See also* specific countries
  Dias and, 392
  Portugal and, 391, 392
  slaves and, 400
African slaves, 597
Age of exploration. *See* Exploration and discovery
Agriculture. *See also* Farms and farming; Rural areas
  commercial, 729
  crops and, 677–678, 729–731
  economy and, 724
  in Germany, 756
  improvements in, 676–677
  peasants and, 520–523, 725–726
  putting-out system in, 726–728
  in Renaissance Italy, 359
  revolution in, 728–731
  in Russia, 627
  in 16th century, 506–507
Aix-la-Chapelle. *See also* Aachen
  Treaty of, 637
Alba, Duke of, 471, 480–482, 483
Albert, Charles, 795
Alberti, Leon Battista, 361, 367–368, 370
Albert of Brandenberg, 436
Albret, Jeanne d', 470, 471
Albuquerque, Alfonso de, 392
Alcala, University of, 433
Alchemy, 530, 585
Alcohol. *See* Drinking
Alexander I (Russia), 716, 768, 769, 771
Alexis (Russia), 626
Alfonso I (Aragon), 372, 376, 377
Alfonso of Portugal, 394
Allegory of Good Government, The (Lorenzetti), 376
Alliances, after Napoleonic wars, 771–772
Almanacs, 681
Alphabet, Russian, 626
Alps, 405
Alsace, 607, 618, 621
Alvsborg, 488
American Indians. *See* Native Americans
American Revolution, 645–646, 686–687
Americas. *See also* Exploration and discovery; New World; North America; South America; United States
  "civilization" and "savages" in, 662
  European expansion into, 619
Amsterdam, 400, 405, 477, 599
Anabaptists, 449–453
Anatomy, 578, 588–589
  childbirth and, 673
Anatomy Lesson of Dr. Nicolaes Tulp, The (Rembrandt), 578–579
Ancien régime (France), 688–694. *See also* French Revolution
Angelus, The (Millet), 764–765
Anglicanism. *See* Church of England
Animal husbandry, 506, 676, 730
Anjou, 415
  house of, 473
Anne (England), 609
Anne of Austria, 555, 571
Anti-Semitism. *See also* Jews and Judaism
  in Spain, 395
Antwerp, 393, 405, 477, 483, 489, 508
Apologetic History of the Indies (Las Casas), 402
Aragon, 395, 406, 416. *See also* Ferdinand of Aragon
Archangel, 487, 625
Architecture, 652, 663
  of Adam brothers, 663, 664
  Italian Renaissance, 364, 365, 367
Aristocracy. *See also* Absolutism; Nobility
  in England, 547
  in France, 690, 691, 692–693
  in Russia, 485–486
  in Spain, 418
Aristotle
  astronomy and, 580–581, 582
  Renaissance and, 370
Arkwright, Richard, 738, 739, 744, 750
Armada. *See* Spanish Armada
Armaments. *See* Weapons
Armed forces. *See also* Military
  in Russia, 625–626
  sizes of, 548
Arouet, François-Marie. *See* Voltaire
Art(s). *See also* Architecture; Renaissance
  bourgeois entertainment and, 666–668
  in 18th century, 652
  Italian, 381
  in Renaissance, 364–369, 370
  romanticism and, 776–778
  in 17th century, 542–543, 578–579

Artisans, 694. *See also* Art(s); Workers
Artois, comte d', 701
Asia, trade with, 595
Assemblies, 407–408. *See also* Parlements (France); Parliament (England)
in Poland, 485
in Russia, 486
Assembly of Notables (France), 691
Assignats (France), 702
Assizes, 547
Astrology, 534, 585
Astronomy, 389–390
Neoplatonism and, 585
scientific revolution and, 580–584
Athletics. *See* Sports
Atlantic Ocean region, 406
Austria, 405, 609–610, 619, 620, 622, 633, 634–637
Charles V and, 418
France and, 638, 703, 712, 713
German Confederation and, 768–769
German unification and, 638
Italy and, 787, 795
legal reform in, 660
Poland and, 640
revolutions of 1848 and, 795, 796
Austria-Hungary
industrialization and, 758, 759
Austrian Empire, 622, 632–633
after Napoleonic wars, 768
Austrian Netherlands, 768
Austro-Hungarian Empire, 496
Autocracies, 787
Autonomy, 792
Azores, 596
Aztecs, 398, 402

Babies. *See* Children
Bacon, Francis, 542, 590–591
Baines, Edward, 740
Balance of power
in Central Europe, 638–640
in 18th century, 618–624
after Napoleonic wars, 771–772
in 17th century, 607–608
Treaty of Utrecht and, 611
Balboa, Vasco Núñez de, 396
Balkan region, 404, 619
Ottomans and, 385
Baltic region, 404, 484, 486, 489, 493, 496, 508, 568, 623
Sweden and, 486–487
Bank of England, 734
Bankruptcy, industrialization and, 744
Banks and banking
Dutch and, 400
Florentine, 379
in France, 714
giro banking, 594
in 17th century, 594–595
Banner of the Shoe, 521
Baptism, Anabaptists and, 452
Barbados, 596
Barcelona, 406, 554
Bascio, Matteo de, 454
Bastardy, 520
Bastille, storming of, 698, 699
Battles. *See* specific battles and wars
Bavaria, 405, 621
Beccaria, Cesare, 631, 653, 659
Beggars, 519–520
Belgium, 618. *See also* Netherlands
independence of, 786–787
Beliefs, in 16th century, 530
Bellarmine, Cardinal, 586
Bellini, Gentile, 354–355
Bentham, Jeremy, 773, 776
Berlin, 633
revolution of 1848 and, 794
Berlioz, Louis Hector, 777
Bernini, Gian Lorenzo, 456, 573
Bible, 428–429. *See also* Luther, Martin; Scriptures
Gutenberg and, 428, 432
Polyglot, 433, 453
translations of, 433
in vernacular, 429
Bilateral trade, 594
Bills of exchange, 594
Bilney, Thomas, 447
Birmingham, 731
Birth. *See* Childbearing
Birth control. *See* Contraception
Birthrate, in 18th century, 674
Black magic, 534–535
Blacks. *See also* Slaves and slavery
Saint Domingue and, 703–704
Black Sea region, 404
Blacksmith's Shop, A (Wright), 735
Blanc, Louis, 793
Blenheim, battle of, 609
Blenheim Palace, 663
Blockade, by Napoleon, 712–713
Blood sports, 682
Bodin, Jean, 543
Body Politic, 515
Bohemia, 404–405, 410, 453, 496, 726
industrialization and, 758, 759
Lutheranism and, 442
revolt of, 490–491
Boleyn, Anne, 412, 447
Bologna, 376
Bona (Poland), 441
Bonald, Louis de, 773
Book of Gold, 517
Book of Hours, 506
Books, 680
for children, 670
printing and, 430
Booth, Henry, 742
Bordeaux, 413, 755
Borgia, Cesare, 381–384
Bosporus, 382
Bossuet, Jacques, 565
Bostonians Paying the Excise-Man, 645
Boston Tea Party, 645
Bosworth Field, battle at, 411
Botticelli, Sandro, 367
Boulton, Matthew, 736, 737
Boundaries
European, 403–407
after Thirty Years' War, 496
Bourbon, duke of, 415
Bourbon dynasty, 469, 474, 609, 621, 717, 772, 786
Henry, king of Navarre, 472
in Spain, 768
Bourgeoisie, 661, 663–671
Engels on, 780–781
in France, 691, 693–694
leisure and entertainment of, 666–668
Marx on, 780–781
urban elites and, 664–666
values of, 666
Boyars, 409
Boyle, Robert, 585–588, 591

Brabant, 405
Brahe, Tycho, 582–583
Brancacci Chapel, 365
Brandenburg, 405, 492, 493, 566, 621
Brandenburg-Prussia, 623–624, 632. *See also* Prussia
Brazil, 392, 393, 397, 596
Breitenfeld, battle of, 492, 493
Bremen, 405
Brethren of the Common Life, 453
Bridgewater, Duke of, 733
Brighton, 666
Britain, 406. *See also* England (Britain)
British Empire, 644
British Museum, 617
Brittany, 415
Broken Eggs (Greuze), 671
Brothels, 509
Brunelleschi, 364, 365
Bruni, Leonardo, 370, 372
Brussels, 477, 482, 489
Buckingham, duke of, 545
Budapest, 423, 795
Bullion, 400. *See also* Trade
Bureaucracy, of state, 779
Burghers, 664
Burgundy, 405, 413–414, 422–423. *See also* France
  Charles V and, 420
  Spain and, 477–479
Burke, Edmund, 772
Business. *See also* Economy; Market(s)
  commerce and, 594–595
  entrepreneurs, managers, and, 744–747
  Florentine, 379
  industrialization and, 733–734
Buys, Cornelius, 519
Byron, Lord, 786
Byzantium. *See* Constantinople

Cahiers de doléances, 695–696
"Cake of the Kings, The: First Partition of Poland" (Le Mire), 638
Calico, 595, 596
Calonne, Charles Alexandre de, 690–691
Calvin, John, 444–446
Calvinism. *See also* Huguenots
  in England, 448–449, 556
  in France, 469
  in Netherlands, 478
  and Peace of Westphalia, 496
Cambio, Arnolfo di, 365
Camões, Luiz de, 400
Campaigne, Philippe de, 545
Canada, 597–598, 611
Canals, 733
  in France, 755
Candide (Voltaire), 655–656, 659
Cape of Good Hope, 392
Capital, industrialization and, 734
Capital city, 542
Capitalism
  Communist Manifesto and, 780
  Italian, 358
Capital punishment, 520, 631
Capuchins, 454
Caravaque, Louis, 624
Caribbean region, 396
  Spanish in, 397
Carmelites, 455
Carnival of the Feast Day of Saint George (Grimmer), 529
Cartesianism, 592
Cartography, 592
Cartwright, Edmund, 744
Casimir IV (Poland-Lithuania), 410
Castiglione, Baldesar, 373
Castile, 395, 406, 416. *See also* Isabella of Castile
  population of, 510
  royal courts in, 547
Castlereagh, Viscount, 768, 769
Casualties, in Thirty Years' War, 496
Catalonia, 417, 548, 554–555
Catalonian Cortes, 554
Cateau-Cambresis, Treaty of, 423
Cathedrals, in Florence, 365
Catherine de Médicis, 469–472, 474
Catherine of Aragon, 394, 412, 432, 446–447
Catherine the Great (Russia), 617, 628–629, 630–631
  legal reform and, 660
  Poland and, 639
Catholic Church. *See* Roman Catholic Church
Catholic League, 472–475
Cattle. *See* Animal husbandry; Livestock
Cavaignac, Louis, 794
Celibacy, 674
Cellarius, Andreas, 581
Census, in Russia, 625
Central America, 619
Central Europe, 405–406
  balance of power in, 638–640
  revolutions of 1840s in, 794–796
Centralization. *See also* Monarchs and monarchies; State (nation)
  in England, 412–413
  in France, 413–416
  of government, 546–548
  in Italian city-states, 377
Cereal crops. *See* Crops
Ceremonies, 513, 528, 529–530
Ceylon, 392, 619
Chadwick, Edwin, 747, 749
Chamber of Deputies (France), 785
Chantries, 435
Charity, 519–520, 679–680
Charivari, 530, 532–533
Charles I (England), 542, 546, 550, 556–558
  execution of, 558, 559, 560–561
  revolution of 1648 and, 558–559
Charles I (Spain). *See* Charles V (Emperor)
Charles II (England), 562
Charles II (Spain), 608, 609
Charles V (Emperor), 418, 433, 460, 461, 476
  Council of Trent and, 459–460
  dynastic wars and, 420–423, 424
  Luther and, 439, 461
  Netherlands and, 478, 482
Charles V on Horseback (Titian), 420
Charles VI (Emperor), 610, 634, 635
Charles VIII (France), 385, 415, 420
Charles IX (France), 469, 471, 472
Charles IX (Sweden), 488
Charles X (France), 785
Charles XII (Sweden), 569
Charles the Bold (France), 414, 419
Charter of the Nobility (Russia), 631
Chartist movement, 788–789
Châtelet, Marquise de, 654
Chemistry, 585–588

Childbearing, 525–526, 527, 669–670, 675, 676
age span of, 674
in 18th century, 672–673
Child labor, 736, 744, 751, 784
Owen and, 747
regulation of, 747
"Child Labor in the Coal Mines," 751
Children. *See also* Child labor
of bourgeoisie, 664
in 18th century, 650–651
in Enlightenment, 668, 670–671
family and, 524, 525
farmwork and, 725
foundling hospitals and, 679
Napoleonic Code and, 714–716
in Renaissance Italy, 359–360
China, tea from, 596
Cholat, Claude, 699
Chopin, Frédéric, 777, 787
Christian III (Denmark), 442
Christian IV (Denmark), 488–489, 492
Christianity. *See also* Monasticism; Theology; specific religions
fall of Constantinople and, 382–383
Galileo and, 583–584
humanism and, 431–432
magic and, 534
Russia and, 408
in Spain, 417–418
Church. *See also* Christianity
French Revolution and, 701
in Geneva, 445–446
in Italian Renaissance, 363
Renaissance thought and, 371
in 16th century communities, 527, 528
Church and state, Luther and, 440–441
Churchill, John (Duke of Marlborough), 609, 611, 663
Church Militant, 458
Church of England, 447–448, 641
Cicero, Marcus Tullius, Petrarch and, 372
Cisalpine Republic, 768
Cisneros, Jiménez de, 433, 453–454, 459
Cities and towns. *See also* Rome; Villages
birthrate and, 674–675
capital cities and, 542
in 18th century, 675
industrialization and, 748
Italian Renaissance and, 356–357
population growth in, 510
poverty in, 519
protests in, 782–783
in 16th century, 507–510
society below elite rank, 518
in Western Europe (1500), 357
Citizens and citizenship
in France, 691
restrictions on, 518
City-states, Italian, 375–385, 405–406
Civil code. *See* Napoleonic Code
Civil Constitution of the Clergy (France), 701
Civil liberties, 703–704, 773
Civil wars
in England, 557–558, 563
in France, 555
Classes
bourgeoisie and, 663–671
in 18th century, 661
in England, 752
Estates as, 691–694
masses and, 671–682
new poor and, 518–519
new rich and, 518–519
nobility as, 661–663
social hierarchy and, 514
Classical culture
humanism and, 431–432
Renaissance study of, 371–373
"Clemency of the Russian Monster, The," 787
Clement VIII (Pope), 468
Clergy. *See also* Monasticism; Popes and papacy; Priests
in France, 691, 701
Climate, 503, 506, 678
Cloth industry. *See* Textile industry; Wool industry
Clover, 730
Clubs, social, 667
Coal and coal industry, 731, 733, 734
child labor in, 751
in England, 734, 735–736
in France, 755
in Germany, 757
Cocceji, Samuel von, 660
Cockpit, The (Hogarth), 681
Codes of law. *See also* Law(s)
Napoleonic Code, 714–716
in Prussia, 660
Coello, Alonso Sánchez, 481
Coffee, 596
Coffeehouses, 667
Coke, 737
Colbert, Jean-Baptiste, 571, 603, 606
Coleridge, Samuel Taylor, 776
Colet, John, 447, 453
College de France, 433
Colleges. *See* Universities and colleges
Cologne, 405
Colonies and colonization
American revolt and, 643–646
in eastern Europe, 511
Portugal and, 391–393
slaves and, 597
Spanish, 397–400
warfare over, 604, 605–606, 610–612
Columbus, Christopher, 381, 393–396, 395, 401
letter of, 396
Commerce, 593–595. *See also* Trade
in Antwerp, 508
Dutch, 598–600
in Florence, 379–380
Ottomans and, 385
in 16th century, 507–508
Smith on, 605
of Venice, 377–378
wars of, 604–612
Committee of Public Safety, 708
Commodities
markets, 599–600
trade in, 595–598
Communication, 420
Communist Manifesto (Marx and Engels), 780–781, 782
Communist party. *See also* Marx, Karl
Engels and, 758
Community life, in 16th century, 527–530

Companionate marriage, 669–671
Compostela, shrine at, 435
Concert of Europe, 796
Concerts (musical), 666–667
Condé, duc de, 469, 555
Condition of the Working Class in England in 1844, The (Engels), 749, 757, 758
Condorcet, Marquis de, 659, 704
Condottieri, 377, 385
Confession, 435
Congress of Vienna, 767–771
Conscription, in Russia, 568–569
Conservatism, after Napoleonic wars, 772–773
Constantinople, fall to Ottomans, 382–383, 384, 385
Constitution
  British, 640–642
  in France, 701–702, 703
Constitutional monarchy
  in England, 564
  in France, 701–702
Consumption
  in Italian Renaissance, 358–359
  and 17th century trade, 595–598
Contagious Diseases Act (England), 747
Continent. *See* Europe
Continental System, 712–713, 716
Contraception, in Italian Renaissance, 360–361
Contract theory of government, 564–566
Convention (France), 705, 708
Conversion, by Jesuits, 458
Conversos, 395, 418
Cook, Thomas, 743
Copernicus, Nicolaus, 581, 582, 586, 591
Corn, 677
Coronation, of Napoleon, 714
Cort, Henry, 736–737
Cortes (Spanish assembly), 408
  of Castile, 549
  in Catalonia, 554
Cortés, Hernando, 397, 398
Corvée (forced labor), 690
Cosmology. *See* Astronomy
Cossacks, 631–632
Cottage industry, 726
Cotton and cotton industry, 596, 734. *See also* Textile industry
  in England, 737–740
  in Great Britain, 750–752
Cotton gin, 740
Council of Blood, 482
Council of Ten (Florence), 373–374
Council of Trent, 459–460, 479
Councils. *See also* Assemblies
  in Venice, 378
  Zemsky Sobor in, 409
Counter-Reformation, 458–460
Counterrevolution, in France, 695, 702
Courbet, Gustave, 779
Courtier, The (Castiglione), 373
Courts. *See also* Royal courts
  in England, 547
Craftsmen, 358. *See also* Artisans; Workers
Cranach, Lucas, the Elder, 439
Cranmer, Thomas, 447, 449
Crayer, Caspar, 552
Crime and criminals, 659
  Bentham on, 773
  prisons and, 773–774
  in 16th century, 520
Crimean region, 404, 484
Crimes and Punishments (Beccaria), 659
Criminal Code. *See* Napoleonic Code
Crompton, Samuel, 738
Cromwell, Oliver, 558, 559, 562–563
Cromwell, Thomas, 412, 447
Crop rotation, 506, 507, 676
Crops, 506
  cereal, 506, 512, 676
  fodder, 729–731
  new staples and, 677–678
Crucifixion (Tintoretto), 454
Cruikshank, George, 785
Crystal Palace exhibition. *See* Great Exhibition (London, 1851)
Cuckold, 533
Cultivation. *See* Agriculture
Cult of the Supreme Court (France), 710
Culture(s). *See also* Renaissance
  bourgeois entertainment and, 666–668
  in 18th century, 616–617, 652–661
  of Native Americans, 401–403
  popular, 680–682
Customs (social), 527–530
Customs duties, 601
  in England, 549–550
Customs union, German Zollverein as, 757

Da Gama, Vasco, 392, 401
Dalmatian coast, 385
Danton, George-Jacques, 705
Darby, Abraham, 736
Das Flötenkonzert, 616–617
Daumier, Honoré, 743
David (Michelangelo), 369
Deaths. *See also* Casualties
  disease and, 362
Death sentence, 707
De Boisdenier, 717
Debt. *See* National debt
Declaration of Independence, 646
Declaration of Rights (England), 563
Declaration of the Rights of Man and Citizen, 697, 703
Declaration of the Rights of Woman and Citizen, 710
Declaratory Act (1766), 644
Dee, John, 592
Defenestration of Prague, 491
Defense of Liberty Against Tyrants, A (Duplessis-Mornay), 553
De Humani Corporis Fabrica (Vesalius), 588
Delacroix, Eugène, 777
"De Missy's Life of Peter," 569
Democracy, French Revolution and, 703–711
Demography
  of cities, 510
  population growth and, 674–676
Denmark, 404, 486, 489, 492, 496, 623
  Lutheranism in, 442
  Sweden and, 488
Départments (France), 701
Depression. *See* Economy
De Quincey, Thomas, 723
Der Pesthof, 678
Descartes, René, 591–592, 654

De Stall, Germaine, 776–777
Devil. *See* Magic; Witchcraft
Devotionalism, 454–455
Dialogue Between the Two Great Systems of the World, A (Galileo), 583, 586
Dias, Bartolomeu, 392
Díaz del Castillo, Bernal, 399
Diderot, Denis, 652, 653, 677
Diet (food), in Italian Renaissance, 362
Diet (Germany), 769
Diet (Poland), 485, 639
Diet of Worms, 439
Dijon, 413
Dimitri (Russia), 486
Dinteville, Jean de, 417
Directory (France), 710, 712, 714
Disasters of War, The (Goya), 712, 713
Discourse on Method (Descartes), 591–592
Discourses on Livy (Machiavelli), 374
Discovery. *See* Exploration and discovery
Disease, 552, 585. *See also* Epidemics; Paracelsus
- in Britain, 749
- disappearance of, 669
- in Italian Renaissance, 362
- population growth and, 675
- sexually transmitted, 783
- spread to Americas from Europe, 398

Distribution of wealth. *See* Wealth
Divine right of kings, 542–544
Divorce, 527
Doctors, 672, 675–676. *See also* Medicine
Domesticity, 668–669
Domestic service. *See* Servants
Donatello, 364, 365, 366
Donation of Constantine, 372
Donne, John, 580
Doré, Gustave, 750, 775, 783
Drama. *See also* Literature
- in England, 542
- of Shakespeare, 542–543

Drinking, 682
Duchies, 406. *See also* Milan
- of Bar, 621
- of Lithuania, 404
- of Savoy, 622–623
- of Westphalia, 770

Dudley Street, Seven Dials, London (Doré), 750, 783
Duplessis-Mornay, Philippe, 553
Dürer, Albrecht, 402
Dutch, 400. *See also* Holland; Netherlands
- colonies of, 619
- commerce of, 593
- exploration by, 393
- independence from Spain, 607
- mercantile wars and, 605–606
- in North America, 605, 619
- shipbuilding and, 593, 594
- in Thirty Years' War, 495
- trade and, 595–596, 598–600, 603–604
- after Utrecht, 620

Dutch East India Company, 601, 602, 620
Dutch Republic, 489, 579, 599–600, 768. *See also* Dutch; Holland; Netherlands
Duties. *See* Customs duties
Dutton Family (Zoffany), 665
Dynasties. *See also* Empires
- in Eastern Europe, 483–489
- in Western Europe, 419–423

Earth. *See* Astronomy
East
- absolutism in, 566–570
- trade with, 391

Eastern Europe. *See also* Europe
- boundaries in, 404–405
- centralized states in, 410
- dynastic struggles in, 483–489
- revolutions of 1840s in, 794–796
- Russia and, 408–410

Eastern Orthodoxy, 660
East India companies, 601–602
East Indies, 599, 620
Economics, 653
Economy
- agricultural revolution and, 728–731
- family and, 524
- farming and, 724–726
- during French Revolution, 702
- industrialization and, 731–760
- in Italian cities, 358
- New World impact on, 512
- rural life and, 503–507, 726–728
- in Russia, 409–410, 626
- in 16th century Europe, 503–513
- in 17th century, 549–550, 552
- Smith and, 660

Ecstasy of Saint Theresa of Ávila (Bernini), 456, 573
Edict of Nantes, 471, 475–476, 573–574, 660
Edict of Worms, 461
Education. *See also* Universities and colleges
- of children, 670–671
- Enlightenment and, 660
- in France, 714
- humanists and, 371–372, 432
- Lutheranism and, 442
- Rousseau on, 658–659
- in Russia, 626, 631
- for women, 432

Edward IV (England), 411
Edward V (England), 411
Edward VI (England), 448
Egmont, Count, 479, 482
Egypt, Greece and, 786
Elba, Napoleon in, 717
Elcano, Sebastian, 397
Eleanor of Portugal, 423
El Greco, 477
Elites. *See also* Aristocracy; Nobility; Upper classes
- classes within, 661–662
- new rich and, 518–519
- popular culture and, 680
- and taxation in France, 690
- in towns, 516–518
- urban, 664–666

Elizabeth (Russia), 628, 638
Elizabeth I (England), 412, 433, 441, 447, 470, 471, 542, 543, 556
- Protestantism and, 448–449
- Spanish Armada and, 477

Elizabeth of York, 411
Emigration, poverty and, 679
Émile (Rousseau), 658, 776
Emperors. *See* Empires; specific rulers
Empires. *See also* Ottoman Empire
- expansion of, 619–623
- of Venice, 377–378

Enclosure, 520–521, 728–729
Encyclopedia (Diderot), 652, 653, 677
Energy sources, 731
Engels, Friedrich, 748–749, 757, 758, 780–781, 782
England (Britain), 406, 410–411. *See also* Parliament (England); Spanish Armada
  American revolt against, 643–646
  banking in, 734
  bourgeoisie in, 665–666
  Chartists and, 789
  child labor in, 747, 751
  civil war in, 556–558
  Congress of Vienna and, 771
  consolidation in, 411–413
  constitutional monarchy in, 564
  cotton industry in, 737–740, 750–752
  elite classes in, 661
  empire of, 610–612
  enclosure in, 729
  France and, 413, 611–612, 712–713
  government of, 640–643
  Hanover and, 621
  Industrial Revolution in, 731–752
  Lords Lieutenant in, 547
  Low Countries and, 621
  manufacturing centers in, 745
  mercantile wars and, 605–606
  nobility in, 515–516
  in North America, 619
  peasant revolts in, 521
  poor in, 519, 679
  population of, 510
  power of, 640–646
  protests in, 552
  Prussia and, 637–638
  Puritans in, 556
  railroad in, 740–744
  Reformation in, 446–449
  reforms in, 784
  revolutions in, 558–564
  romanticism in, 776
  social reform in, 747–750
  taxation in, 549–550
  tea trade and, 596–597
  trade and, 595–596, 601–603
  War of the Spanish Succession and, 609
  wealth of, 740
English East India Company, 601
Enlightenment, 652–661
  masses during, 671–682
  salons in, 652, 663
Enquiry Concerning Human Understanding (Hume), 656
Entertainment
  aristocratic, 663
  of bourgeoisie, 666–668
Entrepreneurs, 726, 744–747
Environment, industrialization and, 748–749
Epic poems. *See* Homer
Epicycles, 581–582
Epidemics, 552. *See also* Disease; Medicine
  in Italian Renaissance, 362
Equality, French Revolution and, 703–704, 705
Erasmus, Desiderius, 433–435
Esch, 518
Essay Concerning Human Understanding (Locke), 658
Essay on Forms of Government, An (Frederick the Great), 634
Essay on the Principles of Population, An (Malthus), 674
Essays (Montaigne), 480
Estates, consolidation of, 729, 730
Estates (France), 517, 691–694
Estates-General (France), 408, 543, 691–692, 694. *See also* National Assembly (France)
  French Revolution and, 694–697
  National Assembly and, 696–697
Este, Isabella d', 364
Esterhazy family, 652, 662
Estevancio, 398
Estonia, 623
Étaples, Jacques Lefevre d', 433
Euclid, 592
Europe. *See also* Central Europe; Eastern Europe; Western Europe; World War I; specific countries
  dynastic struggles in, 419–423
  economy and, 503–513
  in 1815, 766–772
  expansion of, 619–623
  exploration and, 401–403
  in 1500, 403
  formation of states in, 407–419
  geographical changes in, 403–407
  industrialization of, 752–760
  population growth in, 510
  private life in, 523–536
  regional industrialization in, 758–760
  religious divisions of (1555), 461
  in 1714, 618
  society in, 513–523
  unrest in 1830s, 786
  war and peace in (1598-1650), 563
  western, 406–407
Exchange. *See* Trade
Excise taxes, 601
Expansion. *See also* Exploration and discovery
  European, 619–623
  Ottoman, 391
  of Prussia, 632
  of Russia, 623, 624–632
Experiment on a Bird in the Air Pump, An (Wright), 590
Exploration and discovery
  European, 391–403
  Italy and, 381
  legacy of, 400–403
  Portuguese, 391–393
  Spanish, 393–400
  voyages of discovery, 400
Exports
  German, 756
  industrialization and, 733
Expulsion of Adam and Eve (Masaccio), 366

Factories. *See also* Industrialization; Labor; Workers
  cotton, 739–740, 750–752
  in France, 755
  for textile manufacturing, 738–739
Factory Act (England), 747, 784
Fairfax, Thomas, 558
Fairy Tales (Grimm brothers), 778
Faith
  family life and, 442
  Luther on, 437–439
False Dimitri, 486

Families and family life
in 18th century, 650–651
during Enlightenment, 668–669
in Italian Renaissance, 359–362
labor and, 751–752
nuclear families, 359–360, 523
rural manufacturing and, 727
in 16th century, 523–527
Famine, 676
in Ireland, 784
population growth and, 674
revolutions of 1840s and, 792
Farel, Guillaume, 445
Farms and farming, 724–726. *See also* Agriculture; Peasants; Rural areas
in 18th century, 676–677
enclosure and, 728–729
in France, 755
lifestyle in 16th century, 503–507
Federal Diet (Germany), 769
Feeding the Hungry (Buys), 519
Ferdinand I (Austria), 795
Ferdinand I (Emperor), 424
Ferdinand II (Emperor), 490–491, 492–494, 496
Ferdinand VII (Spain), 772
Ferdinand of Aragon, 385, 394–395, 406, 416, 419, 433
Naples and, 420
Ferrara, 376
Fertility, 675
Fertilizers, 676–677, 730
Festivals, 681–682
in 16th century, 529–530
Fichte, Johann, 778
Ficino, Marsilio, 356, 362, 585
Field of the Cloth of Gold, 422
Filipinos. *See* Philippines
Filmer, Robert, 565
Finance. *See* Banks and banking; Economy; Taxation; Trade
Finland, 771
First Blast of the Trumpet Against the Monstrous Regiment of Women, The (Knox), 470
First Consul, Napoleon as, 712, 714
First Empire (France), 714–716
First Estate (France), 691, 696
First Peace of Paris (1814), 767
First World War. *See* World War I
Fishing industry, 597–598
Five powers, in Italy, 375–376, 381
Flags, 698, 778
Flanders, 413, 621
Florence, 377, 379–380, 385, 406, 622
Cathedral in, 365
Machiavelli and, 373–375
Renaissance and, 356, 357, 359, 376
Florida, 619
Florin, Franz Philipp, 727
Flyboat, 593, 594
Flying shuttle, 738, 790
Fodder crops, 729–731
Folk culture, 778, 779
Food(s). *See also* Diet (food); Farms and farming
population growth and, 676–677
production of, 676
supply of, 724
Foreign policy. *See* Balance of power
Forest colonies, 510–511
Forest rights, 520
Fortune Teller, The (La Tour), 516
Foundling hospitals, 679
Fourier, Charles, 780–781, 782
Fragonard, Jean-Honoré, 650, 651, 670
France, 406, 411, 618, 620. *See also* Franco-Prussian War; Huguenots; Peasants; Thirty Years' War
absolutism in, 570–574
Austria and, 638
bourgeoisie in, 665
Calvinism in, 469
Catalonia and, 554–555
constitutional monarchy in, 701–702
Constitution of 1791 in, 701–702, 703
crises in (1715-1788), 688–694
in 1815, 767
in 18th century, 621
empire of, 611
England and, 413, 611–612
Estates in, 691–694
industrialization in, 752–756
intendants in, 547
Italian Wars and, 385, 420–423
July Revolution in, 785–786, 788
Louis Napoleon in, 797
mercantile wars and, 606
after Napoleonic wars, 767–768, 772
Napoleon in, 711–717
nobility in, 516, 661–663
in North America, 619
Parlement of Paris in, 547
persecution of Protestants in, 445
population of, 510, 753
poverty in, 519, 679
revolts in, 552
revolutions in, 694–711, 792–794
Saint Bartholomew's Day Massacre in, 469–472
Spain and, 621
taxation in, 549
trade and, 601–602, 603
unification of, 413–416
wars of religion in, 468–476
Franche-Comté, 607, 621
Francis I (Austria), 771
Francis I (France), 419, 420–423, 544
Francis II (France), 469, 471
Franciscans, 454
Francis of Assisi, 454
Francis of Lorraine, 637
Francken, Frans, 535
Franco-Dutch war, 607
Franco-Prussian War, 756
Frankenhausen, 450, 451
Frankfurt, 405
Frankfurt Assembly, 795
Franklin, Benjamin, 687
Franz Josef I (Austria), 795
Frederick II, the Great (Prussia), 616–617, 633–634, 637, 638
Enlightenment and, 660
Poland and, 639
Frederick III, the Wise (Saxony), 436, 439
Frederick V (Bohemia), 491, 496
Frederick William I, the Great Elector (Prussia), 566–568, 633
Frederick William III (Prussia), 768, 771
Frederick William IV (Prussia), 794
Freedom of worship. *See* Religious toleration

Freeholders, in England, 518
Free trade, 606
French Revolution, 686–687
  Church in, 701
  counterrevolution and, 695, 702
  of 1830, 785–786, 788
  first stage of (1789-1792), 694–703
  guillotine in, 706–707
  industrialization and, 754–756
  peasants' revolution in, 698–700
  second stage of (1792-1799), 703–711
  terrorism in, 705–710
  women in, 700–701, 704, 710
Frescoes, in Sistine Chapel, 369, 370
Friedland, battle of, 712
Fronde (France), 555–556, 563, 571
Fuel, coal as, 733
Furniture
  French Rococo style, 669
  in 16th century, 504
Fur trade, 598
Futures market, 600

Galen, 585, 588
Galicia, 640, 770
Galileo Galilei, 580, 581, 583–584, 586–587, 591
Gama, Vasco da. *See* Da Gama, Vasco
Gare Saint-Lazarre, La (Monet), 722
Garibaldi, Giuseppe, 795–796
Gascony, 413
Gaul, remnants of, 406
Gdansk, 484, 624
Gender
  occupations and, 727
  in Renaissance Italy, 359
  roles in 16th century, 526
Geneva, Calvin and, 444–446
Genoa, 376, 622, 768
Gentleman's Magazine, The, 668
Gentlemen, in England, 666
Gentry
  in England, 641
  in Russia, 626, 627
  in towns, 516–518
Geographer, The (Vermeer), 592
Geographical changes, in Europe, 403–407
George I (England), 642
George II (England), 617, 642
George III (England), 643, 686
German Confederation, 768–769, 773
German Empire, 632, 633
  Holy Roman Empire as, 621–623
Germanic peoples, 407
German Peasants' War, 521–523
Germany, 404, 423, 619. *See also* German Empire; Nazis; Prussia; Thirty Years' War
  Austria and, 634
  Battle of the White Mountain and, 491
  central Europe and, 405
  industrialization in, 752, 756–757
  Luther and, 440–441
  Lutheranism in, 442
  Peace of Augsburg and, 461
  Peace of Westphalia and, 496
  peasants and, 450, 521–523
  population of, 753–754
  Prussia and, 638
  religion in, 468
  revolution of 1848 in, 794–795
  society in, 518
  Thirty Years' War and, 494
  unification of, 638
  Zollverein in, 757
Ghent, 477, 482, 489
Ghirlandaio, Domenico del, 360
Giberti, Gian Matteo, 454, 459
Gibraltar, 610, 620
Gin Lane (Hogarth), 675
Giotto di Bondone, 378
Giro banking, 594
Girondins, 705
Glasgow, 731
Global marketplace, 400
Glorious Revolution (England), 563–564
Gold
  exploration and, 391, 400–401
  Portugal and, 392
  prices and, 512
Golden Horn, 382
Good and evil, Locke on, 658
Göteborg, 623
Gothic architecture, 365
Gouges, Olympe de, 710
Government(s). *See also* Enlightenment; Monarchs and monarchies
  Beccaria on, 659
  of Britain, 412–413, 640–643
  centralization of, 546–548
  contract theory of, 564–566
  in Italy, 377
  Locke and, 659
  Machiavelli on, 373–375
  Montesquieu on, 657–658
  royal courts and, 544–546
  of Russia, 409, 626
  of Venice, 377–378
Goya, Francisco, 712, 713
Grain, 504, 508
Granada, 395, 406, 417
Grand Alliance, 607, 609, 610
Grand Duchies. *See also* Tuscany
  of Warsaw, 769
Grandes, 662
Gravitation, 590
Great Britain, 620. *See also* Britain; England (Britain)
Great Chain of Being, 515, 581
Great Committee (France), 708
Great Exhibition (London, 1851), 743, 752
Great Hunger, in England (1840s), 750
Great Northern War, 623, 624
Great Powers
  France as, 767
  revolutions and, 787
Great Reform Bill (England), 788
Great War. *See* World War I
Greece, 786. *See also* Homer
  Renaissance and, 370, 371, 372
Greek Bible, 433
Gresham College, 590
Greuze, Jean Baptiste, 671
Grimm brothers, 778
Grimmer, Abel, 529
Guilds, 358, 727
Guillotin, Joseph Ignace, 706
Guillotine, 706–707
Guise family, 469, 472, 473–474
Guizot, François, 788
Gulf of Finland, 487, 488
Gulf of Mexico, 398
Gunpowder, 408

Gustav I Vasa (Sweden), 442, 487
Gustavus Adolphus (Sweden), 488–494, 496
Gutenberg, Johannes, 432
Gutenberg Bible, 428, 430

Habeas corpus, 556
Habsburg dynasty, 410, 466, 471, 491–492, 607, 768, 795. *See also* Holy Roman Empire; Thirty Years' War
  in Austria, 633, 634–635, 796
  Bohemia and, 491
  Bourbon family and, 621
  dynastic wars and, 420–423
  Ferdinand, 490–491
  Leopold I and, 622
  Low Countries and, 415
  paintings of, 542
  Peace of Westphalia and, 496
  Philip II and, 476
  Venice and, 378
Hacienda, 398
Haiti. *See* Saint Domingue
Hall of Mirrors (Versailles), 570
Hamburg, 405
Hamlet (Shakespeare), 543
Handel, Georg Friedrich, 666
Hanover, 621, 638
Hanseatic League, 405
Hargreaves, James, 738, 741
Harvey, William, 589
Haydn, Joseph, 652
Haymaking, 501–502
Health
  in England, 747
  in Italian Renaissance, 362
Hebrew Bible, 433
Hegel, Georg Wilhelm Friedrich, 778
Heliocentrism, 580–581, 583–584
Henry II (France), 423, 469, 471
Henry III (France), 469, 473–474
Henry IV (Castile), 394, 416
Henry IV (France), 473–476, 489, 490, 549, 553, 554
Henry IV (Shakespeare), 543
Henry V (Shakespeare), 543
Henry VII (England), 411, 421, 435, 542
  dynastic wars and, 421–422, 423
Henry VIII (England), 394, 411–413, 433, 549
  English Reformation and, 446–448
Henry the Navigator (Portugal), 392
Herder, Johann Gottfried von, 778
Herds. *See* Animal husbandry
Hermetic tradition, 585
Hermitage, 617
Hierarchy. *See also* Classes; Estates (France)
  in society, 514–515
Hispaniola, 401
History of Mehmed the Conqueror, The (Kritovoulos), 384
History of the Cotton Manufacture in Great Britain, The (Baines), 740
Hobbes, Thomas, 564–565
Hoefnagel, Joris, 512
Hogarth, William, 675, 681
Holbein, Hans, the Younger, 417
Holidays, 530, 680–681, 682
Holland, 400, 405, 483, 492, 496, 599, 607, 609, 620, 623. *See also* Dutch; Dutch Republic; Netherlands
  constitutional monarchy in, 564
  Napoleon and, 713
Holy Alliance, 771
Holy Roman Empire, 618–619, 621–623. *See also* Thirty Years' War
  Burgundy and, 414
  central Europe and, 405
  Emperors of, 421
  France and, 460
  German and Austrian, 632–633
  Hungary and, 405
  Italy and, 385
  Lutheranism and, 441
  Protestantism in, 443
  replacement with German Confederation, 769
  split of, 424
  Thirty Years' War and, 490–491
Holy Trinity, The (Masaccio), 366, 367
Homer, 370
Household, in 16th century, 503–506
House of Commons (England), 547, 640, 641
Housing
  of aristocracy, 663
  family life and, 669
Hubmaier, Balthasar, 453
Hugo, Victor, 777
Huguenots, 472. *See also* Protestantism
  persecution of, 573–574
  resistance by, 472–476, 553
  Richelieu and, 571
Humanism, 370–371
  Catholic Reformation and, 453
  Christian, 431–432
  Lutheranism and, 442
  spread of, 381, 431–435
Humanities, 370–371
Hume, David, 656
Hundred Years' War, 413
Hungary, 404–405, 410, 446, 453, 496, 622, 759. *See also* Austria-Hungary; Magyars
  Austria and, 637
  Maria Theresa and, 635
  nobility in, 515–516
  Ottomans and, 385
  peasant revolt in, 521
Hunger, 503
Hus, Jan, 442–443
Husbands. *See also* Families and family life; Marriage; Men
  in Enlightenment, 668
Hutcheson, Francis, 659
Hutter, Jacob, 453

Iberian Peninsula, 406. *See also* *Reconquista* (reconquest)
  uniting of, 476
Ideals, of Renaissance, 370–375
Ideologies, after Napoleonic wars, 772–782
Illiteracy. *See* Literacy
Imitation of Christ, The (Thomas à Kempis), 453, 456
Immigration. *See also* Emigration; Migration
  poverty and, 679
Imperial Diet, 408
Imports. *See* Exports; Trade
Incas, 398–399, 402
Income, poverty and, 679
Independence. *See also* American Revolution; French Revolution
  of American colonies, 645–646

of Belgium, 786–787
of Dutch, 607
of Greece, 786
of Netherlands, 482
India
cloth from, 595
Dutch and, 619, 620
England and, 620
exploration and, 391–392
Portugal and, 392
Indian Ocean, 392
Indians. *See* Native Americans
Indonesia, 392
Indulgences, 436–437, 439, 460
Industrialists, 744–747
Industrialization
of continental Europe, 752–760
environment and, 748–749
in France, 752–756
in Germany, 756–757
in Great Britain, 731–752
railroads and, 722–723
regional nature of, 758–760
steam engine and, 736–737
workers and, 679
Industrial Revolution. *See* Industrialization
Industry, 724
in Florence, 379
in France, 714
Infant mortality, 527, 676
Infantry. *See* Military
Inflation
in France, 702
Price Revolution and, 512
Infrastructure, in England, 733–734
Innocence Undone (Tarabotti), 524–525
In Praise of Folly (Erasmus), 434
Inquisition, 395, 453–454, 479
Galileo and, 583–584
Institutes of the Christian Religion (Calvin), 444, 445, 446
Instruction (Catherine the Great), 631
Instruction of a Christian Woman, The (Vives), 432
Instrument of Government, 558
Intellectual thought. *See also* Art(s); Ideologies; Philosophy; Science; Universities and colleges
Enlightenment and, 652–661
humanism and, 431–435
reformation in, 430–435
Renaissance ideals and, 370–375
romanticism and, 776–778
Introduction to the Principles of Morals and Legislation (Bentham), 773
Inventions
Industrial Revolution and, 731
textile industry and, 741
Investment, 601
in Renaissance Italy, 359
Ireland, 406–407
Chartists and, 788–789
emigration from, 679
famine in, 784
potato famine in, 765
Iron and iron industry, 405, 734, 735–736, 755, 757
Isabella of Castile, 394–395, 406, 416
Islam. *See also* Women
fall of Constantinople and, 382–383
Granada and, 395
Moors and, 406
Spain and, 417–418
Italy, 618. *See also* Rome
Austrian power in, 768
Charles V and, 419
cities and towns in, 356–357
city-states in, 375–385, 405–406
decline in, 385
dynastic wars over, 420–423
France and, 385, 607
humanism in, 381, 431, 432
industrialization and, 758, 759
Napoleon and, 713
after Napoleonic wars, 768
nationalism in, 795–796
protests in, 552
Renaissance in, 354–385
revolution in, 787
Wars of, 385
Ivan III, the Great (Russia), 408, 485
Ivan IV, the Terrible (Russia), 408–409, 484, 485–486, 487, 623

Jacobins (France), 705, 707, 708, 709
Jagiellon family, 405, 410, 484, 485
Jamaica, 597
James I (England), 489–490, 543, 546, 553, 556
James II (England), 562–563
Java, 393
Jefferson, Thomas, 646
Jerome (Saint), 434
Jesuits, 457, 458
Enlightenment and, 660
Philip II and, 479
Jews and Judaism, expulsion from Spain, 395, 406, 418
Joanna of Holstein-Gottorp, 628
John II (Aragon), 416
Johnson, Samuel, 680, 744
Jones, Inigo, 542
Jonson, Ben, 542
Joseph II (Emperor), 617, 636, 637, 660
Josephine (France), 714
Judaism. *See* Jews and Judaism
Judith Slaying Holofernes (Donatello), 365, 366
Julius II (Pope), 369
July Monarchy, 786
July Revolution (France), 785–786, 788, 793
Junkers (Germany), 567
Justices of the peace (England), 547
Justification by faith alone, 438, 445

Kalmar, 488
Kant, Immanuel, 653, 776
Kay, John, 738, 790
Kemble, Fanny, 723
Kepler, Johannes, 583, 585
Ket's Rebellion, 521
Khanates, 404
Kiev, 404
King and the Education of the King, The (Mariana), 553
Kingdom of Italy, 768
Kingdom of the Netherlands, 768
Kingdom of the Two Sicilies, 768
Kingdoms. *See also* State (nation)
of France, 414
Kings. *See also* Kingdoms; Monarchs and monarchies; Queens
divinity of, 542–544
Kinship. *See also* Families and family life
in Italian Renaissance, 362–363

Kneller, Godfrey, 611
Knights, 517
Knox, John, 470
Kossuth, Lajof, 795
Krakow, 770
Kritovoulos, 384
Kunersdorf, battle of, 638

Labor. *See also* Child labor; Strikes; Workers
  cotton industry and, 750–752
  in Germany, 756
  industrialization and, 744
  of men, 526
  mining and, 735–736
  of peasants, 507
  reforms and, 747
  in rural manufacturing, 726–727
  in Russia, 627
  in 16th century, 508–510
  slavery of, 758
  socialism and, 779–782
  of women, 526, 671, 790–792
Labor strikes. *See* Strikes
Ladies' Diary, The (magazine), 668
Lafayette, Marquis de, 687, 695, 698
La Gioconda (Leonardo da Vinci), 368
Laissez faire, 660
Lamartine, Alphonse de, 793
L'Amour au Théâtre Français (Watteau), 667
Lancaster, house of (England), 411
Land. *See also* Crop rotation
  cultivation of, 677–678
  in 16th century, 506–507, 510–511
Landsdowne House (London), 664
Language(s)
  printing and, 431
  in Spain, 418
Las Casas, Bartolomé de, 402
Last Supper, The (Leonardo da Vinci), 368
Latin Vulgate, 433
La Tour, Georges de, 516
Laud, William, 556, 557
Law(s)
  Enlightenment thinkers and, 660
  in France, 714–716
  monarchy and, 543–544
  regulation and, 551
  in Russia, 627, 630–631
  Salic, 414–415
Law courts. *See* Courts
Laws of motion, 589
Learning. *See* Education; Intellectual thought
Le Brun, Charles, 570
Lee, Henry, 543
Left (political), origins of term, 705
Legal system, 547–548
Legislation, poor and, 784
Legislative Assembly, in France, 705
Legislature, Parliament (England) as, 413
Leisure, of bourgeoisie, 666–668
Le Mire, 638
Le Nain, Louis, 526
Leo X (Pope), 439
Leon, Luis de, 506
Leonardo da Vinci, 368, 371
Leopold I (Emperor), 607, 608, 609, 610, 622, 639
Lepanto, battle at, 476
Les Fêtes de l'Amour et de Bacchus (opera), 667
Les Misérables (Hugo), 777
Letrados, 547
Letter from the First Voyage (Columbus), 396
Leviathan, The (Hobbes), 564–565
Liberal arts, in Italian Renaissance, 371–373
Liberalism
  Great Powers and, 787
  after Napoleonic wars, 773–776
Liberties. *See* Civil liberties; Rights
Liberty Leading the People (Delacroix), 777
"Liberty Trees," 708
Libraries, 680
Life expectancy, in Italian Renaissance, 361
Life of Lazarillo des Tormes, 505
Life of St. Theresa of Ávila, The, 455
Lifestyle. *See also* Cities and towns; Classes; Families and family life; Society
  in communities, 527–530
  industrialization and, 748–749
  in Italian Renaissance, 356–364
  product choices and, 595–598
  rural, 503–507
  in rural Russia, 626–627
  in 16th century Europe, 501–502
  in Spanish America, 397–400
Linen industry, 729, 756–757
List, Georg Friedrich, 778–779
Liszt, Franz, 777
Literacy, 681. *See also* Printing; Vernacular languages
  humanism and, 432
  industrialization and, 760
  Lutheranism and, 442
  newspapers, magazines, and, 667–668
  in 16th century, 530
Literature. *See also* Art(s); Drama; Poets and poetry
  humanism and, 431–432
  Lusiads and, 400
  popular, 668, 681
  Shakespeare and, 542–543
Lithuania, 405, 408, 446. *See also* Poland-Lithuania
  Duchy of, 404
Little Pretty Pocket Book series (Newbery), 670
Liverpool, 731
Lives of the Great Painters, Sculptors, and Architects (Vasari), 369, 371
Livestock, 506, 730
Livonia, 408, 409, 484, 487, 623
Liv people, 487
Locke, John, 563, 658, 670, 703
Lombards and Lombardy, 622, 768, 795
Loménie de Brienne, Étienne-Charles de, 691
London, 675, 782
  slums in, 675, 750
London, Treaty of (1827), 786
Long Parliament (England), 557
Lord Protector, Cromwell as, 562
Lords, 506–507
  in 16th century, 527–528
Lords Lieutenant, in England, 547
Lorenzetti, Ambrogio, 376
Lorenzo de' Medici. *See* Medici family
Lorraine, 405, 618, 621
Louis II (Hungary), 419

Louis XI, the Spider (France), 414–415, 417
Louis XII (France), 421
Louis XIII (France), 489, 490, 495, 496, 570, 571
  Catalonia uprising and, 554–555
Louis XIV (France), 570, 571
  absolutism and, 565
  expansion under, 621
  revolt against, 555–556
  trade and, 603
  Versailles and, 540–541
  wars of, 606–610
Louis XV (France), 688–689
Louis XVI (France), 686–687, 701–702, 767. *See also* French Revolution
  Estates and, 692
  Estates-General and, 696
  execution of, 705
  national debt and, 689–691
Louis XVII (France), 767
Louis XVIII (France), 717, 767, 785
Louis-Philippe (France), 786, 793
L'Ouverture, Toussaint. *See* Toussaint L'Ouverture
Louvois, Marquis de, 571
Love, companionate marriage and, 669–671
Low Countries, 620, 768. *See also* Netherlands
  Great Britain and, 621
  Peace of Westphalia and, 606–607
Lower orders. *See* Classes; Peasants
Lower Palatinate. *See* Palatinate
Loyola, Ignatius, 456–458
Ludd, Ned, 790
Luddism, 739–740, 790
Lusiads (Camões), 400
Luther, Martin, 437–439, 449, 451
  Bible and, 428
  Charles V and, 461
  doctrinal issues and, 460
  English Protestantism and, 447
  On Good Works, 440
  Ninety-five Theses of, 436–437, 438
Lutheranism, 439–443, 460–461
Luxembourg, 405, 618
Luxembourg Commission, 793
Luxury
  goods as, 592, 595–598
  in Renaissance Italy, 359
Lyrical Ballads (Coleridge), 776

Macbeth (Shakespeare), 530, 543
Machiavelli, Niccolò, 373–375, 385, 407, 471
Madeira, 392, 401
Madrid, 675
  Treaty of, 422–423
Magazines, 668
Magdeburg, sack of, 493, 494
Magellan, Ferdinand, 397, 401
Magic
  in 16th century, 530–534
  witchcraft and, 534–536
Magistrates, 553
Magyars, 795
Maine, 415
Maistre, Joseph de, 773
Maize, 677
Malay Peninsula, 619
Malinche, 398
Malthus, Thomas, 674, 784
Managers, industrialization and, 744–747
Manchester, 731, 733, 748, 784–785
Man-midwives, 673
Manor lord. *See* Seigneur
Manufacture Nationale (Paris), 754
Manufacturing, 744–747. *See also* Industrialization
  in Germany, 757
  in Italian Renaissance, 358
  rural, 726–728
  in Russia, 626
Manuscripts
  printing and, 430
  Renaissance study of, 371
  in 16th century, 514
  study and translations of, 433
Maps and mapmaking
  Ptolemy's world and, 389–390
  Vespucci and, 401
Marat, Jean-Paul, 707
Margaret of Parma, 470, 471, 478, 480, 482
Marguerite de Valois (Navarre), 441
Marguerite of Navarre, 433, 471
Mariana, Juan de, 553
Marian exiles, 448
Maria of Hungary, 433
Maria Theresa (Empress), 635–637
Marie Antoinette (France), 702
Marie de Médicis, 489, 542, 545
Marignano, battle at, 419, 421
Maritime commerce, 391–392
Market(s), in 17th century, 593
Market agriculture, 677–678
Marlborough. *See* Churchill, John (Duke of Marlborough)
Marriage, 513. *See also* Families and family life
  age of, 675
  birthrate and, 674
  among bourgeoisie, 664
  companionate, 669–671
  in Enlightenment, 668
  in Italian Renaissance, 360–362
  of Luther, 442
  sexuality among married men and, 532–533
  in 16th century, 526–527, 529
Marriage of Giovanni Arnolfini and Giovanna Cenami, The (Van Eyck), 528
Marseilles, 755
Marx, Karl, 758, 780–781, 782
Mary, Queen of Hungary, 470, 471
Mary, Queen of Scots, 469, 470
Mary I (England), 446, 449, 470, 471, 477
  Catholicism and, 448
Mary II (England), 563, 610, 642. *See also* William of Orange (William III of England)
Mary of Burgundy, 415
Mary of Hungary, 441, 471
Masaccio, 364, 365–367
Massacre of the Innocents, The (Poussin), 466
Masses
  during Enlightenment, 671–682
  feeding of, 676–678
  in French Revolution, 704–705
  popular culture and, 680–682
  population growth and, 674–676
  poverty of, 678–680
Massys, Quentin, 513
Materialism, 580

Mathematical Principles of Natural Philosophy (Newton), 589
Mathematics. *See also* Science
 Neoplatonism and, 585
 Newton and, 589–590
 science and, 580
Mathias (Holy Roman Empire), 491
Maupeou, René Nicolas Charles Augustin de, 689
Maurice of Saxony, 636
Maximilian (Bavaria), 493–494
Maximilian I (Emperor), 415, 421, 433
Mazarin, Jules (Cardinal), 555, 571
Mazzini, Giuseppe, 778, 787, 795
Meadow floating, 730
Measles, 398
Measure for Measure (Shakespeare), 543
Mechanistic philosophers, 592
Medici family, 379–380, 385, 420. *See also* Catherine de Médicis; Marie de Médicis
 Cosimo de', 379–380
 Lorenzo de', 362, 368, 379, 380
Medicine, 585, 588–589, 675–676. *See also* Anatomy; Disease; Doctors; Health
 childbirth in 18th century, 672–673
 in 18th century, 678
 in Italian Renaissance, 362
Mediterranean region, 406, 508. *See also* Constantinople; Greece
 Ottomans and, 476
Mehmed II, the Conqueror (Ottomans), 382–383, 384, 385
Memoirs (Catherine the Great), 630
Memoirs (Saint-Simon), 544
Memoirs on the Art of War (Maurice of Saxony), 636
Men. *See also* Husbands
 and family in Italian Renaissance, 361–362
 sex, marriage, and, 532–533
 in 16th century, 526–527
Mennonites, 453
Mercantilism, 601. *See also* Commerce; Trade
 mercantile wars and, 605–606
Mercenaries, in Italy, 377
Merchants, 694
Merici, Angela, 455
Metric system, 714
Metternich, Klemens von, 768, 769, 773, 792
Mexico, 619
Michelangelo Buonarroti, 364–365, 368–369
Mickiewicz, Adam, 787
Middle class, bourgeoisie and, 663–671
Middle Passage, 597
Midland Revolt (England), 552
Midwives, 509, 672, 676
Migration
 to cities and towns, 783
 to towns, 510
Milan, 356, 376, 385, 406, 420, 421, 422
 Florence and, 379
Military. *See also* Armed forces; Wars and warfare
 discipline of, 636
 foundation of states and, 408
 in France, 416
 nobility in, 661
 Peter the Great and, 568–570
 in Prussia, 633, 635
 in Russia, 409, 626
 Swedish, 489
Militia, in French Revolution, 698
Mill, James, 776
Mill, John Stuart, 776
Millet, Jean-François, 764–765
Milliones (tax), 549
Mills. *See* Cotton and cotton industry; Textile industry
Mills, Thomas, 532
Milton, John, 553–554
Minerals and metals
 in Great Britain, 734–735
 industrialization and, 734–735
Mines Act (England), 747
Mines and mining, in England, 734, 735–736
Minorca, 610, 620
Mirabeau, Honoré Gabriel Victor de, 696
Miracles, in Venice, 354–355
Miracles of Saint Ignatius Loyola, The (Rubens), 457
Mirror of the Sinful Soul (Marguerite of Navarre), 441
Miss Goody Two-Shoes, 670
Missions and missionaries. *See also* Conversion
 Jesuits and, 458
 in New World, 400
Mobility, 513
Modena, 768, 787
Mohács, battle at, 419, 423
Moldavia, 404
Moluccas, 393
Mona Lisa. See La Gioconda (Leonardo da Vinci)
Monarchs and monarchies. *See also* Constitutional monarchy; Kings; specific rulers
 absolute monarchy and, 564–574
 in Britain, 640–642
 centralization of government and, 546–548
 crisis of royal state, 550–564
 divine right of kings and, 542–544
 dynastic wars and, 419–423
 of Ferdinand and Isabella, 416–418
 in France, 415–416, 689, 692
 Great Powers and, 787
 law and, 543–544
 royal states and, 542–550
 women as, 470–471
Monarchy of France, The (Seyssel), 414–415
Monastic Hell (Tarabotti), 524
Monasticism, Catholic reformation and, 454–455
Money, banking and, 594–595
Money economy, 512–513
Mongols
 eastern Europe and, 404, 405
 Russia and, 408
Monopolies
 in Italian cities, 358
 trade, 601–602
Montaigne, Michel de, 401, 480–481
Montesquieu, baron de (Charles-Louis de Secondat), 631, 656–658, 703
Montezuma II (Aztec), 398
Moors, 406, 417–418. *See also* Islam
Moravia, 453
Moravian Brethren, 453

More, Thomas, 432, 434, 447, 448
Moro, Ludovico il, 385
Mortality
  of poor, 679
  population growth and, 675, 676
Moscow, 626
  Napoleon and, 716
Mother Goose rhymes, 670
Mothers. *See* Families and family life; Women
Mozart, Wolfgang Amadeus, 652
Mule (cotton), 738
Mundus Novus. See New World
Münster, Treaty of, 607
Müntzer, Thomas, 450–451
Muscovy, 404, 408–409, 484, 496
  laborers in, 518
  Poland-Lithuania and, 410
  Sweden and, 488
  Time of Troubles in, 485–486
  trade of, 487–488
Museums, 617
Music
  in 18th century, 616–617, 652
  romantic, 777
Muslims. *See* Islam
Mysticism
  Counter-Reformation and, 458
  science and, 585

Nancy, battle of, 414
Naples, 356, 376, 419, 420, 622
  kingdom of, 406
  Napoleon and, 713
  occupation of, 385
  revolt in, 552
Napoleon Bonaparte, 711–717
  France after wars of, 767–768
  Saint Domingue revolt and, 704
  Waterloo and, 717
Napoleon II (France), 717
Napoleon III (France), 797
Napoleonic Code, 714–716
Narva, 487
National Assembly (France), 696–697, 698
  abolition of privilege and, 700
  fiscal issues and, 702
National Convention (France). *See* Convention (France)
National debt, in France, 689–691
National Guard (France), 698, 707
Nationalism, 778–779
  Italy and, 795–796
  revolutions of 1840s and, 792
Nations. *See* State (nation)
Nations, battle of, 716–717
Nation-states, 403
Native Americans
  in Caribbean region, 397
  European exploration and, 401–403
  Jesuits and, 458
  missionaries and, 400
Natural laws, 592
Natural resources, Germany and, 756
Natural rights, 564, 703
Navarre, 419
Navigation, 590
  French, 401
  by Portuguese, 391–392
Navigation Acts, 602–603, 604, 733
Navy. *See also* Ships and shipping
  English, 550
  Russian, 623
Nazis, Russia and, 717
Necker, Jacques, 689, 690, 695, 716
Neoplatonism, 585–589
Netherlands, 405, 415, 423, 483, 489, 495, 623, 768. *See also* Holland; Low Countries
  Austria and, 622
  Belgium and, 786
  Calvinism in, 446
  in early modern Europe, 501–502
  independence of, 482
  industrialization and, 758
  revolt of, 480–483
  Spain and, 477–478
Newbery, John, 670
Newcomen, Thomas, 735
Newfoundland, 610
New Lanark, Owen and, 746–747
New Netherland, 605
New Piety movement, 453
Newspapers, 667–668
New Testament, 433, 434, 447
Newton, Isaac, 589–590, 654
New World. *See also* American Revolution; North America; South America
  Charles V and, 419
  European economy and, 512
  exploration of, 393–397
  Spanish in, 397–400
New York, 606
Niccolò da Tolentino at the Battle of San Romano (Ucello), 381
Nice, 768
Nicholas I (Russia), 787
Nijmegen, Treaty of, 607
Ninety-five Theses (Luther), 436–437, 438
Nine Years' War, 607–608, 610
Nobility, 513, 514, 515–516. *See also* Aristocracy
  divisions within, 661–662
  in 18th century, 661–663
  in France, 571, 691, 692–693
  in 16th century, 507, 527–528
Noble savage, 687
Norms, enforcement of, 532–533
North Africa, 406
North America. *See also* Canada; Mexico; United States
  Anglo-French wars over, 611–612
  British colonies in, 643–646
  European colonization of, 619
  France and, 610
  mercantile wars and, 605–606
Northern Europe
  humanism in, 432
  Protestantism in, 442
Norway, 404, 771
Notre-Dame de Paris (Hugo), 777
Nouvelle Héloïse, La (Rousseau), 710
Nova Scotia, 610
Novgorod, 408
Nuclear families, 359–360, 523
Nu-Pieds, 552
Nuremberg, 405, 507, 509
Nystad, Treaty of, 618, 623, 624

Oath of the Tennis Court, 697, 698
Observant Franciscans, 454
Observations on the Effect of the Manufacturing System (Owen), 746
Obstetrics, 673
Occupations (jobs), 727
  in cities, 357–358
  in towns, 508
  training for, 360

O'Connor, Feargus, 788
October Revolution (Russia). *See* Revolution(s)
Oeben, Jean-François, 669
"Of Cannibals" (Montaigne), 480–481
Old Believers, in Russia, 660
Old Man with a Child (Ghirlandaio), 360
Old regime. *See* Ancien régime (France)
Old Testament, 433
Olivares, Count-Duke, 544, 545–546, 547–548
Olmütz, 796
On Architecture (Alberti), 361
On Building (Alberti), 367
On Good Works (Luther), 440
On Liberty (Mill), 776
On the Excellence of the Kings and Kingdoms of France (Bacon), 542
On the Family (Alberti), 361, 372–373
On the Revolutions of Heavenly Spheres (Copernicus), 582
Open-field farming, 724, 730
Operas, 666, 667
Optimism, 659
Oration on the Dignity of Man (Pico della Mirandola), 370
Orders. *See also* Classes; Monasticism
  social, 662
Orléans, 415
Orphans, foundling hospitals and, 679
Osman, 385
Ottoman Empire, 381, 619, 622
  Charles V and, 422
  Constantinople and, 382–383, 384
  eastern Europe and, 404, 405
  expansion of, 391
  Greece and, 786
  Italian decline and, 385
  Spain and, 476
  Suleiman the Magnificent and, 419, 423
Owen, Robert, 746–747

Pacific region
  exploration of, 396
  Magellan and, 397
Pacifism, Anabaptists and, 453
Painting. *See also* Art(s)
  in Italian Renaissance, 364, 365, 367–368, 369
  of Michelangelo, 369
  romantic, 777–778
Palatinate, 491, 493, 496
Palazzo Rucellai, 367
Palmieri, Matteo, 356
Pamela (Richardson), 668
Papacy. *See* Popes and papacy
Papal States, 376, 385, 622, 768, 787
  occupation of, 385
Paracelsus, 585, 588
Parents. *See* Children; Families and family life
Paris, 406, 413, 675
  French Revolution and, 697, 698
  guillotine in, 707
  National Assembly and, 705
  revolution of 1830 and, 785
  revolution of 1848 and, 792–794
Parishes, 528
Parlements (France), 547, 555, 688–689
Parliament (England), 407–408, 412, 413, 517, 547, 562–563, 641
  Charles I and, 557–559, 560–561
  civil war and, 557–558
  colonial taxation by, 643–644
  ministers and parties in, 642–643
Parliamentary government. *See also* Parlements (France); Parliament (England)
  in England, 643
Parma, 768, 787
Partitions, of Poland, 638–640, 769
Passarowitz, Treaty of, 622
Patent of Toleration, 660
Patriarcha (Filmer), 565
Patriarchy, in Enlightenment, 668
Paul III (Pope), 458
Paulette (tax), 549
Pavia, battle at, 419, 422
Peace of Augsburg, 461, 468, 478, 479
Peace of Lodi, 381
Peace of Paris
  First (1814), 767
  Second (1815), 767
Peace of Westphalia, 468, 495, 496, 606–607, 768
Peasant Family (Le Nain), 526
Peasants, 724
  in Austria, 636
  in France, 511, 690, 691, 693, 698–700
  Pugachev's revolt and, 631–632
  revolts by, 450–451, 520–523, 552
  in Russia, 409–410, 627, 631
  in 16th century, 503–507
  taxation of, 690
  uprising in Catalonia, 554–555
Peasants' Revolt, 522
Peerage, 515
Penance, 435
Penitentiaries. *See* Prisons
Pensions, Owen and, 747
People's Charter, 789
Pepper, 595, 599
Persecution, for witchcraft, 535
Persian Letters, The (Montesquieu), 656, 657, 658–659
Peru, 398–399
Peter, Jan, 604
Peter I (Russia), 567–570
Peter III (Russia), 628, 638
"Peterloo" massacre, 785
Peter the Great (Russia), 623, 624–626, 660
Petite bourgeoisie, 664
Petition of Right (England), 556
Petrarch, Francesco, 356, 370, 371, 372
Petri, Olaus, 442
Philaret of Moscow, 486
Philhellenic movement, 786
Philip II (Spain), 424, 471, 476–477, 481, 549, 554
  Netherlands and, 480–481
Philip III (Spain), 489, 491, 496
Philip IV (Spain), 545–546, 547, 608
  army of, 548
Philip V (Spain), 609, 610, 663
Philip of Anjou, 608–609
Philippines, 619
  Magellan and, 397
Philology, Valla and, 372–373
Philosophes, 652–653, 688
Philosophical Dictionary (Voltaire), 655

Philosophical Letters Concerning the English Nation (Voltaire), 653–654
Philosophy. *See also* Enlightenment; Intellectual thought; Science
  mechanistic, 592
  romantics and, 776–777
Physicians. *See* Doctors
Physics. *See also* Galileo Galilei; Mathematics
  Newton and, 589–590
Physiocrats, 660
Piazzas, in Italy, 364
Pico della Mirandola, Giovanni, 370, 585
Piedmont-Sardinia, 768
Piero della Francesca, 367
Pietà (Michelangelo), 368, 369
Pig iron, 737
Pilgrimage of Grace, 448
Pisa, 376, 385
Pitt, William, 641
Pius VI (Pope), 701
Pius VII (Pope), 714, 768
Pius IX (Pope), 795
Pizarro, Francisco, 398–399
Place, Francis, 682
Plague
  in Italian Renaissance, 362
  after Thirty Years' War, 496
Plague in Milan, The (Crayer), 552
Planetary motion, 583–584, 585. *See also* Astronomy
Plantations
  sugar trade and, 596–597
  tobacco, 598
Planting Potatoes (Millet), 764
Plato, Renaissance and, 370
Pleasure/pain principle, of Locke, 658, 659
Pluralism, 435
Poetics (Aristotle), 370
Poets and poetry. *See also* Homer; Vernacular languages
  romantic, 776
Poland, 405, 453, 484–485, 618, 623, 624, 759. *See also* Poland-Lithuania
  Lutheranism and, 442
  Muscovy and, 486
  nobility in, 515
  Ottomans and, 385
  partitions of, 638–640, 769, 770
  revolution in, 787
  revolution of 1846 in, 792
  separation from Sweden, 489
Poland-Lithuania, 404, 408, 409, 410, 442, 483
Political parties, in Britain, 642–643
Political privileges
  of elites, 516–517
  of nobility, 517
Political science. *See* Law(s); Montesquieu, baron de
Politics
  Machiavelli and, 373–375
  after Napoleonic wars, 772–776
  revolutions of 1830 and, 788
  in Venice, 378
Politiques, 472, 474
Poll tax, 625
Poltava, battle of, 569, 625
Polyglot Bible, 433, 453
Pomerania, 770
Poor rate, 519
Pope, Alexander, 661
Popes and papacy. *See also* specific popes
  Henry VIII and, 447
  indulgences and, 436
  in Renaissance, 376
Popular culture, 680–682
Population
  of cities, 665
  in 18th century, 674–676
  of England, 747
  of Europe (1550-1700), 551
  of Europe (1800-1850), 725
  industrialization and, 753–754
  patterns of, 674–675
  poverty and, 784
  in Renaissance Italy, 358–359
  in 16th century, 510–511
  Thirty Years' War and, 496
Portland vase, 745
Portugal, 476. *See also* Brazil
  colonies of, 619
  exploration and colonization by, 391–393
  Lusiads and, 400
  rebellions in, 554
  sugar trade and, 596
  in Thirty Years' War, 495
Posen, 770
Potatoes, 677, 764–765
Pottery
  trade in, 599
  Wedgwood and, 745–746
Poussin, Nicolas, 466
Poverty
  caring for poor, 679–680
  in France, 688, 698–699
  in Italian cities, 358
  levels of, 678–679
  of masses, 671
  new poor and, 519–520
  in towns, 507
  work relief and, 783–784
Pragmatic Sanction, 635, 637
Prague
  Defenestration of, 491
  revolution in, 795
Prayer books, English, 448, 556–557
Predestination, 446, 448
Pregnancy, 525–526
  birthrate and, 674
  childbirth and, 672–673
Presbyterians, in Parliament, 558
Prester John, 401
Price Revolution, 512
Prices, poverty and, 679
Priests, 435–436
  in 16th century, 527–528
Primacy of works, 438
Primavera (Botticelli), 367
Prime minister, of England, 643
Prince, The (Machiavelli), 373, 374–375, 385, 471
Principles of Political Economy (Mill), 776
Principles of Political Economy and Taxation (Ricardo), 776
Printing
  of Catholic works, 454
  revolution in, 430–431
Prison Courtyard, The (Van Gogh), 775
Prisons, 773–774
Privy Council (England), 413
Procession of the Relic of the Holy Cross, The (Bellini), 354–355
Production, agricultural, 724–725
Professions, bourgeoisie and, 665

Progress of the Human Mind, The (Condorcet), 659
Proletariat, 789
Promiscuity, women and, 533
Property, socialists on, 780
Prostitution, 509, 520, 525, 783
Protectionism, 603
Protective tariffs, 603
Protest(s). *See also* Revolts; Riots
by Huguenots, 472–476
right to, 553–556
in 17th century, 551–556
urban, 782–783
Protestantism. *See also* Huguenots; Lutheranism; Reformation; Thirty Years' War; Wars and warfare
alliance in Thirty Years' War and, 492
Anabaptists and, 449–453
Charles V and wars against, 461
Council of Trent and, 460
in Eastern Europe, 483–484
Enlightenment and, 660
gains of, 492–494
Henry IV (France) and, 475–476
in Holy Roman Empire, 443
Luther and, 440
in Netherlands, 482–483
peasant revolts and, 450–451
resistance and, 553
Saint Bartholomew's Day Massacre and, 469–472
Protestant Reformation, 443–453
Proudhon, Pierre-Joseph, 779–780, 782
Proudhon and His Children (Courbet), 779
Provence, 415
Prussia, 404, 566–567, 609, 618, 623, 635, 757, 768, 770, 796. *See also* German Empire; Germany
Austria and, 796
expansion of, 632, 633–634
France and, 712, 713, 716
German unification and, 638
Great Britain and, 637–638
immigration to, 679
law code in, 660
Poland and, 639–640
revolution of 1848 and, 794
Ptolemy (scientist), 389–390, 581
Public Health Act (England), 747
Public opinion, French Revolution and, 697–698
Public works, sanitation systems and, 749
Pugachev, Emelyan, 631–632
Punishment, 659, 773
guillotine as, 706–707
Puritans, 556. *See also* Cromwell, Oliver
Putting-out system, 726–728

Quadruple Alliance, 771
Quakers, manufacturing and, 744
Quantz, Johann, 616
Queens, 470–471. *See also* Kingdoms; Kings; Monarchs and monarchies

Radicals and radicalism. *See also* Communist party; Socialism
Reformation of, 449–453
revolutions of 1830 and, 784–788
Radziwill family, 662
Railroads, 722–723
on Continent, 752, 760
in England, 740–744
in France, 755, 756
in Germany, 757
Raison d'état, 570
Ramillies, battle of, 609
Rationale of Punishments and Rewards (Bentham), 773
Rational thought. *See* Intellectual thought
Ravaillac, François, 554
Raw materials. *See also* Natural resources
Reading, 680, 681. *See also* Literacy
Rebellions. *See* Revolts
Reconquista (reconquest), 395, 403, 406, 417–418
Red Shirts (Italy), 796
Reflections on the Revolution in France (Burke), 772
Reformation
Catholic, 453–462
Counter-Reformation and, 458–460
in England, 446–449
intellectual, 430–435
Lutheran, 435–443
Peasants War and, 450–451
Protestant, 443–453
of Radicals, 449–453
Twelve Articles and, 450
warfare during, 460–461
Regents, in Amsterdam, 664
Regulation, 551
economic, 601
of markets, 602–603
Reign of Terror, 707, 708–710
Relics, 435, 436
Relief. *See* Work relief
Religion(s). *See also* Monasticism; Popes and papacy; Reformation; specific religions
Bible and, 428–429
of Calvin, 444–446
in Europe (1555), 461
French wars of, 468–476
Hume on, 656
of Luther, 437–439
Montesquieu on, 658
Peace of Westphalia and, 496
printing and, 430
Puritans and, 556
reform and, 435–436
science and, 592
Religious orders. *See* Monasticism
Religious toleration, 468
by Dutch, 579
in England, 562
Enlightenment and, 660
of Huguenots, 475
Rembrandt van Rijn, 578–579, 603
Renaissance
in England, 542
Italian, 354–385
Rents, 507
Report on the Sanitary Condition of the Laboring Population in Britain (Chadwick), 747
Representative government, 565
Republic of Rome, 795
Republic of Venice, 768
Research, scientific, 714
Resistance. *See* Protest(s); Revolts
Resistance theory, 553–556. *See also* Protest(s); Revolts

Resurrection, The (Piero della Francesca), 367
Reval (town), 487
Revenue, in France, 549
Revolts, 551. *See also* Peasants
of Bohemia, 490–491
by French Fronde, 555
of Netherlands, 480–483
by Pugachev (Russia), 631–632
in Saint Domingue, 703–704
Revolution(s)
American, 645–646, 686–687
French, 686–687, 694–711
in 1830, 784–788, 793
in 1840-1850, 792–797
in 1648 (England), 558–563, 642
Ricardo, David, 776, 778
Rice, 598
Rich. *See* Wealth
Richard II (Shakespeare), 543
Richard III (England), 411
Richardson, Samuel, 668
Richelieu, Cardinal, 466, 495, 544–545, 547, 553, 570–571
Riga, 487, 488, 489
Rigaud, Hyacinthe, 572
Right (political), origins of term, 705
Righteousness, Luther and, 437–438
Rights. *See also* Equality
natural, 564
of women, 704, 791
Rights of man, 691, 703
Riots, 551. *See also* Revolts
Rituals, 513
Rivers, in Great Britain, 731
Robespierre, Maximilien, 705–710
Robot (monetary payment), 507
Rococo style, 669
Roman Catholic Church. *See also* Christianity; Church; Enlightenment; Huguenots; Protestantism; Reformation; Thirty Years' War; Wars and warfare
ceremonies and, 528
Council of Trent and, 459–460
Counter-Reformation and, 458–460
in Eastern Europe, 483–484
England and, 412, 563
English Protestantism and, 447–449
Enlightenment and, 660
Estates in France and, 692
French Revolution and, 701
humanism and, 432
in Italian Renaissance, 363
Napoleonic Code and, 715
Peace of Westphalia and, 496
reformation of, 453–462
science and, 591
in Spain, 394, 476–477
urban poor and, 519
Romanov dynasty, Michael, 486
Romanticism, 776–778
Rome
Republic of, 795
sack of (1527), 385, 423
Rotten boroughs, 789
Rousseau, Jean-Jacques, 652, 658, 659, 708, 776
Rouvroy, Louis de, duc de Saint-Simon. *See* Saint-Simon, duc de (Louis de Rouvroy)
Royal Academy, 590
Royal African Company (English), 601
Royal courts
courtiers and, 544–546
at Versailles, 572–574
Royal General Farms (France), 690
Royalists (England), 558
Royalty. *See* Dynasties; Kingdoms; Monarchs and monarchies; specific rulers
Rubens, Peter Paul, 457, 542
Rump Parliament, 558, 559, 562–563
Rural areas. *See also* Agriculture; Farms and farming
farm economy and, 724–726
lifestyle in, 503–507
in Russia, 626–627
society in, 517–518
Russia, 484, 618. *See also* Muscovy
absolutism in, 566–570
eastern Europe and, 404
expansion of, 623, 624–632
foundation of state, 408–410
France and, 712, 713
industrialization and, 758, 759, 760
legal reform in, 660
Napoleon's invasion of, 716, 717
Poland and, 639–640, 769
Prussia and, 638
rise of, 486
rural, 626–627
Tsars of, 566

Sack of Rome. *See* Rome, sack of
Saint Bartholomew's Day Massacre, 469–472
Saint Domingue, 597, 611, 703
Saint Helen, 717
Saint-Just, Louis de, 650
Saint Mark. *See* Venice
"Saint Monday" tradition, 751–752
St. Peter's Basilica, 436
Michelangelo and, 369
St. Petersburg, 623, 632
Saint-Simon, duc de (Louis de Rouvroy), 541, 544
Saint-Simon, Henri de, 779, 782
Salic Law, 414–415
Salons, 652, 663
Salutati, Coluccio, 379
Salvation
Calvin on, 446
Luther and, 437–438
Sanitary Condition of the Laboring Population of Britain, The (Chadwick), 749
Sanitation
in Britain, 749
industrialization and, 748
urban, 675
Sans-culottes, 705, 707, 708
Sardinia. *See* Piedmont-Sardinia
"Savages," in Americas, 662, 687
Savoy, 768
Saxe, Herman Maurice de. *See* Maurice of Saxony
Saxony, 461, 492, 493, 621, 638, 770
Scandinavia, 404, 623, 624, 770, 771
Lutheranism in, 442
Sceptical Chymist, The (Boyle), 588
Scholasticism, 370
Schools. *See also* Education
in Russia, 631
Science. *See also* Technology
academies of, 590–591

Science (*continued*)
in France, 714
natural, 584–590
printing and, 431
Ptolemy and, 389–390
religion and, 592
in 17th century, 580–592
Scotland, 406
Calvinism in, 446
Charles I and, 556–558
Great Britain and, 620
Scriptures, 428–429, 460
Sculpture. *See also* Art(s)
by Donatello, 365
in Italian Renaissance, 364, 365
of Michelangelo, 368–369
Sea routes. *See also* Exploration and discovery
Portuguese and, 391, 392
Second Estate (France), 691
Second Peace of Paris (1815), 767
Second Republic, 794, 797
Secularization, of Renaissance society, 372
Seigneur, 506–507
Selve, Georges de, 417
Senate, in Russia, 626
Serbia, 622
Serfs and serfdom, 679, 725. *See also* Peasants
industrialization and, 759
in Russia, 409–410, 627, 631
Servants, 509–510
Settlements. *See* Colonies and colonization; Exploration and discovery
Seven Years' War, 611–612, 638, 643
France and, 688–689, 754
Severus, Alexander, 745
Seville, 512
Sewage disposal, 675
Sex and sexuality
Calvinism and, 446
in Italian Renaissance, 360–361
married men and, 532–533
weddings and, 529
Seyssel, Claude de, 414–415
Sforza, Francesco, 377
Shakespeare, William, 514, 530, 542–543
Shaming rituals, 532–533
Sharecropping, 357
Shelley, Percy Bysshe, 786
Ship Money, 550
Ships and shipping, 593, 594. *See also* Navy; Trade
expansion of, 734
railroads and, 742
Venetian, 377
Sicily, 406, 419
Sieyès, Emmanuel Joseph, 696, 697
Sigismund III Vasa (Poland and Sweden), 484–485, 488, 489
Silesia, 633, 635, 636, 756
Silk industry, 734
trade and, 595–596
Silver
banking and, 594
exploration and, 391
trade and, 400
Simons, Menno, 453
Simony, 435
Simplicissimus, on Thirty Years' War, 490
Sin, 435
Luther and, 437
Single-crop farming, 677
Sistine Chapel, 369, 370
Six Books of the Commonwealth, The (Bodin), 543
Six Months' Tour Through the North of England (Young), 733
Skimmington, 530, 532–533
Slaves and slavery, 401, 597
abolitionist attitudes and, 773
revolts and, 703–704
Slave trade, 392, 400, 597
Slavic peoples, 405
Slums
industrialization and, 748
in London, 675, 750
Smallpox, 398
Smellie, William, 673
Smith, Adam, 604, 605, 653, 660
Smith, J. R., 680
Snatched (Stolen) Kiss, The (Fragonard), 670
Sobieski, Jan, III (Poland), 639
Social classes. *See* Classes
Social Contract, The (Rousseau), 652, 659, 708
Socialism, 779–782
Sociétés, 667
Society
in Italian Renaissance, 362–364
upward mobility within, 665
Society for the Abolition of Slavery, 773
Society of Jesus. *See* Jesuits
Society of Revolutionary Republican Women, 710
Sociology. *See* Rousseau, Jean-Jacques
Soho Engineering Works, 737
Solar system. *See* Astronomy
Soldiers. *See* Armed forces; Military; Wars and warfare
Sophia (Russia), 408
Sophie of Anhalt-Zerbst. *See* Catherine the Great (Russia)
South America
Magellan and, 397
trade with, 595
Spain, 406, 411, 496, 619, 623. *See also* Jews and Judaism
Burgundy and, 477–479
Charles V and, 418–419
conquests of, 397–400
dynastic marriages in, 416–419
dynastic wars and, 420–423
exploration by, 393–401
France and, 621
industrialization and, 758, 759–760
Inquisition in, 395
legal system in, 547
Magellan and, 397
monarchy in, 547–548
Napoleon and, 712, 713
nobility in, 516
Philip II of, 476–477
Portugal and, 554
in 16th century, 510–511
succession in, 608
taxation in, 549
unification of, 394
Spanish America, 397–400
Spanish Armada, 477, 481
Spanish Inquisition. *See* Inquisition
Spanish Netherlands, 606, 607, 608, 609, 618, 620. *See also* Netherlands

Specialization
on farms, 677
of labor, 508–509
Spectator, The (magazine), 668
Spending, in France, 689–690
Spice Islands, 393, 397, 400
Spice trade, 391, 393, 402
Dutch and, 595–596
Portugal and, 392
Spinning, 727
Spinning jenny, 731, 738, 741
Spirit of the Laws, The (Montesquieu), 656, 657, 658
Spiritual Exercises, The (Loyola), 456
Spirituality, 428–429
Sports, 682
Spring (Botticelli), 367
Staël, Germaine de, 716
Stamp Act (1765), 643, 644
Standard of living. *See* Lifestyle
Starry Messenger, The (Galileo), 584, 586, 587
Starvation, 678–679
in France, 698–699
State (nation). *See also* Monarchs and monarchies; Nation-states
centralized government in, 546–548
church and, 440–441
formation of, 407–419
States-General, in Netherlands, 483
Statues. *See* Sculpture
Status, 514. *See also* Classes
Steam engines, 731, 736–737
Steel industry, 754
Stephenson, George, 759
Stockholm, 488
Stock market, 599
Strait of Gibraltar, 406
Straits of Magellan, 397
Strasbourg, 607, 621
Strikes, in England, 789
Stuart dynasty (England), 542, 562
Mary and, 562
Subsistence agriculture, 677
Suffrage, 784–785
Sugar Act (1764), 643, 644
Sugar trade, 596–597
Suleiman the Magnificent, 419, 423
Sun King. *See* Louis XIV (France)
Supernatural, 531. *See also* Witchcraft
Surrender of Breda (Velázquez), 548
Swabia, 450
Luther and, 449
Sweden, 404, 496, 618, 770, 771. *See also* Thirty Years' War
alliances of, 488
constitutional monarchy in, 564
Lutheranism in, 442
Poland and, 484–485
rise of, 486–489
Russia and, 569, 623
after Thirty Years' War, 496
Swiss Federation, 405
Switzerland, 496, 786
Calvin and, 444–446
Protestantism in, 443, 460
Syndics of the Cloth Gild, The (Rembrandt), 603
Systematic Dictionary of the Sciences, Arts, and Crafts. See Encyclopedia (Diderot)

Table of Ranks (Russia), 626, 630
Tabula rasa, 670
Taille (tax), 416, 516, 549, 690
Talleyrand, Charles Maurice de, 768, 769, 770
Tarabotti, Arcangela, 524
Tariffs, 603, 606
Tartars, 409, 484
Taxation. *See also* Peasants; Protest(s)
of American colonies, 643–644
in England, 549–550, 556
Enlightenment and, 660
in France, 415–416, 549, 688–689, 690
increases in, 550–551
manorial, 724
nobility and, 515–516
in Russia, 625
Taylor, Harriet, 776
Tea, trade in, 596
Technology. *See also* Science
European expansion and, 401
foundation of states and, 408
in Germany, 757
Telescope, 583, 584, 586
Tempest, The (Shakespeare), 543
Tenants, in England, 518
Ten Hours Act (England), 747
Tenochtitlán, 398
Tenure of Kings and Magistrates, The (Milton), 554
Teresa of Ávila (Saint), 455, 573
Terra incognita, 390
Territorialism, after Napoleonic wars, 768–771
Terrorism, in French Revolution, 705–710
Tetzel, Johann, 436
Teutonic Knights, 404, 487
Textile industry, 595, 784. *See also* Cotton and cotton industry; Wool industry
British centers of, 738
cotton industry and, 737–740, 750–752
in Florence, 379
in Italian Renaissance, 358
linen industry, 729
Luddism and, 739–740, 790
trade in, 595–596
Theater, 666
Theatines, 455
Theocracy, Zwingli and, 443
Theology, of Luther, 437
Thermidorian Reaction, 710
Third-Class Carriage (Daumier), 743
Third Estate (France), 691–692, 693–694
in Estates-General, 694–695, 696–697
Thirty-nine Articles, 449
Thirty Years' War, 466, 489–496
Austria after, 634
Peace of Westphalia and, 495, 496
Thomas à Kempis, 453
Thornhill, James, 610
Thuringia, 450–451, 461
Tiepolo, Giovanni Battista, 662
Time of Troubles, in Muscovy, 485–486
Tintoretto, 454
Titian, 420, 460
Tobacco, 598
Toleration Act (England), 562
Tolstoy, Lev, 650
Tordesillas, Treaty of, 396

Tories (England), 642
Torquemada, Tomas de, 395
Torture, for witchcraft, 531
Toussaint L'Ouverture, 703–704
Towns. *See* Cities and towns; Urban areas
Townsend, Charles "Turnip," 730
Trade. *See also* Commerce
- agricultural, 678
- Dutch and, 598–600
- with East, 391
- English, 610–611
- industrialization and, 733–734
- long-distance, 400
- nobility and, 692–693
- Portuguese, 392–393
- Russia and, 625
- in 17th century, 592–604
- in 16th century, 508
- Swedish, 487–488
- triangular, 594
- wars over, 604–612

Trade routes, Dutch, 593
Trading houses, 596
Transfer banking. *See* Giro banking
Translations, humanists and, 433
Transportation, 419
- industrial revolution and, 740–741
- railroads as, 722–723, 741–744
- by water, 732–733

Transylvania, 404
Travel
- by bourgeoisie, 666
- in 18th century, 663
- long-distance, 594
- railroads and, 742–744

Treaties. *See* specific treaties
Treatise of Human Nature, A (Hume), 656
Triangular trade, 594, 595
Trismegistus, Hermes, 585
Tristan, Flora, 791–792
Troilus and Cressida (Shakespeare), 514
Troops. *See* Armed forces; Military
True History of the Conquest of New Mexico, The (Díaz), 399
True Law of Free Monarchies (James I), 543
Tsars (Russia), 566. *See also* Russia
Tudor dynasty, 411–412, 433, 542
Tuileries, 702, 705
Turgot, Anne Robert Jacques, 690
Turks. *See* Ottoman Empire
Turner, J. M. W., 777
Turnips, 730
Tuscany, 622, 768
Twelve Articles, 450, 451, 522
Twelve Days of Christmas, 530
Twelve Years' Truce, 483, 489
Two New Sciences, The (Galileo), 587
Two Tax Gatherers, The (Van Reymerswacle), 517
Two Treatises on Civil Government (Locke), 563
Tyndale, William, 447
Type. *See* Printing
Typhoid, 398
Tyrants and tyranny, monarchical, 553

Uccelo, Paolo, 381
Ulm, 405
Unification
- of France, 413–416
- of Spain, 417

Union of Arms (Spain), 548
Union Ouvrière, L' (Tristan), 791
United Provinces, 606, 607, 620
United States. *See also* Americas
- cotton in, 740
- revolt against England, 643–646

Universe. *See* Astronomy
Universities and colleges
- in Geneva, 446
- humanism and, 432, 433

Unskilled labor, 509
Upper classes. *See also* Elites
- revolt in France, 555–556

Upper Palatinate. *See* Palatinate
Upward mobility, 662–663, 665
Urban VIII (Pope), 586, 587
Urban areas. *See also* Cities and towns
- elites in, 664–666
- Lutheranism and, 440–441
- population growth in, 674–676
- protests in, 782–783
- in Renaissance Italy, 356–357

Urbanization, 665
Urbino, 376
Ursulines, 455–456
Utopianism, 781–782
- Peasants War and, 450–451

Utrecht, Treaty of, 610, 611, 618, 623

Vaccination Act (England), 747
Vagrancy laws, 520
Valencia, 406
Valla, Lorenzo, 370–371, 372, 375
Valois dynasty, 413, 414, 466, 472, 474
- dynastic wars and, 420–423

Values (moral)
- of aristocracy, 692–693
- of bourgeoisie, 666

Van Dyck, Anthony, 542, 550
Van Eyck, Jan, 528
Van Gogh, Vincent, 775
Van Reymerswacle, Marinus, 517
Vasari, Giorgio, 369, 371
Vasas family, Gustav I, 487
Velázquez, Diego de, 542, 545, 548
Venereal disease, 783
Venetia, 768
Venice, 354–355, 356, 376, 377, 381–382, 406, 622, 795
- empire of, 377–378
- Ottomans and, 385

Vera Cruz, 398
Vermeer van Delft, Jan, 592
Vernacular languages, 779
- Bible in, 429

Verrocchio, Andrea del, 379
Versailles, 540–541, 570
- court at, 572–574
- Estates-General at, 696–697
- women's march on, 700–701

Vesalius, Andreas, 588
Vespucci, Amerigo, 381, 401
Vice-royalty system (Spain), 619
Vienna, 423, 675, 795
Villages. *See also* Cities and towns
- in 16th century, 503

Villein, 518
Villiers, George. *See* Buckingham, duke of
Visconti family, 376
Visit to the Wet Nurse, A (Fragonard), 650, 651
Vives, Juan Luis, 432

Vladislav II (Bohemia and Hungary), 410
Voltaire, 617, 653–656
Von Grimmelshausen, Hans, 490
Voyages of discovery, 400
Vulgate, 460

Wages
  poverty and, 679
  rural manufacturing and, 727
  in 16th century, 511–512
Wales, 406
Wallachia, 404
Wallenstein, Albrecht von, 492, 494, 496
Walpole, Robert, 642
War of American Independence. *See* American Revolution
War of Liberation, in Germany, 773
War of the Austrian Succession, 637–638
War of the Spanish Succession, 608–610, 621, 623
War of the Three Henrys, 473–474
Wars and warfare
  over commerce, 604–612
  dynastic, 419–423
  foundation of states and, 408
  French Revolution and, 710–711
  French wars of religion, 468–476
  Napoleon and, 712–713
  population growth and, 675
  during Reformation, 460–461
  in 16th century, 466–467
  Venice and, 378
Wars of Italy, 385
Wars of the Roses (England), 411
Washington, George, 687
Water, sanitation and, 749
Water frame, 738
Waterloo, battle of, 717
Water power, 731, 732–733
Waterways, 732–733. *See also* Transportation
Watt, James, 736, 737
Watteau, Antoine, 667
Way of Perfection, The (Teresa of Ávila), 455
Wealth. *See also* Nobility
  distribution of, 747–750
  from explorations, 400
  of Great Britain, 740
  in Italian cities, 358
  new rich and, 518–519
  society and, 513
  status and, 514
Wealth of Nations, The (Smith), 604, 605
Weapons, foundation of states and, 408
Weaving, 727, 739
Wedding Feast at Bermondse (Hoefnagel), 512
Weddings, in 16th century, 529
Wedgwood, Josiah, 745–746, 773
Wesley, John, 668
Western Europe, 406–407
  expansion of, 619–623
  geographical change in, 403–407
  states (nations) in, 410–419
  warfare in 16th century, 466–497
Western Rising, 521
West Indies, 611
Westphalia, Napoleon and, 713
West Prussia, 640
Wetnursing, 650–651, 675
What Is Enlightenment? (Kant), 653
What Is Property? (Proudhon), 779–780
"What Is the Third Estate?" (Sieyès), 696, 697
Whigs (England), 642
White Mountain, battle of the, 491
White Sea, 487
Whitney, Eli, 740
Widows, 527. *See also* Women
Wilhelm IV (Prussia), 795
Wilkes, John, 645
Wilkinson, John, 736
William I (Netherlands), 768
William of Orange, the Silent (William I), 479, 482
William of Orange (William III of England), 562, 606, 607, 608, 609, 610, 642
Wine, 506
Witchcraft, 534–536
Witches Assembly (Francken), 535
Witches' Hammer, 531
Wittenberg, Luther in, 436
Wives. *See also* Families and family life; Marriage; Women
  in Enlightenment, 668
Women. *See also* Families and family life; Wives
  abandoned babies and, 520
  Castilian, in New World, 397
  childbearing and, 525–526, 669–670, 672–673
  domesticity and, 668
  education in Russia, 631
  farmwork and, 725
  in French Revolution, 700–701, 704, 710
  humanists and, 432
  Isabella of Castile and, 418
  in Italian Renaissance, 359, 360–361, 362
  as Jacobins, 708
  literacy of, 681
  Lutheranism and, 441–442
  magazines of, 668
  marriage and, 525–526, 668–671
  midwives and, 672–673
  Napoleonic Code in, 714–716
  perspective of, 524
  rights of, 704
  as rulers, 470–471
  shaming of, 532–533
  in 16th century, 508, 509, 525–527
  status of, 518
  utopianism, socialism, and, 781–782
  witchcraft and, 534–536
  as workers, 671, 736, 790–792
Wool industry, 790
  in Florence, 379
Wordsworth, William, 776
Workers. *See also Communist Manifesto* (Marx and Engels)
  in France, 691, 694, 755
  in French Revolution, 704–705
  living conditions of, 748–749
  poverty of, 679
  as proletariat, 789
  reform and, 747
  revolution of 1848 and, 792–794
  women as, 671, 790–792
Workhouses, 680
Working class, 752, 780–781, 782, 790–792. *See also* Masses
Work relief, 783–784
Workweek, in factories, 751–752

World War I, 756
Worsley-Manchester Canal, 733
Wright, Joseph, 590, 735
Writing. *See also* Language(s); Literature

Xavier, Francis, 458

York, house of (England), 411
Young, Arthur, 688, 724, 733
Young Italy movement, 787, 795

Zemsky Sobor (Russia), 409, 486
Zoffany, John, 665
Zollverein, 757
Zwingli, Huldrych, 443, 460–461

CONTEMPORARY EUROPE
Land Elevation
Feet
Meters
13,123
4,000
6,562
2,000
3,281
1,000
1,640
500
656
200
0
0
Below sea level
Below sea level
0
250
500 mi.
0
250
500 km
30°W
20°W
10°W
0°
70°N
10°E
60°N
50°N
40°N
Arctic Circle
N
S
E
W
ICELAND
Norwegian Sea
FAROE IS.
SHETLAND IS.
HEBRIDES IS.
ORKNEY IS.
KJØLEN MOUNTAINS
SCANDINAVIAN PENI
NORWAY
SWEDEN
L. Vänern
L. Vättern
Scotland
Northern Ireland
UNITED KINGDOM
BRITISH ISLES
IRELAND
Wales
England
North Sea
JUTLAND PENINSULA
DENMARK
Celtic Sea
ATLANTIC OCEAN
Thames R.
NETHERLANDS
RUHR VALLEY
Elbe R.
NORTH E
Oder R.
POL
English Channel
BELGIUM
GERMANY
Rhine R.
BRITTANY PENINSULA
Seine R.
LUXEMBOURG
CZECH REPUBLIC
SLOV
Loire R.
FRANCE
LIECHTENSTEIN
Danube R.
Bay of Biscay
SWITZERLAND
L. Geneva
AUSTRIA
HUN
CENTRAL MASSIF
ALPS
SLOVENIA
Drava R.
Sava R.
Garonne R.
Rhone R.
Po R.
CROATIA
PYRENEES
ITALY
SAN MARINO
BOSNIA
Duero R.
Ebro R.
MONACO
APENNINES
DINARIC AL
IBERIAN PENINSULA
ANDORRA
Adriatic Sea
CORSICA
PORTUGAL
Tagus R.
SPAIN
Guadiana R.
Guadalquivir R.
BALEARIC ISLANDS
SARDINIA
Tyrrhenian Sea
AL
SIERRA NEVADA
Strait of Gibraltar
Mediterranean Sea
Ionia Sea
SICILY
AFRICA
MALTA

Barents Sea
KOLA PENINSULA
White Sea
Pechora R.
URAL MOUNTAINS
Ob R.
N. Dvina R.
L. Onega
FINLAND
L. Ladoga
RUSSIA
Gulf of Finland
Volga R.
Ural R.
ESTONIA
L. Peipus
LATVIA
LITHUANIA
EUROPEAN PLAIN
CENTRAL RUSSIAN UPLAND
Oka R.
VOLGA UPLAND
BELARUS
Volga R.
CASPIAN DEPRESSION
Dnieper R.
Don R.
UKRAINE
Dniester R.
CARPATHIAN MTS.
Siret R.
Prut R.
MOLDOVA
Sea of Azov
CAUCASUS
Caspian Sea
ROMANIA
CRIMEA
TRANSYLVANIAN ALPS
GEORGIA
Black Sea
Danube R.
ARMENIA
BALKAN MTS.
BULGARIA
Bosporus
AZERBAIJAN
BALKAN PENINSULA
TURKEY
GREECE
Dardanelles
ASIA
Aegean Sea
CRETE